THE OTHER SIDE OF WESTERN CIVILIZATION: READINGS IN EVERYDAY LIFE

Volume II: The Sixteenth Century to the Present

FIFTH EDITION

D1416910

THE OTHER SIDE OF WESTERN CIVILIZATION: READINGS IN EVERYDAY LIFE

Volume II: The Sixteenth Century to the Present

FIFTH EDITION

EDITED BY PETER N. STEARNS
Carnegie Mellon University

HARCOURT BRACE COLLEGE PUBLISHERS

*Fort Worth   Philadelphia   San Diego   New York   Orlando   Austin   San Antonio
Toronto   Montreal   London   Sydney   Tokyo*

Publisher	Earl McPeek
Executive Editor	David Tatom
Market Strategist	Steve Drummond
Developmental Editor	Tracy Napper
Project Editor	Laura Hanna
Art Director	Biatriz Chapa
Production Manager	Linda McMillan

Cover credit: Scala/Art Resource, New York. Brueghel, Pieter the Elder. *Landscape with the Fall of Icarus.* Musée d'Art Ancien, Brussels, Belgium.

ISBN: 0-15-507850-X
Library of Congress Catalog Card Number: 99-60750

Copyright © 2000, 1992, 1984, 1979, 1973 by Harcourt Brace & Company

Address for Domestic Orders
Harcourt Brace College Publishers, 6277 Sea Harbor Drive, Orlando, FL 32887-6777
800-782-4479

Address for International Orders
International Customer Service
Harcourt Brace & Company, 6277 Sea Harbor Drive, Orlando, FL 32887-6777
407-345-3800
(fax) 407-345-4060
(e-mail) hbintl@harcourtbrace.com

Address for Editorial Correspondence
Harcourt Brace College Publishers, 301 Commerce Street, Suite 3700, Fort Worth, TX 76102

Web Site Address
http://www.hbcollege.com

Printed in the United States of America

9 0 1 2 3 4 5 6 7 8   039   9 8 7 6 5 4 3 2 1

Harcourt Brace College Publishers

For "the boys"—Luke, Tim, Steve, Pat—with affection and thanks

Preface

Historians often change the understanding of the past, at least in small ways: they find a new specific fact or they launch a different interpretation. In recent decades, however, social historians have done this and more: They have expanded our grasp of what the past embraces and how it helps explain current issues and human behaviors. Our sense of what crime involves, or what consumerism means, has been literally revolutionized. This book, dealing with key examples of social history applied to modern Europe, invites participation in this expansion of knowledge.

When the first edition of this collection appeared, it was necessary to argue the need for a new kind of history, decisively different from the conventional focus on kings, presidents, constitutions, and wars. This argument is still valid to the extent that most textbook history coverage relies heavily, though no longer exclusively, on the old staples. But the new kind of history—social history—is well past its infancy. It has developed a multitude of branches, both in the variety of topics explored and in the interpretations offered. This collection captures the ongoing excitement of the efforts of social historians to widen our understanding of our past and its usefulness in evaluating present, as well as projecting future, societal trends and attitudes. The essays derive from the European experience of the past five centuries, a period of unusually dynamic social change. For between 1500 and the present, along with an abundant assortment of battles and revolutions, the lives of European people were fundamentally transformed.

This Fifth Edition of *The Other Side of Western Civilization,* Volume II, focuses on an unusually rapid series of redefinitions of social institutions and behaviors that have occurred over the past 500 years—as Western society became more urban and industrial and as people, both rural and urban, recast key aspects of their lives. Dealing with these changes and their causes enables us to grasp how different definitions of family, play, or politics shape a larger society. In addition, the book provides an opportunity to measure the considerable progress made by historians in getting to the roots of modern social processes. Unlike most surveys, this volume's major concern is not with the leaders of society, the prominent people whose names and deeds are well known and whose importance is obvious. Instead, it treats the masses of ordinary people, the "inarticulate," whose impact on history has only recently been explored. The intent is to provide some insight into the impact of change on the daily lives of these people, and through this insight to promote a better understanding of the nature and evolution of modern society.

This last point is crucial. Modern society is profoundly shaped by tradition and changes inherited from the past in such basic behaviors as sexuality or illness. We have long been attuned to some understanding of the power of history in affecting political behavior. People are most likely to vote as their parents did; each nation has something of a historically determined political character that shines through even in our day, distinguishing the behavior of, say, the British Labour party from French Communists from American liberal Democrats. We are now coming to understand that other activities have similar historical baggage. What we believe about making love and to an extent even how we do it are partly determined by historical trends that go back at least two centuries. What we think about hospitals is powerfully affected by changes in the position of doctors that began in the later eighteenth century, and more recent changes in hospitals themselves. The history of ordinary people and their daily concerns carries a living freight that helps us understand why we behave and think as we do.

To make valid judgments about our own society and recent trends, we must first analyze and evaluate the nature of premodern society. In addition, we must ascertain the origins of social change: Was change imposed on the masses by forces beyond their control, or did the people actively participate in the construction of modern society? The opening sections represent a number of different interpretations of these issues so that students may assess for themselves the impact of change, the adjustments it promoted, and the resistance it provoked.

Although this collection focuses on only some of the many facets of modern European history, the bibliographies provide numerous suggestions of additional material for further reading.

Some topics in this volume are relatively familiar, for example, the meaning of political involvement in the modern world or the nature of industrial work. Other subjects are only now becoming standard fare: the evolution of the family, the impact of industrialization on women, innovation and continuity in health practices, new attitudes toward madness and deviant social behavior, or new sensitivity to "disgusting" smells. The essays included were chosen with an eye to recent research presented in a stimulating manner and with an awareness of the major analytical problems involved. The purpose is not merely to describe developments in the past, but to assess what they meant and how they emerged. Collectively, the essays suggest important debates over the origins and nature of modern European life. Topics that would hardly have been mentioned ten years ago, such as the history of love, are now supported by a diverse literature. Today the history of women and youth receives more sophisticated treatment as historians reach directly into the lives of women and young people in the past. The history of leisure roles is receiving new attention, perhaps a sign that we are trying to come to terms with the meaning of leisure in our own lives. Work on the limitations of modern attitudes toward death has direct bearing on current reassessments of hospital practices. New topics of this sort offer key insights into the past and vital perspectives on social experiences today, and they are extensively illustrated in the selections in this volume.

Ordinary people are active players in the historical stage. Although the actions and values of most people were undoubtedly affected by the policies set forth by society's leaders (and a number or essays in the book discuss this connection), the masses of people shaped society in part through their own actions. Ultimately, the effort to reach back to the minds of our forebears—to their attitudes toward health, children, death, and protest—represents an exciting chance to place ourselves in context, to understand how, to what extent, and in what directions we are changing beneath the new trappings of an advanced industrial society.

A number of people provided vital assistance in the preparation of this book. I am grateful to those who read and commented on the original plan for this work: J. Kim Munholland, University of Minnesota; James T. Sheehan, Stanford University; Mack Walker, Johns Hopkins University; Edward Shorter, University of Toronto; Donald Sutton, Carnegie Mellon University; John Gillis, Rutgers University; Louise Tilly, The New School; and William Weber, California State University, Long Beach, and Andrew Barnes, Arizona State. Thanks also to the reviewers of this edition: Keith Davie, Nyack College, and Robert Harmon, Elgin Community College. The editorial and production staffs at Harcourt Brace were of great aid. My thanks to Meg for her interest in this project, and for more besides. I am, finally, grateful to the many students, both graduate and undergraduate, at Carnegie Mellon University, who have helped me apply some of the key techniques and interests of social history to the study of the European past.

Peter N. Stearns

CONTENTS

Topical Table of Contents

Women and Gender

Popular Mentalities: Systems of Belief

INTRODUCTION

In the past twenty years, history has become a major source of new knowledge about the ways societies function. In probing unfamiliar facets of the past, social historians add greatly to our understanding of the kinds of human experience that are subject to change, and the wide-ranging effects of such basic forces as new ideas, new technologies, or new population patterns.

ORDINARY PEOPLE IN MODERN EUROPE

Social history involves two major changes in the understanding of the past. First, it focuses on ordinary people as well as elites, because ordinary people have histories of their own which lead to present-day patterns and because ordinary people, by decisions about protest, or birthrates, or witches, help shape the development of whole societies. Second, social history deals with many facets of the human experience—crime, emotion, sex, aging, child rearing—rather than politics, war and formal intellectual life alone. This second aspect of social history expands our understanding of how past trends take shape and affect behaviors today and shows how unfamiliar topics—like the choice of toys—help cause major conventional history events such as war.

Over the past five centuries, Europe has been the scene of fundamental change: The Protestant Reformation, the rise of absolutism, the scientific revolution, the growth of the nation-state, Europe's imperialistic outreach—these are but some of the many markers that dot the historical path. The overwhelming fact is that in the three centuries after 1500 Europe produced the conditions that led to the world's first industrial revolution, while in the two centuries since 1800 the same Europe has been enmeshed in dealing with industrialization's consequences.

These developments are typically handled through a focus on the movers and shakers—the Protestant leaders, the kings, the inventors, perhaps a leading businessman or two. And unquestionably these people were disproportionately involved in Europe's various reshapings. Yet the very scope of the most important changes means that a far larger array of people were involved—not only as victims of changes they could not control, but also as partial creators in their own right. The meaning of basic change similarly extended beyond formal political and intellectual life. The nature of families was altered, so was the nature of work and of play. Emotional standards were also revised, as in the definition of what is disgusting. The essays in this book form an invitation to deal with the sweeping qualities of change in Europe's modern centuries, and to encounter the kind of history that stands near the frontiers of our understanding of how people function amid such change.

Until recently, disregard for most people outside elite ranks and for most activities outside the political sphere left the picture of the past less than half drawn. More to the point, it produced a kind of history that lacked relevance. We do not judge our present on the basis of the doings of the elite and their formal institutions alone, although of course these are vital. When we take our social temperature we think of the stability of families, the condition of women, the fate of the work ethic, the problems of commercialized leisure—in other words, activities whose evaluation depends on knowledge of what various kinds of people, and large numbers of people, are doing. These activities, and the folk who engage in them, have histories. These histories in turn can be as important as, and possibly more interesting than, the narrow accounts of the politics of the past. They can help us to understand ourselves.

Most elites in the past, and most historians until recently, have tended to place ordinary people and their activities in rather simple categories. This does not necessarily mean that they were insensitive to them, but it does suggest that they knew rather little about them. Until the nineteenth century most ordinary people in Europe were peasants, a word that immediately suggests a formless, stolid mass, in terms of the little that most conventional historical surveys say about peasants. According to the simplest definition, peasants normally valued tradition and stability; when they rebelled, as they did occasionally, they did so against change and in the name of the past. But did peasants have a real history, or were they a mindless constant beneath the surface of great events? In fact, from time to time, their economic habits and values, and their definitions of crime and morality changed. Peasant families rose and fell in social standing, often with great rapidity. Many of them were geographically mobile, and welcomed new ideas and methods; some even produced change, despite a certain inclination to resist novelty. We should not be content with merely occasional references to the millions of people who were peasants in Europe as Western civilization developed. Although we cannot know the details of their individual lives and ideas, we must seek to fill in broader generalizations. Simply knowing that a peasantry existed is meaningless unless we also know what trends operated in each major period and area. In some periods peasants regularly practiced infanticide because they could not support their children; in others they were eager to have many children, and not just because of special economic opportunities. Much of modern civilization sprang from the variety and evolution of peasant culture in Western Europe.

In the last two centuries, the masses of people have received more attention, if only because they have impinged more often on the political process. Still, many aspects of their lives are ignored, while others are subjected to judgments by people who are remote from their ordinary existence. Working-class families have decayed, say conservatives who deplore modern times. Many socialists, seeking to condemn the disruptive effects of capitalism, agree. Until recently few scholars even tried to look at the actual evolution of family patterns. With rare exceptions, historians directed their attention to the masses only when the masses rocked the boat, annoying conservatives and giving heart to radicals. But protest, although important, can prove too difficult for people whose lives are so demanding even in the best of times. Consequently, most of the history of people long went unrecorded.

A great deal of historical research is now being devoted to the history of "inarticulate" people. It is now clear that historians have regarded these people as mute in part because they themselves have not tried to listen. To be sure, it is much more difficult to know what "the workers" thought than it is to outline the philosophy of Descartes. Some speculation, some historical intuition is essential if we are to get at popular ideas, which means that there is considerable room for disagreement. The history of the inarticulate remains rife with debate (and it is exciting for this very reason), but already some points are reasonably well established. Aspects of popular behavior can be measured with some precision, even if the outlook that prompted the behavior is more difficult to determine. The common people had ideas, and they left their own kinds of records. In protest, in crime, in family behavior, and in religious practices we can discern the mentality of the masses, even those who lived centuries ago. We can know how many people were born and died, how they structured their families, how often they rioted, perhaps even how they felt about their husbands or children.

Now that historians are looking for them, sources of information about the inarticulate are proving abundant, even overwhelming. These kinds of sources differ from those historians have been accustomed to. Many reveal information only about large groups of people rather than about individuals. But there are individual records as well, which can rescue this new kind of history from impersonality. Criminals, workers, and many others have left statements of what their lives were like and what they thought about.

So we can learn about the common people. But why should we want to? E. P. Thompson has argued eloquently that the common people must be rescued from "the enormous condescension of posterity." He means, among other things, that history, even when written by radical historians, has usually been colored by an upper-class bias that regarded the mass of humanity as a silent lump to be shaped or abused by the elites. This is a valid point, which does not mean that we must appreciate the history of the inarticulate only if we wish to demonstrate democratic or socialist purity.

Because it adds a vast new dimension to what we can learn about people, the history of the inarticulate and of the varied facets of their social lives fascinates many students of the past. To be sure, many historians and history students continue to be most interested in great individuals and great ideas. Some people, however, who could never get excited about the "greats" can now find a new meaning in history through studying the masses and such spheres as work experience or the values of childhood. Others who began with a conventional interest in history may decide that the real meaning of history lies in this new approach and the issues it raises.

Reactions of this sort are personal, of course. But whether or not one is converted to social history as the real channel to the past, there are three reasons why students should know something about it. First, the history of the common people provides one measure of the nature and quality of civilization. Did peasants and artisans gain a new outlook during the Italian Renaissance? Did their lives change, and, if so, did the changes follow the same direction as those that took place in the lives of the political and intellectual elites? Many Enlightenment thinkers believed in humanitarianism and in progress. When and to what extent did such beliefs enter the popular mentality? When the ideas of the Enlightenment were applied to child rearing or the treatment of the insane, did they bring the benefits that "humanitarianism" implies? We cannot fully determine the historical importance of great people and great ideas unless we know what impact they had on the bulk of society. Often the process of disseminating the effects of "greatness" is more important than the initial cause.

Furthermore, we must dispel the notion that the masses of people have not themselves been active agents in history, although perhaps they have reacted to outside forces in many instances. In many of the readings in this volume, this point is implicitly debated. Did the common people adopt more modern attitudes toward work and sex because they were prodded and compelled to do so by forces from above, or did they have, to some extent, their own reasons for changing their outlook? There is no question that the common people had an important voice in determining exactly how they adapted to change. They often resisted change as well, and their resistance was an important historical force in its own right. When masses of people changed their views about their sexual goals or about the number of children they wanted, they played a direct role in altering the course of history.

These arguments apply to the history of the common people at any place and time. There is a final, more specific reason for studying the common people in modern times. The simple fact is that most of us, as ordinary citizens, judge modern society by criteria different from those most historians have used in judging the past. Many of us think of our own time more in terms of divorce rates and crime rates than in terms of, say, artistic achievements. We think in terms of the quality and nature of life of *most people,* and this means that we need histories of precisely these areas. Is the suicide rate rising or falling in modern societies? Has child abuse increased or decreased as families have grown smaller and attitudes toward child rearing have changed? We are approaching the point where we have as much information on patterns of this sort, and as satisfactory explanations for major changes in these patterns as we have long enjoyed for formal political theory and the development of new forms of government.

We return here to the fact that historians long ignored many significant kinds of activities in the past. Until fairly recently, what has been studied in most Western Civilization survey courses, though vitally important, did not provide historical perspectives on many of the features of our own society that are closest to us. Consequently, in a real sense, we could not assess the direction our society is taking. For example, until recently historians have virtually ignored the history of crime, while piling study upon study of the details of diplomatic interchanges. Historians are empiricists. They learn from observation and therefore need sources; sources from diplomats are more abundant than sources from criminals. So historians tend to study diplomats, although it might be argued that criminals are at least as important in shaping society. (Some might even argue that the different labels exaggerate the distinctions between the two groups.)

THE PLACE OF SOCIAL HISTORY

While social history has gained ground steadily in dealing with Europe and other societies, the debate over its place continues. Conservative educators in the United States have been arguing during the past decade that history's task is to pinpoint the great values and great leaders of our civilization, in order to promote consensus among students about political and ethical concepts and to convince them to pattern their lives after history's heroes, who acted rationally to create a better world. The past, in this view, becomes a stable entity, requiring for its interpretation only the filtration system of proper American standards. Social historians, while not denying the importance of dealing with the origins of widely preached values and myths, insist on a wider view that will provide serious historical perspective on a broad array of topics—lest most aspects of our lives seem either timeless or emerging at random. They seek a history that will show society's past warts and all. They argue that exemplary lessons can be found in dealing with the initiatives and reasoned responses of groups of ordinary people as well as with elites.

This is not to say that every fad topic in historical research reflects an important past reality. Some historians who demand that history be "relevant" really mean only that it should reinforce their own views of what should happen in the future. But history is relevant. We can't understand crime today if we don't know about crime in the past, for we will have no sense of direction or means of comparison. We will have no way of knowing if crime is rising, falling, changing in nature, or staying the same. Contemporary comments on crime often assume a historical knowledge. Newspaper accounts, for example, talk about a rising crime rate as an inescapable aspect of modern urban society. This is a historical judgment. But in view of how little is generally known about the history of crime, it is an invalid historical judgment. Modern urbanization has not necessarily produced more crime; the situation is more complex.

The readings in this book stress topics that are not generally considered in historical surveys, such as popular health attitudes and rock and roll, youth, factory workers, and murderers. However it is important to realize that these are not separate strands of history, but parts of a larger social process. Increasingly, social historians, who claim a special interest in the inarticulate and in mundane social activities, are realizing their kinship with students of culture and politics. Topics like crime or the social contributions of housewives should be juxtaposed to more familiar historical phenomena. The modern criminal mentality, for example, may have developed in relationship to Enlightenment ideas about material well-being and individualism. The altered behavior of women in the nineteenth century changed the character of religion; as men left religious activities increasingly to their wives, religion became gentler—less riveted, for example, on condemnation of evil—and certainly more inclined to equate womanhood with purity.

This collection of readings is not, then, merely a sample of interesting insights into the history of contemporary concerns, much less a hymn to unfairly neglected groups in European history. The readings have been selected and organized to relate to some of the larger themes in the history of the last four centuries, amid the transition from an agricultural to an industrial society. The hypothesis used here is that in recent centuries Western society has evolved through a sometimes complex pattern that links various groups, so that some common developments, or at least some common forces, can be seen among paupers and the rich. This pattern also links the various facets of human activity, so that, for example, changes in sexuality bear some relationship to changes in attitudes toward health, and in turn to developments in the world of formal ideas and politics. The idea of some basic modern forces of change gives partial coherence to Europe's recent past and relates it to Europe's present; it might even cast some light on a probable future.

FORCES OF CHANGE IN MODERN EUROPE

The changes that interweave in the development of modern European society can be defined in several ways. Western society became steadily more commercial. Market production stepped up in the sixteenth century, as Europe's position in international trade advanced. More commercial experience and wealth parlayed into outright industrialization around 1800. New technologies responded to market opportunities and spurred production further, and a growing number of workers sold their labor for a market-determined wage. Commercialization entered a new phase in the late nineteenth century with the development of varied consumer interests, as more Europeans sought expression through acquisition of material goods.

Another change involved growing literacy, which altered popular culture in fundamental ways. Europe's printing presses spread reading materials by the sixteenth century, and Protestantism encouraged reading. By the eighteenth century a large minority of Europeans could read, and then in the nineteenth century mass school systems formalized the process. Reading caused habits and methods of thought to change, and allowed for exposure to new ideas.

Expansion of the central state is a third underlying change. By the seventeenth century, governments gained greater ability to regulate economic activity. In the eighteenth century bureaucrats helped prompt agricultural changes, such as the adoption of the potato as a staple crop, in the interest of promoting population growth. Governments turned to mass military recruitment and to the provision of education, from the French Revolution of 1789 onward. By the late nineteenth century they began to develop welfare systems. During the nineteenth century, policing also expanded and state-run prison systems, developed earlier, redefined the state's punishments for crime.

The idea of several basic forces, extending over a considerable timespan, explains some of the common developments of European society over the past five centuries. Commercialization, the cultural impact of growing literacy and government expansion are, however, quite general categories. They changed in specific manifestations in different periods, and they were often supplemented by other basic forces such as massive population growth (as in the eighteenth century) or the technological upheavals of the industrial revolution or, in our own century, the shattering effects of global wars.

At what point did the basic processes of change fundamentally alter the institutions of an agricultural society? We know that it was not until around 1800 that the Western European countries began to industrialize and urbanize, that is, to move away from traditional patterns in clearly measurable ways.

But, increasingly, some historians are claiming that before this, indeed as a precondition for outright industrialization, values were altered; people, or at least some people in key positions, began to think in new ways, to innovate—for example, in the way they raised children. These historians push the processes of basic change back to the seventeenth century or even before. But can one talk of a coherent set of trends spanning such a long and diverse period, that began with changes such as commercialization or shifts in popular outlook so difficult to pin down and measure? A key issue involves the relationship between developments in the sixteenth and seventeenth centuries, like the more commercial economy, and the later formation of an industrial society. Some historians argue that it is better to look at each period of modern European social history, rather than claiming more durable basic trends.

Periodization adds several related issues. Are there definite stages in the key processes of change? The idea of stages of industrialization has some support: A period of early technological experimentation and limited introduction of factories is followed by the fuller application of relevant technology, with appropriate levels of urbanization, business organization, and so on. But the big changes, because they are so much more amorphous in including basic behavior patterns and values, may not lend themselves to this kind of approach. How, for example, does the twentieth century fit after the nineteenth? Are we witnessing continuation of the transforming trends, a souring of the process, or a reversion to older, premodern patterns? The essays in this book offer support for all of these views. Twentieth-century women may be seen as entering the modern world in new ways, and gaining a more clearly modern mentality in the process. Or, as another judgment holds, the contemporary family, after considerable innovation and disruption in the nineteenth century, is returning to something like a preindustrial structure, notably when both husband and wife participate in economic production as they did in the seventeenth century but did not in the nineteenth. A basic pattern of change would seem scarcely applicable in this view, as family behaviors and roles prove more cyclical than anything else.

A definition of the basic forces of change encounters geographical objections as well, even within Western society. How different was the English process from the French or the German pattern? How does one fit specific national phenomena—German Nazism, or the English public school experience—into a single package? The essays in this collection deal with single countries or regions, or with a number of areas, in a variety of ways. In combination, they do suggest that some basic changes still override national boundaries. But it is certainly legitimate to argue, as many historians would, that a region or nation is the key unit for analysis because it puts its own vital stamp on general phenomena such as new cities, factory industries, or the concept of adolescence. To these historians, the trees may be far more important than the woods.

But the overriding issue surrounding Europe's social transformation involves the question of whether trends in diverse areas of human activity relate, or whether it is more accurate to see a number of changes, some of them operating according to distinctive timetables, occurring independently. Leisure is a case in point. Some observers see leisure as a distinctly modern activity, different from traditional recreation in being open to freer choice and based on more immediate gratifications. They view this new leisure as intimately related to other modern characteristics, including the rhythms of work, the attitudes engendered by commercial economic forms, and the personality goals resulting from changes in cultural standards. Other observers interpret leisure differently. Some highlight changes, but see no special connection to other aspects of modern history; leisure history begets its own dynamic. Still others emphasize vast continuities from the preindustrial past, expressing traditional social needs in giving outlets to youth, to male violence, and to community cohesion. Leisure's distinctive history, in other words, cannot necessarily be packaged along with other developments, such as industrialization or an expanding state. But if major trends are not intimately related, and if combinations of change and continuity vary widely from one facet of society to another, can one argue for the existence of any particular pattern amid the complexities of modern European social history?

One approach to this problem suggests a distinction between structural and behavioral changes—that is, between changes in the human environment (urbanization, industrialization) and changes in the way people act, particularly in private areas over which they have the most control, and the values they apply to their acts and to their environment. There is no question that the framework of life has greatly changed since the seventeenth century, and that many of the changes are interlinked. Western society has industrialized, moved to the cities, developed greater wealth, more bureaucratic apparatus, higher literacy and smaller families. Expanded institutions, notably the modern state and the business corporation, try to induce certain kinds of thought in their citizens through education, advertising and other means. Changes result in the values that are judged acceptable. "Modern" opinion also looks down on beliefs in magic or uncouth eating or evacuatory habits. Broadly speaking, each aspect of this structural and opinion-molding change seems to involve the others, although the precise mix may vary from one society or one period to the next.

The essays in this book do not deal primarily with structural changes, however, but with the more complex issue of how, or whether, behavior and attitudes have changed. Here, some theorists, particularly proponents of change labeled "modernization," hold that, as part of structural transformation, people become more rationalistic, individualized, and acquisitive. There is a modern personality that progressively unfolds along with structural changes, both as cause and as result. But how do values of this sort apply to groups such as workers or youth, and to activities such as leisure? Does the structure of modern society compel a particular kind of behavior on the part of women? The basic questions are these: Did modern European history embrace a process by which new standard personalities have been produced over the last few centuries? Is there some coherence to the interaction of various groups in modern society, in their different activities, relating one to another and to modern structures? We cannot expect simplicity. Changes of outlook and behavior may reach some groups before others (the periodization problem again), and may take different, precise forms from one segment of society to another. Will modern men and women turn out to share the same viewpoint and, with due qualifications for biology, behavior forms? Or should we expect distinct gender patterns in modern society? And again, some activities, possibly some definable groups, may best be seen in a different kind of interaction with modern structures, moving in a cyclical fashion, or not changing at all.

Clearly, in addition to issues of variation by time period and geographical location, the course of change in Europe over the past five centuries involves fundamental social differentiations. At key points, men and women become less alike in roles and ascribed character. Even more persistently, there was a division in the social classes between the owners and the wage laborers, and the well schooled and the barely schooled. Lower classes might learn to feign the values expected of them in public, but they hardly changed in lockstep with their social superiors. Modern society's structural trends must then be weighed against a durable tendency to divide, and so to produce distinctive, even mutually hostile, experiences and outlooks.

With all this undeniable complexity, why not just give up on the search for some coherence in the changes that have moved through Europe over the past five centuries? Some scholars clearly have done so. They talk of specific changes, not a grand pattern. They warn of the danger in seeing direction in history instead of the hodgepodge that the past really is. (How, for example, can we speak in the same breath of the expansion of bureaucracy and development of greater individualism in Western personalities?) European civilization, even before modern times, has undeniably tended to see a direction in history, moving toward a final coming of Christ, a better society, new knowledge, improved medicine—the goals vary greatly, but the desire for a goal is deep within us. Perhaps, if we were honest, we could admit that the past gives us no direction or real interconnectedness among our various activities. But there is a longing to see some sense or some pattern to history. And just possibly, a pattern, however complex, really has emerged. A careful reading of the essays in this collection will give some basis for judgment.

THE ISSUE OF PROGRESS

Whether fully coherent or not in long-term direction and mutual relationship, the changes that have described the modern European experience raise obvious questions of causation. Which came first: Did structures change, forcing or encouraging people to think differently, or did some tentative changes in ideas prompt developments such as industrialization? Several of the selections in this book go beyond descriptive summary to an assessment of cause, which includes careful attention to those elements of preindustrial society that could permit change.

Even more pervasive is the issue of the quality of change. Is contemporary Europe a better or a worse place than its preindustrial ancestor? Many historians, again with the partisans of modernization theory in the fore, have been optimists: modern society is not just different from, but better than, traditional society. Many other analysts, while implicitly agreeing that modernization has distinguished contemporary society from past society in coherent and definable ways, are profoundly pessimistic. We have changed, but we have lost in basic human values. Consequently, a study of the impact of basic change on the common people—of Europe or elsewhere—invites some value judgments. Many modern people have been conditioned to believe that change means progress. This is profoundly different from the traditional outlook, which usually looked to the past for standards. Peasants tended to believe that rural society had been better in past ages; artisans looked back to the ideals of the early guilds. Most of the ideologies developed since the eighteenth century, however, including formal socialist thought, look to the future in progressive terms. This means that we may be too quick—in dealing with a change away from rural tradition—to praise, or at least to find the development both natural and understandable. For example, one important aspect of industrialization is the development of a belief in the possibility and desirability of material progress, for oneself as well as for society as a whole. Most Americans probably find this a good change, at least when contrasted with the resignation and stagnancy of a more traditional peasant-like view. A minority—those concerned about the ecological damage that material progress can cause, for instance—would find this aspect of modern history dangerous. But almost everyone would find it natural. It's hard for us to believe that people might think anything else. Economic thought from the early nineteenth century onward has assumed that the goal of "economic man" is to maximize his wealth. Yet, applied to most people even in the nineteenth century, this is not a proper historical view. Interest in material improvement constituted a profound change in the popular mentality. It came slowly and continues to be modified by other goals, some of them profoundly traditional. The question of evaluation, like the historical analysis of change, is complex.

Our focus on the common people may appeal to a different set of values, leading to a condemnation of trends within modern society itself. Arguments over the effects of industrialization and urban growth on the lower classes, for example, began a century and a half ago, and they continue today. Historians still debate whether or not material conditions improved during the first stage of British industrialization—and the topic is significant in the history of any area undergoing the initial stages of an industrial revolution. Conditions in such a formative stage of working-class life may have influenced worker outlook to such an extent that attitudes and behavior persisted even after the material setting changed. If one dislikes contemporary society, it is easy to emphasize how much people have suffered since its inception. In the debates over the British standard of living, historians who favor capitalism and are convinced of the essential soundness of the modern world generally try to show that conditions were improving even during early industrialization. Leftist historians, who dislike capitalism and commiserate with the workers, invariably look for signs of deterioration. Note that the connection between political judgment and historical judgment is not entirely logical. One could well argue that capitalism has proved a good thing in the long run and that modern life is lovely, even for the workers, while admitting that in the first stage of industrialization conditions deteriorated. Or one could urge the need for fundamental reforms in modern life while admitting that conditions have improved somewhat compared with preindustrial times. Obviously, ideological commitments can predetermine an approach—and most of us have an ideology, even if it is not neatly labeled. Changes in fashion can also change our historical perspective. Once, historians viewed medical change as a clear story of progress; now many pick at doctors' exaggerated claims as a new source of enslavement to authority. Perspectives change quickly, as do historical trends, which means that it may be impossible to offer a simple characterization of any development affecting the common people during modern processes of change. A sense of debate over key issues is vital to intelligent study.

The readings that follow present a variety of approaches, some commending the liberating aspects of modern trends, others stressing their deterioration. Few historians who deal with these vital topics content themselves with simply saying that things have changed, which might be the most objective view. They generally try to assess the quality of that change. Try to study the modern history of women, for example, without asking whether their status has improved or worsened. Many now argue that with industrialization and the decline of the family as a productive unit, woman's inferior status became more pronounced, because her economic utility was less obvious and her dependence on her husband greater. Others point to better education and the declining birthrate as indications of improvements in woman's lot.

Students of history must make up their own minds about trends. Several preliminary points should be kept in mind in dealing with the special province of social history. First, most historians drawn to the study of the common people have been sympathetic. Some have tended to dwell on the hardships of their subjects, who they see as having been victimized by some outside force—workers by capitalists, women by men, and so on. In other cases, however, historians have stressed how creatively the common people adjusted to their situations, highlighting values they used and changed in doing so. Social historians generally insist on viewing the common people as an active force, not just in protest—though this is a significant aspect of their lives—but also in shaping family structure, recreational patterns, and so on. This view is quite consistent with an emphasis on the hardships of life, but it goes beyond a dreary catalogue of exploitation. Almost no change is simply imposed on ordinary people without some reaction and mutual adjustment.

The issue of baseline is also crucial: Evaluation of change depends on assessment of prior conditions. Whether or not one is a historian, it is impossible to study modern trends without asking "where from?"—which is of course a historical question. Any journalist or politician who claims that values of behavior patterns are changing, that violence is rising or falling, or that a situation is unprecedented is making a historical judgment. Such a judgment should be made intelligently. Some of the judgments are short-term, of course. It is possible and useful to compare crime rates and patterns of the 1960s with those of the 1920s. But the larger evaluations—those, for example, which concern the nature of industrial life or of urban people—should involve a knowledge of the premodern world. We have no other way to assess the direction of change. We hear of the loosening of family ties. We therefore assume that premodern families were closeknit and jolly—but has the subject really been studied by those who claim a new "modern" collapse? Divorce, for example, is a rather new institution, but does it signify a really new problem in family life or does it represent a new answer to a persistent tension? We must look at the past to find out. We might avoid a lot of nonsense from advocates of the brand new as well as from critics of the present if we required every statement of "never before" or "a sign of these troubled times"—unquestionably judgments of the present in terms of the past—to be backed by solid historical evidence. This book stems from the need to approach key trends in modern life in the only way such trends can really be understood, by examining how they relate to their antecedents.

TOPICS AND PERIODS

The book obviously does not cover all the major topics in the history of the common people during the modern centuries. It largely avoids the study of modern states and institutional structures, vital topics in their own right, in favor of activities normally closer to the common people. Even many of the topics dealt with in this book have only been outlined. There is insufficient information on some of them; there is a great disagreement on others. We are not in total ignorance, however, and the assessment of Europe's transformation from agricultural to industrial society in its various ramifications is so essential that we cannot constantly beg off on grounds of insufficient data. If we are to understand ourselves and our society, we must attempt to establish a genuine historical view of such topics as the evolution of family emotions or the situation of youth. Confusing signals and outright disagreement add spice to our effort to know.

The readings are arranged more or less chronologically, but they can also be grouped into topics that cover essential aspects of the formation of Europe's modern experience. Readings on rural society discuss the nature of preindustrial life and allow an assessment of the changes in the countryside in recent times. A section on modern attitudes presents varying interpretations of our current status. Two large groupings of the inarticulate, women and workers, receive extensive treatment. Children and youth are considered as well. The family is elaborately studied, for, although its nature has changed in a number of aspects, it remains a basic institution in the lives of most people. The family must also be understood if we are to comprehend what values children bring into adulthood: if new personality types emerged as one facet of Europe's successive transformations, then new child-raising practices must be involved. Readings on education and popular culture deal both with the formal values taught to the lower classes and with new and old types of recreation that played a growing role in life outside of work. Health and death practices, a new and exciting area of social history, receive explicit attention. Discussions of crime and insanity consider changes in forms of individual protest and maladjustment and how modern society defines deviance. Readings on protest concern the evolution of the forms and goals of collective action.

The collection of readings focuses primarily on Western and Central Europe, where industrial society first emerged. Patterns of change in Eastern and Southern Europe, though not totally dissimilar, display many different features, in part because they developed at different times and from different traditional bases. Even in Western Europe, however, national and regional variations are extensive at any point in time. The readings that follow do not, for the most part, explicitly compare changes among different nations or regions, for comparative analysis is still in its infancy. The agenda is clear, however, for the bolder students: Are trends in industrial France more French than industrial, and how can the two contexts be sorted out?

The essays in the collection are grouped in several time periods. Each period offers specific features: tensions over religious divisions and witchcraft, fundamental to the seventeenth century, have dissipated by the nineteenth century, when political divisions and the impact of industrialization hold center stage.

It is not easy to pinpoint when key breaks occur because social history remains a fairly recent achievement, and because social historians think in terms of changes in patterns of thought or behavior more than in terms of decisive events. Conventional periodization (1715–1763, 1870–1914, and so on) has little relevance, because most people's lives were not always decisively shaped by the doings of diplomats and politicians. Indeed, we must seek a decade or more in which some measurable change occurred—when rapid population growth began or waned, for example—rather than a single year. The chronological organization of this book is meant to be loose and suggestive, but it does provide a necessary framework. The first section, 1550–1750, allows an understanding of the society and the traditions that were to change. But during the period itself there were important developments that were significant in their own right. Between 1750 and 1850 the confrontation between tradition and change was extremely intense. Industrialization began but was not yet dominant, while the attitudes of ordinary people began to take more modern form. Between 1850 and 1914 the nature of industrial society became clearer. Problems of adaptation remained, but they were more subtle. To many Europeans, at least in retrospect, this period seemed a golden age. However, those who lived through it, outside of the upper classes, may have judged it differently. The period from 1918 to the present opened with the intense dislocation caused by the First World War. The confused nature of European society between the two world wars is important in its contribution to more enduring social trends. But the overriding theme of the twentieth century is the extent to which a new society is taking shape and what kind of society it is. Many observers talk of a postmodern or postindustrial age; we must discover what this means in human terms. There is a strong temptation to see our own age as one of unprecedented change—for modern people are attuned to look for change; but a good historical understanding of prior developments allows us to place these claims in context, for more basic changes may well have occurred earlier. Given a sense of the direction of modern trends we might even forecast future prospects. What, for example, is the probable fate of the family as the contemporary context evolves?

USING SOCIAL HISTORY

While the history of the common people is a new kind of history, it is not a total departure from the traditional study of history. It involves testing many conventional historical themes to see how major ideas and political forms affected the masses. Therefore, although the readings do consider some unusual subjects, they can, and should, be linked to the more obvious developments in modern European history. Rural society was clearly affected by religious doctrine and organization. The spread of popular education involved a deliberate attempt to inculcate in the peasant attitudes such as nationalism, liberalism, and a belief in science and progress. New forms of protest related to changes in political ideology, most obviously the rise of socialism. The world that workers lived in was conditioned by the actions of the state and of employers. These effects can in turn be assessed in terms of liberalism and other political doctrines. Connections of this sort are seldom simple. One cannot assume that liberal ideas about the treatment of workers fully represent the actual ideas of employers, even employers who claimed to be liberal. But the connections are there, and they clearly relate the history of the common people to history in general. Other links can be found as well. We will see how the rise of rationalism changed the definition of madness and, therefore, the attitudes toward the treatment of insanity. Changes in the family or in sexual behavior cannot be understood solely in terms of formal ideas or political activities, but they are not entirely independent either. By the late eighteenth century, people in Europe seemed to have gained a new interest in romantic and sexual love. Surely this must have helped cause the rise of cultural Romanticism, or at least that aspect which stressed human emotions. Historians deepen their understanding of the common themes in political and intellectual history by studying the relationship of these themes with the world of the common people.

One of the challenges many social historians are increasingly accepting involves testing relationships between familiar developments—the rise of science, or the post-World War II economic revival of Germany—and sociohistorical facets such as witchcraft or popular music. They insist only on a two-way street: not just scientists causing the decline of witchcraft prosecutions, but new ideas about witches helping to cause science; and not just the rise of science as the ultimate textbook focus, the criterion for what's culturally important in the early modern period, but changes in views about the poor and women as well.

Students of the basic processes of modern society are trying to fathom what we have become, and why. The quest is one of the most exciting developments in historical study. It is vital not to lose sight of some basic goals. The complexities of analysis, in dealing with Europe's modern transformations, are daunting and the specific topics that now form part of serious history constitute a challenging array. The task of incorporating specific research findings into a larger understanding of the past is not easy. Yet we know that, over the past five centuries, Europe has changed profoundly, and we can agree on some of the key changes. We know also that there are some links, however fragile and debatable, among different facets of change and from one major period to the next. Modern Europe's development pulls different groups in clashing, sometimes contradictory directions. We still cannot be sure whether contemporary society has become too complex in stretching individuals between needs for organizational conformity (one clear modern trend) and urgent promptings to seek individual expression (another clear modern trend). The problem of coherence is not resolved, but, by looking at European social change, we can gain some sense of what the ingredients of the problem are.

More broadly, social history raises significant challenges in dealing with the nature of change, along with a host of specific debates.

The first challenge is the expansion of history's reach to embrace an ever-widening definition of what the human experience is all about and how it has been shaped through the past. In this sense, history becomes a vital source of new social knowledge. The second challenge follows from the perennial need to draw together, to find basic causes and key relationships so that the processes of change remain intelligible. In this case, history becomes a vital source of new synthesis and theory. Advances are being made on both fronts, in what has become an unusually innovative period in historical research—though there is always more to be done. Historical study has become a generator, both of new information and of new understanding about how people and their social institutions move through time. The boundaries expand steadily.

Two final points: social history is a restless type of history, still proving the boundaries. Selections in this edition reflect growing interest in, and knowledge about, gender and beliefs and values—this last a link between social history and a new kind of cultural history applied to ordinary people and a new approach to the growing array of topics social historians have carved out. Subjects explored a generation ago, in social history's first surge, are also being revisited, generating new understandings about the impact of social change: Reinterpretation of the meaning of changing patterns of murder, or the pace of the decline of witchcraft belief, are cases in point. Second, social history is, or can be, impatient with conventional geographical boundaries. Social historians do local studies as often as national—for the nation is not always a real social unit. They increasingly push the definition of Western Europe to include countries like Spain or Denmark, where basic social processes can be examined, as well as in France, Germany, or Britain. And, if too often implicitly, they compare one society with another.

Attention to European social history, including the expanding analyses of past change, is important for understanding the development of one of the world's important civilizations (though not the only one), still widely influential in the contemporary world. It also challenges our understanding of the United States, where closely similar social developments have occurred but not, usually, in exactly the same ways. In addition to analyzing West European society for its own sake, we can use it as a social mirror as we talk about crime, or rock and roll, or changes in women's conditions on our side of the Atlantic.

BIBLIOGRAPHY

A bibliography follows the introduction to each section, to provide further reading on each of the topics covered. A recent survey effort, with rich detail, is George Duby, ed., *History of Private Life*. See also Peter N. Stearns, *Life and Society in the West,* vol. 2 (San Diego, 1988). For the first part of the period, Fernand Braudel, *The Mediterranean and the Mediterranean World in the Age of Philip II* (2 vols), (New York, 1972), constitutes a major study; see also Braudel's *Capitalism and Material Life* (New York, 1974). Henry Kamen, *The Iron Century: Social Change in Europe 1550–1660* (New York, 1971), stresses developments among the lower classes. New work on economic change prior to the industrial revolution introduces the vital concept of "protoindustrialization," which has an important bearing on early modern Europe, is that of Peter Kriedte, Hans Medick, and J. Schlumbohm, *Industrialization Before Industrialization* (Cambridge, England, 1981). Another approach, related to economic development though with different political implications, is Immanuel Wallerstein's world-systems theory, *The Modern World System: Capitalist Agriculture and the Origins of the European World Economy in the 16th Century* (New York, 1974) and *The Capitalist World Economy* (Cambridge, England, 1979).

Important works on industrialization include David Landes, *The Unbound Prometheus: Technological Change and Industrial Development in Western Europe from 1750 to the Present* (New York, 1969), and Peter N. Stearns, *The Industrial Revolution in World History* (Boulder, CO, 1988). A more general survey is Peter N. Stearns and Herrick Chapman, *European Society in Upheaval,* 3rd ed. (New York, 1991). On preindustrial social change, see Sheldon Watts, *A Social History of Western Europe, 1450–1720* (Dover, NH, 1984).

A distinctive approach to modern European history in terms of "big changes" rather than modernization is Charles Tilly's *Big Structures, Large Processes, Huge Comparisons* (New York, 1985).

See also Tilly's essay in Oliver Zunz, ed., *Reliving the Past: The Worlds of Social History* (Chapel Hill, NC, 1985).

Jan Steen, The Egg Dance. *Oil on canvas.*

I

PREINDUSTRIAL PEOPLE

1550–1750

PREINDUSTRIAL PEOPLE

Sociohistorical work on the period 1550–1750 in Western Europe—often called the early modern period—has revealed unexpected richness and complexity. Shaped in part by the more familiar developments in politics, such as the rise of absolutism, and religious and scientific change, ordinary Europeans, in various aspects of their lives, defined a distinctive mixture of old and new features, of anxieties and growing confidence. The period reflected important traditions of a predominantly rural society. It generated some special crises of its own, such as the revealing witchcraft hysteria. Finally, it served as the seedbed for important changes in basic popular habits and beliefs.

With this mixture of currents, Europe between 1500 and 1750 presents a series of fascinating contrasts. European society was traditionally agricultural. Essentially customary patterns of behavior shine through not only in the sixteenth century, but even in the early eighteenth century. By then, indeed, ordinary people were in some ways reviving traditions, such as leisure time, that had been challenged by religious reformers or magistrates concerned with public order.

European society was also changing rapidly, not simply by the early eighteenth century, but even during the sixteenth century. Religious changes counted for more than formal affiliations; they cut into popular beliefs in many ways. Growing literacy and commercialism ushered in important and wide-ranging shifts in social institutions. Some of these changes suggested preparations for more recent developments.

European society, finally, was undergoing some special stresses unique to the era. While the end of major witchcraft trials, around 1700, is an important shift, suggesting a more rational outlook, it is also vital to realize that intense persecutions of witches rose in the sixteenth and early seventeenth century—they had not been part of medieval tradition. Changes in women's work roles resulted from specific features of early modern cities and their still largely precapitalistic economies.

At the same time, positions within the family expanded. In developments of this sort, as in the major series of popular protests that crested around 1648, some distinctive strains developed that must be understood as part of an important and unique period in Europe's social history.

In many ways, the traditional features of Europe's early modern society seem to be the antithesis of trends that took shape later, but even traditionalism must be painted with care. The most familiar terms suggest its distance from modernity: static; wedded to the past; superstitious; and of course, in terms of structure, poor; agricultural; and politically aristocratic and/or monarchical. Can premodern society be characterized so neatly? Many historians, arguing that it cannot, point to great regional variations, even within Western Europe, as well as great periodic fluctuations in the status of individuals and groups. They would find the label traditionalist a vast oversimplifier.

If some complex definition of Europe as a traditional society is possible, however, then other questions follow: Was preindustrial society a pleasant or unpleasant place? Did preindustrial society have characteristics so valuable, perhaps even so natural to the human species, that we should look for attempts to preserve them amid the later structural changes that took shape after 1750? In other words, we might assess our preindustrial past not simply as a contrast to our own day, but as the source of much that remains viable in areas such as family life.

The idea that fundamental changes began to emerge during the sixteenth and seventeenth centuries challenges the static-traditionalist approach, and possibly a nostalgic search for timeless rural values as well. It also raises questions about primacy. Some historians argue for definable, structural shifts as sources of innovations: Europe's new position in world commerce and ensuing internal commercialization, or the growth of the state. Other historians, equally bent on going beyond purely conventional coverage of the period, emphasize changes in attitudes or popular mentalities.

Questions about the real nature of Europe's traditions and about the nature and sources of basic change have focused new attention on the early modern centuries on the part of social historians. Once bedazzled by the obvious link between the industrial revolution and the obvious concerns of the newer kind of history with ordinary people and the diverse facets of social experience, social historians have been extending their chronology. The more subtle issues of early modern Europe draw increasingly sophisticated research. The most obvious task is to discover what was being altered in Europe's social relationships, and what was being maintained; but there is also an eye cocked for the possible links between trends at this point and subsequent upheavals, including those attached to industrialization.

Since the end of the Middle Ages, Europe had witnessed important shifts in population levels, social structure, and popular culture. By the sixteenth and seventeenth centuries, some of the changes began to point toward the formation of modern society. Redefinitions of formal institutions and ideas are familiar enough. Under absolutism, governments became more centralized and efficient. Most of these governments encouraged economic change, if only in the interest of augmenting the tax base for the royal coffers.

During the seventeenth and eighteenth centuries, the tone of intellectual life was dramatically altered. Leading intellectuals, vaunting humanity's power to reason and the possibility of progress, urged further scientific and technological advances. The new world of the intellectuals was aggressively secular. God and religion receded in importance; in some cases, they were directly attacked. The scientific revolution merged into the new general Enlightenment.

Somewhat apart from both government and intellectuals, a variety of businessmen and landowners, primarily in Great Britain and Holland, were experimenting with new farming and manufacturing techniques as well as new forms of economic organization. New crops, drainage methods, and farming equipment began to increase agricultural production. Many landowners—and not just those who directed great estates—began to produce primarily for sales to distant markets. In business, the most spectacular innovators were the merchants who organized great trading companies for worldwide commerce. New systems of investing and accounting developed. Manufacturing changed more slowly, but by the eighteenth century, manufacturers were rapidly extending the systems of rural production, drawing hundreds of thousands of peasants into a new market system. The manufacturers provided raw materials and sold the finished products. Rural workers set up looms or spindles in their homes and produced what they were told to produce. Never before had so many people been involved in a capitalistic production system. Some historians use the term "protoindustrial" to denote these developments, noting how they brought about new consumer and sexual behavior patterns.

Historians still debate the relative importance and interconnections of governments, intellectuals, and entrepreneurs as obvious and significant sources of change. Many new entrepreneurs, for example, knew little about scientific discoveries or the growing belief in progress. They increased industrial production by applying new techniques, but most of the techniques were devised by artisan-tinkerers. It is more likely that the success of the new technology led manufacturers to believe in science and progress rather than the other way around.

The essays that follow, however, deal primarily with groups that were remote from the most obvious sources of change. The majority of Europe's preindustrial people were rural; the peasantry, the archetypical preindustrial group, was wedded to a belief in a stable society. The rural population was diverse, including landowning peasants, near-landless cottagers, and artisans. It was not attached to all existing structures, but was suspicious of outsiders and possessed many deeply rooted traditions. Here, too, however, important changes were taking place. Ordinary people could take the lead too, for example in family life or economic behavior.

Even a brief evocation of Europe's preindustrial people returns us to three vital and related issues. First, in order to assess the impact of change, both in the early modern centuries and later on, we must make a judgment about the nature of preindustrial life. If rural life was in fact comfortable and secure, the advent of industrialization and urban life must have been profoundly disruptive. If, on the other hand, rural life was marked by persistent tension and frustration, perhaps change was welcome. (We need not regard the preindustrial masses as homogeneous; certain areas, personality types, or even age groups may have been particularly restless.)

Second, we must deal with the extent to which the common people of Western Europe actively contributed to change. We might assume that the common people were forced into new political and economic roles by the state, the new philosophers, and the pioneering businessmen, and many social historians do see a new war between elites and traditional masses taking shape by 1650. This approach is presumably most compatible with a belief that change imposed profound dislocation on most people. But perhaps some shifts were spontaneous, stemming from the values of the common people themselves. During the eighteenth century, for example, the spread of domestic manufacturing, although sponsored in part by urban capitalists, found a quick response in the countryside. Rural workers learned new consumption habits. They adopted more urban styles of dress and bought processed food products such as tea and sugar. This was the first step in a new esteem for material acquisitions that would ultimately prove vital to the industrialization process. Family patterns also changed as the family took on new entertainment functions beyond its primary production role.

In other words, the lower classes in preindustrial Western Europe may have been ripe for change. Although no one can deny that disruption was involved—bringing not only material hardship, but intense psychic stress—the common people may have been more than passive victims in the modernization process. Indeed, some of the key innovators stemmed from their ranks. The ancestors of many dynamic factory owners of the early nineteenth century were peasants and artisans. Their rise was unusual, but it may have drawn on a more widely shared openness to change that served to cushion the shock for those who remained in the lower classes.

Finally, there is the question of the extent of change. Historians have uncovered more dynamism in the early modern centuries—the centuries right before industrialization—than was expected. The protoindustrialization concept is one expression of this. Discoveries about the unexpected impacts of religious developments like the Protestant-Catholic split, beyond formal church organizations, form another category—one in which, again, ordinary people are actors, not merely acted upon. Developments once attributed to later decades—the age of political and industrial revolution around 1800, for example—now find initial statements in this previous period.

So we are trying to determine both the distance ordinary Europeans had to travel to accept new trends and the extent to which they launched the process themselves in the seventeenth and eighteenth centuries. Obviously, any discussion of the values of the "common" people is chancy, even for the present day. For the premodern period, historians must use very fragmentary records. In a few cases there is good statistical evidence on behavior patterns—size of families, for example—but the motives and values that gave rise to the patterns are open to speculation.

Distinctiveness as a period—different from more modern times—and significant change are not incompatible of course, but the combination is complex, and most historians end up primarily emphasizing one theme or the other. At the same time, another interpretive angle involves stressing aspects of preindustrial society that are shared with other societies and with the modern West—aspects that relate to more durable features of the human condition, such as urban prostitution or the intensity of love for children. Again, questions of combining disparate vantage points and of overall emphasis provide diverse opportunities for interpretation and the organization of research data.

Consequently, the historian's own preconceptions assume added importance. There has been a frequent tendency to idealize the past. As far back as the beginning of the nineteenth century, many people turned to the preindustrial past for solace from the evils of the present. Even late into the nineteenth century, workers retained a nostalgia for the countryside, although they seldom acted on it. In the United States, as in Europe, "back to the land" impulses continue to appear, based at least in part on a belief in the purity and simplicity of preindustrial life. Not surprisingly, many historians who try to assess this existence have similar yearnings, in contrast to most modernization theorists who point to the drawbacks of traditional conditions and ideas.

Despite problems of adequate evidence and clashing biases, the study of preindustrial society is being actively pursued on a number of fronts. Our knowledge is increasing. We can already draw some tentative conclusions about why a new kind of society began on the shores of the Atlantic, in Western Europe and North America, and what impact it had on the people.

BIBLIOGRAPHY

An excellent introduction to the social history of the early modern period is Sheldon Watts, *Social History of Western Europe, 1450–1720* (1984). See also John Merriman, *Modern Europe* (2 vols., New York, 1996). Studies of preindustrial rural society are varied. For France, classic studies include Emmanuel Le Roy Ladurie, *The Peasants of Languedoc* (Urbana, IL, 1974); Marc Bloch, *French Rural History* (Berkeley, 1970); and Pierre Goubert, *Louis XIV and Twenty Million Frenchmen* (New York, 1969). On England, Alan MacFarlane in *The Origins of English Individualism* (New York, 1979) and *The Culture of Capitalism* (London, 1987) argues for a distinctive English rural history; also, Bary Reay, *Microhistories: Demography, Society, and Culture in Rural England 1800–1930* (Cambridge, 1996). For one aspect of material culture, see Olwen Hufton, *The Poor of Eighteenth Century France* (New York, 1975). Although it deals with the end of the eighteenth century, Charles Tilly, *The Vendée* (New York, 1967), shows the impact of economic change on peasants and the readiness of some to come to grips with it in contrast to the bitter resistance of others—a division that depended on an earlier exposure to a market economy. Finally, for an effort at a general statement on the nature of the peasantry, see Eric Wolf, *Peasants* (Englewood Cliffs, NJ, 1966).

On preindustrial population behavior, see E. A. Wrigley, *Population and History* (New York, 1969); Carlo Cipolla, *Economic History of World Population* (Baltimore, 1962); E. A. Wrigley and R. H. Schofield, *The Population History of England 1541–1871* (Cambridge, MA, 1982); and O. J. Willigan and Katherine Lynch, *Sources and Methods of Historical Demography* (New York, 1982).

For an understanding of premodern attitudes, including popular religion and superstition, see Christopher Hill, *The World Turned Upside Down: Radical Ideas during the English Revolution* (New York, 1972); Alan MacFarlane, *The Family Life of Ralph Josselin* (New York, 1970), and *Witchcraft in Tudor and Stuart England* (New York, 1978); and Natalie Davis, *Society and Culture in Early Modern France* (Stanford, 1975). An interesting effort to connect new ideas with early industrial technology is A. E. Musson and Eric Robinson, *Science and Technology in the Industrial Revolution* (Toronto, 1969).

Key studies in preindustrial mentalities include Keith Thomas, *Religion and the Decline of Magic* (New York, 1971), Peter Burke, *Popular Culture in Early Modern Europe* (New York, 1978); Edmund Leites, *The Puritan Conscience and Modern Sexuality* (New Haven, CT, 1986); David Sabean, *Power in the Blood: Popular Culture and Village Discourse in Early Modern Germany* (New York, 1984); and Robert Darnton, *The Great Cat Massacre* (New York, 1985). On witchcraft, recent work includes Patrick Curry, *Prophecy and Power: Astrology in Early Modern England* (Princeton, 1989) and Deborah Willis, *Malevolent Nurture: Witch-Hunting and Maternal Power in Early Modern England* (Ithaca, NY, 1995).

The position of the elderly and of women in preindustrial society, involved in the witchcraft craze, can be pursued in Peter N. Stearns, ed., *Old Age in Preindustrial Society* (New York, 1983) and R. Bridenthal and Claudia Koonz, eds., *Becoming Visible: Women in European History* (rev. ed., 1988). See also Roger Thomson, *Women in Stuart England and America* (London, 1974) and Carolyn Lougee, *Le*

Paradis des Femmes: Women, Salons and Social Stratification in 17th-Century France (Princeton, 1976). Bonnie Anderson and Judith Zinsser, *A History of Their Own: Women in Europe from Prehistory to the Present* (2 Vols., New York, 1988, 1989), offers a valuable survey. See also Laura Gowing, *Demeter Dangers: Women, Words and Sex in Early Modern London* (New York, 1996) and especially Olwen Hufton, *The Prospect Before Her: A History of Women in Western Europe, 1500–1800* (London, 1995).

The preindustrial family is beginning to receive considerable attention. A pioneering work, with an important general thesis about the development of the modern family, is Philippe Ariès, *Centuries of Childhood: A Social History of Family Life* (New York, 1962). A good summary is Michael Anderson, *Approaches to the West European Family, 1500–1914* (London, 1980). On family structure, see Peter Laslett and R. Wall, *Household and Family in Past Time* (New York, 1972). See also David Hunt, *Parents and Children in History: The Psychology of Family Life in Early Modern France* (New York, 1970); Lawrence Stone, *The Family, Sex and Marriage in England, 1500–1800* (New York, 1987). Linda Pollock, *Forgotten Children: Parent-Child Relations from 1500 to 1800* (Cambridge, 1984), is a revisionist work claiming that parental outlook was little different in 1600 from what it is today. Important recent work includes Wally Seccombe, *A Millennium of Family Change: Feudalism to Capitalism in Northwestern Europe* (New York, 1992) and Joel Harrington, *Reordering Marriage and Society in Reformation Germany* (Cambridge, Eng., 1995).

On the nature of work, leisure, and of changes in both in early modern Europe, see E. P. Thompson, *The Making of the English Working Class* (New York, 1964); W. G. Hoskins, *The Midland Peasant: The Economic and Social History of a Leicestershire Village* (New York, 1957); and three classic studies by J. L. and Barbara Hammond: *The Village Labourer, 1760–1832* (New York, 1970 [reprint of 1911 edition]), *The Town Laborer, 1760–1832* (New York, 1968 [reprint of 1917 edition]), and *The Skilled Labourer, 1760–1832* (New York, 1970 [reprint of 1919 edition]). A vital study on leisure trends is Robert Malcolmsen, *Popular Recreations in English Society, 1700–1850* (New York, 1973).

I

Peasant Rituals

ROBERT MUCHEMBLED

The peasantry was the key constituent of preindustrial society in terms of its numbers and its value systems. Yet it proves an elusive entity when examined with any precision. The peasant world differed greatly from one region to the next—and it changed significantly over time. Even its basic wealth could alter. Too easily we imagine uniform material conditions for the peasantry; in fact, significant gradations occurred within a single region. In Western Europe, the peasant economy usually maintained some contact with the market, even though many peasants produced only enough for their own needs, plus enough to cover tax obligations and landlord exactions. There were peasant owners, peasant employers, as well as peasants who hired themselves out as laborers or sharecroppers.

The following selection deals with the mental world of French peasants, as it related to their material lives, and focuses on patterns of behavior that stretch from the late Middle Ages into the eighteenth century. Attention goes to community forms and groupings of youth and festivals, rather than to peasant divisions and economic calculations. The emphasis is on peasant distinctiveness, as community ties overshadow family life and youth as a phase—though recognizable in modern terms—receives a special treatment.

Robert Muchembled, one of France's current leading early modernists, paints a gloomy view of the peasantry, steeped in poverty and surrounded by fear. This is a crude group, even violent, in compensation for a harsh existence.

Muchembled's interpretation has been challenged by other historians who argue, for example, that reading too much fear into peasant life constitutes a modern value judgment, based more on how modern people would react to peasant conditions, than on evidence from the era itself. Disputes of this sort point out the difficulty of getting at the inner meaning of undeniable behaviors, such as festival activities.

Muchembled's peasantry might certainly be ripe for change, if this would free them from their material and emotional constraints. But this is also a peasantry that does not seem to change much spontaneously. When and from where would a new kind of life come?

From: Robert Muchembled, (Translated by Lydia Cochrane), *Popular Culture and Elite Culture in France 1400–1750* (Baton Rouge and London: Louisiana State University Press, 1985), pp. 94–100.

Birth quite obviously constituted an extremely difficult passage. Terror must often have seized these mothers, bereft of any protection from medical science. For everyone, death came into the world just as much as life did, and the moment of birth was thus particularly distressing. Since death was not considered "natural," it could only be caused by the malevolent efforts of demons as they penetrated the body of the birthing woman or as they emerged with, or within, the child. There were magical rites and baptism to protect the baby; the mother, for her part, underwent a stage of suspension and purification, borrowed from Jewish rite, which in theory lasted forty days. In reality, after a number of days that varied from place to place, the woman "must be purified by the efforts of her priest" and by a churching that readmitted her to the mass and permitted her reintegration into the community of the faithful. The parishioners quite obviously did not view this process as a simple religious ceremony but as an exclusion designed to avoid contact with a woman still inhabited by the mysterious forces set into motion by childbirth. There is, moreover, an obvious comparison with the various taboos connected with women at childbirth and with the ceremony by which they leave the "sacred" state and return to the community in many so-called "primitive" societies. . . .

Groups of young peasants existed all over France in the fifteenth and sixteenth centuries, groups which we should be careful to distinguish from their more complex urban counterparts. . . . All young boys, it seems, must have belonged to such associations at the beginning or at the end of their adolescence. Their role was not limited to charivaris—that is, to ritual reproof of adulterers, of mismatched couples, of the remarriage of widows or widowers, and in short, of all that was not considered normal in sexual matters. They also planted grain and participated in the major holidays, as we have seen, bringing their youth to magical fertility ceremonies.

They also provided the shock troops in punitive expeditions or defensive actions against the youths of neighboring villages. In August of 1450, for example, a young man from Alaincourt, near Laon (now in the département of the Aisne) was courting a young girl from Choigny, a village a league away. The young people of Choigny disliked the idea *que il aloit veoir les jeunes filles de leur ville sans leur en plaire, et dont ilz n'estoient pas bien contens* (that he came to see girls of their town without their permission, and [they] were not very happy about it). A general brawl ensued that left one man dead. . . . The local youth was organized to defend the community's space from any sort of invasion, including matrimonial raids on the part of the inhabitants of nearby villages. The stockpool of young girls of the village was their private hunting grounds. . . .

Unmarried young men also had the privilege of bringing the newlyweds a *chaudeau,* a more or less repulsive brew designed to spur the couple on to greater ardor. . . . The youth were also charged with many other jocose ceremonies such as forcing a cuckolded or henpecked husband to ride backwards on a donkey.

All in all, the *bachelleries* [bachelor groups] and other sorts of rural *abbayes de jeunesse* [youth rituals] fulfilled an important social and cultural role in the village. The adolescent, marginal to society during the long years between childhood and the married state, was in this way invested with extraordinary power. He and his comrades manipulated the sacred during feast days and holidays; on many occasions they reminded the village that it was an entity; they exercised a right of review over matrimonial ceremonies; they stigmatized all deviance and wreaked the community's vengeance on it. The adolescent released his aggressiveness more readily than his elders, and he seems to have wounded, even killed, more than they. He was simultaneously the source of violence and the repository of the sacred in the village. . . .

From the cradle to the grave and even beyond, man, as we have seen, was desperately searching for a security that reality always denied in these iron centuries. At least, the search helped him to construct an oasis of revelry and play in this desert.

REVELRY AND PLAY

Was the Jesuit Father Mariana, who died in 1624, acting as an accurate observer of the popular world in Europe when he claimed that violence fitted into God's plan for transforming the individual into a social and political being? His dictum, in any event, applies perfectly to holidays and to play in French villages of the fifteenth and sixteenth centuries. Events of the sort were extremely "closely tied to social structures and to collective mentalities;" they expressed the culture of the age and, above all, they represented a "basic element of cohesion for these groups."

Festive occasions, in the first place, are a means of reinforcing the internal bonds that define any given group. There was a truly prodigious number of holy days of obligation during these centuries: fifty-five in the diocese of Paris at the beginning of the seventeenth century, for example, besides the fifty-two Sundays of the year. . . . Peasants were obliged to remain idle for what amounted to one quarter of the year, with notable regional variations, however. At that epoch, moreover, they were more apt to spend this free time in drinking bouts and profane pastimes than in assiduous frequentation of the church. Still, the one did not exclude the other, before the sixteenth and particularly the seventeenth century, when the authorities tightened discipline in this regard.

The atmosphere in the village on feast days and Sundays must have been one of contact between kin, friends, neighbors, allies of all sorts, and enemies as well. Just as it did during the six great festive cycles spaced throughout the year described at the beginning of this chapter, the village community found in these lesser times of rejoicing regular and frequent discharge of its inner tensions and a redefinition of its ever-threatened cohesion.

The *fête* [festival] provided an exceptional opportunity for contact within a limited space between persons of all age groups and of both sexes. For the space of one day everyone intermingled and at times for a much longer period: the *ducasses* (celebrations of the anniversary of the church's founding) of northern France mixed laity and clergy and lasted eight entire days from start to finish in the sixteenth century. Wine or beer flowed freely, both on the local saint's feast day and during the Flemish *ducasses* and *kermesses,* at the table of the religious confraternities as at that of the local *bachellerie.*

Although what went on during holidays was far from identical throughout France, and although customs and mores varied greatly from one region to another, the boisterous enjoyment of time passing agreeably could be seen everywhere. But this already worried the civil and religious authorities, for a holiday was a release, a letting loose. With the help of drink, it led to brawls and to killings, like those denounced by the Abbey of Cysoing in 1531, for example. . . .

Accumulated violence, the fruit of unrelenting fears, brought on confrontations at every *fête* during this age. Even when blood did not flow, violence was expressed by a ritual battle, as in the *cournée* in Langres in 1386. This was a game that took place outside the town, near the walls, on all feast days, in which people threw stones at one another. Violence in this case refounded the community by redefining it at the moment in which it had just exhausted itself and no longer risked shattering apart in internecine struggles. Similarly most of the village games and contests that took place during feast days functioned above all as a safety valve. The impact with an outside group made the individual conscious of belonging to his own group.

There was *boules* (bowls), *la paume* (roughly, freestanding handball), archery and crossbow contests, the ever-popular *soule,* both in its soccer-like and its lacrosse form, stone pitching, the game of *le plus prés du couteau* (flipping coins near a knife stuck at table's edge), the *raie du van* (a game like darts using a flat basket as a target), *picquarome* (tossing pointed sticks to send the adversary's stick "to Rome"), sword and shield play, the *jeu de bateau* (juggling and tricks), *les barres* (arena wrestling in teams), *les poulies* (pulleys), *la noiz* (nut toss for odds or evens), *la grille* (sparring with rotisserie spits): all games popular in the fifteenth century, now well known or obscure, and which developed group spirit. (Rabelais was to give an even better list a century later.)

La soule [a kind of football] was typical in this respect. It was played all over France on the major feast days, to the sound of pealing church bells, and it was played in Picardy, Normandy, and Brittany throughout the year. Like many of the other games cited it was played at fever pitch between teams from neighboring parishes or between the married and the unmarried men of the same village. It reinforced the feeling of belonging to a locality or to an age group, and for that reason it was an extraordinarily rough game. It was the peasant equivalent of the nobles' war games, and like them it pushed passions to the limit. Nevertheless, by transferring the rivalries, tensions, and hatreds of daily life to the level of sport, it burned them out in one short brutal competition. *La soule,* like other games, avoided even more frequent bloodshed in every village by purging passions.

The same functions and the same rechannelling of rivalries pertained in archery contests and crossbow matches or in the cruel games of *abattis* that consisted in killing an animal—a pig, a goose, even an ox (much appreciated in Artois and in Champagne)—by throwing sticks, stones, or knives at it. The winner of this sort of contest was proclaimed *roi* for a year, was bathed in glory, and often hosted a banquet and took a leading role in local festivities, both religious and lay. . . .

The *fête,* so frequently reiterated, was not made up of escapism and pleasure alone: it was peasant culture in action. It was that dense living time that enabled men to forget their woes and their fears for a moment, even when it was shot through with fights and killings. It also provided a short-lived oblivion of the dangerous forces on the prowl in the world. Finally, it was the perfect realization of popular magical ritual, since it achieved—only for a moment, to be sure—an exceptional solidarity: mastery of space, time, social relations, and whatever happiness life had to offer.

Under these conditions it is little wonder that sexuality, drunkenness, and gluttony ran riot, or that all manner of human passions found expression in ways that ranged from ritual play to individual murder. All was possible for that short span to man habitually crushed by his environment. Nor is it surprising if the authorities, the Church in particular, began to be concerned about the multiform excesses connected with these festive occasions and began to prohibit certain games or plays, to abolish certain *fêtes,* to prohibit dancing, to limit access to taverns, and so forth—all to slash an overly materialist popular culture at its roots. What is more, the religion of the masses was contaminated by the same spirit and proved to be anything but orthodox.

2

Popular Religion in Preindustrial Society

NATALIE ZEMON DAVIS

The importance of religion in European society before the nineteenth century is familiar enough. Indeed, some portrayals of medieval Europe have focused so heavily on religion that the strong economic and family motives of ordinary people—of the sort discussed in the previous selection—have been forgotten. Nevertheless, there can be no question that religion was a vital part of the lives of almost all people, affecting health care, recreation, and community solidarity as well as spiritual life per se. The Reformation and subsequent Catholic revival of the sixteenth century revealed the strong currents of popular faith.

The following selection deals with popular religion in the growing city of Lyon, at the confluence of the Saône and Rhône rivers in east-central France. Lyon had 65,000 residents in 1560, making it second only to Paris in size and economic importance. The city had been strongly affected by the Reformation, although at least two-thirds of its inhabitants remained Catholic. Relying heavily on concepts drawn from anthropology—an important trend as social historians try to get at popular beliefs—Natalie Davis interprets the symbols of Catholic practice to show how the religion fit intimately into urban life. Religion answered both practical problems—the need for help in sickness, concern about the dangerous Rhône river—and more generalized concerns about the unknown. It was not a separate category of life. While the recognition of religion as a vital element of preindustrial society is well known, this social historical approach adds new ingredients to our grasp of its diverse roles. Popular religion fits into a cluster of beliefs and concerns, like those taken up in the previous selection.

This portrayal raises one obvious question about the future: What could replace religion in ordinary life in a more secular age? The quarrels of the Reformation period helped launch growing skepticism. By 1800, religion in a city like Lyon was much less pervasive than it had been two and a half centuries before. What values and symbols would replace religion in explaining adversity and providing common bonds among people in a complex society?

From: Natalie Zemon Davis, "The Sacred and the Body Social in Sixteenth-Century Lyon," *Past and Present* No. 90 (February, 1981), pp. 40–41, 52–57, 60–61, 64, 67–68.

Where is the sacred in the sixteenth-century French city? We think readily of church towers and spires, which in the old engravings give the town its characteristic profile. We hear the bells ring for terce and nones and other hours of the priest's day, which mark the sacrifice of the mass, which announce the feast's arrival, the neighbour's death and the funeral's passage. We visualize the penitential processions winding through the streets with their relics, statues and great crosses, to appease God's wrath at time of famine or an act of sacrilege. We see the confraternities' processions, more joyous perhaps, banners flying, drums beating, blessed bread held high, all to the devotion of their patron saint. We see the city's poor, in queues or clumps, waiting for their alms of bread in courtyards, at doors and gates. We see Protestant worshippers, dressed in sober clothes, singing the Psalms of David as they move through the town to their preachers; Protestant crowds, breaking idols in the cathedral, mocking the host and threatening the priests; Catholic crowds, throwing themselves on those who have dared affront the body of Jesus Christ and insult his holy mother.

Such scenes are familiar ones, and historians have used them for a variety of purposes: to ascertain whether religious behaviour is or is not bringing people spiritual security and tranquillity, is or is not living up to standards of Erasmian or Lutheran piety. They have been used to describe the conflict between clergy and laity—an important perspective—and to characterize the religious style of different social groups, such as the merchants. But despite a growing documentation on urban piety in the sixteenth century, on urban charitable institutions, on the events of the Protestant and Catholic Reformations in individual cities, and on urban witchcraft and possession, we have come to few conclusions on the ways in which religion formed and gave expression to urban values and mentality in that period. . . .

The space of the Catholic city was not at all homogeneous or symmetrical. The nine parishes, established for centuries and with well-known boundaries, bore no relationship to the distribution of population. The huge parish of St. Nizier, in the heart of the artisanal quarter, had 22,000 communicants at Easter, so it was said in 1534, while the parish of St. Pierre-le-Vieux and St. Romain embraced only a little circle of families. Catholic space was full of special places and sacred spots. The presence of relics—the jaw of St. John the Baptist at the cathedral, the body of St. Irénée (the second bishop of Lyon) at the church on the hill of Fourvière, of St. Bonaventure at the Franciscan church, of St. Ennemond (a seventh-century bishop of the city) at St. Nizier, of one St. Reine, "who did miracles for the health," at the cloister of the Carmelites, among many others—intensified the sanctity of certain locations. Catholic devotion to this sense of space was, if anything, strengthened by the Calvinist iconoclasm of 1562–3; they hastened to purify buildings and to locate and verify relics (such as St. Irénée's head, miraculously preserved among the ruins for ten years) and put them on display.

Catholic ceremonial was also very sensitive to the natural features of the urban environment—the hill of Fourvière, which dominated the city, and the rivers. Processions of the clergy climbed up at least twice a year to the little chapel of Our Lady of Fourvière, and for most of the sixteenth century a "Kingdom" of the newly-wed made a pilgrimage there on Assumption Day. The choir-boys of the cathedral, dressed up as adult canon-counts, went up the hill after Christmas to the heights of St. Just, received a blessing from their boy-bishop and paid their respects to the bones of one of the Innocents slaughtered by Herod. The hill was viewed as a source of protection and help for the city. Often yielding ruins from its Roman past, discovered by gardeners and treasured by wealthy townsmen and humanists, it also contained the blood and bones of the early Christian founders and martyrs.

The slow-moving feminine Saône—the characterization is theirs—was the place for joyous festivals, sacred and popular. In the fourteenth century, in the days before the fairs when the Saône was the central artery of the city, a Feast of Marvels had been celebrated on the river in June, in honour of St. Pothin, first bishop of Lyon, and his comrades. The entire clergy of the city was afloat, praying and singing on the Saône, accompanied by officers, notable citizens and artisans; enormous boats performed a complicated ritual, which started at a rock at the north of the city, centred on the Saône bridge, and moved down to the point where the Saône flowed into the Rhône. This festival had ended in the late fourteenth century, but there still existed on Ascension Day a colourful pilgrimage by boat of laity and clergy up to Our Lady of Île-Barbe, north of the city. In addition to mass at the ancient abbey, which was near the border between France and Savoy, the master of the ports at Lyon and his aides took down the escutcheon of the duke of Savoy and replaced it with the arms of France. On Sundays and feast-days during the summer the boatmen of the parishes of St. George and St. Vincent on either side of the Saône marked their common boundary by jousting on the river. On the eve of the major feast of St. John the Baptist, it was from the Saône bridge that the consulate set off the fireworks.

The Rhône, by contrast, was a powerful, masculine (again their characterization) and dangerous river. As sixteenth-century people still remembered, the building of the bridge over it had initially been commanded by the Lord himself in a miraculous message to a shepherd boy in the mid-thirteenth century. Its difficult construction had had to be preached like a crusade, and financed by the many indulgences that penitents could purchase through visiting the chapel of the Holy Ghost at the Lyon end of the bridge. It was finally completed only at the beginning of the sixteenth century, and people still feared it would collapse—and with reason, for the strong currents often swept away some of the stanchions. As for the Rhône itself, there was constant worry not only that it would be too high or too low for the navigation essential to the fairs, but also that it would overflow. The flood of 1570 was so furious that Catholics claimed that "the water had wished to purge the filth . . . scattered about by the Calvinians," while the Protestants claimed it as a judgment of God against the Catholics for their persecution of his church. In any case, now that the Rhône was so important to Lyon life, Catholic ceremonial took increased note of it and many processions passed by the little chapel on the bridge, especially at Pentecost, the festival of the Holy Ghost. As with the Saône, there were associated popular festivals: at Pentecost young men dressed themselves as horses (more precisely as *chevaux fous,* or horse-fools) and danced through the streets from the end of the peninsula, where the Rhône and Saône "embraced," up to the Rhône bridge. This custom, which exists elsewhere in France and which has been interpreted variously as a fertility cult and a male initiation rite, was thought by some sixteenth-century Lyonnais to signify escape and uncontrollability. In this case, wild horses might well dance and jump towards a barely tamed river.

Catholic processions did not serve only to visit the border points of Lyon, such as the Rhône bridge and the Île-Barbe, but also to unite the two parts of the city cut by the Saône—the Church of Lyon, the king's men at the Palais de Roanne, and the bankers on the side of the hill of Fourvière (Côte de Fourvière) with the town hall, the merchants and the artisans of the St. Nizier side (Côte de St. Nizier). For example, a general procession of the parishes for Corpus Christi Day or a procession of the Confraternity of the Holy Cross for its feast on 3rd May assembled at the cathedral of St. Jean with their monstrances for the holy wafer, their crosses, banners, bells, candles and torches; went north to St. Paul; crossed the Saône bridge to St. Nizier, over to the Franciscans along the Rhône at St. Bonaventure; down to the Rhône bridge hospital, across to the Dominicans at Nôtre Dame du Confort in the midst of the printing quarter; and then, taking the rue Mercière (the main commercial route in the city), returned to St. Jean.

Can we conceive of this fashion of moving through and marking urban space as significant for, as functional in, the economic and social life of Lyon? For the most part, yes. These processions could dramatize the city's identity and give protection to the body of the town, and this effect could last in fairtime and outside fair-time *(en foire et hors foire).* And note that these were not rites to give a sense of closure to Lyon (as did rural processions, when among other activities the parish bounds were beaten and sprinkled with holy water); these processions . . . did *not* go around the enlarged town fortifications constructed in the 1520s. Rather, one visited the Rhône bridge to keep it open.

Furthermore, with the exception of a newly established house of mendicants on the hill of Fourvière, who protested the bellowing of animals at the cattle market across the road, the church objected rather little in the sixteenth century to the proximity of commerce to sacred things. Vintners and candlemakers hawked their wares outside the cathedral door to supply the needs of pilgrims on the feast-day of St. John the Baptist. People selling food came there at other times as well, and the canon-counts made only half-hearted efforts to stop them. Especially illustrative is the quarrel that broke out over the mercers and petty traders who surrounded the church of St. Nizier. The canons had no desire to expel them, so long as they left enough room in front of the doors and four feet between their stalls and the church (canon law prescribed thirty feet, but who cared?). The quarrel of 1559 was between the canons and the city council: who was going to collect the rent for those stalls? The church won, and the tradespeople remained (in fact, they are there to this day). . . .

Catholic ceremonial time was complex, bunched and irregular. Any parish or neighbourhood might have special rhythms of its own; in the area around the cathedral, for instance, from May to mid-August, at least six local feasts were held—for young law clerks, or for the furriers, on in honour of St. Christopher and St. Roch—and this quite apart from the major holidays that fell within those weeks. But the festive calendar for the city as a whole was not homogeneous either. It expanded and contracted, like the diets of the devout, who moved from eating to fasting; like the spirits of the penitent, who moved from carnival to Lent. Putting together the events of the church's liturgical calendar with those initiated by the city council (a procession and mass on Trinity Sunday up to the municipal College of the Trinity; a procession and mass on the Sunday after Easter, of all the poor receiving aid from the municipal charity, and the like) and with those events initiated by parishioners (such as street-dancing at Pentecost), we have periods of high activity in late December and early January; carnival and early Lent; Easter; May and June, a time of intense ceremonial life; and August. Autumn and Advent were the relatively quiet times.

The Catholic city breathed in and out as did the commercial and manufacturing city. How did the rhythms relate? The peak of May and June was not matched by a peak of economic busyness; but apart from that, the festive calendar clustered around three of the four fairs: the Fair of Kings, the Easter Fair and the August Fair. Only the Hallowmas Fair in November, following fast on the sombre Day of the Dead, had rather little liturgical build-up or follow-up. . . .

Having protected the exterior of the body social, Catholic preachers, such as the Jesuit Emond Auger, insisted strongly on the communion and sacred alliance within. Through the mass and the sacrament of the Eucharist, where Christ is really present and ingested, we are joined tightly to our brothers. The fruits of the mass and the prayers accompanying it are numerous, even if the Christian cannot understand the words: one can help the dead, one can help children, one can help those who are absent, the governors of the city and the kingdom, and many others. Auricular confession and the sacrament of Penitence also had social advantages. "How many evil projects," said Auger, "how many domestic conspiracies have been halted by this sacrament! How many enemies have been reconciled!"

The liturgical event which gave the best expression to this Catholic image of community was the rite of conjuration and exorcism. The one that took place in 1582 at the Franciscan convent can serve as our example. The victim was Pernette Pinay, a fifty-seven-year-old widow from a village near Lyon. Through the evil-doing of a witch in her village, she had been possessed by seven devils. Six of them she had forced out of herself by a pilgrimage and by prayers to Mary; now there was left a single devil named Frappan. Pernette had a holy soul and she had struggled with Frappan, so that he had been able to take over only her body. The exorcism, led by a preacher and theologian Jean Benedicti, lasted several days before a large audience. Frappan shouted a great deal, insulted people, and stammered over the name of Jesus Christ. Everyone in the gathering purified herself or himself by prayers, fasts, confession and communion. Everyone prayed for Pernette and vowed to make a pilgrimage to Our Lady at Île-Barbe. Twice during the rite a fountain appeared, distilled from the tears of all the spectators. Finally, Frappan departed during the mass. At that very instant a citizen on the Rhône bridge saw a great flash of fire above the Franciscan church. Thus were refuted the lies of the Calvinists about the mass; thus were demonstrated the power of the priest, the virtue of widows and the direct aid that Christian can give to Christian. Indeed, one could nourish another person spiritually, as the liver and heart nourished the body with blood, natural spirits and vital spirits. . . .

With the Catholics I have pointed to their deep regional roots; their connection with a wide range of occupations, from banking to baking; and their location in traditional collective organization as the elements of experience which, interacting with Catholic doctrine and ritual, perpetuated a distinctive sense of place, rhythm and community in the city. . . .

Sixteenth-century Catholicism could adapt its magic and ceremony readily to the varying character and risks of commercial and banking life in Lyon and could tolerate business practice up to its very walls. . . .

Catholicism had some resources to assist the integration of the different quarters and social groups in Lyon. . . . It could add sanctity to some of the familiar features of the environment, and try to pacify the dangerous ones. For a city with walls, which housed a population that ran from nobles to day-labourers, and an advanced economy as well as traditional economies—for such a city, perhaps this body social, with its changing physical states, its particular organs, its hierarchical order, its arteries, veins and umbilical cords of aid, made some sense.

3

MEN AND WOMEN AT WORK

MARTHA C. HOWELL

Gender relationships, far from forming a stable part of preindustrial European life, seem to have been in considerable flux from the late fifteenth to the seventeenth centuries. Patterns defy any simple generalizations about women's past degradation under patriarchy (in contrast to more recent liberation) or their past potencies (in contrast to more recent degradations). Martha Howell paints a picture of considerable economic success for some women in late medieval northern Europe, followed by declining opportunities and increasing confinement to household domesticity.

This selection is drawn from Howell's sketch of Leiden, a textile production center in Holland. Women, having often won access to skilled craft trades on the basis of their family position, as wives or widows of craftsmen, encountered growing gender exclusion by the sixteenth century. They were particularly excluded by the rise of *Ambachten*—organizations of small craft producers that regulated conditions of the trade as commercial opportunities expanded. *Ambachten* elected officials—almost always male—to help oversee production, purchases, and sales.

Martha Howell describes a clear change based primarily on organizational and occupational registry data. These data do not explicitly demonstrate why change was occurring, or what it meant. Like many social historians, Howell then proceeds to a larger analysis which goes beyond the description of change, while building on its contours. The combination of explicit narrative and general analysis is meant to convey the larger causes and impacts.

Howell emphasizes the subtlety of her picture, because this change is occurring even as relatively small crafts persist; it is not a product of the largest capitalist enterprises. Leiden's craft economy participates in growing commercialization, but not its most advanced or "modern" forms. At the same time, the gender separation that resulted does suggest patterns that would respond to industrialization, over two centuries later. The connection may be no accident, as both men and women had learned some new definitions of the relationship between gender and jobs that they carried into subsequent experience. Again, the link between early modern change and later developments

From: Martha C. Howell, *Women, Production, and Patriarchy in Late Medieval Cities* (Chicago: University of Chicago Press, 1986), pp. 85–94, 151–83.

is tantalizing, as our picture of early modern European society moves away from static stereotypes.

While the focus is on gender, this selection also sketches some larger aspects of the urban world of work—not as important as the peasant world, but a vital area of popular life even so.

In Leiden as a whole, we can estimate that at most only about 25 percent of the medium-to-small drapers were female, or, in total, certainly no more than 100. A few women wove and produced linen and coarse cloth, sold cloth at retail in Leiden, dyed both good and cheap cloth, and did some occasional (illegal) fulling. But these women may not have numbered many more than another 100, so that the total number of women working in textiles who had even moderately high labor-status could have been little more than 200. In sum, only 200 of the female labor force of 2,400, or less than 10 percent, had high-status positions in textiles, as compared to about 25 percent of suburban women.

The second generalization we may make about Leiden's working women requires no modification when the urban and suburban labor forces are compared. In both places, there was a significant correlation between marriage, high labor-status, and high economic status on the one hand, and spinsterhood, low labor-status, and low economic status on the other.

In the city, most women with high-status jobs were married or widowed, and many owed their jobs to their husbands. . . . A significant portion of these married or widowed women were in the same jobs as their husbands. One of the twelve married drapers shared her trade with her husband but three worked in entirely separate businesses; one of the fourteen widowed drapers practiced her deceased husband's trade. One of the two married bakers was her husband's partner, but neither the married peat seller nor the widowed oil presser practiced her husband's trade. . . . The records do not tell us why there was such a strong correlation between labor status and marital status. Common sense suggests that some married women probably helped their husbands in their work, and then took over for them when their husbands died. Others may have benefited from marriage in that it gave them access to capital for setting up their own businesses (for example, for entering the drapery). Possibly, a third factor was even more significant. Labor status and marital status were statistically associated with each other, not because there was a direct causal relationship between them, but because women with a trade or with the money, talent, ambition, health, or intelligence needed to acquire a trade would also have made the most attractive marriage partners. According to this reasoning, single women would have done low-skilled work, not because they were unmarried but simply because they were unhealthy, poor, unintelligent, untrained, very old or very young.

PATTERNS OF WOMEN'S WORK [AND] THE ORGANIZATION OF MARKET PRODUCTION

Women's labor status in Leiden was clearly associated with family position. In both the city and its suburbs, married and widowed women disproportionately dominated the positions granting high labor-status. Because a smaller proportion of these women in Leiden worked, fewer high-status jobs were awarded city women than suburban women. This evidence is therefore extremely good support for the hypothesis that women gained access to high-status work through the family.

For most of these women, the family provided the training they needed, and for many of them the route to high labor-status was as their husband's partner or heir. Women with their own enterprises were concentrated in trades that could be learned in the family; either they practiced skilled crafts like weaving and fulling cheap cloths or they took on managerial functions which required skills any good housewife would have already honed. The evidence also explains why single women had such low labor-status: young, unmarried, possibly immigrants, they were subordinate to the married pair or to the widowed head-of-household with whom they lodged, and consequently they had labor status below that of the senior household members.

With good indirect evidence that the family was the vehicle of women's access to market production, we can now predict that the family's absence from production for the market can account for women's absence from high-status work. . . . An analysis of the relationship [between women's work and Leiden's ambachten system] suggest that two particular features of ambacht organization in Leiden weakened the family production unit and, with that, the labor status of women who had achieved high labor-status through this unit. One feature was the close association between ambacht membership and political status. The trades in Leiden to which women did not belong were those which had links to political bodies, took organized political action, or granted access to government. The artisanal trades in Leiden with these characteristics were its ambachten; although without formal, independent political power, they were organized to carry out municipal policy as agents of the government. . . .

Women did not belong to these ambachten because in late medieval cities political roles were the exclusive preserve of men. Accordingly, women did not weave or full drapery because to do so would have required ambacht status; but they continued to dye cloth and finish it and to weave, full, and finish linens and voerlakens until these trades acquired ambacht status.

The inverse association between the political status of trade and women's place in it held even outside the ambachten. Women drapers, for example, never took on the political roles sometimes associated with the trade. A mid-sixteenth-century document that records the plans of ninety-two drapers to set up a sales office in Amsterdam dramatically illustrates this correlation: although thirty-three of the drapers were women, not one of the association's officers was female. This may be one reason why women did not join the ranks of large drapers. Leiden's large drapers were responsible for negotiating with the Calais wool merchants; they represented the city in discussions with other cities concerned with Leiden's cloth trade; and through the offices they held in the ambacht they supervised manufacturing. Many, as I said earlier, were members of the government.

Important as this political dimension undoubtedly was in making it difficult for women to practice a trade, the process of excluding women from a trade once it had taken on such associations was seldom a straightforward one. In the case of the finishers, the process began with the ambacht's founding ordinance of 1508 which forbade women to train for masterships, but it was some decades before women were written out of the regulations entirely. While the 1508 ordinance referred to a "brotherhood and sisterhood of St. Ursula," the version of 1552 mentioned only the "brotherhood of the dry finishers and trimmers." By then, the reference to women workers in the first article, which had allowed currently practicing female mistresses to continue in the trade, had been eliminated. A new article established burial rights for a "dead brother or sister." Another new article provided that a widow accompanied by a master journeyman who had produced a masterpiece might continue her husband's business, but also stipulated that, should she remarry outside the trade, she would lose her trade rights. By 1563, when the ordinances were again revised, all references to women were gone. Even widows' rights were not mentioned; in addition, the 1552 article that required attendance at funerals had disappeared, and in a new one, requiring aid to sick brothers, women were not mentioned at all, not even indirectly.

With the linen weavers it was the same. As we have seen, the ordinances establishing this ambacht in 1563 explicitly referred to women mistresses. Five years later an announcement by the government implied that women were no longer normally considered when membership and work rules were established. While repeating the requirement that all who produce linen cloth in Leiden must be members of the brotherhood, it, unlike the first article of the founding ordinance, did not refer to female members. The change in language is not easily explained. We have almost no external information about the trade which might tell us more about who actually made linen textiles. It is possible that the first ordinances were simply transcriptions of old, less formalized brotherhood rules which were, in fact, out of date by the time the ambacht ordinances were written. It is also possible that the later omission of women from the ordinance reflected only the attitudes and presumptions of the bureaucracy that formulated trade ordinances; although a few women may still have actually worked in the trade, they were not considered "official" and were not of real concern to the authorities who prescribed entrance standards. . . .

Even when these political associations had drawn work from the family, it did not necessarily follow, of course, that what was now "women's" work had no residual ties to the family and the household. A man's family might well help him in his trade, the family might even succeed to the assets of the trade, and a man's work might very well be located in the household. Nevertheless, because the political system which regulated his work gave him status in his trade that it did not extend to his household or family associates, they were not regarded as having fully shared his work.

Organization as an ambacht seems to have weakened the family production unit in an equally important and more familiar way as well. Ambacht organization almost always involved the establishment of work rules and schedules which were incompatible with family life. For example, weavers and fullers in Leiden's drapery were required to have served one to three years as apprentices and another three as "free journeymen" before they could acquire masterships; weavers also were subject to a daily schedule of work regulated by a clock; fullers labored in terms of one master and two journeymen who were expected to deliver a finished product in a fixed time period and who were paid as a team by the job. None of these arrangements allowed the flexibility needed by someone bound to the rhythms of a household. Because ambacht rules were directed at individuals considered free of household tasks, ambacht membership separated a worker from his household, even if he continued to locate his work in the household.

Records from the 1470s about the fullers help to illustrate how these two aspects of ambacht formation could undermine the family production unit. One document forbade the wives of master fullers to handle their husbands' accounts along with their own. From this evidence we can deduce that women entrepreneurs had once performed certain tasks simultaneously in their own trade and their husbands', for both were considered the family's. When ambacht rules required wives to separate their work from their husbands', the ambacht weakened the unit. Another document contained a complaint by journeymen fullers that the wives of master fullers were infringing on their territory; one of their demands was that fullers' wives no longer remove cloth from the drying frames on which it was stretched and finished, a task the journeymen were presumably claiming for themselves. This demand can be read as a spearhead of the ambacht's attack upon the family enterprise, one prompted no doubt by the journeymen's wish to reduce competition, but one they advanced on the basis that rights to skilled crafts did not belong to families but to individuals.

The large drapers, too, instituted business practices that could have weakened the traditional family production unit and made it impossible for women, even as wives and widows, to work as large drapers. Large drapers in Leiden traveled much of the time: they made at least one annual trip to Calais, and they regularly visited regional markets in cities such as Bergen op Zoom, Amsterdam, and Bruges. Keeping such a schedule would have been difficult for women, who had pressing household tasks and who, in any case, would seldom have found business travel feasible, given the cultural norms they faced and considerations of safety. . . . The pattern of women's work in Leiden also owed something to cultural traditions that defined men's work and women's work as separate. Few of the women in Leiden worked in industrial sectors like construction, metals, or wood, and instead usually performed functions which had grown from the household chores that had been the province of women in the traditional family economy. Widows who carried on their husbands' trades were the sole apparent exceptions to this rule, but in carrying on these trades they were, in fact, upholding the traditional system because they obtained their positions in market production through their position in their family. The traditional sexual division of labor, however, was not responsible for all features of the pattern. Women did not hold *all* the jobs in the market economy that precedent should have awarded them. Leiden's brewers, embroiderers, hatmakers, weavers and fullers of drapery, butchers, and medical doctors—all of them subject to varying degrees of business and political organization—were male.

The data permit one final observation about women's work and the socioeconomic structure. Until the political and business organization of work occurred, women of Leiden's *Mittelschicht*—the group made up of small merchants and producers—were active in market production and did work commensurate with the socioeconomic status of their families. Like the men of the *Mittelschicht*, these women, when young, served as helpers and trainees and as adults took over masterships and proprietorships. During the fifteenth and sixteenth centuries, this pattern gradually changed, however, and such women either retreated from market production to devote themselves entirely to managing their households or, driven by economic necessity, took on low-status work which was incompatible with the social status they once would have had as the wives of artisans.

In summary, then, we can tentatively confirm and refine the working hypothesis of this study. The family production unit was, indeed, the vehicle for women's access to high-status jobs in market production and, so long as it retained its role, women of Leiden's *Mittelschicht* held jobs commensurate with their status in the social hierarchy. But developments directly associated with small commodity production, developments that both secured political control of industry and preserved social order and that enhanced the efficiency of the individual producer, weakened the family production unit. These developments were not capitalist innovations but were products of a system—small commodity production—which even retarded the emergence of capitalism. The effect of these developments was to lower women's labor-status by closing many of the positions that granted high labor-status to women, forcing women of Leiden's *Mittelschicht* to retreat from market production or, more rarely, to take on work incompatible with their social position. . . .

Although women held high labor-status in the European market economy for only a short time and lost it just when high labor-status came to confer unprecedented cultural, political, and economic status, they must have threatened the patriarchal character of Europe's sex-gender system during the period they held it. Such a threat, and its resolution (accomplished by women's withdrawal from high-status positions in market production), must have been perceptible outside the realm of economics, in a realm where attitudes towards gender roles were formed. To explore the connections between changes in women's labor-status or, more generally, the sexual division of labor, and the ideology of gender in this age, we need a great deal more research, but we can be certain that the inquiry will be fruitful. The late medieval and early modern period, as we already know, was an age of great uncertainty, even disagreement, about appropriate gender roles. By its end, the divisions between public and private had been newly and clearly drawn, and women, by and large, were firmly located in the private realm centered on the patriarchal nuclear family. Women's gain and loss of high labor-status in market production has to have been involved in this shift, and the tensions bred by the shift must have been reflected in contemporary sources. To close this [selection], we can look briefly at some of the evidence which reveals associations between women's roles in market production and contemporary struggles over gender relations—and their resolution.

In judicial records that survive from cities very much like Leiden and Cologne, we have straightforward evidence that women sometimes resisted new laws which denied them entry to certain trades. For example, a dyer's daughter in fourteenth-century Ghent sued to inherit her father's place in the guild (and lost); a widow in fourteenth-century Paris sued to keep up her husband's trade as candlemaker. The literature of urban popular culture less directly, but even more eloquently, records such conflicts. Comedies and satires of the period, for example, often portrayed market women and tradeswomen as shrews, with characterizations that not only ridiculed or scolded them for taking on roles in market production but frequently even charged them with sexual aggression. Chaucer's Wife of Bath was an expert at sex—who delighted in playing the aggressor—and at weaving. In Chaucer's words, she "bettered those of Ypres and Ghent," and, as Chaucer undoubtedly knew, the weavers in Ypres and Ghent were men. . . .

The popular literature of late medieval and early modern urban culture seems, then, to express unusual hostility towards aggressive women, women whose aggressiveness in some measure attends their positions in market production, and it seems to equate such aggressiveness with sexual aggressiveness, even sexual misconduct. But are we justified in seeing these implications? Are examples such as these representative of late medieval and early modern urban culture? Do they truly reflect tensions in urban society or do they simply repeat literary conventions held over from other cultures? Are the themes really so transparent? These are difficult questions to answer. If any of them can be answered affirmatively, we can ask yet another: how did the lessons expressed in this literature help to ease women's departure from market production, help to restrict their sexuality and shore up the patriarchy?

It is tempting to suppose that the relationships between work, economics, politics, and law explored in this study were tied to changes in religion, literature, and sexuality, that women's temporary admission to high-status positions in market production seriously threatened the patriarchal order, and that the literary artifacts mentioned above were produced in a struggle to reinforce that order. With the authority granted by their roles in market production, these women may have begun to assert themselves in other spheres, frightening men, other women, and perhaps even themselves, for their actions portended the destruction of the traditional sex-gender system and the institutions based on it. If we accept this reasoning, we can begin to understand why, in the end, women accepted dismissal from commerce and trade, and why men, sometimes with self-conscious deliberation, arranged it. Most often unconsciously—but with unquestionable success—men may have battled to strengthen the traditional order while women may have struggled, as the economic, social, and political order which shapes the meaning of gender was changing, to establish a new gender identity.

The patriarchal order, as we know, was restored, even renewed, where men gained privileged access to high labor-status. In this exploration of women's exodus from the positions in market production which might have overturned the traditional order, we have witnessed an important part of the process of restoration and renewal. While there is much to learn—almost everything to learn—about the other issues at stake as gender was redefined in the late medieval period, we now know, beyond doubt, how important women's roles in economic production were in requiring such redefinition.

4

Pregnancy in Early Modern Germany

ULINKA RUBLACK

The following selection, by Ulinka Rublack, dealing with southwestern Germany from the sixteenth to the early nineteenth centuries, shows the differences between pregnancy in early modern European society and pregnancy today. The contrasts involve beliefs about the body, but also ways in which women are valued and the bases for arguments about attention and care.

The article uses court cases, milking them for information about both private and public aspects of the experience of pregnancy. It draws connections between this family experience and broader issues of the day. Beliefs about pregnancy reflected larger ideas about bodily and what we would call psychological processes, of course. They also related closely to assumptions about witchcraft and magic (see Chapter 6). And they picked up signals from changes in religious culture. Emphases in late medieval Catholicism were echoed in new Protestant discussions about the importance of maternity—a subject Martin Luther wrote about explicitly.

Pregnancy and the culture surrounding it were crucial in defining women's place in the family and in society at large. Rublack shows how women used pregnancy to better their conditions, at least temporarily, and even to win political influence. She also shows, however, how the intensive focus on pregnancy could constrain early modern German women, and even invite social punishments for deviance from established norms—this latter an issue for debate still today, as abortion controversies attest.

Rublack argues that the early modern culture surrounding pregnancy created a special moment, different from medieval conditions but also from the later eighteenth century, in which circumstances were better than they would later become. Here is another crucial aspect of much early modern social history, in pointing out not only the distinctiveness of the period, but also ways in which later developments would run counter to any assumptions of steady progress from then to now. Finally, subtle changes in women's family standing should be juxtaposed with shifts in their position at work, discussed in the previous chapter. What kind of rebalancing was occurring and how would it affect both genders and their mutual relationships?

From: Ulinka Rublack, "Pregnancy, Childbirth and the Female Body in Early Modern Germany," *Past and Present* 150 (1996): pp. 84–86, 87–89, 90, 92–96, 97–100, 103, 108–10.

One summer morning in 1558 a Cologne wine-merchant named Hermann Weinsberg was awoken by his wife, Drutgin, with the frightening news that she had miscarried in the night. In the half-light, she showed him the contents of her chamber-pot; a messy foetus lay at the bottom. Hermann was shocked. He had been unaware that his wife was pregnant, or even that she was still able to conceive. Now he realized that a quarrel he had had with her two days earlier must have disturbed the nurturing flow of blood which the child needed; he should have protected his wife from excitement, he believed. Only later that day did he suspect that Drutgin had tricked him. The foetus in the chamber-pot looked as if it had been fashioned out of wet paper. Hermann understood the bluff's emotional subtext very well, however. The pretended miscarriage was Drutgin's way of voicing her anger at his violence and her claim to respectful treatment.

This article sets out to contextualize a story of this kind. It explores the assumptions common in early modern Germany about women's bodily sensitivity during pregnancy and childbed, and about the connection between their emotional and physical well-being. It also takes issue with earlier approaches to these themes. Attitudes to the early modern female body have hitherto been explored through medical tracts, collections of folk-customs and contemporary literary accounts. Upper-class diaries in particular have suggested that pregnancy, birth and lying in were mainly private experiences, "rough passages" full of danger for the mother's life. One historian adds that, even so, becoming a mother was "suffused with political meaning." A female culture of childbirth enabled pregnant women to resist their husbands' "patriarchal power" by withdrawing sexual services and physical labour. The lying-in chamber was a tolerated but exclusive arena of female gossip, where women forged networks to resist male control.

Clearly, women enjoyed a privileged position during pregnancy and lying in. But I argue that this was not necessarily due to the organization around childbirth of an exclusively female culture. In ways which historians have scarcely recognized, husbands played key participatory roles at times of childbirth. Sharing their wives' understanding of bodily needs, they nurtured, entertained and comforted their pregnant women, and they celebrated safe delivery with them. Moreover, it was understood that women had a right to be cared for by their husbands; and communities supported them as they manoeuvred for more influence within their marriages if husbands failed to do so. This right to protection extended beyond the sphere of conjugal relationships. Pregnant women could also resist political violence by using their claims to protection strategically, and this again with communal support.

I shall attempt to elucidate these themes through sources which have not previously been exploited. They come from south-west German courts, from common people's complaints and demands recorded in council minutes, and from legislation. These sources reflect common people's daily life in fascinating detail (and demonstrate that historians are by no means forced to rely on writings by educated people and on medical discourse to reconstruct the

cultural meaning of early modern physical experiences). Often in the most unexpected contexts, they give a strong sense of the ubiquity of the pregnant
woman in the early modern consciousness, and show that it was a presence deferred to by men as well as by women.

In order to understand this deference, I address an additional theme, and
a key one. It concerns contemporary beliefs about the ways in which social,
physical and emotional experiences were linked—the notion, for example, that
miscarriages resulted, not from organic deficiencies and mishaps, but from socially delivered shocks, or from withheld anger against others. These presumed
linkages made women's emotional well-being during pregnancy highly dependent on public and private support. Pregnancy, childbirth and lying in were experienced by the "unfinished and open body . . . not separated from the world
by clearly defined boundaries" but "blended with the world" and suffused
with the duality of birth and death. A woman before, during or after childbirth
occupied a liminal space in which outer experiences were readily transmuted
into inner experiences which affected both her and the child. She knew that
she could give birth successfully only if her whole body "flowed": she had to
sweat, cry, shout and open her womb wide. Her vulnerability as she prepared
to give birth was recognized and honoured. Gestation and parturition thus
made sexual difference an "ontological category": they gave essentially different meanings to each sex which were rooted in contemporary perceptions of
bodily processes. Moreover, the experience of motherhood could have a wider
ethical meaning. In particular social and political contexts it allowed women
to demand respect for generosity, love and care as the conditions human life
depended on. This article seeks to demonstrate how in these ways beliefs
about women's physical nature could become a source of female strength. . . .

Protestantism, . . . had relatively little regard for lifelong virginity; its
praise of motherhood drew on older traditions. Since the late Middle Ages, de-
votional emphasis had focused increasingly on the holy family, Jesus' childhood and Mary's motherhood. Mystics like Bernard of Clairvaux taught that
Mary, the virgin mother, liberated women from the curse of Eve. Women who
might otherwise be dismissed as weak could prove their toughness by pointing
to the pain they endured during childbirth. Their special needs and desires
were respected: for example, a pregnant woman caught stealing fruit could not
be prosecuted. Similarly, cities passed legislation protecting pregnant women's
health. By 1436, Augsburg supported several lying-in women, and Nuremberg
introduced special alms for such women in 1461. Its 1478 begging ordinance
gave them permission to beg in front of churches wearing a special badge or
to send others to beg in "churches, houses and streets" on their behalf. From
the sixteenth century onwards, most towns seem to have regularly supported
poor women before and after they gave birth if they were citizens. Midwives
handed out "bedding, bread and lard to needy women," ensuring that "clean
swaddling clothes and bandages were ready for the delivery." At the beginning
of the sixteenth century, pregnant women in Hall were also invited to an annual meal of fish, the symbol of fertility. Fish was not to be eaten by virgins;

but pregnant women were believed to crave it. Even though this meal fell into disuse, a "lying-in florin" was routinely granted to the Hall poor during the early modern period. In 1687, for example, a day-labourer told a lower court that his wife had delivered a child, he had nine children, and it was difficult to feed his family because employment in the salt-works was hard to come by; he then asked for the "usual lying-in florin." Wine ordinances similarly drew attention to women's needs after they had given birth. In 1650 the duke of Württemberg outlawed cider-making because many citizens sold home-made cider as wine. "Foreign and poor countrymen" were thus deceived, and the practice "deprived and ruined poor and sickly women in childbed and breast-feeding women, who are unable to get a fair drink of wine." Wine was believed to purify the blood, and together with meat was thought to be an essential part of the diet before and after birth. Durlach watchers risked being fined if they refused to give sick, pregnant and lying-in women cheap roast meat. . . .

The support for women in childbirth was double-edged, however. The child's welfare was increasingly given priority. Luther famously expected mothers to die themselves rather than let their offspring perish, and exalted self-sacrificial motherhood. Motherhood was increasingly policed by secular authorities in both Protestant and Catholic towns and territories. Contraception and abortion were punished and miscarriages monitored. Württemberg women who miscarried because they were reluctant to go into labour were accused as criminals and reported to the ducal supreme council, for such behaviour fundamentally challenged the view that motherhood was natural and sacred. Along with menstruation, lactation and the menopause, women's experience of birth defined identity. The conjunction of fertility and finality was part of their being: the refusal to live through the pain and fear of death in order to give birth challenged views of what being a woman was about. The destructive force of such uncooperative women was feared. They were described as ungodly, suicidal, murderous, Devil-possessed. Both sexes felt this way, male doctors and officials were not on one side, with midwives, mothers and a supportive "female culture" on the other.

The case of a forty-year-old smith's wife in 1698 demonstrated very clearly both this fear and this concurrence. During twelve years of marriage Walburga had had only one child. She never joined other women in spinning-bees, nor spun hemp by herself. She was generally thought of as lazy, even though she sometimes helped her husband at the forge. The pastor had punished her because she had not attended in church during sermons. Everyone knew that she had run away from the village of Nahrstetten several times and wanted to kill herself. Now, having at last given birth to a girl, she suffered from severe melancholy, sighing: "I don't have any linen, everything is torn, and girls are so expensive, how am I going to dress her and give her a dowry?" She stopped eating for ten days. She neither listened nor spoke to other people, and lay immobile even when shaken, splashed with cold water or rubbed with snow. The mayor, schoolmaster and her maidservant suspected that this was unnatural. The maidservant knew that the Devil could be driven out of a body if he was insulted as "chicken-shit" *(Hühnerträckler)*. So she shouted this to Walburga, who suddenly leapt at her and nearly strangled her. After she had stayed in bed for days she got up to cook porridge for her baby girl. Watching the flame, she decided to burn down her neighbour's house. Tried as a possible witch and arsonist beset by the "Devil of avarice," she was found guilty and beheaded. . . . [E]arly modern people believed that shocks, rage, anger and other extreme excitements could cause illness and pain, and this is also why pregnant women were so fearful of terrifying sights or conflicts. Such experiences were dangerous because the ensuing physical symptoms could not be cured in the usual manner. On the one hand, a shock drove the blood away from the limbs to swamp the heart with blood. On the other, anger made the blood flow rapidly into the head, limbs and uterus, where its movement caused convulsions, the cessation of menstruation, and so forth. Women most commonly reported this as a "flux" in their bodies. It thickened the blood, making it impure and causing it to "clog." The concept of health was based on the notion that blood had to be pure and flow. Hence, cures entailed blood-letting in order to re-establish a balanced pace and distribution of blood inside the body. Accumulated blood (for example, in the uterus) was likely to be impure.

Pregnant women could not purify their uterine blood by menstruating. Instead, blood accumulated dangerously, surrounding the foetus for months. In 1573 the Protestant pastor Simon Musaeus imagined how, after God created a living being in the womb, he "moved it from side to side like a midwife, cleaning, so that we should not suffocate in filth." The womb was like a dark cave, but also a dirty one. Christoph Völter, author of the 1679 Württemberg manual for midwives, found it humiliating to reflect that he had developed in what was "almost a cave between many bad smells and filth." Moreover, if a pregnant woman became angry, a hot flow of blood would swamp the fragile cells of the foetus, causing miscarriage; if she were shocked, blood would drain away and the foetus would starve. Thus the borders between women's inner body and the outer world were thin. Even imagined images could affect a foetus. The symbiotic relationship between the body and the outside world was confirmed in the fact that pregnant women craved unusual (or even usual) food, or were unable to eat anything at all. If menstruating women felt confused about food (in 1699 a young woman told her family that she was unable to eat rice or salad because of her period), pregnant women were even more so. A woman would vomit, or want to eat "raw, unnatural things" which, Luther mused, "would shock her, if she was healthy." More than one hundred and sixty years later Völter expected pregnant women to abstain from extremes, since dancing, violent laughing or voluptuous eating might damage the foetus. However, he still recommended that relatives and servants who felt that a pregnant woman was about to behave indecently should withdraw so that she could "indulge in her lust properly without having to be shy or ashamed before anyone."

This precarious state of women's bodies and senses before and after her birth explained a great deal to contemporaries. Just as an English maidservant allegedly gave birth to a cat in 1569, so there were "monstrous" births in Württemberg. Parsons had to report every such birth to the supreme council, and women had to explain any deformity. Usually a shock of some kind was invoked to explain these phenomena. In 1659 a Stuttgart coppersmith's wife "of honourable conduct" bore a child with one foot and without genitals. She said that this could only be explained by the shock she had received from seeing a lame beggar on her way to market. In 1677 a woman in the Hall territory explained that a dog with puppies had jumped up at her while she had been doing her laundry. She had almost fainted and later delivered a child with deformed hands and feet. Shocks explained false pregnancies too. In 1551 Anna Ulmer in Esslingen pretended to have a hugely swollen belly, even though she was a virgin and fasting. Her interesting condition inspired at least three [published] broadsheets, and her mother explained it by telling the court that Anna had been shocked to see a boy who suffered from falling sickness. High and low people flocked to Esslingen to see her until she was imprisoned for life for fraud.

"Shock," then, was a common danger—so much so that in Gryphius's 1658 comedy *Peter Squentz,* those acting Pyramus and Thisbe (like Snug in *A Midsummer Night's Dream*) thoughtfully warned pregnant women in the audience that the lion was not a real one and was played by the local carpenter. There were innumerable recipes for calming mixtures for use when women were shocked. The eighteenth-century Württemberg manual for midwives proposed saffron and wine, or—cheaper and sweeter—wine boiled with sugar and cinnamon. More radically, citizens in the south-west did not hesitate to insist that shockingly ill or ugly residents be removed in order to protect pregnant women. Town councils backed them. A Nuremberg ordinance of 1478 told beggars to hide malformed limbs out of consideration for pregnant women, and other towns followed. . . .

It is apparent from such incidents that the publicly recognized need to protect women during and after pregnancy provided a focus for narratives about disturbed social relationships, just as it mediated women's claims to respect and consideration. Some women used their pregnancy to dramatize complaints about noisy gatherings in neighbours' houses. An Esslingen woman accused a neighbour of stealing meat from her while she was lying in—this to prove his recklessness as well as his dishonesty. Some women skillfully dramatized their demands. In 1711 a pregnant peasant-woman quarrelled with other women about the rank of her seat in church. She asked the parson to decide the matter because she would otherwise be too upset to be able to shout during her labour. She showed him the swaddling-clothes she carried with her lest she give birth suddenly. Since the birth did not take place for another six weeks, the parson not surprisingly felt that he had been duped. The fact that pregnant women claimed protection, care and appreciation as of right, and long lying-in periods too, might help explain why deaths in childbirth were relatively uncommon in Germany up to the eighteenth century. A demographic study of three sixteenth- and seventeenth-century Württemberg villages shows that women gave birth to five children on average up to the age of 38–40. Between 1690 and 1724, an average of four women in a thousand died within forty-one days of giving birth; but between 1760 and 1794 the average rose to eleven. Between 1655 and 1724, a woman would have run on average a 2–3 percent risk of dying in childbed at some point of the procreative cycle; between 1760 and 1829 the risk was 5–6.5 percent. This change might be related, not only to a lower age of marriage, but also to an intensification of female labour during the eighteenth and nineteenth centuries, which forced many women to resume work shortly after delivery and reduced husbands to relative passivity.

During the sixteenth and seventeenth centuries a husband would be affected by his wife's pregnancy roughly every other year. The quality of a marriage was tested in the long weeks before and after the birth, even though the husband would usually be excluded from the birth itself. The physical survival of most couples depended on intensive co-operation in work, with a clear division of labour and little leisure. Between a third and a half of all artisans did not employ a journeyman and depended on their wives' help. Although a maidservant might take over female tasks when her mistress was in late pregnancy, many households could not afford such help. Female work during advanced pregnancy was nevertheless frowned upon, and it was understood that a pregnant woman should not carry heavy objects. In 1602 it was a central point in a wife's complaint that during her pregnancy her husband, a cartwright, forced her to work because he had no journeyman. Husbands had to reorganize the work-load, nourish their wives with meat and wine, buy or hire the bed in which she would lie in, and if possible pay for a nurse. In Constance independent nurses were commonly hired to look after lying-in women. Single women sometimes lodged with a married couple for the purpose. It was also commonly accepted that debts might fairly remain unpaid if a husband expected his wife to be lying in soon. Evidence of this kind suggests that few wives, even in poorer artisan households, resumed onerous duties early.

This impression is endorsed by the case of a Constance tailor, Leehardt Lörer, in 1668. His brother-in-law told the mayor that Lörer had beaten and cursed his wife during pregnancy, thus depriving the foetus of its "food inside the womb," and again after she rose from childbed. He spent everything he earned in drinking, leaving wife and children without bread. Lörer defended himself by saying that he had cursed his wife only because she had lain in for eight weeks: he had wanted to move her bed from the ground floor to the upstairs bedroom to enable him to re-employ a journeyman. (Women always seem to have lain in the main room, for warmth or company.) When Lörer cursed his wife she shouted to make neighbours think he was beating her. She told clients that he did not feed her well enough, and she had spent eight florins clients had given her. The council nevertheless did not believe this tale of a greedy, unruly lying-in woman and banished Lörer from the town. A husband was expected not only to provide for his wife but to be close to her before and after the birth. When in 1525 the citizens of Rothenburg were armed to fight rebellious peasants, one man claimed that his pregnant wife would not let him go; he duly stayed behind. Men were commonly released from prison as their wives approached childbirth. A Sulzdorf peasant was imprisoned in 1686 because he had left his wife for a day while she was lying in. It was emotional support that was needed. A child had to be welcomed by both parents, for this signified their union's strength. A Constance woman in 1562 accused her husband of betraying this union when he stayed in a tavern during her labour-pains. Later he even required her to sell the wedding dress he had given her. In 1620 a Constance woman reported that her lying-in neighbour had only survived thanks to a friend who had looked after her. When the woman's mother had nagged her son-in-law to look for godparents, he had told her he would like to throw her down the steps. Overhearing this shocking response, the man's wife was instantly assailed by "labour-pains" and fears of death. Curses on mother and child were dangerous; they could lead to miscarriages, since hatred destroyed life. In 1614 a Protestant broadsheet attached a different moral to such curses. Mothers were commanded to internalize notions of what was good or bad for unborn children and not to miscarry or risk giving birth to monsters, because babies were God-given, even if unloved by their fathers. It recounted the tale of a pregnant woman who had urged her drunken husband, Hans Lorentz, to leave the alehouse and feed his family. When he started beating his wife, the innkeeper's wife told him to show her respect. Lorentz answered that she was "carrying Devil and hell" and was going to give birth to vipers and snakes. His wife angrily swore by God that she wished this would happen, whereupon Lorentz attempted to kill her with his sword. His wife escaped, but back home her labour-pains started and lasted eight days. Many women attended her and witnessed how she finally gave birth to a child with a long, snake-like tail. Shocked, she died instantly, and the child was killed. This story warned swearing husbands that they would not enter heaven, and pregnant women never to curse themselves; the women had to observe God's word "and read good books". . . . Neighbours were socially involved in all stages of the process, keeping an eye on the mother's condition and supporting her if she was ill-treated. Shouts from women who were pregnant or lying in were monitored and remembered. When in 1600 a citizen of Constance threw a glass at his wife, her nurse reminded him that a lying-in woman was "free" from her obligation to yield to a husband's authority; it mattered less than her and the baby's health. Violence in other types of relationship was similarly outlawed. If a woman was already heavily pregnant, the authorities were even prepared to accuse a violent man of infanticide if the baby died. Violent scenes and deaths were remembered as definitive statements about men's failure to live up to their duty to protect women and children. Descriptions of the consequences of violence against mothers and small children were forceful. One woman, beaten by her stepfather, delivered a dumb child who soon died, and in Constance in 1597, neighbours told how a baby had stopped sucking and died within a week because its mother had been beaten by her husband and father-in-law. Hatred and violence stopped babies from wanting any exchange with the world through speech or food. . . .

In developed economies today, pregnancy and miscarriage, birth and death, are seldom thought to be "rich with meanings which penetrate the whole of social life." Needless to say, a woman's emotional experiences of childbirth retain many private meanings, but—at least in the senses which this article has explored—they do seem to have a diminished "political" relevance. Pregnant women are not granted a privileged voice against political violence, for example; and miscarriages no longer indicate the extent of military aggression. People do discern interconnections between emotional, social and physical experiences, but in no way as intensely, one suspects, as early modern people did. Envy of or grudges against others are seldom now assumed to choke a woman when she gives birth; sick people are not cleared from streets to prevent pregnant women being shocked. Healing and care are the task of professionals, who interpret "disordered experience, communicated in the language of culture . . . in the light of disordered physiology." Medicine has transformed the womb into "a field of operations;" miscarriage indicates that a woman, the foetus's life-support system, has mechanically failed. In the early modern period, by contrast, pregnancy and lying in were highly unstable and risky processes for mother and child—"rough passages" indeed. The threat of death was closely linked to the ability to give life. If it came to the worst, little could save mother and child from death. A body was not a site of predictable processes but of sudden changes. Organs were less prominent in people's perceptions of physical experiences than fluids were, especially blood. Blood could easily clog, become impure, flow too fast or too slowly, or in wrong directions. Social and emotional experiences would affect this inner flow directly. Troublesome experience closed a body off, made women turn inwards instead of outwards, and hindered any open engagement with the material and social world. Boundaries between inside and outside, the individual and the social, the emotional and the physical, were generally experienced as permeable, not firm. This permeability was even more marked during pregnancy and childhood, as a woman dramatically expanded into space, opened to deliver a child, and closed and contracted again. Women's responses to terror and fear during this time generated statements without the role of force in marital, social and political relationships: they affected attitudes, diversely, to the execution of justice and to husbands' abuse. They disclosed the costs of disregard and showed that life depended on care, respect and company. In short, a history of the body has to ask how early modern people gave meaning to their physicality and their needs in social interaction, and how different those meanings were from ours.

5

PROSTITUTION IN SIXTEENTH-CENTURY LONDON

PAUL GRIFFITHS

The social history of early modern Europe offers three possible emphases—not mutually exclusive, but different. The first framework stresses how different early modern beliefs and behaviors were from those of today—perhaps better, perhaps worse, but different. The second emphasizes change within the early modern period itself, sometimes leading to more recognizably "modern" social patterns. The third shows how early modern society may not have been as distinctive in some crucial respect as is often imagined, particularly if one probes beneath the surface of sermons and official proclamations.

The following selection, on prostitution, is definitely of this third type. Prostitution is an obvious topic for social historians concerned with the lives of women and with patterns of sexual behavior. The subject is most often associated with modern, industrial history, and indeed there is good reason to believe that prostitution increased in the nineteenth century as single women moved to the cities, as male sexual appetites possibly increased because of new work frustrations and lower community controls, and as job opportunities for women often deteriorated. But prostitution was part of early modern urban life as well (we know far less about the rural majority, a point that must be remembered in any overall assessment). Even movements like Protestantism and the establishment of special jail sections for prostitutes might have little effect.

Paul Griffiths shows the place of prostitution in London's society, though he provides no estimates or numbers on use. He demonstrates important connections to the lives of powerful men, while arguing that the late marriage age characteristic of urban artisans and businessmen in early modern Europe—an important pattern designed to build up property prior to starting a family—might have increased prostitution's role for other groups as well. Most important, he provides some insight into the motivations, lives and prospects of some prostitutes themselves, and how their choices and lack of choice fit them into the patterns of urban women more generally.

From: Paul Griffiths, "The Structure of Prostitution in Elizabethan London," *Continuity and Change* 8 (1), 1993: 39, 40–41, 44–45, 46–48, 54–56.

This is a different view of women—some women—from the earlier description of family roles. Does it relate to other changes in women's lives and work? Or is prostitution, however important, not too revealing about women in general, at least in the early modern period?

Different types of sources might reveal different constructions of the same social situation. Contemporary perceptions, preoccupations and anxieties give deep meaning to the written record, but they also litter it with characteristic flaws, so that we glimpse life in early modern England through the critical gaze of a contemporary actor (and mediator)—the court scribe, for instance, or the distinguished man of letters, or the composer of doggerel. Every source is the product of a stream of exchanges between experience and prejudice, and we find "fiction in the archives" as well as in the classically versed dramatist and the humble balladeer.

This essay investigates the relationship between archival and literary sources by comparing descriptions of a particular pattern of social behaviour—prostitution in Elizabethan London—in the records of London Bridewell and contemporary prose and drama. The recovery of Elizabethan prostitution from archival sources has only recently begun. Hitherto, authors have often flirted dangerously with contemporary perceptions, relying all too heavily upon the imaginative beings who parade through the pages of Thomas Dekker, John Taylor and other lesser, even anonymous figures. John L. McMullan's *The canting crew* (London, 1984), for instance, consults a body of "broadsides, ballads and companion forms of street literature," to present an anecdotal and arguably sensational account of a highly structured organization with a "distinctive language" and "formal division of criminal roles." In a recent review of trends in the history of crime, McMullan voiced his anxieties.

Contemporary authors depicted the underworld as a real threat to the commonwealth. "Lost women" were obvious enemies to all civility and humanity. These "wretched creatures" were "expelled [from] the society of mankind," and dispatched to the fields to consort with the "filthy," "despicable" and "unclean" beasts. The "sacred word" and "godly books" were distant and bitter memories to these lost souls who never went to church, preferring the satanic promise of "hot desires" and "lawlesse lust," or the illicit lure of such religious deviants as familists and papists. Thus the theme of conversion and regeneration runs through literary representations of the prostitute, touching even the very worst cases. . . .

But salvation was not the only concern. The society of bawds, pimps and prostitutes also disturbed the social hierarchy and the ideology from which it derived legitimacy. The weak husband who visited the "bawdy" broke his marriage contract and created "discord" in the household simply to "satisfy his lust with the love of a base whore." Servants who stole from their master to purchase sex upset master-servant relations, and gave credibility to the near-proverbial wisdom that "whoring is succeeded by robbery," as they began the inevitable descent to the fatal Tyburn [hanging] tree. The civil and pious socialization of youth was a regular theme of plays in the "morality tradition." Bawds and prostitutes "spoiled" the "unwary apprentice," but also themselves.

Prostitutes preferred to live outside the family, free from the claims of "a poor husband and half a dozen of young children." A "shame" to their sex and to virginity, they were "unfit to make a wife" and "unworthy to be call'd a woman." "Grave modest matrons" and "honest women" passed the whore by on their way to "civil gossips feasts," "churchings" and "honest" bridals, from which the whore was excluded. . . .

Both the courtbooks and the literary sources confirm the potential variety of keeper-prostitute relationships. The scale of operations clearly depended upon the size and quality of the establishment: Thomas and Ely Fowles, who kept "very evil rule" in Mutton Lane near Clerkenwell, had a garret and a middle and upper chamber; Anne Wilkes, alias Allawin, had "onelie" a chamber, kitchen and garret in her bawdy house along Northumberland alley; while Tottle's wife kept "iiii or v harlotts," and Alice Dunsley, "ii or iii wenches." The period a prostitute lodged with a keeper ranged from a few months to a few years, though the majority of arrangements which can be traced fall into the three- to twelve-month range. Some prostitutes moved between the "bawdys." One of Dunton's nightwalkers moved around from "every corner of the town." Jane Fuller can be linked with at least 13 prostitutes, and John Shaw with at least 23. Anne Smith informed the Bridewell bench that she had "layen at Wattwood's, M[ar]shall's, Jane Fuller's, Martyn's, Shaw's, and other naughtie howses." Prostitutes were often "fetched" from another "bawdy" if business was brisk. Pimps were the agents in this city-wide shuttle service, and we can occasionally glimpse the relative ease with which whores were ferried across London. One of London's more notorious pimps, Henry Boyer, is recorded fetching at least ten prostitutes to the bawdy houses. Dunton further reports that one keeper "borrow[ed]" prostitutes "from her neighbour bawds. . . . If two or three sparks came in at a time she would send out her pimps for whores."

In the Bridewell [prison] records most prostitutes are described as "laying" at a brothel, generally paying a weekly rent somewhere in the 4s to 6s [shillings] range, though Alice Farewell is recorded giving one Fowkes of Turnbull Street thirty shillings, and Thomasin Breame paid Briary of the Old Bailey "xxs a weeke for the bed of herself, her mayde," Ann Jervis, another prostitute, and Richard Rolles, her servant and pimp. It is likely that the majority of prostitutes handed over additional sums out of a client's fee. Farewell gave Fowkes "in ev[er]y vs. she gained xiid. [pence] for being bawd." More frequent in the Bridewell records is the "keepers" half or "share." Jane Fuller told the governors that Katherine Jones "had to do carnally with many men in her howse" along St John's Street, "and she had her half always of the money for her whoredome." Shaw's wife "had half ev[er]y tyme," while Dorothy Wise "had alwaies half of that . . . given to her girls." "I see others of them [prostitutes],"

Thomas Nash observed, "sharing halfe with the baudes their hostess." Other authors also refer to the bawd's share. Not every keeper was satisfied with her/his half, while others were prepared to settle for less.

It was the duty of the pimp to keep up-to-date with the geography of shady London. Dramatists and other literary observers often restricted comment on the pimp to a bare statement of function and bitter invective. Pimps, "he bawds" or panders, the bawd's "kinsmen," were "chiefly employed abroad, both to bring in customers and to procure such wenches as are willing to be made whores of." We see Boyer and his fellows visiting such spots as the steelyard where merchants and their retinues congregated. Ambassadors' residences were a further source of custom. Pimps also forged close relations with the capital's apprentices. Boyer fetched prostitutes to members of the nobility, gentlemen, a goldsmith, steelyard men, the Portuguese ambassador and a fellow painter. Pimps were not tied to one house. Boyer, "a doyer for mens wyves in London," can be linked with at least nine different keepers; Richard Wattwood, "a bawd to dyverse . . . [who] doth moche harme," with seven; William Mekens, with six; Melcher or "mother" Pelse, "a bawd" who "carryeth very many to whores," with five; and Stephen French, a "bawd and pander," with four.

In their examinations of keepers, pimps and prostitutes, the Bridewell governors were trying to reconstruct the structure of London prostitution, to recover the contacts between the principal characters. . . .

Prostitutes could expect a reasonably high fee. Marie Donnolly was given £10 by a single client over several weeks. Thomasin Breame received the same amount for one afternoon's endeavour with "a good thick sett man with a full brest, and a short statured man," while Elizabeth Foldes earned "x^{li} [power] at the least" in "almost a year" as a servant with Richard Bradshaw in Long Lane. The Bridewell records suggest that women did not work for a standard fee. Breame's £10 was exceptional, though she could also command 10s, Katherine Williams received "sometimes xs., and sometimes more and sometimes lesse," while Katherine Jones was given a range of relatively high fees (3s, 4s, 5s [five times] and 10s [three times]), which reflect her participation in the loose structure around the bawdy houses. Fees were doubtless lower in the alleys, fields and streets where financial expectations and related collective pressure were largely absent. Elizabeth Compe, for example, "a verie lewd queane" and an "old gueste" of Bridewell, informed the governors that she would be "naughtie with anyone for iid [pence]." . . .

Keeping was potentially a lucrative business. Mistress Blunt kept six bawdy houses: three in Garden Alley, two in Bishopgate Street and one in the "Spittle." She collected 20s in weekly rents from each of her establishments. John Shaw kept at least five houses. The Bridewell records show payments to keepers ranging from 10s to 3d, though their share was usually in the eighteen pence to three shillings range. Dekker mentions "twelve-penny" and "two shillings fees." One May's wife of the Three Tonnes without Aldgate was said to have "gotten 3^c li [i.e. £300] by bawdrye within these 3 yeares." Black Luce "had moche gayne by kepinge of" Margaret Goldsmith, while Gilbert East "gott much monye" from lodging Jane Lewis. Keeping was a full-time concern for those like Jane Fuller, who admitted "that she hath used the trade of bawdrye," and had "no other lyvinge;" John Shaw, who had no trade "to lyve by but bawdrye;" John Edward, who kept the Horse's Head at St Katherines, who gave up his job as a woollen draper to devote more time to his "bawdy;" and Richard Wattwood, a grocer and freeman of the city, who had kept a house for eight years and "hath none other lyvinge." Other keepers claimed to be washers or starchers. The majority of keepers who can be traced in the subsidy rolls were assessed at the £3 to £5 rate. Thomas Nash urged his readers to "hoyse uppe baudes in the subsidie booke for the plentie they live in," though at least one keeper claimed that "povertie drew him thereunto." . . .

The Bridewell records tell us little about the social origins of prostitutes, how they viewed their work, and how long they had been in the trade. Such personal detail was glossed over in the hurry to discover the various contacts and links which gave London prostitution a measure of coordination and permanence. My impression is that the majority of prostitutes were single young women, and this is also conveyed by the literary sources, and by the high proportion of prostitutes who were given the significant age-titles "maid" or "servant" in the courtbooks. Such literary sources as Dunton's *The night-walker* contain much greater detail on the roots of their fictional prostitutes, and Dunton's "personal-histories" are drawn from a range of social categories.

The fictional bawds and prostitutes regarded commercial sex as a "trade." Some of the women who told their tales to the Bridewell bench described how they "lived w[i]th the use of my bodye," or spoke of the "trade of bawdrye." Descriptions of commercial sex often resemble the language of the shop counter and exchange: clients had to "deal" with a prostitute, they had "to do with her," or they "had th'use of her." Richard Wattwood "carried" Mistress Mask, "a common harlott, [to] Warran Sellinger's howse to be occupied as a whore." Pimps, after all, are also called "brokers" in the records. Although the descriptive language often appropriates shop-talk, we rarely know how prominent this sort of rationalization was as a compelling "push factor." Again, the governor's preoccupation with rebuilding structures reduces mere personal matters of motivation to an incidental footnote. However, in their own narratives the women often place a telling emphasis upon procurement, which may well have been a strategy, for by shifting the blame they could emerge as victims, while this line of inquiry bolsters the intention to strike a fatal blow at the "bawdys" and the image of the bawd as cruel temptress and manipulator.

A familiar tale in the archives is that of the "honest" maidservant who was "enticed" from her "true" master, only to fall into the world of prostitution by the procurer's trick. In May 1559, for example, Jane Starkey, a skinner's daughter, told her story to the Bridewell bench. Her fellow servant at the house of Mr Willoughby ("a gentleman of the Barbican"), one Margaret "of lewd disposicion," moved in the circle of John Hall, keeper and pimp, who persuaded her to take Starkey to a house in the Barbican. There a "gentleman . . .

so tempted" her with "fayre words and great promises," that he "allured" her from her master, and carried her to Hall's house in Cock Lane where she remained for a fortnight. In that time "dyvers lewd and naughtie p[er]sons," including a character called the "Spanyard," "had th'use of Hall's wife" and others. The "spanyard" offered Hall £10 to take Starkey away with him. Hall's wife tried to reassure her: "thou art a very fool, he is a godly gentleman." Persuaded, Starkey was taken to Blackfriars, given a fresh suit of clothes, and placed in a boat with the "spanyard" at Whitefriars. At some point, the waterman "so admonyshed her of the naughtyness of the spanyard that she cryed out decrying them for the passyon of Christ to carry her back agayne." Hall, his wife and the "gentleman," were all presented at Bridewell, a happy ending to a familiar story.

Other young women were procured by their parents, master and/or mistress, or they were tricked by a false promise of marriage. Marie Donnolly, who admitted that she had spent "her lewd lyfe in whoredome," and was now eager to repent, "for she hath offended almighty God in her wicked lyfe," was first tricked by a porter at the Counter, and then by a Norfolk gentleman, who lured her to Gilbert East at Clerkenwell, a well-established keeper. All of these situations can be discovered in the literary sources, which also paint the prostitute as "the prey of the bawd and debauchee," a figure of misery and pity, "unprotected," "unwary," "ruined" and "enslaved." But another current occasionally runs through these narratives. In keeping with the didactic impulse, the prostitute is not always absolved from blame, and her taste for fine clothes, food and drink and dancing schools, or her folly (and weakness) in allowing herself to be duped, served as a cautionary tale.

Other accounts contain a hint of voluntary participation, albeit by force of circumstance, in the world of prostitution.

In April 1598 Elizabeth Evans told the governors that she was the daughter of Robert Evans, sometime resident of Stratford-upon-Avon. She had called herself "sometime Dudley and sometime Carewe," and had "bin about London for three or foure yeares" living "with th'use of" her "bodye." Like Katherine Jones and Helen Smith, Evans moved in the maze of alleys which were often home to the capital's residual population. Jones and Smith were presented in October 1598, "being taken in whore alley in Morefields in the house of M[ist]ress Brooke," being "vagrant and lewd women" who were discovered "out of service." For some of these migrants it was probably a stark choice between theft or commercial sex. Alice Sharpe, "as bad as the best," who came to London to find a service, was procured by one Green's wife, who informed her that "it is better to does so then to steale." One imaginary prostitute declares "tis better for me, and less hazardous, to get my living by my tail, than to turn thief and steal from other folks." Significantly, perhaps, my continuing research into the marginal world of petty crime reveals a far higher proportion of males among the capital's pickpockets, cutpurses, pickers and nippers.

So prostitution provided some migrants with a tenous niche in metropolitan society. . . .

We are occasionally informed of how long a woman had traded her body: three–four years, three years, eighteen months, and a period in excess of eighteen months. Lawrence Stone has argued that most eighteenth-century prostitutes viewed commercial sex as a short-term option until a husband came along. There are examples of prostitutes having sex with men who they claimed as betrothed, future spouses, though this may have been a strategy to disguise their offence. But many women probably left the "bawdys" behind when they married, though the Bridewell scribe recorded the marriage of Mistress Neale, a keeper: "now married to the Quene's wax chandler in the Old Balye." Some may even have married clients. One of Dorothy Powell's clients, William Delamott, "belonging unto the French embassador," had "lately come from beyond the seas only bycause hys conscience was moved toward her and he means to marry her yf she will go w[i]th him to France." Powell was in fact pregnant. Indeed, illegitimate pregnancy may have forced some women out of the trade, if only for a short interval. Jane Fuller, for example, had two illegitimate children by Sir Edward Baynton's brother "before she was marryed," but this did not prevent her from becoming one of London's busiest late Tudor prostitutes. Fuller is also a rare example from archival sources of movement up the ladder—a prostitute who became a keeper—though the literary sources often reported another sort of occupational progress: the spent and lonely whore is either left prematurely aged and alone, or she sinks ever deeper into a quagmire from which there is no escape, always straying further from civil society and salvation. . . .

So it seems that the Reformation had little impact upon the availability of commercial sex in the capital. Richard Wattwood and Robert Barlow, two pimps who were examined in 1578, offered information about 23 brothels, and claimed "that ther are many other bawdy houses about this cytie." They also reported "that men come to those houses and have harlotts as redely and commenly as men have vittels." Statements of "daily resort" range from six and seven clients, to fifteen and "lx or lxxx men in one daie." The society of pimps, prostitutes and keepers had a social and structural significance in Elizabethan London, and the everyday resort to the "bawdys" induced a certain fatalism on the part of the authorities and moralists.

Despite the moral rigour of the language selected to identify the staff of the brothels, and the petitions and testimony of some "honest" neighbours, London's "bawdys" thrived. Apart from the occasional spectacular purge, such as that in the winter of 1576–7, prosecutions proceeded at the rate of a trickle rather than a stream, which implies a measure of toleration or resignation in the Guildhall and Bridewell. Ian Archer has argued that this apparent "immunity from prosecution" can be related to the protection extended by clients of high social position and influence. Bridewell investigators "often stirred muddy waters near the centre of power." Authors speak of bribery in high places. "Great patrons it [i.e. prostitution] hath gotte," Nash declared, and "almost none are punisht for it that have a good purse . . . can it be so many brothel houses of salary, sensuality and six-penny whoredome (the next doore to the magistrate), should be set up and maintained, if brybes dyd not bestirre them?" Officers laugh at these "abuses," Dekker claimed, or if "not laughed at, yet not looked into; or if looked into, winked at." Other texts fill the "bawdys" with members of the upper classes, young sparks and gallants and "rough roaring roysters" and captains. . . .

The world of prostitution had a clear place in the fabric of London society. Indeed there is a risk in relegating the brothels and their residents to the margins of society and attaching profound labels like "subculture" or "underworld." Some keepers and pimps had a role in the capital's occupational structure. Further, commercial sex provided a social and sexual option for some sections of the "integrated" society. All this has implications for recent studies of early modern London (and urban society more generally), which have presented arguably a rather rosy picture of a stable, consensual society by focusing disproportionately upon the more orthodox *functional* aspects of metropolitan society, including social mobility, poor relief, the guilds and the life-cycle, and upon evidence relating to the more stable and integrated sections of urban life. This reluctance to descend to the basement of early modern London is regrettable, as we can discover much about the character and preoccupations of so-called conventional society by exploring its alleged obverse. The story of prostitution should also be of interest to historians of demography and social structure, as it appears that some young men could not contain their libidos in the long interval between the first stirrings of puberty and the characteristic pattern of late marriage in early modern society, an interval which defined the age of youth itself.

6

WITCHCRAFT

JAMES SHARPE

The explosion of witchcraft prosecutions that spread over many parts of Europe, and New England, in the sixteenth and seventeenth centuries has long fascinated social historians. The phenomenon has many facets. It involved hosts of ordinary people, as accusers and as victims alike. It clearly had great significance to those involved, including those who thought themselves to be witches. At the same time, the persecutions were bounded in time: they departed from traditional social and cultural norms, for few witches had been attacked during the Middle Ages. On the other end chronologically, they lasted in full force for two centuries or less: new laws and growing official disinterest and disdain drew the furor to a close in the early eighteenth century.

Social historians have made several contributions to the understanding of the witchcraft craze, and innovative discoveries continue. First, historians have highlighted the sheer importance of the movement. This was one of the most significance outbursts of post-medieval Europe, easily rivaling wars and the doings of kings in affecting daily life and the nature of European society. If we want to grasp early modern Europe, as it differed from what came before and what would come later, we need to know its witches.

Second, the beliefs involved in witchcraft attacks now receive more sympathetic attention, as we realize that no culture, however different from our own, should be simply condemned without empathic understanding. Against disdainful condemnations of superstition and magic, we now see what a rich culture the beliefs in witchcraft represented. People used magic to manipulate and understand their world—usually with benign intent, hoping to improve fertility or prevent disease. Their patterns differ from ours, but they made perfect sense in context. Someday, if our species survives, historians will similarly look back on our own beliefs and find them comprehensible—but very strange. We gain perspective by thinking about witches, including the people who assumed they had magical power and those who turned to them for help or in fear.

From: James Sharpe, *Instruments of Darkness: Witchcraft in Early Modern England* (Philadelphia: University of Pennsylvania Press, 1997), pp. 15–17, 18–21, 158–63, 172–73, 262–63, 269, 273–75, 284–85, 291, 292–93, 300–01, 302.

Third, two decades of sociohistorical exploration of witchcraft helps us understand why the persecutions broke out. They were new. The beliefs involved—that magic could manipulate the environment—were not novel. But the attacks on witches focused new concerns about poverty, cultural change and certain kinds of women—disproportionately accused—and so converted common beliefs into a frenzy of attacks that would kill tens of thousands of people. Some historians, like James Sharpe, who writes of the craze in Britain, remind us that frenzies are a recurrent feature of human life, even in the twentieth century. But they also help explain why this particular frenzy occurred when, where and how it did. Relationships to shifts in gender roles and work experiences require careful analysis.

Fourth, the frenzy receded. Here is another challenge to analyzing historical causation. Peoples' ideas changed, but not simply because of new science or other obvious developments in the late seventeenth century. New religious controls also played a role. Indeed, the decline of witchcraft belief helped create a friendly reception for new science, as much as reflecting scientific advance. Class relations enter in strongly: officials and the upper class pulled away first, attacking popular "credulity" and renouncing their own earlier participation in attacks. This eroded the basis for further witchcraft trials.

But fifth, the result was no sudden shift in actual popular beliefs. Ideas about magic and witchcraft persisted into the nineteenth century (and they echo even today: Read supermarket tabloids like the *National Enquirer* for an ongoing taste of magical claims). A recent target of social-cultural history involves tracing the long legacy of witchcraft beliefs, as they persisted beneath the official surface of disapproval and scorn. The social historian, if like James Sharpe sensitive to the complexities of a long sweep of time, even provides perspective on Western society today, where witches play a far different, reduced role.

All these themes enter into the following excerpts from a recent treatment of witchcraft in Britain. A final point merits attention as well: what effects did the witchcraft craze have, beyond its tragic impact on many lives and its mirroring a complex crisis in West European society? The focus was on older women (not the traditional European idea of a witch, which had emphasized young female beauty). Did older women learn from this experience and become more retiring and cautious, anticipating a grandmotherly role? Certainly our ideas of the witch still reflect the early modern imagery: Does it have effects on the way we think, about women and fashion for example, beyond favorite Halloween masks?

Our starting point must be that witchcraft, magic and the occult were deeply embedded in European culture, both popular and élite. Such matters had obviously been familiar in the classical world. Apuleius, in *The Golden Ass,* to take a much-quoted example, included tales of shape-changing, a description of Pamphile, a powerful sorceress who could even change the shape of the planets and annoy the gods, and other supernatural elements. Similarly, Ovid's *Amores* includes a description of Dipsas, an old hag of a witch (it has, in fact, been suggested that one of the distinctive contributions of classical literature to developing ideas on witchcraft was the stereotype of the female magician and witch), while the same author's *Metamorphoses* was widely quoted in later discussions of shape-changing. Such references were still of vital importance to writers on witchcraft between the fifteenth and seventeenth centuries. Most educated men and women were steeped in classical literature, and most of the writers of demonological tracts used references from that literature in their descriptions of what witches did.

With the fall of Rome, this literary tradition passed into temporary abeyance, but by the seventh-century A.D. barbarian law codes were demonstrating that witchcraft was still a reality among the population of Europe, although the attitude of the law givers to the phenomenon was clearly somewhat ambivalent. The matter is in need of more systematic research, but for the present it seems safe to claim that the Germanic tribes of the seventh and eighth centuries clearly believed in witches, most frequently in the form of a night-flying cannibalistic female witch known as a *stria* or *striga*. Yet the law codes and moral tracts of the period were anxious to correct such beliefs rather than persecute witches, and to dissuade people from defaming each other with allegations of witchcraft. In the eighth century, indeed, we find St. Boniface declaring that belief in witches was unchristian and Charlemagne ordering the death penalty for those who burnt witches in his Saxon territories, which had just been converted to Christianity. The ninth century saw some Christian authorities repudiating belief in night-flying, metamorphosis and the witch's ability to raise bad weather. This doctrine was incorporated into the *Canon Episcopi*, a theological statement which was to remain a key text for sceptics.

The relatively relaxed official attitude to witchcraft which seems to have characterized the Dark Ages and the early medieval period changed in the wake of a harder line against deviants that set in during the twelfth century, a development which has led to claims for the emergence of a "persecuting society" during the period. This harder line was prompted by the arrival of popular heresy, which was swiftly followed by the formation of the Inquisition. The Inquisition's investigations, coupled with works of clerical propaganda, created an image of heretics as a secret sect which was aiming to overthrow Christian society, and whose mores represented an inversion of Christian values. . . .

Yet at roughly the same time as the "persecuting society" was developing, magical learning among the educated élite was becoming more widespread and more complex. There were a number of influences at work. One was the massive expansion in learning which took place over the twelfth century as Arab texts, among them those containing the works of Aristotle and other Greek writers which had long been lost in the West, became available to Christian scholars. The impact of this accretion of new knowledge (over 100 works were translated from Arabic into Latin during the twelfth century) was immense. And, given that information on medical, scientific and magical matters was heavily intermixed, it became inevitable that those reading them in pursuit of what we would call medical or scientific knowledge acquired deeper insights into the magical and the occult. . . . A second major influence was courtly magic. By the thirteenth century dabbling in magic was apparently common among courtiers, and a number of European courts, notably that of Pope John XXII (1316–34), were riven by scandals arising from the alleged use of magic in pursuit of love or political assassination. . . .

Further shifts in official attitudes were needed before spectacular cases among the élite and scholarly adjustment of theories about demons could be transformed into witch-hunting proper. On a theoretical level, changing notions of the devil were important. The process was a complex one, but it seems that in the centuries which followed the early Christian era the concept of the devil and of diabolical powers slowly changed. By the early fourteenth century, . . . the devil, with his battalions of lesser demon assistants, was becoming clearly identified as a threat to Christendom. . . .

How far there was any witchcraft in reality remains problematic. The fundamental point is that, in so far as they can be reconstructed, the peasant belief systems of the period incorporated numerous "magical" elements which were clearly held to be reprehensible by hard-line theologians. Indeed, it is evident that in the late Middle Ages what we would categorize as magic was a normal part of life for the population of Europe. People went to healers and diviners who used charms and sorcery. Midwives used charms, prayers, blessings and invocations as they officiated. Extensive use was made of protective amulets and talismans, and some insights into the connections between magic and the popular Christianity of the period can be gained from the practice of using fragments of both saints' relics and the eucharist in magical amulets. You could use magical means to attract a partner, while, conversely, one of the things which witches were meant to do was cause impotence among men. And (again here the border between magic and religion is blurred) there was widespread belief in the power of cursing and in the use of charms to do harm.

To some extent the development of the official fear of witches throughout the fifteenth century can be interpreted as a coming together of the demonological models which were beginning to obsess theologians and popular magic of this type. At least some clerical intellectuals became convinced that they were confronted by a heretical sect of witches, the devil's assistants in his struggle against Christianity. The reality of those dragged in before the inquisitors was very different. There were doubtless a few individuals who thought that they had occult powers, and certainly a fair number of people were willing to accuse their neighbours of such. But the existence of an organized sect of witches existed much more clearly in the imaginations of inquisitors and the clerical writers of demonic tracts than in reality, and was essentially a product of the collision between the pure religion of the educated clergy and the folk religion of the peasantry. Most late medieval peasants would have seen themselves as Christian, and would have been familiar with at least the basics of Christian belief and Christian ritual. But this popular Christianity could coexist happily with traditional superstitions which could easily embrace magical elements. The learned inquisitors, increasingly trained to take a severe theological line on what constituted acceptable practices among Christians, and increasingly alert to the need to root out heterodox beliefs, could all too easily reinterpret these more-or-less harmless peasant superstitions as evidence of witchcraft.

Turning from the fifteenth century to a later period, an illustration of how this process might have worked comes from the Friuli, a region to the northwest of Venice. There, from about 1575, the Inquisition uncovered puzzling evidence of what appears to have been a fertility cult. Local beliefs held that during the night the souls of members of this cult (the Benandanti) left their sleeping bodies and went off to do battle with the witches in the hope of defending the fertility of the crops. A handful of cases involving such beliefs were investigated over the years, and it is possible to trace how the Inquisition, whose reaction was initially one of bemused incredulity, redefined belief in the Benandanti as witchcraft. By the 1640s this interpretation was shared by the local peasant population and, indeed, people who thought themselves to be Benandanti . . . had been subjected to inquisitional interrogations. . . . [The] medical dimension of witchcraft is one which still awaits detailed research; what needs to be grasped immediately is that witchcraft was, until well into the seventeenth century, a valid explanation for illness, and that many doctors either realizing the limitations of their own skill or being unwilling to meddle in such a religiously, legally and medically uncertain area, seemed very willing to pass doubtful cases on to cunning men and women. Thus, in 1652, Grace Matthew deposed to the Exeter authorities how, when her husband had fallen sick, supposedly of witchcraft, she had gone to a local doctor named Browne. The remedies prescribed by Browne had proved ineffective and on her return to him he said that "hee could formerly doe something to cure people that had byn bewitched," recommending that she should go "to a woman in Broadclift who was sometyme his servant for that purpose." Matthew went there, and received both medicines and advice as to the identity of the witch.

We have considered the role of cunning men in assisting people thought to be bewitched at an earlier point, and a detailed discussion of their activities in that respect is not needed here. What must be reiterated, however, is that cunning folk were often widely known. Widespread evidence shows how, when suspicions of witchcraft were being discussed or counter-measures against it formulated, local cunning men with a reputation for effectiveness came readily to mind. Edward Fairfax, although rejecting their services, noted how at one point in his daughters' afflictions his household spent an evening discussing the reputation of cunning men in his area of Yorkshire and the success which those resorting to them had enjoyed. Similar widespread knowledge about cunning men was revealed at the beginning of the seventeenth century in another case concerning the daughter of a gentleman, in this instance

Brian Gunter of North Moreton in Berkshire. Having received no effective assistance from physicians, Gunter turned to cunning men, and was particularly anxious to obtain the services of John Wendow of Newbury, "being a p[er]son supposed to be cunning in matters conc[er]ning witchcrafte." Gunter sent his servants to Wendow, who gave good advice but was away from home when the servants were sent again when the girl's fits recurred. Gunter was anxious to send them yet again, but one of them, unwilling to repeat what would probably be a fruitless journey, recommended to his master another cunning man, named Blackwall, who, he assured Gunter, was as competent as Wendow. We return to the conclusion that people knew where to find a cunning man or woman if they needed one.

Apart from doctors, clergymen and cunning folk, there seem to have been odd individuals with a claim to expertise in witchcraft who were called in to assist in witchcraft cases. Edward Fairfax, although unwilling to go to cunning men, was happy to call on the advice of someone he felt to be a legitimate adviser, Robert Pannell, a "mere stranger travelling towards York," who visited the Fairfax household when he heard of the girls' possession. He asked if he could experiment with them to see if they were bewitched, "which," wrote Fairfax, "I did condescend to, the rather for the said Pannell used to serve upon juries at the assizes, being a freeholder of good estate." Accounts of possession frequently refer to interested parties with some knowledge of witchcraft taking a hand, or to people claiming skill in such matters making their way to the house of the possessed. And every witchcraft case must have served a useful educative function. By the end of the Matthew Hopkins trials it is no surprise to find the identification of teats on suspects as proof of witchcraft by "some that were there whoe p[re]tended to have some skill in the discovery of witches."

There were, of course, more direct means of taking action against suspected witches. Despite their reputation for being powerful people, many suffered violence at the hands of those who thought themselves to be bewitched. Oliver Heywood, indeed, noted in 1667 that three men had been hanged at the York assizes for the murder of a Wakefield woman suspected as a witch. Mary Midgely, another Yorkshire witch, was threatened and beaten by Henry Cockcrofte, who believed she was responsible for bewitching one of his children. One of the characters in George Gifford's *Dialogue,* first published in 1593, told how "some wish me to beate and claw the witch, until I fetch blood on her, and to threaten her that I will have her hanged." He added, reflecting what must have been the real experience of many who thought themselves victims of witchcraft, "if I knew which were the best, I would do it."

In fact, the practice to which Gifford referred, the drawing of blood from a witch in the hope of bringing relief to the bewitched person, was very widely resorted to. The logic of this course was summed up succinctly by Richard Browne, the victim of a Yorkshire witch named Elizabeth Lambe, in 1652. He claimed that "he was cruelly handled at the heart with one Elizabeth Lambe, & that she drew his heart's blood from him . . . he desired to scratch her, saying that she had drawne blood of him, & if he could draw blood of her, he hoped he should amend." This form of counter-magic was extremely well known. Depositions and pamphlets dealing with cases from all parts of England attest that it was widely used by the early seventeenth century, while it was one of the practices censured by demonological writers: William Perkins, for example, singled it out for special comment. Witches were frequently compelled to enter the houses of those whom they were thought to have afflicted, and forced to submit to being scratched, ideally on their forehead, until they bled. Thus in the Warboys case of 1593, the parents of the afflicted girls considered scratching the main suspect, Mother Samuel, but desisted after they had "taken advise of good divines of the unlawfulnes thereof." Their afflicted daughters had no such inhibitions, one of them, Elizabeth, scratching Agnes Samuel's hand "and seemed to be marveilous joyfull that she had gotten bloud." Evidence of the effectiveness of the practice was provided after the suspects in this case were imprisoned. Contrary to the belief that incarceration destroyed the witch's power, they allegedly afflicted the gaoler's son. The gaoler brought Mother Samuel to his son's bedside, "and there helde her, untill his sonne had scratched her, and so presently his sonne amended."

Even without scratching, one of the recurrent themes of accounts of witchcraft is that of the dramatic confrontation between the supposed victim and the alleged witch. This could include the deployment of very direct counter-magic against the witch. In 1626 Goodwife Wright was brought before the authorities in the Colony of Virginia as a suspected witch. During a discussion about witchcraft she had apparently shown a suspicious degree of knowledge about the subject: in particular, according to one witness, Wright recalled that when she was in service at Hull

> being one day chirninge of butter, there cam a woman to the howse who was accompted for a witch, whereuppon she by direction of her dame clapt the chirne staffe to the bottom of the chirne and clapt her hands across the top of it by w[hi]ch means the witch was not able to stire out of the place where she was for the space of six howres. After w[hi]ch time good wiefe Wright desired her dame to ask the woman why she did not gett her gone, whereuppo[n] the witche fell downe on her knees and asked forgiveness, and said her hand was in the chirne, and could not stire before her maide lifted up the staff of the chirne.

Another witness deposed how Wright also told how while she was at Hull her dame was sick and thought herself to be bewitched. She directed Wright that when the woman suspected of bewitching her came to the house, she was "to take a horshwe [horseshoe] and flinge it into her dames urine, and so long as the horshwe was hott, the witch was sick at the harte."

The object of other confrontations or meetings between the witch and her supposed victims was either to establish proof or to attempt to effect a reconciliation. Thus late in Elizabeth's reign the grandmother and aunt of Thomas Darling, bewitched by Alice Gooderidge, "making conscience to accuse her till it appeared upon sure proofe, sent for her unto the towne to talke with her privately." Henry Bullock, one of the accusers in the Lancashire trials of 1612, engineered a meeting with Alice Devise, whom he thought to have killed one of his children by witchcraft, at which she fell to her knees and begged his forgiveness. Some years later a Yorkshire woman, Margaret Morton, was thought to have bewitched the child of John Booth of Warmfield. Booth brought her before the child and Morton asked its forgiveness three times. A further confrontation involved Mary Midgely, who, as we have seen, was subjected to a beating and threats by Henry Cockcrofte. Another of her supposed victims, the wife of Richard Wood, went to her in the hopes of negotiating after cattle fell ill. After some hesitation, Midgely accepted six pence from her, "and wished her to go home for the kyne [cattle] should mende and desired her to take for every cow a handful of salte and an old sickle and lay underneath them and if they amended not to come to her again." It is in such meetings that something of the drama of a witchcraft accusation, of the need to confront, negotiate with or browbeat people with occult power, can be most fully sensed.

There were, of course, other less personally confrontational methods of combating the occult power of the witch. There was a widespread belief that burning something belonging to the witch, most frequently the thatch from her roof, would either force the witch to reveal herself or alleviate the witchcraft. It was in such a hope that, during the possession of Brian Gunter's daughter, the thatch of one of the suspected witches, Elizabeth Gregory, was burnt, while in 1621 the clerical author of the pamphlet describing the trial and execution of Elizabeth Sawyer in Middlesex could refer to the practice of burning thatch as an "old ridiculous custom." It was not just the witch's thatch which was in danger. At one point in the Gunter case the supposed victims of Elizabeth Gregory wanted to burn some of her hair "for their better satisfaccons & for their daughter's ease." In the Warboys case it was suggested to Mistress Throckmorton that she should burn some of Mother Samuel's hair and her "hairlace." In a London case of 1599 the parents of a bewitched child were advised by a cunning woman that "for the childe's recovery they should cut of a piece of the witche's coate with a payre of sheeres & burne it togeather with the child's under cloth: which they did, and the childe accordingly was healed." As so often, taking any course of action, either traditionally prescribed or recommended by cunning folk, must have constituted a significant psychological release from the sense of helplessness which being the victim of malefic witchcraft frequently engendered.

Another testimony to the efficacy of fire as a force to counter witchcraft was the practice of burning animals supposedly suffering from witchcraft. Edward Fairfax deplored the practice, common in his area, of following cunning folk's advice "to burn young calves alive and the like" when cattle were thought to have been bewitched, but the usage seems to have been very common. At Warboys in 1593 Mother Samuel was thought to be killing the calves and pigs of Robert Throckmorton of Brampton, who had "dealt verie roughly in speeches" with her. He was advised "that whatsoever next died, to make a hole in the ground, and burne the same." He did this with a cow that died a little later, "and after that, his cattle did well." Here the secret of success was not release from psychological pressure, but possibly something more concrete: such a move may have broken the chain of infection among naturally infected animals. Certainly such practices were not universally conducive to the peace of mind of the owner of the cattle. Anne, the wife of Thomas Harrison, gave evidence to the Lancashire justices in 1629 about the bewitching of her animals by Janet Wilkinson. She burnt one of her oxen, "but in the night whylest the said oxe was in burneing," she was so troubled with thoughts of the supposed witch "that shee could not rest in her bed, shee still thinkinge the said Jennet was at the bedd syde disquietinge her, whereupon this inform[er] fell to her prayers." Falling to his prayers might have saved a lot of trouble for John Crushe of Hawkwell in Essex, who in 1624 was presented to the archdeacon's court for burning a supposedly bewitched lamb alive during Sunday service and accidentally setting the common on fire, to the disruption of the parish's religious devotions.

These are only the more consistently documented forms of counter-magic. Contemporary sources name a wide variety of methods by which persons supposing themselves to be bewitched could attempt either to identify their tormentor or to block the witch's power: hanging amulets around the neck, putting tongs in the fire to immobilize the witch, nailing a horseshoe to the door to prevent the witch's entry and so on. Together these provided forms of relief which, despite the strictures of theologians, were clearly regarded as effective by the population at large. That evidence of such beliefs is so widespread supports the contention that fear of witchcraft was much more pervasive than the number of formal prosecutions surviving in court archives might suggest.

It is evident that witchcraft beliefs and practices were deeply rooted in local society and, we must reiterate, such witchcraft accusations as came to court were more likely to be generated by local tensions within the community than to owe their origins to pressure "from above." It is also clear, despite some evidence of change, that the concerns at village level, the stereotype of the witch and the range of remedies available with which to combat witchcraft, remained relatively stable from the sixteenth to the eighteenth century. It is, of course, all too easy to regard popular beliefs about witchcraft, and popular culture in general, as unchanging and immobile. Popular notions did change, most frequently as a result of the influence of élite ideas. The odd popular voice claiming to prefer prayer to the services of the cunning man, or recognizing the importance of the diabolical pact, is evidence of this, although here, as ever, we are usually having to construct our knowledge of popular attitudes from scattered and imperfect materials. Yet the central concerns of village witchcraft, with *maleficium* performed typically by an elderly, poor woman and which could be combated by a variety of forms of counter-magic, were as clear around 1700 as they were in the early years of

Elizabeth's reign. It is, therefore, all too easy to contrast a monolithic, unchanging set of popular attitudes with the changing perceptions of witchcraft which are all too well documented in the large body of printed works written by the learned.

However, before we accept this clear-cut dichotomy it is necessary to confront a few complications. Perhaps our logical starting point should be the proposition that the early modern English community, whether rural or urban, was a place where gossip thrived, where reputations were evaluated, where discussable news was a welcome entity. In such an environment there is little doubt that witchcraft suspicions were among the more avidly discussed of topics. When suspicions crystallized against the Bedfordshire witch Mary Sutton, who was thought in particular to have harmed the property and family of a gentleman named Enger, so a contemporary source tells us, "the report of this was carried up and downe all Bedford-shire, and this Marie Sutton's wicked and lewde courses being rumoured as well abroad, as in Master Enger's house." Cases of possession were especially prone to attract large numbers of interested spectators, and it was, indeed, thought appropriate that certain stages in the treatment of the possessed were best performed in front of an audience. Thus during the possession of the Starkie children in Lancashire in the 1590s, "all this while the honest neighbours neare about, coming in, the roome filled apace, some holding and tending the sicke possessed, & some sitting by." Mother Samuel, confessing after heavy pressure to witchcraft in 1593, was forced to confirm her words "in the bodie of the church . . . before her neighbours." . . . [A]ny generalizing theory about women and the witch craze encounters a major problem. Modern historians and the more sceptical of early modern observers alike have noted that the women accused of witchcraft were usually a very limited sample of their sex. In theory any woman might be accused of witchcraft, but in practice a disproportionate number of accused witches tended to be old, socially isolated, poor and to have an established reputation in their communities for being troublesome. John Gaule, writing in 1646, was just one of a number of writers who deplored the fact that

> every old woman with a wrinkled face, a furr'd brow, a hairy lip, a gobber tooth, a squint eye, a squeaking voyce, or a scolding tongue, having a ragged coate on her back, a skullcap on her head, a spindle in her hand, and a dog or cat by her side; is not only suspected, but pronounced for a witch.

Recent attempts to explain why such women might so frequently be accused of witchcraft have focused on two, in large measure complementary, explanations. It has been argued that it was the economic marginality of such women which made their neighbours unhappy about them and led to their being accused as witches. We return to the contention that, in a period of harshening economic conditions for the lower orders, and of some moral confusion about how to deal with poverty, the old woman seeking alms was transformed from a proper object of charity to a threat to the stability of the village.

A second strand of thinking would argue that such women, many of them widows or women otherwise living outside the conventional hierarchies of family or household, were not only perceived as poor but also as being outside normal patterns of control. Such women were anomalies in the patriarchal order and thus fit targets for the type of hostility which might lead to their being accused of witchcraft.

Concern over uncontrolled or independent women might have been more intense in this period, irrespective of the phenomenon of witchcraft. It is now a commonplace that the century before 1650 was one in which concern over disorder was running at a high level. Educated contemporaries, many of them convinced that the millennium was at hand anyway, felt that they were living in a period when traditional social and political hierarchies were vulnerable to imminent collapse. Indeed, the cosmic threat that witches, as the devil's minions, were thought to pose to the ordered world fitted neatly into the patterns of thought which such concerns generated. One possible facet of these fears was worry that male domination, that central element of contemporary notions of hierarchy, was being threatened by female insubordination. In an age which was patriarchal, and in which the patriarchal family was seen as the basic unit and (for many) model of political authority, the spectre of the rebellious woman, most often found in the cultural stereotype of the scolding wife, was a disturbing one. It is always difficult to gauge these matters, but there is at least some evidence to support the view that the early seventeenth century experienced an upsurge in misogynistic literature. Thus the notion that the Elizabethan and early Stuart periods experienced a crisis in gender relations, an aspect of a more general concern for the maintenance of social hierarchy and social order, might well have a bearing on why women, and women of a certain type, were accused of witchcraft. . . .

With the coming of the Royal Society [1662], we might be excused for thinking that the rapid triumph of new scientific ideas was assured and the destruction of belief in witchcraft made inevitable. To employ modern concepts, the line between "science" and "magic" would now be clearly defined along lines acceptable to us today. The "magical" elements in early modern science, not least the acceptance of the existence and operation of occult forces, would be marginalized, and hence belief in the reality of witches, apparitions, poltergeists, ghosts and all the other denizens of the spiritual world would be banished from the intellectual framework of the educated. As Charles Webster, one of our leading historians of science, has put it, if it happened, this shift "would constitute one of the major contributions of the Scientific Revolution towards the modernization of belief systems." Once freed from the ancient shackles of demonology, the way was clear for the more scientific investigation of many of the phenomena associated with witchcraft, and the more humane medical treatment of the persons affected. Yet, as recent research by Webster and others has demonstrated, the situation was considerably less clear-cut.

There were two main elements in the new science which have been identified by older generations of historians as permitting a decisive break with existing thought. The first was a rise of an empirical, "experimental" style of scientific investigation, which was held to have made manifest the vacuousness of the traditional method of arguing from existing authorities. The second was that rise of mechanical philosophy to which we have referred. Both these phenomena were of course present, and important, in post-Restoration scientific thinking, but in neither case was their impact quite so decisive as has been argued. Empiricism and experimentalism are both at the heart of what the modern non-specialist would regard as sound "scientific method," but even some initial thoughts on the demystification of scientists suggest a few problems. Ultimately, the emphasis on new methods of validation, on the need for quantitative precision when supporting scientific argument, did represent something novel. Yet historians of science are now aware of the problem of reading into these methodological changes too much of the methodologies of which they themselves approve, while there is also a growing sensitivity over the possible divergence between what seventeenth-century scientists said they were doing as they went about their business and what they actually did. . . .

So even by the 1680s the ideas of the "Scientific Revolution" had not penetrated the educated culture of England sufficiently to allow them to be drawn on to any deep degree by writers on the reality of witchcraft. Yet over the next generation or so, acceptance of this reality became impossible in the best intellectual and social circles, and the positions maintained by More, Glanvill, Casaubon and Bovet were no longer tenable there. But, it must be reiterated, this transition was neither rapid nor straightforward. There was no decisive argument, debate or great work which ended the possibility that the educated man or woman might believe in witchcraft. Indeed, the erosion of the foundations for such a belief seems to have been the result of changing fashion rather than of the triumph of decisive, reasoned arguments. In natural philosophy, as with theology and with concepts of legal proof, such intellectual shifts as did occur are best interpreted as a gradual chipping away at witchcraft beliefs, a gradual process of marginalization, rather than a dramatic overturning of existing belief systems. . . .

For a final indication of the lack of direct evidence between scientific advance and the rejection of witchcraft beliefs among the learned, let us turn to a printed version of a sermon preached in 1736, by a happy coincidence the year in which the English (and Scottish) witchcraft statutes were repealed. Its author was a Leicestershire clergyman, Joseph Juxon, and it was preached after a suspected witch was subjected to the swimming test at Twyford in that county. Juxon was firmly opposed to the practice of swimming witches, and in fact denied the existence of witchcraft altogether. His grounds for so doing are instructive. In part, they were social. He noted, as Reginald Scot had a century and a half before him, that persons suspected of witchcraft were typically "such as are destitute of friends, bow'd down with years, laden with infirmities; so far from annoying others, as not to have it in their power to take care of themselves." Yet "there is so much superstition and fear, and this is so deeply rooted [that] whenever the alarm is given, there is always a party formed, a very powerful one too, against these poor, ignorant and helpless creatures." Accusations against such people had to be nipped in the bud, for though "persons of ill fame be accused at first . . . yet the suspicion may fall at last upon those of unblemish'd character and reputation." Juxon remarked that "in our own country we have in former times had some few instances of terrible executions on this account," and noted one foreign episode of witch-hunting (unfortunately unspecified) where there was "such havock made [that] there was no peace to be had, 'til an effectual stop was put to such unright-eous accusations."

In addition to this disquiet at the social breakdown which might ensue if witchcraft accusations were allowed to flow unchecked, Juxon also mobilized what were by then the familiar theological arguments for scepticism. There was no scriptural basis for the witchcraft beliefs current among the population at large, these being founded rather upon "the very dregs of heathenism and popery" and "such lying legends, which have been propagated only by weak and credulous people, and beleeved by none but those, who are weak and credulous as they." The good man was under God's care and protection and had no need to fear witches. To ascribe too much power to the devil was to deny both divine control of the natural world and the operation of divine providence within it. The evils popularly ascribed to witchcraft, wrote Juxon, "are such as may proceed from natural causes, and are common unto men." The arguments, although voiced in the restrained tones of the early Enlighten-ment rather than the more pungent ones of mid-Elizabethan England, were es-sentially the same as those put forward by Reginald Scot in 1584. There was little sign in Juxon's sermon of any reception of new scientific ideas, or any ap-plication of the new natural philosophy to the problem of witchcraft. The ar-guments against witchcraft to which Juxon had recourse were, by 1736, more or less standard ones; what had changed, for educated opinion if not for the villagers of Twyford, was the willingness to accept them.

Thus, for the generality of the educated public, it would seem that the di-rect contribution of the "Scientific Revolution" to the decline of belief in witchcraft was minimal. Possibly awareness of the advance in scientific knowl-edge helped create an intellectual and perhaps psychological context in which witchcraft beliefs could be steadily eroded and marginalized, but it is difficult to see anything like a direct and open assault. One of the implications of the new physics with which Newton was associated was that the physical uni-verse, the earth included, was now seen as operating under predictable rules, while there may have been a corresponding growth in optimism about hu-mankind's ability to know, and perhaps even control, the natural environ-ment. If this optimism was in existence, it coincided with the growth of a new, more measured form of Christianity, and also, perhaps, with a rather less apprehensive view of the possibilities for the survival of civil society—a shift, as it were, from Hobbes's view of a war of all against all to Locke's notion of a social contract. This latter might have been no less of a fiction than the first, but it was a good deal more reassuring. Such a mental world left rather less room for angels, demons and other supernatural forces, and, perhaps more importantly, was one in which the ubiquitous power of Satan was no longer quite such a matter of concern among educated people. Arguably, the emergence of a recognizably "modern" or "scientific" approach to the study of nature was as much a symptom of these intellectual and cultural changes as a cause of them. But it is undeniable that in the long run, however uncertainly and tangentially, that swirling mass of intellectual endeavour which historians refer to as the "Scientific Revolution of the Seventeenth Century" contributed to the process of the gradual invalidation of witchcraft beliefs. . . .

A belief in witchcraft, it would thus seem, continued to flourish among the lower orders of rural England until the mid- or late nineteenth century. Among their educated betters, so all the evidence suggests, belief in witchcraft, witches and magic collapsed in the early eighteenth century. Yet even here the story is more complex and less certain than might appear at first sight.

There is no doubt that full-scale defences of the reality of witchcraft were rare after 1700. What is generally regarded as the last by a respectable scholar came in 1715, in the shape of Richard Boulton's *A Compleat History of Magick, Sorcery and Witchcraft*. Boulton, a relatively obscure doctor whose other publications included a number of books on medical matters and an epitome of [scientist] Robert Boyle's works, argued along what were by that date traditional lines, and such passages as those describing how the devil came most readily to persons in a state of despair and how magicians were attracted by "too eager desire and pursuit of knowledge" were very similar to their equivalents in demonological tracts of the later sixteenth century. Boulton also emphasized the importance of the swimming test and the witch's mark in establishing proof. . . .

Boulton's work provoked a counterblast that is usually regarded as one of the key English witchcraft texts, Francis Hutchinson's *A Historical Essay* of 1718. Hutchinson, a Church of England clergyman and a future bishop and religious controversist, wrote what was a scholarly and careful piece of work, gathering together a mass of information, which is still a useful historical source. He was anxious to preserve the possibility of the spirit world, declaring that "the sober belief" in spirits was "an essential part of every good Christian's faith," but saw such a belief as something totally separate from "the fantastick doctrines that support the vulgar opinion of witchcraft." And, again, we get a sense of the cultural distancing between the learned churchman and those who might hold "vulgar opinions": "the credulous multitude," wrote Hutchinson, "will ever be ready to try their tricks, and swim the old women, and wonder at and magnify every unaccountable symptom and odd accident." His arguments, apart from these, were also standard: most of what was attributable to witchcraft was, in fact, explicable by natural causes, the references to witchcraft in Scripture were misunderstood and mistranslated, spectral evidence was a nonsense and so on. . . .

And as the late seventeenth and eighteenth centuries progressed, references to witchcraft in literature and on the stage, although by no means absent, demonstrated a shift. In 1689 Henry Purcell, in his opera *Dido and Aeneas,* used three witches to symbolize evil in much the same way as Shakespeare had in *Macbeth.* But the splintering of any consensual view of witchcraft had been demonstrated earlier, in 1681, with the staging of Thomas Shadwell's play *The Lancashire-Witches, and Tegue o Divelly the Irish Priest.* This work took a number of materials, including those relating to the Lancashire trials of 1612 and 1633, but used witches as essentially comic characters in what was an anti-Catholic and pro-Whig satire produced towards the end of the Popish Plot. That the play was staged about fifty times between 1703 and 1729 provides further evidence of how potent the witch image was in early-eighteenth-century politics. But by the early eighteenth century terms like "bewitch" or "enchant" were beginning to lose their sinister overtones and to be used in the more modern but less threatening sense of being fooled or sexually attracted. The language of witchcraft was still part of common parlance, but its resonances had altered. The shift is illustrated neatly in the *Oxford English Dictionary,* which notes that "bewitch" had been used "formerly often in a bad sense," but that it was since "more generally said of pleasing influences." When witchcraft or magic was mentioned, it was usually in a more distanced sense. When, for example, Sir Anthony Absolute in Sheridan's *The Rivals,* a play first staged in 1785, announced, "Had I a thousand daughters, by heaven! I'd as soon have them taught the black art as their alphabet," the effect intended was clearly a comic one. Few people in the polite audience of the 1780s would have taken the allusion in any other way; two centuries earlier, a more ambivalent response may have been evoked. . . .

Yet, as we have suggested, this belief had not disappeared quite as totally as has sometimes been claimed. Or, to put it rather differently, just as the language of witchcraft was changing in its emphasis, so, for the educated, aspects of the occult were being redefined: magic and the supernatural were not so much being rejected as recategorized. Perhaps the clearest clue to this process is provided by the cultural history of astrology. As we have noted, by the eighteenth century astrology had ceased to be treated seriously by polite society and was becoming increasingly an intellectual activity patronized by the provincial middling sort or by the common people. But the repackaging of astrological ideas and the relocating of astrological concerns as a part of popular science meant that the subject never quite vanished from the agenda of the educated, and it was to make something of a comeback from the 1790s onwards. The extent of this comeback is perhaps best demonstrated by the reception of the work of Ebenezer Sibly (1751–99), who combined a belief that modern science should be informed by ancient knowledge with what was, in his period, a very fashionable interest in freemasonry and animal magnetism. The ready market for Sibly's publications on astrology, it has been claimed, was evidence of a middlebrow cultural border zone where sets of interests which might once have been satisfied by natural magic were now being catered to by popular science and redefinitions of Christianity.

Another element in the late-eighteenth-century cultural mix which suggests a renewed interest in the occult was the popularity of the Gothic novel, a literary genre generally considered to have been ushered in with the publication of Horace Walpole's *The Castle of Otranto* in 1765. Obviously, a desire to read Gothic novels should not be equated with a belief in witchcraft, but what the taste for this genre does demonstrate is another episode in that repackaging of the occult which seems to have been a feature of European culture since Roman times. Mary Shelley's *Frankenstein,* published in 1818, is an enduring exemplar of the horror story, but the period saw the publication of numerous other works, now forgotten by all but specialist scholars. And these works contained a number of recurring elements: the Gothic castle, the villain who has pledged himself to the devil, a world of ghosts, apparitions, sorcerers and witches, of a mixture of the spirit and the natural world which, as we have seen, was part of the context for witchcraft beliefs among educated writers in the later seventeenth century. . . .

It is, perhaps, with Hallowe'en that we can end our brief survey of how witchcraft stands at present in our culture. Among the things which everybody knows about witches is that they met in their covens on Hallowe'en, the night of 31 October, in order to weave their spells and practise their satanic rites. Thus children (more so, at present, in the United States than elsewhere) dress up in witch costumes on 31 October and go out trick-or-treating, adults have Hallowe'en parties and occasional cases occur of outraged parents complaining to education authorities about the spread of Satanism when schools hold events to mark Hallowe'en. It would be interesting to try to discover at what point Hallowe'en became associated with witchcraft. On the strength of the materials I have read while putting this book together, if witches met together on 31 October, it is something of which everybody writing about witchcraft, trying witches in courts or physically or verbally abusing them in sixteenth- seventeenth- or eighteenth-century England was totally ignorant. John Brand's *Observations of the Popular Antiquities of Great Britain,* published in 1795, an important early compendium of popular customs and superstitions, while devoting numerous pages to 31 October, makes no mention of witchcraft, while the later and even more comprehensive *British Calendar Customs* of 1940 mentions only one witchcraft-related custom, which apparently could be dated no further back than 1925, amid the numerous ceremonies and beliefs it associates with the last day of October. The notion of Hallowe'en as a witches' feast seems to owe everything to twentieth-century inventiveness and nothing to historical reality, and its current spread in Britain seems to be just another piece of evidence of the insidious Americanization of British culture.

It would seem, then, that history offers little to those currently interested in witchcraft, whether they are the people who are deeply involved in what they consider to be an ancient religion or the children who come trick-or-treating to my door on Hallowe'en. This does not unduly worry me. As far as I am concerned, one of the historian's main functions is to be critical of his or her surroundings, and to be especially vigilant when the past is inaccurately or meretriciously invoked to support present practices. And witchcraft, something which, as I have suggested, is still part of the cultural baggage even of people who have absolutely no belief in any aspect of the occult, is a subject whose past has constantly been misrepresented. . . .

Yet the gulf remains: most people in Britain around 1600 believed in witches; most today do not. Yet explaining why we moderns do not entertain such beliefs is difficult. Perhaps part of the answer does lie in technology. We now have ways of explaining natural phenomena and personal misfortune which do not involve witchcraft, while we are more confident than our early modern forebears of being able to understand and control our cosmos. Part of the answer probably lies in the fact that most of us do not live in the same sort of "face to face" environment as did an Elizabeth villager. And if we accept the once fashionable view that witch-hunting was a form of social scapegoating, it could be argued that later societies have developed other scapegoats and that, to take the two most-quoted examples, Jews in Nazi Germany and Communists in Senator McCarthy's United States fulfilled much the same function as did witches in Europe between the fifteenth and eighteenth centuries. Yet none of these explanations seems to me fully satisfying. The answer, perhaps, lies in some combination of a lack of belief that harm can be done between humans invisibly at a distance, a different set of "explanations" for unusual diseases and the lack of any real notion of cosmic evil. . . .

7

ATTACKS ON POPULAR CULTURE: A CASE FROM JEWISH RITUAL

ELLIOT HOROWITZ

While increasing commercialization formed one basic source of change in preindustrial Europe—affecting peasant structures and gender relations as previous selections demonstrate—shifts in basic outlook form a second dynamic theme. James Sharpe, in the preceding selection, captured one major aspect of the new mentality trends. A second aspect involved growing elite disapproval of popular spontaneity and the celebratory and festival traditions where it was expressed. New fastidiousness was by no means entirely successful; older rituals often survived, at least in part, as this selection makes clear. But there were new constraints, along with new social divisions.

This selection focuses on celebrations among European Jews, surrounding the circumcision of sons. Often regarded as a group apart, and certainly subjected to much prejudice, Jews participated in many wider European trends—including the redefinition of appropriately solemn religious behavior. Jewish family celebrations had shared some of the gaiety of the courtship ritual John Gillis describes for England (see the next selection), but now a new current of propriety sought to reverse their tone. Traditions are here described with considerable, even nostalgic, approval—in contrast to other descriptions of preindustrial emotional life, such as Robert Muchembled's (Chapter 1).

The contrast between day and night which exercised the "troubled imagination" of late medieval and early modern Europe paralleled another which it found increasingly problematic—that between the sacred and the profane. These realms had intermingled with relative freedom during the Middle Ages, often amid the chiarascuristic scenes created by the night's flickering lights. Popular behavior at the vigils held on the eve of a notable feast or parish festival prompted complaints from the clergy that "some dance in the very churches with obscene songs, others play at dice, with oaths denying God and

From: Elliot Horowitz, "The Eve of the Circumcision: A Chapter in the History of Jewish Nightlife," *Journal of Social History,* vol. 23, no. 1 (1989), pp. 45–60.

cursing of the saints." It has been persuasively argued that whereas medieval attempts to curb such abuses seem to have been rather halfhearted, the post-[Reformation] Church was both more persistent and more successful in its efforts to control popular amusements. Although they were not always suppressed, great care was taken to sever their profane elements from the realm of the sacred. By the late seventeenth century, John Bossy has observed, "eating and drinking, like dancing, gaming, and ritual obscenity had everywhere been expelled from the churches."

What, however, of the synagogues? There, too, and in Jewish ceremonial life in general (much of which took place inside the home) the domains of the sacred and the profane had defied neat separation during the Middle Ages. In early modern times, by contrast, the intermingling of these two domains seems to have become increasingly problematic as the dominant religious sensibility turned increasingly austere. . . .

[The] primary emphasis [of this essay] shall be upon the reconstruction of the social history of a Jewish observance—that held on the night or nights preceding a boy's circumcision and known as the "veglia" in Italy and as the "wachnacht" in Central Europe. The changes it underwent suggest certain striking lines of continuity across the boundaries of the religious cultures of Jews and Christians in early modern Europe. . . .

Emerging in the Middle Ages as a night of largely profane festivity in which women, too, played a prominent (and in some cases dominant) role, the precircumcision vigil began, during the seventeenth century, to take on a more sober and sacred character, as well as becoming an increasingly masculine affair. This was due to the intervention of rabbinical or communal authorities, who came to regard as problematic forms of festivity which had previously been tacitly tolerated if not explicitly endorsed. Their initiatives would appear to be rooted in the fundamental shift in European sensibilities discussed above no less than in internal developments in Jewish society. After the seventeenth century the vigil was to retain considerably less of the free and easy atmosphere which had characterized its earlier history, but perhaps not as little as we might imagine. . . .

In his *Synagoga Judaica,* first published in 1603, the Swiss Hebraist Johannes Buxtorf (the elder) described the night of "festival jollity and facetious merriment" observed by the Jews on the seventh night after the birth of a boy, that is, on the eve of his circumcision. It was, he explained, an extended visit with the mother in order to allay her fears considering the possible harm that might come to her child at the circumcision or, following popular belief, during the night preceding it. The visit, however, is described by Buxtorf as an all-night affair, involving, besides abundant food, such amusements as cards, dice, singing, and storytelling, all accompanied, especially among the men, by rather heavy drinking, in which the circumcisor must be warned against overindulging. The account, however, does not neglect to mention, though it does so as a kind of afterthought, that the most learned and pious among the guests also recite several devout prayers. The overall picture which emerges from his description is that of a practice combining both raucous amusement and pious recitation, with the emphasis clearly upon the former. . . .

What actually did go on then during these long nights? Buxtorf, as we have noted, mentioned gambling, singing, and storytelling in addition to the consumption of much food and drink. Sixteenth century evidence from south of the Alps points in a similar direction, with, however, the significant addition of dancing. In 1530 the Jewish community of Padua decided to ban dance celebrations among its members except at specifically stated occasions. One of the exceptions was for "the nights of the 'veglia,' these being the nights preceding the circumcision of a male child, and only in the mother's home." The inclusion of dancing in the "veglia" was undoubtedly part of the Renaissance heritage of Italian Jewry, yet like Renaissance dance in general its actual practice among Jews of the Padua region in the early sixteenth century was sometimes far from chaste. . . .

Seven successive nights of dancing undoubtedly created a rather free and heady atmosphere among those same Jews, conducive to the sorts of amusements not normally engaged in on a regular basis. Gambling, too, seems to have figured prominently in the night's festivities. When, in nearby Cremona, word arrived in 1575 of the impending arrival of the plague, the "health officers" appointed by the Jewish community decided, as a penitential gesture, to ban games of chance. One of the exceptions made, however, was for "the night of the 'veglia' and the day of the circumcision . . . and only in the home of the child's father." Significantly, dancing in Padua was associated with the mother's home, whereas gambling in Cremona was mentioned in connection with the home of the father, suggesting parallel male and female amusements.

The Paduan statute was reconfirmed in 1580, indicating that the communal authorities still regarded dancing as an acceptable form of celebration at the "veglia." In contrast however, to that statute and the aforementioned one in Cremona, both of which treated the festive vigil as an event outside the customary sphere of control, a decade later sumptuary legislation was passed among the communities of the Monferrato which did seek to impose certain limitations on the pre-circumcision celebration. Articles of clothing which women were not to wear in public, it was decreed, were also not to be worn in their homes during the "veglia" festivities (when their homes, presumably, became public domain) and the number of local guests who could be invited to the meal held on that evening was limited to six. A more striking form of control was exerted some three decades later in Ancona where, in 1619, the council of the "Italian" (as opposed to Levantine) Jewish community decreed that on the night before a circumcision "no refreshments, whether food or drink, may be served to the men coming to celebrate with the father but only to the women, as is the custom." The prohibition, however, proved easier to legislate than to enforce, and less than five years later the community decided to nullify it, citing the Talmudic policy against promulgating a decree by which the majority cannot abide.

The Ancona ordinances point, therefore, to two kinds of celebrations on the eve of a circumcision, one in the women's sphere and the other among the men. Only the former was officially sanctioned, which would suggest that it was there the more traditional of the two observances. The men, however, seem to have had a hard time staying away, perhaps enjoying then a night of gambling with the father as had been customary in Cremona. In Venice, too, gambling had been one of the activities associated with the "veglia" until it was banned by the sumptuary regulations issued by the local community in 1616–17 in the interest of maintaining order and avoiding scandal on such occasions. . . .

The silence of both Modena and Morosini, coupled with the testimony from Padua, Cremona, and Ancona cited above, strongly suggests that through the mid-seventeenth century the rite as observed among Italian Jewry consisted of a social gathering on the eve of a circumcision in which the participants enjoyed considerable freedom to pursue a wide variety of amusements. It was a rite essentially profane in content but perceptibly linked, nonetheless, with the spiritual domain through its association with the holy act of circumcision and through its battle, by means of wakefulness, with the threatening spirits. In this respect it was typical of the popular religious culture of late medieval Europe, which saw no reason to sever the sacred from the profane. It maintained itself as a popular tradition, untouched by the religious authorities, and hence an authentic expression of the religion of the people.

One person, however, with whom this tradition did not sit well was . . . the kabbalist R. Aaron Berechia of Modena. If the former attempted to present a tame version of the "veglia" in his *Riti*, the latter sought to create one. In his 1626 work *Ma'avar Yabok,* devoted albeit to the subject of death and its related rituals, the latter proposed a radical reform in the accepted practice. There, while discussing the salutary effects of reciting "pareshat ha-ketoret," the Biblical and Talmudic passages describing the offering of incense in the Temple, R. Aaron added the following suggestion:

> And also on the night before a circumcision how beneficial it would be to recite it before the Chair of Elijah, together with the Psalms of David . . . as against those who spend that night in merrymaking, men and women . . . young and old. Go and observe what the custom was among those of earlier generations who did not interrupt their study for a moment on the night before a circumcision. . . .

Criticism of the popular observance of the "veglia" and [the] attempt to transform it . . . into a more sober and mystical ceremony cannot be seen in isolation from an important trend then gaining force throughout Western Europe. This trend . . . had as its aim the reform of popular culture, whether by means of suppressing traditional practices or by purifying them. The latter, as [Peter] Burke argued, was the path favored by Catholic reformers as opposed to their Protestant counterparts, and would typically take the form of replacing a raucous parade at a parish festival with a solemn procession rather than

attempting to abolish the festival itself. R. Aaron Berechia of Modena's proposed innovation, which sought to purify a popular observance from its more
offensive elements, thus joined a chorus of similar initiatives advanced by the
Catholic clergy of his native Counter-Reformation Italy. His efforts, and others which followed in their wake, suggest that the campaign against popular
culture during this period may be seen as a process whose contours extend beyond the confines of Christian society.

This campaign . . . drew its force from the increasing tendency, especially
on the part of the post-[Reformation] Church, to clearly demarcate the boundaries between the sacred and the profane in an attempt to keep these two domains far more separate than they had been in medieval times. By the end [of
the seventeenth century] the communal authorities of the Venetian ghetto
stepped in to insure that this aspect of the pre-circumcision vigil became its
main feature rather than a mere appendage. The sumptuary regulations of
1697 stated firmly that on the nights before a circumcision a "veglia was absolutely prohibited." By this was meant that no guests could attend the household celebration other than immediate relatives of the mother and father. Exception was made, however, for "the rabbis, to give a lesson." By admitting
them and excluding others the lay communal authorities not only lent their
support to the new pious manner of observing the vigil, but also stepped up
their campaign to tone down the more traditional observance.

It is thus significant that the very term "veglia," which had earlier been associated (like "carnival" among the Christians) with freedom from restraint,
underwent a shift in connotation—to the realm of the prohibited. Whereas the
Venetian sumptuary regulations of the mid-sixteenth century had sidestepped
the issue of the "veglia" and those of the early seventeenth had sought only to
eliminate specific abuses such as gambling, by the end of that century efforts
were made to impose more total control upon the event, and, in effect, to dele-
gitimize its traditional character.

The process of tightening control may also be observed in the Roman
community whose 1661 sumptuary regulations permitted dancing at the veglia only between members of the same sex. Those of 1702 went a step further,
stating that it was prohibited for "men quite as much for women, of any age,
to dance alone as well as with a partner." They did, however, permit some
"public festivities" on such occasions, provided that only Jewish musicians
were to perform and that no comedies involving the use of costumes were to
be staged. The increasing trend to tone down the event is clear, but no less evident through the efforts to contain them are the vital and diverse forms of
Jewish popular amusement which thrived in the Italian Ghetto. An inevitable
tension thus emerged between the intensifying thrust of control from above
and the tenacity of popular traditions.

In Ancona, where the "veglia" had still, in the early seventeenth century,
possessed something of the character of a women's festival, the community's
statutes of 1716 paid considerable attention to the event. One paragraph stipulated that on such nights, as on other occasions when many men or women

gathered together, it was incumbent upon the host to see to it that the pillars of his home were properly reinforced. Another prohibited married or engaged women from dancing except in the course of their lessons, at weddings and on the nights of the "veglia," where they presumably did so unaccompanied by men. A third dealt with the problem of masquerade, forbidding women from attending the pre-circumcision observance while wearing masks or any kind of costume. This paragraph followed directly after one generally prohibiting masks (especially small ones of black silk) for married or engaged women. Its somewhat redundant character, coupled with the absence of a parallel restriction for men, would seem to suggest that it had been especially common, if not customary, for Jewish women in Ancona to attend the "veglia" in masquerade as a sign both of its free and festive character and of the special place they occupied in it. Yet, as in Rome, amusements which had previously been acceptable on such occasions were, in the early eighteenth century, no longer tolerated. . . .

As the pious rite became more widespread so was the popular rite further repressed by the communal authorities. The Roman sumptuary regulations which had, in 1702, permitted Jewish musicians to perform at the "veglia" prohibited even these in 1726, stipulating further that only Hebrew songs (unaccompanied by music) could be sung on the night before the circumcision or at the ceremony itself. In addition to filtering out its profane elements, the community took a further step towards sacralizing the observance by specifying that only the members of the confraternity who had come to recite prayers . . . could be offered coffee and biscuits. Thus coffee, which could be used to extend the night and prolong the traditional festivities, was carefully limited to the practitioners of the pious rite. Theirs was treated as the main event while whatever remained of the popular festivity was banished thereby to the sidelines. . . .

In Italy, as a result of the efforts to repress profane elements in the "veglia" and the increasing emphasis upon the masculine activity of Torah study, the feminine element in the rite was de-emphasized. Whereas, for example, sixteenth and seventeenth century sources described the observance primarily in terms of a visit with the mother, Rabbi Corcos of Rome saw it (unhappily) in the early eighteenth as a party given by the father. In Ancona, where women were first prohibited in 1716 from attending the "veglia" in masquerade, they were, in 1739, effectively prohibited from participating at all, since the sumptuary regulations promulgated in that year limited attendance to officials of the community and first order relatives of the parents. Although men were obviously excluded as well, it had previously been members of the female sex who were the dominant presence at the event and it was they who were therefore most affected by the new regulation.

Beginning with Venetian regulation of 1697, then, a policy emerged in the Italian communities of transforming the pre-circumcision vigil from an open observance into a relatively closed one. This, of course, went hand in hand with the weeding out of its more profane elements, for controlling who goes in has much to do with controlling what goes on. In some instances this took the form of limiting admission to relatives and other privileged individuals, thus toning down the affair considerably. A year after this was done in Ancona, a similar regulation was enacted in Mantua. Both communities, however, eventually abandoned this form of control in favor of that introduced earlier in the community of Rome—the limitation of access to stimulants. By retreating from their earlier position they seem to have recognized that a modus vivendi had to be found in which more tolerance was shown for the popular dimensions of the pre-circumcision observance. Neighbors and well-wishers could not be turned away, but the duration of their revelry could be held in check. In Mantua the sumptuary laws of 1771 imposed no limit on who could attend the "veglia," but stipulated that coffee could be served that night only to the learned men engaged in study around the table. These, rather than the dancing women in Ancona a century and a half earlier, had become the evening's main performers. And if the popular observance could not be abolished entirely, it could be transformed into a prelude to the main event. In an era in which coffeehouses had become perhaps the dominant form of nocturnal entertainment throughout Europe it was understood that only those given access to coffee were given the wherewithal to get through the night. In Ancona itself the sumptuary regulations of 1766 formally divided the "veglia" for the first time into two shifts, at the first of which only sweets could be served and at the second coffee and other refreshments. It is clear that the first of these "mishmarot" was devoted to the traditional festivities whereas the latter consisted of a study vigil. By limiting the use of stimulants to those involved in the more "sacred" of the two ceremonies, these communities seem to have found an effective, if not necessarily subtle, means of placing the new ritual at center stage while at the same time allowing some vestiges of the old rite to survive. . . .

The tradition of gaiety and festivity was not entirely lost upon some rabbinical authorities of the twentieth century, who, while recommending prayer and study on the night before the circumcision, nonetheless saw fit to inform their readers that "in times past it had been customary to dance and to rejoice." If they had any explanation for why this was no longer the case they kept it to themselves. What, however, were their readers to conclude?

8

COURTSHIP RITUALS AND THE BASIS OF MARRIAGE

JOHN R. GILLIS

In this section, John Gillis discusses the emotional and ritualistic atmosphere surrounding courtship and marriage among ordinary people in Britain. He argues, among other things, that many basic habits lasted for a long period, into the nineteenth or even the twentieth centuries, so he traces his subject over several centuries.

Historians dealing with the family have often tried to make big distinctions between premodern and modern types: premodern families, as economic units, were formed from arranged marriages and were emotionally cool; modern marriages, in contrast, result from romantic love and sexual longings. John Gillis is one of a number of social historians who avoid these simple contrasts. He notes that most marriages in the sixteenth and seventeenth centuries had heavily charged emotional content. This may have been particularly true in England, where individual freedoms were unusually great, but it applies elsewhere in Western Europe. At the same time, marriages were not formed on the basis of modern romantic love, defined as intense interaction between two courting people. And community supervision, plus parental determination of marriage timing, remained intense. The relationship of preindustrial to modern courtship, while not a stark contrast, remains complex.

At the same time, Gillis paints a popular culture that is also distinctive in its use of ritual, community ceremony, and magic, and in its distinctive beliefs about the body and bodily manifestations. Europe's ordinary people had a rich arsenal of beliefs, in which magic helped make the environment more controllable, and they had many opportunities for boisterous expression. Some contemporary observers, stressing the more regimented aspects of modern life, wonder how much has been lost with the passing of many of these community rituals and spontaneous gestures. Note that Gillis discusses behaviors similar to those outlined by Robert Muchembled (Chapter 1), but with less emphasis on a larger environment of fear. Like Muchembled, however, he stresses the durability of popular beliefs and symbols.

From: John R. Gillis, "From Ritual to Romance: Toward an Alternative History of Love," in Carol Z. Stearns and Peter N. Stearns, eds., *Emotion and Social Change* (New York: Holmes & Meier, 1988), pp. 87–122.

It is little wonder that historians who view love as pure feeling have had such difficulty recognizing loving situations prior to the nineteenth century. Neither the educated elite nor illiterate folk of the early modern period viewed love as having a separate, disembodied existence. Because we do not have an adequate history of popular ideas of love for this period, I have been forced to impute much about people's perceptions from their behavior, always a somewhat risky enterprise. Nevertheless, it seems fair to conclude that early modern people did not perceive the heart as having a separate existence apart from the mind and body. Psychological and physical healing were closely related; feeling and action, emotion and speech, were regarded as inseparably joined. As we shall see, early modern people were less likely to make the distinction between action and feeling. It would not have occurred to them to dig deep to find emotions. "Feeling" still meant both physical and internal sensation; and, at a time when medical authorities made no sharp distinction between psyche and soma, anger and love were seen as having an actual physical presence in the "cold stare" or the "warm embrace." Love and hate could be transmitted through bodily orifices by emission or ingestion. They were identified with body fluids—blood, urine, saliva, excrement—but also communicated through visible and ritualized body movement. . . . Love was treated more like a script than a drive, something to be negotiated, acted out, worked on, with a public as well as a private dimension. . . .

The best way to comprehend early modern understandings of affection is not through conduct books, sermons, and love poetry, but by observing the way people actually courted, betrothed, and married. These visible behaviors tell us that early modern people viewed love as something tangible, felt in the same way as we feel a blow, savor a taste, or sense a stare. Just as much as they feared the harm that could be transmitted by the evil eye, women and men of the seventeenth and eighteenth centuries reveled in the effects of a potion, a charm, the power of a lover's gaze, kiss, embrace, even a blow. Kissing was not yet a private, intimate activity. It was still more like the modern hand-shake, a public social act signifying a pledge, which, if properly witnessed, was considered legally binding. Our notion of kissing as a private, purely pleasurable activity was unthinkable at a time when sexuality was not yet conceived of as a thing in and of itself. In reality, love kisses were probably not particularly pleasurable. They were more like bites, intended to be felt, to leave a mark, and even to draw blood. Any physical contact, and especially with blood, was believed to have a powerful binding effect. As late as 1906, an Irish boy who had drawn blood from a girl while roughhousing was told by his nurse: "Now you'll have to marry her."

Like kissing, the exchange of body fluids by sharing a meal or drinking from a common cup was "thought to comingle their spirits, and to be made one human life." Similarly, in this still largely oral culture, public speech-acts (as opposed to private or written words) were thought of as having a physical effect, powerful enough to wound or heal, as the case might be. Gestures, body language, and especially the emissions of the body itself had similar powers. In

Wales, a young man proved his love to a girl by urinating on her dress, a practice known locally as *rhythu*. Emotions were so closely identified with the body fluids that blood and urine were also used to drive away rivals and punish evildoers. In this case, the body was not simply expressing emotion; it was emotion itself.

Everything depended, of course, on the intention and social context. A vow had meaning according to the place in which it was made, in what company, and with what degree of publicity. A kiss between friends was not expected to have the same effect as one between lovers. A blow struck in anger was not the same as a love slap. Courting by blows was common in the French countryside throughout the nineteenth century:

> First they exchange glances, then casual remarks, then heavy witticisms. The young man shoves at the girl, thumps her hard on the back, takes her hand and squeezes it in a bone-cracking grip. She responds to this tender gesture by punching him in the back.

Love in the early modern period was not something particularly mysterious or spiritual. As something associated with the body, it was subject to the same control as any other physical function. Love could be worked on, consciously managed in any number of ways, some medical, others magical, but all quite deliberate. Educated elites and ordinary people shared a common corpus of beliefs based on analogical rather than scientific reasoning, and, as a result, many resorted to white magic when faced with physical and emotional problems. . . . In the case of love magic, the body itself often provided both the vehicle for performance and the medium by which love was communicated. Sharing the common set of assumptions about the power of particular gestures or objects, the person to whom the performance was directed thereby was impelled to feel the appropriate emotion.

In the seventeenth century we find all elements of the population, literate and illiterate, indulging in love magic, consulting dream and recipe books, using the same ritual performances to ensure love and exorcise envy and jealousy. They shared a somatic understanding of the emotions that caused them to believe they could cure "lovesickness" just as they could treat the gout or toothache. Even the Puritans, who were otherwise critical of magic, shared the belief that the emotions could be worked on. "Keep up your Conjugal Love in a constant heat and vigor," counseled Baxter. Where the Puritans departed from popular belief was their insistence on the private, inner character of the emotions and the kind of effort necessary to activate and control personal feelings. Whereas they exhorted the lovesick to introspection, other, more orthodox practitioners, like Richard Napier, continued to offer herbal and magical remedies, usually in combination with some advice about the social relationships that were the cause of the emotional distress in the first place. Napier urged his clients to reconcile the conflicts that he perceived as the cause of their anguish. The social side of his practice was essentially conservative. Quarreling couples were told to settle their differences; defiant daughters and prodigal sons were urged to be reconciled to their parents, advice that was ideologically consistent with the current emphasis on family solidarity, even though it was not invariably followed by Napier's clients, many of whom were clearly expressing guilt about their own autonomy.

Magical uses of the body proved such an effective persuasive device because people believed the operations of the body and those of society analogous. . . . Society was perceived organically, and men as well as women were taught from childhood to think of themselves as connected interdependent parts of a larger whole, whether it be the family or community. Boundaries between persons were viewed as porous. The body itself was seen as vulnerable to invasion, but its emissions were also regarded as very powerful. If used correctly—i.e., ritually—body parts and fluids, such as blood, saliva, excrement, hair, urine, the lips, tongue, even the eye, could transmit love or ward off envy.

Wise women and cunning men were sought out in critical situations, but, for the most part, ritual was self-administered. Both men and women were involved in all manner of love magic, including potions, charms, and divination. One seventeenth-century text, which was still being used a century later, advised maidens wishing "to drawe a heart" to put the blood of a young lamb's heart on their left breast. They were then to wash it off, mixing the water with blood from their own fingers and a little wine, before serving it to their sweethearts. Burning dragon's blood, a red resin, was commonly employed, accompanied by incantations:

This is not dragon's blood to burn
But [name of lover] heart I mean to turn
Be he asleep or be he awake
He shall come with me to speak.

In the small town as well as in the countryside virtually everyone knew the arts of divining, had access to love potions and charms, and kept track of those days and months most propitious for lovemaking. White magic was invariably a group activity. The Salem witchcraft panic began with a little innocent divining. Young women had gathered to peer at the white of an egg suspended in water to determine "what trade their sweethearts should be of," when one of them thought she saw a coffin and hysteria developed.

In most cases, however, a conjuring or divining session had much happier results. It was a semipublic event, a time for young men as well as women to make explicit their preferences in a subtle nonverbal manner and, using the persuasive power of magic, to influence the result. Young Welsh women would set a table in hope of conjuring lovers: "The 4 women hideing themselves in ye corners of ye room. The sweethearts will come in & eat, though a Hundred miles off." Divining remained a very popular mode of communication at the village level, where a more direct verbal approach might cause embarrassment or even conflict. Knowing he or she had been conjured, the dream lover could choose to accept or reject without loss of face or hurt feelings to either party, a device which, in a village community where the roles of lover, friend, and coworker overlapped, was essential to preserving communal solidarity.

It must also be remembered that this was a society where marriage was long delayed and premature pairing off strongly discouraged. Courtship in the seventeenth and eighteenth centuries was invariably a polygamous affair, with girls entertaining several suitors simultaneously and boys striving to keep the friendship of many women until such time as an inheritance or trade opened up and they could establish a household. When the time was right, lovemaking occurred with a rapidity that later generations were to find both baffling and repulsive. But, prior to betrothal, care was taken to prevent relationships from becoming too personal, thereby keeping open the options of both men and women. Here both male and female peer groups, with their rich associational and ritual life, also remained very significant in channeling the affections in a homosocial direction. In a period when individual autonomy was discouraged, the ego was permitted a much greater variety of attachments. . . .

Love magic of this kind [like the effort to divine future sweethearts, described above] would have made no sense in a society where choices were dictated by parents or guardians. We now know that it was only among the very rich and powerful that arranged marriage was at all common. Love magic therefore reflected both the freedom of choice and the anxieties that accompanied those liberties. The fact that it was used by men as well as women in Britain suggests that males may have felt some of the same uncertainty and vulnerability as females when it came to matters of the heart. It is significant that in fifteenth-century Venice love magic was used only by plebeian women to secure the attention of more powerful upper-class men, whereas in Britain, where there was greater equality between the sexes, men also felt the need of magical assistance. . . .

We know more about [the] dark side of magic because witchcraft accusations left the most visible historical record. However, white magic was much more pervasive, so integral to the courtship process as to go virtually unnoticed except by folklorists. North Yorkshire women, who went to St. Cedd's Well at Lestingham on magical St. Agnes Eve intending to enhance the power of their love garters by washing them in the waters, understood the social pressures that gossip would put on their young men. St. Cedd's was also the place where a man could test the faithfulness of his sweetheart. To prove herself a true lover, the woman would allow her breasts to be covered with wet linen. If no mark showed, the man was bound to her, but, if a stain should appear, she was proven false. George Calvert reported that "so great was the fear of this trial held that none but a true maid dast venture thereupon. . . ." In North Yorkshire it was thought possible to discover the father of a bastard child by placing a number of basins filled with holy water, each representing a suspected man, around an anvil. A red-hot horseshoe was then struck and the basin in which the sparks landed indicated paternity. Such a procedure was not always necessary, however, because it was said that the very threat of such a test brought about a quick confession from the putative father.

We can see from the examples that, throughout the seventeenth and eighteenth centuries, men experienced a sense of connectedness very similar to that of women. Their sense of self was no less porous; and they thought of themselves not as autonomous individuals but as part of an interdependent whole. Young people were most likely to resort to ritual and magic, but adults also turned to healers like Napier when they found vital relationships—and thus their sense of self—threatened. The body was simultaneously the symbol of their connectedness and the means through which men as well as women managed to secure and repair cooperative connections.

Gifts of clothing, hair, and food all served to bind sweethearts. Love knots were favored virtually everywhere. In North Yorkshire, it was the woman's garter, worn above the knee, which was yielded to the suitor "after that she hath proved him true and it shall hold them both true unto each other." The young man would wear this around his neck during the course of their betrothal, but on the wedding day it was the bride's to give away to a lucky bachelor, thus transferring love's magic to those who would need it in the future. Similarly, garters plaited from the number of straws equal to that of the desired numbers of children were said to guarantee fruitful motherhood. . . .

In the twentieth century, our understanding of the body is so privatized and sexualized that we have great difficulty understanding the magical communicative meaning it holds for other peoples. We think of touching and feeling as sexual "foreplay," when in fact these had quite other, much, more symbolic meanings for the early modern people. Our contemporary "feminized" conception of affection tells us that love must be expressed through soft words and tender caresses. Love must be an individualized experience, best kept quiet and private if it is to flourish. Nothing could be further from the early modern conception, which refused to separate body and feeling, provided little space for sexual intimacy, and insisted that love, defined as cooperation and sharing, express itself through those prime symbols of mutuality, the body social as well as the body biological. The same acute sense of the porosity of self that made magic so potent was reflected in the rituals that accompanied every step of the courtship and marriage process.

Courtship, betrothal, and wedding were all public ritualized events, using the body, the traditional symbol of interdependence, as their principal means of communication. Love was expressed loudly and visibly, not only in a series of formalized speech acts, but also through a grammar of individual and collective body movement. While we go out of our way to give lovers as much privacy as possible, early modern society thought publicity absolutely necessary to the success of any amorous arrangement. Only the very earliest stages of courtship were carried on in secrecy. Couples were very careful not to appear together in public until they were seriously considering marriage. Courtship was normally confined to the hours of darkness until very near the couple's betrothal:

Everyone who knows the ways of country people is aware that courting throughout the night was the custom and a young man going courting was terrified lest anyone should see him in "broad daylight."

Today, betrothal licenses withdrawal from the peer group and the beginnings of the privacy that we associate with conjugal love, but in the seventeenth century the same step plunged the couple into a rite of passage that involved progressively greater publicity and communal involvement. Betrothal was anything but quiet or clandestine. It rivaled the wedding itself in ritual and festivity. Spousals, trothplights, and handfasting—the various regional terms for betrothal—remained until 1753 the legal equivalent of church marriage. Throughout the sixteenth and seventeenth centuries it was a major social event, the beginnings for many people of the real marriage. Couples who had encountered parental or parish obstacles had to resort to "private spousals" or clandestine marriages, but, as a rule, the betrothal was a public event, involving not just family but the larger community. . . .

The body played a very important role in betrothal ritual. In addition to kissing, drinking, and eating, there was also a highly publicized joining of bodies. William Gouge noted that "many make it a very marriage, and thereupon have a greater solemnity at their contract than at their marriage; yea many take liberty after a contract to know their spouse, as if they were married, an unwarrantable and dishonest practice." In interpreting the bedding ceremony as carnal and therefore sinful, Puritans like Gouge mistook for hedonism that which had a meaning that transcended sexual pleasure. In sixteenth-century Leicestershire, it was "common use and custom" for the man to remain "in the house where the woman doth abide the night next following after such contracte otherwyse he doth departe without staying the night." We, like the Puritans, would tend to give a sexual reading to this rite, though seeing it as liberating rather than sinful. However, both interpretations are misplaced, for it is not entirely clear that ritual bedding at betrothal always involved intercourse. In fact, there is no firm evidence that a tradition of trial marriage for the purpose of testing a woman's fertility ever existed in Britain. Some couples may have begun regular intercourse at this point, but most who were bedded probably did not. For the majority, the initial bedding was probably more like the kiss, more magical than erotic, more public statement than private pleasure. If witnessed, as it often was, bedding was the ultimate proof of a couple's claim on one another.

9

Parents and Children in the Preindustrial Period

HERMAN W. ROODENBURG

Capturing the more subjective aspects of family life has been a challenge to social historians. A vital institution, the family cannot be omitted in a social-historical sketch. Preindustrial families had many distinctive features; they were larger and had more economic functions than their counterparts in later centuries. But what about relationships within the family?

As historians began tackling tough subjects like childhood and marriage, they were prone to stress stark contrasts between then and now. John Gillis (see the preceding selection) tried to outline a more subtle view, concerning courtship, in which differences are noted but some emotional aspects shared between preindustrial and industrial-age practices are discussed. Childhood and parent-child relations call for similar subtlety. Children were defined and treated distinctively. Preindustrial parents had worries and standards different from what would develop later, reflecting their culture (filled with magical beliefs and related fears) and also the functions they intended for their offspring, including early work roles. But they could also feel affection for children and identify the individuality of children.

In this selection Herman Roodenburg explores an unusual diary from a relatively obscure Dutch-Flemish woman at the end of the seventeenth century. Isabella de Moerloose, quite literate and city-bred, describes a childhood marked by some special fears and threats by her mother, but with some features common to childhood in other eras—including considerable initial indulgence. Her own sense of how childhood should be handled has an even more familiar ring. Some changes in child rearing standards were underway before 1700, but Roodenburg wonders also if an earlier popular culture, more lenient with children than strict Protestant authorities had been urging in countries like Holland, might have come into play as well. One woman's diary, of course, does not make a general picture, and Roodenburg is at pains to set his evidence in a larger interpretive context—with many important issues, about the nature and direction of change, still open.

From: Herman W. Roodenburg, "The Autobiography of Isabella De Moerloose: Sex, Childrearing and Popular Belief in Seventeenth-Century Holland," *Journal of Social History*, vol. 18 (1985), pp. 520–25.

Isabella's mother . . . was afraid that Isabella was possessed by an evil spirit and it was probably for this reason that she already called her child at an early age "queer."

Apparently, Isabella was called "queer" as a small child because she was born with the caul and also—remarkably enough—because she was always sweet-tempered towards everyone. When Isabella later heard this from her mother, she objected strenuously. It is an interesting passage, because she also tells us something about her upbringing.

Indeed, what child is not sweet-tempered, Isabella felt, if it is petted and caressed by everyone. It is exactly the firstborn—as she was—who receive a lot of love, and they become even more spoiled if the parents are very fond of them and if the grandparents are still alive. Everyone will then want to play with the child. Now, Isabella's grandparents were still alive and her mother also doted on her (mother love definitely existed before 1800). Only her father did not want to pet Isabella too much, as this was not consistent with his "masculine dignity."

These wonderful years ended when, two years later, her mother had a second child. The change was great. Thereafter, Isabella trembled at every harsh word or angry face. And now, no longer because of her sweet temper, but because of this trembling, she was called "queer."

It is difficult to surmise what precisely Isabella's mother meant, but from a subsequent occurrence which Isabella mentions, the mother's belief in spirits and devils becomes clearly apparent. For one or another reason, the mother continually kept her second child near her. This resulted in a ready irritation of that child and her mother and in a situation in which "my mother saw my caresses as flattery and she had a natural dislike of flattering people, whom she considered evil spirits." Such spirits readily scratch and bite, Isabella's mother thought. Once, when Isabella played with another child, and that child stuck its fingers into Isabella's mouth, the mother thought that her daughter would bite the child. In a fury she rushed up and beat Isabella severely. . . .

Isabella's upbringing, we may assume, was determined by the popular belief of the time. For example, Isabella mentions how, in order to get her home on time during her childhood years, she was frightened with a variety of tales about spirits and devils. In this way, she was told the story of "the man with the long coat, of whom it was said that he looked for firstborn children in order to kill them, and that he put a ball in their mouths so they would choke."

Isabella adds that she had heard this story when she played in the streets with other children, and that she thought it was a tale that parents had invented in order to get children to stay home in the evenings, just as were the stories of other ogres, such as the "bullebak" (the bugbear) and "haantje pik [pecking rooster]." Frequently, she even put a ball in her mouth and noted that she could still breathe.

Many readers will work a sexual meaning into this story. That is not completely incorrect. Although Isabella gave little credence to the story when she was small, later—when she was married to the Reverend Hoogentoren—she would think of this tale with horror.

Isabella also talks about such ogres as the "bulbak" and "haantje pik." Even in the twentieth-century Dutch children were still brought up with a belief in such spirits, just as in the supernatural meaning of the caul. Folklorists group these tales together under the term "childhood fears." It appears that children were not only warned to come home before dark, however. The bogeyman or another ogre could take the children with them if they came too close to the water, walked in the corn, or simply cried too much or were obstinate. In order to give more force to these tales, adults did not hesitate to dress up occasionally as bogeymen for them. From the research carried out in the 1960s among older people in the Dutch and Flemish countryside, it appears that as children these people were threatened most with the "bullebak." But they had also heard stories about "haantje pik," the "vleermuis" (the bat), the "weerwolf" (the werewolf), the "tenesnijder" (the toe cutter), the "nikker" (the nigger) and the "Jood" (the Jew).

Unfortunately, Isabella's story of the man with the ball is not reported in this study. Stories of the "bloedkaros" (the blood carriage) as threats against staying out too late seem to be most akin to her story. These were told in eighteenth-century Antwerp. Children who did not come home on time would be taken away in the carriage. There they were killed, after which their blood was presented to a foreign queen. J. J. Voskuil cites a version in which the children were killed with a large knife. Their blood was drawn off into a bathtub, in which the Queen of England would then come to bathe.

Was it only small children who believed in these tales? If we must trust the seventeenth-century Dutch playwrights, that was indeed the case. Famous authors, such as Gerrit Adriaensz, Bredero, Pieter Cornelisz, Hooft and Guilliam Ogier all made fun of such stories. Only children and credulous simpletons still believed in such nonsense, according to them.

Nevertheless, in educational tracts of the seventeenth century such tales were taken very seriously. In his very popular treatise on marriage the statesman and poet, Jacob Cats, devoted at least forty lines to the subject. He describes how people threatened children they wanted to quieten with "spooks" or "bogeymen." But he warns parents that they can make their children too apprehensive and fainthearted with these stories. Even when the children become adults, they will still tend to be startled by nothing. According to Cats, female servants in particular raised children in this way. . . .

Those who strove to combat popular belief, such as the Englishman, Reginald Scot (1538–1599) or the Reformed clergyman, Balthasar Bekker (1634–1698) . . . [agreed in condemning] bogeymen. At any rate, they see in such tales more than the fertile soil in which anxiety in adults is cultivated. It is precisely here that the belief in spirits and devils begins. Scot likewise warned of the role that domestic servants played in this.

With this tour of contemporary authors, we have come to know something more about the seventeenth-century belief in bogeymen. Some, like Bredero, but also Scot, felt that only children and cowards believed in these stories. The other authors are more serious. They are convinced that even adults who are not overly simple could still have anxieties because of this. In this, they probably remained closer to popular culture, because not only children in eighteenth-century Antwerp, but also adults believed in the tale of the blood carriage. It was even the case that, in the summer of 1776, a stranger was suspected of such a horrible murder, and he came very close to being stoned to death by the crowd. Such things also occurred in France. In 1750 the rumour spread that agents in civilian dress roamed through districts of Paris and took children between five and ten years old with them. It was said that a leprous prince could only be cured with their pure blood. The hands and feet of the children were to be cut off and a bath for the prince filled with their blood. In this case as well, an angry crowd rose to its feet. . . .

As is well known, Charles Dickens also wrote of the fear that bogeymen and other ogres could evoke in small children. It would be worthwhile if historians took these tales as seriously as Dickens did. It is clear that not only Isabella but also many other children were made to be obedient in this way. Bogeymen, blood carriages, and other tales formed a large part of the childrearing practices in early modern Europe. Moreover, we get an image of the popular belief of the time, in particular of the fears in many people. Hidden behind the fables, there appears to be a great fear of strangers. It is unfortunate that the French historian, Jean Delumeau, in his book about past anxieties in Europe, said so little about bogeymen ("croquemitaines"). . . .

Childbeating has already been mentioned a number of times. Isabella was severely beaten when her mother despaired that Isabella had been possessed by an evil spirit. Children in school were frequently beaten and Lavater made the interesting observation that striking children is not as bad as threatening them with bogeymen. It is worthwhile to say something more about all this beating, because Isabella not only tells us how she experienced the thrashing her mother gave her, but also how and why, during her later life she continued to oppose these practices.

According to Isabella, the sudden rain of blows she got from her mother made a deep impression on her. She described how, years later, she was still frightened of her mother and would burst into tears if she were unfriendly toward Isabella. To this, Isabella added that she recorded all this "to show the evil beating causes." She may, therefore, have exaggerated.

It is nevertheless not inconceivable that this occurrence continued to haunt her because of the emotions, the fury with which her mother rushed up to her, after she had been petted and caressed for two years. It is well known that children were often beaten in the seventeenth century, although some historians are of the opinion that this happened more frequently in school than in the family. According to proponents of psychohistory, these practices quite simply led to the most severe traumas. Family historians are generally more cautious in their conclusions. However, it is interesting to note what the child psychologist, Jerome Kagan, writes about this. He stresses the importance of the emotions which are coupled with beating. If the beating of a child occurs relatively seldom, he will experience the blows as a sign of hostility, of rejection by the parents. If, on the other hand, the blows are frequent, in a manner of speaking a commonplace occurrence, then the emotional consequences will be considerably less.

Kagan's attention to the emotions which accompany any beating could be useful to family historians. . . . In Isabella's case as well, we can base our assumptions on Kagan's. We have seen that she was seldom beaten; for almost two years, she was petted by everyone. That may have increased the shock when she suddenly received the blows from her mother. Moreover, her mother rushed at her in blind fury, perhaps not to punish Isabella, but to drive out the evil spirit that was to have taken possession of her. With so many emotions in play, Isabella's traumatic reaction was natural. Her later, fierce opposition to childbeating may also be explained in the light of this reaction. . . .

Moreover, later when she had become governess for Hoogentoren and eventually married him, she protected the children against their father. In the second part of her book, which she wrote in the third person, as advice to other women, she describes how she went to stand before him and cried, "I would rather that thee struck me than the innocent children." Hoogentoren answered in return that the children were not innocent at all but ripe for the gallows, and he threatened to give her such a thrashing herself that she would roll aside. And then he would give the children the same treatment. In such cases the only thing that would still help, Isabella advised, was to go away quietly. Perhaps tears would still be able to soften him.

The reasons why Isabella condemned childbeating are interesting. Here again, we may have found a confrontation between popular culture and the learned culture of the elite. Isabella felt that children did not become more virtuous by being beaten. On the contrary, children will beat their parents, because a child does not want to be beaten. It feels it is "likened to the animals," it is "affronted and it is taught by nature not to suffer affronts but to avenge them." Therefore, Isabella felt, "it is not proof of a corrupt nature when children strike their parents but of an uncorrupted nature which is not yet changed by the Scriptures."

The ideas Isabella advanced here are precisely the opposite of the official theories of childrearing of the seventeenth century. Catholic and Protestant moralists alike thought in general that obstinacy and rebelliousness were no less than a sign of a corrupt nature, or worse, a sign of original sin. . . .

We see that Isabella differentiates between the official doctrine of the church, which points to the necessity of beating because human nature is corrupt, and a "natural law," which would be inherent in everyone, as long as one is not corrupted by the "doctrine of the Scriptures." Was this her conviction alone or do we encounter here another aspect of popular culture? Did priests and ministers continuously hammer into their congregations the subject of timely discipline of children because the greater part of their audiences thought differently on the subject? As long as we know so little about practices of childrearing in the lower classes, it will be wise to ascribe this lesson of an uncorrupted nature to Isabella alone.

10

FORMING A NEW MIDDLE CLASS: THE INDUSTRIAL ENTREPRENEUR

JOHN SMAIL

Between the late seventeenth and the late eighteenth centuries, a new breed of businessman arose in Western Europe, particularly in England and Scotland where industrialization would first begin. The new businessman applied capitalism to manufacturing and the employment of labor. Capitalism—the use of investment funds to expand operations and earn larger profits—was not new in Europe. Merchant capitalists, with significant trade operations, had existed since the Middle Ages. Some had run domestic manufacturing operations, buying materials and bringing them to home workers who owned equipment like spindles and looms, and then picking up the products for sale. Capitalism had rarely, however, been applied directly to manufacturing, with owners buying equipment as well as supplies and beginning to treat workers simply as wage employees.

Historians have long emphasized the pioneering spirit of new industrial entrepreneurs who set up new equipment and expanded factories. They explain that special religious values, often associated with intense Protestant sects, or Enlightenment ideals, spurred these giants. And they look for the pioneer entrepreneur mainly from the late eighteenth century onward, when industrialization, in the sense of rapid technological innovation, really began to take off.

Social historians do not entirely contradict this picture. But recent research, applying social history concerns for larger groups to the business classes, reveals a more complex pattern. The new business spirit began to emerge gradually, before the innovators arrived on the scene; relatedly, it predated industrialization by at least fifty years, coming into play around 1700 in parts of England. Numbers of fairly ordinary artisans, taking advantage of expanding markets, moved into a different economic orbit at this point. They ventured no new technology initially, and they had no particularly new ideas or motives. Indeed, they thought of themselves as artisans still, even as they were involved in the changes hereafter labeled protoindustrialization.

From: John Smail, "Manufacturer or Artisan? The Relationship Between Economic and Cultural Change in the Early Stages of the Eighteenth-Century Industrialization," *Journal of Social History* 25 (1992): pp. 791–92, 796, 798–99, 800–01, 803–04, 806–08.

But the process of expansion, accumulating more capital and employing more workers, changed outlook within a generation, leading to a new culture of business and new policies toward workers.

The following selection traces the process of change in the middling business ranks in the Halifax region of Yorkshire, a traditional center for the production of cheap woolen cloth. John Smail shows how economic change responded to new opportunities and then shaped a new kind of middle-class business culture. From this in turn, further changes would result, leading to the attributes of the factory system associated with the industrial revolution of the late eighteenth century. This early period of more modest business change, with the novel entrepreneurial values it gradually generated, constituted the decisive break, even though the more sweeping technological development lay in the future. Here, at least, is one plausible chronology, focused on pinpointing not only the nature but the causes of change, that accounts for the otherwise startling emergence of a new middle class, embracing unprecedented kinds of business ventures and labor policies.

This is a different picture of the early modern period from the world of peasants and witches, but it is no less important. The rise of new kinds of manufacturers occurred, obviously, late in the early modern era, which helps explain its distinctive characteristics. But it had some links to earlier changes in work and family of the sorts discussed in Chapters 3, 4, and 8, some links even to Protestant views of commercial space. It did not arise without prior context, even as it helped bring early modern European society to a close.

In the past few years, a new view of the economic and social changes of eighteenth- and nineteenth-century England has emerged, one which challenges the notion that there was a single event that can be called the Industrial Revolution. Concentrating on the process rather than the event, this recent work shows that industrialization was occurring both before and after the transformative years between 1780 and 1830. For the eighteenth century, scholars have documented the development of large-scale production in several industries, which raises the question of how revolutionary the cotton and iron booms of the late eighteenth century in fact were. If industrial practice appeared earlier in the eighteenth century than expected, studies of the nineteenth century show that industrial practice took hold more slowly than previously assumed. The advantages of the steam-powered factory were apparently not as obvious to contemporaries as they are to economic historians, for scholars have shown that the transition to factory production was still going on in the middle of the century. . . .

One of the strengths of this new interpretation of industrialization is the attention it pays to the social or cultural context of what has traditionally been seen as simply an economic process. Indeed, a focus on cultural change was a point of departure for this new interpretation, for it was through an attempt to explain some of the social anomalies of the traditional Industrial Revolution that scholars realized that industrialization was a process with a much longer and more complex history. . . .

The heroic entrepreneur . . . does not figure in the new interpretation of industrialization. Far from being the property of a few key individuals, entrepreneurship is now seen as a quality possessed by a whole host of petty producers: the countless weavers who adopted and modified Hargreaves's spinning jenny or Kay's flying shuttle, or the Birmingham craftsmen who created so many new styles of buckles and buttons. Given the numbers involved in the process of eighteenth-century industrialization, it is no longer possible to explain innovation as the result of individual genius. Instead, we have to formulate an explanation of industrial innovations in terms of the economic behavior of the numerous little entrepreneurs who made them—economic behaviors that we now recognize were deeply embedded within their culture.

The necessity of a cultural explanation of economic change during the early phases of the process of industrialization thus requires that we understand the relationship between economic and cultural change. In a preindustrial "steady-state," that relationship is clear, for there would appear to be a certain congruence between economic practice and culture. When an artisan made a piece of woollen cloth in his workshop, he did so in terms of his artisanal culture. This culture determined the values and expectations that he brought to his work; it governed the complex web of social relations that made his work possible; and it provided him with the concepts through which he understood his actions. During periods of change, however, the relationship between economic practice and culture is much less clear. In particular, to understand the early phases of industrialization we can begin by describing the ways in which artisans changed their economic practice, but we must also develop an understanding of this change in cultural terms. Did the artisan's culture allow him to engage in new forms of economic practice, or did his culture change at the same time as his economic practice? . . . [O]n the whole, the domestic system worked in practice very much like it was supposed to work in theory; domestic clothiers producing cloth in their own homes made up the backbone of Halifax's textile industry. James Baumforth, for example, falls in the middle of the spectrum of domestic clothiers. His inventory of December 1711 shows that he owned a loom, two spinning wheels, and ten pounds worth of cloth. This was out of a total of just under thirty pounds worth of goods that he had in his five room dwelling, his other major possessions being a horse and three cows. Baumforth's inventory indicates that he made a modest living from his loom, helped out by the cows and what was probably a small garden and pasture. . . . Although domestic clothiers ranged from poor weavers eking out a living in a one room cottage with its garden plot to wealthy yeomen living in large houses and with a substantial farm, they were all engaged in an artisanal mode of production whose characteristics can be defined by independent production and a relatively quick turnover of stock.

In addition, . . . there was a group of manufacturers producing cloth on a substantial scale. In the decades around 1700, this group was not very large; only 32 out of the 211 individuals in the sample of probate records could be called manufacturers. The inventories, of course, do not reveal much about how these individuals got to be manufacturers, for they contain no information about an individual's life history. Nor do they reveal whether this group of individuals constituted the first manufacturers in the parish, for inventories are rare for the period prior to 1690. Yet while it is possible that there were a few manufacturers active in Halifax's textile industry in the generation that preceded the group revealed in the probate sample, the existence of this group of manufacturers in the decades around 1700 is quite significant. It was only from the beginning of the eighteenth century onwards that the manufacturers came to have a vital role in the woollen industry. Moreover, although the process of industrialization in the West Riding was quite varied, it is generally agreed that it was the indigenous manufacturers emerging out of their artisanal backgrounds who played the most important role in bringing industrial production to the region. . . .

From the standpoint of economic practice, the manufacturers' work represented an important change in the organization of the woollen industry, for their mode of production was fundamentally different from that of the domestic system. In some ways, the manufacturer appears to have had a structural position very similar to that of the domestic system's merchant. Both the merchant and manufacturer had a large stock of either raw materials or finished goods. The difference between them concerns their involvement in the production process: the manufacturer was directly involved in the production process, whereas the merchant had nothing to do with it. The difference between the manufacturer engaged in making cloth and the merchant is particularly apparent. Neither the wool merchant who sold the clothier a batch of wool, nor the cloth merchant who eventually bought the piece cloth from him at the market could control what the clothier produced or how he produced it; thus, merchant capital was completely insulated from the production process. In contrast, the manufacturer who put out wool to be woven by his "makers" had substantial control over what was made and how it was made. The difference between the manufacturer engaged in finishing cloth and the merchant also hinges on the manufacturer's active participation in the production process. All of the manufacturers in the sample carried out their operations in workshops attached to the house; even if they did not handle the shears or presses themselves, they would have been present as overseers of the journeymen who did the work. In contrast, the domestic system's merchant finished his cloth by sub-contracting the work to artisanal cloth dressers; it was not done on the merchant's premises nor under his direct supervision.

If direct participation in production separated the mode of production of the manufacturer from that of the domestic system's merchant, the manufacturer's large stocks of raw materials and finished products separated their mode of production from that of the domestic system's clothier. The simplest measure of the difference between the manufacturer and the clothier is the value of the goods associated with textile production in their inventories. In comparison to the clothier's paltry investment in textile production, the manufacturers were giants. Even the wealthier clothiers who might have textile goods valued in the region of twenty to twenty-five pounds were dwarfed by the manufacturers who had inventories of textile goods valued in the region of one hundred to six hundred pounds. . . .

This distinction, in turn, suggests the difference between the clothier's and the manufacturer's mode of production. The clothier's accumulation of stock, either in the form of wool and/or yarn waiting to be made into a cloth or cloths waiting to be taken to market and sold, was determined by the household nature of production in the domestic system. It did not make sense for even a wealthy clothier to accumulate more stock than his household could work on in a fairly short period of time. According to the inventories, they did not do this, for the value of the typical clothier's stock was roughly in proportion to the value of the tools that they owned. On the other hand, the manufacturer, whether he was involved in making cloth, finishing cloth, or both, was in the business of accumulating more stock than his household could work on, either in terms of the labor available in the household or the tools listed in the inventory. He did not do this as an investment; rather, the manufacturer's stock of raw materials and finished goods was part of a large-scale production process that required labor from outside the household. . . .

A [key] aspect of the artisan's attitudes towards work is the nature of the relations between masters and servants in the period around 1700. Artisanal culture did not recognize the existence of enduring social differences between the master and the servant. Obviously the journeyman clothier was younger and less well-off than his master and was therefore inferior to him. Moreover, as a servant in his master's household the journeyman was subject to his authority. However, the journeyman's inferiority was on the whole perceived as a relative condition because of where he was in the artisanal life cycle. Halifax's artisans, for instance, assumed that journeymen and apprentices might one day become independent artisans in their own right, and substantial clothiers often left bequests to this effect. For example, in 1694, Joseph Whewell, a wealthy clothier, left his servant a loom and all the tools of the trade and forgave a debt of forty shillings, "which sum I lent him when he begun [sic] to trade for himself." A similar pattern is evident in the bequests that were left to establish charitable funds. Over the course of the seventeenth century, several Halifax testators left money to be loaned out to poor artisans to help them start out as independent producers or provide apprenticeship premiums for poor children.

Once again, the manufacturers shared these assumptions; despite their wealth and different mode of production, there is no evidence that they perceived themselves as a separate and superior social group with a distinct life-cycle. For example, depositions taken in a testamentary case involving

Jonathan Baumforth show that this substantial manufacturer's relations with the men who worked for him were quite convivial. Anthony Croyser, a clothier who worked for Baumforth, described how he had gone to see Baumforth and asked how he did and inquired what sort of cloth Baumforth wanted made next. Baumforth told him, asked about his stock of wool and, their business done, offered Croyser some food and shared a drink with him. Other depositions give us the vivid image of Baumforth and his visitor—a collier delivering coal, a dyer checking on the next batch of work—"clubbing their two pence" for some ale. From the context of the depositions it is clear that this meant that each man put in two pence and sent a servant out to the local alehouse for four pence worth of beer. Baumforth was not a paternalist; he did not, for instance, pay for the beer himself despite his greater wealth. Rather he was part of an artisanal culture in which drinking beer was a central part of almost any social interaction. Despite being a manufacturer, then, Baumforth still thought of himself as an artisan and did not recognize the social difference that might be implied by his new mode of production. . . .

The inventories of manufacturers show quite clearly that they embraced the cultural implications of [the artisan] style of domestic architecture. It is impossible to differentiate the house of a manufacturer from that of his social equal, a yeoman, on the basis of the number or type of rooms listed in the inventory. Thus, judging by the house he lived in, the manufacturer was a yeoman; indeed, in their wills, manufacturers almost always styled themselves as yeomen, an indication that the cultural designation of status was more important to their self-perception than their economic activities. Moreover, manufacturers used their houses in the same way that clothiers did. In particular, the attached workshop was clearly the central location of the manufacturer's business despite his dependence on labor from outside the household. To give but one example, James Hill, a manufacturer with over £150 of textile goods, had a well equipped finishing shop attached to his house. . . . [I]t is possible to argue that the making of a manufacturer was, if not quite accidental, at least very easy. Given the right conditions, an artisan could accumulate the necessary stock without setting out to transform his mode of production, and the same applies to other aspects of the manufacturer's economic practice. The artisan, after all, already knew how to do almost everything that the manufacturer did. The relative ease with which an artisan could become a manufacturer also helps to explain why there was no cultural change associated with the emergence of these early manufacturers. Since artisans did not set out to become something different, there is no reason to expect dramatic cultural change. In this context, it is relevant that Halifax's early manufacturers were making woollen cloth rather than worsted cloth. In economic terms woollen production did not require the same level of investment as worsted production, so the transition from small-scale to large-scale production was easier. In cultural terms, the continuity in the type of cloth that was produced would have reduced the impact of the changing mode of production.

But cultural change occurred, and the story of capital accumulation also helps to explain that change. Although they may have accumulated their resources as artisans, the Halifax manufacturers were using the resources available to them in new ways. A generation earlier, a clothier with some cash to spare might have bought himself another cow or a cottage and close, for that would have been the extent of his options. However, by the turn of the century, some individuals, the manufacturers, were putting that extra money into cloth production. This was possible because changes in the international market for textiles had made medium- and large-scale production of textiles a viable proposition. These early manufacturers undoubtedly continued to invest surplus cash in the traditional manner, for like their predecessors, buying land or livestock would increase their economic security and social status. What was different was that resources left in active textile production could also yield returns that would increase their security and status. . . . What had begun as the unintentional accumulation of resources in the hands of these early manufacturers, created, as a result of the way that they were used, an economic situation that eventually required the intentional accumulation of capital, and thus a different attitude toward it. Insofar as all manufacturers came to recognize that they needed capital to operate, they had changed their culture. This took time, but a generation after these early manufacturers, a capital market was developing in and around Halifax. From 1730 onwards, for instance, mortgages became much more common, as did the expectation that money would accumulate interest if it was loaned.

The problem of capital accumulation is but one aspect of the more general problem of how to understand the process of cultural transformation associated with industrialization. By focusing on the interactions between behavior and culture, the theory of practice allows us to see how the economic practice of these manufacturers contributed to the development of a new, "industrial" culture. In the same way that their use of traditional networks of debt and credit helped to create an industrial concept of capital, the economic practice of these manufacturers, taken as a whole, helped to create a cultural context which changed the social meaning of their activities. In the 1720s and 1730s, a generation after the individuals discussed here, the cultural implications of the manufacturers' industrial mode of production began to make themselves felt.

For example, in the middle of a depression in the woollen industry in 1736, a large manufacturer, George Stansfield, wrote to his agents in Holland, and complained that because of the bad state of the trade: "[I have] turned off a great many of my makers, and keep turning off more weekly." To the artisan, such a thought would have been impossible, for the relationship between the clothier and the journeyman, for all its exploitative potential, had more to it than simple economic expediency. The logic of the manufacturer's operation, however, made it difficult to maintain this aspect of the social relations surrounding labor. With more and more of his work done outside of his household, the manufacturer employed a larger workforce and was less personally involved with them. This letter exemplifies the impact that this new economic practice could have on those artisanal values. On one hand, due allowance being taken for the fact that he was pleading with his contacts to place more orders, Stansfield recognized the existence of those artisanal values. Even if Stansfield was just shedding crocodile tears for his unfortunate makers, he was acknowledging the existence of a cultural tradition that would have him behave differently. On the other hand, in response to these economic pressures, Stansfield did lay his makers off, breaking with artisanal culture, but making a new one in its place. Stansfield's letter, of course, is but a single example, but it is indicative of the cultural transformation that was taking place. . . .

Carding, spinning and weaving woolen cloth in a colonial household. Drawing, nineteenth century.

(SOURCE: Granger Collection)

II

EARLY

INDUSTRIALIZATION

1750–1850

West Europeans, in various social classes, experienced a wide range of adjustments in the period 1750–1850. Some of them built on previous shifts—like the emergence of new kinds of manufacturers, who now participated in the first surge of industrialization. Others, such as new sexual behavior, broke novel ground. Important changes extended from the ways criminals were treated to expectations of love in courtship and marriage. At the same time, not surprisingly, change occurred differentially, depending on the group and region involved. Some groups actively sponsored change, others clung to old ways, still more shifted readily in some respects but greeted other challenges with reluctance. Finally, changed provoked active resistance. European elites worried about the new sexual behavior among the lower classes. Peasants often balked at efforts toward educational reform. The pace of formal protest stepped up, often in the name of older values and institutions—though the nature of protest, too, would ultimately change as European governments and economies altered the framework of social life.

The selections in this section show the wide sweep of change. They also show differential impact and the many layers of resistance and reactions. Some developments—for example, redefinitions of marriage—related to patterns visible in the seventeenth century. But some earlier issues, like witchcraft, now faded from view, while new developments, from educational reform to consumerism and shifts in popular medicine, began to gain center stage. The period, overall, had its own character, as a sweeping transition from a predominantly agricultural to an increasingly industrial social context.

The rate of social change in Western Europe, already considerable, greatly increased after 1750. The industrial revolution began in England in the late eighteenth century and spread to France and other nearby countries after 1820. Its central feature was the application of power machinery to manufacturing, but it involved much more than this. The introduction of machines and factories necessarily imposed new systems of work. Rapidly rising production required new forms of consumption. Industrialization led to urbanization; many cities grew phenomenally. People were on the move. In the cities they found themselves surrounded by strangers, other new arrivals, and an unfamiliar environment. Urban life had always been different from rural life. More people than ever before would experience these differences, ranging from greater sexual activity to greater literacy.

The industrial revolution was in part the product of other developments affecting the common people. Most important, the population began to increase rapidly in the eighteenth century. This forced people to seek new ways of making a living. Parents at all levels of society had to figure out what to do with and for children who in the past would not have survived. These same children, as they reached adulthood, often had to seek out new livelihoods, for there were not enough traditional jobs to go around. Here was a powerful disruptive force, challenging every social group and institution.

Partly because of population pressure, many economic activities became further commercialized. Domestic manufacturing spread as one means of supporting excess rural labor. More and more peasants became involved with market production. By specializing in cash crops, they could hope to maintain growing families. In the cities, many artisan masters altered their business methods, treating their journeymen as paid employees rather than as fellow craftsmen. Journeymen found it harder to become masters because established masters reserved their places for their own children. This general commercialization of the economy affected far more people than did the early stages of the factory system and was profoundly disturbing to many of those accustomed to more traditional economic relationships. Even the necessity of dealing with strangers, which commercialization required of peasants engaged in market agriculture or domestic manufacturing, may have been upsetting.

The period of early industrialization witnessed a host of developments in popular life and outlook, of which the industrial revolution proper, as it began between 1780 and 1830 through most of Western Europe, was only part. Obviously, then, the leading question for this period of European history concerns the impact of change. Was change simply imposed on the common people? Many peasants entered cities and factories only with the greatest reluctance— population pressure and other economic factors left them no other means of earning a living. A large number of these people endured a massive deterioration in their living conditions before making a move. But other peasants may have been more eager for a change. Tensions with their parents (most migrants to the city were in their late teens or early twenties, an age at which disputes in a peasant household were particularly likely) or an active desire for a better life may have drawn them away from the countryside. Without question, some of the forces of change were beyond the control of the common people, but there may have been positive attractions as well. Changes occurring in rural values may have made some people better able to cope with a new lifestyle. New forms of family life were an important part of Western Europe's history after 1700, and although some of the changes may first have affected the upper classes, other alterations in family functions spread widely across class lines.

Indeed, many of the most striking studies of social change in the decades around the beginnings of the industrial revolution have focused not on industrialization itself, but on other shifts in outlook and behavior beneath the level of formal intellectual or political life. Some of these shifts—for example, in aspects of family or sexual behavior—were genuinely popular; others—like some new attitudes toward schooling or toward physical and mental health—affected middle-class groups more than the population at large. In combination, the shifts suggest a broad pattern of change that soon included the industrial revolution. Factory industry and growing cities would produce changes and dislocations of their own, but they would also build on some of the new uses of the family or new kinds of sexual behavior.

Furthermore, although the industrial revolution caused a huge and rapid transformation, it did not occur overnight. We must not imagine there were modern factory conditions even by 1850. Early factories were small and sometimes rather informal. Many had no more than twenty workers and therefore were not necessarily impersonal or rigidly organized. Actually, most people were not working in factories at all, but rather in agriculture, domestic service, or crafts. Life for peasants and artisans was changing, but traditions yielded slowly. The common people themselves found ways to modify the shock of new conditions. Most people who moved to cities in this early period did so gradually: one generation moved to a village closer to a big city, the next to the city outskirts, and so on. Factory workers found ways to take time off so that they would not have to surrender completely their own notions of work and leisure. Even the middle class, more persuaded of the desirability of progress, harbored many traditional values.

So, along with the shock and disturbance of change, we must consider successful resistance and positive adaptation. Which reaction predominated depended on the particular circumstances—specific economic conditions, for example—and personality types. Few people could adapt to the new life without regret; but probably most people were not completely confused by it either. Even in their outright protests, the common people began to show signs of accepting the industrial system; protest gradually moved away from traditional goals toward demands for greater rewards within the new social order.

Because of the importance of transitional reactions, the following selections relate particularly to the peasantry, still Europe's largest group and the one most clearly tied to traditional structures. In peasants emerged, not surprisingly, some of the most tenacious resistance to change, but also a new variety and new motivations that not only reflected, but also actively caused some of the most striking new developments, from popular literacy to family life.

The century after 1750 saw the most dramatic structural changes associated with early industrialization, although usually still in an incomplete form. Introduction of the steam engine speeded work and production in several branches of manufacturing, while factories subjected both workers and owners to large-scale systems. Industrial technology and organization were accompanied by significant political change, including more representative parliaments, wider suffrage, and government involvement in areas such as education. In addition, the rapid increase in population was a new phenomenon to Europe, and although temporary, it produced great dislocation and an upsurge in the number of young people. The key questions of the period, in terms of human life, relate to the interaction between values and the new structures. What caused change? Impersonal forces and a few social groups such as factory owners and doctors, who had developed new or newly vigorous values, may have imposed changes on the bulk of the population. But some advantages in this first wave of industrialization probably gave even ordinary people a motivation to change. How extensive and how damaging was the dislocation? The thread of persistence must be assessed here. Many groups, although deeply affected by new structures, may not have changed their outlook or their basic hopes and expectations much at all. Their efforts would show in protest, perhaps, but also in an uneven pattern of change. Not only peasants and artisans—still a majority of the population in 1850—but many big-city residents might differ little in their views on health, for example, from their preindustrial ancestors. Against this, others would argue that immense changes, associated particularly with demography and the family, can be seen, suggesting that in the popular mind, the preindustrial world was already lost.

For by many measurements, the scope of change during the later eighteenth and early nineteenth centuries was truly remarkable. Key developments, of course, focused on the new kinds of work developing in the factories, on the redefinition of politics associated with the French Revolution, and on the formation of new social classes, notably the working class and middle class. Selections that follow touch on many of these developments, but they concentrate even more on less familiar facets, ranging from family to suicide to a new kind of consumerism. The link among the changes is, in the first place, the ongoing effects of trends noted in earlier decades, in elite position, popular outlook, and commercial activity, now combined, in the second place, with the wider ramifications of population growth and the expansion of manufacturing.

BIBLIOGRAPHY

For general coverage of the early industrial period, useful treatments include Phyllis Deane, *The First Industrial Revolution* (2nd ed., New York, 1979); Thomas McKeown, *The Modern Rise of Population* (New York, 1976); Eric Hobsbawm, *The Age of Revolution, 1789–1848* (New York, 1962); Peter Kriedte, Hans Medick, and Jurgen Schlumbohm, *Industrialization Before Industrialization: Rural Industry in the Genesis of Capitalism* (New York, 1981); Peter N. Stearns and Herrick Chapman, *European Society in Upheaval* (3rd ed., New York, 1991).

Changes in family life are stressed in Lawrence Stone, *Family, Sex and Marriage in England, 1500–1800* (New York, 1977) and Randolph Trumbach, *The Rise of the Egalitarian Family* (New York, 1978); see also the *Journal of Social History,* special issue, vol. 15, no. 3 (1982). On sexuality specifically, see Peter Laslett, *Family Life and Illicit Love in Earlier Generations* (New York, 1977) and Paul Robinson, *The Modernization of Sex* (New York, 1981). On children, see Ivy Pinchbeck and Margaret Hewitt, *Children in English Society* (London, 1973) and Lloyd De Mause, ed., *The History of Childhood* (New York, 1974).

Recent work includes Hans-Peter Blossfeld, *The New Role of Women: Family Formation in Modern Societies* (Boulder, CO, 1995); John Fout, ed., *Forbidden History: The State, Society and the Regulation of Sexuality in Modern Europe* (Chicago, 1992); Annik Padrailhe-Galabrun, *The Birth of Intimacy: Privacy and Domestic Life in Early Modern Paris* (Philadelphia, 1992); C.J. Barker-Benfield, *The Culture of Sensibility: Sex and Society in Eighteenth Century Britain* (Chicago, 1992); Andrew Blaikie, *Illegitimacy, Sex and Society: Northeast Scotland, 1750–1900* (New York, 1994); Lawrence Stone, *Broken Lives: Separation and Divorce in England, 1660–1857* (New York, 1993); and Simon Szreter, *Fertility, Class and Gender in Britain, 1860–1940* (New York, 1996).

On crime and punishment in the period, see the masterful work by John Beattie, *Crime and the Courts in England, 1660–1800* (Princeton, 1986); Michel Foucault, *Discipline and Punish: The Birth of the Prison,* trans. Alan Sheridan (New York, 1977); Gordon Wright, *Between the Guillotine and Liberty: Two Centuries of the Crime Problem in France* (New York, 1983). Recent work includes Karl Wegert, *Popular Culture, Crime, and Social Control in 18th-Century Wurttemburg* (Stuttgart, 1994); Norval Morris and David Rothman, eds., *The Oxford History of the Prison: The Practice of Punishment in Western Society* (New York, 1995); and Richard Evans, *Rituals of Retribution: Capital Punishment in Germany 1600–1987* (New York, 1996).

Suicide has a slim historical literature. See Olive Anderson, *Suicide in Victorian and Edwardian England* (New York, 1987); and for the U.S., Howard I. Kushner, *Self-destruction in the Promised Land: A Psychocultural Biology of American Suicide* (New Brunswick, NJ, 1989); Roger Lane, *Violent Death in the City: Suicide, Accident, and Murder in Nineteenth-Century Philadelphia* (Cambridge, MA, 1979). Relevant also is work on changes in attitudes toward death; See John McManners, *Death and the Enlightenment: Changing Attitudes to Death Among Christians and Unbelievers in Eighteenth-Century* France (New York, 1981); Philippe Ariès, *Hour of Our Death,* trans. Helen Weaver (New York, 1981).

The topic of popular health and medicine is beginning to receive considerable attention. For this period in European history, see the various works by Roy Porter, ed., *Patients and Practitioners: Lay Perceptions of Medicine in Pre-Industrial Society* (Cambridge, England, 1985) and *A Social History of Madness: The World Through the Eyes of the Insane* (New York, 1988); see also Matthew Ramsey, *Professional and Popular Medicine in France, 1770–1830: The Social World of Medical Practice* (New York, 1988); for an earlier period, Michael MacDonald, *Mystical Bedlam: Madness, Anxiety, and Healing in Seventeenth-Century England* (New York, 1983) is a vital contribution.

See also Mary Lindemann, *Healing and Health in Eighteenth-Century Germany* (Baltimore, 1996); R. and D. Porter, *In Sickness and in Health: The British Experience, 1650–1850* (London, 1989); James Riley, *Sick, Not Dead: The Health of British Workingmen During the Mortality Decline* (Baltimore, 1997); Evelyn Ackerman, *Health Care in the Parisian Countryside, 1800–1914* (New Brunswick, NJ, 1990); Colin Jones, *The Charitable Imperative: Hospitals and Nursing in Ancient Regime and Revolutionary France* (New York, 1989); Hans Binneveld and Rudolf Dekker, *Curing and Insuring: Essays on Illness in Past Time* (Hilversom, 1990); and Ann Digby, *Making a Medical Living: Doctors and Patients in the English Market for Medicine, 1720–1911* (New York, 1994).

Also relevant is ongoing historical work on medical and institutional approaches to insanity; see: Michel Foucault, *Madness and Civilization,* trans. Richard Howard (New York, 1965); Andrew Scull, *Museums of Madness: The Social Organization of Insanity in 19th-Century England* (New York, 1979); George Rosen, *Madness in Society* (New York, 1968); and Klaus Doerner, *Madmen and the Bourgeoisie* (Oxford, 1981). The topic has also been debated in American history; see David Rothman, *The Discovery of the Asylum* (Boston, 1971); Gerald N. Grob, *The State and the Mentally Ill* (Chapel Hill, NC, 1966); and Edward Shorter, *The History of Psychiatry: From the Era of the Asylum to the Age of Prozac* (New York, 1997).

On poverty: Mary Lindemann, *Patriots and Paupers: Hamburg 1712–1830* (New York, 1990) and David Green, *From Artisans to Paupers: Economic Change and Poverty in London, 1790–1870* (Hants, England, 1995); Rachel Fuchs, *Poor and Pregnant in Paris: Strategies for Survival in the Nineteenth Century* (New Brunswick, NJ, 1992). Poverty and family are the subject of Thomas Sokoll, *Household and Family Among the Poor: The Case of Two Essex Communities in the Late Eighteenth and Early Nineteenth Centuries* (Bochum, Germany, 1993).

On old age: Tamara Hareven, ed., *Aging and Generational Relations: Life-Course and Cross-Cultural Perspectives* (New York, 1996) and Peter N. Stearns, *Old Age in European Society* (New York, 1978).

On education and literacy: James Allen, *In the Public Eye: A History of Reading in Modern France* (Princeton, 1989); the classic Eugen Weber, *Peasants into Frenchmen: the Modernization of Rural France* (Stanford, 1976); Harvey Graff, *The Legacies of Literacy: Continuities and Contradictions in Western Culture and Society* (Bloomington, IN, 1987); Gary Cohen, *Education and Middle-Class Society in Imperial Austria* (Lafayette, IN, 1996); and Raymond Grew and P.S. Harrigan, *School, State, and Society: The Growth of Elementary Schooling in Nineteenth Century France—A Quantitative Analysis* (Ann Arbor, 1991).

Changes in emotional standards related to new sensitivities to punishment, new family outlook and new kinds of disgust are treated in Norbert Elias, *The History of*

Manners, trans. Edmund Jephcott (New York, 1982)—a classic study; see also Peter N. Stearns, *American Cool: Constructing a Twentieth-Century Emotional Style* (New York, 1994). On the senses, Alain Corbin, *Time, Desire and Horror: Toward a History of the Senses* (Cambridge, MA, 1995).

Peasant history for the period can be followed in Richard J. Evans and W. R. Lee, eds., *The German Peasantry: Conflict and Community in Rural Society from the Eighteenth to the Twentieth Centuries* (London, 1986); Gregor Dallas, *The Imperfect Peasant Economy: The Loire Country, 1800–1914* (New York, 1982); Pamela Horn, *The Rural World, 1780–1850: Social Change in the English Countryside* (New York, 1981); Judith Devlin, *The Superstitious Mind: French Peasants and the Supernatural in the Nineteenth Century* (New Haven, 1987).

See also Mack Walker, *German Home Towns: Community, State, and General Estate, 1684–1871* (Ithaca, NY, 1971). Recent work includes James Lehning, *Peasant and French: Cultural Contact in Rural France During the Nineteenth Century* (Cambridge, MA, 1995).

Consumerism is just beginning to receive historians' attention. For eighteenth-century Britain, see Lorna Weatherill, *Consumer Behavior and Material Culture in Britain, 1660–1760* (London, 1988) and, for a major interpretation, Colin Campbell, *The Romantic Ethic and the Spirit of Modern Consumerism* (New York, 1987). For later developments, see Michael Miller, *The Bon Marché. Bourgeois Culture and the Department Store, 1869–1920* (Princeton, 1981).

Recent work includes John Brewer and Roy Porters, eds., *Consumption and the World of Goods* (New Brunswick, NJ, 1993); John Benson, *The Rise of Consumer Society in Britain, 1880–1980* (New York, 1994). Issues of middle-class formation (see Part I) and consumerism alike are treated in: Margaret Hunt, *The Middling Sort: Commerce, Gender, and the Family in England 1600–1789* (Berkeley, 1996).

A rich literature has developed on preindustrial and early industrial protest. A good general statement is George F. Rudé, *The Crowd in History, 1730–1848* (New York, 1964). See also Eric J. Hobsbawm, *Primitive Rebels* (New York, 1965). Specific studies include Malcolm I. Thomis, *The Luddites: Machine-Breaking in Regency England* (Hamden, CT, 1970); Eric Hobsbawm and George Rudé, *Captain Swing* (New York, 1968); and Robert Bezucha, *The Lyon Uprising of 1834* (Cambridge, MA, 1974), all of which allow discussion of the persistence of traditional values. Important studies on the transition to new protest goals include John Merriman, ed., *Consciousness and Class Experience in 19th Century Europe* (New York, 1979) and Ted Margadant, *French Peasants in Revolt: The Insurrection of 1850* (Princeton, 1979). Peter N. Stearns, *1848: The Tide of Revolution in Europe* (New York, 1974) surveys a key period. Two important general assessments are Edward Shorter and Charles Tilly, *Strikes in France 1830–1968* (Cambridge, England, 1974) and James Cronin, *Industrial Conflict in Modern Britain* (Totowa, NJ, 1979). For a provocative overview of protest and its limitations, see Barrington Moore, Jr., *Injustice: The Social Bases of Obedience and Revolt* (New York, 1979) and Charles Tilly, Louise Tilly, and Richard Tilly, *The Rebellious Century, 1830–1930* (Cambridge, MA, 1975). See also Charles Tilly, *Popular Contention in Great Britain, 1758–1834* (Cambridge, England, 1995).

11

LOVE AND SEX: A QUIET REVOLUTION

JEFFREY R. WATT

The following selection, based on the Neuchâtel region of Switzerland, deals with two related and fundamental changes in male-female interactions that began in the eighteenth century. Historians have identified shifts in sexual behavior and in the emotional standards of love in courtship and marriage, and they have argued about what both changes—particularly the shift in sexuality—meant to the people involved. Jeffrey Watt uses his local case study to firm up our understanding of these changes, while summarizing key elements of the existing debate.

The basic changes were twofold. Greater sexual license was one. European sexual practices had long been fairly restrained, probably to prevent unwanted birthrates in relation to available rural property. Marriage ages were late, but sexual activity before or outside marriage was also limited—as indicated by low rates of illegitimate births or pregnancies started before marriage. This customary pattern yielded, especially in the groups with less property in countryside and city alike, to higher illegitimacy and prebridal pregnancy figures, from the later eighteenth century onward. Some historians have argued that this quiet revolutionary change reflected greater freedom for women, but predominant opinion now holds that it followed from women's new economic problems, causing them to seek marriage more eagerly, along with greater transiency for male laborers.

The rise of love—the second, emotional, change—embraced all social classes. Evidence from Neuchâtel shows that the law courts that dealt with marriage and divorce issues changed their standards in favor of greater acknowledgment of love as a basis for and goal of marriage, just as individuals did in various social ranks. Love had not been irrelevant in marriage previously, and some change had occurred earlier, as the earlier selection by John Gillis indicates (see Chapter 8). But it was in the eighteenth century that love became more ubiquitous in arguments about why people wanted to get married and, somewhat ironically, about why marriages failed. (The discussions were also less entangled with ideas about magic than Gillis had emphasized for

From: Jeffrey R. Watt, *The Making of Modern Marriage: Matrimonial Control and the Rise of Sentiment in Neuchâtel, 1550–1800* (Ithaca: Cornell University Press, 1992), pp. 178, 187–89, 191–93, 210–13, 215–17, 219–20.

seventeenth-century England.) Here, women may have won some new protections—for example, in being able to argue against arbitrary parental selection
of potential husbands on grounds that there was no love involved, an argument many parents now accepted.

Changes in sex and in love doubtless dovetailed in many instances. But
class differences complicate the picture. Change was greatest in the lower
classes. Upper-class people accepted love arguments but vigorously disap-
proved of more open sexuality, which threatened their values and their desire
to protect family property.

Using a case study like Neuchâtel to test wider sociohistorical issues helps
pinpoint change and sort out the issues involved. Neuchâtel's Protestant
courts, operating under loose control from Prussia, left abundant records
about marriage issues, that reflect both official and popular ideas and practices. Inevitably, local circumstances produced some idiosyncrasies. Illegitimacy did not increase greatly in this particular region, though premarital pregnancies did; the difference reflected a more stable protoindustrial economy. In
the marriage area, Neuchâtel moved well ahead of most European countries in
its redefinition of divorce. Differences of this sort do not contradict larger generalizations, but they require special attention and explanation.

Case studies and general surveys alike, finally, have worked hard at determining causation of such significant shifts. Changes in sex and love both reflected shakeups in village and urban activities as a result of protoindustrialization, which gave young people more independent earnings and a wider
range of personal contacts. Population growth, at the same time, reduced access to property, which made some people more vulnerable—like women seeking marriage but lacking a traditional dowry to help seal the bargain; even
men might suffer from their inability to measure up to older standards of
successful, property-owning masculinity and seek compensation in sexual
prowess. For the rise of love, economic change was supplemented by greater
Protestant emphasis on the family unit, including its emotional centrality, and
by eighteenth-century novels which preached love's glories to an increasingly
avid (though mostly urban) audience. Here was the context in which new standards and behaviors—and new social and gender divisions about emotion and
sexuality—took root, with implications that have lasted through the twentieth
century.

Sexual relations among unmarried couples tell us much about courtship patterns and the formation of marriage, indicating the degree of freedom young
people enjoyed and the criteria they followed in choosing mates. Police actions against illicit sexuality were indeed the most common case heard before
Valangin's consistory in the eighteenth century. For the century, the consistory
subpoenaed 539 persons for having committed adultery or fornication. Accusations of fornication continued to be far more numerous than those of

adultery: 458 to 81. In the city of Neuchâtel, the registers of the Quatre-Ministraux, extant from 1715, reveal 194 actions against people who were at least suspected of illicit sexuality. . . .

In his work on the printed-cloth industry, Pierre Caspard found that the number of illegitimate births remained quite low in certain villages in the principality of Neuchâtel. For the village of Cortaillod, the proportion of illegitimate births was 0.9 percent for 1678–1720, 1.3 percent for 1721–1760, 1.1 percent for 1761–1790, and 1 percent for 1791–1820. In spite of the significant contemporary economic changes, Caspard found that illegitimacy was a marginal phenomenon, normally affecting women of the lower social ranks, such as servants, who frequently were outsiders to a particular parish or even to the principality as a whole—a characterization that holds true for the unwed mothers convoked before the Quatre-Ministraux. In short, though the city of Neuchâtel had a noticeable increase in illegitimate births, the county as a whole did not undergo significant growth in bastardy toward the end of the eighteenth century.

This evidence on Neuchâtel's illegitimate births differs with the findings of many historians who assert that there was a pronounced growth in bastardy in late eighteenth-century Europe. Edward Shorter observes a striking increase in illegitimate births and prenuptial conceptions in the second half of the eighteenth and the early nineteenth centuries, primarily among the lower classes, and he argues that these demographic changes were the result of a sexual revolution that began about 1750. He holds that women who found employment outside the home in protoindustrial and early industrial domains were being freed from the traditional constraints of family and community. Industrial activity liberated these women by providing them with economic independence. They could now indulge in sexual relations without regard to financial gain, as indicated by the fact that the vast majority of these women's lovers were not their employers but rather men of the same social status. Women were not having sexual relations out of hopes of getting married but simply for personal fulfillment, a change in mentality that amounted to a sexual revolution.

Though almost all historians agree that the number of children conceived outside marriage increased in the late eighteenth century, Shorter's provocative thesis has found few supporters. Some scholars deny that there was a general increase in the number of women working outside the home. Moreover, even when women did find outside employment, they generally were not involved in early industrial work. Louise Tilly, Joan Scott, and Miriam Cohen effectively argue that, even though beginning in 1750 more women were leaving their rural homes for cities, their work did not change. In urban settings, women were still employed primarily in domestic service, garment making, and textiles, which traditionally had been the most common forms of nonagricultural work for women. Industrial capitalism did not provide many new opportunities for women; the number of female workers in factories remained low even at the end of the nineteenth century. Women who emigrated to work in cities remained tied to the family economy, often being sent there by their families, and they generally used their wages to supplement their families' income (which was one of the reasons they were poorly paid). Urban working women were no longer protected by traditional constraints—family, community, and church—which could have coerced young men to marry women they had impregnated. Illegitimacy increased during the period 1750–1850 because people had moved out of traditional social contexts, not because they were undergoing a change in mentality or celebrating a sexual revolution. Though scholars generally agree with Shorter that couples who produced bastards were of the same socioeconomic status, they assert that most mothers of illegitimate children had engaged in sexual relations with the expectation of marrying their suitors. Thus, in the words of John Rule, women had become, "not more emancipated, but more vulnerable, as lack of money, unemployment and opportunities for work far afield all kept men from fulfilling promises in conditions where there was no power of enforcing them." As David Levine notes, the increase in illegitimacy in the late eighteenth century was the result of "marriage frustrated," not of "promiscuity rampant." . . .

Even if there was no causal relationship between industrialization and bastardy, economic factors could still have been fundamentally important in the increasing numbers of illegitimate births. Several historians point to changes in courtship practices in the eighteenth century, alterations tied to the growth in wage labor. Many areas of Europe grew in wage labor in the eighteenth century even though they did not industrialize until later. Rudolf Braun found that, with the development of wage labor in the cotton and printing industries, the Zurich Oberland saw a significant increase in illegitimate births and prenuptial conceptions in the eighteenth century. Changes in birth patterns were directly related to new courtship practices made possible by the expansion of wage labor. Braun found that in traditional peasant society personal inclinations had to yield to property concerns in forming marriages. Among wage earners, however, young people enjoyed more freedom from parental influence in choosing mates. This greater liberty in courting was the cause of the increasing numbers of pregnant brides and illegitimate children. Similarly, John Gillis holds that the growth in wage labor in late eighteenth-century England meant that courtship practices became more direct, that go-betweens played less of a role in forming matches, and that betrothal agreements between families decreased. Betrothals and weddings themselves became more private affairs, resulting in fewer traditional weddings in which entire peasant communities participated. . . .

Evidence from Neuchâtel of illicit sexuality gives us good reason to distinguish prenuptial conceptions from illegitimate births. In his study on prenuptial conceptions in the area around Cortaillod, Caspard found that, whereas illegitimate children were rare, pregnant brides became quite common during the course of the eighteenth century. Caspard discovered that before 1760 the rate of premarital conception—defined as births that took place less than eight months after marriage—oscillated between zero and 20 percent of all married couples' first births. Beginning in 1760, however, the rate increased dramatically, attaining in just three decades a level of over 50 percent of first births. Contemporary to the spread of wage labor, this increase in antenuptial conceptions shows that, in spite of the views of pastors and moralists, eighteenth-century Neuchâtelois condoned sexual relations between fiancés.

Caspard concludes that this pronounced increase in prenuptial conception was the result of new matrimonial strategy in the eighteenth century, at least among the nonpropertied classes. For the late eighteenth century, he observes a large gap between the rates of prenuptial conception among the wealthy propertied classes, on the one hand, and the rest of the population, on the other. Only about one-fourth of the wealthy's first children were born within eight months of marriage, a rate 32 percent lower than that for married people in general. Contraception was probably not the cause of this lower rate, since the interval between births was more or less the same for notables as for others. The difference must therefore be due to the fact that premarital sexual relations were less frequent among the propertied classes than among nonnotables. The two groups had different levels of premarital sexual activity because, Caspard argues, they no longer shared the same matrimonial strategies. Up until the mid-eighteenth century, most workers possessed at least a part of their means of production—land and the capital needed to exploit it. As a result, most marriages posed problems of dowries and inheritances for the transmission of this property. By 1760, however, a large percentage of the population was involved in wage labor. Like Braun, Caspard believes that for wage laborers marriage was now becoming less a material venture and more a "union in which instinct and sentiment intervened." It was this new attitude toward marriage that was behind the remarkable increase in premarital relations. Economic concerns in choosing spouses had not disappeared but were now based less on one's property holdings and more on one's professional prospects. At the same time, the sons and daughters of notables remained tied to the traditional material concerns in forming marriages, since their wealth was still in property. . . .

In the absence of a pregnancy, the tribunals almost never enforced a contract, deeming it a lesser evil to annul an engagement than to force an unwilling person into a marriage. Before the eighteenth century most plaintiffs failed to enforce disputed contracts because they did not satisfactorily prove the existence of bona fide promises. After 1700 it became much more common for judges not to require couples to marry because of the unhappy marriage that would follow even though engagements had been properly made.

Parallel to this evolution in the attitudes of judges were similar changes among litigants. In the sixteenth and seventeenth centuries, it was not uncommon to find plaintiffs to contract disputes who blatantly tried to use marriage as a springboard to material wealth. The wage earner who used a piece of sausage to seal a promise of marriage with his employer's daughter and the washerwoman who vowed that a young noble soldier had agreed to marry her are cases in point. In the eighteenth century, cases in which people blatantly sought to capture wealthy spouses, often through deception, were much less common. No doubt material interests were still important to someone choosing a spouse in that century; the evidence from the court records indicates, however, that attempts to use marriage as a means of making dramatic ascents on the social ladder were much less common than they had been before.

Marriage contract disputes also reveal that at least some eighteenth-century Neuchâtelois discovered the love match. Some litigants expressed strong feelings of love for their fiancés, as seen in the case of Madelaine Louise Petitpierre and Abram Barbezat. Madelaine gave birth to a child in 1761 and filed suit in 1764 to force Barbezat, the alleged father, to honor their engagement. The daughter of a Neuchâtel shoemaker, Madelaine had met Barbezat at Caen in Normandy in 1760. Originally from Les Verrières in the county of Neuchâtel, Barbezat was a simple soldier in the French army stationed at Caen during the Seven Years' War. The defendant, like the plaintiff, belonged to the upper fringe of the working class; though he earned very little as a soldier, he possessed property in Neuchâtel worth several thousand livres. Despite the state of war, the troops at Caen were not under attack and had plenty of leisure time, providing Barbezat with ample opportunity to court Madelaine with the knowledge and evidently the consent of her uncle. The child was conceived in January 1761, but later that month Barbezat had to leave Caen to help defend Le Havre from the English. Thereafter, Madelaine saw Barbezat but one time, when he came to Caen for one week in March of the same year. In June she returned to Neuchâtel, where she gave birth to a son who was baptized 6 October 1761.

Appearing before Neuchâtel's matrimonial court in June 1764, Madelaine asked that Barbezat honor their marriage agreement. Since he was still out of the county, Madelaine was instructed to contact his closest relatives and to post her demands at the county's boundaries. In support of her case, she produced twenty-five letters Barbezat had written between 1761 and 1763, twenty-four to her and one to her father. In these letters, as described by Caspard, Barbezat attested to the strongest feelings of love for Madelaine:

> The sentiment of love that Abram Barbezat expresses in his letters is characterized above all by its vehemence: the torrents of tears, oaths to the death, invocations to God or the gods, all of which were part of the contemporary romanesque literature with which Barbezat may have been familiar. Moreover, if the evocation of carnal love is almost totally absent, Barbezat clearly suffered no pangs of conscience concerning the sexual relations he had had a short time ago with his fiancée. He was shocked and indignant about the sanctions the church was taking against her—he seems rather far removed from the "official" morality, expressed in the legal or religious interdicts of the period, whose effect on the daily life of the people we have no doubt overestimated. Furthermore, Barbezat openly avowed his paternity, expressly asking his fiancée to make it known around her. The tone with which he evoked "his fatherly compassion" or "the cries of his dear child" are perhaps also the expression of the sensitivity in regard to childhood which appeared in the course of the eighteenth century.

The theme of the war appeared only as a counterpoint to that of love. In describing his duties as a soldier, Barbezat spoke above all about getting time off to visit Madelaine and eventually being discharged so that he could marry her.

From the first letter to the last, Barbezat never wavered in assuring his affection and devotion:

> How happy I would be if I could be united with the object so dear to me. I repeat to you again that I don't know what in my soul makes me so joyful reading this letter [that you sent me], a letter that gives me so much pleasure. Never do I read it just once per day—as long as there is daylight, never does it leave my hands. I did all I could to come see you again, but they wanted to give me just ten days. How sad for me it would be to have to leave after just ten days, which would be like minutes for me, being close to you. I therefore postponed my visit until the first of next month, when I'll be able to stay with you longer.

In his third letter, dated 17 February 1761, Barbezat wrote, "You alone can bring me happiness, and at the same time you alone, being separated from me, are the cause of my unhappiness." Drawing two interlaced hearts at the bottom of this letter, he proclaimed, "When two hearts are united, they make a paradise." In the eighth letter, written in May of the same year, Barbezat declared that he was devastated by his officers' refusal to give him leave. Sketching teardrops at the bottom of the page, he wrote, "I'll shed tears until I have my felicity."

As the pregnancy progressed, Madelaine evidently grew exceedingly upset with her situation, but Barbezat did not once indicate that he had anything less than adoration for her. Writing in late July 1761, he consoled Madelaine:

> I join my chagrin with your tears, and the most tender feeling grows stronger in my heart from day to day. Yes, I dare repeat to you that this most sincere love will end only with my death. Because I recognize in you the greatest qualities, a spirit who deigns to love me. In a word, I can find nothing great enough with which to praise you. Oh, how happy am I to be loved by the most lovable woman of the century—I who am nothing. . . . Yes, I am favored by the gods. They use their intrigues between you and me, for one cannot find two lovers so tender.

Barbezat had written Madelaine's father in April 1761 to ask for his daughter's hand in marriage, a request that Abram Petitpierre, as yet unaware of Madelaine's pregnancy, at first rejected. When Petitpierre later consented to their union, Barbezat expressed his joy to Madelaine in the following fashion:

> How happy I was to be your servant and to offer my care and to pass moments obeying you. But now my state is so much sweeter since I have the name of husband that you now deign to accord me. Until now my heart was always pining, but this word "husband" makes it the happiest of hearts, most content with the choice that has been given it. . . . Yes, my love is still the same and nothing can change it. . . .

Aside from Barbezat's intimate letters, we have autobiographical material describing how Abraham Louis Sandoz, an eighteenth-century notary, chose his wife. Sandoz was a justiciary in La Chaux-de-Fonds and clearly a devout Reformed Protestant. On 15 April 1756 he described his courting period as a young man. Hoping that he would soon decide to marry, his parents had not interfered in his social life as long as he avoided bad company. During one year, however, he led a rather hedonistic lifestyle with "loud company," but he soon grew weary of this superficial atmosphere. He then began looking for a wife, associating only with those people with whom he could be completely open. Among potential candidates was a woman who openly professed an interest in marrying Sandoz, taking him somewhat by surprise since he did not expect someone as wealthy as she to be interested in him. Though he found this woman agreeable, Sandoz had stronger feelings for another with whom he had not yet broached the subject. Not wanting to reject the wealthy woman's offer quite yet, Sandoz first said that he was indeed honored that she had such feelings for him but needed some time to think it over. She replied, however, that she had brought up the subject of marriage so abruptly because another man—a wealthy man, as a matter of fact—had energetically solicited her hand in marriage. Before responding to this offer, she wanted to tell Sandoz how she felt about him. Surprised and flattered by this revelation, Sandoz was momentarily at a loss for words, but he managed to tell her that she might be wise to direct her affection toward the well-to-do suitor, pointing out the advantages the other man had to offer.

Sandoz then spoke about his marriage prospects with his parents and indicated his preference for Anne Marie Robert, a former member of his confirmation class of 1727. They seemed pleased with his choice of Anne Marie, the daughter of the late Abram Robert. His father noted that in choosing a wife one must not put as much emphasis on wealth as on character. Though young and inexperienced, Anne Marie was deemed capable of making a good living. She was sweet and hardworking, and she came from a good family that was thrifty and had acquired through its labors some property that could be transmitted to their posterity. Their opinion was enough to convince Sandoz to speak to Anne Marie about the possibility of marriage.

Meanwhile, Sandoz had not seen the other woman since the day she had in effect proposed to him. She now wrote him a letter, begging him not to delay any longer in responding to her inquiry. Sandoz was becoming disenchanted with this woman's aggressiveness and accordingly wrote her a letter in which he politely told her that, though honored by her offer, he could not at that time make a decision. Not wanting to be an obstacle to her fortune, he mentioned the good qualities of the wealthier man who had proposed to her and recommended that she accept his offer. Sandoz never again spoke about the subject of marriage with this woman and did not know how this letter was received.

Sandoz then proceeded to discuss the matter of marriage with Anne Marie. She graciously heard his proposal but, wise young woman that she was, refused to make a decision without first conferring with her uncle, who had assumed the authority of her late parents over her. Sandoz then spent a few anxious days waiting for her reply. So nervous was he that his teacher asked him what was wrong. He confided to her what was happening in his life, bemused at the "strange mystery" his feelings could cause him. After a few days, he returned to Anne Marie's abode for their rendezvous, whereupon she accepted the proposal and they touched hands as a symbol of their union. They wrote the announcements in August 1730, and everyone in both families was happy about the match, especially Sandoz himself, who had won the bride he desired. On 11 November 1730 the eighteen-year-old Sandoz went alone to fetch Anne Marie at her home, and together they walked to church where they were wed. The ceremony was followed by a big family supper at his father's home.

Sandoz's narrative is interesting in showing that in early eighteenth-century courtship sentiment could outweigh wealth. Both he and the un-named woman who proposed to him were willing to turn down offers from wealthier people in favor of partners for whom they had stronger feelings. Even though this narrative has no trace of the melodramatic romance that inspired Barbezat, Sandoz, writing a quarter-century after his wedding, nonetheless showed a genuine interest in Anne Marie. While awaiting her response, he suffered a few painful days in which his mood shifted from hope and joy to fear and uncertainty. And when she accepted his proposal, he was thrilled to have won her over. Though flattered that the wealthier woman was interested in him, Sandoz never hinted that he would forswear Anne Marie for her. The frank and earnest inquiries of the woman reveal that she deemed her affection for Sandoz far more important than the riches of her suitor. In short, both Sandoz and this woman were quite ready to trade wealth for affection.

Parents involved in this affair were passive advisers. Unlike some parents from earlier centuries, they did not actively solicit husbands and wives for their children; rather, they let the young people take the initiative them-selves and then gave their approval or disapproval. Sandoz's parents, though hoping their son would soon marry, did not push him toward a particular woman. It was Abraham Louis Sandoz himself who first thought of Anne Marie as a potential wife and then asked his parents' opinion. Anne Marie's uncle did not actively seek an advantageous marriage for his niece but simply gave his approval when she received an offer that pleased her. Likewise, the more aggressive woman acted on her own initiative independent of her parents when she revealed her feelings to Sandoz. From all sides, this affair supports the view that young people were able to pursue marriages relatively independent of parental pressure in the eighteenth century.

Like their sons and daughters, parents also valued sentiment more than wealth in the process of choosing spouses. Though noting that Anne Marie's hard-working family had acquired some property, Sandoz's father explicitly recommended character over wealth. He was quite content with his son's choice and did not in any way try to pressure him into accepting the more financially attractive offer. For the previous one hundred fifty years, numerous instances can be found in which parents vigorously encouraged their children to marry certain individuals for financial reasons. In contrast to such practices—clearly exceptional even in the sixteenth and seventeenth centuries—more eighteenth-century parents simply advised, rather than directed, their sons and daughters in choosing spouses. Even though the young people of Neuchâtel could not marry without parental consent until the age of twenty-two, mothers and fathers who served as matchmakers were rarer than before; the vast majority of parents, like Sandoz's, allowed their children freer rein in choosing mates. . . .

During the course of the eighteenth century, the most dramatic changes in matrimonial disputes took place in the area of divorce. Whereas at the beginning of the century judges for the first time recognized cruelty as a viable ground for dissolving marriages, cruel misconduct was not commonly cited in divorce cases until the late eighteenth century. Toward the end of the century of Prussian rule, the justices further promoted companionate marriages by taking the unprecedented step of accepting incompatibility as sufficient grounds for divorce. These innovations promoted domestic harmony and served the interests of women more than men.

While divorce cases changed qualitatively, their numbers also increased dramatically vis-à-vis other forms of litigation. For the first time in the history of these courts, divorce suits displaced contract disputes as the most common type of marital dispute. The increase in the quantity of divorce suits is remarkable, far surpassing the rate of the contemporary population increase. The consistory of Valangin had heard a scanty 41 divorce cases for the years 1622–1706; a total of 426 requests for divorces were made during the eighteenth century: 227 in Neuchâtel and 199 in Valangin. Of these, only 78 suits were heard during the first fifty years of this period; 348 such cases were heard from 1757 to 1806. If we compare the statistics for the first and last decades of this century, the increase in court activity is still more dramatic: only 15 persons petitioned for divorce in Neuchâtel and Valangin from 1707 to 1716, whereas Neuchâtelois filed 128 divorce suits from 1797 to 1806. Over all, while the population of the principality increased by 70 percent during this century, the volume of divorce cases heard in the same period increased by roughly 750 percent.

Several factors account for this increase in divorces. To a certain extent, the increase in marital breakdown was likely due to a greater emphasis on emotion and sentiment in marriage. As Lawrence Stone suggests, the more marriage is based on sentiment, the more common marital breakdown becomes. As love matches became more common in eighteenth-century England, Stone argues, women grew less tolerant of their husbands' infidelity and increasingly asked and received judicial separations. Eighteenth-century French novelists and pamphleteers strongly advocated the love match as opposed to the marriage of convenience, and they eloquently argued in favor of divorce in order to maintain happy, loving marriages. Residents of Neuchâtel may have been influenced by this literature; at any rate, eighteenth-century jurists and litigants put more importance on the personal compatibility of spouses than had Neuchâtelois of earlier centuries. . . .

12

OLD AGE: TRADITION AND CHANGE

DAVID G. TROYANSKY

The history of old age is a relatively new frontier in social history, spurred by the general research interest in capturing all significant facets of past society and by the growing importance of the elderly in our own day. Social historians have already revised established views in ways that improve historical accuracy and provide useful perspective on current problems. Most obviously, conventional ideas that the elderly were rare before modern times or that they were uniformly venerated have simply been disproved, particularly in Western history.

The following selection deals with the elderly among French peasants in the eighteenth century. It highlights some traditional issues in Western rural society, involving tensions over property as children reached maturity and as the work capacity of older parents might falter. It indicates the importance of the old age segment, despite the huge numbers of the very young in a society in which deaths in early childhood ran high. It also emphasizes the extent to which dealing with old age was largely a family matter, with no government or extensive charitable resources to draw upon. Careful strategies were required, but they might cause serious intergenerational tensions. David Troyansky notes some common assumptions about veneration, but shows they did not always prevail in practice. There were no automatic bonds of love or respect, though individual relationships varied.

While basic attitudes and strategies were not changing rapidly in the eighteenth century, there were important new developments. The number of the elderly increased, thanks to more abundant food supplies. Soon, population pressure would create larger groups without significant property, though this development had not yet transformed the French countryside. Change was already putting new strain on the traditional system, exacerbating hostilities to the elderly and creating new vulnerabilities for old people themselves. As one social historian has put it, "There was no golden age for age"—and the eighteenth century introduced some additional problems for those advancing in years.

From: David G. Troyansky, *Old Age in the Old Regime: Image and Experience in Eighteenth-Century France* (Ithaca: Cornell University Press, 1989), pp. 125–26, 130–33, 135–37, 139–40, 141–42, 149–50.

Approximately 85 percent of the French population in the eighteenth century lived outside the cities. There the past "was visible in the shape of white hairs, of ancestry, of physical resemblances, and of inherited deformities and diseases." Village life—family and communal existence—gave individual life its significance, and in the best of circumstances the community acted as a defense against rapid deprivation.

Work often lasted until death, but a gradual disengagement could be arranged. In parts of rural France, when younger workers went on annual treks along traditional routes of transhumance, some of their elders might stay behind and find themselves in positions of continued authority and even some leisure. Others were less fortunate; in villages in the center of France, when younger men migrated to Provence, the aged did the fall planting and, in winter, journeyed to Lyon and Clermont to beg. Elsewhere, the aged too continued to migrate with the seasons, sometimes trying one last time to earn enough for a settled retirement.

Retirement, when it could be afforded at all, required negotiation. Rather than a bureaucratic arrangement between an individual of a prescribed age and an institution, it was a notarized act between, say, a retiring father and his children, who granted his pension. It did not depend solely upon age but upon the person's relations with his or her successors.

Gerontologists have called the forced inactivity of the aged a social death that precedes biological death. If today's social death is characterized by a contradiction between a slower biological aging and a more sudden retirement decided by employer or state rather than family, the older form of withdrawal was characterized by a network of concerns, sometimes adverse, sometimes supportive. The timing of retirement involved the interests of a household: the marriage of children and the transmission of property. In order to understand the process throughout the country, we must look to inheritance law and practice. . . .

A good place to explore old age in the rural family is Provence [Southern France]. A land of Roman law, it placed property relations in the hands of the father and his chosen successor. Moreover, the high rate of coresidence of parents and married children provides a precise physical setting for the succession of generations. Much of this chapter is derived from a study of the life of parents after the marriage of their children in the Provençal village of Eguilles in the eighteenth century. A sample population of parents alive at the signing of their children's marriage contracts was traced through the notarial archives until the parents' deaths were announced in the parish register.

The farming *bourg* of Eguilles, perched on a hill surrounded by fields producing grain, grapes, and olives, numbered 2,333 inhabitants in 1765. Despite its proximity to Aix-en-Provence (10 kilometers), where the Boyer d'Eguilles family owned an *hôtel* (now a museum of natural history), the village was socially and ecomomically isolated. *Eguiléen* married *Eguiléenne* and stayed put, transmitting land or profession from generation to generation. Even the plague that devastated Marseille in 1720 left Eguilles untouched. The only "outside" influence that seems to have affected it was the dechristianization that swept Provence in the eighteenth century. Eguilles too experienced a decline in piety. Inheritance and property arrangements stand out in the secularized testaments, while requests for masses disappear. Concern for earthly reality overrode questions of the soul.

At the beginning of the eighteenth century virtually every testament notarized in Eguilles had opened with the remark that death comes without warning to young and old alike. By the 1740s that sentiment appeared in only 13 percent of the total; then it disappeared completely. Death was still certain, but its hour was becoming more predictable. People of Eguilles had realized that surviving one's childhood enormously improved one's chances of reaching old age. Anyone who lived to acquire property and exercise authority had a good chance of holding on for a long time.

According to Charles de Ribbe, nineteenth-century historian of the family, authority bred respect, and respect guaranteed support in old age. After reading family registers (*livres de raison*) kept by noble and bourgeois fathers, he delightedly reported that chapters were often entitled "memoirs of the births of children that it has pleased God to give to my son"—evidence that the grandfather ran the house. The *livre de raison* is not a likely place to find records of family conflict. It only confirms the legal status of the head of the Provençal family, the *chef de famille*.

In theory a widow could inherit her late husband's role, and the notarial archives include examples of widows wielding considerable power over their children. But such phenomena were exceptions in male-dominated Provence. Aged fathers, and a few mothers, signed contracts along with their adult children. Children under their parents' authority had to be emancipated by notarial act in order to sign for themselves. This relinquishment of parental authority, though relatively uncommon and normally involving sons who left the village, is indicative of power relations; it occurred in the presence of notables and amid considerable feudal pomp. As parental longevity increased, however, emancipation even of adult children staying home became more common.

On November 16, 1745, Jean Reynier emancipated two younger sons, his eldest having died and left four daughters and a son behind. Before the ceremony took place the father convinced the notable witnesses that he had not been "seduced" into the act. The sons knelt before their father, their hands in his; then the father bade them rise, symbolizing their freedom from his authority. In the same document Jean Reynier gave them his house, stable, attic, and cellar along with specified furniture and furnishings, including a bed each and linen. But the father retained the use of a furnished apartment of his choice in the house and the right to storage of his personal effects and goods for the rest of his life.

The role of the community in protecting authority within the family indicates that public status and power were at stake. Indeed, the head of the family had the right to exercise his power outside the household in the municipal council, whose records permit a view of village authority.

An analysis of attendance on annual election days (the council's best attended meetings) for the years 1716–88 yields the names of 203 different persons, of whom only sixty-nine showed up more than four times. Every family head had the right to vote (one of the reasons that nostalgic nineteenth-century historians wrote of a patriarchal village democracy in the ancien régime), but clearly not everyone bothered. The council was not representative of the village household structure; those who attended regularly were the local notables, the large landowners and the surgeons. Though it was in a sense patriarchal, it was not gerontocratic. Of the sixty-nine persons who attended more than four times, the dates of death of forty-one have been recovered; of these only seven participated in an election within a year of their death, and only one elected official actually died in office. An average period of over seven years passed between last ballot cast and death. There was no institutional framework for retirement; a man just stopped attending and was succeeded by a son or nephew. Thus, local affairs were governed by a council of middle-aged oligarchs, not a council of elders. Class took precedence over age, but even among the local governing elite extreme age brought on a form of public inactivity. . . .

It is often said that in preliterate societies such faith in the wisdom, or at least the memory, of the aged in general—whether doctors or other venerable sages—is of great importance. In semiliterate Eguilles a long memory played a role in court testimony involving customary boundaries and rights of passage through certain fields. Mathieu and Louis Joye claimed in a suit against Mathieu Artaud in 1744 that "since time immemorial man and beast had passed in the land and meadow concerned." They gathered expert witnesses whose ages (in order of testimony) were 85, 82, 80, 73, 73, 85, 57, 60, 58, 48, 46, 43, 41, 38, and 43. Pierre Giraud, "townsman aged about 85 years," remembered practices of the past seventy years, but his competence did not derive solely from age: he was the same influential man who had founded the hospital the previous year. But even if his words constituted the wisdom of the aged, they were only oral testimony. In a village where a clerk took notes at council meetings, where orders from either the monarchy or the Parlement de Provence came in printed form, where the *curé* was dutiful in recording baptisms, marriages, and burials, and where contracts and testaments were carefully written by notaries, little room remained for illiterate memory.

Records of public life yield only glimpses of the aged. The elderly retired from office; they did not go to the hospital in great numbers; only a few went to the *hospice* when granted charity by the *seigneur* (local nobleman); they were called upon only occasionally to remember the past. One must seek them out where most of them remained: in the household.

A census of 1765 counted 2,333 inhabitants of Eguilles living in 397 households. How they were actually distributed is unknown, as no detailed

Table [1] Eguilles census, by age and sex, 1810

Age	Male	%	Female	%
0–25	629	48.7	639	50.2
26–59	524	40.6	493	38.7
60–91	138	10.7	142	11.1
Total	1,291	100.0	1,274	100.0

census exists from before 1810. Nevertheless, the 1810 census provides an approximation of the eighteenth-century household structure. The ages of all but one (a servant) of the 2,566 residents are given (see Table [1]), showing a young population, almost half of it twenty-five years of age or less. Yet it included a high number of survivors for its day: 10.9 percent were sixty and over . . . and the senior group evidently played a significant role in the village economy. Of the 319 persons whose titles and professions are indicated in the census, 68 were at least sixty years old: 15 of 49 large landholders, 27 of 101 small farmers, two of six masons, two of three carders, one of two blacksmiths, one of two priests, and both cloth weavers, plus the builder, lawyer, mayor, rural policeman, tax collector, and plasterer. Whether they were all still actively pursuing their careers in 1810 is unknown; however, they were all identified by profession, whereas their sons were generally not. Such a barrier to professional advancement of the young is more eloquent than the turnover of seats on the ill-attended municipal council.

Conspicuous sexagenarian participation in the work force indicates activity in old age but equally implies a fear of dependence. It was risky to test the respect owed by a generation coming to power. Peasant proverbs certainly made that point: "One father can support one hundred children, but a hundred children wouldn't know how to support one father" was common wisdom in Provence and elsewhere in the Mediterranean world. Central European peasants quoted similar warnings, "To hand over is no longer to live"; "To sit on the children's bench is hard for the old"; "Do not take your clothes off before you go to sleep." But the barrier to the young that protected the aged took a psychological toll, for it undoubtedly tended to estrange the generations. . . .

Though "old" is not synonymous with "retired," the two states are clearly related. In the village setting, withdrawal from control of the patrimony indicated retreat from the world of adult activity and power. Folkloric sources suggest that it was foolish to pass on property before death, but the family did have to consider its long-term interests. It would have been equally foolish to hold onto power one was incapable of maintaining physically or to withhold authority from adult children eager for their due. Individuals had their demands, but so did household units, and the prospect of a classically restful retirement coupled with a growing belief in the generosity of the family probably induced parents to overlook some of the evidence of selfishness among their adult children.

The marriage of children normally provided the first opportunity for fathers and mothers to look to their own old age. The marriage contract foreshadowed the future course of the household, making gifts and promising subsequent ones in return for support in retirement. . . .

Most marriage contracts also outlined a future transmission of the patrimony. On August 10, 1761, Jean Baptiste Davin and Marguerite Pelenqui stated the conditions of their son Jean François Davin's marriage to Clèrc Aillaud. The father agreed to house the couple, and the mother offered a gift (*donation entre vifs*) of a house upon her own and her husband's death; the only condition was that Jean François house his brother until he too should marry. Antoine Artaud, a maker of pails, took in his son's bride on November 10, 1755, and provided the couple with one room. Upon the parents' death the younger couple would receive two more rooms. . . .

How reliable was the family? Melchior Gros, a farmer with wealth to distribute, provided a comfortable pension for his second wife, but one clause of his bequest is troubling: "She will be permitted to walk in the vineyards, pick and eat grapes from the vines." Gaspard Marroc in his testament of January 29, 1746, granted the same right to his wife Jeanne d'Eyme, and the clause also appeared in the contract of Agnès Cauvet. . . . Such an act demonstrates the ambiguity of relations between generations in this society. On the one hand, it shows a recognition of the sentimental—as well as biological— attachment of an older person to the land. On the other hand, the need to notarize permission to help oneself to grapes from one's children's field indicates a certain weakness of affective relations. . . .

The seigneurial court of Eguilles heard some cases of battles between households: neighbors feuded at the village fountain, and plaintiffs argued that particular individuals had developed demonic hatreds. Accusations of *vieille masque* (old hag) and *vieille sorcière* (old sorceress) were reminiscent of the days of witchcraft, an activity associated with old women. But the individual household rarely exposed itself to the courts, though in-law problems— occupying a middle ground between family and outsiders—were common. In testimony concerning a nuisance of a mother-in-law who lived above her married daughter and persisted in pouring water through the cracks in her floor to put out the couple's fire, it was said that her sons-in-law had never set foot in her apartment; separate housing was truly separate.

Testimony about an eighty-year-old man and his sons who fought with the man's son-in-law yields conflicting images of the father. On the one hand he is the powerful patriarch, leading his sons into battle and striking the first blow; on the other hand he is the weak old fool, shouting in the middle of the street, "I'll kill him myself," but "get me a stick so that I can stand." Theater may describe one old man as a respectable patriarch, another as a ridiculous graybeard, but in the street the same person could play both roles on the same day. It depended upon who was watching.

If conclusions about individual cases are ambiguous, historical generalizations about affective relations can be problematical. Nevertheless, some tentative conclusions can be drawn. The frequent recourse to contract in Eguilles indicates that although people did retire, there was no harmonious pattern of retirement. Family assistance was not something that was assured without contract, and individual measures resulted from particular attachments and resentments. Eighteenth-century Eguilles was far from being an ideal *Gemeinschaft* (community). Indeed, what is striking about the old person is his or her individuality. Retired from the council and challenged in workplace and household, a man may have found himself estranged in a supposedly "communal" world. "Community," as Tönnies would have it, existed before there was a need for contracts, but we have seen every detail of household finances spelled out and notarized. In a curious way, the elderly awaited the coming of a national bureaucracy to form a well-defined, albeit segregated, community of the aged. . . .

13

A REVOLUTION IN PUNISHMENT

PIETER SPIERENBURG

During the eighteenth and early nineteenth centuries, European society redefined its reactions to deviance and violations of the law. This redefinition may have been linked to new emotional reactions toward punishment, whether of children or criminals. The following selection, like the two that follow, calls attention to the wide range of social change during the period when an industrial society was just beginning to take shape.

Using primarily Dutch evidence but dealing with a general European trend, Pieter Spierenburg traces the attitudes underlying a major shift in the way criminals were treated and the masses were instructed. During the eighteenth century public executions were abandoned. New sensibility had begun to develop in the previous century, as part of earlier emotional change; now it was simply too disgusting to allow executions or torture to be public spectacles.

The changes in criminal punishment primarily involved the attitudes of the elites, an ongoing part of the new campaign to discipline mob passions and uncontrolled emotion. Did ordinary people change their outlooks in similar ways? If not, what happened to the kinds of community passions that public executions once expressed?

Historians like Spierenburg do not see the shift in punishment, away from torture and public execution and toward the growing use of imprisonment, as a pure gain for humanitarian progress. Prisons allowed the state to exercise more durable controls over many criminals than torture had once done. Whether the net result, particularly given the ongoing difficulties of modern prison systems, has been a boon either to criminals or to society at large is by no means clear. The fact remains that a key transformation occurred, focused on the eighteenth century, that has lasted, in some respects, to the present day.

After the mid-eighteenth century, confidence in public punishment began to crumble. In the Netherlands the earliest signs of a fundamental change of

From: Pieter Spierenburg, *The Spectacle of Suffering: Executions and the Evolution of Repression; from a Pre-Industrial Metropolis to the European Experience* (Cambridge: Cambridge University Press, 1984), pp. 183–96.

attitudes can be traced back to at least the 1770s, although the completion of the transformation of repression was a long way off. The actual abolition of public executions took another hundred years. A similar chronology characterized most European countries. The transformation of repression was a far from sudden transition, which began in the middle of the eighteenth century and ended towards the close of the nineteenth century. It comprised changes which took place both on the ideological and on the institutional level. At least three phases can be distinguished: first, there is the quest for legal and penal reform which began during the Enlightenment. It is relatively well known and has been analyzed in several studies of the period. Second, there is imprisonment: not the "birth of the prison," as is sometimes stated, but the rise of confinement to a more prominent position within the penal system and the emergence of the penitentiary. . . .

What is of concern here is the change of mentality implicit in [these phases]. The aim is to present the following argument: first, the transformation of repression, before and after 1800, was not a matter of political and legal changes alone, but primarily a consequence of a fundamental change in sensibilities, and, second, this change in sensibilities preceded the actual abolition of public executions. This abolition constituted the "political conclusion," only drawn at the end. . . .

The term "sensibility" should not be misunderstood. It refers to verifiable expressions of anxiety or repugnance and the question of whether these reflect a genuine concern for the well-being of delinquents or for that matter of anyone at all is left aside. . . .

This process of identification proceeds along two lines. More categories of persons are considered as "just like me" and more ways of making people suffer are viewed as distasteful. . . . Even in the Middle Ages spectators sometimes experienced sadness at the sight of an execution. When the audience in Paris wept in the early fifteenth century, it was because the person on the scaffold was a nobleman and an Armagnac leader. Not many other people would have been the object of pity. When an intended execution in Seville around 1600 "provoked the compassion of all" it was because the condemned was seventeen years old and believed to be innocent. Around the same time a few Amsterdam magistrates stated that the house of correction should serve to spare juvenile delinquents who were not real rogues a scaffold punishment. They identified with them enough to want to avoid a physical punishment. But it was only after the mid-eighteenth century that the pain of delinquents who had committed serious crimes and whose guilt was not in doubt, produced feelings of anxiety in some of the spectators. This implies that a new threshold was reached in the amount of mutual identification human beings were capable of. . . .

The disappearance of most forms of mutilation in the early seventeenth century has been discussed. Commentators from the later eighteenth century already took their absence for granted and often considered it as a sign of the greater civilization of their own times. Writers who commented on the esoteric, physical punishments still in use on ships felt obliged to excuse them-selves for confronting the reader with a tale of "cruelty and inhumanity." Again it is only around 1800 that certain groups among the elites considered all forms of public, physical punishment as "uncivilized."

Thus, the process certainly covered many centuries. Around 1800, however, it accelerated. Before that date human identification was only extended to the few or, to put it differently, a large amount of suffering was considered accept-able. Yet another way of putting it is to say that the system of public repression met with no significant opposition. Rejection increased from the 1770s on-wards. If delinquents were made to suffer, it should at least be done privately. . . .

In the sixteenth century most Dutch towns had a permanent scaffold with a gallows on it. It was often made of stone. A characteristic shape of the exe-cution place was that of a so-called *groen zoodje:* a square surrounded by a low fence and grass verges. In the middle the floor was elevated or a small scaf-fold built. These execution places seem to have disappeared in the course of the seventeenth century.

We saw that Amsterdam had a removable scaffold. According to Wagenaar, the wooden poles and planks were ready-made, so that the scaffold could be erected and dismantled "in a very short time." The city had perma-nent places of execution in the sixteenth century. The shift must have occurred in the early seventeenth century. It occurred in other towns as well. The city of Leiden had been executing its delinquents on a *groen zoodje* for centuries. This was pulled down in 1671–2 and from then on a wooden scaffold was erected in front of the Papestraat before each execution. In Maastricht the stone scaf-fold on the Vrijthof, which had stood there from about 1300, was removed in the middle of the seventeenth century. In Haarlem, however, the reverse hap-pened. As part of a project to rebuild the town hall in the 1630s the old wooden—but permanent—scaffold was replaced by one made of stone. This stone scaffold on the east wall remained there until 1855. Although this is clearly a counter-example, it should be noted that the new scaffold had the ap-pearance of a classical balcony and that the equipment of justice was normally kept inside the building.

The case of Haarlem calls for caution. Nevertheless, the shift from per-manent to removable scaffolds must have been common in the seventeenth century. The Court of Holland made such a decision rather late, but in this case it can be clearly observed that the shift was an expression of changing sen-sibilities. Constantin Huygens had already lobbied for the destruction of the stone scaffold in the 1670s. . . .

A few seventeenth-century writers pleaded for the abolition of torture. The movement became widespread and international in the second half of the eighteenth century. The actual abolition of torture was the first visible expres-sion of the transformation of repression. Although we are not dealing with a public feature, torture is still typical of *ancien régime* repression because in-fliction of pain is the essence of it. Its abolition in some states was the only re-form of criminal law which was carried through under the *ancien régime*.

Torture was practiced privately because secrecy during the trial itself was a guiding principle of criminal procedure. But the authorities were quite open about its existence as such. The sentences recited during an execution often began with the standard formula that the prisoner had confessed "outside of pain and chains." Apart from this, they occasionally contained references to concrete acts of torture. Thus the sentence of a burglar in 1661 adds to the account of his crime: "and the court did not take the other accusations into consideration, which he, prisoner, impertinently denied even during torture at the post." Similar passages, with only one erasure, slipped into other sentences, also in the early eighteenth century. . . .

A major change in sensibilities occurred in the second half of the eighteenth century. It is most clearly expressed in the fact that the defenders of torture felt obliged to display feelings of repugnance as well. Characteristically a writer would open with the announcement that he too found it an unpleasant method. Thus the Amsterdam lawyer Calkoen acknowledged a "humanitarianism" towards delinquents but wished to bestow his compassion in the first place on "the body of respectable citizens." He advocated "humanitarianism without cowardice and severity without cruelty." The opening remarks of the Viennese professor Josef von Sonnenfels' "On the abolition of torture" are the exact opposite of Calkoen's argument and therefore reflect the general sensitivity of the age just as well. "Many people," he said, "reproach the opponents of torture because they only appeal to their readers' feelings, while they fall short of convincing them rationally. Therefore I renounce all the advantages which such an appeal to emotion and pity for the suffering could provide me with. I am treating the topic with the cool indifference of the lawyer, who turns his face away from the twitchings of the tortured; who closes his ears to their cries and sees nothing but a scholarly debate before him." Thus Sonnenfels took feelings of repugnance for granted. He wished to attain a new detachment from these feelings, if not, his opening represents a covert emotional appeal after all.

Torture was abolished in Prussia in 1754; in Saxony in 1770; in Austria and Bohemia in 1776; in France in 1780–8, in the Southern Netherlands in 1787–94; in the Dutch Republic in 1795–8. The rise of sensitivity with regard to torture had prepared the way for other elements of the transformation of repression. The next step was the abolition of exposure of corpses.

The display of the dead bodies of capitally punished delinquents was discontinued in Western Europe around 1800. It antedated the abolition of public executions by at least half a century. There can be no doubt that increased sensitivity moved the authorities to act. Abandonment of the custom was usually motivated by calling it a relic of the "barbarity of former times." . . .

In the middle of the nineteenth century sensitivity towards executions is taken so much for granted that, just as with torture three generations earlier, the defenders feel obliged to show their revulsion too. Thus, in 1847 a Utrecht physician takes care to explain that he also dislikes them. Nevertheless, he argues, whipping cannot be abolished yet because of the low standard of civilization and moral development of the lower classes. A year earlier a lawyer from the same town had pleaded for the abolition of physical punishment. According to him, the appearance of recidivists on the scaffold proved that public executions only made people more obdurate in their ways. He found the spectacle a "barbaric" one and wished to see it disappear in the name of "civilization" and "enlightenment."

This sensitivity was largely confined to the upper and middle classes. They comprised polite society of the time, who formed public opinion and whose members expressed themselves in writing. The lower classes continued to be attracted to the event until the end. The elites had frowned upon their fascination from the middle of the seventeenth century onwards. Two hundred years later some people still thought that control depended on a display of toughness. Many others, whose forefathers had fully approved of the spectacle, now considered the eagerness of the lower classes to watch it as a sign that they were not yet as civilized as themselves. . . .

14

CHANGING REACTIONS TO SUICIDE

MICHAEL MacDONALD

Historians are just now taking up the challenge of dealing with suicide as a historical phenomenon—that is, a development rooted in specific periods and likely, at some point, to change.

In this selection, Michael MacDonald deals with a redefinition of attitudes toward suicide in eighteenth-century England, and its treatment in law and ritual, resulting from reconsideration of traditional religious fervor and magical beliefs. He points to areas in which elite decisions played a key role, but attitudes among ordinary folk, who served on juries or decided burial practices, were involved as well. Clearly, new mentalities were beginning to have sweeping impacts, from punishment to medicine to suicide, and the relationship between leaders and ordinary folk in this pattern of change was both mutual and complex.

The selection deals with changes in outlook and policy, and their gradual and uneven course from the late seventeenth century and well into the nineteenth century. It embraces not only suicide and religion, but new ideas about medicine and psychiatric disturbance, that could apply to other areas as well. The selection does not deal with the impact of change on suicide itself: Was suicide facilitated? Would other factors, such as the nature of industrial life, play a more important role in determining any new patterns here?

Suicide was a heinous crime in Tudor and early Stuart England, and it merited condign punishment. The word "suicide" itself was not coined until the 1630s, and it did not pass into general circulation until the eighteenth century. Before then there were no terms with which to describe self-destruction that did not brand its perpetrators as criminals or madmen. Self-killing was a species of self-murder, a felony in criminal law and a desperate sin in the eyes of the church. "For the heinousnesse thereof," observed Michael Dalton, "it is an offence against God, against the king, and against Nature." Self-murderers were tried posthumously by a coroner's jury, and if they were found to have been

From: Michael MacDonald, "The Secularization of Suicide in England 1600–1800," *Past and Present* No. 111 (May 1986), pp. 52–55, 58–60, 64, 84–85, 87–88, 93.

responsible for their actions savage penalties were enforced against them and their families. They were declared to have been *felones de se,* felons of themselves: their chattels, like those of other felons, were forfeited to the crown and placed at the disposal of the king's almoner or the holder of a royal patent. Their bodies were denied the usual rites of Christian burial. By ancient custom, based on popular lore, the corpses of suicides were interred at a crossroads or in some other public way, laid face down in the grave with a wooden stake driven through them. The state of mind of self-killers at the time that they committed their fatal deed was crucial. Men and women who slew themselves when they were mad or otherwise mentally incompetent were not guilty of their crime. Edmund Wingate explained concisely that suicides had to be sane and to take their lives intentionally to be guilty of self-murder: "He is *felo de se* that doth destroy himself out of premeditated hatred against his own life, or out of a humour to destroy himself." Idiots or lunatics who were insane when they killed themselves were judged *non compos mentis* by the coroner's jury and spared both the secular and the religious punishments for suicide.

Abhorrence of suicide was deeply rooted in English history and custom and it was very powerful. Despite the reluctance of many medieval theologians to condemn suicide unequivocally, self-murder was a crime in common and civil law long before the sixteenth century. The practice of confiscating the goods of suicides dates from the thirteenth century. Elaborate rituals that dramatized the disgrace of suicides were prescribed by civil law, but these seem to have been little regarded in England. The rites that were used when burying the bodies of self-murderers in this country were based instead on popular, supernatural beliefs, which were sanctioned by the church both before and after the Reformation. Suicide was spiritually perilous. The souls of self-murderers were restless and malevolent, and the custom of burying them away from the community and piercing their bodies with stakes was supposed to afford some protection against their wandering ghosts. The clergy taught that suicide was literally diabolical. Latimer warned that some men are so vexed by the assaults and temptations of the devil that "they rid themselves out of this life," The principal causes of self-murder, the Puritan John Sym declared almost a century later, are the "strong impulse, powerful motions, and command of the Devil"; and he added that Satan sometimes appeared to a suicidal man, especially if he were also plagued by melancholy, "speaking to and persuading a man to kill himself." . . .

These views were shared by men and women of every rank and calling. It is impossible to know if churchmen originally implanted among the common people the belief that suicide was the handiwork of Satan and his demons or if they merely validated an ancient popular conviction. English Protestant preachers certainly redoubled their medieval forebears' effort to incorporate many popular beliefs about the supernatural into a Christian theological context, and they emphasized the devil's role as a tempter in their sermons on suicide and despair. There is in any case no doubt that Satan had become the leading supernatural figure in the popular lore of suicide by the sixteenth and early seventeenth centuries. The rector of Great Hallingbury in Essex wrote in his register in 1572 that "the enemye of mans salvayon on off the devylls angells" appeared repeatedly to one of his parishioners and succeeded at last in making him hang himself. Richard Napier noted that 139 of his mentally disturbed patients were "tempted" to kill themselves between 1597 and 1634, and some of them actually saw or heard the tempter or one of his demons. "A Pious, Credible woman" told Richard Baxter that one day when she was unhappy the devil had appeared in her parlour in the shape of a big black man, holding a noose in his hand and pointing to the lintel. Coroners' inquests on the bodies of self-murderers, like other felony indictments, alleged that the crime had been committed "at the instigation of Satan," and at least until the late seventeenth century the legal formula expressed the almost universal belief that suicide was literally diabolical.

Attitudes to suicide changed profoundly in the century and a half following the English Revolution. Judicial and ecclesiastical severity gave way to official leniency and public sympathy for most people who killed themselves. This transformation was a complex phenomenon. The views of particular classes and groups altered at different times and for different reasons; the actions of officials and institutions did not simply reflect public opinion. Moreover the laws against suicide were not altered until the nineteenth century. The savagery of the traditional reaction to suicide was mitigated by the increasing suspension of the law on a case-by-case basis, rather than by reforms promulgated by parliament or by the officials at Westminster. The locus of change was therefore the coroner's jury, which became increasingly reluctant in the later seventeenth and eighteenth centuries to enforce the penalties for self-murder. The decisions made by coroners' juries are especially significant and revealing. They were influenced by the changing attitudes of the governing élite as well as by the moral conservatism of local communities. At the same time the verdicts that juries returned determined what the community's response to suicidal deaths would be. Neither the official penalty of confiscation nor the popular sanction of ritual desecration could be performed unless a jury brought in a verdict of *felo de se*. The mysterious alchemy of the coroner's inquest transmuted the insubstantial stuff of attitudes and beliefs into the tangible matter of collective action.

Coroners' juries meliorated the societal reaction to suicide in two ways. The first way was to frustrate the claims of lords and the crown to the goods of self-murderers by undervaluation and deliberate negligence. Undervaluation is obviously impossible to detect in individual cases unless the offenders were caught at it, but the trend in the numbers and size of forfeitures indicates that it became increasingly prevalent. Because so many people who committed suicide were poor or female, forfeitable goods had always been reported in less than half of inquisitions on self-murderers. Between 1485 and 1659 they were mentioned in only about 40 per cent of the inquisitions returned to King's Bench. After the Restoration, however, the percentage of inquisitions reporting goods fell inexorably until, at the end of Queen Anne's reign, property of any value at all was mentioned in less than 8 percent of inquisitions returned to King's Bench.

And when juries reported goods to seize, they set their worth at figures that were lower and lower. In the 1660s about one-third of the forfeitures reported in inquests to King's Bench were valued at sums higher than £1, and some of them brought the crown hundreds of pounds; by the period 1710–14 only 6–7 per cent of forfeitures were worth more than £1, and there were no windfalls of £50 or more at all. In the last decades of the seventeenth century and in the reign of Queen Anne juries were declaring openly that yeomen and even gentlemen whom they judged to have been self-murderers either possessed no chattels or owned goods that were worth only trivial sums. In other words, the proportion of cases in which suicides were supposed to have had no goods at all or in which juries simply ignored the matter grew as the value of the forfeitures that did take place shrank. Even allowing for the distortions that are caused by missing inventories and by procedures that were inconsistent and shifting, the king's right to the goods of suicides was obviously severely eroded by noncompliance between the Restoration and the accession of George I.

The second way that juries effectively decriminalized suicide was to bring in increasing and finally overwhelming numbers of *non compos mentis* verdicts. Less than 7 per cent of the suicides reported to King's Bench were declared to have been insane in the early 1660s, but the proportion more than doubled in the next two decades [Table 1]. In the 1690s around 30 per cent of suicides were brought in *non compos mentis*, and lunacy verdicts exceeded

TABLE 1 **Goods of Suicides Reported to King's Bench 1660–1714***

	Numbers of suicides	Goods reported	Per cent reporting goods
1660–4	334	122	36.5
1665–9	293	97	33.1
1670–4	241	72	29.9
1675–9	219	55	25.1
1680–4	256	68	26.6
1685–9	177	44	24.9
1690–4	256	59	23.0
1695–9	216	43	19.9
1700–4	181	30	16.6
1705–9	170	17	10.0
1710–14	156	12	7.7
Totals	2,499	619	20.9

*Notes and sources: Public Record Office, London. The figures given for "goods" include only those inquisitions in which chattels were valued (i.e., were assessed at a sum larger than nothing).

40 per cent in the early eighteenth century. Unhappily, the practice of returning coroners' inquisitions to King's Bench declined in the eighteenth century. But there are some records from local jurisdictions that illustrate the growing tendency to bring in verdicts of *non compos mentis* in the otherwise poorly documented years between 1714 and about 1740. The long run of inquisitions for the city of Norwich is perhaps the best set of such records for the period. *Non compos mentis* verdicts exceeded *felo de se* there even in the early eighteenth century. By the 1720s 90 per cent of all suicides were judged insane. . . . Several runs of coroners' inquisitions and bills from the second half of the eighteenth century tell a similar tale. Regardless of the character of the locality, from remote Cumberland to London itself, *non compos mentis* had become the usual verdict in cases of suicide by the last third of the century. . . .

Enlightenment rationalism certainly contributed to the demystification of suicide, but the appeal of philosophical and medical arguments cannot be ascribed to their novelty or logical superiority. The ideas of the free-thinkers and physicians who advanced more liberal attitudes to self-slaughter were strikingly unoriginal. The philosophers' defences of suicide were based largely on classical sources and had been familiar to sixteenth- and seventeenth-century writers. The physicians made no notable contributions to the understanding of suicide in the late seventeenth and eighteenth centuries. When they mentioned the subject at all, they were content to repeat the Renaissance commonplace that melancholy (sometimes rechristened the vapours or the spleen) often led to self-destruction. The chief difference between the treatment of the psychiatric causes of suicide before and after the Civil War is that later writers no longer insisted that its medical causes, such as melancholy, might be amplified by supernatural ones, namely Satan and his minions. Except for clerical writers, Georgian authors who discussed the medical psychology of suicide assumed that its causes were entirely physical or psychological. Even very pious doctors like the famous Cheyne no longer invoked the devil as the author of self-murder after 1700. It is notable as well that the medical and philosophical approaches to suicide contradicted one another. Medical apologists presumed that suicide was the action of a demented person: anyone who committed it was therefore innocent of their own murder because they were insane. Philosophical apologists argued that suicide was sometimes permissible because it could be defended as a rational course of action in certain circumstances. Juries acted increasingly on the former assumption while the press and pamphleteers debated the correctness of the latter point of view. . . .

By the middle of the eighteenth century the ruling élite generally had come to regard suicide as the outcome of mental illness or a moral choice, not a diabolical act. The views of the common people changed more slowly than fashionable opinion, though. Ordinary men and women were reluctant to abandon beliefs that reinforced their view of the universe as a theatre of spiritual warfare between the forces of good and evil, and they continued to fear the power of Satan and malign spirits throughout the eighteenth century.

Allegations of possession and witchcraft were made long after exorcism and witchcraft prosecutions had ceased officially, and there seems to have been considerable popular support for the ritual burial of the minority of suicides condemned as self-murderers. Orders to bury them in the public highways were observed, and huge crowds attended the interment of some celebrated *felones de se*. Stories collected in the nineteenth century show that country folk still dreaded the spirits of suicides. The practice of burying suicides who were judged *non compos mentis* on the north side of churchyards where excommunicants, unbaptized babies and executed criminals lay seems in the eighteenth century to have satisfied a strong, lingering antagonism to the legitimation of self-destruction: "We are all aware," commented a Scottish correspondent to *Notes and Queries* in 1852, "of the popular repugnance to permitting the bodies of suicides to be interred within the 'consecrated' or 'hallowed' precincts of a churchyard." Even in the late eighteenth century attempted suicides sometimes implicated Satan or evil spirits in their deed, and these malign figures still made appearances in dying speeches and suicide notes. . . .

The practice of ritually burying the bodies of criminal suicides continued well into the early nineteenth century. By that time the very rarity of their use in other circumstances added to their dramatic value as a method of defaming notorious malefactors. The burial of the famous murderer John Williams, who committed suicide while awaiting trial in 1811, was organized as a macabre entertainment. Williams's body was exhibited to the huge crowd that attended the rite. His countenance was "ghastly in the extreme": the maul and ripping cord with which he had killed his victims were displayed beside him. A procession led by several hundred constables stopped at the houses of the families he had murdered and brought his body at last to a crossroads, where it was staked in the grave. The grave-diggers sold small bits of wood cut from the stake to spectators as souvenirs. Williams's crimes and his punishment were highly publicized at the time and were the subject later of Thomas De Quincey's essay, "On Murder Considered as One of the Fine Arts," and a number of less notable literary efforts. Williams's interment was the most famous ritual burial of the nineteenth century, but it was not the last, and other criminal suicides were occasionally desecrated in similar ceremonies until the 1820s. Ironically, in this final phase of its enforcement the law against self-murder was restored to its original function: the *felo de se* verdict seems to have been invented in the middle ages as a means of punishing offenders who killed themselves to escape justice. The principal achievement of the theologians and preachers who had condemned suicide in the Tudor and Stuart age had been to fuse the civil, religious and folkloric sanctions against self-murder into a single stereotype. By restricting the *felo de se* verdict to criminals and deviants, eighteenth-century coroners and their juries very slowly drained the rites of desecration of the last vestiges of supernatural significance and completed the gradual secularization of suicide that had begun soon after the Restoration.

15

THE ORIGINS OF CONSUMERISM

NEIL McKENDRICK, COLIN BREWER, and
J. A. PLUMB

Historians have begun to pay serious attention to consumerism as a major facet of modern European society only recently. The results have involved some striking adjustments in our understanding of the social past: Consumerism increased with industrialization but it also, we now realize, predated it and helped cause it. Obviously, consumer behavior changed as a result of increased industrial production; new outlets like the department stores, first introduced in Paris in the 1830s, expressed this relationship. Definite consumerism, however, predated the industrial revolution and indeed helps explain it, for a growing demand for nonessential goods set the context in which new production methods made sense. Consumerism emerged in the English middle class in the eighteenth century, and the following selection details some of its key manifestations. What did early consumerism focus on? What was distinctive about it? How did it differ from more traditional attitudes toward material goods?

Debate about the causes of new consumer interests continues. Earlier commercialization helped set the stage; English people at several social levels had been participating more actively in the marketplace and enjoying a rising standard of living for some time. But commerce does not guarantee a consumerist passion. Imitation of the aristocracy; the lures developed by manufacturers such as Wedgwood, the porcelain magnate, or Boulton, the fashion-button maker; and larger shifts in attitude, including openness to new emotions such as romantic love—all have been invoked, and all may have been involved in one of the big changes in behavior and values of modern history.

Consumer expressions were, even in the eighteenth century, highly contagious, spreading to some degree among various social groups (particularly in London, England's commercial mecca) and certainly to both women and men. This too is a sign of the importance of this new interest.

From: Neil McKendrick, Colin Brewer, and J. A. Plumb, *The Birth of a Consumer Society: The Commercialization of Eighteenth-Century England* (Bloomington: Indiana University Press, 1982), pp. 1, 11, 12, 44, 47–48, 49, 53–54, 60, 75–77, 93–94, 316.

There was a consumer revolution in eighteenth-century England. More men and women than ever before in human history enjoyed the experience of acquiring material possessions. Objects which for centuries had been the privileged possessions of the rich came, within the space of a few generations, to be within the reach of a larger part of society than ever before, and, for the first time, to be within the legitimate aspirations of almost all of it. Objects which were once acquired as the result of inheritance at best, came to be the legitimate pursuit of a whole new class of consumers.

What men and women had once hoped to inherit from their parents, they now expected to buy for themselves. What were once bought at the dictate of need, were now bought at the dictate of fashion. What were once bought for life, might now be bought several times over. What were once available only on high days and holidays through the agency of markets, fairs and itinerant pedlars were increasingly made available every day but Sunday through the additional agency of an ever-advancing network of shops and shopkeepers. As a result "luxuries" came to be seen as mere "decencies," and "decencies" came to be seen as "necessities." Even "necessities" underwent a dramatic metamorphosis in style, variety and availability.

Where once material possessions were prized for their durability, they were now increasingly prized for their fashionability. Where once a fashion might last a lifetime, now it might barely last a year. Where once women had merely dreamed of following the prevailing London fashions, they could now follow them daily in the advertisements in the provincial press, and actually buy them from the ever-increasing number of commercial outlets dedicated to satisfying their wants and their needs. Where once consumers eager for new fashions were dependent on the chance of rumour and the impressions of gossip, they could now rely on the accurate details of the illustrated fashion print or ring the changes for themselves on the endless combinations made possible by the English fashion doll; instead of what a quick eye and a retentive memory could glean from the dress of the rich or a visit of the fashionable, there were now precise details minutely recorded in the pages of the fashion magazines for a new and larger market to pore over. Where once the ability to wear such fashions was limited to the very few, now rising real family incomes brought them increasingly within the reach of many. . . .

Both commercial activity and the consumer response to it were feverish. Uncontrolled by any sense of commercial decorum men advertised in unprecedented numbers—whole newspapers were taken over by advertisements, and a very large proportion of all newspapers was filled with advertising. And the customer had plenty to choose from. For, spurred on by rampant demand, designers produced both fashions of outrageous absurdity and styles of lasting elegance. Fashion in hats and hairstyles, dresses and shoes and wigs and such like, arguably reached even greater extremes than ever before and certainly changed more rapidly and influenced a greater proportion of society.

As early as 1711 we find Addison writing ironically of "the ladies" that "the whole sex is now dwarfed and shrunk into a race of beauties that seems almost another species. I remember several ladies who were once near seven foot high that at present want some inches of five." He comforts himself that "most are of the opinion that they are at present like trees lopped and pruned that will certainly sprout up and flourish with greater heads than before." They did. Men and women's wigs were caricatured as needing special openings in the roofs of their carriages in the 1770s. Women with enormous swollen hoops found it difficult to negotiate narrow doorways, and announced their presence through wide ones with several feet of swollen skirt before they arrived themselves. Hats sprouted upwards and sideways, and such was the rage to follow fashion that even labourers in the fields were recorded by Stubbs and Blake in graceful wide-brimmed picture hats.

Styles in furniture, silver and pottery and the like were (by the nature of their market and the nature of its demand structure) less susceptible to annual or even monthly change in taste, and they achieved an enviable serenity which we still cherish two centuries later. Despite the conflicting claims of Gothic, Chinoiserie and Neo-Classical, some designers managed to impose a remarkable uniformity of style on all classes in the last decade of the century—the rich had Adam and the rest had Adamesque. Even Gothic and Chinoiserie were adapted to classical proportions (apart from occasional extravaganzas like Beckford's Fonthill or the Pagoda at Kew). But within those limits objects of the most marvellous quality and variety were produced for the higher ranks of society. Unworried by any sense of the impropriety of ample profits, manufacturers were able to exploit what they called this "epidemical madness" to consume, this sickness to buy even at inflated prices, this "universal" contagion to spend. They felt such "infections" should be cherished. They felt that the compulsive power of fashion should be pandered to. They made sure that this obsessive need to consume was constantly titillated and encouraged. . . .

But as the range and variety and amount of English manufacturing developed, as the evidence for increased domestic consumption of the products of these manufacturers grew, so some writers "responding to the obvious, if uneven economic growth, began to speculate upon the dynamic effect of increased demand. The word "markets" in their pamphlets subtly changed from a reference to the point of sales to the more elusive concept of expandable spending."

It was, in fact, one of the first examples of the unleashing of latent home demand (in the face of suddenly prolific cheap calico and muslins from India) which stimulated the new recognition of both the elastic nature of domestic consumption and its benefits. As a result many of the underlying causes of the consumer revolution of the eighteenth century were explicitly recognized for the first time. For in the 1690s the taste for the cheap, colourful fabrics imported by the East India Company reached "epidemic proportions." It was then "when the maverick spirit of fashion revealed itself in the craze over printed calicoes [that] the potential market power of previously unfelt wants came clearly into view. Here was a revolutionary force. Under the sway of new consuming tastes, people had spent more, and in spending more the elasticity of demand had become apparent. In this elasticity, the defenders of domestic spending discovered the propulsive power (and the economic advantages to the nation) of envy, emulation, love of luxury, vanity and vaulting ambition." . . .

Although the first fashion magazine appeared in France in the 1670s, and even fashion drawings have been found as early as 1677 in *Le Mercure Galant*, "it was in England that the systematic and . . . widespread production of fashion prints began." The time was the last three decades of the eighteenth century.

The Lady's Magazine brought out its first fashion print in 1770, and it was at this time that an enterprising advertiser started to insert a page of the latest hats and dresses into ladies' pocket books and almanacs. These were specifically devised for the guidance of "ordinary young gentlewomen, not the extravagant few." . . .

The first coloured fashion print is dated 1771 and appeared in *The Lady's Magazine* described as "a fine Copper-plate beautifully coloured," but within a few years, "when much greater elaboration had been attained and the circulation of such journals was far larger," whole teams of colourists (each member handling only a single colour) worked on assembly line principles passing the page along until it reached its multi-coloured completion.

These fashion plates were, in fact, trade plates, designed as commercial propaganda. Their intention was to stimulate demand, to spread new fashions, to encourage imitation of the "taste-makers." As the earliest editors assured their subscribers, they would no longer have to rely on the French fashion dolls, those "puppets always inadequate and yet extremely dear, which give at best merely a hint of our new modes." . . .

Mrs. Bell held a fashion show for her novelties on "THE FIRST DAY OF EVERY MONTH" as the banner headlines of *La Belle Assemblée* announced it. But as the London source of a flow of monthly fashions which were taken up and celebrated in the provinces she was merely the culmination of a process typical of the eighteenth century. The stay maker of North Walsham who advertised in the *Norwich Mercury* of 1788 "that he is *just returned from Town with* the newest Fashions . . . in Stays, Corsetts and Riding Stays" knew what his customers wanted to hear. His assurance that "their Orders [will be] executed in a Height of Taste not inferior to *the first Shops in London*" offered to his female customers the confidence that even the least displayed part of their clothing would be in the latest fashion. What was invisible to the world at large would be seen by her maid, and, in the closely stratified society of provincial England, demonstrating the modishness of even one's underwear to one's maidservant was a sufficiently desirable event for the local tradesman to insist on the fashionability of each and every undergarment. And Mrs. Bell played a vital role in keeping the provincial world supplied with a constant flow of such London prototypes to copy.

In the last thirty years of the eighteenth century the fashion plate and the fashion magazine offered wholly new means of spreading fashionable contagions. Unprecedentedly accurate, they and the fashion doll in the last ten years, marked the culmination of the commercialization of fashion which had been developing so rapidly in the rest of the century. But their novelty at the end of the century must not distract us from other agents of commercialization and other manipulators of fashion which had been effectively at work earlier in the century. . . .

Clothes were the first mass consumer products to be noticed by contemporary observers. It is often forgotten that the industrial revolution was, to a large extent, founded on the sales of humble products to very large markets—the beer of London, the buckles and buttons of Birmingham, the knives and forks of Sheffield, the cups and saucers of Staffordshire, the cheap cottons of Lancashire. Beer was arguably the first mass consumer product to be mass produced under factory conditions and sold to the public for cash at fixed prices by pure retailers. But the sales of mass-produced cheap clothes understandably excited more attention. When *The British Magazine* of 1763 wrote that "The present rage of imitating the manners of high life hath spread itself so far among the gentle folks of lower life, that in a few years we shall probably have no common folks at all," it was the imitation of fashionable dress that it was complaining of.

Dress was the most public manifestation of the blurring of class divisions which was so much commented on. Social expectations rose with family income. The standards of what Veblen later called "pecuniary decency" rose too as succeeding layers of English society joined the consuming ranks. The effects excited much comment, "It is the curse of this nation that the labourer and the mechanic will ape the lord," wrote Hanway, "the different ranks of people are too much confounded: the lower orders press so hard on the heels of the higher, if some remedy is not used the Lord will be in danger of becoming the valet of his Gentleman." Dibdin complained that "the Tradesman vies with my Lord." Tucker made the same point when he wrote that "the different stations of Life so run into and mix with each other, that it is hard to say, where the one ends, and the other begins." The *London Magazine* for 1772 reported that the classes were imitating one another so closely that "the lower orders of the people (if there are any, for distinctions are now confounded) are equally immerged [sic] in their fashionable vices." In 1775 it complained more specifically that "whenever a thing becomes the mode it is universally and absurdly adopted from the garret to the kitchen, when it is only intended for some very few Belles in the first floor."

Writer after writer notes the "absence of those outward distinctions which formerly characterized different classes." Somerville, writing in the early nineteenth century, reflects on the changes which had taken place in his lifetime. "At that time various modes of dress indicated at first sight the rank, profession and the age of every individual. Now even the servants are hardly distinguishable in their equipment from their masters and mistresses?" Davis, in his *Friendly Advice to Industrious and Frugal Persons*, drew attention to the same phenomenon: "a fondness for Dress may be said to be the folly of the age, and it is to be lamented that it has nearly destroyed those becoming marks whereby the several classes of society were formerly distinguished." . . .

On every side contemporaries rushed into print to explain the phenomenon. It was the result, they all agreed, of the downward spread of fashion, and of the imitation by the poor of their social superiors. As early as 1750 Fielding complained that "an infinite number of lower people aspire to the pleasures of the fashionable." In 1755 *The World* complained of "this foolish vanity that prompts us to imitate our superiors . . . we have no such thing as common people among us. . . . Attorneys' clerks and city prentices dress like cornets of dragoons . . . every commoner . . . treads hard on the heels of the quality of dress." . . .

The expansion of the market, revealed in the literary evidence, occurred first among the domestic-servant class, then among the industrial workers, and finally among the agricultural workers. The servants were the most readily observed group seen by the articulate middle and upper class observers who dominate our records, but from the 1750s and 1760s onwards

> the accounts of increasing luxury among the labourers—both urban and rural—were becoming much more frequent. These continued through the next thirty years and by the end of the century what had previously been looked on as a luxury for the worker was thought of in terms of being a decency or even a necessity.

Contemporaries complained that more and more classes and more and more occupations were being sucked into the pursuit of fashion. Even the watermen of London were described as wearing silk stockings. Even the women labouring in the fields were described as succumbing to fashionable hats and other accessories. . . .

Throughout the 1770s and 1780s watches were the height of fashion. Source after source tells us that two watches, or one watch and one miniature, suspended from ribbons or watch chains, were the prevailing mode. "Two watches *were universal* unless a picture was substituted for one of them" said the *Ipswich Journal* of 1788. But by 1792 the *Lady's Magazine* firmly pronounced their death knell: "Watches, trinkets, etc. quite mauvais ton." To the Birmingham toy trade advance warnings of such changes were vital. With that advantage production could be switched, and the favourable trade wind of the demand for the new fashion could be successfully exploited. With time for preparation it could be further puffed along by newspaper advertisements, new pattern books and eye-catching displays all fulsomely promoting the new fashion; while the products of the old production lines "much seen and blown upon" could be rapidly switched to the distant provinces, or better still dumped abroad.

Wedgwood constantly begged Bentley for news of any new opening—"Ise [sic] make you new Vases like lightning when you think we may do it with safety"—and thanked him warmly when it arrived—"since your wants have been made known to us we have been at work night and day." Bentley not only had to decide "the time & way of ushering in the Grecian vases," he also had to warn Wedgwood when a new fashion was imminent. He had to act as both social oracle and the barometer of fashion. Accurate social judgements and accurate fashion readings were both necessary if the correct decisions were to be made about the numbers that could be sold, and the price at which they would sell, and the designs chosen first to please the few and then to attract many. Such accurate fashion decisions were vital to prevent even the highest quality goods failing to sell, or remaining the concern of merely an exclusive aristocratic *cul-de-sac* which offered no opening into the beckoning mass market—and that alone could sustain the demand which could make full use of the assembly line production. . . .

Wedgwood needed immediate information about *any* changes in consumer demand. He needed prompt news of market saturation lest [his] highly efficient assembly line should churn out more than could be sold, and thereby build up "an enormous old stock [which would] Gorgon like, stir [sic] me in the face & chill me into activity." He needed prompt news of any new fashion like women's craze for bleaching their hands with arsenic which gave such a boost to black basalt tea ware during the general down-turn in home demand in late 1772. Few knew better than Wedgwood that he could not rely simply on quality as a guide to what would sell. After one of their rare failures to read the needs of the market correctly, he sadly rehearsed the reasons for their failure with Bentley: "We will make no more Gorgons Heads—But *these things being some of the finest things we have, & not knowing they did not sell,* we ventur'd to make a few more of them when we did not know what to make. We stand in need of *Negative* as well as *Positive* orders, & it is always of the first consequence to us to know what *does not,* as well as what *does* sell."

But once men like Wedgwood and Boulton had got first wind of a new fashion, or by careful stage management had whipped up a powerful demand for a new product of their own, they needed to push home their advantage if it was not to be wasted. When "a violent Vase madness broke out amongst the Irish" Wedgwood took decisive measures to cherish the disorder and to encourage the contagion to spread. Wedgwood developed a whole battery of commercial techniques to exploit such openings. Boulton was the master of a similar array of aggressive selling devices. Like Wedgwood, Boulton accepted special individual orders for the sake of prestige and publicity, offered free carriage of goods to London, and made flexible use of credit facilities. He too used a London showroom, spectacular sales and exhibitions, widespread advertisement and judiciously placed puffs, he too sought royal patronage and the support of the fashionable. He too gave gifts to ambassadors and their wives in the hope that "the prejudice of the Italian Ladies" to buckles would collapse "at the feet of Lady Hamilton" if her ladyship were *"to set the Example."* He too built a display room to attract aristocratic visitors to Soho where they could buy his latest inventions direct just as Wedgwood did. . . .

For want of the required research little is known about the individual techniques of the smaller shopkeepers. We know of course that many advertised their royal patronage as eagerly and prominently as Wedgwood and Bentley. Many used local newspaper advertisements, others used their own colourful personalities as an advertisement to attract trade. Martin von Butchell, one time pupil of John Hunter, earned himself an "enormously lucrative" practice (as a doctor-turned-dentist and seller of medicine) by advertising *himself*—the eccentricity of his manners and his extraordinary costume. We are told by contemporaries that he "astonished all beholders" by his methods of self advertisement. It was "his custom to ride on a white pony which he sometimes painted all purple and sometimes with spots." In Hogarth's *Execution of an Idle Apprentice* of 1747 one can see another individual salesman who used his own extreme of fashion to advertise his wares. To attract attention to the gingerbread he was selling he appeared in an imitation of court dress, lace ruffled shirt, gold-laced and feathered hat. These were little more than individual exploitation of the traditional street cries or the public advertisement of age old skills—like the ratcatchers and itinerant gelders who advertised their services with special shoulder sashes (ornamented with rats for one and horseshoes for the other) to make sure they were not overlooked.

Many shopkeepers did better than this, inundating their customers with specially printed trade cards, shop bills and individual advertisements of surprising ingenuity and imaginative quality. Not all sales techniques were as obvious as the use of a purple pony. Some of the more subtle ones were meant to be concealed from their customers and have as a result all too often remained hidden from historians—even those which were practised very widely. Even the humble eighteenth-century shopkeeper can be shown to have been the master of methods of boosting sales which are, all too often, confidently attributed to the ingenuity of twentieth-century commerce.

The concept of the loss leader, for example, was well established amongst eighteenth-century shopkeepers. As Campbell wrote in 1747, "A custom has prevailed among Grocers to sell Sugars for the Prime Cost, and [they] are out of Pocket by the Sale." The losses were not inconsiderable: "The Expence for some Shops in *London* for the single Article of Paper and Pack-Thread for Sugars amounts to Sixty or Seventy Pounds *per Annum,*" and there was also the cost of "their Labour in breaking and weighing it out." The intention (as it still is today) was to attract customers with this loss leader and then induce them to buy "other Commodities" (thereby boosting the shop keeper's turnover) on which they would have to "pay extravagant Prices" (thereby boosting the shopkeeper's profits). . . .

During the eighteenth century extraordinary economic and social changes swept through Britain and brought into being the first society dedicated to ever-expanding consumption based on industrial production. For this to succeed required men and women to believe in growth, in change, in modernity; to believe that the future was bright, far brighter than the past; to believe, also, that what was new was desirable, whether it was the cut of a dress, the ascent of a balloon, or a new variety of auricula. Novelty, newfangledness, must be matters of excitement for an aggressive commercial and capitalist world: ever-increasing profit is not made in a world of traditional crafts and stable fashions. Appetite for the new and the different, for fresh experience and novel excitements, for the getting and spending of money, for aggressive consumption lies at the heart of successful bourgeois society. These must be its dominant moods.

16

THE RISE OF MODERN MEDICINE

JEAN-PIERRE GOUBERT

Without question, changes in the attitudes and practices associated with health formed a major part of the development of a new mentality during the eighteenth and nineteenth centuries. We think of sickness as something to be cured scientifically; we define good health with growing rigor; and we worry about health increasingly. These changes in our approach to health began to take shape a few decades before 1800.

Shifts in popular attitudes toward medicine are receiving growing attention as we seek to understand our own attitudes toward doctors, health, and death. In one sense, medicine seems a clear success story for modernization. Doctors uncovered more and more scientific information about the human body and how to treat it; people learned to use doctors, and health improved.

The actual story, not surprisingly, is more complex. Doctors' new claims certainly represented change. As early as 1780, they claimed sole access to scientific truth, and they did indeed know that a lot of popular medical practices were dangerous. But their own knowledge of new treatments was limited well into the late nineteenth century. Also, their attacks on the medical habits of the past (including remnants of witchcraft) were far from a complete success. They had little to do with major health gains until the twentieth century (and, some would argue, even beyond), and the gains themselves, stemming mainly from improved nutrition, were not substantial. Consequently, doctors often relied on government support to bolster their position, as when they used the state to ban unlicensed practitioners.

The following selection, dealing with doctors' attitudes in the late eighteenth century, captures a particularly dramatic early phase of the rise of modern medical attitudes. Based on state-sponsored surveys of doctors in 1786 and 1790 by groups like the Committee on Health (Comité de Salubrité), the selection reflects official medical opinion above all. Although they had no new means for treating illness, doctors were mounting new claims to science and attacking other popular healers who could not make these claims. Their campaigns suggest the richness of popular medical culture, relating to the

From: Jean-Pierre Goubert, "The Art of Healing: Learned Medicine and Popular Medicine in the France of 1790," in Robert Forster and Orest Ranum, eds., *Medicine and Society in France* (Baltimore: Johns Hopkins University Press, 1980), pp. 1–2, 5–6, 8–9, 11–12, 18–19.

longstanding role of religious and superstitious faith in dealing with health problems. New understandings of magic and religion suggested in readings on the sixteenth and seventeenth centuries emphasize the active range of choices preindustrial Europeans had maintained concerning types of healers. Doctors were now attacking this range of choices—this "medical eclecticism," to use the common term—with new vigor.

In the long run, however gradually, the doctors won, although more than vestiges of popular cures and charlatanism remain. We now ask two related questions: How much has the doctors' victory improved health, and at what social and financial costs? And how have popular attitudes—our own attitudes, not just those of "the masses"—changed with regard to treatment for disease? Doctors have clearly taught us to expect more cures, and to pay more for them. But Jean-Pierre Goubert, a leading authority on the social history of medicine, asks whether or not the dilemma first suggested by the rise of modern medicine—doctors' claims to authority unsupported by corresponding scientific advance—continues to underlie the modern outlook. Have people simply been encouraged to transfer older faiths and superstitions to new practitioners? What, indeed, is a "modernized" outlook toward health?

Goubert also suggests a major use for schematic history that has been applied to areas other than health. Take a basic paradigm in the early stages of industrialization—in this case, doctors' claims to authority. Then assume that this paradigm still applies to modern society and is as fundamentally hollow as it was in the first place. The result of this kind of analysis suggests a need to adjust key portions of the modern outlook—to downgrade doctors for example. But it also suggests the difficulty of doing this—precisely because of the power of initial claims and assumptions. If someone believes that modern medicine has moved away from simple assertion of new scientific authority to a more complex and useful role in society, how could that person develop a different historical picture?

At the end of the eighteenth century, the effectiveness of medicine—whether preventive or therapeutic—was not the indubitable fact it is today but, rather, a goal to be pursued, despite certain advances that had recently been made. Recourse to the physician, the surgeon ("the poor man's physician"), or the midwife remained the prerogative of a minority that asserted its enlightenment, even though a concerted effort was made by the medical elite and the royal government to train midwives or to provide care for the poor in times of "epidemic disease." For the most part, of course, the French population practiced self-medication; it also consulted quacks, bonesetters, and matrons, listened to ambulant charlatans, and followed the course of treatment prescribed by the sorcerer-healer of the village.

Although the enlightened physicians of the eighteenth century took much of their inspiration from Hippocrates and Galen, they had come to question the set patterns of their learned tradition and to stress the prime importance of firsthand observation. Yet one wonders whether they were also able to understand the practices of popular medicine and to grasp the causes of its expansion and increasingly broad appeal. In view of the profusion of written documents they felt obliged to pass on to posterity, and of their zeal in denouncing charlatanry, which they viewed (in the years around 1789) as one of the four evils afflicting the "art of healing," one might be carried along by their self-assurance and their unanimity. To decide this matter on the basis of concrete evidence, certain testimonies left by the physicians and surgeons of the time must be carefully analyzed. These testimonies are to be found in the replies to the official surveys made in 1786 and 1790 and form the documentary basis of the present study.

For this reason it is important to stress the mythical character of the opposition between learned and popular medicine. If there was really a break between these two arts of healing, it was to be found at the end of the eighteenth century more at the level of collective notions than in the area of medical learning and social practice. In this respect, medicine was one, for all of its diversity and even its cleavages, except perhaps in the minds of the several thousand men who shared the social view of the Enlightenment. In fact, these two "worlds" of medicine were so close to each other that they were in constant contact, both hating and penetrating each other. For one and the same patient might well turn successively or simultaneously to a physician, to a surgeon, and also to his healer—to the Devil but also to the Lord.

Consequently, the questions asked of the representatives of the surgical profession by the Comité de Salubrité tell us something about the manner in which these men perceived the so-called popular medicine. Under these circumstances it would be absurd (even if it were possible) to try to measure the extension or the actual density of the network of charlatans. It would mean to accept the question asked in 1790 by the members of the Comité de Salubrité as entirely valid, without recognizing the fact that the committee transferred to a realm where it was not applicable a question that was valid for a preselected population, namely, the officially certified practitioners.

Actually, the question had been asked earlier by the controller general's office of the provincial administrators in a survey of 1786. This survey attempted to ascertain the medical statistics of the country as a whole and to assemble information concerning the professional quality of its physicians, surgeons, and midwives. The statistical analysis of the results of this survey concerning the physicians and surgeons (especially the latter), within the limits of northern France, leads to the following conclusion: if the vast majority of the French population, especially in rural areas, only rarely consulted a physician or a certified surgeon, it was not because the medical network was lacking in density. In other words, the "medical desert" evoked by certain correspondents of the Société Royale de Médicine does not correspond to the actual facts; it only expresses—and this is not surprising—the refusal of an elite to include in the medical profession the masses of "second string" surgeons and popular therapeutists. The success of "charlatanry" in the France of 1780–90 was indeed a matter of concern to the medical profession of that period; especially the success of the category of surgeons who regularly treated a more rural, less "enlightened," and generally more modest clientele than their colleagues, the physicians.

PHYSICIANS AND CHARLATANS

How, then, could a well-designed "medical policy" fail to ensure the future of the profession and also bring relief to a suffering humanity? The physicians' discourse, whether in 1790, around 1900, or even after 1970, constantly expresses the same obsession: "to confound [sic] charlatanry and bring enlightenment to so useful an art. . . ."

In any case, and with respect to the late eighteenth century, the social border between "physician" and "charlatan," between learned and "popular" medicine, was not clearly drawn, however shocking this may seem to us. A few examples will briefly demonstrate this fact. The first set of testimonies is taken from the responses to the survey of the Comité de Salubrité concerning the practice of surgery (1790); the second comes from the survey of the kingdom's physicians and surgeons the intendants were ordered to conduct by the controller general's office in 1786.

At Montdidier the deputy surgeon reported "a charlatan admitted to the surgeons' guild." The deputy surgeon at Lyons-la-Forêt thundered against two "charlatans" who wanted to join the surgeons' guild. Better yet, the deputy surgeon of Tonnère notes among the "empirics" "only one or two experts in urine, although they are not masters of surgery." At Domfront, the deputy surgeon declared, speaking of "charlatans, empirics, and purveyors of nostrums": "there are many of them here, . . . even a physician and a surgeon who judge their patients' water by sight and give them medications from behind."

Whether admitted to a surgeons' guild or not, these "surgeons-empirics" appear to have been very numerous in rural France in 1790. And yet, if we are to believe the statements analyzed here, they were actually on the side of the patented surgeons and physicians, for they "borrowed" or sought official recognition, practiced a "natural" medicine based on bleeding, purging, emetics, and simple or composite remedies, and followed—albeit from a distance—the sociocultural model imposed from "above." Thus, the official surgeons found themselves in an understandable quandary: should they reject these semisurgeons, or should they try to absorb them? Officially, of course, the outcome was rejection, expressed again and again in the various royal edicts and declarations, in the name of *competence* and with a view to the *monopoly* over which henceforth the medical profession wanted to keep full control with the help of diplomas. This is why most of the deputy surgeons were distressed at their "inability to curb the country's empiricism. . . ."

The unanimity and ferocity with which the surgeons lashed out against their colleagues the "semisurgeons" are all the more understandable as the latter took many patients away from them, thereby threatening their livelihood and diminishing the practices of those who, often of modest origin, had been obliged to pay for their education, examinations, and admissions fees.

These studies show that the potential clientele of the surgeon (and of the physician as well) was not very considerable, nor even elastic, despite the demographic growth of eighteenth-century France. The existence of two cultures, the patients' need to trust their therapeutist, the existence of a "wall of money"—all of this contributed to making the ascendancy of the official medical profession much less extensive than it considered desirable. And it is because they sensed—not too clearly at times—the importance of such obstacles to their advancement that the patented physicians and surgeons avidly seized the opportunity held out to them by the state to be recognized as the obligatory source of help and as the sole "specialists" in human sickness. This explains to a large extent their crusade against "empirics," "charlatans," and "purveyors of nostrums." . . .

The majority of the surgeons (47 percent) denounced, first of all, the *itinerant* charlatans, but also those with a fixed residence, the "empirics" and "purveyors of nostrums." Among the settled charlatans were the "traditional village healers," and here the bonesetters occupied a prominent place. In fact, certain surgeons' guilds had admitted them and recognized their existence, to the keen regret of the surgeons of 1790, who already favored an unqualified monopoly. This, whether they admitted it or not, was the reason why they excluded the bonesetters from their guild.

The other practitioners cited (see Table 1)—dentists, oculists, hernia experts, pedicurists—were excluded in a similar manner. The surgeons treated them as a kind of subcategory of the paramedical type, thus foreshadowing the official medicalization of these occupations and their eventual inclusion in the health professions.

In the second rank of the accused we find the representatives of charitable medical organizations. For the most part, these were ecclesiastics, the majority of them regular clergy, primarily—as one would expect—nuns, and the Gray Sisters in particular. Better tolerated as a group in consideration of their "estate," they were nonetheless almost always designated as empirics, even charlatans, and sometimes as purveyors of nostrums "of the worst kind." Such statements mark the dividing line that was supposed to separate those whose professional concern was with the body and with health from those whose professional concern was with the soul, with poverty, and with charity. It was, of course, in the name of the Enlightenment, in the name of their professional competence, and in the interest of the common good that the patented surgeons of 1790 rebelled against the interference of these "benefactors of the poor."

Lastly, the deputy surgeons leveled charges of charlatanry against certain of their colleagues, namely, in ascending order, physicians, apothecaries, and

TABLE 1 Gamut of "Charlatans," According to the Words Used by Surgeons (77 Statements)

Stated Category	Number of References	Percentage of Total
Charlatans and healers		
Bonesetters	11	
Dentists	6	
Oculists	5	
Hernia specialists	4	
Spice mongers	3	
Pedicurists	2	
Straighteners	2	
Redresser	1	
Restorer	1	
Total	35	47%
Representatives of charitable medical organizations		
Nuns	10	
Secular Clergy	8	
Monks	3	
Lay persons	2	
Total	23	30%
Members of the medical profession		
Surgeons	13	
Apothecaries	3	
Physicians	2	
Total	18	23%
	Total	100%

surgeons. To be exact, these accusations applied only to the more or less "empiric" "semisurgeons" of the countryside. The physicians and apothecaries, for their part, were accused of encroachment, that is, of the illegal practice of surgery. This was no longer a matter of medical men lashing out against charlatans, but rather of infighting within the medical profession.

In the final analysis, the vocabulary used by the patented surgeons is remarkably narrow and confused: narrow to the extent that these surgeons perceived and designated the various types of charlatans in terms of their "enlightened" culture, and confused, since the term "charlatan," which in the surgeons' minds was highly charged with emotion, became a vengeful epithet used to encompass and to exclude. In other words, they did not seem to know what it meant.

The "charlatans" were thus considered, on the first count, as actual or potential criminals. According to the expressions of the surgeons' representatives, they constituted a "scourge of humanity," a "poisonous horde," a "[special] race," and a "sect of cannibals." The deputy surgeon of Tartas, steeped in physiocratic thinking, spelled out the meaning of this accusation:

"charlatans and empirics contribute to the country's depopulation. . . ." This accusation also frequently flowed from the pens of intendants and subdelegates in their responses to the survey of 1786 and appears in the correspondence concerning "epidemic diseases," although it was leveled more often against the matrons and "so-called wise women." In this manner the charlatan, the empiric, and all nonprofessionals appeared to be eminently harmful, if we follow the opinions of the masters of surgery and physicians, who judged the learning of the "charlatans" totally irrational and more than inadequate, considering them "a separate race," "barbarians," and savages. It was in the name of a learned culture bent on asserting its superiority that the medical profession—and in this instance the surgeons in particular—loudly voiced its claim to the monopoly of health care.

The second count of the accusation (mutilations, accidents caused by imprudence and incompetence) concretely expresses the grievances and the reproaches directed against the "charlatans" by the surgeons. The deputy surgeon at Nuits (Côte-d'Or) wrote in this connection: "We have women and men, both in our town and in the surrounding countryside, who meddle with treating the sick and giving them remedies. . . . We even have a woman oculist, well-versed in producing one-eyed and blind people, as well as individuals who claim that they can straighten cripples." At times some compassion is expressed for the "unfortunate ones who are *martyred* by the charlatans."

Given their animosity and their lack of understanding, the surgeons had no qualms at piling up the crimes and acts of malfeasance with which they charged the "charlatans." The logic underlying their hatred seems to proceed as follows: (1) the charlatan is incompetent, for he has not studied; (2) since he is incompetent, the charlatan causes accidents or, worse, commits crimes: and (3) under these conditions, charlatans are "knaves who dupe the people, . . . swindlers in fact, who try to mislead others about their health." All this because the learning of charlatans and healers did not proceed from a rational logic, founded upon a specific set of therapeutic procedures that were already seen as the only "scientific" ones!

Yet in the responses analyzed here the surgeons do not place all the blame on the regime, old or new. They felt—and explicitly said so—that the fundamental cause of charlatanry was to be found in the "credulity of the people," which, according to their testimony (9 out of 12), was more widespread in rural areas than in towns. The surgeons of Strasbourg, for example, stated: "The people of the countryside are more credulous than those of the towns." At Boiscommun and also at Cognac, the deputy surgeon felt that this popular credulity was due to the lack of enlightened education. At Mont-de-Marsan the local deputy depicted "a people impressed by the marvellous . . . devoid of the faculty of discernment," which for this reason is easily deceived by charlatans. Clearly, the various explanatory factors invoked by the provincial surgeons fit into the typical ideology of the adherents to the second Enlightenment. As we now know, these explanations did not correspond to the social realities in the specific area of literacy and primary education. Most importantly, however, the explanatory schema itself, proposed by diploma-holding and city-dwelling surgeons, is unconvincing, for a culture does not have to be founded on a narrow or short-sighted rationalism.

Pursuing their analysis of charlatanry, some of the surgeons saw it as more than a breach of trust committed by one kind of swindler or another. The deputy surgeon of Saint-Omer wrote, "The people . . . like to be deceived." According to the deputy surgeon of Tours, "It even seems that the wretched class derives a kind of satisfaction from being deceived. . . ." The deputy surgeon of Beaufort came to the following conclusion: "And with a heavy heart, we say to ourselves: the public wants to be deceived. So be it!" What more is needed to show the discouragement, or perhaps the conscious or unconscious wisdom, of the surgeons faced with a "new world," inhabited by "savages" who refused the benefits of the Enlightenment?

Finally, the surgeons whose responses are recorded have spoken of the deepest cause of their failure; but since they felt that they represented a rational, learned, and (therefore) superior culture, the only "true" culture, they were unable to carry their analysis very far. Here is one indication, found in the response sent by the surgeons' guild of Cognac: "The number of purveyors of nostrums is also very large. They talk of *chaple, vertaupe,* and a lot of other foolishness of this kind, which surely is not part of the *nomenclature of diseases. Chaple,* according to them, is any mucous tumor appearing anywhere on the body. Scrofulous tumors are called *vertaupe* by them." Here we have the expression of "two interpretations of the world, two systems . . . that had become more alien to each other than ever before." These statements also manifest—notwithstanding the translation proposed by the "enlightened" surgeon—the dismissal of a popular nomenclature of diseases. At the very time when they asserted the need for observation unhampered by any preconceived system, the surgeons adamantly refused to consider a different language, a different body of knowledge, because they felt that these were tied to a "popular" culture inferior to their own.

The analysis of the responses to the surveys of 1786 and 1790 has provided a series of revealing testimonies about the mentality of the French medical profession concerning the relationship between learned and "popular" medicine. It has brought to light certain problems of interpretation involved in reading a set of documents of learned origin and character. First of all, it confirms the assumption that the ideology of the Enlightenment had reached the group of masters of surgery as a whole as well as their urban elite. When it came to "charlatanry," their "discourse" deviated very little from that of the "enlightened" correspondents of the Société Royale de Médecine or of certain Parisian master apothecaries. The irresistible ascent of surgery and pharmacy in professional and scientific terms was in part responsible for the establishment of closer ties between some of the surgeons and the physicians; it was a *rapprochement* that foreshadowed, albeit from afar, the eventual unification of the medical profession that was to take place in 1892.

The second testimony provided by the *corpus* examined here is this: better administrative techniques for taking a survey (which had been perfected in the course of the eighteenth century) tended to reinforce the preconceived notions of an elite that meant to stress its enlightenment. The medical elite also expressed, very forcefully indeed, its "will to power," its will to monopolize the vast field of health care, from which it excluded all nonprofessionals with a grim determination that was rooted in a centuries-old tradition and strengthened by the ideology of the Enlightenment.

Altogether, then, the medical elite clearly outlined the undertaking it was to pursue throughout the nineteenth and twentieth centuries, namely, a veritable crusade against charlatanry and a struggle to impose medical control upon the body social as a whole. During the 1780s a group of men, asserting their superiority, laid claim to the exclusive practice of an art that was itself considered the fruit of superior learning. This, among other things, explains the masculine image of the therapeutist in the discourse of the enlightened surgeons, not only on the level of the images projected (sorcerers were designated as such, but nothing was said about witches) but also on the level of social realities, as exemplified by the increasing numbers of physicians practicing obstetrics and surgeons demonstrating the techniques of delivery.

This was the attitude of a conquering power; it was also a lazy and ultimately unwarranted attitude, for it side-stepped the authentic problems raised by the existence of a popular culture, problems that must be faced by the historian as well as by the anthropologist or the physician. In our own time the scientific, professional, and social success of medicine and the medical profession is so great that in the present medical elite one can observe the reappearance of the feeling of superiority and the same self-assurance that pervades the enlightened texts of the eighteenth century. In order to stress the superiority of its learning, the medical profession has reduced or denied the veiled kinship, the mere nuance of difference, the sigh [of mutual attraction] that existed—and still exists—between "legitimate physicians and charlatans." And this nuance is due not only to the increasing (and that means both dangerous and beneficial) effectiveness of medical knowledge, but also to two different systems of understanding the world. It also involves the matter of personal identity. As for the denial of this nuance, it has its source in the peculiar relationships obtaining in the social and the natural order, where the first [group], once it has detached itself from the second, attains a sovereign position, thanks to mankind's adaptation to that segment that holds the tools of power.

17

Poverty in the Early Nineteenth Century: An Italian Case

Paola Subacchi

Historians have long been interested in tracing the history of poverty, a subject which links economic and social considerations. The following article, using data from a municipal survey in the medium-sized town of Piacenza, sketches the constituents of poverty in a particularly bad year, 1815. Conditions in this year were shaped by a major recession in manufacturing, in turn related to the perturbations caused by the final wars of the Napoleonic era.

Several decades ago, a vigorous debate focused on issues of poverty and the standard of living in Britain during the industrial revolution. Some historians claimed that material life deteriorated in the early industrial decades—up to the 1840s—while others pointed to improvements. Both sides used their arguments to assess the quality of industrial capitalism. The debate was vigorous but inconclusive (in part because conditions varied by year and by particular groups of workers and types of cities), and by the 1970s attention turned to other topics, including the quality of the work experience and the formation of working-class culture.

Interest in poverty as part of urban life before full industrialization has expanded, however, with the realization that many early modern cities faced growing numbers of poor people as property ownership declined and wage labor grew, and as population pressure increased. The following selection uses and contributes to this discussion. Distinctions between endemic poverty and poverty relating to recurrent economic downturns, or conjunctures, have been increasingly refined, as has analysis of the stages in the family lives of working people in which poverty was particularly likely.

This selection deals with the framework of poverty, though it touches on the strategies of poor people themselves. It sheds light on family conditions and on the lives of women and the elderly.

The article is based on quantitative data. Social historians have gone through several phases with regard to quantification. Quantitative methods were extremely fashionable in the 1970s, but they have receded as the focus

From: Paola Subacchi, "Conjunctural Poor and Structural Poor: Some Preliminary Considerations on Poverty, the Life-Cycle and Economic Crisis in Early-Nineteenth-Century Italy," *Continuity and Change* 8(1); 65–67, 68–70, 72, 74–75, 77–78, 81–82.

on values, on beliefs—on cultural issues—has increased. But for topics like poverty, quantitative data remain essential—for example, in determining the relative weight of various causes of poverty.

The selection sketches a common urban pattern, before significant factory industry developed. It invites comparison with subsequent impacts of industrialization and the development of more recent social policies. Like much social history, the selection also invites consideration of the role of geographic place in framing key aspects of the social period. It focuses on a particular location, but the city and its Italian characteristics have little to do with the analysis, which seeks to draw broader, more widely applicable typologies.

INTRODUCTION: DESCRIBING THE POOR

The purpose of this article is to define the concept of poverty in the light of a specific case study and to consider to what extent its dimensions were affected by life-cycle squeezes, economic fluctuations and personal circumstances. The focus of this discussion will concern the situation of the poor in a North Italian town, Piacenza, at the beginning of the nineteenth century. Various theoretical models of the nature of poverty will also be used to guide the interpretation.

Seebohm Rowntree in his work on poverty in York was one of the first to associate poverty with certain specific stages of the life-course, arguing that a poor person might experience a state of deprivation several times during his life. According to Rowntree, there were three critical periods in the life of a poor person. First, an individual could experience a state of deprivation very early in life, as a child, when his parents had to support the whole family. Then, once he grew up, between 30 and 60, he could be driven into poverty after marriage as a parent, before his children had started work. Then he could decline into indigence in old age, when he was unable to carry on working, and his children had married and left home. . . .

Any attempt to discuss poverty raises the fundamental question of its definition. For the purposes of the present article poverty has been defined as the condition of those who, lacking property or capital, are forced to work in order to make a living. Unless they were employed in certain favoured industries, such persons could hope for no improvement in their lifetime: they could, in fact, only expect a deterioration in their position. From the late Middle Ages until a fairly mature stage of industrialization, their income and their means of subsistence were strictly linked to the rhythms and crises of pre-industrial agrarian and manufacturing economies. In periods of economic downturns or family hardships, or when some unfavourable personal events occurred, the individual could easily fall below the subsistence line and experience indigence, meaning the state of anybody unable to provide his own living and that of his family. . . .

On this matter the conceptual distinction introduced by [J.P.] Gutton and [Brian] Pullan in relation to urban poverty offers a useful approach. They define as "conjunctural" or "crisis" poor all those whose indigence was strictly linked to fluctuations in bread prices and to economic or demographic hardships. As long as these were able to work, indigence was recognized to be a cyclic event, more likely to occur at certain phases of either the economic cycle or the life-cycle. On the other hand, the "structural" poor were people incapable of earning a living by reason of age, illness or physical handicap, and hence wholly dependent on assistance or begging. This condition was not at all related to economic fluctuations, but to unfavourable personal events occurring in the individual's life. Since it was recognized as a permanent condition, we can talk here of structural poverty.

To assess the concept of conjunctural and structural poverty, extensive use will be made here of an enquiry ordered in 1815 by Piacenza's mayor, the *podestà*, to determine the extent of urban deprivation. This document consists of reports drawn up by the parish priests on their own parishes. The compilers were requested to distinguish between citizens who were able to work but were currently unemployed or whose wages were insufficient for their subsistence and that of their families, and those who on the other hand, were unable to work because of illness or old age. . . .

In 1815, the population of Piacenza was given as 27,949, distributed over 34 parishes. The number of the poor reported by the priests was 11,609, which represents 42.3 per cent of the city's population. Distinguishing between structural and conjunctural poor we can see that the [latter] made up at the time 9,548—34.8 percent of the population—while 2,061 were structural poor—7.5 per cent of the population. A statistical survey compiled in 1857, which, again, distinguishes between conjunctural and structural poor, records 30,599 people living in Piacenza in that year: 3,103 were conjunctural poor and 2,078 structural poor. In this case, the former made up 10.1 per cent of the population, and the latter 6.8 per cent, together 16.9 per cent of the urban population. We can see that while the percentage of the structural poor was similar in these two years, the numbers of conjunctural poor were very dissimilar. This difference probably reflects the different economic conditions prevailing in each year and shows to what extent the local economy could provide adequate livelihoods for people living from their labour. . . .

At the end of the eighteenth century there had been a number of bad harvests that forced up cereal prices and consequently the prices of other goods. This agricultural crisis affected most of Europe and lowered wages and reduced employment opportunities for all those who worked as agricultural labourers. Moreover, 67 per cent of all the people previously employed in the local industries became unemployed. In these conditions the high numbers of the conjunctural poor listed in 1815 are not surprising. The stagnant economy was still suffering from high food prices and, at the same time, it could not keep people employed. This year clearly represented the low point in the downturn in economic trends from which the town had been suffering since

1808. The reports made by the parish priests were probably a response to the government's need to know the real dimensions of poverty in Piacenza in order to support the needy.

The occupational pattern of people listed in the poverty survey shows both a high degree of adaptability and a willingness to change occupation frequently, in what Olwen Hufton has defined as an "economy of makeshifts." The poor had previously been employed variously as servants, labourers, bricklayers, carpenters and shoemakers. They were journeymen and worked for a master; very few of them ran their own businesses. Others, especially women, were employed in textile manufacture: "bombasari, filatori, tessadri, lavori donneschi quali cucire e fare calzette" ("spinners of silk and cotton, weavers, seamstresses and stocking knitters"). No merchants or shopkeepers were included in the list of the poor. Women in particular had an even more marginal occupational pattern. In fact, besides the work provided by local agriculture and industry, they were mostly employed in odd jobs and casual labour. . . . Women headed 41 per cent of all poor households. Of these 62.5 per cent were widows and 26.3 per cent were unmarried, while 11.2 per cent had been abandoned by their husbands. They very often had small children to raise; others were ill or unable to work because of some infirmity, or because they were too old. Their average age was 51 years. This meant that women would become heads of their families late in life, normally after the death of the husband or of another male who was in charge of the family. In a few cases we find young women heading their households: these were young widows with children, single women and children, and orphans. . . .

This analysis of household structure has highlighted the fact that the conjunctural and structural poor had rather different household sizes and forms. In particular, the structural poor had above-average proportions of "solitaries" and "no family" households. . . . Given the importance of the domestic unit for the economy of the poor, we can argue that, especially for elderly or handicapped people, having a family on whom they might rely might help them avoid a permanent state of indigence. When, for instance, a son or daughter's family was able to support an elderly parent he or she escaped permanent indigence, even if this put extra pressure on the family. So the structural poor were more likely to be the victims of the dissolution of the family unit; in fact, they were at the mercy of all the hardships produced by the interaction of chance and the high-risk phases of the life-cycle. Of course, the family represented a protection against poverty insofar as the principle of people staying in the household formed at the time of marriage was strong enough to keep an individual inside the family when economic hardships were on the increase. In the case of Northern Italian towns, where neolocal rules prevailed, the percentage of "solitary" households in a community was strongly affected by the percentage of elderly people living on their own, most of whom had high probabilities of becoming structural poor. . . . [I]t has been possible to identify the main turning points in the family economy in terms of the surpluses and deficits which occurred as the domestic unit developed. In particular, couples were able to sustain themselves and two children for the first five years of their marriage. Then, from 7 to 19 years after marriage the family economy went into deficit with an excess of current consumption over production. It would remain in deficit through[out], to the moment when the first-born child began to make a significant contribution to the family economy. Finally, married children would frequently find themselves entering their first family "deficit" phase between approximately the ages of 35 and 45, reaching their peak family deficits just as their parents were entering their own second "deficit" period in their late 60s. . . . It can be argued that the temporary indigence experienced by age groups who were in surplus according to the model was likely to arise from the economic downturn. For instance, there were some persons aged 47–59 whose family economies were running a deficit although this period of the life-cycle is supposed to have been, together with the early years of marriage, a period of considerable cumulative surplus for the family. In fact, children began to work and to contribute to the family budget when their fathers were aged between 47 and 60. But, as happens in this particular case, the capacity of children to contribute to the common pool could be reduced in periods of economic crisis, when unemployment and the rising price of necessities lowered the standard of living of those who in normal times were living on the edge of subsistence.

Unemployment and lower wages were likely to be responsible for the deficits in the family economy experienced by the age group 27–33 years, which is supposed to be another period of relative prosperity when earning capacity should exceed current consumption. In fact, normally in a pre-industrial economy at the moment of marriage, which was the most important turning point in the life of an individual, a young couple probably possessed more than they would ever again possess, unless the death of a parent brought them a small property. . . . The majority of households . . . whose head was older than 60 were composed of married couples without the children who had presumably already left the parental home. According to the life-cycle model, such children would not be able to help their parents because they were also moving through a critical period in their lives. Many of them would be aged between 34 and 46 years and would still be raising their own children. In very few cases could we find children still living with their elderly parents. . . .

Illness as a cause of impoverishment became more marked with increased age, while the percentage of those with inadequate wages was progressively diminished because the size of the household was reduced.

18

A Divided Peasantry

PAVE OVE CHRISTIANSEN

Many historians and social scientists have tended to see the peasantry, in Europe and elsewhere, as an undifferentiated group. They have increasingly recognized some divisions of wealth in the peasant class, between substantial landowners and more marginal cottagers, but they have often assumed a common community structure and worldview. This is the impression conveyed in the treatment of peasant culture in the Muchembled passage in the previous section (Chapter 1).

Without fully contradicting the idea of "peasant values," social historians are increasingly taking a closer look. Many argue that peasants appeared unified only to the upper classes and urban groups, who tended to disdain them but also largely ignored them. In fact, according to this new analysis, vital differences existed.

The following passage, dealing with Danish peasants still working on a manorial estate south of Copenhagen, owing work service (*corvée*) and dues to the landlord, carries this analysis to the point of arguing that two distinct personality types had emerged by the late eighteenth century. Interactions between the two peasant groups were vital, but so were mutual incomprehensions and hostilities.

The analysis should be placed in a larger, though still speculative, framework of historical change. The more active peasant group was clearly expanding or at least becoming more ambitious, introducing specific innovations in village agriculture often at the expense of the more hedonistic group; in turn, this latter group was becoming even more disorganized, with drinking on the rise. But was the basic division new or had it long existed in rural life? What might have been causing change?—the author mentions a growing urban market for agricultural production, which could spur change, and also population expansion, which could disorganize some families but goad others toward new endeavor.

Finally, what might be the consequences of this kind of rural division, for overall food production and for the generation of new social classes in the

From: Pave Ove Christiansen "Culture and Contrasts in the Northern European Village: Lifestyles Among Manorial Peasants in 18th-Centruy Denmark," *Journal of Social History* 29 (1995): 275–76, 279–80, 283–84, 284–86, 288–89.

cities, as rural people began soon to migrate to urban centers. What urban social classes would the two peasant groups fit into? what attitudes would they
bring to industrial life? The peasant divisions discussed here predate Danish
industrialization and even the full commercialization of Danish agriculture in
the mid-nineteenth century. They may, nevertheless, help explain why such
later changes occurred. In this sense, this chapter should also be compared to
the following, on south German peasants a bit later in time, where a balance
between change and continuity is more explicitly assessed.

This study deals with the reconstruction of peasant life in an East Danish
manorial estates region seen in a cultural and social perspective. Even when a
population could not write, it may be possible to reconstruct the cultural order in people's closest environment—usually their village. Such a presentation
can be built up against the background of normal repetitive sources, where ordinary people appear so frequently that it is possible to identify the "features"
of otherwise anonymous individuals so they emerge as socially distinctive. . . .

The article contends that we are not, as assumed in most of the rural
research, faced with just one, but two different lifestyles among the inhabitants of the same peasant villages. Through the sample study it should be possible to see that we can get closer to the relations among people's actions, routines and perceptions of the world than one normally does in historical
interpretations.

By *lifestyle* I mean the principle of people's everyday activities and their related cultural perspective on life, articulated in relation to their material conditions and in contrast to other lifestyles. Some peasants lived from day to day,
more or less resigning themselves to their fate, while at the same time their
neighbours might be occupied with the rational management and planning of
the future.

The two co-existing lifestyles I want to compare structurally must be seen
in contrast to the attempts to identify one particular Continental European
peasant type, often normatively described as refractory, simple-minded, sly,
and sensual. The forward looking Holstein-born civil servant August
Hennings, for example, described the Danish Zealand peasant and his English
equivalent as follows: "There [i.e. in England] the farmer, in a [half-timbered]
wattle cottage which, for want of windows, looks like a prison, enclosed by
filth. . . . There creeps from the filth a small, bent, sleepy figure, in degree of
civilization more like . . . a helot than a citizen shaped for the tilling of the soil
and the protection of the state." Estate steward Troyel, from the Crown estate
in Odsherred, in 1784 wrote somewhat less ironically: "The in general simple
and unlettered estate peasant, whose intellectual abilities are quite uncultivated, cannot be expected to be able to be persuaded as others who have a cultivated reason. He is not accustomed to thinking and to agreeing and being
moved by inferences, but is driven merely and wholly by the senses. He

cannot test the strength and reason of arguments as he never acted from convincing grounds, but only from habit and example."

Statements like these are not so much descriptions of what the peasants were like, as expressions of how the agrarian world could appear from a progressive bourgeois or aristocratic viewpoint. The characterization of the peasants' cultural differentness corresponds entirely with the Enlightenment's foe-images of savage peoples. The strongly degrading phrases are further put into perspective by the fact that before 1800 most people were in fact peasants in the broadest sense of the word. With the exception of the regions around the Channel, the Netherlands and northern Italy, villagers made up 80% of the population of Europe. Most of these people have left us no testimony of their own beyond fields, hedges and some houses in our present-day landscape. . . . If we want to get closer to this culturally diverse, but until 1850 largely anonymous group of the inhabitants of Europe, we must attempt to overcome these difficulties. . . .

In a world where crop failure and cattle disease were uncontrollable quantities, there was a constant struggle to keep a level of production that was stable and sufficient for the needs of the ever-increasing number of people in the eighteenth century. Because of the changeable Scandinavian climate and the poor resistance of the crops to bad weather and disease, the yield from the various crops could fluctuate from sixfold down through the normal fourfold or fivefold to as little as twofold—which meant crisis. The villagers also often had great problems obtaining sufficient fodder for the cattle, and for the many horses which it was found necessary to keep on account of corvée.

It has emerged that even slight climatic irregularities could make it hard for many peasants to do the preparatory spring work on the areas of the village that could theoretically be sown. It might be impossible to drain off the water from the land, the horses might be too weak to plough enough, and the seed grain stored from the previous year might have been eaten up.

For many peasants, these dilemmas in the communal village developed into problems because the peasants were also burdened by the farm dues. On Giesgaard [a landed estate] most of the peasants had to till what corresponded to about a third of their own fields. Compared with many Eastern European conditions, corvée [required labor] of about 300 man-days a year for each farm was not harsh, yet it could have striking consequences. The extra wear on the peasants' own implements and horses was palpable, and to this one must add the 3–6 kilometre transport of ploughs etc. to the demesne [landlord's] fields. Moreover, the peak period for agricultural work on the demesne and in the villages was the same. This meant that the work for Giesegaard directly detracted from the peasants' own farming, and exhausted the horses and manpower of the households in the most pressing periods.

In other words there was a relationship between the demands of the estate and the bottlenecks in the ecological/economic situation of the villages. Yet it is misleading simply to speak of the destructive consequences of corvée labour and its generation of a general sense of despair among the peasantry.

Simplistic explanations like this are well known from both the contemporary debates and our own historiography. Corvée and the other payments and services due to the lord and king seem to have had different effects depending on the "peasant profiles" we focus on. Some peasants slowly but steadily consolidated their positions, while others at the same time lived in a situation of almost permanent resignation and often suffered want. These were the peasants who were hit hard by Giesegaard's corvée labour.

Even without having to pay an entry fee, some of the landless inhabitants of the village might refuse to take over a fairly large tenant farm, while others were willing to pay substantial amounts to subject themselves to the lord. Some young unmarried farmhands almost had to be compelled to become tenants by the estate. Other strong young men were apparently exempt from this pressure, while at the same time Giesegaard complained that there were not enough young people in the area!

We are faced with a kind of paradox. In the period after 1750, with grain prices rising regionally and internationally and a growing population, the studies show that the peasants expanded the cultivated areas fairly substantially, and that both their stocks and the amount of valuable furnishings increased *on average*. At the same time, as mentioned before, we see a tendency for both unmarried farmhands and cottagers to exhibit a negative attitude to becoming tenants. Extreme drunkenness was widespread. To the surprise of the observers of the Enlightenment, many people—even in an apparent boom period—had a very reserved attitude to "striving" (*at stræbe*), as an enterprising peasant called it. They preferred to "stay merry" (*holde sig lystige*). Even though in the same period the estate intensified corvée labour, the overall rent paid by the villagers was, in relative terms, less than before if one views it in the context of increased production and better prices. The potential seemed great, yet many still drank. . . .

What seems most extreme, however, are the situations where farmers from the "forward-looking" category had annoyed other villagers for years by letting their own pigs run loose (and into neighbour's gardens), and where the village council does not appear to have dared do anything about it; or where people from the same group directly appropriated resources for themselves at the expense of the village as a whole. In 1792 three of these powerful farmers even organized a full-scale relocation of the house and land of a cottager family, solely so they could get a longer, more rational ploughing shape for some of their own fields. This meant fewer turns of the wheel plough and thus a little extra soil to plough. Instead, the cottagers, with the approval of the estate and the "men of the village," were assigned an alternative area elsewhere in the village, to the detriment, however, of the *common* pastures. This was a real small planning coup executed by a small section of the elite, with negative consequences for the common grazing of all the peasants and cottagers. For the sake of individual gain, these peasants ignored the time-honoured social patterns of action of the village. Yet influential individuals like these were able to force the arrangement through. . . .

The forward-looking peasants were tenants just like the inadequate ones. But the interesting thing is that the provident ones on the whole managed to avoid direct interference from the estate. They do not seem to have been under constant pressure. They avoided sanctions, received no help, and they also had the resources to give the steward any small bribes that were necessary.

It would appear that their view of the concept of seigneurial dues was different from that of the "merry" or "failing" group. For both groups the dues were very much a presence, but as an extension of the Giesegaard policy, the forward-looking peasants appear *externally* (i.e., vis-à-vis the estate) to have used fairly full and punctual payment of their dues as a means of avoiding interference in *their* administration of their farms. They may well have considered the dues a burden, but also as economic contributions that could patently exempt them from the most restrictive ties with the estate—ties which certainly existed, but which did not to any great extent have to be visible or a real nuisance in their everyday life. This strategy required an already-stable production apparatus and the development of their own innovative features. If one could honour these requirements—unlike those who could not—one could avoid direct interference from Giesegaard. Here, some people had better initial conditions than others. If the estate was paid its full rent on time, it was willing to a great extent to leave people to their own devices. This was precisely what this category of peasants was interested in, if they were to lead a life that was meaningful for them in terms of accumulation and succession in their households. It was probably these people the steward was referring to in a letter to the lord when he used the characteristic expression: "those who think ahead, who [in times of crisis] can see how reasonable it is to maintain a thrifty household. . . ." These were the ones who had "courage" in life. For the estate, they were the easy peasants to manage.

This variation in the forms of manorial practice had its counterpart among the other peasants. For the ailing farming households it was a relatively greater effort to produce the necessary surplus, but the attitude to the very concept of *dues* was also clearly different. Those who would anyway have difficulty constantly meeting their full rent would see the dues as something they should pay as sparingly as possible. Their logic was that they could pay just enough rent to ensure that they were allowed to continue farming. The lower limit for many payments was the point where the arrears had become so high, or the exploitation of the farm's resources so disproportionate, that the estate showed the family the road. Up to this limit it was a matter of living so that, in the here and now, this peasant category had as much enjoyment out of it as possible. The face presented to the estate was often a pathetic one. On the other hand, these peasants could count on the help of the estate in crisis years. For the sake of the corvée and taxes, if for no other reason, it was important from Giesegaard's point of view to keep the farms running somehow, especially if there were no immediate prospects of alternative tenants. This was a clear requirement, if the life expectations of these peasants were to be fulfilled. In a 1778 report to the Ministry of the Interior on cereal farming in the area, it must have been this kind of farmer that the steward called those who did not "think ahead," but were characterized by "slavish thinking, under the influence of which they . . . doze off in a flood of sighs." In his eyes they suffered from "refractoriness and indifference." . . .

These two forms of manorial peasant practice thus did not exist because of the absence of the estate in the village, but by virtue of its presence, combined with the competition among the peasants for the resources of the village. Through *fæste* [tenancy] and its administrative practice, Giesegaard erected a quite definite framework for the kinds of life that could be lived.

If the peasants' views of the meaning of rent were as different as claimed here, it is because they must have been associated with diverging views of fate. For the peasants, fate was their perspective on existence, including the purpose of their daily life. Whereas payment of full rent was what gave the "strivers" peace to realize themselves in agricultural work organized as much as possible by themselves on their constantly improving farms, what we can perhaps best call the barely adequate rent, combined with least possible rebellious behaviour, was what enabled the other peasants to have enjoyable hours. For these people the farm and the agricultural work were hardly ends in themselves. The adequate work on the estate (under the corvée) and in the village made possible the degree of survival necessary to "live life" culturally.

The forward-looking peasants concentrated on their work with the resources to stay "free" of the steward, and thus on having the scope to improve their farms further, so they could in the longer term buy better horses, furnishings, etc. This must have been a meaningful life for them. It demanded ambition, thrift and planning. For these people, it seemed that fate could be influenced by sufficient personal initiative. In their consciousness, their own disposal of the resources meant they could exploit new opportunities, as some of them showed for example in the removal of the cottager's house. They were people who exhibited an individualistic thinking. They scheduled their lives in terms of a plan for the future. Their organizational form indicates what I call the *aspiring lifestyle* of the village.

For the peasants seen as "dozy" by the estate, the situation was more or less the opposite. They considered any thought of getting out of their treadmill as utopian. Even if they tried to save something up, their investments would not go far on a run-down farm, and before that the steward would probably have claimed an installment on their arrears. The work on the farm was probably considered necessary, but is unlikely to have been seen as particularly meaningful. In the circumstances, these peasants would feel that personal initiative did not lead to any tangible advantage. Fate was simply what came to you. It was not something to be sought out. Their strategy seems to have been to pursue short-term goals. Much time was spent on sociability. When one year was largely like the next, the purpose of life must be to make everyday existence as tolerable as possible. So one looked for merry company when money occasionally came to the house. Consumption was immediate. I will call their organizational form the *fatalistic lifestyle* of the village.

This lifestyle could manifest itself in rather different ways. On the one hand there were those who lived more or less in a vicious circle of misfortune, illness, resignation and drunkenness. Their conditions were such that some more or less gave up hope in life. They lived for the day, gave highest priority to small pleasures and are unlikely to have thought of the world as something that could be changed. There were also peasants who muddled through without attracting much attention from the outside world, perhaps with a little help from the estate.

Inwardly in the village the two lifestyles were the preconditions for each other's existence. Within the organizational structure of the village, the strivers exploited the often poverty-stricken situation of the fatalists, although they did so with their consent. They rented parts of the fatalists' pasturage quota cheaply—the parts *they* did not have enough cattle to exploit. This way the strivers could increase *their* cattle stock beyond the ordinary size. The cattle represented the road towards expansion for the peasants. Similarly, they often sowed some of the poor peasants' fields, which the latter could not keep cultivated because of their lack of seed and ploughing power. They might also buy from the weaker neighbour, in order to resell it, the wood that he had been granted by the estate to make harrows and wagons from. One could say that within the hierarchy of the village, the fatalists—to be allowed to live *their* life—had to stand by and watch the strivers helping themselves; just as, *outwardly,* they had to satisfy a minimum of Giesegaard's requirements for corvée labour, taxes and a certain superficial obedience.

This way the strivers within the communal system helped to keep the weaker peasants in their vulnerable economic position, while at the same time complaining that the fatalists, for example, did not have the punctuality, implements and drawing power (which required fodder) to keep up their end of the collective work of the village. However, if the strivers had been unable to draw on these extra means of production, they would hardly have achieved *their* level of material wealth.

Conversely, the richer farms were essential to the fatalists. The constant economic competition of the strivers in principle provided opportunities for the different priorities of the fatalists in life. At a pinch they could borrow small amounts of grain for bread from the strivers—for example, for funerals, for which one could not ask the estate for help. They probably attempted to maintain positive formal relations with the strivers by asking them to be godparents to their children. This could later be exploited in a tight situation. . . .

To the "striving" peasants, the fatalists must have seemed like people who did not know what was good for them, who held back the economic management of the village, and whose sloppiness attracted the attention of the estate to the life of the village. They really did not deserve help, as their condition was to a great extent their own fault. Often they squandered the aid they were given anyway. Perhaps some saw them as people who did not have the self-discipline necessary to plan for the future. On the other hand, they did understand how to enjoy themselves, they were inventive when it came to stealing wood from the forests, and they had the ability to give the steward amusing, pithy answers. However, since the strivers themselves depended on them in the village work, there was much indignation over their sluggishness. At times some of the fields were flooded because some of them did not clean out their fallow ditches in time, and the often late sowing and harvesting of the fatalists delayed everyone else in the village.

Conversely, the fatalists must have had difficulty understanding the point of the work-fixated life of the strivers.. They must have seen them as self-righteous, puritanical individualists, with an "I'm all right, Jack" attitude. Their enterprise broke into the cultural rhythm of the village, and in some cases directly paralysed the village council. Through their position they were able to seize privileges at the expense of the community in general (individual cultivation of the common), and by renting uncultivated fields cheaply, to exploit poor fellow villagers without seed or enough drawing power. The strivers are unlikely to have been loved for their greater wealth, yet many people were often able to go to them for small loans. On the other hand, the fatalists would have been capable of understanding the really poor people in the village. They might end up among them themselves if the arrears became too high, or some extra misfortune occurred. For this reason, and out of fear of misfortune, they were also willing to give a wandering beggar something, although they had little to give themselves. . . .

19

THE RURAL WORLD: BAVARIAN PEASANTS AND PEASANT FAMILIES IN THE EARLY NINETEENTH CENTURY

ROBERT LEE

An obvious but important problem in dealing with changes in early industrial European society is their uneven quality. The following selection shows how little Bavarian family and village life altered—despite massive changes in commercial structure, state functions, and certain behaviors, such as premarital sexuality. Indeed, in some respects life in the countryside may have been changing in directions opposite to those of many urban areas. Bavarian peasant families and villages held firm to tradition. They either ignored change—like many state edicts—or they actually tightened traditional structures in response to new market opportunities for agricultural goods (using more family labor given scant technical innovation) plus the decline of rural manufacturing.

Bavaria was a somewhat backward part of Germany. Population growth, for example, was unusually low. So rural stability, or even reactions against previous changes, may not have been typical of the rest of rural Germany, much less Western Europe. Still, the fact that in some ways Bavaria in the 1820s fits a "traditional" peasant family model better than England in the 1620s reminds us of the complexity of change, as well as Europe's regional diversities. When would change come to rural areas like Bavaria? What reactions would it bring? How did peasant values and behaviors here compare to those of Danish peasants, described in the previous chapter? Clearly, it is vital to understand the complexities of peasant life as the pace of change in European society more generally began to accelerate.

The opening decades of the nineteenth century, according to many historians, constituted a critical transition period as far as the function and role of the

From: Robert Lee, "The Family and 'Modernisation': The Peasant Family and Social Change in Nineteenth-Century Bavaria," in R. J. Evans and W. R. Lee, eds., *The German Family: Essays on the Social History of the Family in Nineteenth- and Twentieth-Century Germany* (Totowa, NJ: Barnes and Noble, 1981), pp. 84, 94–99, 104–109.

Western European family was concerned. Edward Shorter, for example, in attempting to compress the transformation of the family and family relations within the framework of modernisation theory, has argued that the beginning of the nineteenth century witnessed the end of "traditional society." This view has been accepted by other historians. This period coincided with the end of a formerly static village society and was characterised, even in rural Bavaria, by "an immense dynamic of social, economic and cultural change." The first half of the nineteenth century was a time of "partial" but nevertheless significant change in the daily life of rural society. Indeed superficial evidence of radical social change prior to any industrial take-off in Germany is relatively easy to find. The dramatic rise in illegitimacy rates, particularly in many areas of South Germany, has been taken as signifying the onset of sexual revolution which was ultimately to transform sexual attitudes and family roles in general. . . .

Even before the onset of industrialisation, secularisation and agrarian reform had fostered the "breakdown of authority in traditional rural society." But if the extension of the capitalist mode of production to German agriculture had undermined traditional values in rural society, the process of social change was reinforced by the increasing manipulative power of the State over most aspects of peasant life. . . .

The continued prominence of the nuclear family in nineteenth-century Bavaria also reflected the degree to which the peasant family had retained its primary economic function. The concept of the family was largely dependent on the economic significance of the holding. The unifying bond which provided an important element of stability in rural society was the family holding rather than a complex of personal relationships. Within this framework, work-orientation determined the relationship between parents and children and the role obligations of all household members. The social role of women, with its attendant ramifications for the socialisation of children, was also determined by this factor. The sexual division of labour played a central part in the organisation of both the family and the household, and the role of peasant women during this period continued to be determined by the nature of the rural economy. Financial considerations, particularly the dowry of a future bride, were very important in the choice of a marriage partner. It is not surprising, therefore, that as far as the social background of marriage partners was concerned, rural society evinced a high degree of class endogamy. However, this pattern was just as prominent in the first half of the nineteenth century as it had been in the final decades of the preceding century. Economic considerations, rather than feelings of personal love and affection, were still predominant in Bavaria, despite the alleged impact of reform legislation and the partial "modernisation" of both social and sexual attitudes. For the same reason many men continued to seek older and more experienced brides with a larger personal dowry well into the nineteenth century.

But if economic factors continued to determine the choice of brides in rural society, they were even more apparent in the treatment of women within the family unit. Despite the increased discussion of female emancipation in the eighteenth century within enlightened circles, the position of women in rural society remained subject to the mode of production of material life. This was embodied in the attitude of peasants to their womenfolk. Wife-beating in Bavaria was apparently commoner than the ill-treatment of horses and this picture confirms available evidence from other parts of Western Europe. Even well into the twentieth century peasant women were frequently subjected to a strict domestic rule. But the specific role of women was most clearly apparent in the degree of economic exploitation. Like his Swiss counterpart, the Bavarian peasant was relatively slow in applying a rigorous division of labour and the traditional division of work between the sexes persisted well into the late nineteenth and early twentieth centuries. Not only was the overall workload of the wife in excess of that of her husband, but if his was relatively well defined and bound by routine, the wife was expected to modify her labour input in accordance with changing economic needs and circumstances. Her work was seldom limited to household duties, but often encompassed domestic clothing production, the preparation of flax, and agricultural labour at certain times of the year. The role of women was vital in terms of the continued functioning of the family holding. This often precluded any necessary period of rest either during pregnancy or immediately after child-birth. The reform legislation of the early nineteenth century and the significant reduction in Church authority associated with secularisation did not impinge at all on the underlying economic factors which determined the sexual division of labour in rural society and the role performance of women as a whole. Indeed, once again, the form that agrarian development took in Bavaria may well have reinforced existing attitudes. The initial increase in the total demand for labour necessitated by agricultural reform was met by an enforced extension in the workload of peasant women. The rise in infant mortality rates and adult female mortality, together with a further deterioration in the observance of the traditional year of mourning following the premature death of peasant brides, provide tentative evidence of the real cost in human terms of such an economic system. The work role of women in rural Bavaria and the existing sexual division of labour which affected sexual attitudes and relationships within the family remained unaffected by the period of reform. Agrarian reform merely exacerbated the existing state of affairs.

The socialisation of children, both within the first five years of life and during childhood as a whole, was also determined by the primacy of the economic function of the peasant holding. By and large parental attitudes towards children continued to be determined by the economic utility which could be gained from additional family members. Until the child had received some training in a particular, if rudimentary, skill, or had proved its economic usefulness for the domestic household economy, it was seldom accepted either economically or emotionally as a full family member. The amount of attention given by parents to young children and particularly to infants, remained minimal. Young children were rarely regarded as a benefit to the family and once the future of the holding had been secured by the successful rearing of one or two children beyond the critical period of early childhood, the parental attitude to later offspring noticeably deteriorated. In Mittelfels, for example, it was rumoured that a farmer would rather lose a young child than a calf. Peasant indifference to the fate of infants was arguably legitimised by contemporary Catholic ideology. Childhood innocence and early death invariably secured the attainment of lasting salvation. Further evidence of this negative pattern of parent–child relationship can be found in the custom of naming children. The same Christian name occurs with monotonous regularity in parish baptismal records, until it was finally retained within the family through the survival of a particular infant. On this basis, children in Bavaria, at least in the first few years of life, seldom enjoyed a personal existence. The excessively high infant mortality rates in early nineteenth-century Bavaria, the absence of breast-feeding and the fact that children under the age of five years rarely received qualified medical attention prior to their final illness, is further testimony of the prevalence of this general attitude to young infants and children.

However, once a child had survived the perilous rigours of early infancy and had shown both resilience against disease and a potential economic usefulness for the family holding, parental attitudes noticeably changed. But even at this stage, the treatment of children and their socialisation within the family was dictated by economic considerations. Children were employed as soon as possible on menial tasks associated with the management of the holding and incorporated at an early age into the household's economic function. If the family tenement was relatively large, then each child in turn would be employed, perhaps until marriage, in such a capacity. But in the case of small-holdings, which were increasingly predominant in many parts of Bavaria during the early nineteenth century, most surviving children would be employed at a comparatively early age outside the family holding. The Freising census of 1803, for example, reveals the employment of children of only six and eight years of age as domestic servants. The relationship of the child to the parental home and to the family unit as a whole was not only affected by the relative size of the holding and its immediate labour requirements, but also by the presence of other offspring. In peasant legal settlements governing the inheritance of holdings a distinct pattern is observable, both in the late eighteenth and early nineteenth centuries. If only one child was present, in the majority of cases the child retained the right to stay on the holding and to receive food and accommodation in return for labour beyond the age of 16 years. As soon as further children had to be taken into consideration, these rights diminished sharply. In every case, therefore, the position and function of the child were determined by immediate economic considerations.

The reform legislation of the early nineteenth century which contributed, it is claimed, to the partial modernisation of Bavarian society and the transformation of sexual and social attitudes, did not alter the primacy of economic factors in the determining and moulding of inter-family relations. Although the adoption of a more labour-intensive system of production in the primary sector should have re-emphasised the importance of family labour, any radical impact of such a development was minimised by the trend to small-holdings and the collapse of agricultural prices in the late 1820s and 1830s. As a result there was no significant shift in the treatment and socialisation of children in Bavarian rural communities. . . .

Agricultural production in Bavaria remained dependent on residential farm labour and not wage labour. The increasing predominance of small-holdings reinforced the production function of the peasant family. Indeed not until the late nineteenth century, with the gradual introduction of mechanisation in the primary sector, was there any change in the traditional production role of the family unit. Under these conditions, therefore, the socio-economic reform legislation of the early nineteenth century could not have produced any radical transition in peasant attitudes and relations.

Given that the mode of family production was the critical factor in determining both the sexual role of women and the socialisation and treatment of children, it is not surprising that educational reform in the early nineteenth century had such a limited impact in rural society. Engelsing has argued that the penetration of new educational theories was a major factor in providing the preconditions for social change in nineteenth-century Germany. In Bavaria, however, a wide gulf continued to exist between the aims of official reform and their impact on peasant consciousness. Despite some improvements in literacy rates, probably between 40 per cent and 50 per cent of peasant society were still illiterate by the late 1840s. Deficiencies in central administration and inadequate funds for educational provision were just two factors which limited reform at the local level. However given the importance of child labour within the rural economy, it was inevitable that the introduction of compulsory primary education would conflict with local labour requirements. The production function of the family remained the prior consideration. School attendance rates were often poor, particularly during the harvest period and until the end of threshing. Many children only attended for part of the year and truancy rates were high. It is clear, therefore, that increasing State control over the teaching profession was not synonymous with greater manipulative powers over peasant society as a whole. Educational reform in the early nineteenth century may have been successful, at a general level, in inculcating loyalty to the ruling house of Bavaria, but in terms of the socialisation of peasant youth and the forming of social attitudes it was largely a failure. The traditional function of the family in the socialisation of children and the reproduction even at an early age of the sexual division of labour, remained unaffected by educational reform imposed from above. . . .

The village community had been an important mechanism for the inculcation of a collective mode of behaviour in the late eighteenth century, to a large extent it retained this function in later decades. The closeness of a village community was expressed in face-to-face contact, the commonalty of purpose and personal familiarity. In the absence of rapid population growth during the first half of the nineteenth century, the average size of villages in Bavaria remained small. . . .

Personal contact under these conditions would have remained both frequent and normative during the period under consideration. Community contacts continued to be important as a direct support to the functional role of the family. At one level, the powers of the local communities had been considerably strengthened. The tighter regulations governing marriage and settlement of 1825 were to be enforced by the *Gemeinde* [communities] and with the abolition of all seigneurial jurisdiction in 1848 the local authorities were now empowered to exercise the right of guardianship previously reserved for patrimonial courts. Such an extension in the powers of the local authority, however, was not synonymous with greater State control over rural society. Quite the contrary. The strengthening of community powers facilitated the retention of indigenous patterns of behaviour. Far from acting as the State demanded, the *Gemeinde* frequently failed to fulfil their official role, whether in combating rising illegitimacy, introducing an improved midwifery service, or in promoting better educational facilities for the local population. Increased local autonomy, even allowing for the re-drawing of local authority boundaries, more than compensated for the limited enclosure of common land that took place in early nineteenth-century Bavaria.

At a more personal level the local village community still performed its traditional function. Group contacts had always provided important support for the individual in rural society, and this continued to be the case after 1800. . . . These obligations, which constituted important communal bonds between rural families and within individual communities, continued well into the late nineteenth century. At most central family events, such as weddings, during sickness and at burials, immediate neighbours continued to be assigned distinct functions and roles. Equally god-parents were selected with care and were expected to visit the family on every Sunday and public holiday. In many cases, both before and after 1800, god-parents were selected from outside the local parish, but from within the same administrative areas and frequently from neighbouring villages within a radius of 5 to 10 kilometres. . . .

Moreover the village community as such continued to be involved in a general sense in family events. The whole village normally participated in marriage festivities and this also signified communal involvement in the integration of young people within the adult world. Whether in the context of traditional feast days and public holidays, irrespective of the degree to which they were general religious festivals or limited to particular groups within rural society, community involvement in Bavaria continued to be paramount throughout the early nineteenth century. . . .

The economic changes in the primary sector during the first half of the nineteenth century did not affect the underlying production function of the Bavarian peasant family. Indeed the exact nature of agrarian reform in Bavaria, although viewed officially as a contribution to the economic modernisation of the State and to the development of market-oriented capitalist production, merely served to reinforce the existing mode of production. Technological innovation was limited and increased agricultural output was achieved primarily through a more intensive utilisation of existing resources. Land redistribution and the enclosure and subdivision of common land only served to underline the importance of the peasant family economy. The end result was the creation of a peasantry dependent on either medium- or small-scale holdings, which became even less diversified, in terms of economic function, with the later decline of domestic craft production. Agrarian reform in Bavaria, by emphasising the inherent production function of the peasant family, thereby confirmed the traditional sexual division of labour in rural society and the existing attitude towards children and other family dependents. The labour-intensive nature of agrarian reform only served to exacerbate the sexual role of women and the socialisation and treatment of children. . . .

20

POPULAR EDUCATION AND ITS LIMITS

MARY JO MAYNES

One of the great changes in modern social history involves the spread of education to all sections of society and the redefinition of childhood from a time of work assistance to a time of schooling. In Western Europe, the nineteenth century was the crucial point of change. Schooling and literacy had been gaining ground gradually since the sixteenth century, but the majority of people—and the vast majority of women—remained unschooled in 1830. By the 1880s, when compulsory education laws were introduced to complete the process of change, the majority were encountering school at least briefly in childhood and majority literacy (however rudimentary) had been achieved. This shift was especially significant for women, previously laggard in educational opportunity; gender differences remained but narrowed.

The following selection, dealing with Baden, in southwestern Germany, and the Vaucluse region of southern France, considers the beginning of this process of change. The impulse to spread education now came from above—from governments and middle-class reformers, with new ideas about childhood, with a desire to attack traditional beliefs and superstitions through schooling, with a burning interest in creating more loyal national citizens and more skilled workers and soldiers. Popular reception to the educational push reflected what a huge change it was, in terms of family economies and the customary view of children. There was much resistance, some of which also had gendered aspects. But change did begin to break through, partly because of steady pressure from above, partly because certain groups of peasants and urban residents altered their own thinking about children and their service to the family, which caused them to see some new advantages in the process. Actual individual results, ironically, were not always predictable, in societies that still presented substantial barriers to advancement. Mary Jo Maynes captures this complex mix of reform pressures, resistance, shifting motivations and ambiguous results.

Early nineteenth-century developments in education connect to other social history themes for the period. Government and elite initiatives, seeking to

From: Mary Jo Maynes, *Schooling for the People: Comparative Local Studies of Schooling History in France and Germany, 1750–1850.* (New York: Holmes and Meier, 1985), pp. 101–07, 109–10, 112–14, 115–16, 124, 128–31, 132–33.

alter social patterns for ordinary people, had previously shown up in reforms in criminal punishments. The state, in both cases, was becoming a more active social agent. Peasant response in the educational area related to other aspects of rural life and culture, including often hesitant reactions to change (see Chapter 19). Here was one reason that government measures, though capable of inducing social change, usually encountered unexpected delays and complexities.

Two other features of the selection deserve emphasis. Unlike many historians who deal with a single place, Maynes focuses on two regions, in different national areas. But the emphasis is on common processes and reactions, rather than French-ness or German-ness. Baden (a separate state at the time) and the Vaucluse were different in many ways, but some social developments and reactions were impressively similar—not an uncommon finding in social history, and one that forces some reconsideration of traditional assumptions about conventional geographic definitions in history. Only after the basic social situation emerged can the interesting differences in detail between Baden and the Vaucluse gain meaning.

Finally, the social history of educational change holds both richness and complexity compared to conventional treatments. The fact of educational advance, through measures like the French Guizot law of 1832, which required each district to set up primary schools, is well known. But conventional historians tended to announce a law and assume that such top-down initiatives were the whole story. They also tended to treat educational change as clear progress, the advance of knowledge against traditional ignorance. Obviously, social historians agree that efforts from the top did have effects, and they may even agree that the results were mostly good. But the interaction with popular traditions and assumptions was not easy, and there were losses as well as gains as customary ideas and family roles gradually gave way. How different is the view of the modern "education revolution" when viewed from below?

The hostile response to school reform on the part of many local notables was perhaps predictable. But educational authorities may well have hoped that once good schools were available, the people would take to schooling with enthusiasm. That turned out not to be the case. Many parents, apparently more in Vaucluse than in Baden, seemed to be strangely indifferent to the potential blessings of education. The reports of inspectors and teachers record a litany of complaints on the topic and a persistent official effort to describe and account for this presumed obstinacy or irrationality. Certainly a number of possible explanations came to mind and appeared in educational communications: because the people were as yet unenlightened and unrefined, they were unable to appreciate the value of the improved schooling offered them; because they themselves were so poorly educated, they were unable to perceive the advantages for their children of the new institutions; precisely because of their long history of moral inferiority, the people were trapped in a vicious cycle of ignorance rooted in a popular culture for the most part indifferent to learning. The cycle needed to be interrupted through intervention on the part of the educated. In Vaucluse, where reformist educational officials encountered hostility, suspicion, or indifference at every turn, authorities were nonetheless constrained in their response to it by their own reluctance to coerce. Badenese school officials had more direct means at their disposal for circumventing or countering obstinacy in the populations they administered, but they, too, have left records that suggest that parents were sometimes recalcitrant, despite the penalties, when it came to sending their children to school.

These recurrent official complaints about parental attitudes toward schooling do offer some entry into popular interests. To be sure, the perspective is a distorted one and must be interpreted with due caution. Still, the evidence supplied by administrators suggests that many of the people must have held views about schooling that diverged from the official view. And, what is more, this divergence of opinion became increasingly troublesome to authorities as their commitment to universal schooling increased.

There was a certain irony in the popular response to the call to universal schooling. During the ancien régime, the campaign for improved popular education had been directed as an appeal to monarchs and aristocrats on behalf of the uneducated masses. It was the elite who needed convincing that they had nothing to fear from popular schooling. Now that the state was openly committed to the spread of schooling, the campaign had shifted ground. One inspector of the académie of Nîmes noted in 1837:

> For a long time now the poor and humble classes of society have asked to be permitted to enlighten and better themselves, to grow intellectually and morally; [those in power] always pretended not to understand needs of this sort, and refused to satisfy them. . . . [Now] the words Instruction, Popular Education are on all lips. The movement, the impulse, as they say, comes obviously *from above*. Is it the case that the classes who are the object of so lively and so general a solicitude understand the value of this benefit whose enjoyment we want to assure for them? Do they accept with enough rapidity and gratitude the sacrifices that are made for them in the name of a goal so elevated and so selfless? Now, does not the resistance come *from below?*

As efforts to provide wider access to improved schooling began to have some impact, the resistance from below became more apparent and more troublesome. This inspector, like many other *universitaires* "could not help being profoundly affected by the coldness with which our own people still accepts that for which it has so pressing a need and which is so generously offered." Early efforts to reform the schools and to bring all of the children into them produced a discouraging realization: the people could not be counted upon to be voluntary and enthusiastic partners in what school reformers regarded as their intellectual and moral improvement.

Popular indifference to schooling had troubled school administrators for as long as authorities had regarded schooling as a duty incumbent upon all.

Records of the drive toward universal attendance, already under way in the late eighteenth century in southwestern Germany, reflect the running disagreement between parents and school officials. An ordinance proclaimed in the Kürpfalz in 1751 berated Catholic parents who "out of pure stinginess, in order to save school fees and firewood, condemn their children to irreversible damage to body and soul" by keeping them out of school. The edict set stricter punishments for truancy. As efforts to corral children into schools became more intense in the following decades, Reformed and Lutheran authorities issued similar ordinances condemning parental negligence of schooling. The pastor of Heddesbach reported that in 1807 parents were still abusing and exploiting their children by making them tend flocks during church and school hours. The pastor of Daisbach complained several years later that truancy was inordinately high in his parish, and that the payment of truancy fines was not being properly enforced. Still, despite the persistence of complaints of this sort into the nineteenth century, it is clear that most Badenese children were enrolled in school by the early nineteenth century and attended class for at least part of the year.

In Vaucluse, on the other hand, school administrators encountered a population singularly unresponsive to the attraction of primary schooling. One inspector lamented in 1837:

> One of the biggest obstacles to primary schooling is the lack of enthusiasm for sending their children to classes which the poorer classes of the villages and the rural population exhibit. . . . There are parents who, even though aware of the usefulness of instruction, still prefer to put their children to work for even a small profit rather than to send them to school. For these people, the present moment is everything; the future of their families is nothing because they don't see it or are afraid they won't profit from it.

School inspectors in Vaucluse continued to complain throughout most of the nineteenth century about the apparent shortsightedness of peasant parents. Often, inspectors were convinced, parental indifference toward schooling was more the product of benightedness than of poverty. One inspector noted that *cultivateurs* from Pertuis refused out of sheer "insouciance" to see the need for schooling; very few parents could actually demonstrate the need for the pittance their children were capable of earning. In La Tour d'Aigues, the small *cultivateurs* who comprised the majority of the population "couldn't begin to understand" the importance of schooling. Local supervisors in the community of Jonquerettes reported in 1834 that the reasons for absenteeism were the "negligence, ignorance, and greed" of parents. Their findings were echoed in a départemental survey of the late 1840s, which found that the overwhelming cause of persistent absenteeism in Vaucluse (cited in the cases of 760 of the 1101 absentees in the arrondissement of Avignon and 371 of 778 in Apt) was "parental indifference."

Negligence of the education of daughters was even more common than that of sons, even if the explanation for it was similar. The inspection reports of the 1830s claimed, for example, that in Cabrières "the inhabitants, believing that instruction [was] unnecessary for their daughters, put them to work at home from their early childhood on." In St. Saturnin, "the mothers, who all [belonged] to the agricultural classes and, having no education themselves, [didn't] know how to appreciate the advantages of knowing how to read their own language," were opposed to sending their daughters to school.

These complaints, in an almost identical language, persist into the Second Empire. The Inspector Rouossi reported even as late as 1856 on the continuing struggle to get the children of Vaucluse into the schools. Among the difficulties he cited were:

> the poverty of the inhabitants; the too great avarice of some families who, without being constrained by need, want to make some profit from their young children; the indifference of some parents who do not want for their children a benefit whose advantages they cannot comprehend because they themselves are deprived of it. . . .

Even where parents did send their children to school, they did not seem to understand the importance of regular attendance. They sent the children at their convenience, apparently unaware that such a pattern was considered to be subversive of the intellectual development of their children. Again, these sorts of complaints can be detected as early as the late eighteenth century in southwestern Germany. The Reformed Council of the Kürpfalz reported in 1765 that "Parents [were] not industrious enough in sending their children to school . . . [many children] spent hardly a quarter [of the year] in school." A similar complaint the following year from the Lutheran Diocese of Heidelberg attributed to irregular and infrequent attendance the consequence that "children soon forgot what they had just learned during the short time in the classroom." Officials in this region fought the common practice of summer truancy throughout the late eighteenth and early nineteenth centuries, but even as late as the 1830s there persisted complaints about communities like Bockschaft, where no one attended school during the summer semester.

In Vaucluse inspectors saw "the desire, the need to make money [as] the cause of the fact that there [existed] not a single agricultural *commune* in which the majority of parents [consented] to deprive themselves of their children during the rural work season, or if a few [sent] their children to school during this time it [was] because they [were] too young to be of real use to them." In one hamlet in the commune of Gordes, the teacher was reportedly annoyed by the practice of children "coming at different hours of the day, only to pass a few moments in school."

The pattern of complaint suggests that many parents did not share the convictions of school authorities that regular school attendance was necessary for their children's well-being and did not see the role of schooling in their children's lives in the same light as the educational reformers. Parents themselves rarely left direct statements about their visions regarding schooling. Still, the shreds of evidence that do survive about what parents thought and how they behaved when it came to sending their children to school allow one to go a bit beyond the suggestive, if prejudiced, views of school authorities.

One useful approach is to reconstruct the "family economy" of the popular classes—that is, to examine the constraints within which families lived their lives and made choices about the allocation of collective resources. The decision to send a child to school was ultimately a family decision. It was so more clearly in France, where there was no legal compulsion to send children to school before the end of the nineteenth century, but even in the German states, where such laws impinged upon family prerogatives earlier, parental compliance was by no means assured. The laws, and their enforcement agencies, as well as changing social and economic conditions, altered the context in which choices were made, but families were the final arbiters where the behavior of their children was concerned. And in this period of transition to industrial capitalism, accompanied as it was by economic dislocation and periodic crises that left many families on the margins of indigence, simple survival was the dominant goal influencing family strategies. In order to increase the number of family members able to contribute to the collective income, children, particularly older siblings, were usually set to work as soon as possible. The evidence suggests that in both Baden and Vaucluse patterns of family economy in the early nineteenth century left most families dependent to some extent on the labor of their children. For these families, work and schooling must have appeared as competitors for their children's time.

In Vaucluse nearly every rural family had a small plot of land for subsistence, but probably two-thirds of all peasant families had to supplement the living provided by their plots with income from work on more substantial farms or from cottage industry. Although the rural work force was not wholly dependent on wage labor, the prevailing low wage levels did depress living standards throughout the first half of the nineteenth century. The salaries of day laborers varied according to season, reaching a maximum at harvest time, when a man could earn 2 francs or more in a day and a woman or child could earn 50 centimes or even a franc. During the rest of the year, however, wages for agricultural labor were lower, plummeting during the wintertime, when work was unavailable. Yearly incomes were constrained by the rhythm and length of the agricultural work season, which varied in Vaucluse between 200 and 280 days in length. At these rates, a bachelor *journalier* could just about support himself through the whole year on his earnings from wage labor, and he would have had to spend a full four-fifths of his income on food. Obviously, women and children workers could not be self-supporting, but were paid wages that presumed them to be contributors to a family wage. A smallholding *cultivateur* could manage somewhat better by raising food on his own plot, but at the sacrifice of time worked for wages or of longer workdays. Male *cultivateurs* often relied on family members for either the work on the family plot or the supplementary wage labor, and census returns attest to the universality of farmwork of some sort on the part of women in *cultivateur* families. Some rural families in Vaucluse still drew income in this period from domestic industrial work, especially in textiles, but returns were meager and diminishing as the rural industries confronted competition from goods produced in mechanized mills in northern France and abroad. . . .

Although a general, if slight, improvement in living conditions occurred gradually over the first half of the nineteenth century, most agricultural and industrial workers continued to live close to the margin of subsistence. The average diet was composed of grains, potatoes, and occasional vegetables and salt. With bread costing 30 or 40 centimes a kilogram, and meat more than 1 franc a kilogram throughout most of the period, the wage of a single male adult could not support a family. The bulk of the family income was spent on food, and the amount needed increased with family size. There was a built-in pressure on family members to work as soon as their need for food was significant. In fact, with the exception of the families of fully employed skilled artisans and the wealthiest peasants, families of the popular classes were dependent on the earnings of women or children simply to survive. . . .

Rural children in Baden had work routines as well. Some children's poetry, written at the turn of the nineteenth century for inclusion in a primer, refers to their tasks: guiding the reins of horses and mules during plowing; gathering, tying, and stacking sheaves during harvest. The poems also allude to the industrial side of the rural economy. A poem entitled "The Evening" illustrates the complex economic roles played by various farm family members:

The shutters are closed and the evening work brought out:
The maid peels a turnip, the lad carves a wheel,
Mother sews a seam in my coat, then teaches us spinning while she spins
    along,
Father makes nails as though he were a smith.

These poems are obviously idealized presentations, but more prosaic sources like the reports of *Industrieschule* inspectors verify the image of intense levels of economic activity of various kinds on the part of children. One inspector wrote in his report of 1808:

> The Odenwald communities are small, dispersed and usually poor. Woodworking serves as an occupation for boys while girls drive the spindle. In the regions of viniculture, carrying night soil into the vineyards keeps boys busy on good winter days while girls spin at home. Where the woods are interspersed with fields, the girls occupy themselves in winter with women's work [i.e., the needle trades] for which the growing of hemp and flax provide a natural opportunity, while boys make benches, baskets and pots during the time when they are not taking care of the cattle and the pigs. . . .

By the 1830s a new opportunity had appeared. In addition to working in the crafts and in domestic industry, urban children were beginning to find work in the new factories in both regions. A Vauclusan school inspector attributed the absenteeism of more than three hundred boys and girls of the community of L'Isle-sur-la-Sorgue "principally . . . to the fact that this *commune,* because of its waters, [held] a large number of factories. Children [managed] to find profitable work there and parents [preferred] sending their children to work to having them educated." At the end of the 1830s, the *conseil de prud'hommes* of Avignon prepared a report on child labor in that city in anticipation of forthcoming governmental regulation. Their report noted that

> Girls, for the most part, are employed from their childhood on in the silk factories. They find work suited to their capacities and enter at the age of ten or twelve. Their salary is ordinarily forty or sixty centimes a day. The length of the workday is thirteen or fourteen hours, of which two to two-and-a-half hours are used for moments of rest and meals. The children employed in the factories generally belong to the workers who work there, to which others are added according to the needs of the different shops. Their education is generally quite neglected. They rarely go to school from the time they are capable of earning a small daily wage to help in their maintenance.

Factory work had also begun to attract school-aged children in Baden. Industrial statistics collected by the state indicate that by the late 1830s there were already more than ten thousand factory workers in the state, of which some two thousand were children. Mechanized industry located in small shops employed an additional four thousand or so workers, most of whom were women and children. In both regions factory children were a dilemma for school authorities. Their visibility and the inflexibility of their work routines made it especially difficult to combine their work with schooling. But most urban children who worked earned their pittances in ways that were less visible, less regular, and less lucrative. Street peddling of small items (matches and thread were common commodities sold), sweeping chimneys, pilfering were all methods of adding to the family purse. It should not be overlooked that older siblings, especially girls, were generally expected to watch over younger brothers and sisters to free their parents for other work. And in front of the churches in Vaucluse, at the taverns of Baden, the common presence of beggar children was a public reminder of the persistent poverty of many families. Still, the evidence suggests that, despite all of these possibilities, and despite their ingenious efforts to find sources of income, it was the case that urban children, unlike their rural counterparts, were generally hard pressed to find employment, which no doubt lowered the opportunity cost of schooling in most urban communities.

Since the cost of sending an employable child to school was greater than that of sending one unable to work, patterns of child employment are reflected in a predictable manner in school-enrollment patterns. First, the sex typing of child labor made the work of girls less valuable than the work of boys. Some of the jobs boys commonly did—construction labor and field work, for example—were done outside the home and were relatively well paid. Among girls, except for those employed in the textile mills, most child workers worked at home at occupations with flexible hours and very low pay, or helped with household chores. In other words, from the simple perspective of their potential contribution to the family pool of labor or income, sending girls to school was generally less costly than sending boys. There was an opposite pressure operating as well, since it is clear that schooling was generally considered more valuable for boys, and the anecdotal evidence at least suggests that, where choices had to be made, applying resources for boys' schooling took priority over that of girls. This would certainly help to account for the consistently lower literacy among women in both of these regions, but most markedly in Vaucluse, prior to the school reform era. What is interesting to note is that once fines and other punishments for truancy were applied systematically and equally for the truancy of boys and girls—as they were in Baden around the turn of the nineteenth century—the old pattern was reversed. It became more costly for parents to keep their daughters home than to send them to school, since their earnings were not high enough to offset the truancy fine. The tendency for enrollments of girls to catch up with those of boys and in some communities even overtake them during this period is probably at least in part a result of the increasing application of truancy fines. This is even clearer in the scattered truancy records . . . which suggest that girls were truant less often than boys.

In Vaucluse, where school attendance was voluntary, enrollment patterns continued to reflect the prevailing greater concern for the education of sons. This was especially marked in Vaucluse, which displayed a typically southern French pattern of extreme divergence between male and female literacy patterns. If anything, parents in rural communities perhaps relied more heavily on daughters than on sons for domestic labor, in order to make schooling possible for their sons. In any event, it was in the rural communities that sex ratios among enrolled pupils remained the most unbalanced. . . .

In the agrarian economy, children were put to work at a very young age during the times of intense demand for labor. Full-time work was taken up only after a child had had several years' experience with occasional labor. The most commonly cited age of entry into full-time agricultural employment is twelve or thirteen. In France the *première communion*, a religious rite of early adolescence, seems to have served as a rite of passage with regard to economic status and dress as well; its completion signaled the entry into adulthood. In Baden the *Konfirmation* played a similar role, marking the end of schooling and the beginning of adulthood. The school system in Baden was specifically oriented around this turning point; a decision had to be made at the time of the *Konfirmation* between work and advanced schooling of some sort for those "not required to devote themselves at this age to a practical occupation." There was a lot of flexibility in practice, of course, especially in Vaucluse, but it was certainly customary in both regions permanently to withdraw most children from school by early adolescence and start them to work full time. The legal school-leaving ages in Baden were established with an eye toward practice: thirteen for girls and fourteen for boys. Early-nineteenth-century registers suggest that school leaving often occurred somewhat earlier.

In Vaucluse the employment of adolescents played a role in shrinking their schooling time, if inspection reports are accurate. The level of instruction in the village of Jonquerettes was low in 1802; the inspector attributed this to the practice of permanently withdrawing children from school at the age of ten or twelve. Half a century later, children in this farming community were still leaving primary school early to take jobs in the fields. The school inspector reported in 1843 that in another village the children of the upper two divisions had left school, while those in the third, who were seven or eight years old, "were probably destined to remain on the benches for another few years." At the end of the 1850s it was still reportedly the case that "fathers were impatient to put their children to work, and those who [sent] their children to school rarely [left] them there after the first communion, the time at which they [were] employed in fieldwork." . . . Among the middle class and even for wealthy peasants, educating a son was one prerequisite to setting him up in a profession or in the church. Still, for people to accept the claim that schooling assured a more solid future to most children, they had to be convinced, first, that planning for the future of their children made sense at all, and second, that educational accomplishments could be converted into enhanced opportunities. This would have entailed a reorientation in the general population of attitudes about childhood similar to that which Philippe Ariès demonstrated among the upper classes beginning in the seventeenth century or so. The transformation of attitudes was related to simple demographic realities, for, as Charles Tilly has pointed out in his commentary on Ariès, it was difficult for parents to be calculating about the future of children whose survival was by no means secured. High infant and child mortality rates discouraged the adoption of Malthusian attitudes toward procreation; it seems likely that they would also have discouraged a calculating approach to schooling. . . .

Furthermore, access to schooling, even theoretical access, cannot be equated with access to careers. In the early industrial world (and even today, if these criticisms are valid) access to a particular career had very little to do with skills or certification acquired through schooling. A child's future was largely settled by his or her family on the basis of its needs, its aspirations, and its capacities to invest in expensive and time-consuming training that was a prerequisite for many futures but not a guarantee of entry into them. In general, schooling made sense as an investment only for those to whom the desired future was already open. For the rest, mere schooling was a downright waste of time if not an impossibility from the investment perspective.

For that majority of the early industrial population that still drew livelihood from the land, the path to the future was largely marked by the social and demographic situation of the family. Children who were in a position to inherit land from their parents could expect to follow the pursuit of agriculture; nonheirs could expect to change occupations. The children of the landless and land-poor were, of course, less motivated to follow in their parents' footsteps, but the dearth of resources in these families made any investment in alternative training unlikely. In either case, learning to farm entailed work alongside elders, which began early in life. This does not mean that peasants had no use for schooling, but only that they did not rely on it as the primary source of information about how to do their work, nor did they regard it as a prerequisite for the running of a farm.

There is some suggestion that peasants were becoming more interested in some aspects of schooling for reasons connected with the changing conditions of the agricultural economy. Inspectors' reports in Vaucluse note at times the apparent interest of peasants in skills that could help in the management of property and in the mastery of the increasingly intrusive market. Peasants in Vaucluse were in general little concerned with the niceties of grammar—not too surprising in a population whose everyday tongue was different from that taught in the schools. On the other hand, they reportedly "held a great store in arithmetic because they made use of it more frequently . . . there [were] a lot of children interested in it." One inspector was surprised to find during his 1836 rounds children who (despite their absenteeism for farm work during six months of the year) "could read passably [and], although little learned in grammar, the usefulness of which they couldn't appreciate, were applying themselves more diligently to arithmetic." This same interest in arithmetic apparently even encouraged adults to return to school, as, for example, in Gadagne in 1838, where ciphering was the principal interest of the evening pupils, many of whom were "fathers of families who sense each day the need they have to know how to keep accounts." These testimonies suggest that even if the agricultural classes of Vaucluse were as yet unwilling to cooperate with the government's program of full-time elementary education, it is apparent that certain sectors of that population, particularly peasants with property to manage and market dealings to master, were showing some interest in the acquisition of basic literacy and numeracy skills through occasional schooling.

It should be noted that this early evidence of peasant interest in schooling was largely limited to schooling for sons. Discriminatory behavior with regard to the schooling of boys and girls continued in Vaucluse, particularly in rural areas. This was in part the result of the old and new taboos against coeducation; where a separate girls' school was not available, girls were not sent as frequently as where there was one. But it does seem to have been the case that schooling was considered to be less valuable for girls. The sexual division of labor within the peasant household allocated the tasks of management and marketing of major crops to the men. Comments suggest that the education of girls was usually the domain of mothers, and these usually, though not always, decided that schooling was unnecessary. In St. Saturnin d'Avignon, for example, there was a girls' school for teaching reading and writing, but no grammar was taught, since "mothers of families, all belonging to the agricultural classes, [were] opposed to having their children devote themselves to studies which they believed [served] no purpose but to make their children waste their time." In Beaumont the female pupils were reportedly not making much progress because their attendance was too often interrupted by excessive parental demands on their time. Families in Vauclusan rural communities continued to be less likely to send their daughters to school even after they began to send their sons. Still, the evidence is not unambiguous. According to the testimony of Agricole Perdiguier, who came from a family living from farming and industrial work, the picture was not so simple. He recalls his father deciding that schooling was a waste of time for girls. His mother, however, felt differently and she decided to send her daughters to school, paying the tuition money herself from her earnings from the sale of small amounts of farm produce and handicrafts.

Although the evidence suggests that in the late eighteenth century girls in Baden were less likely to be in school than their brothers, the old pattern of higher enrollment of boys had largely disappeared by the early nineteenth century. Even if schooling was considered to be less important for girls from the point of view of their work expectations, the enforcement of fines for truancy, coupled with nonmaterial interests in schooling, was sufficient to encourage parents to send their girls to school even more frequently than their boys. . . .

Children who were not in a position to inherit land or to invest in training of any sort, those under pressure to begin their work lives young, drifted without resource into whatever unskilled or semiskilled work was available, in the mills and mines, in construction and transportation, in service. The occupations of the popular classes were not taught in the schools. This was not true in the same way for the middle classes. For them, even if specific techniques for each profession were learned on the job, the certification required for entry into the careers they followed was indeed provided through the classical schools and the universities. But by and large, these educational institutions were closed to the children of the people. Primary schools were their schools, and they were the most they could expect.

One cannot help concluding that the reform of the primary schools did little, in the short run at least, to improve the prospects of the children who attended them. The somewhat enhanced access to basic skills was a boon to those subsectors of the population formerly cut off from them, even if that group was smaller than the school promoters' claims would suggest. But the direction of most of the early reforms—geared as they were toward making schooling a more engrossing experience and making its lessons more responsive to state than to parental concerns—actually had the effect of making schooling less compatible with the demands of the family economy of the more marginal families. The ways in which universal schooling clashed with the family economy became clearer only as authorities tried to fulfill universal attendance goals. Conflicting expectations about how children should employ their time caused reformers to rethink the practicality of establishing a single common elementary school. . . .

A REDEFINITION OF DISGUST

ALAIN CORBIN

Alterations of emotional reactions continued in the early nineteenth century. The following selection deals with shifts in the standards of smell and cleanliness, based on a combination of new sensitivities developed in the eighteenth century and the fears and pressures of life in the growing cities.

Disgust, of course, was not new, and at the same time a full exploration of this human expression has yet to be offered. What is clear is a transformation in the focus of disgust toward manifestations of the body—redefining the role of the body in the process.

In this selection Alain Corbin uses a variety of evidence, including comments by contemporary doctors and other observers, and changes in behavior and law, to show how standards of odor and cleanliness changed, both in the area of social relations and in personal grooming. Led by the middle class, in France and elsewhere, the new sensitivities to smell set a basis for radical (if often amusingly gradual) changes in personal hygiene and for attacks on popular and working-class habits as well.

The focus thus rests on a crucial passage in the development of middle-class hygiene standards in relation to the framework of industrial society. Have the standards formed at this point changed significantly in more recent times? Did the initial class divisions over these standards persist beyond the early industrial period?

The stress on the repulsive smell of the proletariat appears clearly in the accounts by doctors and visitors to the poor. This was a new intolerance. Hitherto, doctors had seemed impervious to disgust; only fear of infection appeared to motivate precautions. During the second third of the nineteenth century, repulsion toward the smell of the masses was openly acknowledged, without any real recognition whether this represented a new intolerance or a new frankness. The patient's domicile became a place of daily torture for the doctor. "One positively suffocates there," Monfalcon and Polintère stated. "It

From: Alain Corbin, *The Foul and the Fragrant* (Cambridge, MA: Harvard University Press, 1986), pp. 150–59, 176–81.

is impossible to go into this center of infection; often the doctor who visits the poor cannot bear the fetid odor of the room; he writes his prescription by the door or the window."

Unlike his wretched clientele, the doctor no longer tolerated animal effluvia. "On entering this house," noted Dr. Joire in 1851, "I was struck by the foul-smelling odor breathed there. This odor was literally stifling and unbearable and seemed like the smell of the most fetid dung; it was particularly strong around the patient's bed, and was also spread through the whole apartment, despite the outside air that came in through the half-open door. I could not remove from my nose and mouth the handkerchief with which I protected myself the whole time I stayed with this woman. Yet neither the inhabitants of the house nor the invalid seemed to notice the inconvenience of the miasma." Adolphe Blanqui, assailed by the stench of the Lille cellars and by the odor of filthy men emanating from them, recoiled in shock at the entrances to these "ditches for men"; only in the company of a doctor or a police officer did he "hazard" descent into this hell where "human shadows" tossed and swirled. . . .

The flood of discourse on the habitat of the masses and its stifling atmosphere revealed the new preoccupation after the 1832 cholera morbus epidemic. "The atmospheric swamp of the house" had replaced the cesspools of public space in the hierarchy of anxieties about smells. In towns, complaints concentrated on the stench of the communal sections of the dwellings of the masses. The basic theme of the diatribe was a denunciation of the odor of excrement and refuse, which had not yet been privatized in these sections of society.

The odor of stagnant urine, congealed in the gutter, dried on the paving, encrusted on the wall, assailed the visitor who had to enter the wretched premises of the poor. The only means of entry was through low, narrow, dark alleys. These formed channels for a fetid stream laden with greasy water and "the rubbish of every type that rained down from all the stories." Gaining access to the poor man's stinking dwelling almost amounted to an underground expedition. Adolphe Blanqui moved through the Lille courtyards or the Rouen slums with the fascinated caution that earlier had driven Parent-Duchâtelet to cross the sewers of the city. The narrowness, darkness, and humidity of the small inner courtyard into which the alley opened made it look like a well, the ground carpeted with refuse. Here, garbage rotted, laundry- and dishwater-formed pools; stenches amalgamated and rose to nourish the fetidity of the upper stories. Within this order of perception the staircase acted as an overflow; a foul-smelling cascade rushed down it, checked at every floor by the landing, fed by the latrines, which revealed through open doors the obscenity of the privy full of excrement. Dr. Bayard retained the aural memory of the "gurgling household water" on staircases in the IVᵉ arrondissement of Paris. The stench of these premises formed an ensemble. The odor of excrement predominated; it varied only in strength from one place to another. There was no subtle division into different categories of smells here. . . .

[The] idyllic vision of the peasant and the life of the fields survived into the nineteenth century. Picturesque journeys, and particularly iconography, helped to keep it alive. Unlike the everyday contact of medical practice, which involved the senses of touch and smell, ethnology via observation allowed distance; it permitted scales of revulsion. The artist's brush easily transferred reality into symbolism.

Nevertheless, the village was soon perceived as the antithesis of the mountain summit bathed in the purity of the ether, and was painted in dark colors. Social emanations fermented in the depths of valleys; travelers should not leave the slopes of hillsides. Obermann fled from low ground; Dr. Benassis set out to curette it. This was no hopeless undertaking: as early as 1756, Howard successfully transformed Cardington peasants' "mud huts," where in his opinion they lived like savages, into cheerful cottages.

Charles-Léonard Pfeiffer has cataloged the manifestations of Balzac's repugnance to the smell of peasants. Here is just one example: "The strong, savage odor of the two habitués of the highway made the dining room stink so much that it offended Madame de Montcornet's delicate senses and she would have been forced to leave if Mouche and Fourchon had stayed any longer."

When Balzac wrote *Le Médecin de Campagne* (1833) and *Les Paysans* (1844) the stench from villages had been feeding a steady stream of writing for some years. No report read to the Conseil de Salubrité from whatever rural department, no medical thesis about the peasant environment, no report on an inquiry under the July Monarchy or the Second Republic failed to denounce violently the poor hygiene of the habitat of rural space. Thus, every book about the social history of the French countryside at that time gives considerable space to this complaint. Most of the authors—including myself—have rather naïvely used the copious discussions by bourgeois observers for their own purposes. It would have been more valuable if they had tried to unravel the tangled systems of images and, above all, shown that the basic historical fact was not the actuality (which had probably changed little) but the new form of perception, the new intolerance of traditional actuality. This sensory change within the elite and the flood of discourse it provoked were to bring about the revolution in public health, the road to modernity.

A reversal thus took place at the level of perceptions. Filth and rubbish, so greatly feared by refined city dwellers, invaded the image of the countryside; even more than in the past, the peasant tended to be identified with the dungman, intimate with liquid manure and dung, impregnated with the odor of the stable. Hitherto, the public stenches of the town had been under fire; now, the town was—slowly—cleared of its refuse; half a century later it had almost succeeded in cleaning up its poor. Its relationship with rural space was reversed: it became the place of the imputrescible—that is, of money—whereas the countryside symbolized poverty and putrid excrement. The power of agrarian ideology was not sufficient to challenge a perceived reality, which the negative welcome given to immigrants from the countryside and the attitude of travelers or city-dwelling tourists bore out for more than a century. A new relationship between the images of town and countryside was not established until the arrival in the latter of water supply, mechanization, household equipment, and ecological propaganda. . . .

In the town, overcoming the uncleanness of communal conveniences and draining off the filth from the courtyards seemed the most urgent requirements. Progress occurred via the semiprivatization of latrines and the distribution of keys to families whose dwellings opened onto the landing. In this environment the advance in "privacy" consisted chiefly in protection against other people's dirt and odors, in the achievement of an approximate familialization of excrement, and in protecting modesty against potential dramatic interruption. Abolishing the promiscuity of latrines, keeping doors closed, and installing blowoff pipes were indispensable preliminaries for that disciplined defecation deemed essential to the elimination of stenches. It was also important to keep watch against individuals who urinated in alleys: this was a task for the good porter. If necessary, Passot noted, he could set up a small barrier outside and cover the gutter with a slab. In short, the venture aimed at progressively transforming communal conveniences into private conveniences. Frequently, whitewashing and painting to eliminate impregnation of walls completed the arsenal of measures advocated. Obviously, the advance involved a subscription to the water company; the manifold obstacles that blocked the extension of this practice are well known.

In the country and in a number of small towns, the struggle against the stench of excrement sustained the interminable battle between municipal officials on the one hand and the owners and users of dung on the other. Opposition to abolishing smells was keen, sometimes savage, because it was desperate. The sanitary reformers most often lost the fight; they never succeeded in getting dung buried in trenches. Other measures expected to disinfect the rural house included using lime, opening new casements, and knocking down party walls. . . .

More important to the present argument was the attempt to inspect the habitat of the masses. Once again, it was the terrible epidemic of 1832 that prompted new tactics. District commissions were set up when it was announced that the scourge was imminent; their function was to visit every house, detect the causes of insalubriousness, and force the landlord to comply with police rules. These commissions performed their task thoroughly; the one in the Luxembourg district visited 924 properties in less than two months. The prefect Gisquet claimed that he received about ten thousand reports from these organizations. . . .

The new control of odors that accompanied the increased privacy inside bourgeois dwellings permitted a skillful change in the way women presented themselves. A subtle calculation of bodily messages led to both a reduction in the strength of olfactory signals and an increase in the value assigned them. Because, in the name of decency, women's bodies were now less on show, the importance of the sense of smell increased astonishingly. "The woman's atmosphere" became the mysterious element in her sex appeal. However, exaltation of the young girl's virginity and new perceptions of the wife, her role and her virtues, continued to forbid any open advances. To arouse desire without betraying modesty was the basic rule of the game of love. Olfaction played a crucial role in the refinement of the game, and it turned primarily on the new alliance between woman and flower.

New medical arguments were invoked to justify practices aimed at eliminating putrid filth so as to diminish the risks of infection. Since the time when Lavoisier and Séguin had precisely measured the products of cutaneous perspiration, there had been increased concern that perspiration not be impeded. Broussais's physiological approach to medicine called for greater attention to the hygiene of the secretory organs, which ensured that the body was freed from impurities. Medical theory indicated the "geography" of the body that governed the ritual of the toilette. The key was to supervise cleanliness of hands, feet, armpits, groin, and genital organs. The importance that Broussais accorded to the concept of irritation strengthened the ban on oxymetallic cosmetics. Sensualism, which still had considerable influence though it was now questioned, enjoined sensitivity and lightness of touch by means of a scrupulous toilette.

The canons of bodily aesthetics urged the most scrupulous hygiene. Cosmetics were governed by the aristocratic ideal of pearly skin, through which the blue blood could be seen pulsing. For nearly a century the supreme reference points remained the brilliant whiteness of the lily and of the Pompadour's complexion; the aesthetic code decreed that all visible parts of the body be washed—as it also prescribed a sedentary life, the cool shade of trees, and the protection of gloves for "soft, white, firm, plump hands."

Removing the dirt from the poor was equivalent to increasing their wisdom; convincing the bourgeois of the need to wash was to prepare him to exercise the virtues of his class. Cleanliness was the tenth of Franklin's thirteen principles of wisdom, coming just before moral balance and chastity. "Hygiene, which maintains health, which nurtures the mind with habits of order, purity, and moderation, is for that reason alone the soul of beauty; because this precious advantage depends more than anything else on the freshness of a healthy body, the influence of a pure soul." Vidalin put his finger on the unexpected link between economy and cleanliness. Cleanliness, in its widest sense, reduced waste of food and clothing and facilitated the identification, control, and even possibly the salvage of waste; it became another method of fighting loss. From this point of view, the best preventive measures consisted in learning not to get dirty, to avoid contact with the putrid, and to get rid of all excreta on the skin.

The stress on the requirements of modesty, as we know, both favored and restrained the practice of bodily hygiene. Olfaction was caught up in the network of intertwining prohibitions. Richard Sennett has cited the physiological and psychic disorders that fear of farting in public caused the Victorian bourgeoisie. Do not require your servant to do anything repugnant to her senses, the comtesse de Bradi advised in 1838; except in case of illness, "do not have your shoes taken off."

Nevertheless the progress of bodily hygiene encountered numerous set-backs; the most important was the slowness with which houses were equipped, authorized by doctors' persistent distrust of immoderate use of water, as is evidenced by the long list of prohibitions and precautions that larded public health discourse. Menstrual frequency still ruled the cycle of bathing. Few experts advised taking more than one bath a month. Hufeland was notoriously bold in prescribing a weekly regimen, and Friedlander even more so for permitting children to take baths two or three times a week, although he still denounced immoderate use of water.

Plunging into water involved a calculated risk. It was important that the duration, frequency, and temperature of baths be adapted to sex, age, temperament, state of health, and season. Baths were thought to exert a profound effect on the whole organism, because they were not an everyday event. Mental specialists and sometimes even moralists pinned their hopes on them; gynecologists feared them. Delacoux noted that the courtesan owed her infertility to her excessive preoccupation with toilette. According to him, numerous women had been deprived of the joys of motherhood by this "indiscreet attention." Even more serious, baths endangered beauty; women who overused them "were generally pale and their fullness of figure owed more to fleshiness than to the bloom of the skin." Young girls who bathed too much risked debility.

Tourtelle advised against immersion after meals, during times of weakness, and, of course, during menstruation. Rostan recommended that the bather wet his head in order to prevent congestion of the brain. One must get out of the water at the occurrence of the second shiver, dry promptly, and then stretch out on a bench for a few minutes to rest from the fatigues of the bath, without running the risk of making the chamber damp.

Until the triumph of the shower, which shortened the time spent in bathing and rendered self-satisfaction harmless, baths aroused suspicion. The ban on nudity acted against the spread of baths. Drying the genitals posed a problem. "Close your eyes," Madame Celnart ordered her readers, "until you have completed the operation." Water could become an indiscreet mirror. Dr. Marie de Saint-Ursin described the young girl's confusion in the bath: "Inexperience descends, blushing, into the crystal of the waves, meets the image of its new treasures there, and blushes even more." In affected phrases, the author confirmed the synchronism established between female puberty and initiation into the practices of bodily hygiene. "Bathe, if you are ordered," concluded the comtesse de Bradi; "otherwise take only one bath a month at the most. There is an indefinable element of idleness and flaccidity that ill becomes a girl in the taste for settling down on the bottom of a bathtub in this way."

These attitudes account for the obvious disparity that grew up between the volume of discourse and the scantiness of practice. Bathing still required therapeutic justification. It is therefore not surprising that the ritual was complicated. Transporting the water and filling and emptying the tub, bucket, or metal bath entered, like laundry or seasonal housework, into the timetable of major domestic rites.

Accordingly, the major innovation was an increase in partial baths, as shown by the spread, still limited it is true, of footbaths, handbaths, hipbaths, and halfbaths. The concern to avoid getting dirty, the new frequency of ablutions, and the stress on the specific requirements of washing shaped the bourgeoisie's apprenticeship in hygienic practices. The physiology of excretion, which appeared even more important in the light of Broussais's theories, governed the fragmented ritual of the toilette in the same way that it obsessed both the actual practices and utopian fantasies of municipal policy. The same rationale underlay both the insistent hygiene advocated for the bourgeois body and the ceaseless evacuation of urban waste that was the sanitary reformers' aim: the abolition of the threat from excrement, no longer so much determined by the risk of infection as by the risk of congestion.

A proliferation of lotions accompanied the increase in ablutions. This was the result not only of a process of substitution encouraged by the disrepute of perfumes, but also of the alliance between lotions and friction, highly recommended for its energizing properties. The other activities of the toilette ritual can be quickly listed. The fashion for plastering pomade on hair had disappeared. Hair hygiene consisted of periodic untangling with a fine comb, brushing, and plaiting before bed. . . .

Mouth hygiene was becoming more specific; Londe advised daily brushing of all the teeth to deodorize breath, and not, as was most often the practice, only the front ones. Madame Celnart prescribed the use of aromatized powders.

Fresh bodily odor depended even more on the quality and cleanliness of underwear than on scrupulous hygienic practices. Development in this area too moved at an accelerated pace. Sanitary reformers endeavored to institute weekly changing of underwear. The new timetable for changing clothes and the new appreciation of the pleasant odor of clean linen were incentives to perfume washtubs, chests, and drawers. These practices spread long before those of bodily hygiene proper.

In fact the new behavior patterns were accepted only slowly even by the bourgeoisie, as the rareness of bathrooms attests. The bidet was popularized only at the very end of the century. The use of the tub, imported from England, long remained a sign of snobbishness. In 1900 a Parisian bourgeoise of good social standing was still quite happy with periodic footbaths. Inventories suggest that contemporary doctors may have possessed a fair number of halfbaths, but this was because they formed an avant-garde responsible for encouraging hygiene.

For the time being there could be no question of obliging the masses to follow a ritual that the elite was still neglecting. Consequently, they remained condemned to steep in their oily, stinking filth, unless they braved the putrid and immoral promiscuity of public baths. Practices of bodily hygiene became commonplace in the Nivernais only after 1930, according to Guy Thuillier.

Until then, the apprenticeship in cleanliness carried out at school, barracks, and youth organizations aimed at scarcely more than external appearances; the battle over the use of the comb, the ritual cleanliness inspections carried out by schoolmasters, and the advice dispensed by Madame Fouillée in *Le Tour de la France par deux enfants* were clear proof of this.

Nevertheless, several segments of the population were already confronted with the norms formulated for the bourgeoisie. Prisons rather than boarding schools were serving as the laboratories for personal hygiene. As early as 1820, Villermé ordered that convicts comb their hair before washing their faces every morning, and that they wash their hands several times a day and their feet every week. He advocated a weekly review of cleanliness; he wanted new arrivals to be bathed and the administration to insist on short hair. Sanitary reformers asked no more of school children a century later. . . .

22

POPULAR PROTEST

CHARLES TILLY

Protest movements have long formed a major interest for historians trying to fathom the nature of European society. In such movements, ordinary people speak out directly, and may have explicit contact with more familiar political developments. Interpreting popular protest is not, however, an easy task. Workers faced many barriers—the treatment of police, the retaliation of employers, divisions in their own ranks, and earlier protest traditions that had once made sense but now proved organizationally inadequate—as they tried to formulate responses to the growth of factory industry and the new powers employers gained over their living and working conditions.

The following selection deals with the area around Lille, in northern France (the Nord), which had been a stronghold of craft manufacturing, but after 1815 rapidly converted to factory production. The selection describes various kinds of protest actions, the constraints protesters encountered, and changes in goals and organizational form that gradually developed as a result. The role of the Revolution of 1848 and the ensuing Second Republic, until 1851, proved crucial both in demonstrating how old protest impulses persisted and how new directions, including political directions, captured growing attention.

The Lille area did not produce many dramatic outbursts as a first response to industrialization, and this selection helps us understand why. It did generate rebellion, however, and worker evolution was a seedbed for the more formal kinds of labor action that emerged later in the nineteenth century.

By the end of the Middle Ages, the common people of western Europe had developed a standard form of protest—they rioted against deteriorating economic conditions and against more general encroachments on their rights. With the onset of industrialization many groups stepped up their rate of protest, but did not initially change its nature. Protest still largely took the form of riots in the name of past rights and standards, a reaction against changes imposed by the outside world. The protesters sought the restoration of a previous price or wage level. Some of the most dramatic passages in nineteenth-century history, such as the French revolutions of 1830 and 1848,

From: Charles Tilly, *The Contentious French* (Cambridge, MA: Harvard University Press, 1986), pp. 260–71.

resulted in part from these reactions against change. Typically, the groups most involved were not new factory workers, but peasants or artisans, who still had a sense of traditional community and past values on which to base protest as a reaction.

But protest did change, often suddenly, for some groups. The new kind of protest could be vigorous, bitter, and certainly violent. The demand for expanding rights—to vote, to demonstrate, to strike—encouraged more frequent protest than ever before.

Yet we must ask whether or not motivations changed as much as did the form of protest. In the following selection, protest is labeled very neatly, but organization is stressed more than human content. Many people may have accepted new organizational form as a necessity of industrial life, while still harboring traditional sentiments. Others may have turned away from the most overt forms of protest because massive organization was itself unacceptable. The human meaning is more difficult to find in modern protest than it is in traditional protest—which may caution us against accepting too simple a categorization or too optimistic an assessment of the ability of protest to express grievances in modern society.

The twin concentrations of capital and coercion framed nineteenth-century contention. The holders of capital began with a decided advantage. Their control of growing capital in a time of capital intensification helped them become masters of the sphere of production. But the Revolution and Empire had also given them great power in the sphere of coercion. Their access to the state helped them establish a public definition of workers' organization as a threat to public order, of strikes as "disorders" or "troubles" or at least as "violations of the freedom to work."

Workers, furthermore, had carried over from the old regime a principle of organization and collective action that concentration made obsolete. In general, skilled workers in a trade organized at the level of a community, sought to make a common front against the [other] workers of that community, and tried to control the entry of workers into their trade anywhere in the community. To control actual and potential workers in the trade, they deployed a variety of sanctions: sharing of rituals and secrets, pooling for mutual aid, withholding of information and support from nonconformists, plus ritual mockery and direct coercion for blacklegs, ratebreakers, strikebreakers, and other undesirables.

Early nineteenth-century workers likewise had a number of means for putting pressure on employers. The word "strike," which we now associate inevitably with firm-by-firm action, conveys badly their usual mode of action. The British word "turnout" fits better: the routine in which a group of aggrieved workers in a trade assembled to talk over their grievances, then went from shop to shop in that trade throughout the community, made a hullabaloo, called the workers inside to join them, continued their march through the streets until they had assembled as much of the trade as they could muster, moved off to a relatively secure public place (such as a field at the edge of town), debated their grievances, demands, and actions, then sent a delegation to bargain with representatives of the employers.

As employers built large plants employing many workers in different trades, and as the number of workers in a community began to number thousands, the old scale and type of organization no longer served workers well. In skilled crafts employing relatively small numbers and giving their members control of irreplaceable, crucial skills, adaptations of the old forms survived; indeed, with strikes and trade unions illegal, nineteenth-century workers' politics long depended on secret, militant organizations built on craft models. But in the growing remainder of the labor force the old organization atrophied or never formed at all. The growth of large firms and semiskilled industrial labor eventually threatened the artisans on their own ground; through competition or through their direct employment by large capitalists, artisans and skilled workers faced proletarianization.

During the nineteenth century, as capital concentrated, and as the alliance of capital and state became more obvious, workers fashioned new forms of organization and action: the politically active workers' association, the trade union, the public demonstration, the firm-by-firm strike. . . . The Nord took a while to recover from the rigors of the Napoleonic wars. The region bore the brunt of enemy occupation in 1815, then slowly rebuilt its industrial strength. . . .

In Roubaix employers had been cutting wages on the ground that (despite protective tariffs) English competition was doing them in. At the same time they had been recruiting Belgians who were willing to cross the border and work for low wages. They had also been building high-density housing for the workers, deducting the rent from their pay, and evicting workers who proved to be troublesome. Those *coureés* and *forts,* as people called them, were becoming heavily Belgian. On Bastille Day 1819, according to the royal prosecutor,

> rather serious disturbances broke out in that populous and entirely industrial city. . . . Politics has nothing to do with the affair . . . it is a sort of coalition among French workers for the purpose of expelling from Roubaix and the surrounding area the Belgian workers who have settled there, and whose competition brings down a wage that the French would like to see rise. The fourteenth of this month, between eight and nine in the evening, when the workers were leaving their shops, a crowd of four or five hundred people gathered in Roubaix. The aim of that gathering was to attack and expel the foreign workers employed in the same shops. The local police stepped in, and order was restored.

On 15 July three gendarmes on horseback frightened off another gathering, but a rock hit one Belgian; he was said to have shouted, while under the protection of the gendarmes, "You Frenchmen can't do anything to us. We're the bosses here now!" The gatherings continued for days.

The fact that the prosecutor ruled out "politics" meant that no organized group making claims on the national structure of power—republicans, supporters of Napoleon, or anyone else of that ilk—had a hand in the events. In fact Flemish-French hostility as such played only a small part in the local politics of Roubaix and other frontier towns. For the next two decades, workers' politics in the Nord concerned labor markets, wages, and working conditions.

The transition from the Restoration of 1815–1830 to the July Monarchy of 1830–1848 made little difference to the tone or tempo of workers' politics in the Nord. True, a moment of absorption into national politics arrived in 1830; during the July Days, as the news of insurrection arrived from Paris, workers streamed out of the factories of Lille and rushed through the streets breaking windows and shouting "Long live the Charter!" When the cavalry tried to break up the crowds, people stoned them. When the infantry fraternized, the shout changed to "Down with the cavalry! Long live the line!" In Douai, young people "of the working class" went through the streets forcing people to light their lights in celebration of the Revolution.

The struggle with employers, however, continued to preoccupy the Nord's workers. The night of 10 August 1830, for example, workers in Roubaix gathered in large numbers and asked employers for a raise. More precisely, they demanded restoration of the four sous per yard of finished cloth employers had cut from their pay the year before. For resisting that decision by undoing the cloth then in their looms and disassembling the looms themselves, in October 1829 the merchants' court of Roubaix had sentenced several workers at the Motte Brédard plant to two days in jail and court costs. Ten months later, in August 1830, Roubaix weavers "broke the windows of the principal factories," wrote the royal prosecutor, "and entered in force to ask for written agreement to the raise." Although *Le Moniteur Universel* of Paris blamed the action on "foreign workers," the chief division clearly followed class lines.

In general, until the 1840s the Nord's workers relied on the local organization of their trades and made little effort to form unions and other special-purpose associations. More broadly, associations did not begin to play major parts as vehicles of collective action—working-class or bourgeois—until well after the July Revolution. In 1834 the prosecutor of the arrondissement of Lille provided an inventory of associations in the city. He enumerated 106 workers' mutual aid societies, providing sick benefits from pooled funds and named for saints. . . .

To the thinness of formal organization among workers corresponded a near-absence of strikes. Workers in textile towns did occasionally use the informal structure of their trade to keep others away from their jobs, to sanction workers who broke ranks, and to organize an occasional turnout. But on the whole, considering their wages and working conditions, the Nord's textile workers mounted very little collective opposition to the region's capitalists during the 1820s and 1830s.

For serious, long-term strikes during those decades, we must turn to the Nord's miners, especially those who worked for the big Anzin Company in its pits at St.-Waast-la-Haut and Anzin. Citing fierce Belgian competition, the company had begun cutting wages in the early 1820s. At the same time it tightened surveillance and discipline in the mines. The economizing paid off; in 1833 the company's stockholders were receiving an 8 percent return on their investment. The miners complained not only of the four sous in daily pay they had lost in 1823, but also of being treated with contempt by the Anzin Company's officials.

Periodically the miners struck back. Shortly after the July Revolution, for example, they had risen briefly and unsuccessfully. In May 1833 it was a different story. The so-called Four Sous Riot (*émeute des quatre sous*) made its mark in national labor history. When the Anzin Company's governors met in Anzin on 10 May, word spread among miners that the governors were finally going to give back the four sous they had taken away ten years earlier. Nothing of the sort happened. After the disappointing meeting, a new story went the rounds: the company was actually considering another wage cut, and Charles Mathieu (pit supervisor at St.-Waast, whose brother Joseph was mine inspector and mayor of Anzin) had been cashiered for favoring a raise. The story gained credibility from the fact that, shortly after the governors' meeting, Charles Mathieu did leave the company to take a job elsewhere.

On 17 May two or three hundred people—men, women, and children—gathered before the company offices in St.-Waast. They demanded their four sous, called for the firing of three overzealous supervisors, and sang songs whose refrain ran "Down with the Parisians, long live the Mathieux of Anzin!" Some of the miners went to the lodgings of Monnier, one of the three unpopular supervisors, where they broke furniture and tore up clothing.

After the company's general agent, Englishman Mark Jennings, met with members of the crowd, the mayor and the curé of Anzin persuaded the miners and their families to disband. In the meantime, however, company officials had called the police. That evening detachments of gendarmes, cavalry, and infantry, plus 150 national guards, converged on Anzin. During the following days gendarmes made a few arrests, and support for a work stoppage developed in a number of nearby coal mines, but few direct confrontations between miners and troops occurred. Philippe Guignet summarizes the events:

> From 17 to 22 May the miners unquestionably kept the lead; the movement spread, the "forces of order," which were numerically inferior to the massed workers, being unable or unwilling to stop the strikers. That is why the authorities decided to put a stop to the movement on the twenty-second by calling on regular army units. On the twenty-seventh, in a region placed under a state of siege, the miners decided to return to work.

The national authorities who sent in massive force were probably remembering the 1831 silkworkers' strike in Lyon, which turned into a general insurrection; they were not going to let Anzin get out of hand.

As insurgents, the miners of Anzin were remarkably nonviolent during the Four Sous Riot. But as strikers, they looked remarkably like insurgents. In fact during the 1830s the miners and their employers had no established routine— by striking or otherwise—for collective negotiation over employment, wages, and working conditions. Every work stoppage therefore took on a tinge of insurrection.

The increased tempo of industrial conflict during the 1830s and 1840s normalized the strike, at least to some degree. Miners kept up their losing battle for wages and job control. Anzin itself produced another small strike in December 1833, and standup battles in 1837, 1846, and 1848; in these confrontations miners typically tried to stop the pithead machinery, and mine owners typically called in troops to protect their property. During the same period the mines of Denain, Fresnes, Vieux-Condé, and Abscon joined the ranks of major strike producers; in most of their strikes, a walkout from one mine incited a work stoppage in at least one more.

In the later 1830s textile workers of Lille's region began to organize strikes as never before. In the spinning mills of Lille, employers cut the piece rate in 1839. The senior workers of dozens of plants started meeting to plan their defense, first establishing a pool of money to aid the unemployed, then edging toward transforming it into a strike fund. The first full-fledged work stoppage came in August. After a quick settlement of that first dispute, which ended with city officials intervening to cancel the wage reduction, the "elders" of the trade started drafting a citywide agreement.

By mid-September workers were responding to rising food prices by calling for wage increases. Paris' *Le Constitutionnel* clipped this account of the events of 20 September from the *Echo du Nord*:

> Groups of cotton spinners who had left their shops went to various spinning mills to persuade those who were still working to follow them. In some of these plants the rebels started disturbances by throwing stones at the windows. The national guard eagerly took arms; a number of patrols organized at once and spread out through the city, especially toward the threatened places. About nine o'clock that night the groups, which had previously been separated, met together in the main square; one heard incoherent yells, or rather jeers, that the national guard had the good sense to ignore. A police officer read the mayor's edict forbidding riotous assemblies. Immediately afterward, he gave the required three calls to disperse, and the national guard started clearing the square. Heavy rain helped scatter the groups. The following morning at five the national guard was out; its mission was to assure the entry into shops of those workers who didn't want to follow their comrades in rebellion. There were still a few attempts at disorder and a few arrests.

As we might expect, the national guard drew its troops especially from Lille's bourgeoisie.

Although the spinners of Lille did not strike again on any scale until 1848, the series of conflicts in 1839 showed the substantial class division within the city as well as the capacity of its textile workers for collective action. In nearby

Tourcoing, Roubaix, and Fourmies, similar strikes—most often incited by employers' attempts to cut wages, and again typically ending with the authorities' use of armed force against the workers—occurred repeatedly between 1839 and 1848.

During the same period, small signs began to appear that workers were identifying their cause with opposition politics at the national scale. In the Nord those glimmers of political opposition often took on a republican tint but sometimes colored themselves Bonapartist. In 1840 the prosecutor at the royal court of Douai began to report incidents in which people sang the semiseditious *Marseillaise* in the streets or at the theater. In 1841 republicans of Lille and Valenciennes joined the resistance to the national census, seen widely as a government maneuver to extend its control and to clear the way for tax increases.

In 1846, when workers of Roubaix gathered to protest curtailment of the Mardi Gras celebrations, they turned to attacking well-dressed young men as "sons of industrialists," shouting "Down with the industrialists!" and breaking the windows of bourgeois cafés, police stations, and homes of manufacturers. They sang the *Marseillaise* as they marched through the streets. When the radical bourgeois of Lille organized their part of the national campaign for political reform in 1847, a few workers actually joined them. With the news of the February Revolution in Paris, many of the activists in Lille's streets were workers. The theme song of those days was, of course the *Marseillaise*.

Once a provisional republic took power in Paris, workers of the Nord underwent a remarkable mobilization. In Valenciennes, Tourcoing, and especially Lille, workers' marches through the streets became commonplace. Almost immediately after the February Revolution, furthermore, a new round of important strikes began. During 1848 Anzin, Lille, Roubaix, and Tourcoing all had significant strike movements. Then, as Louis Napoleon's government tightened its control, moved to the right, and began its deliberate dismantling of the radical republican movement in the country as a whole, the Nord's workers demobilized.

The experience of Lille shows that process of mobilization and demobilization clearly. When the news of revolution first reached Lille on 25 February 1848, groups of workers entered the prefecture, seized rugs, wall hangings, and a bust of [King] Louis-Philippe from the prefect's dwelling, burned the household goods in the city's Grand'Place, paraded the bust through the streets like a severed head, and threw it in the canal. Groups of workers likewise burned the suburban railroad station at Fives and attacked the interim central station in Lille. Noisy gatherings in the streets continued for several days. The National Guard of Lille took on the task of containing them.

Two weeks later, Lille's workers were again marching. This time, however, they were protesting cuts in the workday (hence in total pay). The city's textile manufacturers, under pressure from the Nord's revolutionary commissioner, Delescluze, had agreed upon the cuts as a way of getting unemployed workers back on the job. A group of workers sought to organize a citywide turnout but failed to bring out all those who had accepted the reduced scale. Strikers gathered outside the working shops, shouted their call, and tried to block the entries. Workers ("accompanied by women and children," according to *Le Siècle,* 20 March 1848) set up barricades and fought the national guard in the streets. But their main business was with employers and strike-breakers. The evening of 14 March, for example, about four hundred men, women, and children had assembled in Lille's Grand'Place and marched off toward the city's spinning plants, singing the *Marseillaise.* . . . At the same time that some workers were in the streets, however, others were attending the Société des Ouvriers, which collaborated with the Société Républicaine des amis du Peuple in the first phases of the revolution at Lille. Although employment, salaries, and working conditions remained the centers of workers' politics, they had once again connected directly with national politics. . . .

Contention in the Nord during the Second Republic combined forms of action that strongly recalled the eighteenth century with other forms that remain familiar today. Attacks on Belgian workers, for example, reached their nineteenth-century peak between 1848 and 1851. Around Denain especially, manufacturing workers tried repeatedly to force the firing and expulsion of Belgians. But Denain was not alone: in May 1848, workers in Tourcoing and in Semain called for Belgians to leave town. Where the workforce in a trade was relatively small and compact, resident workers could still hope to control the local labor market. In time of contraction, that often meant calling for the expulsion of "outsiders," even those who had been at work for a long time.

Similarly, textile workers continued to act via the communitywide turnout: trying to get the entire trade to stop work by marching from shop to shop and by blocking the entrances to unstruck shops. That tactic was becoming decreasingly effective in the towns with large shops and many workers, such as Roubaix. There, the one-firm strike was becoming common.

Struggles over food showed the combination of old and new forms most clearly. The term "food riot" gives a specious sense of continuity; in the nineteenth century, it covers routines as different as blockage of the shipment of grain, seizure of stored grain for placement in the public domain, forced sale of grain or bread below the current market price, direct attacks on presumed profiteers, and demonstrations urging public officials to control prices, distribute food, or punish profiteers. During the Second Republic all of these occurred at one time or another in the Nord.

Blockages occurred fairly often. In April 1848, for example, workers in Dunkerque stopped the departure of a shipload of grain from the port while people in Trélon, Anor, and Baives, on the Belgian border, blocked the shipment of grain out of France. In Anor people also confiscated eight sacks of flour from a merchant and deposited them in the town hall, asking that the municipality distribute the flour free. . . .

In addition to these classic actions, people also organized in ways that broke with the eighteenth-century grain seizure. On 19 May 1848, for instance, "troublemakers" in Villers-Outréaux, near Cambrai, "assessed a contribution in bread and money on those landowners whom they singled out as giving nothing or too little to the poor"; a detachment of gendarmes and fifty cavalrymen soon put a stop to that popular organization of charity. The demand that wages be adjusted to match the price of food, or vice versa, figured repeatedly in the workers' demonstrations in larger cities. . . .

Meanwhile the strike, the demonstration, the election rally, the public meeting had become the standard forms of popular involvement in open struggle. During 1848 and 1849 ordinary people—especially workers—of the Nord had helped combine these newer forms into their part of a national political movement. The repression of 1849 and thereafter checked that variety of popular involvement for twenty years but did not stamp it out entirely.

Golfing on Munchinhampton Common: A hazard on the ladies' course.

III

MATURE INDUSTRIAL SOCIETY

1850–1918

With industrialization well established in central and western Europe, some of the more dramatic social dislocations eased in the later nineteenth century, if only because a smaller percentage of the population was moving from countryside to city—that is, from a traditional to a dynamic environment. Major problems of adaptation remained, however; rural people had only just begun to be brought into industrial economies and political structures. Many workers were still new to the factory setting. Even some older workers, who had successfully preserved elements of a traditional approach to work during the early stages of industrialization, had major problems of adjustment as industrialization became more firmly entrenched.

And the nature of industrial society continued to change. For factory workers and artisans, the introduction of new techniques and the rise of big business organizations created obvious difficulties. Women in many social classes felt the impact of change more acutely in this period than ever before, as new stresses and new opportunities combined. In the early industrial revolution, middle-class women preserved many traditional goals. They worked closely with their husbands in business and expected to bear many children. Working-class women faced a less familiar situation, particularly when they worked outside the home; but again their outlook probably retained important traditional elements. They expected to marry, after which the vast majority would stop working outside the home, and to define their lives through service to their families and a family-based economy. In the later nineteenth century a declining birthrate gave women more free time, and as most women were now exposed to schooling—a minority to advanced schooling—rising levels of education produced new expectations. In some cases expectations outstripped opportunity because the definition of a woman's "place" changed only slowly. Particularly in the middle class, problems of adjustment became increasingly obvious. By the 1900s, one result was an intense feminist movement in many countries.

Issues of gender—the qualities and roles assigned to men as well as women—loom large in this period of European history. The subject is always important in social history. Some periods, however, involve more contest and uncertainty about gender than others. Advancing industrialization, and the culture that accompanied it, tended to separate men and women in the workplace and in attendant movements such as trade unionism. Yet because women were gaining more education and the birthrate was falling, the situation was ripe for social debate. Reassessments occurred at the political level, with feminism, but also at the personal level with discussions of who should do what in the family or how leisure should reflect, or not reflect, specific gender characteristics. Men had their own issues, aside from women's demands, as work became increasingly regimented and, in some cases, sedentary; it seemed important to find some new badges of masculinity. Selections in this section ranging from sports to labor protest to toy preferences to crime show the extent of gender issues, as tensions were both reflected and promoted in a spectrum of basic activities, in all the urban social classes.

The class structure of industrial society solidified. Peasants and artisans were still important, but social inequality increasingly focused on the cities, and on the components of middle and working classes, respectively. Both had origins earlier, but their full definition, and their frequent mutual conflict, took hold as industrialization matured. Probing the values, behaviors, and interactions of the key urban classes offers a vital entry into European social history in the decades around 1900.

The class and gender structures developing at this point were not immutable, but many of the attitudes formed during this period of maturing industrialization proved quite durable. Although many workers were new to their situation and the nature of industrial life continued to change, a recognizable working-class culture began to emerge—one major outgrowth of the general industrialization process that endures in some respects to the present day. Persistent changes in the nature of protest form one aspect of the new popular culture, as earlier experiments turned into a full-fledged labor movement. Many of the new ambiguities in women's lives also persisted.

Along with new definitions and standards for the major social classes—middle class, peasants and workers—and for women, the decades of maturing industrialization also saw an explosion of new leisure forms for all urban groups. Rising standards of living and more time free from work created the opportunity for new leisure; the need for distraction and also for new ways to socialize children and to provide social cohesion guided the actual process of innovation. A new interest in sports arose, soon to become a consuming passion for many people. Other mass leisure forms also took shape, some confirming, some bridging class and gender lines.

The outlines of industrial society were becoming clearer. Most people in western Europe were now accustomed to change, so questions arising from the sheer confrontation between tradition and innovation gave way to more subtle issues. Was the new interest in leisure, for example, an expression of alienation, a desire to escape monotonous labor and recover, if only vicariously, some of the aggression and passion of humanity's primitive ancestors? Or was the rise of leisure a more positive sign, an indication of growing affluence and leisure time and an expression of the desire to develop new fields of individual achievement? The changing position of youth might be seen as an application of modern values to a new age group or as an expression of stress caused by modern institutions and family life, forcing isolation of age segments that did not readily fit the mold. Similar questions apply to more familiar topics: Did the rise of socialism signify a growing belief in progress and an orderly political process on the part of working people? Or did it betoken the institutionalization of class warfare and periodic acts of violence? Was imperialism the product of a confident, dynamic society or of a society that translated its insecurity into aggression abroad? With change established as an inescapable part of modern life, the need to assess its meaning became paramount.

BIBLIOGRAPHY

Despite the currency of generalizations about the middle class, there have been surprisingly few real studies of this group. Charles Morazé, *The Triumph of the Middle Classes* (New York, 1968), interprets modern history in the light of middle-class ascendancy. See also W. J. Reader, *Professional Men* (London, 1966) and R. S. Neale, *Class and Ideology in the 19th Century* (London, 1972). Social mobility studies bear heavily on the middle class; see Hartmut Kaeble, *Historical Research on Social Mobility* (New York, 1981). An excellent overview on middle-class development is E. J. Hobsbawm, *The Age of Capital 1848–1875* (New York, 1975). The key issue of contacts between middle-class values and those of the lower classes is taken up in Reinhard Bendix, *Work and Authority in Industry: Ideologies of Management in the Course of Industrial Labor* (New York, 1956); Sidney Pollard, *The Genesis of Modern Management* (Cambridge, MA, 1965); Peter N. Stearns, *Paths to Authority* (Urbana, IL, 1978); Stephen Crawford, *Technical Workers in an Advanced Society: The Work, Careers and Politics of French Engineers* (New York, 1990); David Blackbourn and Richard Evans, *The German Bourgeoisie: Essays on the Social History of the German Middle Class from the Late Eighteenth to the Early Twentieth Century* (New York, 1991).

The history of women is receiving growing attention. J.A. Banks has written *Prosperity and Parenthood: A Study of Family Planning Among the Victorian Middle Classes* (New York, 1954), and with Olive Banks, *Feminism and Family Planning* (Liverpool, 1964). Good general introductions to the history of women are Martha Vicinus, ed., *Suffer and Be Still: Women in the Victorian Age* (Bloomington, IN, 1972), and *A Widening Sphere: Changing Roles of Victorian Women* (Bloomington, IN, 1977). An important introduction to recent writing and theory is Joan Scott, *Gender and the Politics of History* (New York, 1989). Other valuable collections are Lois Banner and May Hartman, *Clio's Consciousness Raised* (New York, 1974), and Renate Budenthal and Claudia Koonz, eds., *Becoming Visible: Women in European History* (New York, 1976). Bonnie G. Smith, *Ladies of the Leisure Class: The Bourgeoises of Northern France in the 19th Century* (Princeton, 1981) is a vital monograph. Some key trends among working-class women are discussed in Margaret Hewitt, *Wives and Mothers in Victorian Industry* (New York, 1958). William L. O'Neill, *Woman Movement: Feminism in the United States and England* (Chicago, 1969), is a good brief survey of this important movement at the turn of the century. An important survey is Joan Scott and Louise Tilly, *Women, Work and Family* (New York, 1978). See also: John C. Fout, ed., *German Women in the Nineteenth Century: A Social History* (New York, 1976) and Edward Shorter, *A History of Women's Bodies* (New York, 1982); Judith Coffin, *The Politics of Women's Work: The Paris Garment Trades, 1750–1915* (New Jersey, 1996) and Anna Clark, *The Struggle for the Breeches: Gender and the Making of the British Working Class* (Berkeley, 1995).

On masculinity and its recreational and military implications, J.A. Mangan, ed., *Manliness and Morality: Middle-Class Masculinity in Britain and America, 1800–1940* (New York, 1987); Peter N. Stearns, *Be a Man! Males in Modern Society* (rev. ed.,

New York, 1990); Scott Myerley, *British Military Spectacle: From the Napoleonic Wars Through the Crimea* (Cambridge, MA, 1996).

Studies that deal with work as opposed to formal protest movements by labor, are not overabundant, but they cover substantial ground (see also above, Part II, Introduction). For Britain, E. P. Thompson, *The Making of the English Working Class* (New York, 1964), Eric J. Hobsbawm, *Labouring Men: Studies in the History of Labour* (New York, 1964), and John Foster, *Class Struggle and the Industrial Revolution* (New York, 1975) are works of major importance; for the years around 1900, see also Standish Meacham, *A Life Apart: The English Working Class 1890–1914* (Cambridge, MA, 1977). Daniel Walkowitz and Peter N. Stearns, eds., *Workers in the Industrial Revolution* (New Brunswick, NJ, 1974) covers several countries; see also Stearns, *Lives of Labor: Work in Maturing Industrial Society* (New York, 1975). On France, see Michael Hanagan, *The Logic of Solidarity: Artisans and Industrial Workers in Three French Towns 1871–1914* (Urbana, IL, 1980). A fine German case study is David Crew, *Town in the Ruhr: A Social History of Bochum 1860–1914* (New York, 1979). A major survey, with good bibliography, is Dick Geary, *European Labour Protest 1848–1939* (New York, 1981). For other recent works, see Vernon Lidtke, *The Alternative Culture: Socialist Labor in Imperial Germany* (New York, 1985); Donald Reid, *The Miners of Decazeville: A Genealogy of Deindustrialization* (Cambridge, MA, 1985); Patrick Joyce, ed., *The Historical Meanings of Work* (New York, 1987) and Lenard Berlanstein, *The Working People of Paris, 1871–1914* (Baltimore, 1984).

To follow continuities in working-class culture into our own time, see John H. Goldthorpe et al., *The Affluent Worker in the Class Structure* (New York, 1969). See also Robert Blauner, *Alienation and Freedom: The Factory Worker and His Industry* (Chicago, 1964).

Key studies in the history of crime are: J. J. Tobias, *Crime and Industrial Society in the 19th Century* (New York, 1976); Howard Zehr, *Crime and the Development of Modern Society* (Totowa, NJ, 1978); Abdul Lodhi and Charles Tilly, "Urbanization, Crime and Collective Violence in 19th-Century France," *American Journal of Sociology* 49 (1973), 296–318; and V. A. C. Gatrell, Bruce Lenman and Geoffrey Parker, *Crime and the Law: The Social History of Crime in Western Europe Since 1500* (London, 1980). Louis Chevalier, *Dangerous Classes and Laboring Classes* (New York, 1972) deals with perceptions, rather than firm statistics; also interesting is Mary S. Hartman, *Victorian Murderesses* (New York, 1975). Michel Foucault, *Discipline and Punish: The Birth of the Prison*, trans. Alan Sheridan (New York, 1977), is an important interpretation. For some of the changes in twentieth-century criminal patterns that so complicate a modernization model for this topic, see F. H. McClintock and N. Howard Avison, *Crime in England and Wales* (New York, 1969). Recent work includes Eric Johnson and Eric Monkhonen, eds., *The Civilization of Crime: Violence in Town and Country Since the Middle Ages* (Urbana, 1996) and Eric Johnson, *Urbanization and Crime: Germany, 1871–1914* (New York, 1995).

The history of leisure is another of the important subjects that have until recently not been given much attention by serious historians. For specific treatment of youth, see J. A. Mangan, *Athleticism in the Victorian and Edwardian Public School* (Cambridge, England, 1981); John R. Gillis, *Youth and History* (New York, 1974). Other studies of youth are cited in this text in Part 4, on the 20th century.

On the leisure phenomenon generally, see Peter Bailey, *Leisure and Class in Victorian England* (Toronto, 1978): For a brief general interpretation, see Michael Marrus, *The Rise of Leisure* (St. Louis, 1976), and *The Emergence of Leisure* (New York, 1974). Peter C. McIntosh, *Sport in Society* (New York, 1963), and *Physical Education in England since 1800* (London, 1969), are useful. See also William J. Baker, *Sports in the Western World* (Totowa, NJ, 1982); James Walvin, *Football— the People's Game* (London, 1975) and *Leisure and Society, 1830–1950* (London, 1978); Richard Mandell, *The First Modern Olympics* (Berkeley, 1976). Hugh Cunningham, *Leisure in the Industrial Revolution* (New York, 1980) has a rich bibliography. On France, see Richard Holt, *Sport and Society in Modern France* (Hamden, CT, 1981).

On changing demography, in addition to materials on women's history suggested above, see Etienne Van de Walle, *The Female Population of France in the Nineteenth Century* (Princeton, 1974); John Knodel, *The Decline of Fertility in Germany, 1871–1939* (Princeton, 1974); and Ansley Coale and Susan Watkins, eds., *The Decline of Fertility in Europe* (Princeton, 1986). On birth control developments, see Angus McLaren, *Reproductive Rituals: The Perception of Fertility in England from the Sixteenth to the Nineteenth Century* (New York, 1984) and *Sexuality and Social Order: The Debate over the Fertility of Women and Workers in France, 1770–1920* (New York, 1983); an excellent discussion for the United States is James Reed, *The Birth Control Movement and American Society* (Princeton, 1983).

23

THE MIDDLE CLASS

LENARD R. BERLANSTEIN

Europe's middle class was by no means an entirely novel product of industrial society. It drew on older positions and beliefs of merchants and preindustrial professionals, plus the emergence of new kinds of manufacturers at the end of the protoindustrial decades (see Chapter 10). It was in the nineteenth century, however, that the middle class gained new numbers and new economic, political and cultural ascendancy. In the process, key values were refined—as in the almost missionary fervor about the moral quality of work. We have seen the importance of changing views in such areas as cleanliness, and later selections will discuss distinctively middle-class contributions to the formation of gender standards and modern leisure.

The following selection addresses a basic question, surprisingly rarely handled by historians: How did middle-class people work? The focus is on executives in a Parisian gas company (the PGC) from the 1870s to 1900. This was a corporation, beginning to sketch a new kind of reliance on corporate hierarchy and professional engineering expertise. Yet it touched base with older middle-class attitudes, which helps explain how some members of the middle class (in France at least, the process may have been more troubling in Britain) could adapt to new organizational forms. Middle-class beliefs in the later nineteenth century undergirded a devoted, possibly a rather constrained, existence. They also shaped reactions to workers and worker demands. This case study shows much about the middle-class contribution to the growing class tension of the final decades of the century.

Whatever their deficiencies, the [French] technical schools performed an invaluable service to companies like the PGC. In countries like Britain, where such institutes did not exist, filling managerial positions was a great problem. Owners refused to trust salaried executives to use their capital honestly and efficiently, so kinship and friendship played a large role in hiring. The engineering schools of France provided the guarantees of probity and expertise that

From: Lenard R. Berlanstein, "Managers and Engineers in French Big Business of the Nineteenth Century," *The Journal of Social History* (Winter 1988): 218–23, 225–30.

personal familiarity did across the Channel. The PGC relied on the recommendations of the school directors more than any other source of recruitment. Faith in the excellence of the alma mater, reassurances provided by shared experiences, and established contacts made managers draw their new colleagues from their own schools. The factory chief Arson recommended one engineer after another from the École Centrale, from which he graduated in 1841. As his influence waned and Paul Gigot, his assistant, took charge, appointments gravitated to the École des Mines, Gigot's alma mater.

More than excellence of training, the schools offered the PGC a cadre of managers with the proper attitudes and firm character. Despite minor variations in curriculum, all the institutes sought to impart an ideology of sobriety, discipline, and assiduousness. Standards of accomplishment were very high, and the schools worked the students mercilessly. Consciousness of class rank, continuously re-assessed, ritualized the view of life as a constant struggle. Any student who did not embrace hard work and constant application left the program. Those who remained developed a sense of intellectual and moral elitism. For good reason one historian of the École Centrale has labeled it a "factory of the bourgeoisie." Although not all graduates attained the schools' ideals, the PGC found among them a group of men with ample aptitude for science, a passion to apply it, and a commitment to the work ethic. Satisfied with the graduates of these institutes and loyal to them, the PGC failed to support the creation of more practically-oriented schools at the end of the century. The students of Centrale . . . did what they had to do and accepted what they had to accept on the job. . . .

The company placed extensive demands upon them. It taxed them to assume responsibility in areas far removed from the engineering problems they had studied. It transferred them to new departments which required a new round of learning. That many managers spent nearly all their waking hours on the job, either by choice or necessity, seems likely. Much of this labor was self-directed, putting to the test the work ethic their training had sought to instill.

Managers at all levels had to master four areas of performance—daily operations, planning, financial oversight, and personal research. . . . Even top management supervised or intervened in the details of daily routine. Most of such burdens fell on lower managers, however, and the PGC was probably understaffed at this level. The chief of the by-products department ran by himself an operation that involved revenues of some two to three million francs and 250 workers. Several superintendents directed plants with nearly a thousand laborers and millions of francs in equipment with the assistance of, at most, one other engineer.

Apart from the duties posed by current and future operations, the managers undertook individual research and improvement projects. They were usually self-directed, and the director was poorly informed about them, so the company did not gain the benefits of coordinated research and development. Nonetheless, the handiwork of the engineers occasionally proved very useful to the company. It was common for managers to do their work in areas that were not directly related to their duties within the firm. The assistant head of the factory division developed a crucial device which improved gas distribution. A chief of the coke department was responsible for important innovations in street lighting. The chief of factories worked on creating new gas engines. The managers undoubtedly conceived of their projects as the most noble aspect of their work, the most befitting their role as engineers.

Such duties left little room for leisure or, indeed, any meaningful distinction between free time and work. Managers did task-oriented labor, and there were no fixed hours on the job. Factory superintendents and their assistants lived at the work site so were on duty at all times. Sunday labor, at least on personal projects, may have been normal. When the owner of the Rossini Theatre bestirred himself early one Sunday morning to have gas restored to his establishment, he found the chief of the lighting department at his office. The chief sent the impresario to see the director, who was also at work and assured him that both executives would be on the job all day. As far as we can discern from the incomplete records, vacations were not part of the annual calendar. Starting in the late 1880s, there were requests for a week's leave during the slow summer season, but these came from a minority of engineers. It was not only for their laborers that the management conceived of hard work seven days a week, 52 weeks a year, as natural and inevitable.

Beyond constant application, the company also demanded a rare combination of moral qualities from its executives. They had to be eager to accept new challenges and grow on the job. The self-confidence to make decisions on matters that were not susceptible to mathematical logic was a basic requirement of their work. It was a virtue they did not seem to lack. However, self-confidence had to be tempered by self-effacement when necessary. The company was not especially sensitive to the egos of their executives and assumed their pride was expendable. The director once sent the assistant factory chief, Servier, to examine an electric pressure regulator which competed with his own invention. The mission was still more delicate in that his competitor had accused Servier of copying. Arson, his superior, found that Servier had nonetheless carried out the task with "the most perfect impartiality." . . .

For all the burdens the company imposed on its executives, relations between it and the managers were more familial than contractual. Paternalistic policies extended to areas beyond life-long employment. If a manager died on the job, the PGC assumed responsibility for the education of his children. It welcomed the engineers' sons into the firm and, when the children were competent, delighted in having them succeed their fathers. Corporate symbolism and celebration exalted long service to the firm—perhaps above all other virtues. When the superintendent Cury retired after 58 years with the PGC and with one of the pre-merger gas companies, an elaborate banquet was held in his honor, and he received his full salary as a pension. None of the engineers who made more fundamental contributions to the prosperity of the firm received such recognition. Thus, the culture of paternalism encompassed executives as well as the subordinate personnel, but with this difference: The company would always regard its workers as children needing stern guidance whereas it expected managers to assume all the duties of their high positions. . . .

Managerial salaries at the PGC were probably in line with those at other large firms—that would help account for the career-long commitments on the parts of most engineers—but the pay was by no means munificent. . . .

Modesty of horizons was a key feature of most managers' work experience. Their rigorous training completed, they began their careers in humble posts—draftsmen, secretaries to middle managers, assistants to assistant plant superintendents—for a few years at the very least. Even Charles Boisière, a graduate of the Polytechnique as well as the École des Mines, spent three years as a draftsman with the company. When he had become chief of the coal department and was recommended for the Légion d'honneur, his file did not even mention that phase of his career. The *centralien* Théodore Bouffé began as nothing more than a chief foreman in the gas distillation plant. Engineers did not usually remain at such lowly posts for more than two or three years, but the position of assistant factory superintendent—not too glorious nor remunerative in itself—could be more enduring. Several managers were stuck as assistants for ten years or more. One graduate of Centrale entered the PGC in 1879 and was still assistant superintendent of the Passy plant in 1902. Moreover, such unassuming starts were not usually purgatories inevitably leading to grander positions. After twenty years the typical engineer climbed from assistant plant supervisor to superintendent, from technician to assistant department chief, from a salary of 2,400 francs to one of 6,000 or 8,000 francs.

Blocked channels of advancement were inevitable. The volume of business of the PGC expanded rapidly, [but] . . . middle and top management positions hardly grew more numerous. Opportunities were further constricted by the paternalistic policies of the company. A department head remained on the job until his retirement with his successor chosen at an early age. The firm did not remove him even when aptitude or capacity had diminished. The prospects of a young engineer were thus dominated by patient waiting. . . . Thus, the take-off into industrial capitalism in France did not produce a situation of openness, fluidity, and dramatic mobility for most in this emerging category of salaried managers. Patient anticipation of small advances characterized their careers.

It is easy to believe that the modesty of horizons facing the majority of engineers caused some disappointment, and perhaps even distress; but the outward response was resignation to that fate or purely individualistic efforts to improve their situation. Rarely did managers draw enough attention to their problems to make the corporation reconsider its policies. . . .

Drawing a psychological portrait of French managers, Charles Kindleberger mentioned elitism, arrogance, and the incapacity for human relations as outstanding traits. To be sure, the engineers of the PGC did uphold the formality of a bourgeois social code and were well aware that they constituted an elite. Nonetheless, their acceptance of modest horizons and the loyalty they accorded to an organization which demanded so much and rewarded so sparingly reveals other, more deeply grounded, characteristics. Duty and hard work were the most prominent features the engineers used to represent themselves—and perhaps they were correct. A useful point of departure for exploring their personalities and attitudes would be their successful completion of training that exalted effort, discipline, and conformity to hierarchical rules. While many excellent students could not endure the strains, the managers of the PGC had thrived in this demanding environment. All but three of 48 graduates of Centrale and [the school of] Mines had ranked in the top half of their classes; 47 per cent were in the top quarter. As students, they had nearly always received favorable reports on conduct and attitude. Making noise in study hall was about the worst sin any of them had committed. Ultimately, we can find very few documents shedding light on the managers as people; yet, the eulogy describing one former superintendent of the machinery department as "cold, feeling all the weight of the responsibility he bore" rings true. Similarly, the eulogy for the factory manager Biju-Duval stressed his serious and reserved demeanor; music and family had been his only refuges from work. Charles Monard of the coal department was reportedly a "stranger to worldly distractions" and someone with few interests outside his labors.

Circumstances give such testimony a note of verisimilitude. The engineer-managers, from wealthy families, had been raised in or sent to Paris at a young age for serious study. They had resisted all the temptations of that modern Babylon and had fulfilled parental expectations by passing through a clearly charted course based on rigorous selection. Deferred gratification and self-control allowed them to attain the qualifications necessary for employment at the PGC. Their acceptance of prospects within the corporation was an exercise of habits they had developed early in life. . . .

However, such familiarity with the rhetoric of industrial paternalism and abstract approval for initiatives to engender social peace did not make the managers of the PGC into model bourgeois reformers. The engineers' commitments to paternalism were both limited and opportunistic. Their interest in housing, pensions, profit-sharing, and other such schemes may have been sincere but always emerged as part of a wider plan for social control. Plans to offer workers these benefits arose when subordinates challenged their authority in a serious manner and waned the moment the threat had passed and the expense began to appear as unnecessary. Ultimately, the managers gave a much higher priority to thrift as a virtue for its own sake than to paternalism. While their attention to improving the workers' lives (as they saw it) came and went and usually foundered on the question of cost, their striving to save the corporation money was constant and serious, even when profit rates soared and the public griped about them. The engineers of the PGC were too conscious of being stewards of other people's capital to be good paternalists.

It has sometimes been suggested that engineers were strategically placed to serve as mediators between industrialists and labor, that they were active agents in making capitalism more humane. The case of the PGC does not sustain the claim. Its managers were unable to transcend the perceived conflict of cultures between themselves and workers. In the end, they proved unable to be genuinely generous toward their underlings. Their motives for introducing gestures of good will were transparent, and understood as such. Quite possibly, these limits were another legacy of the engineers' own background and experience. Schooled, literally, in deferred gratification, they learned that life was a struggle from which even their privileged births did not preserve them. They were intent on living by the principle that meeting obligation was its own reward. Expecting mediocre compensation, working most of their waking hours, and living frugally, engineers could have little sympathy for demands for shorter hours and higher pay. The workers' refusal to see things their way only confirmed their worst fears and reinforced their prejudices. If such stern precepts were, in fact, the outcome of their training and career experiences, then the engineers' culture was one more reason for troubled industrial relations in France.

24

MIDDLE-CLASS WOMEN

PATRICIA BRANCA

There has never been much question that the middle-class woman of the nineteenth century was in a novel position, but there has been great debate over what the novelty consisted of. Some historians see the woman trapped in an essentially idle domestic role, praised for her purity and lack of sexual desire, pampered as an ornament, but given no effective life functions other than demonstrating a few social graces and bearing children. They note that this woman participated in some important changes. The middle class pioneered birth control, though this can be seen as a decision by sexless women to limit their responsibilities still further or by harried husbands to reduce the drain on the family budget. From the middle class, unquestionably, came women reformers and ultimately feminists, but they are seen as rebels against the middle-class way of life, its vacuity and boredom, not as positive products of it. Indeed, in this view, the Victorian woman has only a negative impact on modernization, symbolizing values and constraints against which really modern women had to fight and must fight still.

Patricia Branca takes a different view. Dealing with British women around 1850, at the height of Victorianism, she admits the primacy of the household for women, but sees the middle-class wife and mother as a key agent of change. Far from functionless, she was burdened with huge responsibilities, many of which were newly defined. Motherhood, for example, became much more arduous with fathers at work outside the home. Moreover, with a new sense of concern for children's health and well-being, changes in the concept of the child became central to the life of adult women. As mothers and housewives, women worked in novel urban surroundings, amid intense criticism for failures ranging from sloppiness to inadequate child care. On the whole, despite great anxiety, women met the challenge by applying much the same mentality that their husbands were developing in the business and professional worlds. Above all, this fostered a desire to gain new dominion over their lot. Birth control, stressed again as a middle-class innovation, here stems from women's modernized outlook, their openness to new techniques, and their desire for satisfactory self-expression.

From: Patricia Branca, *Silent Sisterhood: Middle-Class Women in the Victorian Home* (Pittsburgh, PA: Carnegie-Mellon University Press, 1975), pp. 95–96, 108–109, 114, 137–38, 144–53.

Ending with the late nineteenth century, Branca leaves open the question of women's future. Would they be able to apply their new mentality to a wider sphere, or did their horizons remain too purely domestic even to cope with the implications of birth control itself in reducing the domestic function? Was their adaptation, in other words, part of the larger social process, or was it distinctly female, leaving women changed but still trapped in a set of gender roles that would find them ill-prepared for the twentieth century? In recent decades, more obvious changes in women's situation have occurred than took place in the nineteenth century, but Branca would view such changes largely as a continuation of the trends launched in the Victorian era, not simply as a rebellion against this era as many believe.

The Victorian woman's life would never be quite the same with the birth of her first child. Most of her thoughts, her worries, and her energies would revolve around her child, and with each child the responsibilities grew more and more intense. She did not feel confident in the adequacy of her maternal instincts and so she worried continually about her child and its care. Her major concern was for the child's health. With every sickness of childhood, the mother's anxieties heightened. Even the most basic aspects of child care, for example, feeding and discipline, were to create serious problems for her. She continually sought advice on the best method of care for her child. But in the end, as was the case with her own health, there was very little she could do to improve the child's situation given the limited means available and the traditionalism which still maintained a strong hold on this part of her life.

With each new birth, the Victorian mother experienced many anxious moments wondering if the babe would live or die. The fate of thousands of infants dying prematurely every year was to become a burning issue in Victorian society. The outcry against the needless tragedy of infant mortality continued throughout the century. The sentiment expressed was similar to that concerning the state of maternal mortality, but more intense because of the greater numbers involved and the helplessness of the victim. A declining sense of fatalism and a growing determination that this tragedy need not be, were again much in evidence. A typical reaction was that of Dr. Alfred Fennings, author of *Every Mother's Book: or the Child's Best Doctor* who noted that

> The OMNISCIENT GOD never intended that nearly half the babies born in this country should die as they now do, before they are five years old. Carelessness . . . and a general ignorance of simple and safe remedies to cure their peculiar diseases have been the fatal causes.

Dr. R. Hall Bakewell, who wrote a series of articles on "Infant Mortality, and Its Causes" for *The British Mothers' Journal,* was of the same belief.

> We cannot deny that there must be something wrong in the management of children during the early years. Children are not sent into the world to die,

they are sent to live to a natural term of man's life; and a system by which one-fifth of all who are born never see the first anniversary of their birth, must be radically wrong somewhere.

These are just two examples of the growing concern over infant care. There were hundreds of books published and articles written specifically on child care. The books were widely publicized: for example, Dr. Fennings' book was advertised regularly in *The Mothers' Friend,* a monthly magazine. One of the advertisements made the following claim:

> Do not let your children die. Fennings' *Every Mother's Book* contains everything a mother ought to know about her child's Feeding, Teething, Sleeping, Weaning, also Hints, Cautions, Remedies for all diseases, and Secrets worth 500 Guineas. Mothers and Fathers, save your child's life by reading it. Its instructions have already saved thousands.

However, in spite of the intense concern, in spite of the sage advice, infant mortality remained a perplexing problem for the Victorian mother. The infant deathbed scene so popular with the religious writers, the grief of a bereaved mother at the loss of her child, which was a regular feature in many of the women's magazines, reflected grim reality. . . .

> "Doctors . . . gave it eight calomel powders, applied one leech to the chest, one blister to the chest, six mustard plasters, and gave it antimony wine and other medicines in abundance. Yet the poor thing died!" The friend in amazement replied, "Died! It would have been a miracle if it had lived."

It is difficult to say when women sought medical attention for a sick child. Judging from the mortality rates it would appear that it was not often enough or soon enough. Traditional ideas about childhood illnesses were still very strong, as indicated by Dr. Bakewell in his last article on infant mortality. His warning was that

> I would caution my readers against the notion, too prevalent among mothers, that ailments will get well of themselves when the child has cut all its teeth. Very frequently we see children suffering from scrofulous and other constitutional diseases, who are undergoing no treatment, because their mothers "fancy" it is nothing but the teeth.

He also noted that many children died of bronchitis because their mothers failed to take them to a physician soon enough. Mothers ignorant of the disease treated it as a cold, but even a delay of twenty-four hours could make the case hopeless because of the rapid progress of the disease in infants. But in many cases even when a doctor's advice was sought it was of little use, because of the lack of knowledge of pediatric care. Traditionalism and the state of medical practice supplemented each other.

Hence the growing concern about children's health enhanced anxieties on the mothers' part and at the same time, in public discussions, produced a barrage of criticisms of maternal care. Not yet would the concern produce the kind of knowledge about the infant's health and care that was needed. As with the advice on women's health, the advice for child care was too general, based in fact on the same three principles of general health: regulation of diet, proper clothing and plenty of fresh air and exercise. There was little concrete assistance for the mother faced with serious illness and the prospect of frequent infant death. The middle-class mother, no longer resigned to infant mortality, had to feel an acute sense of helplessness and frustration when she realized that despite her efforts and intentions the fate of her child was still so very precarious.

Along with the growing concern for the physical health of the child a profound interest developed in securing the child's mental and moral health. Here too a new attitude toward children was beginning to make strong inroads among the middle-class, by mid-century, and was to alter child-rearing methods significantly by the end of the century. The child was beginning to be viewed as an individual with very particular needs which only a loving mother could fulfill. The ramifications of this new concept of the child for the Victorian mother were indeed great, as they increased her responsibilities to the child even more. . . .

The deliberate limitation of family size was one of the principal contributions of middle-class women to the modernization process of women generally. This decision flowed not only from the new definitions of childhood and motherhood; it represented the only means available in the mid-nineteenth century of resolving several key problems arising from the new situation and new consciousness of women. As manager of the household the middle-class woman, confronted with limited means, was acutely aware of the expenses involved in maintaining her children in the new fashion. Also birth control was the most practical means of coping with the unresolved problems of maternal mortality.

The positive aspects of the decision to control births were perhaps the most compelling for the middle-class woman. As we will see, the middle-class woman's new image of self involved a new sexuality—one of more intense personal enjoyment. In order to maximize sexual enjoyment, it was necessary to prevent the traditional consequences of sex—pregnancy. Through the adoption of birth control the middle-class woman found the most important ingredient to liberation. . . .

It is probable that the most significant devices involved in the middle-class birth rate decline were the sponge, the douche, and the vaginal diaphragm. One cannot ignore the fact that all the other methods—abstinence, *coitus interruptus,* and the condom—were well-known before the nineteenth century, yet it was not until the introduction and development of the three new methods of birth control that the birth rate began to drop significantly. The fact that the newer methods were designed for the female at a time when she was beginning to exert more and more control over her body also cannot be ignored. Just as the woman rejected the fatalistic attitude related to pain in childbirth and sought chloroform, just as she rejected the fatalistic attitude toward the discomfort and burden of nursing and sought artificial feeding methods, so she rejected the fatalistic attitude to the inevitability of pregnancy and sought contraceptive devices. Is it mere coincidence that as the burdens and responsibilities of motherhood increased the demand for and production of birth control methods particularly for the woman also increased? Overall, the array of available contraceptive devices makes it abundantly clear that the woman was an important factor in the decision-making process. This is not to imply that the husband had no part to play, though the advertisement for the Check Pessary suggested that this might sometimes be the case. The mutuality of decision-making so commonly invoked by the marriage manuals may well have operated in this area. We can reasonably be sure that the woman was no passive partner and that her changing values and situation—even more than economic factors—heavily influenced the decision taken, whether by husband and wife together or, as was technically possible, by the wife alone.

The Victorian middle-class woman experienced dramatic changes in her role as mother. She challenged the traditional attitude toward infant mortality and maternal mortality by seeking advice on better care for herself and the child. Unfortunately, until very late in the nineteenth century, the challenge was successful only in so far as she was able to limit the number of children she had, and thereby lessen the risk of death for herself and her child. Here again, the development of birth control is a vital feature of the history of Victorian motherhood.

The Victorian woman took her role as mother seriously. She realized the importance of the new emphasis on the intimate relationship of mother to child, which added significantly not only to the physical work involved with child care, but also to the mental strain on the mother's part. She assumed complete responsibility for the future health and happiness of her child. The new birth control methods aided her in meeting her responsibilities as mother and helped eliminate an important threat to her life and health. . . .

After an examination of some of the more important aspects in the life of the middle-class woman, one begins seriously to question if the Victorian woman, as she has so long been depicted, ever really existed. Certainly, the woman whose life was characterized as leisurely, dependent, prudish, and boring was not the married middle-class woman of the nineteenth century. Whether or not the image applies to upper-class women remains to be investigated, and it is a task worth undertaking in nineteenth-century English social history. The woman portrayed in this study perhaps lacked some of the glamor and romantic flavor of the woman in the image. However her life, viewed in terms of realities, in terms of the problems she encountered, gives the Victorian woman more meaning and substance than ever before. Within the context of the family, her role was not only functional but central and crucial. One could not possibly understand anything about the Victorian family without understanding the woman in the family, who nurtured it, who managed it, who comforted it. In her role as mistress of the house, in her relationship with domestics and most importantly, in her role as mother, the middle-class woman of the nineteenth century defined herself.

Yet the middle-class woman's historical role transcended the boundaries of the family during the nineteenth century, for she was caught up in the broader transformation of English society. In her daily functions she began to develop attitudes and behavior patterns that form part of the process of modernization. The evolution was incomplete, even well after the 1880s, for the middle-class woman retained important links with traditional values. And assessment in these terms is complicated by the failure, heretofore, to apply any but economic criteria of modernization to the history of women. Nevertheless, the stresses and problems with which this study has been concerned cannot be understood without relating them to a more fundamental evolution, in which middle-class women led the way. If other women, many of them unmarried, seem as individuals closer to a modern set of values during the nineteenth century, the married middle-class women constituted the first large category to undergo the modernization process, precisely because they applied it within the context of the family.

Before proceeding with this discussion, it is necessary to elaborate the precise definition of modernization. Modernization involves industrialization and urbanization on a broad scale. Concentrated population centers replace isolated rural communities as the normal human environment. The nature of work obviously changes and the bulk of the populace is removed from the land. And modernization brings about not only changes in work and style of living, but also a new attitude of mind, which in the long run is probably its more significant feature.

Modern man has conventionally been defined as possessing a mentality that, for the most part, is open to innovation and new experiences. This involves belief in planning and organization in every aspect of life, in the benefits of science and technology, and a conviction that one's environment was calculable, that it could be improved. The modern mind rejects fatalism, and it is present- and future-oriented rather than backward-looking. Characterization of modern man in many ways defines the new middle-class man of the nineteenth century, and in combination the modernization theme and progressive middle-class values are familiar enough. But what about modern woman? Since this study claimed from the outset that the Victorian middle-class woman was the first modern woman, it is necessary to apply the definition of modernization to her life. Did she follow the same pattern? Did she share the same outlook?

The process of modernization was never a voluntary process for women (nor was it for men). It was more a result of outside forces, the new pressures of urban industrial society coming together and making their impact in the nineteenth century, first on the values of the middle class. More than her upper-class sister or her working-class sister, the middle-class woman, in order to maintain herself in this period of great transition, had to adapt to new economic means and a new environment. The working- and upper-class woman long maintained more traditional life styles. For example, the upper-class woman never encountered the economic pressures which continually perplexed the middle-class woman in her effort to maintain an appropriate living standard. The upper-class woman could still afford her retinue of servants and enjoy the society and seasons of the fashionable world during most of the nineteenth century. While the working-class woman shared more of the experiences of the middle-class woman, on the whole, and was certainly deeply affected by industrialization, her life was restricted by a number of factors. Her material means were long insufficient to enable her to alter greatly her lot in life. Her education and outlook were not the same as those of the middle-class woman. Her attitudes toward ordering her home and children remained tradition-bound for the greater part of the nineteenth century. In some respects, in the initial reaction to industrialization the working-class woman developed a special function in preserving as many traditional familial values as possible, to cushion the shock of change. In contrast, the middle-class woman was ultimately able not only to react to change but to initiate some changes on her own. The primary impulse toward modernization stemmed from the middle-class woman's accession to a modest level of prosperity which ultimately brought about a new life style—a life style defined by middle-class values and goals—which neither imitated the aristocracy or attempted to throw up purely traditional defenses against change within the family.

The impact of urban living was profound for the middle-class woman of the nineteenth century. The problems of urbanization—overcrowding, polluted waters and air—were not of great concern for upper-class women, who maintained control of the better sections of the city during most of the century. Also the upper-class woman was able to maintain her traditional rural ties by keeping a place in the country. However, urban society was the only life for the new middle-class woman and in this she shared many of the problems of urbanization with the working-class woman. But in contrast to the ability of many working-class wives to recreate a supportive family network, the middle-class woman was more on her own. Admittedly, until a serious investigation is made into the demographic changes of the middle class in the nineteenth century, we have to rely upon impressionistic evidence. It appears from the literature of the day that one of the special problems for the middle-class woman was the frequent changing of residence. The results of this constant state of flux was that the middle-class woman had no sense of roots, no sense of belonging to an established community, and often lacked strong extended family ties. It is interesting to note that in all the various sources used for this study, there is no mention of any type of family relationship beyond the nuclear family. Never once was there a reference to the role of grandparents, aunts, uncles, or cousins. This lack of relationships beyond the immediate family was particularly striking in the discussions on pregnancy. It would seem likely that at this very important event in a woman's life she would have her mother or sister or some other close relative assist her. However, the middle-class woman was advised to seek the aid of a friendly neighbor. The absence of guidance from experienced kin could have accounted for the middle-class woman's need for such fundamental advice on child care. Also the middle-class woman would be able to innovate in child-rearing more easily without the more traditional-bound influence of her mother. She was certainly freer to adopt artificial feeding methods and contraceptive techniques.

Another important aspect of the modernization process in the lives of married middle-class women, which must be viewed as both cause and result, was the declining influence of religion in their lives. Historians have generally accepted and documented the overall decline of religion in the nineteenth century. It is well known that the returns of the Religious Census of 1851 indicated severe limitations in the numbers attending church, for approximately half the population was not present at religious services. Contemporaries claimed that widespread absenteeism was due mainly to a waning of religion among the working class, and subsequent historians have generally accepted this position. However, more recently, it has been noted that "there was proportionately as much conscious unbelief, if not indifference, in the Victorian middle-class as amongst the workers. . . ." Yet even if this point is accepted it is tempting to assume that indifference was confined to men only; and the image of the Victorian middle-class woman as extremely pious and religious continues to persist. However, there were some indications of changes in women's outlook during the nineteenth century which suggest, at least, a growing modification of traditional religious beliefs. There is no need to claim complete separation or a defined anti-religious sentiment; but religion lost some of its meaning for middle-class women.

One indication of the declining influence of religion was the increasing secularism of the material read by women. In the early years of the century, the printed matter for women was primarily of a religious nature. By the second half of the century, the literature was almost completely lacking in religious inspiration. The few religious magazines, such as *The British Mothers' Magazine,* constantly bemoaned the decline of religion among the fairer sex. One example of the new trend of secularism was found in the editorial policy of the very popular *Englishwoman's Domestic Magazine,* which stated that it was the policy of the magazine to exclude all religious composition from its pages. It would not answer any theological questions, or even publish poetry of a religious nature. Looking through the hundreds of magazines printed in the nineteenth century for women, one is left with the impression that women were more concerned with the condition of their wash or the nature of their complexions than the state of their souls.

In sum, middle-class women shared with other groups many of the general pressures of urbanization. They shared also a decline of religious interest, and this may have had a distinctive impact on them because of their exposure to secular reading materials. Their ability to modernize was particularly enhanced by an unusually nucleated family structure and by the ability to forge a standard of living above the subsistence level. Other causes may have been involved, for we are in a better position to describe the modernization process than to assess the reasons for its special applicability to middle-class women, but even this short list suffices to explain why middle-class women were able to innovate in response to new pressures.

But not all middle-class women could adapt. Even for most, as we shall see, modernization should not be regarded as a triumphant conquest of progress over tradition but as a painful, often confusing, reaction to change. Some women could not manage even this, especially given the real physical burdens that still defined their lot. As with most social groups, middle-class women divided between adapters and nonadapters, although we are not yet in a position to suggest the size of the latter group and the boundary line is admittedly unclear.

The rapidity and vastness of change could cause a sense of bewilderment, which was especially difficult for many women to cope with because they had very little outlet for their tensions. The growing sense of insecurity seen in the many letters asking for advice is one sign of the tensions modern society produced in the life of the middle-class woman. Forced into the mainstream of a new style of living, the middle-class woman developed anxieties, as we have suggested in the study of her various roles in the family. The changing concept of motherhood is a case in point. The middle-class woman believed that she could be a better mother so she ventured new methods of child-rearing. However, she was still very insecure about the new ways; hence the continual seeking of advice, perhaps as a source of reassurance. In some respects aspirations changed more rapidly than reality, as in the desire for better health or for an orderly improvement in the standard of living, which added frustrations to anxieties.

Not surprisingly, given the tensions of initial modernization, some symptoms of disturbance emerged among some middle-class women. There is evidence that some women sought refuge in alcohol and drugs. The subject of alcoholism among women was discussed a number of times, indicating that it was a serious problem for some. In 1870 a letter appeared in the *EDM* from "A Sufferer of Low Spirits," asking advice from other women on her problem with depression and alcohol. Especially in the health manuals, women were often warned about the ill effects of alcohol. In the manual, *The New Home; Or Wedded Life,* the story was told of a young girl who came to realize the folly of taking a little gin, or brandy, or beer every time she was low, overworked, or simply out of sorts. The relief it offered was very brief, but the destruction it wrought upon her health was lasting. Another indication that women might have resorted to alcohol is suggested by the article "Intemperance in Women, with Special Reference to its Effects on the Reproductive System," which appeared in *The British Medical Journal.* The author noted that one of the principal causes of alcoholism among women was domestic problems.

Drugs were commonly used in the nineteenth century and were readily available, as was seen in the discussion of infant mortality. There is, again, no direct evidence about the use of drugs by women, but some contemporary observers noted a problem here too. For example, Dr. Robert Dick, in his health manual, made the following observation on the need of drugs by women:

> Many women would pass the most indifferent night; many would be inade-
> quate to the task or duty of entertaining their guests or meeting their friends:
> in others the chagrins of life would prey too severely; regrets and disappoint-
> ments and painful reminiscents would visit them too acutely did they not
> deaden the poignancy of suffering, actual or remembered, by the "drowsy
> syrups"; . . . or by something analogous.

He remarked that many women, because of the pressures of society, needed artificial sedatives or stimulants, such as opium, morphia, hyoscyamus, prussic
acid, camphor, musk and valerian. Further indication of the probability of
considerable drug use comes in the many home remedies found in the manuals and periodicals for headaches or sleeplessness which included strong
dosages of drugs. The following is a preparation recommended for use as a
sedative: orange flower water—2 oz., laurel water—1 oz., syrup of poppies—
½ oz., acetate of morphia—½ grain. A teaspoon of the above was to be taken
every hour.

All of this, obviously, involves impressionistic evidence. There is no reason
to suggest that alcoholism or abuse of drugs were the normal lot of middle-
class women or even that they necessarily followed from the tensions of modernization in every case. The extent of the phenomena cannot presently be determined, but they must be taken into account both because they suggest an
interesting group of women who could not cope with their lot and because
they emphasize some of the pressures that women more generally encountered
during the period.

The more durable impact of modernization on the life of the middle-class
woman can be seen more directly by looking back upon the discussion of mistress of the house. It was shown that the middle-class woman's most important considerations here were time and money. She never seemed to have
enough of either, so they required of her careful planning and organization.
Admittedly, she was not totally successful in meeting these requirements, but
she did display a willingness to accept and try the new concepts. She was the
major purchaser of the proliferating manuals that proclaimed the new science
of domestic economy. She seemed to realize that she had novel problems which
required new solutions.

One of the clearest illustrations of the middle-class woman's willingness to
participate in the mainstream of modern society was her acceptance of innovation and technology into her home. The sewing machine is one very important example. Objections were voiced concerning the sewing machine, similar
in many ways to the objections roused early in the century over the introduction of machines into industry. There was a lament that the sewing machines
would destroy the long-valued skill of hand sewing—that element of personal
touch associated with the craft and womanhood. However, the criticism was
never persuasive enough to deter the middle-class woman as she readily

adopted this new invention and eagerly sought information on it. No doubt the primary reason women welcomed this advance in technology was necessity. There were just so many hours in the day, and so much time to spend on sewing. With the sewing machine, the middle-class woman was able efficiently and economically to come to terms with both problems. However, one cannot neglect the fact that she was willing to give up, almost overnight, a long tradition of hand sewing in favor of a machine which did take away much of the personal touch. One could further suggest that the sewing machine was, in some ways, an expression of the woman's growing sense of individualism within the household. In buying the machine she acquired a new piece of property that was hers, as well as one that worked primarily to her own benefit. This does not mean that she was the heroine of passive consumerism as depicted in the conventional image—the manifestation of the paraphernalia of gentility—but in her own sphere she was trying to define herself, as well as make her life easier, in new ways.

Viewed in the light of modernization, the familiar list of other household innovations that gained ground in the later nineteenth century assumes new importance. One could argue that if the middle-class woman had not been so receptive to innovation, the process of modernization, which depended on mechanization, could not have progressed as rapidly as it did. As was noted in the earlier discussion of the mistress of the house, the middle-class woman was the prime consumer of many of the new products of industrialization. She was the only woman who both needed and could afford the advances in technology. The upper-class woman with her retinue of servants did not necessarily need the innovations, while the working-class women could not afford them. Other major industries, such as advertising and women's magazines, depended heavily on the middle-class woman as consumer. In other words, because of her new attitudes and her decision-making power, the middle-class woman emerged as a significant force for consumer-related economic development.

There are other aspects of the process of modernization in the life of the middle-class woman which are not as easy to recognize but equally significant. In the discussion on health it was shown that the middle-class woman was intimately involved with many of the changing attitudes now associated with modernization, such as sanitation. Also, the middle-class woman more and more rejected the traditional, fatalistic attitude toward death, especially where infant and maternal mortality were concerned. By seeking advice about her health and that of her children, she demonstrated the belief that her world could be ordered and improved. She expressed a growing reliance on science; first through her purchase of health manuals which were generally written by doctors, and second by her increasing use of doctors to tend to her health problems. There was some evidence that she clung more to traditional ways in this particular aspect of her life than as mistress of the house. The reliance on quack medicines was certainly based to a great extent on tradition, but we have noted that the key to success for many of the patent medicines in the nineteenth century was the claim to innovation and scientific expertise, most often in the forms of bogus testimonials from doctors. It was also pointed out that one major reason for apparently traditionalist behavior lay with the reluctance of the medical profession to implement available innovations rather than with the woman.

The Victorian woman's personal life was profoundly altered by modernization. This was seen very clearly in her receptiveness to chloroform, artificial feeding and contraceptive devices. In all three cases, especially the last, there was evidence of the middle-class woman's growing desire to order her own personal comfort, thereby demonstrating a sense of strong personal autonomy. In the discussion of contraception the development of a modern mentality was most evident. Women accepted contraceptive devices for selfish reasons in part, to insure their own physical well-being by limiting the number of children they bore, and to increase their opportunities for sexual pleasure and gratification.

There were, of course, ambiguities in "modern" attitudes themselves. For example, the woman's desire for greater personal autonomy was juxtaposed with the equally modern notion that as mother she should devote herself intensively to the care and attention of her child. This is a dilemma in the modernization of women that has even yet to be resolved. And these and other modern attitudes did not win complete acceptance by the 1870s, for the hold of traditional values was still strong. The period covered in this study emerges as an important transitional stage. The advent of birth control is perhaps the most obvious sign of the development of new attitudes, and by releasing some energies from traditional functions it sets the stage for other developments. But we can now see that this change was part of a larger modernization package, which saw the middle-class woman seeking to define herself, albeit within the family, as an individual and to gain new control over her body.

The changes in behavior and outlook that did occur in this transitional period were both marked and confused by the constant carping from contemporary publicists, which has in turn tended to mislead historians dealing with Victorian women. Contemporary observers found the middle-class woman a convenient vehicle for criticism of modernity generally. They sensed her desire for new things and therefore exaggerated her indulgence in luxuries. Many critics, some of the strongest of which came from among the religious spokesmen, found an audience among middle-class women themselves. This undoubtedly reflected an uncertainty among many of these women about the new ways, even as they largely persisted in them. There was also some unintended coincidence involved: reading matter that was sought primarily for recipes or patterns often contained a lament over the decline of true womanhood. And this raises again the question of the impact of the criticism in heightening the middle-class woman's sense of insecurity and anxiety. Victorian society, in terms of its official culture, was very demanding of its women. It expected them to be perfect ladies, perfect wives, and perfect mothers. The Victorian woman was to have an observing eye, a calculating head, a skilful hand, concise speech, a gentle step, external tidiness and internal purity. She was expected to exercise constant patience and forebearance, in spite of narrow means, inconvenient houses, crying children and preoccupied husbands. Her responsibilities were indeed overwhelming, and if she failed she had only herself to blame:

> . . . on you *fair* and amiable creature who was born to assuage our sufferings, dispel care, wipe away the tears of grief and to exalt all our enjoyments, much more depends than you commonly imagine. For, if we so frequently remark that marriages of attachment end in anything but cordiality and happiness,— if it be obvious that indifference has crept in where all was once love and respect,—it is (we are sorry to state) but too probable that the lady has originated this fearful change. The angel has become a demon of domestic strife.

To be sure, middle-class men encountered some criticism of their life style as well, but it was never as intense as that directed against women. For women, the adverse public culture could not only cause feelings of guilt about new patterns of behavior but could inhibit a consciousness of the significance of this behavior. Women were seeking more autonomy and control but they may not fully have realized their own goals, because they lacked public sanction. Here is another complicating factor that requires consideration in an understanding of the modernization of women.

Clearly, the middle class needs renewed attention if we are to grasp the dynamics of change in nineteenth-century Britain, and indeed elsewhere. The study of Victorian women suggests that the middle class had not only its own life style but a complex series of problems that have rarely been appreciated in the cursory treatment the class has received from historians. Its men have been too often dismissed as exploiters or conquerors; its women as useless ornaments barely deserving a serious history. In fact, while the social historian cannot point to the stark misery that has lent drama to many of the treatments of the working class, the problems with which the middle class was grappling have at least as much enduring significance. Aspirations were often unmet in a life that remained rigorous in many ways. The class did advance, and Victorian women did benefit from the modernization process. But the changes were hard-won, for new ideas were the product neither of leisure nor of luxury. Most middle-class women had enough margin to avoid taking refuge in traditional family functions alone, but they suffered considerable anxiety as they tried to develop a new life style. That many of the behavior patterns they developed ultimately became part of the modernization of women more generally is a tribute to their ingenuity as well as their influence. But the complexities of the transitional period have enduring significance as well, for they have by no means been shaken off. Here is where middle-class women, like the middle class as a whole, deserve a careful historical assessment, and not merely a characterization.

25

WORK AND WORKERS

Changes in the nature of work and the rise of a new working class were crucial features of European industrialization, a pendant to the new middle classes. Beginning to emerge before 1850, particularly in Britain, the characteristics of industrial labor, and the class subjected to it, became clearer toward the end of the nineteenth century.

There had been manufacturing workers before, as earlier readings demonstrate, but they were fewer in number and more concentrated in the craft sectors. From the beginnings of the industrial revolution until quite recently, the manufacturing labor force grew steadily, becoming for a time the preponderant group numerically in industrial society. At the same time, the workers' position in the social power structure was weakened, compared to the urban-artisanal past, by their lack of property and by the erosion of many traditional skills. Some workers reacted by trying to cling to as many traditional patterns of behavior as possible, particularly during the early decades of industrialization when some workers could directly recall village and guild traditions of work and leisure. Gradually, however, workers began to change. They learned to protest in new ways, and also to develop new goals. They also generated new patterns of consumption and family life—a working-class subculture off the job (see Chapter 15).

The varied facets of working-class life raise obvious issues of focus. Some historians see the essence of a modern working class in the new protest forms. Pointing to the situations and groups most capable of militancy, they assert that this militancy went to the heart of the industrial power balance. Workers were not simply interested in better pay or shorter hours; they wanted to determine their own working lives. Other historians, recognizing the importance of radical groups and of periods of militancy, also consider other kinds of worker adaptation to modern conditions. Indeed, some stress ways in which workers tried to imitate middle-class habits, a process known as *embourgeoisement*. More commonly, the creative and adaptive features of working-class culture are emphasized, as workers learned to shape something of their own world.

Despite important points of agreement—including the recognition of the importance of innovation in defining the modern working class—there is important dispute about what the essential trends in modern working-class development are. Some differences relate to the stop-and-go quality of technological change and to fluctuations in material conditions—workers calm at one point, might be irate five years later. Some differences unquestionably reflect variations stemming from place and type of employment setting. But differences also flow from the aspects of the worker experience considered—whether family life is evaluated along with strike action—and from the extent to which militant workers are taken to represent the whole class. These differences affect the judgment of what workers were in the recent past, and they also relate to continuing disputes about the position of workers today.

The following selections, dealing with German workers in the period 1870–1911, focus on work itself, and the attitudes and protests workers developed around this experience. Here is a central aspect of workers' lives over which they had incomplete control at best. Could they find any satisfaction in their labor? If so, did this require major adjustments in traditional assessments of what characteristics a job should contain? If workers increasingly endured their labor, rather than committing to it, what off-the-job compensations would they be able to find? Most historians (and many others, including many workers) agree that there were major points of deterioration in the modern experience of work, despite big disputes over the extent to which these deteriorations poisoned working-class life overall. These selections allow some evaluation of what industrial work was coming to mean, during Germany's extraordinarily successful industrialization process.

The first selection outlines general changes in the conditions and political position of German workers in the later nineteenth century, following the severe economic depression of the 1870s. The second selection focuses on conditions in a metals factory in Dortmund around a bitter 1911 strike. Both selections emphasize disorienting changes in the nature of work, combined with management and government attempts to isolate working-class response. Working-class protest patterns, already evolving, continued to change in this setting, though not always in consistent directions: German workers supported the most rapidly growing socialist movement in Europe, but also sought more spontaneous outlets for their grievances, including acts of sabotage that accompanied the Dortmund strike. In Germany, and elsewhere, the development of the working class in mature industrial society involved growing class conflict; these selections explain some of the key ingredients for this conflict (see Chapter 22).

I. TRENDS IN GERMANY

MARY NOLAN

The Great Depression of 1873–1896 brought in its wake a restructuring of Germany's economy, a transformation of its political parties, and a refounding of the Reich. This reorientation of state and society set the framework within which the working class and workers' movements developed. Of equal importance, the working class and workers' movements were central elements of that new framework. They were both the objects of repressive and paternalistic state policies. . . .

The Great Depression involved the entire industrial capitalist world, but its impact on Germany was particularly pronounced, testifying both to Germany's new integration into the world economy and to the instabilities and vulnerabilities generated by rapid industrialization. For Germany this prolonged crisis entailed three periods of intense economic downturn—1873–1879, 1882–1884, and 1891–1893—interspersed with tentative and short-lived upswings. It abruptly ended two decades of rapid growth and prosperity and . . . the authoritarian state institutions established in 1871 encouraged and reenforced the animosity of the dominant classes toward the working class and workers' movements. The German state, like the process of unification it crowned, was the product of a conservative revolution from above, not a popular uprising from below. The impotent parliament threatened neither the autonomy of the right-wing military and bureaucracy nor the power of the prime minister. Universal male suffrage for the Reichstag, conferred by Bismarck in an effort to win the loyalty of the lower classes, promoted mass politics without empowering the masses. . . .

If the authoritarian state structure made democratic reform and working-class integration unlikely, the state policies adopted during the depression made them impossible. The refounding of the Reich was a complex process, affecting all classes. The state sought to bolster its legitimacy and benefit its supporters by means not only of tariffs but also of colonial policy, social imperialism, and the purge of liberals from the bureaucracy. The state also intervened actively in an effort to shape working-class formation and defuse activism. Only if the latter strategy complemented the former could the authoritarian state and conservative social order be permanently stabilized.

From: Mary Nolan, "Economic Crisis, State Policy, and Working-Class Formation in Germany 1870–1900," in Ira Katznelson and Aristide R. Zolberg, eds., *Working-Class Formation: Nineteenth Century Patterns in Western Europe and the United States* (Princeton, NJ: Princeton University Press, 1988), pp. 335, 359–60, 364–66, 380–81.

Although the government had devoted relatively little attention to workers prior to 1873, it made them a prime object of policy thereafter. Repression, aimed at containing both workplace unrest and the political potential of social democracy, was the dominant strategy adopted. Beginning in the mid-1870s the police and judiciary intensified their harassment of the still insignificant socialist unions and political organizations. Persecution of the fledgling workers' movement culminated in the passage of the Anti-Socialist laws in 1878. This legislation, initiated by [Chancellor] Bismarck and widely supported by other parties, simultaneously singled out social democracy as the "enemy within" and, in conjunction with the tariff bill, rallied Liberal industrialists and Conservative agrarians behind the Bismarckian state. Under the terms of the Anti-Socialist laws, the Social Democrats could legally run for political office, but all Social Democratic political organizations, publications, and activities were declared illegal and in practice the ban applied to Social Democratic cultural associations and trade unions as well. The laws, whose application was accompanied by vituperative antisocialist and anti-working class rhetoric from the state and other parties, proved ineffective in curbing the workers' movement. In 1890 parliament, which recognized the failure of the Anti-Socialist laws but was unwilling to strengthen them, re-legalized the Social Democratic party. But twelve years of institutionalized repression were to shape the ideology, strategy, and organization of the working class profoundly . . .

If the structure of the work force changed, so too did the nature of the work being performed. Industrialists' desire to cut costs and increase productivity in order to expand operations and maintain profits in a time of crisis led to significant changes in the labor process. Concentration and intensification were the general strategies pursued. Factory expansion and integration meant that the percentage of employees in firms with a labor force of fifty-one or more (that is, in what were then labelled large firms) increased from 22.8 percent to 33.5 percent between 1882 and 1895. Productivity per worker rose 54 percent in the two decades after 1875, while hours generally fell slightly.

Mechanization, dequalification, and new forms of supervision and wage payment were capital's preferred means to attain its ends, especially in larger factories. Recent research suggests the extent and variety of attacks on more traditional labor processes. In Bochum's large-scale basic metal industry, mechanization was increased, the work pace was intensified, piece rates were lowered, and two twelve-hour shifts per day were introduced in iron and steel. In a Bielefeld sewing machine factory, productivity per worker nearly doubled between 1868 and 1889 due to mechanization, the simplification of tasks, and the introduction of piece rates. The factory, which had initially been like a large Handwerk [craftwork] shop, came to resemble a textile mill. From the late 1870s on, machine makers in a Württemberg machine factory saw their skill and prestige eroded. As management became bureaucratized and rationalized, it increased its control over individual workshops. Apprenticeship was restructured so that youths were given narrow training for specific factory jobs rather than wide-ranging artisan expertise. Piece rates were steadily lowered to the point where the wages and lifetime earning prospects of skilled workers were scarcely better than those of the semiskilled and unskilled. If such an extreme narrowing of wage differentials was exceptional, the general pressure on the earnings of the skilled was not. At Siemens, the major producer of electrical equipment, more flexible forms of supervision, resembling those of journeymen by masters, were replaced by increasingly strict and detailed factory ordinances and sharper surveillance for laxity, theft, and the like. At least formally, although not always in practice, foremen gained complete control over the labor process, workers' access to materials, and their relationship with other workers. Not all capitalist initiatives were, to be sure, immediately successful. In a Berlin machine factory, internal subcontracting was eliminated and piece rates were introduced but worker opposition led to the reinstitution of hourly wages in the early 1890s. After the turn of the century, however, the premium bonus system was imposed to increase productivity and intensify work.

The same general processes were operative in mining. In the 1870s, Ruhr mine owners responded to the crisis by cutting wages and firing workers; in the 1880s, by rationalizing and intensifying work. Although mechanization was not introduced, the average size of mines grew from 234 workers in 1870 to 722 in 1890. As a result, the division of labor increased, miners were more isolated from one another, and supervision became more formal. Owners sought to increase productivity and lower labor costs by eliminating the traditional eight-hour day, violating work rules, imposing arbitrary fines, and manipulating company housing and welfare programs to ensure acquiescence to these harsher conditions.

The situation in the artisanal sector was more varied. Construction, for example, remained immune from mechanization and concentration, allowing workers to retain their skills and control of the labor process. Woodworking shops remained small, but some mechanization and specialization occurred. Less fortunate branches of Handwerk were fundamentally transformed as employers sought to cope with the depression and compete with factories by cutting labor costs. In cigar making, for example, the position of the skilled male was destroyed by ruralization, feminization, and simplification of tasks as a once-thriving artisan trade moved not into the factory but into the home. Similarly, shoemaking was transformed from Handwerk to home work, but it then shifted to factory production, with its labor force becoming increasingly female.

Both skill hierarchies and the meaning of skill were modified by these changes. The numerical preponderance of the skilled in manufacturing persisted. Indeed, in 1895 there were roughly three skilled and semi-skilled workers for every two unskilled. But such global statistics mask the disproportionately rapid rise in the unskilled as well as the emergence of that amorphous category, the semiskilled, who were recruited from the dequalified skilled workers, from independent artisans, and from formerly unskilled manual laborers who became machine operatives. Although some highly trained workers retained or even upgraded their skills, others saw their autonomy and expertise limited by transformations in the industrial labor process. Those limits were evident in wages, hours, and forms of supervision. Language also reflected the growing similarities in the condition of all wage labor. In government statistics and social insurance programs, skilled and unskilled alike were treated as part of the universal category "workers" (*Arbeiter*). At Siemens "the use of the collective designation 'worker' for all non-clerical and non-managerial employees became ever more widespread" from the 1870s on. Although in some sectors of Handwerk skill was simply destroyed, in others it was not skill per se but rather the link between skill and independence that was eliminated. Rather than an age-specific and temporary status, the position of journeyman increasingly became a lifelong situation of dependence. Those in declining trades, like shoemaking, where capital requirements were low and tools simple, might make the "flight into independence" but they seldom succeeded in escaping wage labor in the shop or factory permanently.

The demands of strikers, which included backward- and forward-looking elements, reflected the growing realization that craft exclusiveness and residual corporatism were unsuitable to new conditions. Workers' demands centered on increased wages and shorter hours. The form of payment was seldom attacked, for although trade union leaders insisted that "piecework is murder," skilled workers objected more to the unilateral lowering of rates than to piecework itself. Workers' demands sometimes represented the defense of tradition, as with the Ruhr miners, who had once had a state-guaranteed eight-hour day and privileged pay, and at other times the logic of subsistence. Increasingly, however, these demands were justified in terms of the right to a normal workday and the need to compensate for increased intensity and to combat the manipulation of piece rates. As late as the early 1880s protesting journeymen accompanied their demands with appeals for cooperation between masters and men in the creation of a harmonious workplace. By the decade's end, however, the conflict between capital and labor, even in Handwerk, was unequivocally acknowledged.

Tactics, like demands, were a mixture of the old, new, and the old used in new ways. Although journeymen's strikes in the eighteenth century had been rationally timed, thoroughly organized, and strategically sophisticated, in the early nineteenth century journeymen's organizations had declined and with them the earlier effective strike tradition. By the 1860s and 1870s strikes were largely local and spontaneous affairs, undertaken by one occupation with relatively little regard to the state of the economy and the size of strike funds. Gradually they became more carefully planned and executed by local organizations, which increasingly preceded and promoted protest. With growing frequency strikers appealed to workers in other occupations and locales—a clear indication of diminishing craft exclusiveness and developing links between local issues and wider class concerns. Throughout the period, Ruhr miners resorted to their time-honored tactic of petitioning government officials for the redress of grievances and the restoration of privileges. Other workers, however, used such petitions both to promote union organization and to demand more general rights, as in the ten-hour workday petition movement of 1882. In addition, they looked not only to the state but also to public opinion for support. Even the Ruhr miners, who painfully discovered that capital was intransigent and the state hardly neutral, learned the necessity of supplementing traditional petitions with strikes and ultimately with ongoing union organizations.

II. A 1911 Metal Workers' Strike

DAVID F. CREW

When employers in certain industries—coal-mining, the iron and steel industry and, eventually, engineering—began to rationalise production, the privileged position of the "specialised worker" was undermined. Now skilled workers increasingly were replaced by a new class of unskilled and semi-skilled workers, many of them women and youths, who experienced none of the conditions of work or of life that had given rise to the peculiar mentality of the "specialised worker." . . .

In the German steel industry, the creation of the new "mass worker" began with the introduction of the Bessemer-Thomas process after 1880. With this new technology at their disposal, German employers could rapidly reduce the level of skill required to make steel. Working conditions consequently became even worse than those in the mining industry. The trade unions and the SPD [Socialist party] were able to do little to protect skilled steelworkers, such as puddlers, against this onslaught. Nor could they later gain any ground in the massive, new, autocratically managed steel mills of the Ruhr. . . .

The impotence of the official trade union movement thus prompted rank-and-file steelworkers to develop novel forms of resistance to their employers. The sabotage incident [involving shutting off factory power systems] during the 1911 Dortmund "Union" strike provided a spectacular example of this new activity. . . . The insufficient education of the worker for responsible positions is not restricted to the "Union" steel mills. For reasons of profit, there is no real period of apprenticeship at all. In the reports of the factory inspectors for 1909, the following can be found [for the administrative district of Arnsberg]:

> The larger steel works, in particular those that have a high turnover of workers, often shorten the apprenticeship of some workers to a few weeks, even a few days, and allow them to take on even the most difficult tasks after such a short trial period, if they seem to be capable.

This deprivation of skill (in the sense that this term was understood by the SPD and the Free trade unions) stripped the worker of his individual and collective capacity to resist capitalist depredations. Consequently, iron- and steelworkers were subjected to daily physical torment for the sake of ever-increasing profits, a torment which itself further contributed to their collective impotence:

From: David F. Crew, "Steel, Sabotage and Socialism: The Strike at the Dortmund 'Union' Steel Works in 1911," in Richard J. Evans, ed., *The German Working Class 1888–1933* (Totowa, NJ: Barnes & Noble Books, 1982), pp. 110–13, 120, 127.

> The extraordinarily hard physical labour and long working hours often destroy the foundry-man before his time, and deaden him mentally, so that far too frequently he allows himself to be misused by his enemies against the interests of his own class.

To this physical devastation were added psychological and social disorganisation. The individual worker's fear, anxiety and suspicion blocked the emergence of any strong sense of collective interest. A report published by the German Metalworkers' Union in 1912 contended that it was not uncommon for workers to be offered bonuses for reporting on the trade union activities of their colleagues. Indeed, the *Arbeiter Zeitung* [Worker's Press] claimed that in most iron and steel works an extensive spy system existed and whoever came under "suspicion" was quickly denounced and thrown out of work. . . . Often it was only by changing their profession that steel workers could avoid starving to death. Hand in hand with this spy system went the most nauseating toadyism—to ensure one's job it was often useful to have a pretty wife willing to perform the appropriate services [for the foreman]. The iron- and steel-workers knew of many masters and other works officials who reportedly would ensure an extra shift and a good wage packet for this sort of consideration. . . . The management showed no signs of being willing to negotiate collectively with the striking workers. After the strike began, they broke off all discussion with the unions and concentrated their energies upon procuring enough strikebreakers to keep the plant in operation. Striking workers were sent dismissal notices by registered post and those who were living in company housing were evicted. Efforts to involve the state as a mediator failed completely. Near the end of the strike, the national chairman of the Centralverband der Maschinisten und Heizer [Machinists' Union], Franz Scheffel, along with the union's regional secretary from Cologne, petitioned the Lord Mayor of Dortmund to intercede. The company curtly answered the Lord Mayor by stating that "it could not consider [his] mediation because of the violent manner in which work had been halted." . . .

Faced with this level of intransigence, the SPD and the Free trade unions could only hope that by encouraging the strikers to resist returning to work for yet another day, they might perhaps wear management down to the point at which it would at least recognise their existence. . . .

But none of this prevented the strike from coming to an abrupt and inglorious end. Perhaps all it did achieve was to make that ending somewhat unexpected and hence all the more debilitating for the rank and file. . . .

26

WOMEN WORKERS

PAMELA RADCLIFF

Historical treatment of women factory workers has undergone striking changes in the last two decades, as part of the growing sophistication of sociohistorical and feminist research. Conventional historical coverage of the industrial revolution long focused on shocking accounts of women in the factories, exploited by long hours and low pay and kept away from their homes. This picture has by no means been replaced, but it has been supplemented in important ways. First, it is now realized that an overriding issue for women in Europe's industrial revolution was a loss of job opportunities and an increase in economic inequality in relation to men. Women did work in factories, often performing vital service, but machines steadily displaced the number of jobs they had held in more traditional rural and protoindustrial economies. The most common urban occupation for women was as domestic servants, not factory workers—partly because domestic service was viewed as more appropriate for women, partly because factory jobs were relatively scarce. Second, and relatedly, historians now emphasize how male workers frequently tried to drive women from the labor force, keeping them out of unions and supporting laws that would restrict women's hours of work—on humanitarian grounds but also as a means of making them less employable. Only a minority of working-class women were able to hold factory jobs beyond a few years in adolescence prior to marriage.

Differences between the male and the female work experience also underlie discussions of women who did work in factories—an important if not typical group. This selection deals with one group of these women, the cigarette workers in the Spanish city of Gijón. The author argues that analytical schemes designed to assess the protest of male workers—schemes visible in earlier selections in this book by Charles Tilly and by Mary Nolan and David Crew—are not fully applicable, for women had distinctive protest situations, motives and goals. This, along with the hostility of male labor leaders, helps explain the special position of women in union and socialist movements. This argument should be assessed in terms of the situations the author describes: Do they demonstrate that women workers were defined more by gender than by shared conditions in their social class?

From: Pamela Radcliff, "Elite Women Workers and Collective Action: The Cigarette Makers of Gijón, 1890–1930," *Journal of Social History* 27 (1993): 86–87, 88–89, 100–01.

One other feature of the passage deserves comment: its focus on Spain. Spanish history has long seemed different from the rest of European history, because of Spain's unusually fervent Catholicism and its frequently unstable politics. Social historians, however, looking beneath the surface of events and cultures, increasingly argue for including Spain in some common social patterns, including developments in a modern working class. Spanish history thus becomes less separate—just as Spain itself becomes less separate from other European currents in the twentieth century. In this passage, certainly, the issues emphasized are not Spanish at all, so much as those flowing from gender and class in reaction to the conditions of factory life.

On May 2, 1898, the Spanish industrial city of Gijón witnessed perhaps the most dramatic riot in its history, when thousands of angry consumers took to the streets in protest against an unpopular food tax. Adding to the drama was the fact that the protest was instigated and carried out by women, whose violence and disregard for property shocked local officials. It began in Cimadavilla, the oldest working-class neighborhood in the city, when a customs official confiscated two fish from a woman fishmonger who had not paid the new tax (*consumo*) on seafood. Immediately the other sellers in the fishmarket closed their posts and marched behind their banner to the city hall. When the mayor did not appear to talk to them, they took to the streets again, and walked up the hill to the tobacco factory. There they convinced the cigarette makers to join in solidarity. The fact that over 1,800 women worked in one place made them very easy to mobilize and added immediate power to any demonstration. The entire crowd of over 2,000 women and children returned to the city hall, stopping on their way at the jail to shout their support for the editor of the republican daily newspaper (*El Noroeste*), who had been recently arrested for libel. After more silence from city officials, the crowd marched by other factories calling on all of their women workers to walk out.

The demonstration had been peaceful up to then, but in the afternoon, with still no response from the authorities, it turned violent. From the original issue of the fish, the cry broadened to include the other necessities made expensive through the hated tax. When the focus turned to the price of bread, the women went to Zarracina's flour factory, threw rocks and broke all of the windows. A clerk tried in vain to get a commission of the demonstrators to express their demands "reasonably." Instead they entered and tore open sacks of grain. Afterwards they headed towards Zarracina's own house (he was an important republican leader), pelting it, too, with stones. The next stop was the office of *consumo* administration, where documents were brought out and burned in the street. Other symbols of tax collection received similar treatment. Finally, local officials called out the soldiers to "calm them down," but their shots into the air only increased the excitement. When darkness fell, the women went home of their own accord, probably to cook dinner and rest.

The next day the rioting began again, with a violence never before seen in Gijón, according to the newspapers. First the women shut down the office where farmers registered their produce. Then they sacked several bakeries (one owned by another noted republican) and Zarracina's chocolate factory. They took the sacks of cocoa, coffee and cinnamon to the streets and sold them for a fraction of their market price to any passer-by. Although the chocolate factory was the first target unrelated to the *consumo* issue, it formed part of a clear pattern. From the rioters' point of view, food, whether basic or luxury items, should be made available to everyone at affordable prices.

By this time the city and regional government had finally coordinated a response, and the Civil Governor, speaking from the balcony of the City Hall, told the crowd that the *consumos* would probably be dropped. There were further shouts that the mayor should be sacked, and a committee of women presented a petition to the mayor demanding his resignation. With such a loss of confidence in his leadership, the mayor agreed to step down. The announcement of his resignation drew cheers from the crowd, which finally went home peacefully.

This story offers a fascinating glimpse at one face of working-class women's collective action in turn-of-the-century Gijón. The episode also poses interesting questions about the deeper process of politicization that informed the rioters' behavior. For most of the participants of the riot, these questions are impossible to answer, as they left no other historical footprints. Nevertheless, one group of rioters, the cigarette makers, left a more visible trail of their collective activities. . . .

Although the evidence of the cigarette makers' collective presence in the city is sporadic, the pattern that emerges suggests a new approach to understanding not only the 1898 protest but also the broader question of how working-class women forged and expressed a collective identity. Aside from these implications, the compelling drama of the cigarette makers' lives makes theirs a story worth telling.

Since the early 19th century, the female cigarette maker has been a powerful image in Spanish popular culture. In the 1840s, folklorist Antonio Flores extolled the *cigarrera* as the epitome of "spanishness," with her "graceful figure," her "black eyes that shoot daggers when they are open," and a set of teeth "whose whiteness the snow could not compete with." Bizet, of course, immortalized the picturesque version of the cigarette maker in his story of Carmen, the feisty heroine who works in a tobacco factory. This popular image of the *cigarrera* fostered the myth that they were more independent and, as a result, more dangerous than most working-class women. The pervasiveness of this myth is revealed in a manifesto issued in 1919 by the cigarette maker's union in Gijón: "it is time to destroy the legend that cigarette makers are common rabblerousers, earn high salaries and enjoy complete liberty in their work."

The cigarette makers' complaints reflected the decline in their position in the Spanish economy after the 1870s, a decline fostered by long-term processes of mechanization, deskilling and the stagnation of wages. And yet, throughout the period, Gijón's cigarette makers retained their image as privileged and independent workers. More importantly, they translated this privilege into a powerful collective voice that defended their concerns in the political community at large. Their strong and independent voice is even more remarkable in the context of the highly politicized atmosphere of early twentieth-century Gijón. After 1900, Gijón evolved into the quintessential worker's city, dominated by construction, shipping and metallurgical industries, and infamous for its contentious politics. In a political sphere crowded with the voices of male republicans, anarchists, socialists and monarchists, the *cigarreras* transmitted one of the few public, collective female voices. Thus, the unusual position of the *cigarreras,* both as workers and as community activists, provides an excellent opportunity to examine the complex ways in which gender shaped the formation and expression of political consciousness.

In many ways, the *cigarreras'* work experience was similar to that of male artisans in other industries. With relatively high wages, a lifelong job commitment, pride in their skilled labor, and the possibility of promotion up to the lower levels of management, these women aspired to an artisanal elite. With the effects of mechanization, and their concentration into large factories, they were also classic proletarians, skilled workers exposed to mechanizing work processes that reduced their autonomy. These job characteristics set the *cigarreras* apart from the majority of women workers, who either worked in cottage industry, domestic service, or in low-status jobs within male-dominated industries. They also stood out by generally remaining in the workforce after marriage. Thus, for the *cigarreras,* wage earning did not comprise a phase in the female life cycle, but a permanent fixture in their lives. Simply put, the cigarette makers' work experience shared more with that of other male artisans than with that of the average female worker.

And yet, as is evident by the gender composition of the *consumo* protest, the cigarette makers' collective action looked very different from that of their activist male counterparts, who invested their political energies more heavily in formal trade union associations. The context of male working-class politics in 1898 makes this juxtaposition very clear. Gijón's first trade unions were formed early that year, but no women workers joined the burgeoning movement. The male workers most likely to unionize first were those in skilled and artisanal trades, but among women workers even the skilled cigarette makers did not respond. With the apparent discrepancy between their elite work status and their collective action, the *cigarreras* present a paradox, one that puzzled both their contemporaries—who saw them as politically inconsistent—and historians who might expect them to act like their male counterparts in the work force. Since their artisanal work experience did not translate into typical artisanal political behavior, the cigarette makers confound existing models and open the door to a more flexible interpretive framework that incorporates nuanced gender distinctions.

More specifically, the cigarette makers seemed to have formed a collective identity rooted in their varied roles in the factory, in the community, and in the family. Since they continued to work after marriage, most of them had immediate family responsibilities as well as workplace concerns. Beyond the confines of the factory and the home, the cigarette makers also emerged as community leaders in the neighborhood in which the factory was located. Thus, during the protest of 1898, the *cigarreras* were recruited from the factory by their neighbors the fishmongers, but were also motivated as mothers who had to buy food for their families. While working-class men's collective identity had similarly complex origins and motives, the prevailing division of labor in the society created different sets of possibilities for men and women. As a result, the cigarette makers followed a collective agenda that distinguished them from their unionized male colleagues. Even when the cigarette makers eventually unionized, in 1915, they continued to chart an independent course. . . .

In fact, while the cigarette makers' collective activities represented a blend of workplace and extra-workplace roles, these roles do not necessarily correspond to private and public compartments—at least as we presently articulate them. The cigarette makers' understanding of their extra-workplace duties appeared to be rooted in their specific domestic settings but their actions clearly indicate that their sense of responsibility often transcended an exclusive concern for individual families. Women maintained a strong sense of responsibility to care for their families, but the same obligations could push them into defending the larger community. Thus, a consciousness rooted in the family division of labor could also dictate a public role for working women, regardless of their relationship to the work force or to official political institutions. In other words, from their "obligation to preserve life," women have been able to carve out positions as community leaders. While the cigarette makers never articulated any of this, and it is especially difficult to get a glimpse into their family life, their public collective behavior makes more sense if we infer a consciousness shaped by family and community as well as workplace concerns.

The gendered political formation of working-class women like the *cigarreras* suggests the possibility of a distinct philosophical vantage point. The "obligation to preserve life" created, in the words of historians Deborah Valenze and Ruth Smith, an alternative political theory based on an "ethic of mutuality" that contrasted with the dominant political values of liberal individualism. In addition, working-class women's often broad construction of the extent of mutuality could conflict with the socialist-influenced labor movements' evolving class-based understanding of the concept. As a result, evidence of working-class women's collective action frequently has been marginalized because it appears to stand outside the dominant philosophical traditions of the nineteenth and twentieth centuries. While it is difficult, given the evidence, to assert that the cigarette makers acted according to such an ethic of mutuality, it is apparent that their actions were marginalized because their male contemporaries couldn't understand the logic behind them. If we at least acknowledge the possibility of alternative theoretical starting points, then we are forced to piece together their own agenda and analyze it on their own terms. . . .

While working-class women rarely got involved in party politics, they continued to practice a street politics often centered around the provision of market goods and rooted in their domestic obligation to feed and provide basic comforts for their families. Women's prominence in these types of protest has already been noted. . . . The problem is that the market tradition has been treated implicitly as a stage in the modernization of protest, in which there is an appropriate evolution of collective action, in its forms, its motives and its participants. In this scheme, 18th-century bread riots by consumer mobs give way to workers' strikes and political demonstrations; the politicized worker replaces the consumer, who increasingly targets power at its central source, the national government. Once a timeline is in place, historians view certain types of protest as meaningful only in specific contexts.

This scheme ignores, however, the fact that working-class women, whether "workers" or not, retained a powerful interest in consumer issues and continued to organize most effectively at the local level. As a result, they continued to take to the streets when they felt cheated by hoarders, shop owners, or an indifferent government. And, as evidenced by the cigarettes makers' participation in the *consumo* riot in May of 1898, wage-earning women shared this perspective with their housewife neighbors. In fact, although the immediate instigators of the protest were sellers, not buyers (the fishmongers), its escalation depended to a large degree on all of the women's common concerns as household managers. The dismay of government officials and the incomprehension of trade unionists in the face of the May riot illustrated that men often failed to understand women's language of protest. Once again, the cigarette makers and other working-class women's gendered identity created a collective agenda that set them apart from their male counterparts.

As the narrative of the riot makes clear, Gijón's working-class women capably defended their "private" sphere concerns in public. Moreover, they accepted the use of extreme measures to force the government to reconsider the policies that affected the lives of themselves and their families. Why, then, did they not join the emerging union movement, which, by the following year had gathered together the majority of the city's male workers? As stated earlier, the cigarette makers, with their visible corporate solidarity, were the first women to organize, but not until 1915, almost twenty years later. Women's ambivalence toward the labor movement did not necessarily mean that they were too conservative or apathetic to join. The cigarette makers were clearly anything but apathetic, and all the evidence points to their ongoing political and cultural activism. And yet the style and content of their activism did not fit neatly into the trade union model of progressive politics. This divergence in agendas led the cigarette makers, and perhaps other women, to remain on the margin of the mainstream labor movement.

27

THE WORKING-CLASS HOUSEWIFE

JOANNA BURKE

Along with women as workers, and the special forms of protest they might develop, roles as housewives loomed large, in all urban classes, at the end of the
nineteenth century. The roles were and are hard to interpret. At present, many
Europeans and Americans view housewifery as confining, and assume it was
pressed upon women (even when they seemed to consent) by men who were
bent on maximizing their economic and family power. At the time, observers
worried that working-class housewives, at least, were insufficiently skilled at
their tasks, often responsible for families that spent beyond their means, suffered from poor sanitation and unnecessary disease, and failed to inculcate
proper values in children.

While social historians often point out exploitation of key groups, they
usually find that the groups have some voice over their lot. Hence a purely critical or pejorative view of working-class housewifery in maturing industrial society is unlikely to fit the facts. The following selection emphasizes records and
voices of British working-class housewives themselves, as they explain what
their goals were and how they judged their roles and their relationships with
husbands. Housewives clearly have a history, though it has received less attention than other aspects of women's lives. This passage should be compared
with the treatment of women in the middle-class domestic sphere (Chapter 24,
above), and with other accounts of the working-class family (Chapters 31 and
32). It also should be juxtaposed with the analysis of women who worked, in
the passage immediately preceding: Why would some women choose one emphasis, some another—at least when choice was available?

In 1939 Frank Steel looked back into his youth and remembered the following discussion:

> "Listen, Dad!," I recollect saying once, "didn't you say this woman on the
> money—the one with the helmet—is Britannia? What is she doing?"
> "Why," said father, "she's ruling the waves, of course . . . ."

From: Joanna Burke, "Housewifery in Working-Class England 1860–1914," *Past and Present* 143
(1994): 167–69, 171–74, 179–81, 188–91, 194, 195–96.

"But, Dad!," I persisted, "it isn't a ruler she's holding; it's a toasting fork! . . . ."

"Oh, ah, yes!," said Dad, after considering the matter a moment, "this must be one of the days when she rests from ruling, and stays home making toast."

This exchange took place between a small boy and his father in a working-class area of London in the 1870s, at a time when increasing numbers of married working-class women were redefining themselves primarily as housewives—with paid employment as a second, and less desirable, option. In Steel's story, Mother England "rests from ruling" to make toast. Is this what working-class women at the end of the nineteenth century were doing when they began to concentrate their labour in the domestic sphere? The speakers in the reminiscences are a boy and a man. What were married working-class women thinking and speaking? . . . In 1911, 90 per cent of [British] wives were not engaged in paid employment compared with only one-quarter in 1851. With the collapse of the home-employment system, and the development and expansion of industrial, commercial and factory systems outside the home, working-class married women were hardest hit. Although most such women continued to spend some time engaged in paid employment (usually at the lower echelons of the market and frequently on a part-time or casual basis), they increasingly came to define themselves primarily as housewives. Further-more many seemed pleased to do so.

Today we seem less pleased with their choice. Working-class women are portrayed as creatures buffeted about by a nebulous, oppressive ideology or by dominating fathers, brothers and husbands. Historians speak of the "growing exclusion [of women] from waged labour outside the home" as though some economic demon was forcing them into the domestic sphere. . . .

Whatever explanation is adopted, this movement of women into the un-paid domestic sphere is generally assumed to be one of the great oppressive changes in history. Ann Oakley contends that the role of the housewife in the nineteenth century was a demeaning one, consisting of monotonous, fragmented work which brought no financial remuneration, let alone any recognition. . . .

The chief aim of this article is to let working-class housewives between 1860 and 1914 speak for themselves. My interest is in social agency, or seeing housewives not simply as determined, but also as determining their own history. In the words of Jean Comaroff, we need to see working-class housewives as human beings who "in their everyday production of goods and meanings, acquiesce yet protest, reproduce yet seek to transform their predicament." There are three parts to my argument.

First, if full-time housewifery entailed a reduction in the power of the individual woman, why did so many working-class women from the end of the nineteenth century wholeheartedly embrace this new identity? What is striking is the fact that many women thought that housewifery was a good—even the *best*—option. The intensification of the two spheres of labour was acceptable to women in this period because it was seen as a better and less risky way of increasing their power over their own lives and the lives of their families. This is not to argue that the search for a better life was what *motivated* women moving into full-time housewifery; rather that it was not *against* their interests to make the move. There was a price to pay for the movement; but the benefits were perceived as being cheap at the price.

Secondly, there were serious risks involved in devoting one's time to unwaged housework. The family is a confrontational unit; husbands may beat up wives; women may get a smaller share of the household goods. By not earning a wage, women were more vulnerable to the power of wage-earners within the home. Housewives tackled these risks directly. As the nineteenth century drew to a close, working-class housewives attempted to consolidate their power within the home. They did this by adopting and adapting a language of domesticity and by domestic education. Married women in working-class homes attempted to recreate the world in their own image. Their actions involved a consciousness of themselves as a group with shared values and special needs. The actions of these housewives to improve their status from within the domestic sphere have been ignored or belittled by historians for a number of reasons. To begin with, there was no revolutionary change. Then, their actions do not coincide with the class-based analyses many historians find congenial. Furthermore historians do not generally share the values of housewives they are studying, and they have trouble taking these values seriously. We need to ask what is the meaning of housework to housewives; they did not disparage it as we do.

Thirdly, these quiet, individualist and educational attempts to create a powerful, comfortable space for women-as-housewives were not unambiguously successful. Married working-class women forced to earn a wage because of the collapse of household finances entered the employment market from a worse position. Many husbands continued to act in oppressive, domineering ways. Working-class housewives maintained their neighbourhood-based consciousness of their group as a group and actively resisted male power over them. Strategies for asserting one's power within the household ranged from passive methods of subversion to physical violence. Whatever the strategy employed, the site of conflict was the home: the kitchen, the bedroom. Domestic production is intimate; it is not surprising that housewives should want to protest in personal, individualized ways. This said, the striking feature about the resistance of housewives was the degree to which the conflict was arranged around a set of values shared by women-as-housewives and either opposed or ignored by men-as-"breadwinners." Resistance requires expression in language and symbols. Analogies with statecraft provided the language; capitalism the symbols.

. . . By the end of the nineteenth century, many working-class women had come to view full-time housewifery as an ideal, and one which was increasingly attainable. Most working-class married women did not want paid employment . . . [one wife] explained, "It never answers for a woman to go out to work; if you earn 1s. you lose 1s. 6d. [shilling and pence]. I used to go to work, and then had to sit up at nights to wash." Furthermore employment could be more expensive than not being employed. Besides paying for wear and tear on clothing and shoes, childcare costs had to be considered. Mrs Cawthorn, wife of a labourer in Epworth (Lincolnshire), argued:

> I don't think wives ought to go out at all. When a wife goes out they can't put their victuals to the best. Then there's the clothes. I've been out many a day when I should have saved money by staying at home, what with paying 2d. and 4d. for my babies to be taken care of.

The "free" child-care provided by older children was often unacceptable. The fear that one's child would be injured through carelessness or ignorance was prevalent, and this fear grew with increased investment in children. Mrs Hoskins's husband was a labourer in Michel Troy (Monmouthshire). In 1867 he was in bad health and some weeks earned less than 2s. To her dismay, she was often forced to undertake labouring jobs:

> When I go out I am obliged to leave the children to take care of themselves; one is only a few months old, and none are old enough to take any real care of the others. I lock them into the kitchen, and they play about. Must leave a bit of fire because of the supper, but it is dangerous, and I am always afraid they may come to some harm. Still we are so poor, must go out to work.

A female agricultural labourer and mother of thirteen children in Studley (Wiltshire) had similar worries:

> I think it a much better thing for mothers to be at home with their children, they are much better taken care of, and other things go on better. I have always left my children to themselves, and God be praised nothing has ever happened to them, though I have thought it dangerous. I have many a time come home, and have thought it was a mercy to find nothing has happened to them.

When all the costs of wives and mothers working for money were calculated, it was frequently decided that female labour lowered the household's standard of living. Poor women in a number of different counties repeated the saying, "Between the woman that works and the woman that doesn't there is only 6d to choose at the year's end, and she that stays at home has it" . . . .

The housewife gained status by her management of scarce resources. The movement into full-time housewifery enabled the special needs and tastes of the individuals within the household to be catered for—and it was the housewife who created this collective identity. The great symbol was the parlour where the relationship between the housewife and her family, as well as the relationship between the family and the wider community, were symbolized and structured in subtle yet distinctive ways. The parlour was a symbolic space. In working-class England, it came to represent the housewife's power and control over her family. The parlour was a confirmation of the housewife's preeminent role in the management of resources, and symbolized her success as the domestic manager.

By investing time in the household, housewives experienced the pride and sense of well-being that comes from creating beautiful things. Cooking a variety of dishes was important. One of the pleasures spoken about by women moving into full-time housewifery was the joy of spending more time nurturing children. Mrs Mary Cole, wife of a shepherd in Ingoldisthorpe (Norfolk), had fourteen children. Believing that her children would have "suffered" if she had taken a paid job, she spent her time looking after them, rather than trying to boost her husband's low wages. Child-rearing was her chief pleasure (or so she told the commissioners):

> They were her happy days when she used to hear their innocent prattle when they used to come home from school. [She] Remembers the time when flour was 3s. 6d. a stone, and she had nine children at home, and nothing coming in but her husband's wages, which were then "heined" (raised) to 12s. a week. They were hard times, surely, but by the blessing of God she struggled through, and never had a penny from the parish.

The point that not all pleasures have a money price was not always understood by middle-class commentators on working-class life. In 1895 one landowner in Norfolk showed a lack of appreciation of domestic beauty when he complained:

> If you build a cottage with a good living room, and a kitchen containing a copper, oven, etc. they insist on living in the kitchen, and shutting up the front room as a "drawing room" to be entered probably only once a week. You put in patent ventilators and they promptly shut them up. They block up the windows of the sitting-room with a blind curtain and flowers.

Although my main argument is that domestic arranging and rearranging had a function in creating a human environment which was both pleasurable to "make" and pleasurable to "consume," there was some economic purpose to actions intended to keep up a good "front" in the eyes of the neighbours. Maintaining acceptable standards of beauty and order were crucial to achieving good credit levels with the local shopkeeper, the pawnbroker and the neighbours.

All this domestic work took a great deal of time, energy and skill. Furthermore, relative to the other members of the household, the housewife did not get her "fair share" of leisure. In one sense, *her* work facilitated *their* leisure. It was the housewife who was doing the work necessary for leisure; she made the comfortable kitchen in which the family could talk; she packed the cold lunch for the trip to the seaside; she budgeted for the special fête. Yet the full-time housewife reaped more of the benefits of increased leisure in comparison with women working a double shift in the factory and the home. . . . Attempts by women to improve their status by education were not an absolute success. Working-class housewives maintained consciousness of their group identity and actively resisted male power over them. This resistance was carried out within a system of shared values. A husband was a "good" man if he let the housewife do her work without interference. He was a "bad" man if he attempted to oversee or intervene in the home. When this happened, the housewife was liable to express resentment and resistance. This is not to deny that the housewife was less powerful than her husband. Clearly the housewife had relatively less power to coerce and, when it came to the crunch, the husband's superior physical strength and financial bargaining power gave him a considerable advantage. However, the bullied housewife may not have felt ill-treated or oppressed. For her, there was an important distinction between legitimate and illegitimate uses of power.

Subversion is at the centre of all oppressive structures. In 1974 E. P. Thompson wrote: "The same man who touches his forelock [shows deference] to the squire by day—and who goes down in history as an example of deference—may kill his sheep, snare his pheasant or poison his dogs at night." A woman may express contradictory opinions about her husband and family depending on the audience, the issue being discussed and the immediate circumstances. One moment she may be heard approving; the next, denying. To one person she may express resentment; to another, merely a desire to see things slightly modified. Occasionally (though not rarely) she uses violence to fight for what she considers to be her rights. Furthermore subversion and resistance were part of the accepted reality of marital relations and were explicitly promoted in female-dominated media. Thus, women's magazines published articles entitled "Strategy with Husbands," "The Kingdom of the Home and How to Rule It" and "Are Men Inferior?"

Housewives sometimes physically fought men who did not appreciate the subtle balance between the rights of husbands to a degree of symbolic authority and the rights of wives to rule the household. In the words of one poor London woman in 1906, "I chastise my husband like a child." Violence was most frequently adopted by women in response to a man's attempt to assert his will aggressively. Women would fight back when beaten up by husbands. Thus, in 1908, when the district nurse, M. Loane, expressed dismay on hearing that a certain husband hit his wife, a working-class neighbour explained: "She isn't a bit afraid o' he. If he do give her a good smack, she do give he another"; on which Loane commented: "I gathered that this was the usual custom in the neighbourhood if husbands so far forgot themselves, which was rather rare." Sometimes violence was only used after a wife's patience in "talking him down" was used up. Then she might "go berserk and clump the old man for all she was worth." She would threaten to "brain him"; a threat which always worked since no one doubted that she would do it. Husbands were liable to find heavy bass mats, irons, trays of toffee, brooms, loaves of bread, boxes of buttons, shovels, sheep's heads and whatever else was at hand thrown at them, if they arrived home late ("more foolish than when they went out") or drunk or were unappreciative of the wife's efforts in the home. A girl in the East End resented the fact that her husband took his time coming to bed ("He seemed to forget he had a wife with a lovely little fanny just waiting for him"), so she threw a book at him. More dangerously, knives could be waved in front of stubborn husbands.

Less aggressive, but still daring, ways of resisting included lying about money or stealing from husbands. A correspondent in the *Pawnbrokers' Gazette* mentioned a wife who stole her husband's wooden leg while he slept. She pawned his leg, saying "now he'll have to stop at home until he shells out." A domestic servant in London at the turn of the century justified the fact that she lied to her husband about how much profit she had made from a certain bargain with the words, "Now, if I do say I'll do a thing, I do do it, and everyone that do know me will tell you the same. Now me husband, he's not straight. If anyone do act fair with me, I do do the same with them." Or, in the words of another poor woman, "If anyone tries to do me, I does them." In other words, certain forms of "stealing" were legitimate, because wives have a right to the income earned by household members, and they have a right to be treated fairly and honestly.

Language could also be used in a confrontational manner. A noisy argument might help a housewife get her own way within the household. A man could be rebuked for being a few minutes late for dinner, "after me slavin' away all mornin.'" The use of swearing is another example. When Jasper's mother was angry with her husband, she would call him all the "miserable old gits" she could remember and these words would "start a real bust-up." Men—and husbands in particular—considered swearing as a deliberately provocative action. Nancy Tomes's analysis of wife-beating shows that swearing was generally mentioned by wife-beaters as the "final straw."

These forms of open insubordination were, however, often dangerous and counter-productive. It is not surprising, therefore, to discover that the most common forms of resistance for housewives were non-confrontational: manipulation, slander and disdainful silence. . . .

Different forms of address were adopted if a husband needed to be persuaded—forms such as "my dear," "love," "darling" and so on. Housewives may use appropriate linguistic forms of deference to get their own way, but this should not be taken to mean that they believe in the superiority of the "master." To his face, they may cajole; behind his back they may sneer. In working-class Salford at the turn of the century, Robert Roberts's mother responded to a visitor's question "An' is the master at home now?" with "I haven't one . . . but my husband's out." To get a man to do the housework while the housewife is ill, they might beg for his "help" and praise his "goodness," while knowing behind his back that it was his duty. To make a husband stop beating his wife, neighbouring wives could use the language of chivalry, but that does not mean that they believed in male superiority. Significantly, when all other protests had gone unnoticed by the "male head," a woman most commonly resorted to arguments based on an ideology of women's weakness. . . .

We should not dismiss small acts of resistance as somehow less "political" than mass movements of resistance. Risk-averse protests were not lower forms of resistance; they were the *preferred* response to oppression. For the housewife, the personal (sometimes anonymous) character of her resistance was not only an integral part of her position within society and the family, but also an integral part of the very value system she was defending. Her goals were not to overthrow the family, but to protect it from the threats posed by "breadwinners," not to drive away her husband, but to consolidate her role as housewife. It was no less radical for all that.

28

THE RISE OF SPORTS

JAMES WALVIN

This selection and the one immediately following deal with new leisure forms emerging around 1900, forms that attracted all the urban classes. Modern leisure involved commercial organization and widespread spectatorship, but they embraced other values as well, including values that mimicked work routines and military virtues along with new forms of display and honor.

The emergence of sports as a key leisure outlet, particularly, though not exclusively, for men in both middle and working classes was a fundamental development in the later nineteenth century. Sports served all sorts of interests; they recalled traditions, and most of the new games that spread out from England were based on older rough-and-tumble team play. Updated through new rules and standardization, sports meshed with working patterns by providing examples of speed, coordination, and competitiveness. Sports helped form new community ties, recapturing some qualities of earlier festivals. They also lent themselves to commercial exploitation, as companies could sell sporting equipment and form professional teams.

Enthusiasm for specific sports multiplied steadily. Soccer-football teams developed on both amateur and professional levels, first in England and then elsewhere. Cricket, tennis, track and field, boxing—the list expanded. Local teams and pick-up games combined with team play in newly built mass stadiums, before tens of thousands of screaming fans.

The following selection deals with some of the initial bases of sports enthusiasm and, through this, what the rise of sports meant. It emphasizes links with wider loyalties in England, including the race to expand the empire. It also stresses the initial importance of sports in serving middle-class interests to find new ways to control and socialize male youth, now that periods of schooling expanded. First applied to middle-class children themselves in exclusive public schools, the sports regimen seemed appropriate to deal with what the middle class perceived as problems and ill-discipline in the working class.

The cross-class basis for the rise of sports was vital to the new role athletics gained, but the selection makes it clear that sports were transformed in

From: James Walvin, "Symbols of Moral Superiority: Slavery, Sport and the Changing World Order 1800–1950," in James Walvin and J. A. Mangan, eds., *Manliness and Morality: Middle-Class Masculinity in Britain and America 1800–1940* (Manchester: Manchester University Press, 1987), pp. 247–58.

working-class hands. Sports as discipline, as an interest that transcended class, and as a means of class expression—all these facets combined during the seed period of one of modern society's abiding institutions.

Finally, the selection must be judged in light of other aspects of middle-class development in the later nineteenth century. Sports and their justifications help explain how the class could move into leisure interests despite, or rather because of, its work values. The selection should be compared with the treatment of work habits (see Chapter 23), noting also that the English middle class moved into the sports enthusiasm earlier than its French counterpart.

Writing in 1888, a commentator on football remarked: "Health, endurance, courage, judgement, and above all a sense of fair play, are gained upon the football field. A footballer must learn, and does learn, to play fairly in the thick and heat of a struggle. Such qualities are those which make a nation brave and great. The game is manly and fit for Englishmen; it puts a courage into their hearts to meet any enemy in the face. . . ."

In retrospect it is easy to minimise the physical dangers and hardships of life on the imperial frontiers. Contemporary travel and hygiene, the infancy of tropical medicine and the simple newness of so many colonial and overseas Europeans settlements determined that a life of "duty", in the imperial or trading cause, would be arduous and difficult. And how were young men to be trained and conditioned for the physical rigours of such a life? Fortunately, British schools had developed the perfect tool for perfecting and honing the physical and collective qualities needed in such a venture—school games. The playing field—later the playground in the state schools—was as important as the class room in inculcating a number of attitudes and in encouraging the physical fitness which imperial life demanded. Moreover, it was at games that the British excelled like no other people, not surprisingly perhaps since they were the pioneers and originators of many of the games which, though new at the time, have subsequently come to dominate modern mass leisure pursuits.

The ideal of public school athleticism began earlier in the century in the idealised world of Thomas Hughes. . . . The playing fields were the place where public schools put into practice their own distinctive brand of Social Darwinism; in games, only the fittest survived or triumphed. One public school man argued that the rigours of the school system forced its pupils to be "broken in to many things, and hardened simply by a process of friction to endure, to suffer, to be patient, to bide his time . . . to take care of himself, to hold his own, to fight his way, to trust to his best, his own determination, and coolness, and pluck." . . .

The history of modern team games is the history of the nineteenth-century public [elite private] school. There, the games were codified, rationalised and disciplined. The natural instinct for play among the young was given a new focus and purpose. Games became an agency for disciplining the young and addicting them to a number of important individual and collective qualities: obedience, physical commitment, accepting rules and authority and to give one's all for the good of the team (or house, or school, or country). They also of course involved the universal lessons of endurance and fortitude, and give and take and striving to win, but team sports in particular also encapsulated a number of important ideals about rank, social role, class and race—all of which had important ramifications for Britain's role in the wider world. Endurance and toughness—finely tuned in the Social Darwinism of public school games—were clearly important (as contemporary boys' magazines regularly told) in the world of imperial conquest and administration.

The two games which dominated the lives of public school athleticism (and later the board schools)—football and cricket—were highly structured and disciplined. If their pre-modern folk roots were indisciplined and informal, by the late nineteenth century they were formal and disciplined, with their own codes of behaviour and governing bodies and impartial officials (on and off the field). Both were subjected to the determining regulation of the clock and both demanded of their players an acceptance of a given role within the team. A player's role and value were subsumed to the greater needs of the team itself (notwithstanding the fact that the games' best-remembered players are men whose distinctive athletic genius allowed them to flout team play). As teams, cricket and football had a chain of command which reached from the playing field into a higher structure of authority (house or school captain). Playing these games, like working in many of the newer industrial occupations, was a means of accepting that structure of authority; obedience to betters/superiors, obeying orders and a commitment to pursuing the interests of the team—all of these had abiding importance in the broader conduct of British life at home and abroad. Games were, in some key respects, an illustration of contemporary Social Darwinism but they were equally instrumental in establishing a broadly-based discipline whose consequences transcended the mere playing of games.

The key issue however is not that the British simply played games but that they were *better* than others at those games. British athleticism—original, manly and pioneering—was but another illustration of the superiority of the British. Sports and games seemed to confirm the abundant evidence which was available on all hands—economic ascendancy, imperial prime, diplomatic assertiveness—that Britain was the world's pre-eminent power. Moreover, that global pre-eminence was to be found in the personal and collective qualities of her people. If Britain was the world's leading power, it was because her people were superior. There is again a welter of evidence to illustrate the fact that the British *believed* themselves to be superior. . . .

There were, however, distinctly worrying dimensions to this interpretation, especially when, from the 1860s, it came to be applied to *domestic* British life; when sociologists and anthropologists in analysing British life began to speak of the lower order as a race apart. While it was possible to claim that the upper and middle orders held sway because of their racial superiority over the poorer classes, what did these racial fissures do to the alleged claim of an *overall* British racial superiority? How could the British be so superior if, by the same criteria of natural selection and racial categorisation, a substantial part (perhaps a majority) of British life itself consisted of racially-inferior beings? In 1864, the *Saturday Review* wrote: "The Bethnal Green poor, as compared with the comfortable inhabitants of western London, are a caste apart, a race of whom we know nothing, whose lives are of a quite different complexion from ours." . . .

Lazy, stupid, ignorant, unwilling to work unless compelled; the urban poor shared a racially-determined category remarkably like colonial blacks, and few British people were so frequently denounced in racial terms as the Irish, hundreds of thousands of whom lived the lives of helots in major English and Scottish cities. . . .

Awareness of material deprivation among the urban poor had been one inspiration behind the urge to encourage athleticism and manliness among the young. The reasons for the development of manliness among public school boys is clear enough. More bemusing is why this concept—specific to a particular educational and social *milieu*—should be extended among working class boys. As we have seen, from the mid-nineteenth century, there was mounting concern about the "condition of England" as evidence came to hand, from diverse sources, of the human wretchedness in urban life. Moreover, it was equally clear that the young suffered from many of the physical ailments and afflictions worse than adults. Indeed, lingering and fatal illness among the young was an inescapable fact of Victorian society. An increasingly professional medical world steadily accumulated—and published—a mass of ghastly evidence about the physical weaknesses and shortcomings of urban children. Moreover, that data was added to by evidence more broadly available after all the urban young began to attend schools in the last quarter of the century. In 1870 medical observers began to call for physical exercises—drill— among school children as an antidote to a number of widespread ailments. In the last twenty years of the century, physical education made great progress throughout English elementary schools. Of course, there were the years of the extraordinary explosion in mass leisure pursuits in Britain when the British turned to organised games and commercial pleasures to a degree, and in numbers, which amazed contemporaries. With a little more spare cash available and with entrepreneurs actively creating varied commercial entertainments, millions of people now spent their free time at organised leisure—at football, music hall, seaside and the like.

There was, in effect, a congruence of forces propelling people, especially the young, towards a number of leisure forms which had the virtues of being enjoyable and apparently healthy. Games were actively encouraged among working class children by those public school men whose calling—in the churches, schools or simply as voluntary workers drew them into working class life. Ministers and curates, keen to help their flock to lead a better, fuller life and committed to the view that "the laws of physical well-being are the laws of God", established games, teams, leagues and competitions. Indeed, a substantial number of modern soccer teams began life as church or Sunday school teams. This was a development paralleled in the new school system. Again, the public schools led by example as their ex-pupils—now teachers, heads and administrators—actively promoted their old schools' games in working class communities. There followed a pattern which had been noticeable in public schools a generation earlier. Competitions proliferated among plebeian boys' teams, between schools, leagues and later even between different towns and cities. By the end of the century thousands of spectators paid to watch the finals of schoolboy football matches. How many of those tens of thousands of committed spectators and players knew that the games, the competitions, the trophies and the very enthusiasm were, like the FA [Football Association] Cup itself, inspired and founded by the public schools?

By the turn of the century, the commitment to manly pursuits among working class boys had begun to worry some observers who appreciated its obvious risks: "Our school competitions in football and other sports have now become a severe tax on the strength of any boy and particularly on the poorly-clad and ill-fed."

What made football so abidingly popular with young working class boys was, however, its basic attraction: the ease with which it could be organised and played, in most urban areas, with indeterminate numbers. This was, in a sense, a return to the popularity of the game as a *folk* custom though, by the late nineteenth century, overlaid with a new structure and meaning. Boys playing football in the street was a common complaint and a cause of regular and numerous non-indictable juvenile offences. This basic enthusiasm was tapped by energetic and enthusiastic teachers, anxious to direct their pupils' energies into useful channels and to put youthful zest to good ends. When football established itself in schools it often became an attraction, luring boys to, or keeping them at, school. Gradually this enthusiasm persuaded even the most resistant of educationalists that vigorous team games were of great educational and social importance. By 1900, members of staff were instructed to "teach the most skilful method of play, and should encourage orderly behavior." In 1904 the New Code of Regulations for Elementary Schools—prefaced by Robert Moran, himself an ex-Winchester pupil—stated: "The corporate life of the school, especially in the playground, should develop the instinct for fair play and for loyalty to one another which is the germ of a wider sense of honour in later life." The physical facilities available remained, in general, poor but could occasionally be supplemented by neighbouring municipal facilities and open spaces, encouraged by associations devoted to acquiring and maintaining public playing fields.

However ill or well-endowed, the playing field or playground was the place where new plebeian footballers were expected to acquire those qualities long familiar to the public school player, and time and again the late century working class game was extolled for the same virtues. In 1893 the headmaster of Loretto thought football and rugby a "means of testing the manly prowess of representative teams of schools, colleges, clubs, villages or other communities. . . ." A letter in the *Glasgow Herald* a year later claimed that football developed "physical strength and agility, swiftness of foot, self-control, courage and manliness." Lord Rosebery, presenting the FA Cup in 1897 claimed that the game encouraged those "splendid characteristics of the British race—stamina and indomitable pluck." By the end of the century, major football matches attracted leaders of the main political parties; in a democracy, elected teachers needed to associate themselves with the games of the people. Furthermore, it was even argued that the game healed political divides: "all Englishmen meet upon common ground for the furtherance of every pursuit which can add to the manliness of the people, or to the available strength and resources of the country." On the eve of World War I, proponents of football in particular (and of competitive sports in general) imputed to the game a host of extraordinary personal and collective qualities. It was viewed as the elixir of personal and social ills—regular doses from an early age would work magical cures—and, in the process, the national good was greatly enhanced; national unity, physical well-being, social harmony and cohesion would be furthered. . . .

Sport offered the comforting illusion of continuing effortless superiority and of the means of restoring the nation to good health and mental security. It was reassuring to believe that the cult of manliness which underpinned the development of public-school and popular games was a key agency in this process. There is no doubt that it was a quite remarkably powerful force—an inspiration and belief among successive generations of public school men, who took their proselytising commitment to games and manliness throughout Britain and around the world. . . .

29

Mass Culture in Paris

CHARLES REARICK

Here is a second view of the rise of modern leisure in the decades around 1900. Sports figure in, but the emphasis in this case is on leisure as entertainment and escape, and on new commercial exploitation of leisure forms, including deliberate efforts to draw unprecedented audiences through low ticket prices.

Parisian mass leisure in the late nineteenth century had many facets, including famous stage shows, fairs, working-class cabarets, street entertainments and—by 1900–early movies. Variety was a hallmark, as was change.

The earliest forms of the new leisure allowed working-class audiences some voice over content. Themes in the small popular theaters evoked earthy, spontaneous expression—somewhat reminiscent of older festival or courtship approaches from preindustrial society. Some historians have even argued that the new entertainment showed how lively preindustrial popular culture had remained, underground, since its heyday. Middle-class observers, predictably, were often appalled, but some elements of the middle class joined in, finding popular expressions a way to indulge their own growing but somewhat constrained sense of fun. Leisure forms were not entirely class specific.

At the same time, some public disapproval, plus the desire of commercial organizers to win large audiences through common entertainment denominators, did limit the ability of working-class groups to use this leisure as a direct expression. The rise of movies, though reflecting earlier mass entertainment styles, further reduced audience involvement. Was the new mass leisure ultimately manipulative and hollow? What did working-class participants want from their leisure—and did they get what they sought?

A French workingman visiting the Paris Universal Exposition in 1889 could find before him an expanse and variety of amusements that no king or noble had ever commanded. That the common man should have such opportunity was fitting, since one of the purposes of the fair was to mark the centenary of a revolution against privilege and inequality. Anyone could enter that

From: Charles Rearick, *Pleasures of the Belle Europe* (New Haven, CT: Yale University Press, 1985), pp. 83–84, 90–93, 95–96, 101–104, 110, 189–90, 193–95.

wonderland for half the low official admission of one franc and sometimes for even less, for many holders of twenty entry-packets were competitively hawking their extra tickets. Or if he chose not to go to the fair, the clerk or carpenter could go out on the town and, for a franc or two, hear and see the best professional singers and comics and acrobats in the land. New places of entertainment flourished by serving worker as well as bourgeois, particularly in the center of Paris.

Most numerous and accessible were the cafés-concerts, of which there were an estimated 264 in the capital around the turn of the century. Most of them charged no admission and made money only on drink and food. At the most basic they were simply cafés with a small stage and some singers, providing entertainment for the ordinary price of a beer. The cafés-concerts were the "democratized theater," declared Jules Claretie, journalist and director of the Comédie-Française. They were the "theaters of the poor," noted expert André Chadourne in his book on cafés-concerts. In the last decades of the nineteenth century some of these places broke with the "temple of song" format and became English-style music halls with richly varied programmes and showy theaterlike interiors. . . .

Under an ochre and gold ceiling of ruffled and tasseled fabric, amid allegorical statuary and rattan divans, customers could watch a trapeze duo, ballet dances, a juggler, a snake charmer, wrestlers, clowns, and such novelty acts as a kangaroo boxing a man—or an array of other spectators throughout the well-lighted hall. No matter where one sat or stood, one's ears were filled with a medley of waltzes and polkas and finale chords blaring over the cries of program hawkers and shoeshiners, audience chatter and applause. Everywhere the air was laden with perfume scents and the acrid odors of cigar smoke, beer, and dusty rugs. The miscellany of sensations mixed together as promiscuously as the prostitutes, *mondaines* [sophisticates], and their admirers in the famous *promenoir* (gallery-lounge) with its elegant bar that Manet's painting has immortalized. "It is ugly and it is splendid," concluded Huysmans; "it is of an outrageous and exquisite taste." In the Folies-Bergère as in the Scala or the Eldorado, the "worker, employee, the bourgeois, the *flaneur* of every profession by means of one or two 20-sou coins is as entertained as an emperor of the One Thousand and One Nights at the height of power, magnificence and idleness," asserted the Comte d'Avenel, a scholarly observer who devoted a whole book to the subject of the "leveling of enjoyments" in modern times. . . .

In 1893 clients of the Moulin Rouge for a small sum could hear the best and latest Edison phonograph available in France playing the music of a New York orchestra, the greatest singers of the day, the Plébins reciting monologues. At the Fête de Vincennes in April 1901, seamstresses and butchers could, for a mere four sous, take a ride in an automobile.

Or for only a franc they could watch the horse races. Once a sport confined to the rich and aristocratic, the racetracks in the 1890s drew new clients from lower social levels. Up to 40,000 people went to the Paris track on

Sundays at the turn of the century, and the greatest part of them walked there and paid the lowest admission of one franc to watch from the standing area, the *pelouse*. In the 1870s Longchamp races, which consistently drew the largest crowds through the entire period, were attended by never more than 200,000 a year on the pelouse; by the 1890s, attendance there was in the 500,000 to 600,000 range. One of the reasons was the establishment of a regular pari-mutuel system of betting, which allowed small bettors without particular expertise a greater chance of winning something; "the people" increasingly indulged in betting alongside counts and millionaires at Longchamp, if not at the more distant Chantilly and Deauville. The growth of racetrack attendance and sums wagered is perhaps the best evidence for democratic leveling of amusements in the belle époque. . . .

In plebeian places of amusement, social mixing occurred when the well-to-do and socially prominent dropped in to sample lowlife. "It is well known that the height of refinement for *mondains* is to come mix themselves in these popular amusements," journalist "Jacques Lux" observed of street fairs in 1907. At the end of the Old Regime the nobility had enjoyed rubbing shoulders with the rabble at fairs and Italian comedies; similar excursions downward became fashionable again in the 1880s. At the Folies-Bergère or the Cirque Fernando, middle- and upper-class spectators could relax and indulge in unpretentious common tastes. In the cafés-concerts, Georges Montorgueil testified, there reigned a "kind of freedom and openness in the American manner": men kept their hats on, dressed as casually as they liked, and smoked cigars. "It's the ideal of 'no bother' and it is the only [ideal] that people in these places of distraction want in reality." To join the rabble *(s'encanailler)* from time to time was apparently a refreshing flight from the predictable rituals of a restricted upper class. . . .

The workers and poor had their own cafés-concerts that attracted few others, not just out in the proletarian zone around Paris, but also in the center of the city. In a special issue on cafés-concerts, the *Paris illustré* noted in 1886 that workers made up the regular audience at the Ba-Ta-Clan and the Epoque, halls on the Boulevard Voltaire and the Boulevard Beaumarchais, respectively. At the Pépinière, Rue de la Pépinière, one found soldiers from nearby camps and domestic servants of the neighborhood. "These domestics come to the concert every evening: the *valet de chambre* correct, freshly shaved; the coachman, giving his arm to Madame's chambermaid." At the Concert-Cluny, butcher boys and other workers predominated; their singing drowned out the voices of the performers. Working-class clients also filled the Grand Concert de la Presse on the Rue Montmartre. At the Folies-Rambuteau, "a sort of barn," one found "a poor public, coming from everywhere, and the little Jewish France of the Faubourg du Temple." The Concert de la Gaîté Montparnasse also served its immediate neighborhood, especially the local shopkeepers, tradesmen, workers, and their families. Like most theaters, most music halls served primarily a neighborhood and a quite limited range of social classes. . . .

Despite the vogue of occasional slumming, suspicion and hostility toward newer popular entertainments festered in the middle and upper levels of society. Minister of Fine Arts Jules Simon fulminated in 1872 against "these base shows [of the cafés-concerts] which spread and sell poison around us"; from that moral point of view the situation continued only to deteriorate through la belle époque. In 1886 in a special issue devoted to cafés-concerts, a *Paris illustré* article blasted them as "the wonderland of the ugly, the obscene, and the grotesque. . . . it's degradation [*abrutissement*]." "Nothing is more grievous for the sincere friends of art than the growing success of those establishments which at this century's close threaten the downfall of good taste and the lowering of the intellectual and moral level of the masses," wrote a historian of Marseilles in 1891, as he noted the spread of "splendid cafés-concerts in the style of the Parisian Folies-Bergère, . . . pernicious products of the unlimited liberty of theaters." "In sum, the inquietude of the belly and the-below-the-belly composes almost all the repertory of the café-concert," lamented writer Gustave Coquiot in a book on the subject in 1896. Even music hall star Paulus railed against "the invading march of filthy licentiousness" in café-concert songs.

The subjects of songs and jokes that drew the biggest and surest laughs. Montorgeuil reported, were diarrhea and constipation, beans, and breasts—their smallness or ampleness. In the early 1890s the enormously popular Pétomane threw Moulin Rouge audiences into hilarity by playing "Au clair de la lune" on a flute attached by a hose to his anus, not to mention his farting both like cannon fire and like a bride on her wedding night and then the day after. The hefty singer Dufay amused by cracking nuts on her robust chest, which she explained was "made of iron"; her rival Demay broke them by sitting on them. She also sang such ditties as:

I am married to a man
Who has the sweet name of Victor,
But what annoys and wears me out,
Is that he has the fault of snoring loudly.
Sleeping he makes so much noise
That he frightens the people of the neighborhood
And to calm their alarm
I am obliged to repeat to them:
It's Victor who is snoring, the precious thing,
It's Victor who is sleeping,
It's from his nose that it comes out.

Female singers also won favor with a startling frankness about money and sex, expressed in such remarks as "to love equals to pay, give and take/cash down [*donnant donnant*]" and "I find men perfect if they are generous."

Alongside love songs—tragic or happy, and an occasional artsy classic chanson for which Yvette Guilbert became so famous—went the chauvinist swagger of a Paulus, the drunken gestures of Bourges, the nonsensical rhymes of comic soldier Polin, and the inane saws of Dranem (for example, "Les P'tits pois" [small peas]). Mixed throughout was violent slapstick; "always delighting," noted Montorgueil, was the liberal distribution of blows and cuffs to the ear and mouth, breaking teeth and noisily knocking them out. The chahut, or cancan, also delighted many, but to some, including even a music hall insider like André Chadourne, the dances of La Goulue (Glutton) and Grille d'Egout (Sewer Grating) were "appalling exhibitions of women snatched from the lowest gutters." From 1894 on, Victorian-style striptease acts, involving more display of petticoat and chemise than nudity, became part of the music hall repertory, bringing new outcries of disgust and condemnation. Dancers like Violette entered the stage to calls of "Take your pants off" and "higher, show it." A lascivious taint derived also from reports that some directors forced women performers to make themselves available after the show—for the directors themselves or for select clients. Spectacles such as women's wrestling (borrowed from the fairs) and sometimes fatal daredevil stunts brought further reproach—and eager crowds—to the flourishing establishments.

Such places were also notorious for their excesses of smoke and noise. "People came there to make a row [*du potin*]," recalled Yvette Guilbert. "People came there to make some chahut"—that is, uproar, rowdiness. So "loud-mouthed singers were hired to cover the everyday noise with their voices." . . .

The old intimacy between popular crowds and [entertainers] was further strained as the street-show entrepreneurs became bourgeois, big businessmen with considerable capital investment and a genteel manner of speaking and living. The individual fairgoer was left to a more strictly visual experience when strolling by the booths. At the same time proliferating mechanical rides absorbed customers in their own sensations and turned them into moving objects in orbits apart from the milling crowd.

The most thoroughgoing transformation of life into captivating spectacle took place through the new magic of the movies. Though they separated audience from performers definitively, they also created transitory new publics sharing the same view of the same scenes and sometimes sharing reactions of laughter, hisses, and applause. But critics of the cinema observed that in the darkened halls (darker than other spectacle halls) where the new vivid images held sway, there was strangely little audience reaction. Were the moving images so entrancing that they turned people into gaping badauds [idlers]?

Cinema was born and nurtured in the badauds' stamping ground, the Paris boulevards. On that cold night of December 28, 1895, when Louis Lumière gave the first commercial show in the basement of the Grand Café at 14 Boulevard des Capucines, only the most inveterate boulevardiers turned out. Thirty-five customers paid a franc each to see the new spectacle. Though the press virtually ignored the debut, word did spread quickly; audiences grew rapidly and competing entrepreneurs scrambled to get into the new business. Within weeks the music halls were incorporating the novelty into their catchall programs. The Folies-Bergère showed "American Biograph" movies between song and dance and acrobatic numbers. By April 1896 the Eldorado and the Olympia were competing with their own movies, and the Théâtre Isola was screening a color film of Loïe Fuller doing her serpentine dance. Also as early as April 1896 magic-show impresario Georges Méliès had introduced kinetograph-animated photography into his Robert Houdin Theater on the Boulevard des Italiens, and soon he began to make and show his own creations. In a large department store on the Boulevard Barbès, Dufayel featured movies near his furniture gallery. The street fairs were also quick to adopt the new entertainment. Pétomane, the enterprising Pujol, ran a movie booth in Paris fairs for three years beginning in 1899, and by then the fair showmen were major providers of the new entertainment. By the turn of the century another forain named Charles Pathé had turned from playing popular novels on a phonograph to the movie business, establishing a dozen fairground theaters, some of which held as many as a thousand seats, in the foire du Trône and the fairs of Neuilly, Clichy, and Batignolles.

Like the spectacle of the boulevard, film fascinated with external appearances, visual sensations, available for little cost and with little formality. As in any successful boulevard and street-fair entertainment, prices were low—from fifty centimes to one franc usually; some small baraques charged as little as twenty centimes. And customers did not have to bother with dressing up or observing any particular etiquette modeled by their social superiors. In short, it was entertainment for the common people, and they responded to it unhampered by any precedent making for stuffiness or pretensions.

At first moviegoers, like ordinary badauds, watched not only the most banal scenes of public life—a train pulling into a station (Louis Lumière, 1896) and Lumière workers leaving the factory in Lyon—but also the exceptional sights that always drew crowds: a parade, the Czar's visit to Paris in October 1896, President Faure in Russia in August 1897, and the Festival of Flowers at the 1900 Exposition. Like the badauds of the boulevards, moviegoers gave their attention to moving subjects not requiring long concentration. The first films lasted only about a minute or two each; the entire program of ten different films lasted about twenty minutes. Such visual experiences were unusual only in that the scenes were being mechanically reproduced with movement in a way never seen before. With unprecedented visual verisimilitude, life was recreated by machine as spectacle. The spectators ready to appreciate it—practiced badauds, if you will—were numerous and primed for cinema well before its invention. . . .

Contemporary observers recognized the invention's extraordinary power. . . . They noted that movies dealt in primitive gestures and simple images, a universal language that even the simplest, most uneducated, and fatigued spectator could follow. And the "living pictures" brought actors close up, producing an impact that players on a stage could not, especially for spectators in the poorer, distant seats. Further, movies required little reflection and little imagination—only looking, looking, looking, as one particularly unsympathetic critic remarked of the silent films. Their special power over audiences aroused significant worries and objections from a variety of critics. Movies could be propaganda, it was noted, powerful influencers of behaviors. Like a drug, movies dulled and warped spectators' sense of reality, reducing human dramas to a primitive simplicity. Movies were moving some young people to go out and imitate the action just seen on film—most alarmingly, to commit violent crimes, it was widely reported. . . .

The new magic of moving images in darkened halls perhaps better countered the isolation and ennui of spectators; apparently it allowed them to escape more easily their everyday constraints and to identify with heroes and a piquant variety of experiences beyond their usual ken—more effectively than did panoramas, the illustrated press, vaudeville sketches, or theater melodramas. Powerfully captivating through the primary visual sense, movies could "enlarge the horizon of spectators in a surprising way," providing vicarious adventure and revealing the interiors of palaces, distant lands, or tumultuous wars, wrote Max Nordau just before the outbreak of the war.

If movies were liberating, they were also controlling. More than any other entertainment, they subjected people to mechanical, industrial, highly centralized power. They were standardized, mass-produced spectacles, each unvarying and unresponsive to audiences, each easily repeated anywhere and everywhere in uniform fashion. They were "image factories," as one contemporary critic wrote. Perhaps they created new habits and needs (the habit and need of going to the movies, at the least), but they also reinforced behavior already entrenched in industrial, urban work life. Treating spectators as inert and uniform parts of a grand machine—or system of production and consumption— the "image factories" extended modern work life into leisure, as Theodor Adorno has observed. In taking people beyond old horizons, the movies took them farther from the festive community of the past.

30

TOYS AND WAR

KENNETH D. BROWN

The following article uses a number of social history topics, some of them
quite new, to help explain one of the great historical events of European and
world history in the early twentieth century: World War I. The data this new
research uncovered are blended with a sense of historical change, and an admittedly loose interpretation of psychology, to produce a distinctive sociohistorical contribution to historical causation.

The history of childhood is a difficult but challenging facet of social history. Childhood is by no means an unchanging experience, though information is sometimes hard to come by because children themselves leave few
records. With modern consumerism, new commercial influences and products,
including toys, help shape what children do and what they carry on to adulthood. In this article, changing patterns of toy production are blended with
other evidence of growing militarism among children and the adults who particularly shaped boys' activities. The link with leisure forms, including masculine sports, is obvious and important, as play took on new meanings.

Two other, familiar analytical staples enter in. Social class is one. With
consumer production and sweeping cultural influences at play, class boundaries might combine with some crosscutting attractions—including the attraction of toy soldiers. Inevitably, we know more about what upper-class boys did
with and thought about their toys than about the experiences of the lower orders; but consumption figures strongly suggest important common ground.

Gender looms large. Toy soldiers appealed for reasons beyond availability: meaningful consumer products rarely spread without contributions from a
wider social and cultural context. Boys, and the men who guided boys, had
new reasons to establish their masculinity, and military interests, along with
sports, could serve vital functions here. With work increasingly prosaic for
many men, and with women demanding new rights and functions, it seemed
both vital and comforting to establish some new canons of gender, beginning
in boyhood. Here also was a reason to carry boyhood delights over into adulthood. Grown men, including cabinet ministers, played with toy soldiers, and
some looked forward to playing with real war too.

From: Kenneth D. Brown, "Modelling for War? Toy Soldiers in Late Victorian and Edwardian
Britain," *Journal of Social History* 24 (1990): 237–41, 243–47.

Toys did not cause war. A host of factors, including well-known diplomatic and industrial rivalries, enter in. But innovative social history has its contribution to make. Toys, and the factors that promoted new interest in war toys and war games, help explain the readiness for war—and this readiness played a major role in the conflict that engulfed Europe and the world in 1914.

[Historian] Geoffrey Best once observed that it was the prevalence of militarism in Europe, rather than alliances and assassinations, which was ultimately responsible for the outbreak of the First World War. While such a suggestion cannot be empirically proven it is certainly difficult to see how, in the absence of just such a deeply engrained militarism, Britain was able to sustain its armed forces on a voluntary basis for well over a year of the most demanding war in its history. In the first two months of the conflict a fifth of all the men aged between 20 and 35 joined up. By the time conscription was introduced in 1916 a staggering two and a half million men had volunteered for the army alone.

In recent years social historians have identified many of the elements which served to create and sustain the environment which produced the fervent response of 1914. Thus the author of a popular general survey on the origins of the Great War has remarked that "schoolbooks and speechday orations, rifle corps and cadet groups, newspaper leaders and popular novels, Navy League pamphlets and military drill instructions books, import-export tables . . . have all become source materials for the serious investigator." These and other features of contemporary social life, it has been suggested accurately, albeit in a somewhat unlovely phrase, "constituted self-generating ethos reinforcement." In two stimulating books, the same writer has also drawn attention to the "cultural ephemera of imperialism"—post cards, board games, cigarette cards, jigsaws and even commercial packaging—all of which frequently had strong military and imperialistic themes. Also among such artifacts of everyday life which consciously or otherwise shaped the thought patterns and expectations of a generation were toy soldiers which, it has been argued, were "even more significant as recruiters for the armed forces." This may seem an excessive claim but in the two decades prior to 1914 there certainly was a toy soldier craze in Britain, although its historical significance has not perhaps been fully appreciated. It is the dual purpose of this paper, therefore, to establish the dimensions of the phenomenon and to examine some evidence concerning its likely contribution to the growth of contemporary militarism.

Toy soldier manufacture had a long history although the earliest products tended to be expensive and purchasers restricted to the relatively wealthy. In Germany strips of lead figures dating from about 1250 were found at Magdeburg in 1956. The earliest known survivals in France date from the thirteenth or fourteenth centuries and a valuable collection belonging to the French royal family perished, along with its owners, during the revolution of 1789. In Britain, too, the first known miniature soldiers appeared in an aristocratic context, the Rolls at Alnwick Castle, home of the Percys of Northumberland, containing references from the turn of the sixteenth century to monies spent for "tryminge of 4000 leaden soldiers." By the early nineteenth century the growing availability of new metals and the consequential cheapening of production combined with the growing public awareness of professional standing armies in Europe to widen considerably the toy soldier market. Some German towns, notably Nuremberg, were already well-established as centres of toy production and it was not surprising, therefore, that it should be German makers such as Johann Hilpert and Ernst Heinrichsen who emerged as Europe's first mass producers of toy soldiers. But the appeal and manufacture of these flat, two dimensional *Zinnfiguren* remained confined largely to continental Europe. They were not popular in Britain where such toy soldiers as were available tended in the main to be made of wood. The figures which the Bronte sisters had in their nursery, for instance, were of this type. These, too, however, usually came from Germany since there were very few toy makers at all in Britain. Thus when Captain William Siborne was commissioned in the 1830s to make a diorama of the Battle of Waterloo, it was to Germany that he sent for the 190,000 half-inch metal figures with which he made the model. . . .

What really caused the mass expansion of toy soldier production in Britain, however, was a technological breakthrough pioneered by a well-established British toy manufacturer, William Britain. In 1893 his firm marketed the first hollow metal soldier, produced by a process which adapted to metal casting a technique long used in the manufacture of wax doll heads. Because the resulting figure was hollow it was naturally cheaper to make than its solid European rivals. This had the added advantage of reducing domestic transport costs as well, since contemporary railway practice was to relate the charge for carriage to the value of freight. It has been generally accepted that William Britain was able to undercut German prices by about fifty percent in the British market. This, combined with their superior accuracy and finish, enabled his figures, therefore, to penetrate the market much more widely. Within two years of the first models appearing the domestic trade press was exultant, referring to their "well deserved popularity." Six months later another journal declared boldly that the Germans were no longer "in it" because of Britain's "unqualified success." By 1900 the firm was producing over 100 different models, mainly though not exclusively of British regiments. In 1907, the year after William Britain died, his five sons turned the enterprise into a private company with a capital value of £18,000. By 1910 about 200,000 figures a week were leaving the firm's small north London factory. . . . From the 1890s a toy whose appeal had been somewhat restricted by both price and availability, found its way into a much wider social range of homes. Naturally enough they appeared in vast quantities in the wholesalers and toy shops visited and described by the correspondents of the trade press. W. H. Gamage's popular department store was a major retail outlet which also sold by mail order. Woolworths carried a cheaper line of figures made especially for them by Britains after 1912. But the toys turned up in unlikely places, too, for example in the premises of a small town optician who capitalized on contemporary enthusiasm by selling them as a profitable, if somewhat unlikely, sideline to his main business. The toy soldier was also a stock feature in juvenile literature as a perusal of publications such as *Little Folks* reveals, while in 1910 one of the most popular comics, the *Boy's Own Paper,* thought Britains sufficiently important to run a substantial article on the firm. It was a justifiable decision, for there is no doubt that small boys provided the biggest market for the soldiers. Doubtless this was why "two large boxes of soldiers, and some artillery" were the means by which Galsworthy chose to console his fictional creation, the eight-year old Jon Forsyte, when his childhood nurse was paid off. They "co-operated with his grief in a sort of conversion, and . . . he began to play imaginative games, in which he risked the lives of countless tin soldiers . . ."

In 1901 thirty-two percent of the population of England, Wales and Scotland was aged under 14 years. Almost exactly half of them, slightly over six million, were boys. Some allowance should perhaps be made for the fact that both Charles Booth and Seebohm Rowntree estimated roughly a third of the urban population were living in primary or secondary poverty, although it should not automatically be assumed that toys were an unknown luxury for such unfortunates. Most commentators agree that even the poorest families made some effort to provide gifts at Christmas, even if birthday presents were comparatively rare. It is also relevant in this context to emphasize again that while most firms sold boxed figures, all of them produced cheaper models which were retailed singly. Indeed, one modern collector, Shamus Wade, found more Johillco figures in working class homes, largely, he suggested, because they could be purchased in this way. Assuming an even age distribution between nought and fourteen, about another two million boys were aged under five years and should also perhaps be discounted on the grounds that toy soldiers were not appropriate for them, although it is clear that then as now parents entertained unrealistic notions as to the suitability of toys. Thus one educationalist complained that "I have seen toy soldiers given to little boys before ever they had seen real soldiers or even heard of them." Some parents probably refused to buy toy soldiers for their children on religious or ethical grounds as well, although it is worth noting that by the turn of the century nonconformity, which by tradition was strongly anti-militarist, was becoming less overtly so. But even if we ignore all the poor and all those under five, and also make some allowance for religious sensibilities, we are still left with a minimum of some two and a half million small boys as potential customers—and it should not be forgotten that at least one popularizer of toy soldier games suggested that they were quite suitable for "the more intelligent sort of girls," as well. . . . [W]e know that military subjects were a favourite feature of boys' comics while oral evidence attests to the popularity of the imperial adventurings with which the army was intimately associated. Furthermore, it is important to note that toy soldier games were essentially home-centred, private activities, characteristics which, it has been argued, were becoming increasingly typical of leisure patterns, particularly among the working classes. . . . We know, for instance, of Harry Sweeting and John Walker who first acquired toy soldiers from parents in 1906 and 1908 respectively. There was also C. W. Beaumont, who, spying a box of Britain's Soudanese infantry in a shop window on his way to school, saved up his pocket money until he had the shilling necessary to make them his own. Subsequently, his Christmas present included one of Britain's larger boxes, containing two regiments each of cavalry and infantry and a 4.7 naval gun. Similarly, H. E. D. Harris, who later became a collector of some note, laid the foundations of his collection in childhood, receiving a weekly box of Britain's soldiers from his father as a reward for good conduct. . . .

It is generally the case that in all ages toys have been used not only for amusement but also as instruments of socialization and instruction, a way of introducing children to the realities of the adult world. Such was the tendency in late Victorian society to emphasize this educational aspect of toys that one contemporary psychologist was moved to protest in 1898 that the whole idea of "transforming play into an educational instrument has been carried quite far enough." His complaint went unheeded, however, and *Games and Toys* was able to claim in 1914 that during the previous twenty years it had become axiomatic that the toy dealer came "next to the parents . . . as a factor in the education of children." As far as toy soldiers were concerned, this educational role had a long pedigree among the upper classes. Joseph Strutt's early nineteenth century study of popular pastimes contained an illustration of a pair of toy jousting knights and the text pointed out that "persons of rank were taught in their childhood to relish such exercises as were of a martial nature, and the very toys that were put into their hands as playthings were calculated to bias the mind in their favour."

From the end of the century the vast extension of toy soldier production greatly increased the number of children who were exposed to this type of influence. The miniature figures took their place as part of a complex web of educative influences, both formal and informal, which linked the games of the nursery floor to the adolescent and adult worlds. Dearth of adequate evidence and the variability of social and economic circumstances make it virtually impossible to trace how this web operated to influence a particular individual. Rather, all that can be done is to suggest the possible nexus of relationships which may have existed within it. For the relatively privileged, playing with toy soldiers must sometimes have provided an appropriate background or stimulus for membership of the public schools' cadet corps or the various specialist classes which some institutions organized for intending army entrants. It is relevant perhaps in this connection that toy soldier production accelerated at exactly the same time as the cadet corps were being established in growing numbers in the public schools—after the Boer War. Even before this however, Winston Churchill had decided upon a military career and entered Sandhurst from Harrow's army class. This was a decision which he himself attributed to the influence of his toy soldier collection. "The toy soldiers turned the current of my life," he wrote later.

Lower down the social scale, there may have been a progression through the toy soldiers to one or other of the uniformed youth movements. The earliest of these, the Boys' Brigade, had distinct militaristic overtones which were manifested in the styles of its uniforms, its command structures, its bugle bands, and above all in its drilling with rifles. Similarly, the emphasis within the boy scout movement on outdoor pursuits, tracking, camping and the like, stressed a rather different and arguably newer set of military skills deriving from the experiences of the founder, Baden Powell, in the South African War [the Boer War]. . . .

In all of these ways, then, toy soldiers may have inter-acted with other aspects of Edwardian society to contribute to the growth of militarism, that "system of images, symbols, and rituals designed to express the character of the warrior," which was so prevalent in Britain following the debacle of the Boer War. In seeking to explain its growth, historians have rightly stressed the importance of youth movements, popular art, public schools, amateur soldiering, and the popular press. Yet it might be argued that with a minimum annual output of some ten or eleven million figures a year by 1914 toy soldiers were, potentially at least, much more significant than most of the other elements. Only a very small minority of boys attended public schools, the Boys' Brigade and the scouts had respective memberships in 1910 of 61,660 and 106,937, while the Volunteers numbered, together with the Yeomanry, about 280,000 in 1906. Furthermore, the appeal of the toys, as we have seen, cut across all class barriers. . . .

The importance of such games [with the toys] was that implicit in all of them were the ideas of enemy and conflict. Here perhaps the toys may have contributed to that buildup of aggression which, in some commentators' view, explains the rush to the colours in 1914. Most of William Britain's output, for example, came in sets of opposing armies, and their production provides a virtual catalogue of European and extra-European conflict between 1895 and 1914. Spanish and American infantry were made at the time of the Spanish-American War, for example. Existing figures were hastily converted into Boers to set against their readily available British counterparts when the South African War broke out. The various Balkan conflicts which preceded the First World War saw Turkish, Greek, Montenegrin, Serbian, and Bulgarian armies marching out of the Britains' factory. "Nine out of every ten boys until they are twelve years of age at least want to be soldiers," observed the *Toy and Fancy Goods Trader*, "and the desire is much greater if there is a war in progress in some part of the world. The Balkan War caused an increased demand for play soldiers and the market was fairly swamped with orders for these." . . .

Yet there is at least one school of modern psychological thought which traces the origin of men's aggressive instincts to the influences of upbringing and there were those in the late nineteenth century who were already making such a connection in the context of toy soldiers. This was why Oscar Wilde's wife felt it necessary when she addressed a meeting of the women's branch of the International Arbitration and Peace Society in 1888 to discuss the proposition that toy soldiers should be kept away from children. Even earlier, in 1871, a journalist, noting that "military toys come mainly from France and Germany," had suggested that "in the former country they probably serve as a sort of elementary training to fire the war spirit of the nation." Some years later, by which time the balance of military power in Europe had shifted significantly eastwards, a French toy expert made a similar comment about the Germans. "Nos voisins . . . ont fait du soldat de plomb un amusement en quelque sorte nationale destiné à échauffer leur patriotisme et à entretenir dans leur coeur les plus nobles traditions de l'honneur et du courage." Another Frenchman, the writer Pierre Benoit, shared this view, suggesting in his novel, *Axelle,* that toy soldier collectors were nothing more than "frustrated warmongers, seeking to transform the theory of the war game into practice. . ." Certainly his countryman, Charles de Gaulle, was one avid devotee of toy soldiers who subsequently followed a military career, as did Winston Churchill. Here perhaps is evidence of the fear expressed by Elsie Parsons that "the toy soldier, long after he has been put away with other childish things lives on unchallenged by reason." Similarly, H. G. Wells had no doubt that many of those with whom he had developed his war game before 1914 "remained puerile in their political outlook because of its persistence. I like to think that I grew up out of that stage . . . and began to think about war as a responsible adult should." Even more convincingly, one of the papers produced as part of the great University of Chicago study on the causes of war concluded that "men who fought frequently in childhood are more favourable to war than those who did not . . . people are favourable to war in proportion to the amount of military education and military service they have had."

In explaining the causes of war psychologists have been much attracted by the drive-discharge model, in which war is seen as a welcome release for aggressions denied valid outlets in the increasingly constrained contemporary world. . . . It seems likely that the Edwardian toy soldier boom both by its scope and implicit nature was an important part of the web of educative influences which helped to create and sustain the militarism which undergirded that initial enthusiasm for war. There was a significant output by a growing number of producers, a substantial market, both popular and elite, and there existed several obvious routes through which the soldiers marched into the mainstream of popular consciousness.

MURDER AND THE FAMILY:
SIGNS OF INDUSTRIAL CHANGE

ANNE PARELLA

Crime is an obvious social history topic, though attention to it has oscillated over time. Crime reveals much about social relationships—the motives of criminals, the reactions of respectable society at large capable, among other things, of redefining what constitutes crime and how it should be identified and punished (see Chapter 13).

Studies of crime trends have uncovered important, often unsuspected patterns. It is well established that, in Western history, in both Europe and North America (despite higher rates in the United States), crimes of violence have declined over time, between the early modern period and the twentieth century, on a per capita basis. Even subsequent increases, often widely noted and sometimes exaggerated, did not recapture earlier levels. Greater discipline and formal policing cut into traditional levels, and many criminals focused increasingly on thefts or confidence tricks rather than violence. Another important finding involves the development of new crime categories, like juvenile vandalism or, more recently, sexual harassment, that used to pass as acceptable if annoying human behaviors.

Renewed interest in crime in recent years has highlighted another important development: a shift in the framework for murder, in the later nineteenth century, even as murder rates declined overall, rather dramatically, on a per capita basis. The following selection explores these changes in the north of France (the Nord), a concentrated industrial area, and offers an explanation of the new patterns in terms of radically altered marital relationships and, ironically, an increase in the emotional importance of the family over other contacts such as male fellowship in taverns. Interestingly, similar findings have been uncovered, in precisely the same time period, in U. S. cities like Chicago. What do the new patterns mean? Does murder, a rare event, suggest general issues in family contacts around 1900, or an anomalous exception to more standard interactions between families and industrial society? This discussion

From: Anne Parella, "Industrialization and Murder: Northern France, 1815–1904," *Journal of Interdisciplinary History,* XXII:4 (Spring, 1992): 627–28, 630–33, 635, 637–39, 641, 647–49, 650–51, 653–57.

of changes in family configurations should be juxtaposed with the following selection, also dealing with family change but in terms of more widely adopted behaviors; and with Chapter 27, on the expectations and tensions associated with a growing commitment to housewifery.

Analysis of aggregate crime data has shown that rates of murder in preindustrial societies were sometimes extremely high compared to those in industrialized cities of the nineteenth century. Modern industrial societies exhibit high levels of crime in general (property damage and various other offenses, including "victimless" crimes), but relatively lower rates of criminal homicide.

By the nineteenth century, murder was already an infrequent crime in many European societies. If the overall murder rate were low, then industrialization would not necessarily have had any notable impact on the rate. Furthermore, there is another way in which industrialization could affect violent crime, not in the total frequency, but in the relative frequency of different kinds of murder. Examination of individual cases of murder in the premodern period indicate that most murders occurred outside the family, between acquaintances, neighbors, and strangers. Criminologists report that twentieth-century murder is primarily a crime within the family and between intimates. . . .

By the nineteenth century, this northern department of France had one of the lowest rates of murder in the country. The average annual rate of murder in the Nord was .97 per 100,000 inhabitants. On a yearly basis, the rate for the Nord varied from 24 to 86 percent of the national rate . . .

On the other hand, an initial survey of court documents preserved in the departmental archives offers a startling insight into the changing nature of homicidal conflict during the nineteenth century. Before the triumph of industrial capitalism, 62 percent of all murder indictments between 1815 and 1824 occurred in conjunction with theft, or in the midst of a dispute over money, on inheritance, or some other material interest. By the 1870s, mercenary homicide declined to 13 percent of all cases (see Table [1]). After 1900, despite a small increase in the number of murders with theft, disputes over material things no longer precipitated homicidal violence.

The disappearance of material disputes was especially significant in cases of family murder. Most family murders in the early nineteenth century appear to have been highly charged disputes over an inheritance, or rivalries which centered upon conflicting material claims. None of the cases pitted husband and wife against each other. By the 1870s, family murder became the single most frequent type of murder. Not one case involved an inheritance or property dispute. Couples now fought over the emotional terms and durability of their relationship. As we will see, most murders of the preindustrial period occurred between virtual strangers in public settings such as the cabaret or at the French/Belgian border, or on public roads at night. The less personal the

TABLE [1] **Rates of Murder According to Type**

Type of Murder	1815–1824		1870–1879		1900–1904	
	Number Accused	Rate per 100,000	Number Accused	Rate per 100,000	Number Accused	Rate per 100,000[a]
Intra-Familial	21 (16%)	0.23	32 (30%)	0.21	40 (37%)	0.42
Cabaret	22 (17%)	0.24	25 (25%)	0.16	14 (13%)	0.15
Theft	44 (34%)	0.49	13 (13%)	0.09	22 (21%)	0.24
Workplace	4 (3%)	0.04	7 (7%)	0.05	4 (4%)	0.04
Border	15 (12%)	0.17	1 (1%)	0.007	0 (0%)	0.00
Random	14 (11%)	0.15	22 (22%)	0.14	15 (14%)	0.16
Unknown	9 (7%)	0.10	2 (2%)	0.013	12 (11%)	0.10
Total	129 (100%)	1.42	102 (100%)	0.67	107 (100%)	1.15

Note Comparison with the period 1845–1854 is not made because court records for these years did not contain enough detail to distinguish between types of homicide.

[a]Rates adjusted to correspond to ten-year period.

SOURCE *Chambre des mises en accusation, Archives départementales du Nord* (Lille, 1815–1904).

conflict, the higher the tendency for people to act in concert with others. Conversely, the more intimate the relationship in which violence occurred, the less likely a person was to kill with the aid of an accomplice. This shift toward murder as a single act of violence committed by an individual coincided with the movement away from public, nonintimate violence to private, intensely personal violence.

These data suggest that twentieth-century patterns of homicidal conflict originated in a period of social change from a pre- or protoindustrial to an industrial order. The most significant change occurred in the nature of family murder, especially in the decline of mercenary conflicts and the rise in emotional disputes. Changes in other types of murder, although evident, were less dramatic.

The case studies presented below will approach murder within a general framework that defines murder as a way that people deal with intolerable situations when other ways of coping are, for whatever reason, not available. This framework delineates where murder is situated on a spectrum of possible methods of managing conflict with others. Through this conceptual device, we may study murder as an extreme method of control which is historically specific to certain identifiable situations (relationships and conflicts). The analysis seeks to reveal the historically relevant features of changing homicidal situations independent of the individual personalities or motives of the murderers. . . .

Violence was least personal in theft-related murders. All of the available evidence suggests that assailants selected their victims in this type of murder primarily on the basis of vulnerability, *rather* than personal antagonism. Death of the victim was not the primary aim, but was instrumental to the completion of a successful robbery. Victim-assailant relationships in cabaret murders of the early nineteenth century were also superficial. Fatalities resulted when men engaged in violent brawls in locations where there were few external controls to prevent the fighting from escalating. Alcoholic consumption contributed to an atmosphere in which people were loud, less inhibited, and more likely to give and to take offense. Violence was spontaneous and impersonal. However, in the category of family murder (which also includes murder between sexual partners), this act of violence occurred in the context of an emotionally charged relationship. Murder was a passionate event. Death of the victim was the desired end. . . .

The rise of factory labor had its most disruptive impact on working-class families. Under the domestic system, families had formed a unit in which productive tasks and domestic activities were interrelated. Home-centered production allowed men and women to fulfill both their economic and familial responsibilities in accordance with traditional expectations. The removal of productive labor from the home destroyed the ground upon which family coherence and solidarity depended. The working-class family survived and remained the single most important relationship in workers' lives; but, the dispersal of family members from the home each day placed a new stress on the relationship between men and women. Cases of spouse murder during the 1870s reveal the significance of these changes in terms of individual family lives.

The percent of family murder increased by the 1870s (see Table [1]), and became more concentrated in cities. During that time, 46.4 percent of all family murders occurred in four industrial cities: Lille, Roubaix, Valenciennes, and Anzin. Urban development had been an inseparable part of northern industrialization. . . .

Theft-Related Murder, 1815–1824

The single most frequent murder indicated during this period (34 percent of all cases) occurred in connection with theft (see Table [1]). The majority (81 percent) of theft-related murder cases occurred between 1815 and 1817. Thirty-six percent occurred in 1817 which was the most difficult year because of the poor harvest the previous spring. If these bad years are excluded, then the rate for the years 1819–1824 is 0.13 per 100,000—much closer to the rates for the later periods. The majority of crimes occurred at the peak of the crisis in the Nord; yet, those indicted for theft-related murder were both employed and housed and sought to steal cash. They appear less directly affected by the crisis than others who were indicted for simple theft of food. . . . It is possible that these cases represent efforts by people to take control of their lives during times of enormous stress when all else was out of control, and when circumstances created situations in which ordinary people are pressed to commit desperate acts. Weakened political and social authority, combined with the food crisis, had created a climate of opportunism in which people were more prone than usual to take advantage of the presumed helplessness of others as a way of looking after themselves.

Violence facilitated theft. Death of the victim allowed the amateur thief to steal with impunity. The instrumental nature of violence in these cases might have seemed so obvious to contemporaries that examining magistrates never explored the problem of motive for violence independent of the theft. Jean François Frémaux was responsible for organizing a small band of people to murder and rob his employer, an elderly widow. According to his own testimony, Frémaux had no complaints against his employer. He had already accepted work at another farm when he began to consider the money box under the old woman's bed. For weeks he mulled over the idea of taking the money box with him when he left. He concluded that he would have to kill her first, presumably because he did not have free access to the bedroom. But, as he explained, he did not have the "heart" to kill her himself. He embarked upon a search throughout the cabarets on the outskirts of Lille for someone who would be able to carry out the murder. Eventually, he enlisted the aid of four other men and his girl friend. Frémaux's anxiety remained so great that he continually postponed the crime. Finally, on the night of April 23, 1815, while the men stood by, Frémaux's girl friend smothered the victim to death. Following the murder, Frémaux might not have had any clear understanding of his own feelings. His original feelings could have changed as a consequence of the murder. The examining magistrate did not pursue these issues at all.

The people accused of theft-related murder were not professional thieves but first offenders. Almost 60 percent of the accused were either artisans or domestic weavers. Their crimes did not represent a decision to embark upon new careers as outlaws. The desire to protect themselves from the consequences of theft may have led them to kill the people that they robbed. . . .

Cabaret Violence, 1815–1824

Local writers and antiquarians never fail to comment on the well-known association between cabarets and violence. According to popular lore, drinking and brawling were almost inseparable. In earlier centuries, cabaret fighting broke out nightly in the city of Lille. Cabarets served a vital social function in the Nord, meeting people's need to warm themselves in the company of others, sheltered from the damp and cold northern air. People conducted business, closed deals, and hired workers in cabarets; *mutualités* and other organizations held their meetings there; people drank, ate, sang, danced, met friends, played cards, and gambled. Court cases suggest that in the preindustrial period, the cabaret was a freewheeling place where people could express themselves without censure. Drinking was the most important form of sociability in the Nord. It was one of life's few pleasures, to be indulged with gusto. Drinking beer was respectable. When they wanted to express themselves with others, they drank beer. When northerners wanted to "drown their troubles," they drank gin. But uninhibited self-expression could become offensive to others and could provoke fights. . . .

Family Murder, 1870–1879, 1900–1904

A series of closely interrelated changes had, by the 1870s, made family murder a crime of passion between men and women. By this time, family murder became the single most frequent type of murder (30 percent of all murders, double its proportion from the period 1815–1824). As family murder became a more prevalent form of murder, it ceased being a mercenary crime between relatives and became an emotionally motivated crime between couples. Eighty percent of all family murder in the 1870s occurred between men and women, in contrast to 35 percent in the earlier period.

Court records suggest that extended kinship ties remained an enduring part of one's life. In-laws, aged parents, and siblings were there to help a wife seeking refuge from an abusive husband, or to listen to a young man's distress over his wife's infidelity. Other cases point to the isolation of couples in communities of strangers as a result of urban renewal. Uprootedness and isolation of migrants and Belgian immigrant workers to the industrial towns of the Nord are suggested in several cases. The importance of migration as a factor cannot be assessed because records do not provide enough information on the timing of people's movements.

The shift in the locus of tension in family murder away from in-laws and siblings, and toward spouses coincided with a shift in homicidal conflict away from disputes over inheritance and material interests, and toward the emotional and physical durability of the marriages. Material interests did continue to be a source of tension within families, but fights over money did not directly lead to any of the murders during the 1870s and early 1900s.

Decline in violence over material disputes within the family is part of a more general trend in homicidal conflict away from material disputes during this period. It was a reflection of the declining importance of the patrimonial family in the Nord. This changing socioeconomic structure is reflected in the new occupational profile of family murderers. By the 1870s the social base of family murder had broadened to include nonpropertied groups: factory workers (10 percent), day laborers (13 percent), agricultural workers (13 percent), artisans (13 percent), peasants (10 percent), and retail merchants (16 percent). By the early twentieth century, factory workers and day laborers made up 58 percent of those accused; artisans, retail merchants, and peasants comprised 34 percent of the accused. The changing occupational profile of family murderers coincided with the transformation in the family economy. It reflects the decline in household production and the emergence of the wage-earning family. The decline in disputes over patrimony is in part explained by the changing occupational profile of family murderers.

The rise of the wage-earning family gave a new centrality to the nuclear unit. Relationships with extended kin remained significant, but now spouses became exclusively dependent upon one another for their economic survival. The wage-earning couple emerged as an important unit in itself. Yet, at the same time, the separation of the work place from the home undercut a couple's ability to integrate and to control the flow of work and family life. As Accampo has emphasized, the removal of productive labor to the factory was a critical change which disrupted daily routines in such a way that basic familial roles could not be maintained as before. The relationship of men and women to each other, and their respective familial roles had to be redefined.

For women, the separation of paid labor from the home created a conflict between the need to contribute to the family income and the demands of child-rearing. Work at home became one solution for married women with children.

The separation of the work place from the home created a new source of anxiety for men. Even if wives worked at home, men's absence from the home during the day undermined their authority over wife and children. Factory workers were not at home to supervise their wives' daily activities. They no longer held the central position in the household by making day-to-day decisions and transmitting skills and values to children.

All of these changes heightened the material and affective importance of interpersonal relationships within marriage. The inadequacy of economic resources and the separation of work from home, however, was disabling to men as "providers and patriarchs." Incidents of spouse murder now often occurred when women abandoned the relationship. It is not possible to determine if women were leaving husbands more frequently than in earlier periods. Disaffection within marriage was not new. Women's departure from the home remained contingent upon the willingness of other relatives to shelter an estranged wife. It is the husband's homicidal attack in response to the abandonment that, in the context of earlier patterns of murders, appears new. Out of seven cases of the earlier period in which men killed women, only one pertained to abandonment. . . .

By the 1870s, this basic pattern had completely changed. These new cases suggest that men were less able than earlier to withstand the rejection and loss of a spouse. For some reason, their ability to cope in a nonviolent manner diminished. Alexis Perette's wife left him about a month before the crime occurred. She complained of his drunken, lazy, and abusive behavior; Perette countered that she had lovers. After she left him, she sought to obtain a legal separation. Perette tried to persuade her to return to him. One day he went to meet her after work, and told her, "You're making me very unhappy." He had hoped to arouse her feelings for him, but when she smiled with satisfaction (as he saw it) at this statement, he pulled out his knife and killed her. He then threw away the weapon and went to the police station to confess.

One interesting difference between spouse murders of the 1870s and early 1800s stems from the degree to which the men themselves were possessed by the meaning they had created for the relationship in the later period. In the 1870s, murderers became obsessed with the women who left them. They were unable to work, eat, or sleep. They stalked the women for days, pleading with them to return. Although these murders were usually premeditated, they were not premeditated in secret. François Dheyne went around telling all of his friends that he was going to kill his wife if she did not return. This behavior was another aspect of the emotional despair experienced by these men. The plans they revealed usually included some thoughts of suicide. Others poured out their troubles and plans to one and all, from mothers to bartenders, to prostitutes. In the end, failing to go through with suicide, they surrendered voluntarily to the police.

In the 1870s, infidelity, alcohol abuse, and physical mistreatment were all important themes in cases of spouse murder, but women's rejection of men was the single most important circumstance that led directly to the crime. All of these problems were far more widespread at this time and contributed to the increasing frequency of domestic homicide after the mid-nineteenth century. Yet, these factors alone would not have made spouse murder more frequent. These relationships ended in murder because of the new meaning of the relationship itself—especially for the man. In 1902, a thirty-five-year-old *journalier* [day laborer] from Tourcoing stabbed his wife because of her infidelity. She forgave him and interceded on his behalf before the *Tribunal* and returned to live with him upon his release from prison. In 1903 she decided to leave him again. From the time she left he became obsessed with the need to find her, and began an exhaustive search that took him everywhere he thought she might be. A month later he met her at the hospital where their daughter was being treated. As soon as he saw her, he begged her to return to him, throwing himself on his knees, telling her he could not live without her. When she refused, he stabbed her. This time he killed her. He threw away the knife and took his daughter in his arms while he waited for the police. . . . Murder was an unusual event in the Nord. The low aggregate rate of murder in this part of France was indicative of a disciplined culture. Before the advent of industrial capitalism, discipline was more likely to fail at specific weak points. These weak points were located in the community where groups of people engaged in impersonal, spontaneous murder, often in pursuit of pragmatic, mercenary values. At this time, murder within the family was also characterized by mercenary interest. Significantly, spousal relations were relatively immune to this type of fatal violence.

An important break with this pattern of murder coincided with the development of industrial capitalism in the Nord. By the 1870s, a reversal of earlier patterns became notable. Mercenary, impersonal, and spontaneous murders declined dramatically. Fatal violence in intimate relationships increased to become the single most frequent type of murder.

Industrial capitalism had transformed the economic meaning of the family for individual members. The decline in the patrimonial family among artisans and peasants, and the rise of the wage-earning family were important manifestations of this transformation. Analysis of murder cases, however, suggests that this economic transformation had emotional ramifications for individual family members. Although intergenerational conflicts over wealth declined in intensity, new sources of tension emerged between spouses. In wage-earning families, the separation of work and home created new conflicts between couples. The dichotomy of rationalized work in pursuit of material interests in the marketplace, and family life at home with expectations of emotional fulfillment required new adjustments. The double identity of wage earner and head of family created special tensions to which violence was one response. Case studies after 1870 showed that the rise in spouse murder was related to a new pressure on industrial male workers in their domestic roles. In general, we would expect the separation of work and family to have a similar impact on family violence in other societies during the initial stages of industrialization.

32

CUTTING THE BIRTHRATE: THE DEMOGRAPHIC TRANSITION IN THE WORKING CLASS

WALLY SECCOMBE

A key change in European society in the decades around 1900 involved a dramatic reduction in the birthrate, as all social classes followed the middle-class lead (see Chapter 24) in cutting back on reproduction. Europe (along with the United States) provided the first example of a society reducing birthrates so dramatically—though it must be remembered that European traditions had emphasized considerable control over population growth through late marriage and other arrangements, prior to the great demographic surge of the eighteenth century.

The following selection explores how and why British workers embraced the new birthrate pattern, from the 1870s into the early decades of the twentieth century. Wally Seccombe draws on demographic statistics and worker responses to polls and other qualitative material, including letters to an expert on sex, Marie Stopes, to discuss the motivations and the methods used.

In the process, key aspects of working-class family life are explored—sexuality obviously (findings here should be compared to earlier discussions of lower-class sex—see Chapter 11); and also gender relations and initiatives within the family. Working-class families resisted certain middle-class standards but assimilated others. Inevitably, the resultant patterns are complex—doctors provided multiple messages, husbands, wives, and marriages had diverse qualities. Given a change of this magnitude, with huge impact not only on population size but on women's lives and family functions, the complexity matched the impact. Motivation finally involved several ingredients, including important new views by women about children, and changes in these areas explain the timing of the modern pattern.

The British fertility decline got under way in the late 1870s. There is evidence that specific upper-class and urban professional strata were limiting family size

From: Wally Seccombe, "Starting to Stop: Working Class Fertility Decline in Britain," *Past & Present*, No. 126 (1990): 126, 153–54, 160–62, 165–66, 170–71, 173, 175–76, 184–86.

earlier in the century, but reductions in these groups were offset by buoyant and slightly rising fertility trends among the labouring classes. In the last two decades of the nineteenth century, however, the birth-rates of all social classes began to decline. Yet the descent was uneven; proletarian fertility edged down gradually, while the reduction ran much deeper among the urban propertied classes. . . .

In England and Wales the descent was primarily due to a reduction in marital fertility. Although women's mean age at first marriage rose by one year from 1881 to 1911, the contribution of marital delay to the overall decline was a small one. While births out of wedlock subsided concomitantly, this contraction accounted for a tiny fraction of the overall decline. The reduction of marital fertility was achieved almost entirely by means of "stopping," the deliberate cessation of childbirth prior to menopause. In England and Wales there may have been a slight rise in women's age at first birth, but it is doubtful that intervals between births were lengthened. The fertility decline was thus a historic watershed in two respects: the birth-*rates* of entire societies reached new lows, and the stopping *mode* of fertility regulation within marriage was established as a mass practice for the first time. How was stopping accomplished? There is evidence of change in four practices: (a) a rise in the incidence of induced abortion; (b) more frequent resort to coitus interruptus; (c) a decline in coital frequency by deliberate abstention; and (d) increased use of contraceptive devices.

The weight of evidence points to coitus interruptus as the most popular method in the first phase of the decline. Yet the Stopes correspondence and the clinic data suggest that prolonged abstinence was not negligible and may well have been underestimated in the Lewis-Faning survey. Historical demographers generally assume that couples trying to limit births before the widespread use of contraceptive devices would naturally practise coitus interruptus, as a less stressful method than prolonged celibacy. But withdrawal was also much less secure, and this generated another kind of stress, the fear of pregnancy, mentioned by several female respondents who favour abstinence for this reason. Perhaps most women writing to Stopes failed to mention withdrawal because they did not take it seriously as a birth-control option. The technique depends on male commitment and control; it is likely that many women did not have much faith in being able "to push him out of the way when I think it's near." As one woman explained in a letter pleading for contraceptive devices:

> My husband had been withdrawing all that time and the only time I had any suspicion he was not so careful was on his birthday and [nine months later] my second boy was born . . . I make my Husband and myself miserable by always worrying in case I have another baby. Please do help us.

While abstinence was probably *women's* preferred method of limitation, most could not enforce it consistently for any length of time; they feared the consequences of trying or simply felt that it would be unfair to their husbands to deny them their "marital dues." "I cannot always refuse my husband as it only means living a cat and dog life for both of us." The Stopes correspondence indicates that wives *were* able to reduce coital frequency through dissuasion, deferral and evasion. Some developed the habit of "staying up mending," retiring after their husbands had fallen asleep. But they could not steadfastly refuse a cohabiting husband his "conjugal rights"; to do so would have been to deny one of the basic purposes of Christian marriage. Without his active co-operation, total abstinence was out of the question. As it was, avoiding intercourse and insisting on withdrawal wracked marital relations with tension, bitterness and alienation. "Our love seems to bring us more suffering than anything else . . . The result is our married life is spoiled and we are gradually drifting apart". . . .

Given the widespread desire to limit, why were barrier methods and spermicides not used more often? Respondents wrote bluntly of their own lamentable ignorance concerning the most elementary matters of human reproduction and contraception. Most had heard tell of various "remedies," many had tried devices and drugs that "put you right" offered for sale by charlatans and quacks. Contraceptives were often confused with abortifacients, an impression that was undoubtedly reinforced by unscrupulous advertisements for various products in the penny press. Repeatedly, respondents complained that these commodities were injurious or ineffective, often both. Fears of physical injury and mental disorder were often blended with deep moral reservations and aesthetic distaste; many regarded contraceptives as "repulsive and unnatural." Condoms had an unsavoury reputation, being associated with prostitution, extra-marital liaisons and the prevention of venereal disease, which probably *was* the principal context of their use at this time. People's compunction in this regard was buttressed by the major Christian denominations, Protestant and Catholic, which "viewed with alarm the growing practice of the artificial restriction of the family," urging "all Christian people to discountenance [such means] . . . as demoralizing to character and hostile of national welfare". . . .

People's fear of contraception was partly based on a well-founded suspicion of bogus products, but it was also due to misconceptions as to the harmful side-effects of "preventatives." The advice of doctors was a major source of such misapprehensions. Leaders of the British Medical Association condemned contraceptives as unnatural and warned that all sorts of maladies would befall their users. Espousing semen as a cure-all elixir for women absorbed through the vaginal wall, they opposed anything which interfered with the intermingling of secretions. Many doctors felt it was their duty to impede the dissemination of contraceptive knowledge and devices. "When the last baby was born the doctor said can't you finish up but when I asked him how . . . he just laughed. What's the use of saying finish up when they won't tell us poor women how to." Thirty-five respondents in *Mother England* mention such rebuffs, often with a good deal of anger. The refusal to assist patients in need was not the work of an unrepresentative rearguard of doctors. The editor of the *British Medical Journal,* authoritative organ of the British Medical

Association, wrote in 1901: "the medical profession as a whole has set its face against such [contraceptive] practices which are unnatural and degrading in their mental effect, and oft times injurious to both husband and wife in their physical results." By the 1920s increasing numbers of doctors were becoming uncomfortable with their profession's embargo on prophylactics, and a minority risked their reputations to offer patients practical assistance. But medical schools still taught nothing at all about contraception, and the conviction that all such devices were deleterious to health persisted in the profession.

While doctors led the resistance, respondents also accused public health nurses, maternity home matrons, pharmacists and government officials of spurning requests for birth-control information: "as for the ministry of health they would rather learn us how to have them rather than tell us how to avoid it. . . . The health visitor said it was very wrong to do anything to stop yourself from having children . . . I don't care if I never see her again they are no good to us."

One woman commended Stopes on:

> your outspoken fearless comments on a government that won't release Birth Control knowledge . . . If only some of the fatheads . . . could come and live here for awhile, I am sure out of pure pity for the little ones and the poor harassed mothers, they would soon agree with you and release the Birth Control knowledge.

Several letters reveal class resentment at the withholding of information desperately needed by the poor. "The rich seem to think a working woman has no right to know anything, at least that has been my own experience," wrote a woman who wanted Stopes to address her reply to "the lodge" lest her mistress see it and disapprove "of my trying to prevent being pregnant." "I feel it a great injustice and unchristian like to think that rich women should have this knowledge and a poor woman should live in ignorance of it." "We absolutely cannot afford any more children and its a sin to know the poor are to be the oppressed because of the wealthier classes. I don't begrudge wealth but I do its value of knowledge". . . .

Demographers conventionally present the desire to control fertility in marriage as arising from the cultural formation of an ideal family size, with couples striving to stop once they have successfully borne the planned number of children. There is no doubt that the two-child family became a common target for middle-class couples in the post-war [1918 ff] era. Was such a goal prevalent among the first generation of proletarian limiters? Evidently not. In the Lewis-Faning survey 84 per cent of working-class women marrying from 1910 to 1924 report that they did not plan to have a definite number of children at marriage. Family-planning norms strengthened over time, with 43 per cent of the 1940–5 cohort indicating that they did plan in this way. The Stopes correspondence corroborates this impression. Several women insisted that they had "done their duty" ("to the Race," "to my Country," "as a woman") by having a certain number of children. "I am 35 years of age and have up to the Present given Birth to Seven Children six of which are Living so that I do not think I am asking Advice before I have at least Done my Duty as a woman." This is, however, a different mentality from that which underlies the modern objective of fulfilling a planned family size.

What reasons *did* respondents give for wishing to cease childbearing? . . . Stope's correspondents [refer] . . . most frequently to the husband's wage or irregular employment, implying that his was the primary and often sole income. Employment opportunities forgone by wives in the event of pregnancy were also mentioned, but this was in a minority of cases; a near total reliance on the income of the male bread-winner appears firmly entrenched. Male writers, feeling the strain of these responsibilities, mention the family's economic difficulties almost invariably, and for women as well, financial worries were seldom far from their minds. Overcrowded households impressed several respondents who insisted they had no room for any more.

Concern about the mother's health was the second reason, cited by one woman in four in Lewis-Faning's survey. The most immediate impression left by the Stopes correspondence is of women's dread of future pregnancies and their fierce determination to bear no more children. . . .

So far as women bear most of the direct burdens of repeated pregnancy, childbearing and childcare, we would expect them to be more determined than men to call a halt. The correspondence bears this out. While most men agreed on the need to stop, women were the driving force behind family limitation. Where differences arose between spouses on the risks of unintended conception, what were their nature? Hypothetically, disagreements might focus on three related issues: the desirability of having another child; the optimal frequency of coitus and other aspects of sexual conduct; or the use of birth control. The correspondence indicates that the latter two were the primary bones of contention. Simmering tension arose from men's sexual impulsiveness or indiscipline, based on the reckless assertion of their conjugal prerogatives, rather than deriving from a difference between spouses on the desired number of children.

There were a variety of attitudes among unco-operative men. A minority were intensely hostile to the use of contraceptives of any sort, and were resigned to accept the number of children that Nature, or God, provided. Others were ambivalent or simply indifferent to the prospects of another pregnancy; Stopes's female correspondents complained frequently of their spouses' insouciance. "My husband doesn't care if we have a dozen, so long as he satisfies his own selfish desires."

The prevailing view of social historians is that working-class women in the past disliked sex and wished for as few encounters with their husbands as possible. Jane Lewis finds "copious evidence . . . of women who felt no sexual pleasure because of the fear of pregnancy, and there is here some indication that working-class women may have internalised middle-class ideas of passionlessness and its correlate: male sensuality." In her oral-history interviews with working-class women in Preston and Barrow, Elizabeth Roberts reports that "sexual intercourse was regarded as necessary for the procreation of children or as an activity indulged in by men for their own pleasure, but it was never discussed in the evidence as something which could give mutual happiness. No hint was ever made that women might have enjoyed sex."

The Stopes correspondence is not nearly so bleak in this regard. While several writers confirm the conventional stereotype, many others present a more balanced and mutual picture, with female passion apparent. (The following authors are all women.) "When two people are so fond of one another as we are, as I have one of the best, you like to get the best out of life." "At certain times of the Month we nearly get beyond control . . . it is strange for us to go 4 years without proper connections." "My husband tells me to control and hold myself in check, well I can, but we do without kisses, and oh, lots of other little things that help make life pleasant." "Its impossible to put passion entirely out of our lives, for its the love I bear my dear husband that makes me yield to him at such times." "I am very passionate as well as he, and we have been so wonderfully happy and I do so want to make this happiness last." While most respondents who mention the subject portray men's sexual desire as being stronger than women's, wives who receive no pleasure from sex are in a minority. . . .

Many men empathized with their wives' fear of pregnancy and were evidently willing to waive their conjugal rights when there was a serious risk of conception. "After this child is born I feel I will have to leave her alone as we are both frightened that we may have another and I don't know what we would do if there was." Men also had their own reasons for seeking to limit family size. [With] the arrival of another child, breadwinner responsibilities weighed heavily on their minds. "I don't want to be the cause of bringing children into this world and not being able to keep them." "I am only a working man it take all my time to feed and clothe them if there should be any more I don't know what We should do."

Even if men's determination to stop was not as intense as their spouses', all that was necessary to avoid numerous conceptions was that husbands be willing to accede to their wives' wishes and not to override them in bed. Spousal co-operation did not make withdrawal and abstinence secure methods: "moments of weakness" and "slips" were commonplace, as the letters attest. But a very considerable reduction in birth-rates was none the less achieved through a determined application of methods that remained notoriously haphazard on a personal level. To continue the descent, reaching the low levels which have prevailed in the developed world since the collapse of the post-war baby boom, it has been necessary for the great majority of reproductive couples to replace "natural" methods with the regular use of contraceptives. But in the first phase of the transition, withdrawal and abstention were sufficient to produce a dramatic reduction in the birth-rate. . . .

A third fundamental impetus [in addition to issues of growing use of doctors and some feminist influence] to the spread of birth control was the underlying shift in the family economy, inducing a convergence in the reproductive interests of men and women. When referring to children in economic terms, both the Guild women and Stopes's correspondents treated them as a net cost. Very few anticipated a substantial monetary contribution from children through their teenage years or looked forward to their eventual material support in old age. Yet these advantages had existed for their Victorian grandparents, holding up longest among the labouring poor where child labour persisted. These were liable to be the same parents who resisted sending their children to school, following the introduction of compulsory legislation in the 1870s. "Of course we cheat the School Board," a Shoreditch matchbox-maker informed Lady Dilke in 1893. "It's hard on the little ones, but their fingers is so quick—they that has the most of 'em is the best off."

The contrast between the late Victorian and Edwardian generations can best be appreciated by looking at the difference in the dependency ratio at that point in the family cycle when the question of stopping first arose—when parents were in their mid- to late thirties and their oldest children were reaching their teenage years. Throughout most of the nineteenth-century working-class youth took paid jobs from the age of eleven or twelve, earning their keep and beginning to recoup parents' investment in their labour power. If they remained at home until their early twenties, remitting their wages faithfully (as most did), the supplementary income of the eldest would ease their families' economic pinch, just as mothers entered the final phase of childbearing. By the Edwardian era, the eldest children were still in school, attending fairly regularly, when a mother reached her mid-thirties and had to determine whether to go on conceiving or to try to call a halt. Parents could not anticipate any substantial income supplementation from children for another two or three years. Furthermore the tradition of young people remitting their full wages to their parents had weakened by this time, particularly for boys in their late teens; even when they did go out to work, their income was not as secure from the parents' standpoint. Older daughters were not nearly as likely to be available to mind the young ones, freeing mothers to seek employment. The delay and dissipation of children's economic contribution was accompanied by higher costs associated with prolonged schooling and regular year-round attendance. Facing these prospects, increasing numbers of working-class parents concluded that their living standards would deteriorate if they had any more children. . . .

By the early twentieth century the continued prosperity of families in the upper strata of the working-class became increasingly dependent on limiting conception and terminating unwanted pregnancies. Taking control of one's fertility became a mark of self-reliance and respectability, while the prolific poor were pitied or ridiculed. Formerly, fecundity had been associated with masculine virility; now it was considered in excess to be foolish insouciance, a self-inflicted source of poverty. Life expectancy from the age of one onwards had improved in the Victorian era, and infant mortality finally began to abate at the turn of the century. These trends raised the potential supply of surviving children very considerably, widening the disparity between the desire for smaller families and the old procreative regime, making it all the more urgent to cease childbearing well before menopause. As the costs of additional offspring rose and the potential benefits declined, the family's primary breadwinner was increasingly inclined to share his wife's view of the need to quit childbearing.

Beach scene in Europe, circa 1929.

IV

THE TWENTIETH
CENTURY

1918–Present

Social changes in mid- to late twentieth-century Europe built on patterns already established in mature industrial societies, but with a host of novel twists and surprising directions. Many experts argue that Western Europe in fact began building a new kind of society, based now not on classic factory industry so much as a host of service occupations. Certainly some older commitments, like the notion that women should choose home over work, were almost stood on their head. Other trends, like commercially based leisure, persisted and intensified, but with important embellishments such as a growing emphasis on youth culture and the growing influence of fads first launched in the United States. In a climate of innovation, gender relationships within the family were revisited, while characteristic class tensions assumed different dimensions. Brand-new ingredients, such as an unprecedented wave of immigration from outside Europe, added to the mix. The result, clearly, was a new social period, linked to but differentiated from the turn-of-the-century decades.

This period was itself divided in part. Europe in the wake of World War I suffered severe dislocations, enhanced by the Great Depression of 1929 and then the tensions that would lead to a second great war. Specific movements, such as Nazism, responded to this important moment of social disarray. After World War II, a different atmosphere took shape, with far more uniform economic advance and a blurring of some of the political fault lines that lingered from the interwar years. Yet connections existed beneath the surface between these two subperiods. Changes in women's social roles surfaced in the 1920s, before the revolution in work patterns. The new sources of immigration, though more massive from the 1950s onward, had interwar precedents as well, with groups like the Algerian workers who began to trickle into France around 1930.

Analysis of European society in the past seventy years must handle two themes. In the first place, a number of vital developments were specific to Europe—including the rise of major political movements such as Nazism and Communism that had few echoes on our side of the Atlantic. Many of these movements took root during the 1920s and 1930s, Europe's difficult decades between the world wars. At the same time, Europe continued to develop as an industrial society, mirroring developments common to such societies, including the United States. Indeed after 1945, Europe underwent a major revival in which it began to surpass the United States in such areas as national income growth and available leisure time. Both European themes—the responses to tensions between the wars and the continued redefinition of industrial society—drew from the activities of ordinary people, as basic social change persisted. Even novel responses like Nazism continued such trends as the concentration of economic organization and increasing social mobility.

Contemporary Europe began to emerge from the strictures of its past during the horror of the First World War. The war severely damaged Europe's morale. Staggering death tolls distorted the population structure. Economic dislocations induced, or at least intensified, two decades of economic insecurity, culminating in the Great Depression. The war set other disturbing trends in motion. For example, Great Britain's crime rates in the early 1920s began to rise and have continued to mount to the present day, although they have not reached the levels of the late eighteenth century. When compared with nineteenth-century European history, it is not hard to portray twentieth-century European history in gloomy terms. Certainly any history that focuses on the two decades between the world wars must stress the extreme social and political chaos that prevailed throughout most of the continent.

Along with interwar dislocations and new political extremes, other developments built on previous industrial trends. For example, youth continued to move into greater prominence as a stage of life, with differences in the youth experience reflecting the still sharp distinctions between the middle class and the working class. Europe's recovery after World War II also showed a continuation of some earlier features of industrial development. Countries like France were able to realize older goals, like intense productive work, more fully than they had before the war. Europe contrasted interestingly with the United States, where concern about work values increased by the 1970s.

However, European trends also developed some new directions. As in the United States, the role of women changed markedly. Attitudes concerning health and medicine showed new features, resulting among other things in a novel approach toward death. In these respects, and also regarding leisure behavior, Europeans moved further away from nineteenth-century patterns than Americans did.

Some observers believe that the whole society that has emerged since the 1940s is radically new; they call it "postindustrial" or "postmodern." Has the basic process of industrial maturation given way to a new set of values and institutions? The question deserves serious consideration, particularly with regard to the lives and outlooks of the major segments of European society. The status of the family, for example, suggests that, although nineteenth-century patterns differed from traditional ones (as in the "modernization" of childhood), today's society is heading in a different direction. In general, the increasingly common references to "postindustrial" society raise the question of whether we have entered a new period *within* the industrial process or whether we are developing yet another social framework, so soon after industrialization began.

It is certain that Europe continues to change rapidly and that, within a recognizably common range, its developing blend of the old and the new differs, in some cases, from other advanced industrial countries. Compared with the United States, Europe is less violent. European family life is more stable, despite important changes in family values. At the same time, Europeans express less religious belief and engage less commonly in religious practice. Politics in Europe tends toward greater diversity and extremes. The possibilities for social mobility in Europe and the United States are approximately equal, but because Europeans tend less to emphasize it, European society at least appears to be more stratified. Similarly, the position of women may seem more rigidly controlled (in some countries it is demonstrably inferior in law); but how great are the real differences between Europe and the United States in this area?

It is not easy to determine major trends in the very recent past, and the essays that follow cover only a few of many possible topics. We do, however, have something of a head start in interpreting key features in the development of contemporary European society. We know some of the basic responses to earlier transformations. We can compare recent patterns with these responses to see if ordinary Europeans are reinforcing values established earlier or creating new ones. We can even try to assess the strengths and weaknesses of the society Europeans have developed.

BIBLIOGRAPHY

Age groups are just beginning to catch historical interest. See, for the United States, Joseph Kett, *Rites of Passage: Adolescence in America, 1790 to the Present* (New York, 1977); and John Modell, *Into One's Own: From Adolescence to Adulthood in America, 1920–1975* (Berkeley, 1989). On Europe, John Gillis, *Youth and History* (New York, 1974) is a splendid treatment of the nineteenth century. . . . A set of oral histories on English adolescence is found in Thea Thompson, *Edwardian Childhoods* (London, 1982); see also J. A. Mangan, *Athleticism in the Victorian and Edwardian Public School* (Cambridge, England, 1981). See also Mark Roseman, ed., *Generations in Conflict: Youth Revolt and Generation Formation in Germany 1770–1968* (New York, 1995) and David Fowler, *The First Teenagers: The Lifestyle of Young Wage-Earners in Interwar Britain* (London, 1995).

Most of the studies of Nazism deal purely with the movement itself. Alan L. Bullock, *Hitler, a Study in Tyranny*, rev. ed. (New York, 1964), well exceeds the confines of biography and is an excellent survey. Karl D. Bracher, *The German Dictatorship: The Origins, Structure and Effects of National Socialism*, trans. Jean Steinberg (New York, 1970), deals extensively with the bases of Nazi strength. Ernst Nolte, *The Three Faces of Fascism* (New York, 1966), is an ambitious interpretation, but is written mainly from the standpoint of intellectual history. A valuable specific study of Nazism's causes and impact in a small German town is W. L. Allen, *The Nazi Seizure of Power* (Chicago, 1955). See also Herman Lebovics, *Social Conservatism and the Middle Classes in Germany* (Princeton, 1969), Peter Pulzer, *Anti-Semitism in Germany and Austria* (New York, 1964), and Jürgen Kocka, *White Collar Workers in America 1890–1940: Political History in International Perspective* (Beverly Hills, CA, 1980). For ambitious interpretations of the effect of Nazism on German society, see Ralf Dahrandorf, *Society and Democracy in Germany* (New York, 1969), and David Schoenbaum, *Hitler's Social Revolution* (New York, 1968). Hannah Arendt, *The Origins of Totalitarianism* (New York, 1973) is an important interpretive statement.

Seymour Lipset, *Political Man, the Social Bases of Politics* (New York, 1959), studies the variety of modern political attitudes from a liberal viewpoint. John E. Goldthorpe et al., *The Affluent Worker: Political Attitudes and Behavior* (New York, 1968), based on data from a detailed study of the British working class, offers important interpretations of workers' political values. On French communism, see Robert Wohl, *French Communism in the Making* (Stanford, CA, 1966); on later changes in communism, see George Schwab, ed., *Eurocommunism* (Westport, CT, 1981).

Probably the most sensitive study of modern women, with careful attention to historical background, is Simone de Beauvoir, *The Second Sex*, trans. H. M. Parshley (New York, 1953). See also Betty Friedan, *The Feminine Mystique* (New York, 1953). A vigorous survey is Evelyne Sullerot, *Woman, Society and Change* (New York, 1971); see also R. Patai, *Women in the Modern World* (New York, 1967); Patricia Branca, *Women in Europe since 1750* (London, 1978); and S. B. Kameran and A. J. Kahn, eds., *Family Policy: Government and Families in Fourteen Countries*. Vital recent work includes Penny Tinkler, *Constructing Girlhood: Popular*

Magazines for Girls Growing Up in England 1920–1950 (Pennsylvania, 1995); Mary Louise Roberts, *Civilization Without Sexes: Reconstructing Gender in Postwar France, 1917–1927* (Chicago, 1994); and Victoria de Grazia with Ellen Gurlough, eds., *The Sex of Things: Gender and Consumption in Historical Perspective* (Berkeley, 1996).

On the twentieth-century family, Colin Rosser and Christopher Harris, *The Family and Social Change* (New York, 1965), is an excellent detailed survey based on a study of a Welsh city. See also P. Willmott and M. Young, *Family and Class in a London Suburb* (New York, 1960). Michael Anderson, *Family Structure in Nineteenth-Century Lancashire* (New York, 1971), offers valuable background material. Richard Sennett, *Families Against the City* (Cambridge, MA, 1970), based on a study of a Chicago neighborhood, is a pessimistic view of modern family trends that deserves comparison with the European studies; so is *Haven in a Heartless World: The Family Besieged* (New York, 1977), by Christopher Lasch. An important thesis, derived from France, is J. Donzelot, *The Policing of Families* (New York, 1979); this book offers even greater pessimism about the autonomy of the contemporary family.

New work and leisure behaviors are discussed in Stanley Hoffmann, ed., *In Search of France* (Cambridge, MA, 1963) and John Ardagh, *The New French Revolution* (New York, 1969). Michael Young and Peter Willmott, *The Symmetrical Family* (London, 1976), focus on work values while offering an important theory on the contemporary family's place in modern history.

On immigrant workers, see Michael Marrus, *The Unwanted: European Refugees in the Twentieth Century* (New York, 1987) for historical perspective, and Gary Cross, *Immigrant Workers in Industrial France: The Making of a New Laboring Class* (Philadelphia, 1983). On postwar immigration, see Robert Miles, *Racism and Migrant Labour* (London, 1972); and particularly Michael Piore, *Birds of Passage—Migrant Labour and Industrial Societies* (Cambridge, England, 1979) and Stephen Castles and Godula Kosack, *Immigrant Workers and Class Structure in Western Europe* (London, 1973).

Studies of the modern history of death include John McManners, *Death and the Enlightenment* (Oxford, 1981); David E. Stannard, *The Puritan Way of Death* (New York, 1977), and *Death in America* (Philadelphia, 1975). Related studies of health attitudes include Ivan Ilich, *Medical Nemesis: The Expropriation of Health* (New York, 1976); and René Dubos, *The Mirage of Health* (New York, 1959). A recent study that combines social history and sociology in the evolution of European health attitudes is Claudine Herzlich and Janine Pierrot, *Illness and Self in Society* (Baltimore, 1987).

33

WORKING-CLASS YOUTH

J. ROBERT WEGS

The experience of youth changed considerably in the later nineteenth and twentieth centuries. School edged into work, which meant that youth had a new kind of dependence on parents and other adult authorities. New social standards, as in the area of sexuality, also earmarked youth as a time of stress.

Concern about youth—including invention of a new word, adolescence—developed first in the nineteenth-century middle class. Youth as a special experience, or at least as a new kind of special experience, emerged more slowly among workers.

The following selection deals with worker youth in Vienna between the world wars. It raises a number of important themes. How and to what extent was the experience of youth changing? How much and in what ways did middle-class standards affect youth experience, and how did youth react? The selection clearly indicates important class differences still remained, but it also shows divisions within the working class and some acceptance, however grudging, of certain middle class concerns. The role of socialist leadership (some of it middle class in origin) must also be assessed.

Worker youth clearly maintained an interest in distinctiveness as they embellished older habits to differentiate themselves from the middle class and from adults. However, they also had to change and to develop new kinds of adaptations and resistances to adult authority. Was youth becoming increasingly tamed, and what effects would this have on adult behavior and family institutions?

Naturally, working-class children had far fewer personal possessions than middle-class children. The son of a carpenter told me, "When a child had a tricycle, he was looked up to." Few working-class children had more than one pair of shoes. Forced to go to an orphanage at the age of six when his father died, he remembered that "we each had one pair of shoes and they were

From: J. Robert Wegs, *Growing up Working Class* (University Park: The Pennsylvania State University Press, 1989), pp. 66–81, 86–91.

ripped. When we were able to buy something, we went to the *Dorotheum* [pawn shop] and bought used clothing." The son of a galvanizer recounted that a neighboring family of a ditch digger with twelve children, obviously lower stratum, could not even provide their children with shoes: "They didn't even have shoes in the winter. Directly across from the apartment house stood the school. Before school began, they stood barefooted on newspapers. When school began, they ran fast across the street and into the school since it was heated." He went on to point out that "all of these children became respectable." Again, dealing resolutely with scarcity in the working-class environment was essential if one did not want to lose the respect of other inhabitants. For most working-class families it was not how much one had but rather how one dealt with scarcity that was important. . . .

Crowded housing was not a totally negative experience for the working-class family. Against the indisputable health and educational disadvantages of cramped quarters, the crowded tenement houses provided plenty of other children for playing and often brought parents together to care cooperatively for the children. The common feeling among inhabitants of the *Zinskaserne* [tenements] that they were one large family was partially a result of children's playing together in the hallways and courtyards. Wives often looked after the children of the next-door neighbor and sometimes cooked for them when their parents were unable to. As the son of a bakery worker remembered, "Every family had from two to four children in our building . . . and the doors were open on the hallway. The children bumped into each other . . . for example, at *Jausezeit,* someone's mother cut bread, spread lard on it and gave every kid a piece. The next day another mother did the same." Many I spoke with remembered how they came to know many of the other occupants of their building through the children. Often, the economically better-off or those with jobs in the food industry shared some of their food with their neighbors. The daughter of an Anker Bread Factory worker remembered how the neighborhood children used to always drop by for bread, which her family was amply supplied with.

This sense of community often extended beyond the hallway to the streets. But a sharp division existed between those working-class families who restricted the amount of time their children could play in the streets and those who did not. It became a mark of respectability among some working-class families, as well as a precaution against injury, to keep their children, especially daughters, out of the streets. A woman reared in Favoriten [a working-class district] remembered that "my mother paid very close attention to me. She was very strict. When I slipped away, I went into a park and fooled around like the devil." The daughter of a furrier worker who was reared by her grandfather, a railway worker, recalled, "Everything had its rules. I couldn't play with the street kids. The parents of the street kids were not so proper; they lived down below in the cellars." This division between those who played in the streets and those who did not reflects somewhat that division between the respectable upper stratum and the remainder of working-class society discussed [previously]. Normally the children from the upper reaches of the working class, especially the daughters, were supervised while playing in the streets, or they played in the apartment courtyards or parks. Except for the lowest stratum, parents usually refused to let their daughters go into the streets at night alone once they had reached puberty.

But most working-class boys did spend much time in the streets. As the son of a plasterer in Ottakring recalled, "After school, we did our lessons and then we were in the streets." The daughter of a locksmith in Favoriten remembered the mothers being happy when the children were outside, since it provided some relief from the noise in the crowded living quarters. She told me, "They were happy when the children, all sixty children in the building . . . were outside." Although playing in the streets was against the law, it normally was not enforced by the police. This plasterer's son remembered a policeman who did try to keep kids out of the street: "We said, ow, the lightning flash is coming, because it was like lightning flashing when the sun shone on his helmet, it glittered." Some working-class children tended from an early age to play outside the family circle due to their parents' absence at work and the more communal nature of working-class housing. Hetzer [a social researcher] found that a 3- to 5-year-old working-class child spent 16 percent of his time with his play group. Thus they were bound to be more influenced than middle-class children by their peer group. By the time working-class children reached school age they had a much greater independence than the children of higher social classes, who were "ängstlich kontrolliert" [anxiously controlled] according to Hetzer. A recent study points out that in the bourgeois family any "spontaneous and unplanned meetings with other children were strongly discouraged."

Children's play activities best exemplify the importance of group variation and continuity rather than change over time. Through all the difficult times of World War I and the depression, children's play changed very little within a particular social stratum. The major changes resulted from the fewer possible playmates brought about by the demographic transition [lower birth rate] and the emergence of a multifaceted Social Democratic youth program that kept some children occupied in more structured activities in the interwar period. The enormous number of possible playmates available in the prewar *Zinskaserne* simply did not exist in the thirties. Games such as soccer, which had been played in the streets by large numbers of children at the turn of the century, were played on a reduced scale in the thirties. Most youth in a working-class district took advantage of SDAP-sponsored activities, although their parents never became avid [Social Democratic] party supporters. Some youth could now swim in SDAP-built baths rather than swimming in the ponds in the outlying districts, or they could take part in SDAP-sponsored hikes or myriad other activities. But it remained the practice for lower-stratum children to spend much more time in the streets than others and to play the same games they had played prior to World War I. Also, more lower-stratum youth had the opportunity for play in the interwar period due to the reduced use of child labor in the more mechanized plants. The emergence of the cinema began to have an impact on leisure among the upper reaches of the working class . . . but it was too expensive for most lower-stratum youth.

Youth games reflected children's social milieu. In Favoriten, many games were the direct product of the crowded conditions and the streets. One game, called corner spying (*Eckengucken*) in Favoriten, required that one player run around an apartment building while another followed peering around corners and upon catching sight of the one being sought yelled "Is schon wer!" (Here he is). *Strawsack* was another favorite street game. Players first stood on a sewer cover in the middle of a street crossing, counted off, and then hopped away on one leg. A catcher waited until one player put down both feet and yelled "strawsack," after which the latter became the catcher. Players were permitted to hop only on the sidewalk or along the curb. One game, robber and policeman (*Räuber und Pole*), characterized children's attitudes toward the police. All wanted to be robbers rather than the policeman. When a robber was caught, the policeman hit him three times and yelled "police hit" after each time. Another game that was tied closely to working-class areas was *Drei Handwerksburschen* (three handicraft workers). In this game three children split off from a fourth youth and chose an occupation. After choosing they had to tell the first letter of the occupation and then describe it through movement while the others guessed what it was. But the game most often played in the streets was soccer. It was played with a homemade ball (*Fetzenlabrl*) constructed from one of their mother's stockings and anything they could find to stuff inside it that had some bounce. A favorite game was opening one shop door after the other and then watching the shop owners come out to search for the perpetrators.

As the children grew older, street games became more violent. Loosely organized youth groups often established dominion over a certain street or area and drove non-neighborhood children away. Through a number of interviews with former inhabitants, it is possible to reconstruct how youth groups operated. From an early age youth marked off their turf and exercised control over it. To a certain extent it was merely a way of preserving the streets around their apartment buildings as their playgrounds. Not only were all sorts of games played in the streets, but it was also the place where the majority of personal relationships developed and were played out. One of the severest punishments parents could impose was to refuse to permit their children to go into the streets. When 60 interwar, primarily proletarian, higher-elementary-school children were asked what the worst punishments of their life had been, many cited not being permitted to play in the streets. Rada found that 42 percent of the 120 12- to 13-year-old girls she observed found their enjoyment in the streets. This percentage probably dropped considerably during the subsequent years as these girls would soon be experiencing puberty.

In Favoriten, competition took place between youth from different streets and areas. . . . Battles between the *Müller* and the *Weber* [gangs] reminded some of those I interviewed of the conflict among youth groups they had seen in the American film *West Side Story*. Although the battles did not reach the gravity of those depicted in the film, since the major weapons were stones rather than knives or guns and the youth groups lacked the organized leadership typical of the contemporary gangs, the potential for more serious violence existed. . . .

The most compelling explanation for youths' sometimes violent street activity is that the streets provided a place where youth were not dominated, except for the occasional policeman, where they were in control. Here they could give free rein to their innermost feelings, to a spontaneity that was not permitted in their cramped working-class quarters where the authority of their parents was normally unquestioned. They were also not subject to societal divisions in the streets, since the major requirement for participation was not one's social background but one's willingness to share in the common youth street culture. Their identification with the local area gave them a basis for collective action. Former Favoriten residents remembered identifying with a prominent tavern *(Müller)* and housing area *(Weber)* in their neighborhood. That youth sometimes resorted to violence points to the greater emphasis on masculinity within working-class culture. Conquering an opponent is much more important than one's ability to articulate. The stronger members of the youth groups were invariably the most respected. . . .

While there is no denying that difficult conditions existed in Vienna's working-class districts in the early twentieth century, it is also difficult to deny that a relative stability, rather than disintegration, characterized life for most of the working class there. While World War I and the depression brought hard economic times, the smaller families typical of all strata in the interwar period reduced the economic suffering. Of course, those children of often-unemployed lower-stratum workers experienced the greatest want. No doubt their desperate conditions forced them to reduce their number of offspring below that of the other two strata during the interwar period. The prewar crowding and resultant lack of attention experienced by lower-stratum children undoubtedly influenced them as parents in the interwar period to limit family size. With fewer children and with the help of neighbors and relatives, these families managed to scrape by during the depression. Youth play had changed somewhat by the interwar period due to the many activities provided by the SDAP and the fewer children competing for facilities, including park and street space. It was possible in the interwar period for the children of lower-stratum parents to experience greater affection since they had fewer siblings competing for their parents' attention. . . .

Working-class family attitudes toward the schools were both practical and psychological. While many parents were apparently hostile because schools reduced family income by preventing their children from working, some viewed schools as possibly erecting intellectual barriers between parents and children and thereby stripping parents of their rightful role as educators of their children. Most of those parents who were not outright hostile still did not believe that schools equipped their children for the real world of work or suited the working-class environment. Such studies have explained the high attrition rate among students from working-class homes as resulting from the essentially middle-class status and career-oriented values characteristic of the schools. Youths' attitudes toward the schools have been explained as either outright hostility, as indifference, or as a desire for learning that was thwarted by family needs. Those who adopt the hostility thesis argue that youth viewed schools as part of the dominant culture and therefore opposed, sometimes violently, the acceptance of their value system. Others fail to see any group or class solidarity in resistance to the schools and therefore reject this class interpretation. What, then, were the reasons for Viennese working-class acceptance or rejection of schooling, and to what extent did their attitudes change between 1900 and 1940?

In Vienna, working-class opposition to schooling began with the preschools. Not one of the 70 persons I interviewed, all but four born before World War I, attended a kindergarten. Ludwig Battista, a ministerial adviser for education and author of several studies on the Austrian schools, determined that as late as the 1930s only one-seventh of eligible children attended a kindergarten. Only 19.4 percent of the women workers with children studied by Leichter sent their children to the free city kindergartens or socialist *Kinderhorte* (day-care centers with some instruction), even though their children were given preference for the existing openings. Since many of these mothers were members of labor unions and the socialist party, and therefore presumably were more aware of the purpose of the *Horte,* and since many were in need of some sort of child care (17 percent of the children were left at home without any supervision), the response of all working-class mothers must have been even less enthusiastic. This study led two students of the working-class experience to claim that the working class viewed preschools only as a necessary evil, which they would utilize only when home supervision of children was impossible. The reasons they offer for this attitude—that parents believed preschools were not places where children could obtain a desirable collective education but were only places of supervision—describe the motivation only of those who were politically involved.

Avoidance of preschools was tied closely to workers' lives. Writing in the socialist magazine *Die Unzufriedene* in 1929, Gerda Kautsky determined that working-class parents opposed kindergartens because, in the parents' opinion, they increased the possibility of infectious disease, exposed their children to bad influences, and robbed mothers of the responsibility of educating their own children. Kautsky rejected the first argument because she did not believe it possible to protect children from disease unless they were kept at home constantly. This reason may have been an excuse that concealed other, more important reasons for avoiding preschools, as Kautsky argues, but it is consistent with the working-class desire to avoid sickness and should not be dismissed as a reason among some working-class families. As a mother of three recounted, "No, my kids didn't go to kindergarten. My husband said 'no, they'll only bring sickness home.'" Leichter's study of 1,320 working mothers also found that fear of sickness was an often-cited reason for keeping children at home. Any additional sickness in the family could spread to other wage-earning family members and result in reduced income and hard times. Therefore, what may have appeared to Kautsky to be irrational seemed logical to them. . . . [To mothers, care of children seemed] their most significant responsibility and their reason for being. Kautsky recognized an attitude that much subsequent research has shown was common to all classes in Central Europe: a reverence for private family virtues over public (communal for socialists) values. The typical "respectable" proletarian family, as discussed earlier, valued nurturing in the home nearly as much as the bourgeoisie. Despite the most industrious efforts of Vienna's socialist administration in the 1920s to instill public virtues in the working class—common kitchens were the most glaring failure—most working-class families continued to shun police organizations and functions other than those in their immediate neighborhood. As we will see, these attitudes continued to influence working-class attitudes toward education well into the twentieth century. . . .

While most working-class parents resisted the schools, government and private agencies worked to institutionalize youth in order to provide "in industry and trade a morally predisposed, efficient, intellectually and physically sound generation and to protect against *errors* [italics mine] in the interest of the state and society," according to Josef Meixner, president of the Imperial Federation of Youth Defense *(Jugendwehren)* and Boy Centers *(Knabenhorte)* of Austria. Meixner headed the Department for Welfare Work for Industrial Employed Youth in the Ministry for Public Affairs. An alleged 86 percent increase in crime among 10- to 14-year-olds between 1880 and 1905, cited in Meixner's article, provided much of the impetus for the private and government actions to control youth. Although much of the crime attributed to youth could have resulted from a broadened interpretation of criminal activity, fear of an uncontrolled street culture with possible damaging social and military consequences lurked in the hearts of the authorities. Military leaders warned about the lack of discipline and physical fitness among street youth and the consequences this could have for military preparedness. . . .

Socialist party leaders tried to counter the street milieu as resolutely as did the government. Convinced that traditional working-class culture was responsible for the educational deficiencies of the lower classes, the predominantly middle-class SDAP leadership sought to fashion a new working-class consciousness by reforming youth behavior. By creating "new beings" *(Neue Menschen)*, socialists hoped to bridge the social-cultural gap between SDAP leadership and most workers severely hindered attempts to transform working-class behavior. For example, the socialist *Horte* established to care for children after elementary school hours were only partially successful in their mission to keep working-class children off the streets and provide them with some supplemental education to help keep underprivileged children abreast of the privileged. . . .

In opposition to these attempts to institutionalize youth was the indifference, and in some cases hostility, of most working-class youth and parents toward the schools. Oral interviews reveal that few respondents could remember much, especially anything positive, about their school experience. Certainly very few remembered it as being an especially pleasant experience. Children could speak only when spoken to by the teacher and had to sit upright with their hands on the desk and pencil at the ready. Peukert's description of the German schools during the Weimar Republic as places of detention more than learning centers rings true for many of the Vienna schools as well. It is little wonder that most yearned to escape to the streets and their own less oppressive world. Alfred Molnar wrote in his autobiographical study, *Unstet und Flüchtig,* that he skipped school ten days during the first half-year of the 1911–12 school year so that he could play with his peers. Parents were especially opposed before World War I to learning other than the basic reading, writing, and arithmetic. They did not consider education useful unless it had some occupational importance. Wenzel Holek's mother told him, "Those who learn and study a lot will go crazy, will end up in an insane asylum." Adelheid Popp, an Austrian socialist leader and former factory worker, wrote that her parents thought that three years of school was enough and those who had not learned anything by the time they were ten would learn nothing after that. Humphries argues that the English "saw it as an imposition with little relevance or application to the world of the working-class child."

Even those with outstanding elementary school grades knew that they would not be able to attend a secondary school. As the son of a mason and agricultural worker related, "I had very good report cards in the *Hauptschule* and *Volksschule*. I was always an excellent student. But it was not possible for me then, although the teacher offered it to me . . . I should study further, attend the *Gymnasium*. But it was naturally not possible since my father was only a mason by training and we had a very simple household. I had two brothers, my mother was in the home, and we had to live from my father's income alone." Family considerations continued to take precedence over individual goals far into the twentieth century. This attitude was not unique to Austria. Elizabeth Roberts found family considerations to be dominant among the English working class throughout the entire period 1890–1940. As she wrote, "The children learned early to subjugate personal ambition to their parents and to care, on a daily basis, for the needs of other members of the family."

Working-class parents preferred to get their children into an apprenticeship so that they could either aid the family financially or at least cease to be a financial burden. This traditional attitude predominated among all workers before World War I but began to subside among the two upper strata of workers in the interwar period. While children of middle-class families could concentrate on schoolwork, working-class children often had to divide their time between education and work. Many elementary school students worked before and after school and on weekends. A 1913 report from the Austrian

Labor Statistical Office showed that large numbers of Austrian school children were employed while still in school and had been employed at a very early age. One-third (148,368) of the school children surveyed were gainfully employed, and three-fourths of them had begun work before the age of 9. Over one-third worked more than three hours a day during the winter months and 42.9 percent worked on Sundays and holidays. Another survey of 80,859 Austrian school children in 1908 had similar results: 23,016, or 28.5 percent, were gainfully employed. Figures for other European countries paint a similar picture. Bray calculated that 25 percent of all London school children were employed after school hours as late as 1910. . . .

A common obstacle encountered in school by working-class children was the necessity to learn "book" or formal German. Since few Viennese youth ever left the working-class areas, where only Viennese dialect was spoken, they seldom encountered anyone speaking "book" German. It was almost as if they had to learn another language. A woman who had moved to Ottakring from the first district during her youth told me, "I came out here and the children laughed at me. For the school it was wonderful [knowing formal German] . . . my friends . . . they all had difficulty in school because they didn't speak formal German at home. They couldn't. They had to learn it first. For me it was second nature." But outside the school, and especially in the streets, dialect held sway. Rada related how one of her students who tried to speak formal German was embarrassed by her brother when he sarcastically responded, "Look at the goose, she wants to act high-born [*will nobel tun*]." A woman who grew up in Favoriten recalled that "we spoke 'book' German when we went walking . . . it was a lot of fun. We were refined girls then." It was therefore difficult outside the schools to speak "book" German even if one knew it.

Rada further noted that her students disliked subjects such as history because they were embarrassed to recite in class since they knew little "book" German. In order to overcome this language barrier, a few schools used the Viennese dialect to instruct pupils in language classes. The objective was to make use of the home environment to introduce students gradually to "book" German. A survey of 90 female *Bürgerschule* students in the interwar period showed that gymnastics (19 percent), drawing (18 percent), and German (17 percent) were the favorite subjects. Religion, geometry, and foreign language were not selected by any of the students as their favorite.

Working-class parents' lack of concern about "advanced education" for their children could change to open hostility toward subjects and activities they considered to be culturally and psychologically damaging, impractical, or time-consuming. As studies for England and Germany have found, working-class parents feared that advanced learning would separate their children from the family and, in effect, the child would be lost to the family. Children would be educated "out of their estate [*Stände*]." One former resident of Favoriten recalled his mother telling him not to waste his time reading poetry. When he attempted to read poetry to her, she angrily responded that he should stop such "nonsense." Another remembers not being permitted to read newspapers until she was fourteen. The socialist leader Anna Maier wrote that "when a comrade loaned me the *Arbeiterinnenzeitung* [*Working Woman's Press*], I had to hide it, for at home I wouldn't dare read it in front of my mother." Rada found that 56 percent of her students were forbidden to read newspapers. One told Rada, "I most like to read about legal trials, especially murder trials, and the weather. My father forbade that I read the newspaper, but I found the time to do it." Part of the parents' objection was certainly that knowledge of destructive behavior might promote similar behavior among their children, but, more important, such time could be better spent helping with housework, working in part-time jobs to aid the family economy, or learning some skill that would be more "useful" later in life. Essentially the family came first, and parents opposed too much independence and anything that would enhance it. Reading introduces independent ideas and reduces the parents' control over their children. . . .

34

Nazism and the Lower-Middle Class

HEINRICH AUGUST WINKLER

The rise of Nazism in Germany, and of similar movements in other countries, is the outstanding characteristic of the two decades between the world wars. How could such a movement take shape and win substantial support? Social scientists have developed a number of approaches to deal with the phenomenon. Some see Nazism and other totalitarian movements as endemic to the condition of modern society. Robbed of traditional values (such as religion) and close community ties, the modern person stands alone and fearful, easily yielding to the solidarity and discipline of movements such as Nazism. Others view Nazism as a specifically German phenomenon, seeking in the German past an acceptance of authority and militarism. Still others emphasize more temporary factors, maintaining that Nazism was the product of a massive and unexpected defeat in war and of a variety of severe economic pressures, all of which had much greater impact in Germany than elsewhere. Even amid unprecedented social and political stress, Nazism did not really gain popularity until the Great Depression.

Interpretation of support for Nazism is further complicated by the sheer opportunism of the movement, which tried to appeal to almost all groups and was quite capable of switching stands to win support. Relatedly, the reasons Nazism won popularity differ considerably from the results of Nazism in practice. No one has yet clearly assessed the extent to which Nazi anti-Semitism and aggressive nationalism won support: all we know for sure is that these ideologies did not deter the Nazi voters. But Nazism's promises of support for farmers and small businesses and its suggestion of a return to a more traditional Germany, were directly contradicted by the actions of the regime once it gained power. It has even been argued that, horrible though it was, the Nazis ultimately helped make Germany more genuinely modern and therefore less susceptible to similar movements after Nazism itself was defeated in war.

The following selection points to the conditions and outlook of small businessmen as a crucial ingredient in the growing popularity of Nazism after 1930. It also stresses a larger social context in Germany, in which a modern

From: Heinrich August Winkler, "From Social Protectionism to National Socialism: The German Small-Business Movement in Comparative Perspective," *The Journal of Modern History*, Vol. 48, No. 1 (March, 1976): 7–18.

economy had arisen without destroying key ingredients of a premodern social structure that included a powerful traditional aristocracy. Some historians would accept this kind of social analysis as part of the explanation for Nazism, but would also look at less clearly social factors, such as the German national character and characteristic ideology. Some historians would also point to other social groups, along with the property-owning lower-middle class, who contributed to Nazi success; rarely can a major political movement be explained solely in terms of one-class adherence.

Nevertheless, in seizing on the lower-middle class *[gewerblicher Mittelstand]*, Heinrich Winkler is dealing not only with a major ingredient of Nazism, but with an important social group in the ongoing industrialization process. The industrial revolution initially expanded the ranks of small tradesmen. They displayed a distinct and conservative version of the larger middleclass ideology, including a vigorous desire to remain separate from the working class and working-class politics. Later industrialization attacked this same group via new business forms. A new lower-middle class arose simultaneously, composed of clerks and salespeople who owned no property. These developments altered both the position and the attitudes of small businessmen in many countries. This aspect of industrialization—creating a major social group and then attacking it—is being repeated in our own day as the position of factory workers is eroded in the advanced industrial societies of Western Europe and the United States. Consequently, the reactions of the traditional lower-middle class—called *Mittelstand* in Germany—have a bearing on an understanding of modernization beyond the interwar years themselves.

Yet Winkler emerges with an ironic conclusion about the old lowermiddle class itself. Further development of the industrial economy, in part encouraged by the Nazis when they were in power, changed the situation of the small businessman and integrated him within modern society in new ways. Winkler's analysis—unlike some more foreboding analyses of German character which hint that the beast might still be lurking—suggests a literal repeat of Nazism is unlikely in Germany.

The revolution of November 1918 forced the artisans and the retailers to reappraise their political options. No doubt, only a tiny minority of impoverished small businessmen felt sympathy with the revolution or supported it actively. For the bulk of the *Bürgerlich* [middle-class] population, the paramount interest was the restoration of law and order. Their organization hence pleaded for the immediate election of a National Assembly. When the election took place, on January 19, 1919, most small businessmen voted for the left-wing liberal German Democratic party (DDP). The reason was obviously not a late conversion to the cause of liberalism but a tactical consideration. The DDP was the presumptive coalition partner of the Social Democrats; a strong liberal party was thus seen as the best guarantee against socialist experiments.

The vote for the DDP was the beginning of a long migration through the party system of the Weimar Republic—a migration from left to right. After years of social and political unrest, of revolutionary and counterrevolutionary assaults on the Republic, middle-class sympathies shifted in the Reichstag election of 1920 to Gustav Stresemann's German People's party (DVP), a right-wing liberal party with an originally monarchist tendency. In May and December 1924, they turned to the extremely conservative and avowedly antidemocratic party, the German National People's party (DNVP). After the rampant inflation and the Rhineland crisis of 1923, and after renewed Communist insurrections and Hitler's Munich putsch, a majority of the middle-class voters were prepared to protest against the parliamentary system as such. The vote for the DNVP was an expression of political nostalgia. The middle classes were longing for the world of the *Obrigkeitsstaat,* the authoritarian system of the Empire.

The DDP lost popularity for the same reason which had made it so appealing in 1919: its alliance with the Social Democrats. For a brief time, the DDP appeared to be indispensable, but it soon became a political liability. The German People's party disappointed the small businessmen because of its undeniable dependence on powerful industrial circles. It did not serve as a bridge between the interests of small and big business. Neither the industrialists nor the artisans and shopkeepers realized that they needed each other politically. The DNVP, while more successful than the right-wing liberals in combining heterogeneous interests, also had dominant groups: the agrarians and certain exponents of heavy industry. Thus, after a brief flirtation, the craftsmen and shopkeepers who had identified themselves with the Nationalists became disillusioned once again. It was particularly artisans and landlords who turned, in the mid-twenties, to a pure interest-type party, the Business party (Wirtschaftspartei), which in 1925 was renamed the Reichspartei des deutschen Mittelstands.

The growing alienation between the small businessmen and the traditional nonsocialist parties has to be seen against the background of the process of industrial concentration which culminated in the second half of the 1920s. The more corporations extended their power, the more helpless the small-scale producers felt. Feeling squeezed between big business and big labor, many small businessmen voted for the Business party in order to protest against the political and economic system of postwar Germany. The Business party never polled more than 4.5 percent of the total vote (1928), but it was highly symptomatic of small business's disgust with political parties. By mobilizing resentment against parliamentary democracy, the Business party helped prepare the ground for the biggest mass movement of the 1930s, the National Socialists.

The Weimar party system continued to reflect the social segmentation so characteristic of the Empire. The logic of the parliamentary system called for social integration within the parties, but there was, in the last analysis, only one party which learned this lesson sufficiently well: Hitler's extremely antiparliamentary NSDAP. In the mid-twenties, however, it was by no means clear that this party would win massive middle-class support. The pseudoso-cialist rhetoric of the Nazis, especially strong in the formative years of the party, frightened off industrialists, small businessmen, and peasants. The com-bination of nationalism and socialism as it was proclaimed by Hitler's party was only attractive to white-collar workers, members of paramilitary leagues, and some intellectuals. For many years the *Bürgertum* [middle class] took the Nazis—as a right-wing handicraft weekly in Hanover put it in 1924–for "bol-shevik poison in a black-white-red wrapping."

The shift finally came in 1930. It took a basic change in Nazi propaganda and a panic, caused by the great economic depression, to bring about heavy *mittelständisch* [middle-class] support for Hitler's movement. As early as 1927, the Nazis had tried to shed their proletarian image and to woo leading industrialists in private and the lower-middle classes in public. During the years of stabilization between 1924 and 1929 they were not very successful. After the outbreak of the economic crisis they intensified their efforts to win middle-class support. Their "socialism" was now interpreted as just another version of the party's slogan, "Service not self" (*Gemeinnutz vor Eigennutz*). As the small-business organization of the party, the Kampfbund des gewerblichen Mittelstandes, put it in December 1932, socialism meant the "deproletarianization of the German worker." "The purpose of the socialist idea is the creation of property for those who have none. This means that Adolf Hitler's socialism contrasts most sharply with the mendacious pseudo-siocialism of the Marxists which aims at the expropriation of the Proprietors."

The attraction of the Nazis for the lower-middle classes—and it was these groups that provided the Nazis' strength in the elections—cannot be explained by a single element in the Nazi ideology. Neither their extreme nationalism nor their violent anti-Semitism accounts for the rise of the NSDAP after 1930. Both issues were, though in differing degree, traditional aspects of right-wing movements in Germany. My proposition is that the combination of two ele-ments made the Nazis so appealing to the lower-middle classes: first, their per-sistent adoption of the protectionist demands of the lower middle classes and, second, their readiness to eliminate radically all ideologies, institutions, and groups which the lower-middle classes blamed for their miseries.

Thus, the craftsmen were promised compulsory guilds and obligatory masters' examinations, and the shopkeepers were attracted by the campaign against "Jewish" department stores. The peasants were told that they would become the "first estate" in the Third Reich and that the goal of autarky made it necessary to introduce higher tariffs for agricultural products. The civil ser-vants, emotionally linked with the tradition of a strong authoritarian state and deeply embittered by Chancellor Brüning's deflationary policy of salary cut-ting, expected Hitler to restore law and order and to recognize their vested place in the social hierarchy. The white-collar workers were the group which was most afraid of proletarianization. As mentioned before, they had been treated as a special group, separated from the working class in German social security laws since 1911. In their majority, they regarded themselves as part of the *Bürgertum*. No political party appealed more convincingly to their status concerns than the Nazi party. No group was more impressed by the specific Nazi combination of leveling and hierarchy than the white-collar workers, who felt both resentment toward the old elites and superiority toward the *Proletarier*.

The promise to eliminate the enemies of the *Mittelstand* aimed not only at the Communists but at the specter of "Marxism" as a whole, including the trade unions and the Social Democratic party. Moreover, no party was more convincing when it came to promising the destruction of parliamentarism, political parties, and majority rule than the Nazis. The preservation of the existing social order and the liquidation of its political superstructure, which obviously no longer guaranteed the status quo, was the service the Nazis were expected to perform for the German middle class. It was this very same promise which motivated leading industrialists, particularly in the coal and iron sector, Prussian Junkers, and conservative politicians to support, directly or indirectly, Hitler's seizure of power. This was just as crucial a contribution to his final success on January 30, 1933 as the millions of votes for the Nazi party. The conservative Kartell still functioned in 1933.

Nazism and fascism have been described as an "extremism of the center." Lipset, who first formulated this proposition, maintains that mainly former voters of the liberal parties turned to the Nazis. This is true, but it should not be overlooked that most of these voters had already shifted to the conservative camp before they eventually supported the Nazi party. Though [the] strategy and tactics of the Nazis differed clearly from the traditional conservative right, their attacks were predominantly directed against the left. If there was a mass basis for right-wing extremism, it was the middle classes.

But fascism was not simply a form of middle-class extremism. (I should add, at this point, that I regard nazism as a Fascist movement, though its violent anti-Semitism was not shared by the Italian Fascists and is, in fact, not a "necessary" element of Fascist ideology.) Fascism, if I may use the generalizing term, has to be analyzed on three different levels, depending on whether its social basis, the expectations of the traditional power elites, or the strategic objectives of its leadership are being considered. Fascism cannot be adequately described by unveiling the economic interests of its social basis and of the groups which supported it either financially or through collaboration after the seizure of power. The Fascist power elite acted with remarkable independence. Its final goals were not economic ones. Its domestic alliances had only a tactical character. It wooed those social forces which were indispensable for the achievement of its final objectives: in the case of the Nazis, hegemonical expansion without discernible limitations, and an inexorable fight against the Jews—*Lebensraum* and *Lösung der Judenfrage*. Other interests were unhesitatingly subordinated to this particular "primacy of politics."

It is well known that, in the last analysis, the *Mittelstand* belonged to the dupes of the movement it had helped to bring into power. Some of the traditional demands of the craftsmen and shopkeepers, such as obligatory masters' examination, the compulsory guilds, and prohibitive measures in favor of the retail trade, were fulfilled. With regard to the surtax on the turnover in department stores and to other discriminations against large-scale retail business, the Nazis continued the small-business politics of the presidential governments of the early thirties. But the Nazis never began the promised destruction of department stores and postponed action on the abolition of the consumers' cooperatives until 1941. Both types of enterprises proved to be useful instruments in regulating the distribution of goods. But more importantly, during the first years of the Third Reich, a liquidation of the larger retail enterprises would have meant an unacceptable increase in unemployment. The corporatist order, of which the craftsmen were particularly in favor, never came into being. Bureaucracy as well as big business thwarted all plans that would have led to a new parastate hierarchy and to economic stagnation.

The few concessions to small-business interests which were actually achieved were due more to the pressure of the conservative allies of the Nazis than to the Nazi party itself. After the proclamation of the Four-Year Plan in 1936, it turned out that small business was not seen as particularly essential to the war effort. The economic weight of small business sank, handicrafts and retail trade were "combed out," the chambers of handicrafts as instruments of corporate self-administration were dissolved under the impact of total war, and Nazi propagandists blamed the *gewerblicher Mittelstand* for its notorious selfishness. When in 1941 the Reichsstand des deutschen Handwerks complained about the allegedly ruinous competition between the construction industry and the construction crafts, Heinrich Himmler, the *Reichsführer SS,* comforted the craftsmen by pointing to the social opportunities offered to them in the newly conquered territories in eastern Europe. No *Lebensraum* perspective, however, could compensate for the material losses of small business. A privileged position in the Third Reich was only available to those who were indispensable for rearmament and war. The *Mittelstand* did not belong in this category.

Social protectionism for small business was no German invention. Discriminatory measures against department stores were taken in other countries too. France was the first when she introduced a special tax on large retail turnover. Further interventions of that kind followed at the end of the nineteenth and the beginning of the twentieth century. Under the impact of the Great Depression, a law was passed which made the expansion of certain types of large-scale retail business illegal. Belgium and Switzerland chose similar forms of protection for small retail business. Handicraft chambers existed not only in Germany but also in some other countries; France introduced that institution in 1925. Only the reestablished artisan guilds, the *Innungen,* with their roots in the Middle Ages, can be seen as a specifically German phenomenon.

It is certainly not the guilds, however, that account for the difference between the political behavior of the *gewerblicher Mittelstand* in Germany and that in other European countries. In Germany, social protectionism was an integral part of an authoritarian system of mutual social reinsurance. The protection of small businessmen was intended to promote their identification with the existing social and political order. This was generally a successful strategy. The bulk of the craftsmen and shopkeepers became interested, in the wake of social protectionism, in the preservation of a nonparliamentary authoritarian state which sheltered them against the danger of being outvoted by consumers and workers. Soon after the revolution of 1918, the Empire began to look to small business as paradise lost.

The antidemocratic tendency of the *gewerblicher Mittelstand* was a cause as well as a consequence of the longevity of the *ancien régime* in Germany. In countries with a long democratic tradition—and this means, in most cases, countries that had experienced a successful middle-class revolution—protest movements of small business did not take an openly antidemocratic or Fascist but rather a populist direction. This applies in particular to the movement around Pierre Poujade in France during the 1950s. The attacks of the Union de défense des commerçants et artisans centered on department stores, banks, corporations, and unions; they were directed against the economic and political establishment as a whole. At the same time, the Poujadists claimed to be the true heirs of the French Revolution of 1789. Poujadism was late-Jacobin radicalism, nostalgic and backward, but certainly not totalitarian, as were the Fascist movements of the interwar years. The petit bourgeois allegiance to the ideals of the Revolution has solid material roots. By enabling the wealthier peasants to buy land, the French Revolution had indirectly also strengthened small shopkeepers and craftsmen. There was no large "industrial reserve army," formed from a rural proletariat, which could have been absorbed by big industrial enterprises. The retardation and incompleteness of the Industrial Revolution meant the lasting predominance of small-scale production in France. Moreover, the Revolution had destroyed that social class which in Germany helped to form the antidemocratic *Mittelstandsbewegung:* the feudal aristocracy. It was, thus, the Revolution which in the last analysis determined the political development and the ideology of small business in France—a development and an ideology which clearly differed from those of the *gewerblicher Mittelstand* in Germany.

The development of small business in Britain and the United States was basically different, but at least in America some parallels to the French case exist. The classical countries of capitalism have produced political cultures which have not offered many opportunities for openly protectionist *Mittelstand* politics or for a protectionist *Mittelstand* movement after the German model. In England, small-scale entrepreneurs possess only a rudimentary interest organization. Consumers' cooperatives and department stores have drastically reduced the economic weight of shopkeepers and artisans, particularly in the food business. This had not led, however, to a Poujadist-style protest movement, and it is questionable whether one can speak at all of a political profile in connection with the small shopkeepers and artisans of England. In the United States, too, small business, of which craftsmen and retailers form only a small minority, is characterized by an organization lag. Interest groups for small-scale producers and retailers were not created on the national level until the 1940s; these, however, represent only a minority of small business. Small businessmen tend to identify themselves with independent entrepreneurs as against "anonymous" corporations. Small business distrusts "big business," "big government," and "big labor." It is antiurban and antiintellectual, it is in favor of all that it takes to be originally "American," and it is against such "foreign ideologies" as socialism. American small business wants security in the face of the "unfair competition" from chain and department stores. It glorifies the virtues of "rugged individualism" and the American Revolution. Many parallels exist to the mentality of small business in continental Europe. In some states, there is strong pressure toward public regulation of interest fights between different professions (e.g., the recent clash between barbers and cosmeticians in Iowa) and a legal demarcation of their respective spheres of activity that looks almost like a *zünftlerisch* (guildlike) restriction of industrial freedom. Nevertheless, it seems that there are still signs of a common business ideology in the United States. At least until the 1930s, the National Association of Manufacturers epitomized a basic consensus among businessmen. Trust-busting belonged, of course, to the credo of the independent entrepreneurs, and the resentment against bigness still has its populist ring. It is important to note, however, that small business in America is basically antistatist. The German *Mittelstand,* by contrast, expected everything from the state and nothing from itself.

A disposition toward moral indignation at different value orientations, an inclination toward collective panic, a readiness to demonize all forces which threaten the traditional social order—these seem to be characteristics of the mentality of the lower middle classes. Such a mentality, however, is obviously not enough to bring about fascism. Fascist movements have come to power only in those societies which have never experienced a successful middle-class revolution, in societies where preindustrial power elites such as landed aristocracy, military, bureaucracy, and church have been able to preserve their privileges beyond the threshold of the Industrial Revolution and to exert decisive influence on the political behavior of other social groups. Not just capitalism alone, as vulgar Marxists assert, produced fascism; equally, if not more important, was a burdensome legacy of feudalism and absolutism.

Precapitalist forces worked together both with leading industrial groups and with the middle classes. In Germany, the Prussian Junkers, a class accustomed to governing, played a decisive role in the destruction of democracy. They were much more skillful than conservative industrialists in the mobilization of mass support for their political objectives, and they had, once Paul von Hindenburg had become president of the Reich, immediate access to the executive—a fact of crucial importance in the last weeks of the Weimar Republic.

The existence of powerful preindustrial groups seems to be a *sine qua non* for authoritarian or Fascist regimes. Wherever the business elite can resort, in times of crisis, to the political support of older social classes it is not forced to compromise with the rest of the middle class or with the workers. Obviously, different national conditions exist for the mobilization of the middle class as a mass basis for a Fascist movement. In Italy, the economically independent parts of the lower middle class prior to Mussolini's seizure of power were hardly organized. Owing to the retardation and defectiveness of the Industrial Revolution in Italy, small business had not yet experienced a real confrontation with big industry. In the early twenties, small shopkeepers supported the Fascists because they regarded them as determined allies in the battle against consumers' cooperatives and other "socialist" enterprises. The political influence of small business under the Fascist regime was as weak as it had been prior to 1922.

According to Rudolf Hilferding, the famous Social Democratic theorist, competitive capitalism was succeeded, at the turn of the century, by "organized capitalism." Hilferding aimed at replacing a competitive economy, operating within the framework of general conditions set by the state, with a highly concentrated and bureaucratized economy based on interest groups and propped up by permanent state intervention. The German bureaucratic tradition of a patriarchal social commitment was the main reason why the shift to "organized capitalism" took place earlier there than in most other countries. If, thus, "organized capitalism" has such obviously deep roots in German society, it is so much the truer for "organized precapitalism," as the regulated small business economy may be called by analogy. Whether with respect to industry or to handicraft and retail business, the state was expected to protect the economy against economic crises and their social consequences, regardless of the costs which consumers had to bear. The protection of small business as practiced by the Empire became the basis of *Mittelstand* demands in the First German Republic. This was particularly true for the handicrafts, whose very organization had been made possible by Imperial laws. Price regulation through the guilds, already demanded prior to World War I, was a plank with which the parties and the governments of Weimar were confronted time and again. The artisans' argument was simple: if cartels were seen as a legitimate institution for big industry, why should they be unacceptable in the case of small business? The consideration of the vital interests of the consumers, which kept the Weimar governments from meeting such demands, was a permanent source of frustration for craftsmen and shopkeepers.

The experience of massive protection for small-business interests, granted by the patriarchal Empire as part of its quest for social stability, provided *one* condition of the growing *Mittelstand* support for an antiparliamentary movement such as the Nazi party. The social protectionism of the prerevolutionary regime had promoted the segmentation of German society. Ironically, it was the beneficiaries of that policy who assisted in a movement which finally, in the name of the *Volksgemeinschaft* [national community] and despite all previous promises to the *Mittelstand,* proceeded to abolish many of the corporate privileges so typical of the traditional social order. To be sure, many objections can be made to the proposition that the Nazi regime brought about a "social revolution." With regard to small business, however, it can hardly be denied that the abolition of protectionism, which was pushed through after the late thirties, has had a modernizing impact on that part of Germany's social fabric.

Modernization was certainly the very last objective of the National Socialists. And it was, in fact, their total collapse and not any positive action of their regime that caused a real break with Germany's social traditionalism. After World War II, the Allied occupation, and its assumption of supreme political responsibility, made the situation decisively different from that in 1918. In short, there was much less political, administrative, military, and social continuity after World War II than after World War I. The disappearance of the landed aristocracy of Prussia is a factor which can hardly be overestimated, and it remains the most striking break in the social as well as political sphere.

Small business, in the Federal Republic, has undergone tremendous structural change. It has used the chances which the economic reconstruction offered. The number of small-scale production enterprises has continuously decreased, whereas the number of employees per entrepreneurial unit has grown. The contribution of crafts to the gross domestic product is rather stable: it amounted to one-tenth in 1968 (one-twelfth in 1936). Small business has altogether a more stable structure today than in Weimar Germany, though parts of it are largely dependent on the decisions of the industrial concerns from which smaller entrepreneurs get their raw materials or for which they work on the basis of delivery contracts. A result of this relative stabilization is a decreasing exposure to political extremism.

The contribution which National Socialism made to the development of postwar Germany is thus predominantly an indirect one. It was its failure which destroyed many of the social, political, and ideological traditions that had helped bring it to power. In this sense, it seems safe to say that the Third Reich constitutes the most cynical and costly example of what Hegel called the cunning of reason.

35

INDEPENDENT WOMEN
AND A NEW CONSUMERISM

MARY LOUISE ROBERTS

The following selection deals with important changes in women's styles, the reactions they provoked, and the vital issue of what both change and reaction meant—in France in the 1920s. The focus is on a new culture and form of expression, as women began to use consumerism in novel ways to express interests and needs. The language, urged on them by fashion gurus, emphasized independence, but historian Mary Louise Roberts notes that a host of constraints were in fact being accepted in the process. Yet conservative, largely male response suggested that the gesture struck home: women, to many observers, were simply no longer looking like women, and the change was deeply disturbing.

This selection should be juxtaposed with earlier assessment of middle-class women (see Chapter 24)—here is one clue to the new meanings of consumerism. And of course consumerism was not in itself novel (see Chapter 15), so some analysis must be devoted to why it could be turned to additional, gendered uses at this point.

Women of fashion were disproportionately young and disproportionately middle- and upper-class. Yet their gestures resonated more widely, setting standards that other women might aspire to. The following selection (Chapter 36), dealing with French working-class women a decade later, shows the reverberating impact, which still carried complicated political messages.

Attention to France captures some developments widely shared among women between the wars, in terms of new styles, new body imagery, and new devotion to cosmetics and other consumer products. There were, however, some French features to the process. French women did not get the vote after World War I, unlike their counterparts in Britain and Scandinavia; yet, like their sisters elsewhere, they turned away from exclusively political goals toward this wider concern for changes in lifestyle. France was also a country with an exceptionally low birthrate and greater concern—the natalist

From: Mary Louise Roberts, "Samson and Delilah Revisited: The Politics of Women's Fashion in 1920s France," *American Historical Review* 98 (June, 1993): 657–62, 664–65, 670, 674–75, 677–81.

movement—about inadequate population levels. The country led, finally, in high fashion, which the new developments both reflected and furthered.

The basic analytical issue, however, remains the problem of interpreting consumerist gestures and their relationship to more explicitly political goals. Here, French women developed patterns that were quite widely shared: in a period when most women still did not work, in the sense of formal, lifelong employment, and when political power was elusive, radical uses of consumerism most clearly defined the ongoing change in gender relations.

In France during the 1920s, fashion was a highly charged issue. In 1925, an article in *L'oeuvre* jocularly described how the fashion of short hair had completely overturned life in a small French village. After the first woman in the village cut her hair, accompanied by "tears and grinding of teeth" on the part of her family, the fashion had quickly become "epidemic: from house to house, it took its victims." A gardener swore he would lock up his daughter until her hair grew back; a husband believed that his wife had dishonored him. A scandalized curé decided to preach a sermon about it, but "unfortunately he had chosen the wrong day, since it was the feast of Jeanne d'Arc." As he began to condemn bobbed hair as indecent and unchristian, "the most impudent young ladies of the parish pointed insolently at the statue of the liberator." By claiming the bobbed-cut Joan of Arc as their mascot, these young women grounded their quest for "liberation" in the rich, tangled mainstream of French history. They appealed to the ambivalent yet strongly traditional image of *Jeanne la pucelle* (Joan the Virgin), at once patriotic, fervently Christian, and sexually ambiguous.

The fashion among young women for short, bobbed hair created enormous tensions within the French family. Throughout the decade, newspapers recorded lurid tales, including one husband in the provinces who sequestered his wife for bobbing her hair and another father who reportedly killed his daughter for the same reason. A father in Dijon sought legal action against a hairdresser in 1925 for cutting the hair of his daughter without his authority. "At present, the question of short hair is dividing families," argued Antoine, one of the hairdressers who pioneered the bobbed cut. "The result," according to journalist Paul Reboux, "was that during family meals, nothing is heard except the clicking of the forks on the porcelain." One working-class woman, who was in her twenties during the era, remembered that her mother-in-law did not talk to her sister-in-law Simone for almost a year after the latter bobbed her hair. René Rambaud, another hairdresser who helped to popularize the cut, recalled the story of a newly married woman who cut her hair, believing that she had the right to do so without consulting her parents. Her mother and father in turn accused her husband and his parents of the monstrous crime, leading to a rift so severe that the two families did not reconcile for twenty years.

The outcry concerning the fashion of bobbed hair can be explained in part by its novelty and unfamiliarity. Short hair exemplified the dramatic, provocative changes sweeping the world of French fashion. Notions of female fashion had undergone a profound transformation since the beginning of the century. According to the journalist René Bizet, for example, every aspect of female dress had not only changed but become the mirror opposite of what it had been in 1900. Both before and during the war, as the ideal of the voluptuous, curvaceous woman gave way to a sinuous, smooth, "modernist" one, the compressed structural lines and highly ornamental fashions of the previous century were radically simplified. Paul Poiret pioneered the new minimalist style within the elite world of *haute couture* in the first two decades of the twentieth century. Working-class and middle-class women began to adopt the more efficient approach to fashion during the war. In the early 1920s, designer Coco Chanel created a sporty, casual mode by further simplifying Poiret's style. Mass-produced and meticulously imitated throughout France, the Chanel style reached its peak of popularity by 1925 and held sway until 1927 or 1928.

The craze for short hair typified this chronology of change in the fashion world. At the fin-de-siècle, excessive, baroque hairstyles had dominated, and, in the pre-war years, only a few actresses, such as Caryathis and Eve Lavallière, cut their hair short. Precisely who was responsible for popularizing the bob is a matter of dispute. Coco Chanel, who cut her hair in 1916, is often credited with the revolution in hairstyles, as are two hairdressers, Antoine Cierplikowski and René Rambaud, who pioneered the style in professional circles during the early 1920s. In any case, between 1918 and 1925, short, bobbed hair "à la Jeanne d'Arc" or "aux enfants d'Edouard," grew in popularity and by mid-decade was sending shock waves throughout France. Important to the popularity of the bob was the 1922 publication of Victor Margueritte's novel *La garçonne*, about a young "modern woman" who rejects her bourgeois family, cuts her hair, adopts male dress, and leads a hedonistic and "liberated" life in Paris. According to René Rambaud, the novel, which became an overnight best seller, inspired young women throughout France to cut their hair and to follow the new style "à l'allure garçonnière." After 1922, the new styles were associated particularly with the young, sexy, independent "garçonne" or "femme moderne."

The fashion styles that emerged in the 1920s differed dramatically from those at the turn of the century. Since the new look emerged gradually, however, the controversy it inspired cannot be explained solely in terms of its novelty. Memoirists, in looking back on the decade, invariably described the new styles as central to the spirit of the era, suggesting the broader cultural significance of fashion. "Short hair was not only a fashion, it was an epoch. It was a particular sign of a time," argued Rambaud in his memoir. The "epoch" of short hair began immediately after the war when the new bobbed cut first became an object of widespread controversy. If we are to believe the radical feminist Henriette Sauret, the bob already preoccupied the French in 1919, when relatively few women were actually cutting their hair. During that year, Sauret made fun of male journalists who, faced with major stories such as the Paris Peace Conference, demobilization, and the Bolshevik "threat," still concerned themselves with women's hair. "This urgent question," Sauret sarcastically observed, occupies "a good third of their daily remarks." Short hair, she wrote, "holds a certain interest for men which has gone undetected by us, because they deign to devote to it the precious emanations of their brains." Although Sauret was obviously exaggerating, her remarks raise an interesting question. What "undetected interest" did short hair hold in order to become the focus of so much emotion and anger? If fashion was a sort of text, a complex visual language that postwar observers "read" in various ways, what was it about the new style that gave offense? How did postwar observers—journalists, clergy, pamphleteers, designers, feminists—explain its dramatic and explosive power?

I will argue that postwar observers interpreted the new fashion in two ways: as a visual language for the war's social upheaval and as a visual fantasy of female liberation. The new styles emerged during the war and postwar periods—years of dramatic change in French gender relations as well as in fashion. In this context, a first set of postwar observers, especially natalists and Catholics, interpreted fashion as evidence of a refusal among women to pursue traditional gender roles. Fashion bore the symbolic weight of an entire set of social anxieties concerning the war's perceived effects on gender relations: the blurring or reversal of gender boundaries and the crisis of domesticity (*la crise du foyer*). The belief that women were becoming more like men and rejecting their traditional domestic role existed as early as the fin-de-siècle period but was greatly exacerbated by the war's disruption of the normal hierarchies of status between men and women. One of the most commented on of the war's effects was its blurring of sexual difference. Although the entry of women into higher education and traditionally male professions had begun in the 1890s, the war accelerated this process, as women took over male jobs and often had sole charge of the family. Even after the war, many bourgeois women continued to work outside the home, in great part because of the devastating economic effect the war had on their families.

In this age of social and cultural transformation, issues of gender roles and identity concerned, worried, and even traumatized French men and women. Such anxiety found expression in the increasing attention to female identity in the fictional, theoretical, and periodical literature of the years 1917 to 1927. A preoccupation with gender issues was also articulated in fears concerning the crisis of domesticity and the growth of the natalist movement during the same period. Natalist rhetoric warned of a widespread *crise du devoir maternel,* an unwillingness on the part of women to have children, despite the fact that little evidence exists to suggest that women were, in fact, scorning motherhood. The mother as an image of female identity inspired a comprehensive array of social policies, such as legislation on abortion, military and financial privileges for large families, and the establishment of state-run maternity institutions. Natalist values were so pervasive in postwar France that only the most politically marginal figures, such as socialists and radical feminists, dared to denounce them openly. While historians usually associate the deep anguish connected to the crisis of domesticity with postwar natalist rhetoric, the same sentiments shaped the debates over fashion.

A second set of postwar observers, among them, fashion designers and feminists, interpreted the new look differently. For these people, fashion became the means by which women gained a necessary freedom of movement—and thereby were liberated. According to the feminist Henriette Sauret, the new fashions were not created by men to fulfill or further their ideal of female desirability; rather, they were created by women themselves "to respond to our personal aesthetic or our need for convenience." Sauret described short hair as "a gesture of independence; a personal venture." This second reading of fashion in turn raises questions concerning fashion, feminism, and politics worth examining in greater detail. What did it mean politically to argue that these new styles gave women some measure of independence? Did they, in fact, allow women more freedom of movement, and what connection, if any, did this physical emancipation have to more general feminist aims? What, in other words, were the politics of postwar fashion?

The political significance of fashion in postwar France has not been adequately explored by historians, perhaps because of theoretical assumptions concerning the relationship between fashion and social change. Many historians interpret the change in female fashions during these years as nothing more than a derivative expression of social changes already under way. They explain the trend among women toward short hair and a looser, more carefree style of clothing as a reflection of a new freedom of movement women enjoyed in both professional and social circles that was itself brought about by the war. Fashion is thus denied a historical dynamic of its own; it becomes a "marker" but not a "maker" of social change. . . .

Furthermore, one can scarcely ignore the political role that dress has played in French history. During the upheaval of 1789, for example, men and women signaled their allegiance to revolutionary change by demanding the elimination of aristocratic and religious distinctions of dress and by wearing *sans-culottes*, the *bonnet rouge*, or the *cockade*. A law for an official revolutionary costume, adopted in 1795, was given this rationale by [the revolutionary priest] Grégoire: "The language of signs has an eloquence of its own; distinctive costumes are part of this idiom for they arouse ideas and sentiments analogous to their object, especially when they take hold of the imagination with their vividness." Revolutionary fashion was invested with political significance inasmuch as it acted as a language of signs capable of presenting a "vivid" (visual) image of the new republican citizen. . . .

As clothing became commercialized into fashion, it became political in a more subtle and less conscious way than in the revolutionary period. Nevertheless, postwar fashion—the short hair and scandalously abbreviated dresses of the modern woman—acted as a political language of signs in the same manner that Grégoire had outlined in 1795. Feminists, designers (both male and female), and the women who put on the new fashions interpreted them as affording physical mobility and freedom, in short, as a visual analogue of female liberation. When the new fashions were widely interpreted in this way, they became invested with political meaning. To wear them was to challenge traditional notions of gender difference and to arouse sympathy for freedom and autonomy for women. In other words, fashion constituted a semi-autonomous political language that served as a maker as well as a marker of the modern woman. Postwar fashion figured in a larger struggle for social and political power. . . .

. . . [T]he new tendency of women to "disguise themselves as men" was not met with humor but with serious observation and invective. "Smoking, wearing short hair, dressed in pyjamas or sportswear," complained the writer Francis de Miomandre, "women increasingly resemble their companions." In 1925, an anonymous Catholic author declared, "Modern women shouldn't try to 'masculinize' themselves, and thus to lose their sex.—A woman becoming a boy: Oh no!" Some critiques were grounded in fashionable scientific discourse, such as that on sexual perversion inspired by the translation of Havelock Ellis's work into French. "The species feels itself endangered by a growing inversion," the literary critic Pierre Lièvre argued in 1927, "no more hips, no more breasts, no more hair." Evolutionary theory linked fashion trends to an ominous biological future. "I myself don't know if Lamarck had foreseen this transformation of the species," wrote the poet Jean Dars in a 1925 survey on the *jeune fille*. "It is not written in his *History of Invertebrate Animals* that young girls were supposed to take on the appearance of boys so soon."

Supporters produced a notion of fashion as "emancipatory" by equating the new look with the aesthetic of modern consumer culture. The rise of mass culture, the adoption of new forms of transportation and communication, and the growth of consumerism were socioeconomic developments well under way by 1914 but were intensely accelerated by the war. Fashion was by nature visual and dynamic, a constantly changing marketable mass of images and a mark of the capitalist commodification of the body; thus it became integral to the new aesthetic of mass consumer culture. Bonnie Smith has argued that "fashion made women at once more desirable, more efficient, and in need of new goods." The fashions of the modern woman were often associated with the new palladiums of pleasure in the postwar world—the tea dances (*thé dansants*) and jazz clubs—as well as American consumer culture.

The fashionably dressed modern woman was also linked to the new consumer plaything of the decade: the automobile. At mid-decade, advertisers, novelists, and social observers pictured women (much more than men, it seems) behind the wheel of the car, creating a visual image of female mobility and power. In *L'aventure sur la route* (1925), a popular novel about a modern woman who tours France in her new car, the heroine is described as a beautiful, sleek animal who moves effortlessly in the clothes she wears: "An astonishing ease accompanied all of her movements. It seemed as if her clothes imposed no servitude upon her; she moved with the glorious animal independence of gymnasts in their tights." In 1927, the dramatist "Rip" described the new position of the modern woman: "Athletic as well as capable of exercising most male trades, *la femme moderne,* firmly installed behind the wheel of the *torpédo* which takes her to her office, store, or factory, has understood the superiority that severity of dress confers upon a man." These advertisers and writers created the image of a woman who leads a busy, fast-paced, and independent life, and who is empowered by the "mannish" fashions she wears. . . .

Although the origins of such images are impossible to determine, feminists were using them to describe fashion in the early 1920s, several years before they were adopted by the designers quoted above. As we have seen, the radical feminist Henriette Sauret described short hair in 1919 as "a gesture of independence; a personal venture." According to Augusta Moll-Weiss, a well-known feminist and founder of the household rationalization movement, when women of all classes were working, they demanded fashions "which one can put on easily, rapidly." Complicated fashions were no longer popular, she argued in 1921, because women "no longer tolerate impeding their freedom of movement for the benefit of laws whose omnipotence they no longer recognize." In 1922, feminist journalist Jane Misme, editor of *La française,* praised the new, more abbreviated swimsuits worn by young women for giving them ease and freedom of movement in the water: "anything which stands in the way of the harmonious and necessary development of the body can only be a false kind of grace and modesty." By describing the old swimsuits as "false," Misme implied that the new ones more faithfully expressed a woman's "natural" self. Maria Vérone, a prominent postwar feminist leader and the editor of the bourgeois feminist monthly *Le droit des femmes,* agreed with Misme. "The women who have preceded us," she maintained, "gave us the bad example of fake hair, false sentiments, marriage without love." By contrast, she argued, "we wear short hair, dresses which are not constricting and we want to have a profession, in order to be independent." Like Grégoire, Vérone believed that dress constituted a symbolic language that, through its vividness and ability to excite the imagination, "arouse[d] ideas and sentiments analogous to their object." Fake hair encouraged duplicity in one's life as well as one's appearance, leading inevitably to "false sentiments" and loveless marriage. Likewise, the "non-constricting" clothes of the modern woman created a visual analogue of liberation, encouraging an "independent" life. . . .

The new style was no more carefree than it was physically liberating. According to the historian Marylène Delbourg-Delphis, a new concept of beauty arose in the 1920s, particularly after mid-decade. This concept was based on faith in the body's malleability, its ability to be shaped and improved. As a result, she points out, women began to use more make-up and invest greater amounts of time and money in beauty products for face, skin, and hair. An article in *Vogue* during 1923 commented on how long women were spending in "instituts de beauté" and insisted that to achieve the look, the modern woman must "greet with a smile the incessant admonitions, the harsh instructions of the trainer, masseuse, professor: "Stand up straight, don't slump your back, eat little, don't drink, walk, get up, lean over . . . think of your health, of hygiene above all." Several such *instituts de beauté* were begun during the 1920s, especially in the later years of the decade. Although women claimed that the new bob cut was "practical" and easy to care for, one commentator asked in 1924, "who will be persuaded that a few minutes every day devoted to the maintenance of long hair in the intimacy of the home can be compared to the interminable periods of waiting at the hairdresser's?" The political writer François de Bondy agreed in 1927 that women now spent their lives at their hairdresser's and remarked that "to pretend the contrary would be a little like saying that it was more practical for us men to shave every morning than to grow a beard."

In addition, after 1920, the style of dress required excessive thinness, which could only be achieved by continuous, strict dieting. A panoply of new products appeared on the market to help women shape their sometimes unwilling bodies into conformity with the new silhouette. These included such panaceas as Dr. Duchamp's *l'Iodhyrine,* "approved and recommended by the French and international medical body," Dr. Jawas' "Mexican tea," "L'ovidine-Lutier," which promised a "marvellous result, without diet or danger," the Gigartina seaweed sugar-coated pills (*dragées*) designed to thin the chin, thighs, and waist, "Galton pills," also to rid women of double chins, and "Tanagra *dragées,*" containing thyroid to dehydrate women and produce "in no time an elegant and supple silhouette." With a tone of great pity, a 1924 *Vogue* article described the regime of "*la malheureuse* who has resolved to maintain an ideal weight": "Hours passed in the gym, mornings devoted to the brutal hands of *masseuses,* thyroid pills taken despite the risk of permanently ruining one's health, masks or rubber girdles to slim down waists or faces." Although traditional types of corsets were abolished, most women still wore constraining undergarments of some kind, such as the straight elastic girdle or bust bodice. Poiret himself admitted in 1921 in *L'Illustration* that the new look demanded some kind of girdle. As *Vogue* exclaimed in 1923: "how seductive the straight line of our winter dresses is, how revealing the *sveltesse* of the female silhouette! But how ungracious when the waist is not shaped [*moulée*] by a corset-girdle, the indispensable complement of contemporary fashion." Dr. Monteil's *ceinture-maillot*—cheerfully called "The Goddess"—was made entirely of rubber and cost a walloping 150 francs. There were also girdles for a woman's face, neck, and ankles, those for the latter advertised as "invisible even under the sheerest stockings."

From this perspective, the new fashions look like an elaborate marketing ploy to feed the growth of a burgeoning beauty industry, including make-up and skin-care manufacturers, owners of *instituts de beauté,* hair salon owners, diet specialists, and the *hauts couturiers.* In this sense, postwar fashion can be understood as a sort of modern consumerism that exploited women in the pursuit of profit, as feminist historians have claimed. Far from enjoying freedom, women who bought into this quest for beauty found themselves locked into a relentless and time-consuming set of physical and financial constraints.

But if postwar fashion was not as "liberating" as it appeared, why did feminists and the women who wore the styles present them as affording enormous mobility and freedom? According to the journalist René Bizet, who wrote a treatise on fashion in 1925, it was the illusion of freedom, if not freedom itself, that was the objective of the new look. In Bizet's words, "there was a tyranny of liberty in current fashion." Women went to desperate lengths in order to produce "the illusion of being free" through their clothes. The fashion writer Jacqueline de Monbrison supported this notion in 1926 by referring to Princess Irène, a woman who took no less than two hours with her maid to prepare for the evening. But the desired effect, according to Monbrison, completely disguised this effort: "The effect of extreme elegance that she produces would hardly lead someone to suspect that it took two hours to achieve, so much is it dependent on the triumphant appearance of simplicity."

36

THE COMMUNIST MOVEMENT AND WOMEN

SUSAN B. WHITNEY

The rise of strong communist parties in the 1920s and 1930s, in West European countries like France, constituted a striking political change. Communists represented far more hostility to existing economic and political structures than the more reformist socialist movement. Historians continue to debate the political results. On the one hand, communists put new pressure on moderate regimes and terrified the conservative elements, thus contributing to political instability of the sort that would paralyze France and several other countries during the later 1930s. Even communist willingness to ally with other parties in popular front movements, against the growing Nazi and Fascist threat, did not suffice to calm the waters. On the other hand, however, communist fervor expressed massive worker grievances, especially after the onset of the 1930s Depression, and communists provided the core of later resistance movements against Hitler's occupation forces.

Social historians have tried to determine what types of workers and peasants were most likely to support communism, thus exploring the causation and meaning of the movement to the groups involved. Certain industries particularly radicalized workers, while some regional cultures seized on communism as a protest vehicle.

The gender factor also deserves emphasis, as the following article demonstrates, looking at changes in the Communist party's approach to women before and after the popular front adjustment. Communist leaders had decided views about women before 1936, which reflected both the movement's militancy and more standard worker ideals of masculinity. Seeking broader appeal, the movement shifted gears in the popular front era. Working-class women were now seen as consumers, devoted to distinctive family interests and femininity. Why did this approach prove more realistic? What image of women did it reflect? Along with consumerism, the new approach may have touched base with some special traditions and assumptions about women's community- and family-oriented protest ideas—a topic pursued in the earlier

From: Susan B. Whitney, "Embracing the Status Quo: French Communists, Young Women and the Popular Front," *Journal of Social History* 30 (1996): 29–32, 33, 34–36, 37–38, 43–45.

selection on Spanish women workers, by Radcliff. At the same time, the communist emphasis may have had significant long-term effects. It anchored many working-class women to the movement, as it grew into post-World War II decades, helping to explain its unusual durability and fervor in France. At the same time, the emphasis may have confirmed women's inferiority in French society and their preoccupation with consumer interests and personal attractiveness. Here, a gender-sensitive social history exposes some surprisingly conservative ingredients in Europe's new radical force.

The French Communist Party's adoption of a Popular Front strategy during the mid-1930s involved a radically new approach to French politics and culture. By 1935, the party had abandoned its almost exclusive focus on organizing the working class at the workplace and reconfigured its appeal in an attempt to mobilize a range of new constituencies within a broad anti-fascist coalition. As part of this strategy, the party embraced French revolutionary symbolism for the first time, recast itself as the defender of France and French culture, and adopted new approaches to leisure, tourism, and commercial culture. In the process, the party created new models of Communist political activism and positioned itself centrally within French political life for the first time. But if the broader contours of the party's Popular Front politics are increasingly well-known, there has been no scholarly attention to the ways gender functioned in this political strategy. This is unfortunate, as new approaches to young women and female gender roles played a central if heretofore unremarked upon role in Communist Popular Front politics.

As part of its Popular Front strategy, the party abandoned its previous, always ambivalent efforts to mobilize young women within the Communist youth organization, the Jeunesse Communiste, and created a separate organization for young women in 1936. The seasoned Young Communist veterans put in charge of the new "L'Union des Jeunes Filles de France" (U.J.F.F.) [Union of Young Girls of France] worked to construct an organization whose activities and publications would appeal to the masses of young working women. To this end, they designed activities, such as fashion shows and cooking and sewing classes, thought to be particularly attractive to young women, and published a newspaper, *Jeunes filles de France,* meant to resemble the commercial women's press. Encouraged by party leaders, the organization and its press devoted considerable attention to love, fashion, and the cinema. Danielle Casanova, the U.J.F.F.'s leader, set the tone for the new organization when she announced that it would link its program to "the life and even the dreams of the young woman."

If the U.J.F.F. represented a political and strategic effort to mobilize young French women through their perceived interests and desires, it also represented an attempt to create new models of Communist femininity and female political activism. Within the U.J.F.F., Communists replaced the ideal of the Young

Communist woman as comrade in the working-class struggle which had reigned in the 1920s and early 1930s with one who was at once a charming, modern young woman *and* a future wife and mother. This new Young Communist woman was characterized less by a commitment to gender-neutral revolutionary action than by moral probity, a commitment to marriage and motherhood, and gender-specific public activism. This is not to suggest that the U.J.F.F. removed young women from the political arena but rather that it sought to politicize them in ways deemed more consonant with accepted notions of femininity. This effort to redefine Young Communist femininity and reconfigure models of female political activism was central to the party's attempt to reposition itself as integral to French politics and culture. By emphasizing these young women's roles as potential mothers, for example, Communists underscored their new commitment to raising the birthrate and safeguarding the future of the French "race." Moreover, by promoting the idea of charming political activists who restricted themselves to activities deemed appropriate for young women, the party countered attacks on Communism which made repulsive women the very embodiment of the revolutionary threat. Thus the new Young Communist woman served to highlight the extent to which the party had foresworn revolution and embraced a new, more centrist approach to French society and culture. In the Communist effort to build and sustain a broad Popular Front coalition, therefore, the refeminized young women of the U.J.F.F. simultaneously symbolized and furthered the party's integration into French society and political life.

COMMUNIST APPROACHES
TO YOUNG WOMEN, 1920–1934

The newness of the party's approach to young women and female gender roles after 1935 can best be appreciated in the context of the party's earlier ambivalent attempts to enlist young women. During the 1920s and early 1930s, French Communists focused almost exclusively on mobilizing the working class at the workplace. They did not consider young working women to be a distinct political constituency but rather to fall within "working youth." As such, they were to be mobilized within the Jeunesse Communiste (J.C.), or Young Communists. In its first decade, the J.C. was a determinedly revolutionary organization. Not content to be part of an auxiliary youth organization, the Young Communists viewed themselves as a revolutionary youth cohort and claimed for themselves a vanguard role in the construction of French Communism. . . .

The nature of J.C. political action and organizational life during the 1920s tended to marginalize young working women. This was especially true of anti-militarist agitation, which formed the centerpiece of the organization's revolutionary action for much of the decade. In this campaign, the Young Communists worked to persuade French conscripts to oppose "capitalist" wars and support revolutionary struggles in Europe and throughout the French Empire. To this end, they attempted to distribute propaganda to conscripts (both before and during their military service), transform soldier discontent into revolutionary agitation, and sabotage defense production. Although civil and military authorities monitored J.C. anti-militarist activities very closely and the Young Communists rarely succeeded in making much headway among the majority of French conscripts, the anti-militarist campaign helped gender the organization in ways that limited young women's participation. Most obviously, the focus on anti-militarism meant that the primary site of J.C. revolutionary action occurred within the broader confines of an institution that excluded women. As a result, Young Communist women could only participate in certain aspects of the anti-militarist campaign, such as the production and civil distribution of anti-militarist literature. Moreover, young women as a group were largely ignored by an anti-militarist campaign which aimed to mobilize male conscripts. Equally importantly, the anti-militarist campaign—which celebrated Young Communists arrested and jailed for their activities—helped construct the ideal Young Communist as fearless and tough and the J.C. as an organization willing to wage revolutionary war. As J.C. general secretary Maurice Laporte boasted in 1921, "We do not moan about war and its horrors as those in the Second International·do. Down with snivelling and humanitarian pacifism. As we declared recently in *L'Avant-Garde:* war itself does not frighten us at all." This emphasis on a kind of revolutionary virility helped shape the J.C. into a highly masculinized sphere, one in which young women could only participate on limited, male terms. . . .

As new types of less skilled, lower-paying work were created, industrialists often brought in inexperienced male workers and female workers, especially those who were young, to fill the newly created positions. As a result, the number of female workers increased in industries like metals, chemicals, and electricity which, until recently, had been the province of men. In fact, the new, prototypical semi-skilled worker of the period ("l'ouvrier spécialisé") was often a woman. As female workers uniformly earned less than male workers (regardless of age), Young Communists joined their adult male counterparts in the C.G.T.U. to interpret the increased presence of women as a threat to male wages and employment prospects. In 1928, for example, *L'Avant-Garde* explained how young women's low wages allowed them to be pitted against adult workers as well as against young male workers; this resulted, the newspaper continued, in the dismissal of male workers and their replacement by young women.

The perception of the threat to young male workers not surprisingly affected the organization's approaches to young female workers. When young women workers were singled out, it was often to equate their exploitation with that of young male workers and to urge them to see their real interests in terms of common struggle with young male workers and the "working class" more generally. Moreover, J.C. demands concerning young women workers—namely a shortened, six-hour day and equal pay for equal work—functioned, as they had in the past, as a double-edged sword: they were designed to lessen the threat of female youth labor as much as they were designed to improve the lot of young female workers themselves. . . .

By constructing a model of gender-neutral political activism in a mixed sex, avowedly revolutionary organization, the J.C. disregarded attitudes concerning acceptable behavior for young working women in ways that complicated female involvement in the organization. Although the 1920s have often been viewed as a time when young women enjoyed a range of new freedoms, they were also a time when young women's behaviors were vigorously contested *and* when young women's movements and activities remained considerably more restricted than those of young men. This appears to have been especially true of female workers in their teens and early twenties, who often continued to live at home under the careful surveillance of parents and brothers even after joining the workforce full-time at age twelve or thirteen. Indeed, parents frequently prohibited their working daughters from going out unchaperoned at night and discouraged them from taking part in mixed sex organizations, which were considered morally suspect. Not surprisingly, parents were sometimes particularly aghast when their daughters ended up at the police station after a day of Young Communist activity. To join the J.C., therefore, young women were often forced to accommodate themselves to or flout a certain number of conventions concerning appropriate behavior for young women. One J.C. militant, Josette Cothias, remembers being accompanied to J.C. meetings by her father while another, Lise London, remembers taking advantage of the absence of her ever watchful brother to join the J.C. (As she relates it, he would never have allowed her to join for fear that she would "lose her soul.") Still another militant could only attend J.C. meetings after the cell moved its meetings from weeknights to Sunday afternoons to accommodate its one female member. . . .

THE POPULAR FRONT APPROACH:
LES JEUNES FILLES DE FRANCE (U.J.F.F.)

The Communists' Popular Front project radically altered French Communist approaches to young women by making them a distinct political constituency, one which merited a separate organizing strategy within a revamped Communist youth federation. Prompted by the Communist International leadership, French Communists began to abandon their earlier focus on organizing the working class at the workplace in an effort to mobilize a range of new constituencies against fascism in late 1934 and 1935. In this effort, Communists focused especially on "youth," whom they considered particularly susceptible to fascist appeals. To mobilize French "youth" (which, because of the particular configuration of interwar generational politics, included young men and now women from their teens to their early thirties), the Young Communists worked to create a youth front which would complement and parallel the adult Popular Front. This involved making new overtures to non-Communist and even Catholic youth organizations and restructuring the J.C. itself. Taking its cue from the Communist Youth International, the J.C. shifted its focus from anti-militarist agitation and revolutionary action at the workplace to a strategy which combined the defense of new, more centrist youth demands with the provision of a broad range of leisure activities. To reach the largest possible numbers of "youth," the J.C. also moved to create separate organizations for students, young peasants, and young women. . . .

The women chosen to head the new organization exemplified the earlier model of the Young Communist woman as comrade in the revolutionary struggle. Casanova, who would go down in history as *the* female Communist martyr of the Resistance, was tough, committed, and long experienced in J.C. politics, having served on the J.C.'s central committee since 1932. Those who worked with Casanova at the helm of the U.J.F.F. had followed similar trajectories. For example, Claudine Chomat had been a student at the Leninist School in Moscow during 1934–1935, while Jeanne Vermeersch (who would later marry party leader Maurice Thorez) arrived at the U.J.F.F. with an arrest record and extensive experience in J.C. politics. Given these women's extensive involvement in J.C. politics, it is not surprising that many Young Communist women disagreed at first with the decision to form a separate organization for young women. Whatever their initial skepticism, however, leading J.C. female militants quickly rallied to the new organization.

As part of the Communists' broader Popular Front youth strategy, the U.J.F.F. resembled the newly revamped Young Communist organization in important ways. Both the new J.C. and the U.J.F.F. were based in neighborhoods, rather than in workplaces, and both ceded responsibility for workplace organizing to Communist-affiliated trade unions. Moreover, both the J.C. and the U.J.F.F. abandoned the J.C.'s previous tight focus on revolutionary political action in favor of a heavy dose of leisure activities designed to appeal to youth. For the first time, in the words of Communist Youth International leader Michael Wolf, Young Communists attempted to speak "the lively and fresh language of youth." The two organizations also endeavored to appeal to a broader range of young people. No longer would the Communists focus exclusively on young workers from a narrow range of industries. Instead, the J.C. and the U.J.F.F. now reached out to young people from a range of occupations and socioeconomic backgrounds, and *Jeunes filles de France* featured articles on the lives and working conditions of *midinettes,* secretaries, and teachers as well as female factory workers. Finally, the U.J.F.F., like the J.C., took great care to emphasize the commonalities that united young women.

But if the U.J.F.F. took its lead from the J.C.'s new direction, its approach to young women was particularistic. The U.J.F.F. quickly mapped a strategy which not only redefined young women's relationship to politics but also reconfigured Young Communist models of femininity and public activism. Casanova first outlined this new approach in her report to the J.C. congress in March 1936. According to Casanova, interviews with young women pointed to their uneasiness within the Young Communist organization: some felt uncomfortable in the cells; some were not interested in Young Communist activities; and others objected to being treated like one of the boys. To win young women over to the Popular Front struggle against fascism, Casanova declared, the Communists would have to radically transform their methods. They would have to educate young women in the spirit of Marxism-Leninism "by taking into account the distinctiveness, the character, and the aspirations and needs of young women." . . .

Determined to take into account the "dreams" of young women, those building the U.J.F.F. created an organization that differed from its male counterpart in important ways. First, the U.J.F.F. highlighted its role as a friendship organization. As *Jeunes filles de France* announced, "Friendship and solidarity are our watchwords. We are friends above all, and if animosity sometimes exists, we will get rid of it." Within the U.J.F.F., it was clearly the bonds of friendship—not a commitment to a larger revolutionary struggle or the fight against war and fascism—which would unite young women. Of course, this is not to say that the U.J.F.F. removed itself totally from the fight for better conditions for young women at the workplace. It called vaguely for rights to apprenticeship and work for young women and applauded the Young Communist women who participated in the massive strike movement of May–June 1936. However, friendship and leisure were clearly the movement's focus. Such a focus was underscored by the U.J.F.F.'s response to attempts by the employers' association in the fashion industry to roll back many of the gains made by the *midinettes* during the strikes of 1935 and 1936. Instead of attempting to rally young women against these changes, the U.J.F.F. urged young women to take advantage of its "Maison de la Midinette." Here, the *midinettes* would be able to relax, exercise, and benefit from the special prices negotiated with doctors and merchants. It was clear that the U.J.F.F. would not be the center of the struggle to make a new world but rather a refuge from the troubles of the old. . . .

Reflecting the dramatic reversal in Communist attitudes towards commercial culture which occurred during the Popular Front period, the U.J.F.F. embraced the style and idiom of commercial culture in its effort to appeal to the life and dreams of young working women. During the 1930s, young working women were ardent fans of cheap popular romances and the mass women's press. They were also thought to go to the movies as often as their meager paychecks would allow and to devour the magazines devoted to screen stars and their lives. To appeal to these interests, the U.J.F.F. created a newspaper-cum-magazine—*Jeunes filles de France*—which was designed to resemble the mass women's press in both style and content. In contrast to the J.C.'s *L'Avant-Garde,* which continued to resemble the adult political dailies even as it devoted more space to leisure, sport,and mass culture during the Popular Front era, *Jeunes filles de France* had a strikingly different format. Sized somewhere between a magazine and a newspaper, *Jeunes filles de France* offered many photographs, as well as regular features on the cinema, fashion, and romance. And as the paper and movement matured, *Jeunes filles de France* moved ever closer to the style of commercial women's magazines. In May 1937, for example, the publication introduced a letters to the editor section, thus replicating a popular feature of the commercial women's press. The summer of 1937 also witnessed the introduction of the regular page-two feature "Song of Love." Situated directly following the often textless cover, this became the first item encountered by the reader. From a Communist stance that had been by turns dismissive and contemptuous of "bourgeois" commercial culture, then, the U.J.F.F. had arrived at a point where it embraced both the form and content of the women's press.

The U.J.F.F.'s embrace of ideas promoted within commercial culture was especially apparent when it came to *Jeunes filles de France*'s approach to the female body. Like commercial women's magazines, *Jeunes filles de France* helped young women negotiate the new practices associated with the female body and interwar notions of beauty. So at a time when the use of makeup and the practice of tanning were becoming more widespread throughout French society, *Jeunes filles de France* instructed young women in the art of applying makeup and dispensed advice about the proper way to tan. It also encouraged young women to remove hair from their arms and legs. As *Jeunes filles de France* noted cheerfully in "Always Pretty!," this practice "demonstrates a desire to be stylish that is not only natural but perfectly commendable." Throughout, *Jeunes filles de France* emphasized cultivating the youthful, specifically female approach to the body and style promoted within the commercial women's press and an emergent consumer culture. Whether urging young women to exercise or reminding them not to wear their mothers' clothes—however fashionable they might be—, the emphasis was on being young and modern and on finding a style suitable to twentieth-century young women. . . .

One typical letter printed in the page-two feature "Song of Love" read in part, "I'm now nineteen years old. For many years, I have been dreaming of love. Because for me, love is not simply an accessory but the foundation of my life." Countless other letters exhibited the same sentiments. In its presentation of these letters, *Jeunes filles de France* rarely editorialized or attempted to move these young women away from their focus on love. . . .

In its approach to social problems, the U.J.F.F. never engaged in a critique of capitalism and instead rooted its action in what it considered young women's special talent for nurturing. As *Jeunes filles de France* noted at one point, it was responding "to women's and young women's deep-seated need to soothe the distress and misery of the most unfortunate." With such an approach, the U.J.F.F.'s program of social assistance differed little from that undertaken by the Catholic organization of young working women, the "Jeunesse Ouvrière Chrétienne Féminine." Not surprisingly, the U.J.F.F. found itself in the position of having to fend off criticism that its work among the needy was nothing more than philanthropy. In its defense, the U.J.F.F. asserted that such work was necessary to "bring together all its forces, without losing a single one, in order to move ever more numerous down the path to the complete emancipation of youth." . . .

[T]he U.J.F.F.'s calculated appeal to young women through their perceived interests and desires succeeded in attracting them to Communism. By the end of July 1936, for example, the U.J.F.F. claimed 5,000 members; by the end of December 1937, that number had soared to 19,411. Of course, the U.J.F.F.'s success was not unique; it came at a time when membership in the party and the J.C. also rose dramatically. Nevertheless, it represented a striking shift in the Communists' ability to mobilize women, one that hinted at the more dramatic successes to come in the post-World War Two period.

To what can we attribute the organization's effectiveness among young women? First, the U.J.F.F.'s status as a single-sex organization seems to have appealed to both parents and their daughters. Among working-class parents, for example, the U.J.F.F.'s single-sex status was considered so important that some Socialist fathers apparently encouraged their daughters to eschew the mixed sex Young Socialists in favor of this new Communist organization. But the U.J.F.F.'s status as an all-female organization also offered important advantages to its members. If the young women of the J.C. had often been relegated to the periphery, those of the U.J.F.F. found themselves at the center of a burgeoning national movement. They alone assumed responsibility for the organization at the local, regional, and national levels, and their work became a source of great pride to at least some within the movement. As activists in a national movement, moreover, many were able to travel in ways that remained rate for young working-class women, who were excluded from the sporting associations and military service which drew young provincial men of modest means beyond their towns and villages. For the two hundred provincial delegates to the U.J.F.F.'s first Congress in December 1936, then, the Congress not only provided an opportunity for all-female political action, but also for a trip to Paris; one can only imagine how many besides Cécile Ouzoulias-Romagon were enchanted first-time visitors to the capital that December. Finally, the U.J.F.F.'s success testified to the leaders' ability to create an organization whose embrace of commercial culture and attention to young working women's private, as well as public, lives clearly resonated in a society where young working women had few opportunities for associational or political life. . . .

Although the U.J.F.F. clearly succeeded in mobilizing many young women on behalf of Communism and, later, France itself, the Communist approach to women and femininity it exemplified also contributed to the widespread acceptance of decidedly conservative discourses regarding women and the family. These discourses helped structure subsequent French policy regarding the family and women's place within it. Indeed, by construing the young woman's role as mother to a threatened French family, French Communists lent their support to a conservative vision of the family that would be enshrined in the Family Code of 29 July 1939 and in the Vichy government's subsequent family policies. These policies—as well as the continued postwar emphasis on motherhood by parties across the political spectrum—helped lay the groundwork for a postwar family and welfare policy which cast wives as dependents within French families. The Communists' politically successful decision to embrace the status quo was not without long-term implications for the status of French women.

37

MODERN FAMILIES: PATTERNS OF CHANGE IN THE TWENTIETH CENTURY

R. E. PAHL

Most evaluations of modern life require passing reference to the family; the more critical ones dwell on the subject. The decline of the family has been a constant theme in European history since at least the early nineteenth century. Indeed, its collapse has been suggested so often that it is a wonder there is anything left still to decay. Clearly, many who have found modern life distasteful have exaggerated their laments about the breakup of the family. But this does not mean that they have not correctly identified trends, for no one denies that great changes have taken place in family structure.

There are several key problems in dealing with modern family history, aside from the difficulty of obtaining adequate information. To begin with, any valid judgment requires an evaluation of the quality of family life before the modern age. Most assessments of the modern family reflect, if only implicitly, deeply held beliefs about the premodern family. Those who find family life deteriorating and the modern individual bereft of the solidarity he or she needs, point to the strength and diverse functions of the premodern family. Yet we have seen that the premodern family structure may have had serious inadequacies, so that changes in family structure may conceivably have been good, not bad.

Judgments of the twentieth-century family must [also] be compared to assessments of family change earlier in the industrialization process. We have seen that important trends concerning household, affection, and sexuality began over two centuries ago. Where have these trends taken the family in recent decades? Have new trends intervened to complicate the process? How much does the twentieth-century working-class family owe to earlier changes in emotional expectations? How many of the heralded problems of contemporary families are due to these same changes?

The question of interpretation remains crucial. We can easily agree that, although its importance as a unit of consumption has increased, the family is no longer a key production unit. What does this mean for the family? For

From: R. E. Pahl, *Divisions of Labour* (London: Basil Blackwell, 1989), pp. 89, 100–105, 110–111, 213–214, 222, 227, 219–220, 231.

some observers it suggests decay, a loosening of ties, because many family members now work outside the home. For others it suggests a reduction of the tensions and bitterness that family economic relations once involved. No longer, for example, are twenty-five-year-olds normally under their father's economic control, unable to marry before he retires or dies. With this kind of family friction reduced, the family can become a closer emotional unit, with more affectionate ties between husband and wife and between parents and children.

Evaluations of the modern family typically reflect the standards of each analyst as to what the proper role of women is, what kind of care children deserve and need, and so on. Many students of the family, heirs to a long line of pessimists (and some optimists) who have been proclaiming the decay of the family since the onset of industrialization, find it teetering on the brink of a new communal or individualized existence. Some simply believe that the conditions of modern society have proved progressively less compatible with family life: parents drawn outside the home to work, children forced into schools, and people encouraged to replace familial with individualistic motivations. Others now see the first reactions to industrialization in the nineteenth century as immensely fruitful. They point particularly to the strength and intensity of the middle-class family, with the strong direction it provided for children. They find the twentieth century far different and far less appealing (thus implicitly rejecting modernization as a schema covering family history, by stressing a distinction between industrial and postindustrial society).

Still others find the family alive and kicking, even healthier than it once was. They see developments in the twentieth century, particularly after World War II, as hopeful and encouraging. They emphasize the discontinuities between family history over the past half century, and family history under industrialization. They point to the major changes in women's roles, but they see family adjustments that go beyond this one change and that defy any simple claims about destabilization. Some argue, indeed, that families in recent decades have regained a range of functions, and a sense of shared roles among at least adult family members, that recall preindustrial characteristics.

The following selection, based on both quantitative and case-study data on working-class and middle-class British families, and combining sociological analysis with historical perspective, focuses on one main aspect of family life: the definition of household activities and adult roles in these activities. What kind of change is emphasized? How do these families compare both to industrial and to preindustrial households? What might be causing the efforts to widen some of the functions assigned to family life?

The selection obviously suggests that family trends remain complex, and not easily captured by a single decline model. Are contemporary families reflecting a growing privatization of interests, away from earlier commitments to a more collective culture and a more active political sense? What relationship do family trends have to social class division in late twentieth-century Europe? Family history must be measured against wider social change, as

Europe's main social classes continue to adjust to modern economic and political life.

First, it is irrefutable that the pattern of work in the formal economy is changing: full-time employment, particularly for men in manufacturing industry, is declining, and this has been offset only partly by an increase in part-time employment, mainly for women in the service sector. . . . While men outnumber women as full-time employees by more than two to one overall, for both full-time and part-time employees, the differential is narrowing as the number of women employees declines less rapidly than that of male employees. . . .

There are indications that from around 1973 there was a substantial increase in certain forms of self-provisioning among British households. A substantial amount of production once again took place in the home by household members, which earlier in the century might have been done by employing another individual or firm. . . . A number of reasons were adduced for this substantial increase in domestic work. First, the sale of local authority houses and the encouragement of owner-occupation by the Conservative government, which came into office in 1979, helped to maintain demand; second, middle-class home owners found that the combination of lower disposable incomes and higher labour costs squeezed them into doing more work for themselves; third, both manual and non-manual workers were reducing their hours in employment, thus giving them more time for other activities. . . .

The growth in this particular area of self-provisioning is obviously related to a number of factors not all operating together. To begin with, new tools and cheap, readily available materials encouraged experimentation in providing domestic comforts and improvements, such as draught exclusion and the like. Later, as inflation rapidly grew in the early 1970s, people saw the advantage of improving what was their strongest hedge against inflation; and, since the cost of labour for building and services was also escalating, it seemed good sense for people to paint their own houses and even to attempt more ambitious work. The political impetus to increased home ownership has already been noted, and many local authorities began to encourage tenants to maintain their own homes after 1979 as they reduced their direct labour operations. Finally, the growth of unemployment and perhaps an increasing awareness that *whom* you know was coming to matter more than what you know contributed to a tendency for people to move houses less frequently: whatever the reason, between 1980 and 1981 there was a reduction of 7 per cent in households moving from one area of the country to another.

Furthermore, according to market research data, women were said to be increasing their share of such work. It was suggested that married women working part-time in the service sector, often in pleasant, well-decorated surroundings, would adopt a more critical approach to their own domestic environment. . . . Interestingly, 59 per cent of the women felt that they could do jobs themselves just as well as their husbands and only 21 per cent said they would rather get someone professional in to do the job.

It is likely that, while men are doing more non-routine work in terms of domestic maintenance and improvement, their contribution to the routine domestic tasks is still in the order of "helping" rather than any substantial shift to true role reversal. In the early 1970s, while there was a growth of interest in what was generally referred to as housework or domestic labour, little interest was shown in the domestic self-provisioning done by men. Rather, it was held by many commentators that "housework is an activity performed by housewives within their own homes." . . .

With the decline in servants, members of households have to do much of their everyday work for themselves. Friends, relatives, neighbours and the official home help service may do anything from making the bed to washing up for those who are elderly or incapacitated. Not all of these may define doing such a task as work: clearly the woman in the home help service will do so, but the dutiful son or daughter may be "helping mum". . . .

Not only are richer households more likely to do more work, they are more likely to do tasks with their own labour. Thus, 74 per cent of the home maintenance and 39 per cent of the home improvement and renovation are done by members of "high"-income households. The same category is also most likely to use household labour in domestic production and car maintenance. Those with cars, children, their own homes and high-household incomes appear to do a very great amount of work. There is little sign that households with higher incomes are that much more likely overall to use formal service provision—or, indeed, to use more informal sources of labour for which they have the means to pay. In every cluster, the higher-income households have the lowest percentage of informally paid sources of labour. By contrast, the poorest households use informal sources, most particularly *unpaid* informal sources of labour. It is important to bear in mind the degree of unreality produced by this aggregation of tasks, but it does provide some clarity at a high level of generality. . . .

However, if the economic activity of the female partner apparently makes little difference, the total number of adults employed in the household certainly does. Employment in the formal economy as a factor determining what other sources of labour are used may be more a matter of numbers than of gender: in almost every task the likelihood that it will be done (if it is done) in the household increases with the number of adults in employment. This applies particularly to tasks connected with home renovation or extension. The proportion of households in which painting is done at home, for example, increases from 78 per cent of households with no workers to 100 per cent with three. Couples with unmarried employed offspring living at home and with school-age children old enough not to inhibit the female partner from taking employment *need* more tasks done and are busiest doing them. The position of the household in the domestic cycle is one of the chief determinants of the sources of labour that are used. What needs doing differs throughout the life cycle, and the source of labour varies substantially between youth and old age and between households based on couples and those with only a single adult. The latter, typically, do not have the income to use formal provision of services (although, of course, local authority and welfare provision are important); hence, single-parent households and old people are obliged to use informal sources of labour. . . .

In terms of patterns of work and sources of labour, household structure, particularly as that reflects the number of earners and the domestic cycle, appears to be more significant than social class. It is one of the main themes of [analysis] in this book that this has always been so. One recognizes that sociologists will be accused of rediscovering the wheel once again—or at least recognizing the force of history. In the same way that late medieval households . . . needed someone of the opposite sex in order to get by and to help to get the work done, so the exigencies of the domestic cycle and the demands of capitalist consumerism make couple households with multiple earners the best unit for getting by in the late twentieth century, albeit for different reasons. . . .

This approach emphasizes the convergence in goals and aspirations of a large section of society, which in recent years has become the majority in most Western societies. The resulting households, more privatized, inward-looking, home-centered and autonomous, are consumption-oriented and consider that they can achieve their individual goals more readily through private plans than through collective action. This large "middle mass" comprises between 55 and 65 per cent of all households in Britain, with a deprived underclass of between 20 and 25 per cent in poverty beneath them and a well salaried or capital-owing bourgeoisie of about 12–15 per cent above them. Most of these households in the middle mass own their own homes and, judging from the wSheppey Survey, gain substantial satisfaction from creating a style of life based on small-scale domesticity.

38

WORK AND PLAY

JOHN ARDAGH

European society has changed greatly in the decades since 1945. Levels of productivity have soared in comparison with both the European past and the performance of the United States in the same decades. Change has been particularly striking in countries like France, which was not previously known for zealous economic behavior and which suffered from severe dislocation during the years immediately following World War II. Government and corporate officials, often dubbed technocrats because of their devotion to planning, have worked hard to promote economic growth and technological change.

This economic surge has involved other sectors of the French population. The following selection discusses styles of work and leisure in Toulouse, a regional center in southwestern France. It focuses on patterns in the 1970s, after twenty years of rapid economic growth and rising living standards. The description of work goals and patterns invites comparison with nineteenth-century middle-class behavior. In some ways, the French are adhering more closely to the classic middle-class ethic now than they did in the nineteenth century when the cultural example of the traditional aristocracy bore more heavily on society. Inevitably, changes in postwar France invite comparison also with the United States. "Americanization," in the form of new drugstores and new eating habits, has been an important phenomenon in contemporary Europe. In the 1950s the term often brought derision, when the Europeans feared American domination. By the 1970s, the French seemed sufficiently comfortable with aspects of an affluent consumer society that the sense of foreignness had declined.

Inevitably, change in contemporary France brings losses as well as gains. Many observers mark with regret the passing of some eating customs that marked the good old days, at least for the well-to-do. But change is not simply in the direction of American standards. Note that while French eating habits seem to be moving in some American directions, they do not merge entirely. And the French enthusiasm for hard work developed in a period when Americans were developing new worries about their own devotion to labor; yet the French also maintain a devotion to lengthy vacations, in contrast to maintenance of the long working year in the United States. Contemporary

From: John Ardagh. *A Tale of Five Cities* (New York: Harper & Row, 1979), pp. 336–41.

Europe, in other words, displays some patterns in work and leisure that differ from their counterparts in other advanced industrial countries. Within Europe, a sense of national and regional lifestyles persists.

In their daily lives, at work and leisure, Toulousains are struggling to reconcile the traditional French ways with a newer, more international style of consumer living. Are the evenings still for long leisurely talkative meals, or for a quick snack followed by thrillers and quiz-games on television? Does an employee still make his way home every noon for the ritual family lunch, despite commuter problems that make this habit ever less realistic?—or will he opt for the canteen? Does his wife hold out for fresh farm produce, or stock up with tins and frozen packets from the new hypermarket [supermarket] down the road? In these and many other ways, Toulousains are torn between old and new.

Their living standards rose steadily in the 1945–75 period, especially in housing. Twenty or so years ago, the average family ate well and knew how to enjoy itself, but accepted a low level of home comfort. In 1954, only 44 per cent of homes had inside flushing lavatories and a mere 11.4 per cent had bath or shower. This latter figure has now risen to well over 50 per cent, since for some years all new homes have been built with modern plumbing. But most lower-income flats are still equipped with no more than a shower or hip-bath, and their living rooms are very small: despite the improvement, Toulousains remain noticeably less comfortably housed than [German] Swabians, or even [British] Geordies. Yet they manage to fill up their cramped little dwellings with every kind of modern gadget—levels of ownership of washing-machines and refrigerators are higher than in Britain. Toulousains are finally becoming more house-proud, and their patterns of domestic budgeting are gradually moving closer to those of northern Europe with a relative decline in the high percentage devoted to food and entertainment.

It was claimed to me by Dr. Brouat that the true Toulousain disdains hard work and lives for his pleasures, but I think that today this is only partially true. Much of the city's working life has become infected by the new work mania of the French, imported here by the newcomers, notably the Parisian executives and the energetic [returned colonists. Officials] and businessmen work with more eagerness and dynamism than in Newcastle, and for longer hours, often staying at their desks till 7 or 8 at night: if they were better at teamwork, the results might reach Swabian levels.

One management consultant told me that he and all his staff work from 8 A.M. to 7 P.M., though this does include the two-hour lunch break that is still the norm in Toulouse despite its growing impracticability. "Many of us," he said, "would like to move over to the Anglo-Saxon short break and go home an hour earlier in the evening. But this would be hard to adopt unless other firms did the same: many of my clients do their busiest work after six and expect me to be here at the end of the 'phone." Most shops, banks, offices, hairdressers, still close from 12 till 2—"By staggering my staff, I could easily stay open," said the owner of one big store, "but there's not the public demand for it. My customers are not used to shopping at midday, they expect to be home eating a big lunch." This is still the main meal of the day for most families. Schoolchildren as well as their fathers go home for it, even though the growth of the city is making it less convenient: as people move out to new suburbs, they may have to spend half their two-hour lunch break on travel, and rush-hour traffic-jams occur four times a day. In Paris and many northern French cities, there has been a steady move towards the Anglo-Saxon system, which the French call *"la journée continue"*: but Toulouse, conservative in so many things, has been slow to follow this trend, and only in the past few years have some larger stores and banks begun to remain open over lunchtime. On the other hand, supermarkets stay open till 8 P.M., often later, whereas in Newcastle they close at 5:30 or 6. This English practice is also tiresome, though in a town of commuter proportions it seems more logical.

Since they stay at work so late, Toulousains set less stress than Geordies or Swabians on evening leisure activities during the week. They have few hobbies, they are not great club-joiners. But they live for their weekends and their holidays—the French take the longest holidays in Europe. Most families now own a car, and their first aim at the weekend, summer or winter, is to get out of town, for Toulousains adapt little better than Parisians to the new tensions of urban living, and they feel an urgent need to regain contact with nature. Since many are ex-peasants, or the children of peasants, at weekends they go to relatives in the country, or else they retain the old family farmstead for use as a weekend and holiday cottage. People of all classes, including workers, spend money on buying some little rural *résidence secondaire*. Or else they go walking or skiing in the Pyrenees, or for trips to the Mediterranean or Atlantic. And the vast traffic-jams on the roads into Toulouse every Sunday evening bear witness to a weekly migration that is largely responsible for the dearth of social and community life in the city. In the old days, before mass car ownership, most Toulousains were forced to rely on each other's company at weekends: the new mobility has encouraged privacy, hence unsociability. In addition, the average family takes at least four or five weeks' holiday a year, and in the wealthier classes it may be much more. They go to the sea or their country cottage, or they tour abroad, mostly to nearby Spain.

Toulousains spend more time on outdoor sports than most Europeans. All classes go hunting, shooting and fishing on their country weekends; in town, they play tennis or *pelote* (a kind of outdoor fives or squash, Basque in origin) or, above all, *boules*. So popular are sports that the city council has recently built four large new recreation centres in the outskirts, complete with lakes for boating, swimming-pools and playingfields. The latter are essentially for rugby, which was imported here by the English in the last century and is today more popular than association football throughout the south-west. In Toulouse, rugby is a proud tradition almost on a par with *bel canto* and *cassoulet:* the town has 30 teams, two of them of international class. One of these, the Stade Toulousain, has seven times won the French national championship. When it plays at home to one of its major rivals, such as Bordeaux, the crowd gets almost as excited as Newcastle soccer fans when their team is at home to Liverpool.

An important part of local leisure is good eating. . . . Toulousains may care less for gastronomy than in former days, yet the tradition remains in their bones: they eat well as a matter of course, without thinking twice, and with the innate good taste that a Bolognese, for instance, shows over dress or a Stuttgarter over music. A housewife will spend time and care on choosing just the right cut of meat, or cheeses of perfect ripeness, or the correct fresh vegetable to go with a certain dish, and even an ordinary weekday family lunch is a carefully planned affair. A middle-class family might start with some neat array of *hors d'oeuvres* including *crudités* and *terrine* of duck, then go on to garlicky roast leg of lamb with properly-dressed salad, followed by a cheese tray including the local Roquefort, then a home-made *clafoutis* (a kind of sweet Yorkshire pudding filled with cherries), a regional specialty. Wines are also likely to be local—say, a red from Cahors or Gaillac—for only on special occasions will Toulousains drink a more expensive wine from another region.

Admittedly, the gastronomic tradition is now under pressure, as younger housewives find less time for careful home cooking, as a new generation turns its attention to other things, and as the French food industry begins to adopt the mass-processing habits of other countries. Much later than in Britain or Germany, frozen foods made a cautious appearance in northern France in the 1960s and are now percolating to conservative Toulouse. Some hurried housewives may now accept to buy frozen or tinned vegetables rather than fresh ones, or put some processed ingredients in their soups, casseroles and cakes. Or they may as soon toss a steak under the grill as spend hours preparing some local stew such as *cassoulet* or *boeuf en daube* as their mothers would have done. Gastronomy suffers. Yet there are some bright signs—one, that when the French do go over to processed foods, they often ally them to their own complex classic dishes. Go into a Toulouse hypermarket, and you will find the deep-freeze full of packets of pre-cooked *cassoulet, coq-au-vin, bouillabaisse,* and so on, as well as frozen snails, quail and frogs' legs; and the French are more ready to buy these costly delicacies than staple frozen items such as peas or fish-fingers, so popular in Britain. In fact, many experts believe that the French, after a difficult transition phase, may succeed in preserving their traditional quality within the context of modern techniques. Already one finds instances of how modern mass catering can retain gastronomic flair: in the canteen of the Motorola factory in Toulouse (American-owned!) I had a delicious *cassolette des fruits de mer* (seafood casserole), the *plat du jour* (daily special). I found no such refinement in the works canteens of Stuttgart or Newcastle.

Toulouse's restaurants are in much the same transitional phase as home cooking, and many have lowered their standards, as they struggle with rising costs, staff shortages, and the temptation to cut corners by using tins and packets. It used to be possible in almost any *bistro* (tavern) to find for a modest price an honest *cassoulet,* the famous rich stew of haricot beans, port, mutton, Toulouse sausage and preserved goose. I know a few places in Toulouse where the *cassoulet* is still superb, but in most others the vital ingredient, *confit d'oie* (liver goose),will have come straight out of a tin and the dish will lack flavour. Another local speciality, as in all the southwest, is truffled *foie gras,* often served hot in a sweet sauce with tiny grapes—delicious, but pricey.

Inevitably, Toulouse has its "Le Grill-Pub," pseudo-smart, with expensive hybrid menu and plush décor hopefully imitating some imagined Victorian pub—one of scores of such places in France today. For a few years recently it also had "Le Drugstore." So-called "drugstores" first appeared in Paris in the early '60s and soon spread to the provinces, Toulouse's being one of the first. They adopted an American name because of the naif fashion for *franglais* words: but the French "drugstore" is a purely French invention, owing little to American ones. In France, a drugstore is a modernised *brasserie* with a ritzy Paris/New York air and a number of boutiques attached, all open till late: Toulouse's sold books, newspapers, cosmetics, sweets and tobacco, till about midnight, and very useful it was too. Its two restaurants served rather good food. It was a favourite haunt of the younger affluent society, and on a small scale had something of a metropolitan Champs-Elysées air. Unfortunately it lost money, and closed in 1976, to re-open as a simple steak-bar. One or two newer places also call themselves "drugstores," but they have no boutiques, and entirely lack the old ambiance.

39

IMMIGRANT WORKERS AND CHANGES IN THE SOCIAL STRUCTURE

STEPHEN CASTLES

Assessing contemporary European society is not merely a matter of sweeping evaluations; it also involves pinpointing some specific developments. Since the 1950s, Western Europe has recruited and attracted a growing number of immigrant workers—"guest" workers as the Germans ambiguously term them—from non-Western nations such as Turkey, North Africa, the West Indies, and Pakistan. These immigrants for the most part form part of a new underclass, separated from the native-born working class not only because of race and culture, but also because of high rates of unemployment and low skill levels.

The following selection covers important aspects of the lives of this substantial segment of Europe's social structure. The treatment is objective, but the tone ominous. Whether Europe can assimilate the new immigrants through mutual accommodations remains uncertain, and the prospects if assimilation does not occur are even more so.

Issues of immigration relate to changes in Europe's economy, whereby many workers have been able to move into better jobs and more comfortable incomes while a new unskilled, largely immigrant residue is also drawn in. They also relate to Europe's altered position in the wider world, as European diplomatic and military power and its own birthrate have declined. A dynamic Europe has emerged even so, fueled in part by this new immigrant labor, but some obvious challenges remain.

Minorities make up 5 to 14 per cent of the total population in the industrial countries of Western Europe, but their regional distribution is very uneven, so their impact is much greater in certain areas. The original migrant workers came to the growing industrial conurbations, where their labour was needed, but where problems of urban stress, overcrowding and lack of amenities were greatest. In Britain, black communities have become established mainly in

From: Stephen Castles, with Heather Booth and Tina Wallace, *Here for Good,* (London: Pluto Press, 1987), pp. 117–20, 164–70.

London, the west Midlands and the industrial areas of the north-west and north-east of England. In France, foreign residents are heavily concentrated in the Paris area, and around Lyons and Marseilles. . . .

The pattern in West Germany is similar. . . . In some districts foreign residents make up less than one per cent of the total population. Foreigners are concentrated in the industrial growth areas of the post-war boom; the Ruhr, the Rhine–Main conurbation around Frankfurt, the newer industrial areas around Stuttgart and Mannheim, and in southern Bavaria. Half of all foreign residents are to be found in cities (officially defined as towns with over 100,000 residents), where they often make up a large proportion of the total population: 24 per cent in Frankfurt, 18 per cent in Stuttgart, 17 per cent in Munich, 15 per cent in Cologne, Remscheid, Mannheim and Düsseldorf and 13 per cent in West Berlin. The distribution of nationalities varies. Over half the foreigners in Berlin, Cologne, Duisburg and Bremen are Turks, while Yugoslavs are the largest single group (but not the majority of the foreign population) in Frankfurt, Munich and Stuttgart. Sometimes these patterns result directly from employers' recruitment preferences; between 1960 and 1973 Volkswagen hired mainly Italians, so today over 70 per cent of the foreign population of Wolfsburg have that nationality. The Ruhr mines recruited mainly in Turkey, so Turks are now the most numerous group in towns like Gelsenkirchen, Hamm, Herne, Duisburg and Bottrop.

Within the cities, foreign residents are anything but evenly dispersed. In West Berlin, for instance, Turks have become so highly concentrated in the old working-class area of Kreuzberg, that politicians and the media speak of a "ghetto." In Frankfurt, the city with the highest foreign share in population (24 per cent on average), foreigners only make up 8 to 10 per cent of residents in outer suburbs like Nieder Eschbach or Harheim, or in the middle-class areas like Dornbusch and Eschersheim. In the district around the main railway station, foreigners make up 70 to 80 per cent of the population and, in the industrial districts, over a third of the total population.

Concentration in the inner cities is typical for the new ethnic minorities throughout Western Europe. It is in part due to their recruitment by manufacturing industries sited in the major conurbations. It is also a result of the way the housing market has reacted to immigration. In Britain, as the white working class moved out of the inner cities into suburban estates (both council and owner-occupied), low standard inner-city accommodation became available. The newcomers had no choice but to accept such housing, initially as private tenants. Employment patterns, together with fears of racism and discrimination, have kept the minorities largely in such areas, even when they have been able to finance the shift to home ownership.

In West Germany, most foreign workers were initially housed by their employers, usually in huts or hostels on the work site. This accommodation had two major drawbacks: it allowed employers to control their workers' private lives, and it precluded family reunification. Indeed there were cases in which husband and wife, both recruited as workers, were forced to live in separate hostels. Most foreign workers got out of employers' accommodation as quickly as they could. In 1972, 38 per cent of male foreign workers and 24 per cent of female foreign workers were still housed by employers. Since then, this type of accommodation has declined considerably, although no figures are now available. . . .

Foreigners find themselves the victims of a double process of discrimination. On the one hand, owners of better quality housing in areas with reasonable environmental conditions often refuse to rent to foreigners. On the other hand, landlords of poor quality housing in areas of urban stress exploit foreigners' weak position to demand extortionate rents. As a result, some inner-city streets and districts become predominantly minority housing areas. Overcrowding and pressure on social amenities in such areas further encourage better-off Germans to flee to the suburbs. Those remaining belong to socially disadvantaged groups. The West German inner cities are not purely foreign housing areas, but concentrations of the social groups at the bottom of the socioeconomic ladder.

Inner-city concentration has disadvantages for the minorities. Most obvious is the material deprivation. An officially commissioned survey in the late seventies showed that 15 per cent of the foreigners interviewed had no toilet in their dwellings (compared with 4 per cent of the Germans); 42 per cent of the foreigners had no bath or shower (6 per cent of the Germans had none); 45 per cent lacked running hot water (15 per cent of the Germans had none); and 58 per cent had no central heating (25 per cent of the Germans had none). The survey also showed that foreigners pay more rent than Germans for comparable housing, and concluded that foreigners' inferior housing was in part due to discrimination and in part to foreigners' low occupational status. Lack of such amenities as schooling, medical care and recreation facilities is most marked in inner-city areas. This is a special handicap for foreign children since their schooling and therefore their future occupational opportunities are severely jeopardised. The problem hardly affects Germans, for most of those remaining in the inner cities are elderly. The situation is growing worse in the current fiscal crisis of the cities which, in turn, is partly a result of the decline of the inner cities. As better paid Germans move out, the cities' tax income falls, while at the same time demands for social amenities and welfare benefits increase. There is less money to meet more needs, and the quality of inner-city life deteriorates yet further.

The trend towards concentration and semi-segregation in the inner cities also has advantages for the minorities. It offers them protection from racism and discrimination, and makes it easier for them to maintain and develop their own cultures, and informal networks of mutual aid that are vital both to newcomers and to other members of the community who find themselves in difficulties. Ethnic shops, cafés, cultural centres, mosques, churches, sports associations, parents' groups, political organisations and the like can be set up. At present, such institutions are developing rapidly in West German cities. They are the focal point of growing minority communities, and although they improve cultural, social and political life they also confirm and reinforce segregation by West German society. . . .

This dichotomy gives rise to the idea that migrants suffer a "culture shock," which makes it hard for them to cope in the new country, while their children are "torn between two cultures." However, these notions are misleading, for they imply that migrants move between two intact, coherent and homogeneous societies. The reality is different. In response to the spread of capitalist farming and industry, the social and economic framework of the countries of origin is going through dissolution and change. Traditional forms of production are collapsing, and family farms and handicraft enterprises can no longer provide a livelihood. Internal migration, political conflict and shifts in family and social structures correspond with this process. Also, many of the migrants come from the more developed areas of the countries of origin, and have already experienced such transformations.

Recent research indicates that the extended family is no longer dominant in Turkey. It is being replaced by the nuclear family, so that many Turkish workers have decided to bring their children to West Germany for lack of child-care facilities in Turkey. While traditional family and community structures dissolve, their modern counterparts—social insurance schemes, health care, pensions—are developing only slowly, if at all. Emigration is indeed the most obvious expression of this process of economic and social change. It is highly misleading to think that migrants have intact, extended families to return to in case of need. A specific sort of migrant or "guest worker family" develops, leading a marginalised existence during the migratory process. This insecure family is a temporary phenomenon, but it has been the essential unit of primary socialisation for the foreign children now growing up in West Germany. . . .

Rather than being "torn between two cultures," migrant youth are part of a new and evolving "culture of migration." This is not just a combination of various aspects of the culture of the countries of origin and of immigration. It embodies the dynamic response of migrants to the experience of migration, and to the problems of working-class existence in the inner city. The culture of migration is contradictory and volatile at this formative stage, for it has to try to incorporate elements of experience which are in themselves irreconcilable.

At the present time, the situation of many foreign children is still characterised by a high degree of mobility and insecurity. When the father or mother originally migrated, the children were often left with relatives in the country of origin, and only brought in after some years. Later on, children (including those born in West Germany) are frequently sent back to the country of origin to attend school. When children reach school-leaving age (11 in Turkey) they are brought back to West Germany and continue schooling there. Yet others are left with grandparents until they get close to working age, or until they reach the maximum age for entry as dependents (15 at present). Young men often to return to the country of origin to do their military service, and then return to West Germany (if permitted to do so).

Movement between country of origin and West Germany may be for more personal reasons. There are more foreign boys than girls in West Germany, indicating a preference to leave girls in the country of origin. In other cases, girls are brought over to look after younger brothers and sisters. Some children are sent home because the family cannot find an adequate dwelling, and may be sent for later on if better housing is found.

It is impossible to say how many children have experienced this oscillation between the two countries, but it is far from unusual. The effects on children's mental development, social relationships and school success are often negative. Underlying the problem is foreigners' lack of security of residence, and the resulting impossibility of making clear plans for the future of the family. Most migrants still want to return to the country of origin at some time, or expect that they will be forced to do so. So they are not sure whether it is more important for children to learn German and succeed in the German education system, or to maintain full knowledge of the language and culture of the country of origin. Insecurity is a constant source of worry for both parents and children.

Migration and the conditions of inner-city, working-class life often lead to considerable stress for foreign families. The parents' own upbringing has rarely prepared them adequately to cope with this situation. Marital relationships are often strained by long periods of separation, or by the need for both parents to go out to work. Cramped housing conditions and lack of social amenities make matters worse. Where foreign families live in isolation, lack of support from relatives and the community can be a serious problem. Often the need to work long hours means that parents have little time and energy left for their children, who are left to their own devices in a strange and sometimes hostile environment.

Family strain is exacerbated by the breakdown of the gender-roles of the countries of origin, especially where migrants come from strongly patriarchal societies, like Turkey. Where the father is no longer the sole breadwinner, his dominance over wife and children is weakened. Working mothers may demand more say in family affairs and begin to reject male authority, especially when the husband is unemployed and the wife becomes the sole earner. Some men try to reassert their authority through emphasis on traditional values, through return to patriarchal religion, and sometimes through violence towards wife and children. Wives who do not work, on the other hand, are frequently isolated, do not learn the language, and can do little to guide their children in the new environment. Children often take on the role of interpreters and mediators between parents and bureaucratic institutions, weakening parental authority.

Despite these strains and conflicts, it would be wrong to see the foreign family in West Germany as a "pathological family," which is somehow responsible for foreign children's educational failure. The idea of the "pathological black family" has been advanced in Britain as a convenient explanation of continued social disadvantage of black youth. There is no evidence that foreign families break down more frequently than German families. On the contrary, the rate of divorce among Germans is higher. Foreign families are at least as likely to be able to provide emotional support and refuge for the children. It is not the family that is pathological, but the conditions under which migration and settlement have taken place, and the constant pressure of discriminatory laws that often split families. The establishment of closely knit, inner-city minority communities and the trend towards cultural separateness are mechanisms of defence against such conditions. . . .

Young foreigners also share the problems encountered by all working-class children in an educational system geared to the language, norms, values and behavioural patterns of the middle class. Success in education for working-class children often means rejecting their origins and accepting middle-class cultural dominance as a pre-condition for selection for higher levels of education. This class selection system is highly effective in West Germany; less than 10 per cent of university students come from working-class homes. . . .

Large-scale entry of foreign children was not anticipated nor desired by the state, and the fact of settlement is still not officially recognised. Policies towards foreign youth have therefore been fragmentary, contradictory and belated, and apparently guided by the hope that they would go away if life were made uncomfortable for them. . . .

The aims of the 1976 Decision of the Standing Conference of Education Ministers were defined as follows:

> It is a question of enabling foreign pupils to learn the German language and to obtain German school-leaving certificates, as well as allowing them to keep and improve their knowledge of their mother tongue. At the same time, educational measures should contribute to the social integration of the foreign pupils during the duration of their stay in the German Federal Republic. They also assist in the maintenance of their linguistic and cultural identity.

Again we see the "dual strategy": schools were to help foreign children integrate into West German society and at the same time prepare them for return to the country of origin. The Decision was to be implemented through setting up special "preparatory classes" to give intensive language instruction to prepare foreign pupils for entry to normal classes, and "native-language classes" to maintain knowledge of the language and culture of the country of origin. The contradictory aims of the dual strategy and the isolation and strain caused by the special classes are at the root of many of the difficulties experienced by foreign youth.

40

Music and Gender in Postwar
Germany: Rock 'n' Roll

UTA G. POIGER

This following selection discusses the significance of the spread of rock 'n' roll music from America to Western Europe, and particularly Germany, from the late 1950s onward. It argues that the music had profound implications, even though teenaged consumers were not fully aware of them, and it shows that hostile reactions by adult media implicitly recognized the new values and behaviors involved. Radical new music styles, in sum, were wrapped up in more fundamental social changes of age groups and gender, and at the same time encouraged these changes. Yet ultimately, outside of communist East Germany, authorities came to terms with the new music, and what it represented, but also contained some of the extremes involved.

The article focuses on trends of obvious social importance: a new wave of consumerism and the new influence of American popular culture, itself changing rapidly. It also picks up the rise of youth culture at a very different stage from that described in Chapter 33.

After years of fascination with Nazism and related facets of German social and political history, historians have recently turned to the postwar experience. They find that for the most part basic social structures and assumptions remained surprisingly unchanged in the first decade after World War II. Gender values, among other things, remained quite stable, as Germans sought continuities in part to protect themselves against the huge political and military shifts that they had to contend with in the wake of Nazism and defeat in war. But in the later 1950s, new adolescent behavior, first in the working class, new women's awareness and even changing child rearing styles betokened more serious change, in an atmosphere of Cold War tension but also intensifying economic prosperity.

Using shifts in music styles as a serious marker for social history is not uncontested, as the author of the following selection recognizes. Some shifts in fads, in a consumer society in which style changes are regularly promoted as a means of selling goods, are not particularly significant. But the rise of

From: Uta G. Poiger, "Rock 'n' Roll, Female Sexuality, and the Cold War Battle Over German Identities," *Journal of Modern History* 68 (Chicago, 1996): 577–80, 586–87, 589, 594–96, 598–99, 607–08, 610–11, 615.

rock 'n' roll and partial cultural Americanization in clothing styles and other behaviors do need sociohistorical interpretation—even when many participants were not particularly aware of what their enthusiasms meant in terms of larger social standards. The social historian dealing with popular culture needs to assess effects, as the following selection emphasizes, but also causes: Why were young Germans so ready for this kind of outside influence?

When rock 'n' roll crossed the Atlantic to Germany in the second half of the 1950s, it dramatically—and relatively suddenly—brought young women into the public eye as consumers and sexual beings. In 1956, a cartoon in the East Berlin daily *Berliner Zeitung* showed a small, emaciated Elvis Presley performing under larger-than-life female legs in front of a crowd of girls much bigger than he was. They were throwing off garter belts and bras and licking their thick lips in obvious sexual excitement. The accompanying article identified girls as the main consumers of American "nonculture" and commented that rock 'n' roll appealed to primitive humans. West Germans had similar worries: According to one commentator, the behavior of female rock 'n' roll fans illustrated the dangerous "sexualization of the 15–year-olds." Another West German saw rock 'n' roll dancers as "wild barbarians in ecstasy."

In this article I will locate the rebellious actions of female rock 'n' roll fans in the context of cold war struggles over East and West German national identities and explore how their public behavior at dances, at concerts, and in the streets challenged the traditional norms of female respectability that authorities in East and West Germany had made central to their respective reconstruction efforts. Both East and West German authorities, albeit in increasingly different ways, politicized the actions of female rock 'n' roll fans.

Two interrelated concerns shaped East and West German reactions to rock 'n' roll: worries about uncontrolled female sexuality on the one hand and about alleged racial differences on the other. Commentators linked consumption, sexuality, and femininity. While these links had characterized discourses on consumer culture since the nineteenth century, alleged connections among the consumption of mass culture, the oversexualization of women, and the feminization of men were particularly worrisome to East and West Germans in the 1950s. After the defeat of National Socialism and in the face of the cold war, authorities in both states saw the success of reconstruction as dependent on reconfiguring and revalidating Germanness; defining normative gender roles was important to these reconstruction projects. Although East and West German officials differed greatly, for example, in their approval of female employment, both sides relied on the image of the asexual female caretaker and the controlling and controlled male protector in their construction of ideal gender roles. In the mid-1950s, young male and female rebels with a penchant for American music and fashions challenged these norms and exacerbated East and West German concerns about the consumption of American popular culture. Indeed, worries about the actions of female rock 'n' roll fans were intimately linked to concerns about male rebelliousness. Authorities in East and West Germany invoked American and German women as instigators of, victims of, and solutions to the problems they associated with consumer culture.

The need to affirm racial differences between Germans and African Americans also emerged in East and West German discourses on rock 'n' roll. Although many attacks against musicians and fans employed racial slurs and stereotypes, race has hardly been used as a category of analysis in histories of the German post-Nazi period. Debates about rock 'n' roll reveal that after World War II Germans continued to define Germanness in racial terms. Since the nineteenth century, race had clearly been central to German identities. German conceptions of racial hierarchies had manifested themselves most forcefully in anti-Semitism, but many Germans also saw blacks, along with other groups like Sinti and Roma ("Gypsies"), as racially inferior. For example, hostilities toward blacks were pronounced in the 1920s when the French occupation army in the Rhineland included many Senegalese. The Nazis forced the children that German women had by these soldiers to undergo compulsory sterilization. Anxieties surfaced again when black soldiers came to Germany as part of the American occupying forces after World War II. Yet Germans have not needed black people within their own country in order to make blackness a quality against which to define their Germanness. Rock 'n' roll in 1950s West Germany was radical precisely because of its associations with blackness; unlike many Americans, Germans did not perceive it as "whitened" music. . . .

When the West German weekly *Der Spiegel* ran a cover story on Elvis Presley in December 1956, it described his American fans as girls steeped in "orgiastic hysteria." According to *Der Spiegel,* the American music industry had pushed Presley after "the first symptoms of collective erotic eruptions" appeared. In late 1956 and in 1957, many more West German newspapers reported extensively on female American teenagers who were said to swarm around Presley wherever he showed up and who would even go so far as to tear his clothes off in ecstasy. The West German press thus made a clear connection between rock 'n' roll and white American female sexual aggressiveness.

Just two months earlier, West German papers had evaluated rock quite differently—namely, as instigating male rebellion. In September 1956, *Der Spiegel* reported in an article on Presley's success that riots had occurred at American rock 'n' roll concerts; here *Der Spiegel* treated Presley's fans as male delinquents. This resonated in both Germanies. Since 1955, youth riots with mostly male participants had also shaken many West German and some East German cities. In the West commentators worried about a rebellion of the *Halbstarke*—literally, the "semistrong," a term that connoted working-class male delinquents. East Germans preferred the English word "rowdies" to describe young males who, like their counterparts in the West, roamed the streets attacking policemen and destroying public property. When the American movie *Blackboard Jungle* brought Bill Haley's song "Rock around the Clock" to Germany in December 1955 (and implied a connection between the song and the juvenile delinquency shown in the movie), some commentators in Germany began to make rock 'n' roll into the culprit that instigated male misbehavior. These fears were exacerbated by reports of riots after Presley concerts in the United States and violence after showings of the movie *Rock around the Clock* in London and Oslo in the summer of 1956. . . .

West German commentators again harnessed alleged racial characteristics to criticize Presley and his fans, but this time they used them to support the notion of *female* aggression and male weakness. Some West German reports on Presley drew a clear connection between his gender and racial ambiguities: Presley's way of moving put not just his male gender but also his racial origins in doubt. Newspapers in the West suspected that Presley must have black blood in his ancestry to be able to move and sing in this extraordinary fashion. In another attack, one West German paper directly referred to Presley's thick lips as an attribute of the ideal man in the United States—a country described as run by women ("Frauenstaat Amerika"). Such statements used references to racial stereotypes, like thick lips, to underline the notion that in the United States gender norms were reversed. Gender and racial ambiguities on Presley's part elicited and required gender and racial transgressions on the part of his female fans. Unlike earlier writers who associated rock 'n' roll with male overaggressiveness and blackness, commentators now turned against female aggressivity: they reported that in the United States Presley's female fans attacked policemen and exhibited active sexual desire toward this feminized man with what they described as stereotypically black features. West German commentators thus conflated male weakness with blackness and linked both to female desire. These associations of blackness with both male overaggression and male weakness reaffirmed Western stereotypes of black men. . . . Perhaps because of their specific fears, many West German commentators still hoped, in the spring of 1957, that the American "mass hysteria" around Elvis Presley would not take hold in Germany. In spite of evidence to the contrary, they contrasted the "hysterical" behavior of American teenagers with the "more rational" reactions of their German counterparts. Journalists thus praised German girls who, confronted with the movie *Love Me Tender,* allegedly urged Presley to get rid of his makeup. One West German paper expressed relief that German women, unlike their American contemporaries, would not "melt" when they saw Elvis's wide, soft—and, implicitly, unmanly—face. Allegedly, German women were not swayed by Elvis's American brand of eroticism.

However, as other reports indicate, East and West German girls did like rock 'n' roll. In October 1956, a local Berlin newspaper reported that "rock 'n' roll reigned in the Hot-House," a West Berlin club. According to the article, women were the more accomplished rock dancers and preferred to buy their cokes themselves rather than have some guy step on their fashionable shoes. They would even turn their backs on clumsy young men and grab their girlfriends to "rock" on the dance floor! Rock 'n' roll dancing provided a dramatic contrast to traditional dance styles in which the man led and the woman followed. Consequently, one West German commentary in 1956 described rock 'n' roll dancers as "wild barbarians in ecstasy" and worried that their dancing "degenerated" into "vulgar and erotically expressive movements." Women and men threw each other through the air. Also, rock 'n' roll dancers often held each other just by the hand and thus were able to design their movements individually. This "open dancing" even made it possible for women to dance with each other in public. Thus the new dynamic dance style associated with rock 'n' roll changed gender codes dramatically, as women asserted their independence in ever greater numbers and rejected the male control that older dance styles so effectively symbolized.

The West German youth magazine *Bravo* now showed less hostility toward the black origins of rock 'n' roll and even referred to these black origins to market the music. When advertising the first German rock 'n' roll dance championship, *Bravo* stressed that rock 'n' roll came into existence among "Negroes": "They played it hotter, more convincingly, and danced it better, more freely and more elegantly." Comparisons with "Negroes" certainly served to underline the outrageous character of the new musical style, yet *Bravo* valorized black styles exactly because they were outrageous. It now urged German teenagers to try for themselves the dance styles developed by African-Americans.

The shocking fashions of female rock 'n' roll fans further exacerbated fears in both East and West Germany. For critical contemporaries, their looks signified a loss of femininity. A West German critique of an outspoken female Presley fan imagined her this way in 1958: "half-long pants, funny jacket, sauerkraut figure like a toilet brush." Others commented on the boyish looks of girls with ponytails. In the East, too, young women sported jeans, tight pants, and short sweaters, and they emulated Western models. As one paper put it: "Female creatures of this kind distinguish themselves from the males only in their hair, which is eaten regularly by rats, so that one ultimately doesn't know where these rodents wreak more damage—in or on the heads." In an East German youth magazine, a report on East German male delinquents featured girls with tight pants and short jackets prominently among the boys. Wearing men's clothes in public had formerly been reserved for women in times of emergency, like the war and the immediate postwar period. With their new fashions, many East and West German girls now directly countered the images of female respectability available to them: the model of the "clean" German woman with no makeup and with her hair in a German bun that the Nazis had promoted so forcefully and that West German cultural conservatives still saw as an ideal, as well as the model of the asexual East German worker/mother. . . .

As more and more female rock 'n' roll fans clearly challenged the East and West German ideals of female (sexual) passivity after 1956, the East and West German press oscillated between ignoring them and raging against them. Thus East and West German papers did not report that there were female rioters at a Bill Haley concert in Berlin in 1958, although pictures in the press clearly showed both boys *and* girls throwing chairs. At the other extreme, one West German paper mobilized the image of the (usually male) delinquent *Halbstarke* against female rock 'n' roll fans, criticizing a young West German woman who had spoken out in Presley's defense as a "typical female *Halbstarke*" with "an open mane, a face full of pimples, a purple loud mouth, and black eyeliner."

In their most publicized challenges to dominant gender norms, young women often made use of their status as potential girlfriends and wives. Publicly making Elvis Presley into a male ideal, women in East and West Germany redefined norms of both masculinity and femininity. A female fan wrote a letter to the editor of a West German newspaper concerning a negative review of a Presley movie in which she accused the reviewer of being "a fat, old, nasty dwarf, a jealous dog and an old sack." Also in 1958, girls from a West Berlin fan club from the upper-class district of Wilmersdorf announced that Elvis had more success with women than his critics did. East Berlin girls stated their support for Presley by wearing his name on the back of their jeans. These young women went public with their (sexual) desire, asserted their right to choose their mates and, further, constructed Elvis into a "softer, [more] understanding man." Thus they opposed the male machismo prevalent in the *Halbstarken* subcultures and rejected the image of the self-restrained, controlling man that had been the accepted ideal in East and West Germany. Authorities in both German states were promoting such men as ideal citizens and soldiers in the mid-1950s, at the same time as they began rearming. The spread of rebellious behavior from the working class to a wider circle of young women from middle- and upper-class neighborhoods certainly threatened ideologies that, in both Germanies, had sought to confine women's sexuality to the sphere of marriage and motherhood.

It was exactly this double resistance to bourgeois norms of both male and female respectability and the transgression of racial boundaries that made rock 'n' roll an attractive dance style and Elvis an important figure for East and West German girls. In spite of, or perhaps because of, the negative reporting about American and German female rock 'n' roll fans in the press, many German girls made it known publicly that they liked Elvis. In Germany as in the United States, Presley's female fans supported his challenge to respectable masculinity; at the same time, their association with blackness through Elvis and rock 'n' roll made their own challenges to norms of female respectability all the more radical. Adopting styles with connotations of blackness was a radical act for young women in the German context, where blacks (along with Jews, Sinti and Roma, and Asians) had been portrayed as sexual aggressors under National Socialism and into the postwar years.

While it is difficult to determine exactly what young women in the 1950s thought about their actions, the effects of their behavior were certainly subversive, clearly undermining the gender norms and sexual mores propagated by parents and state officials. Female rock 'n' roll fans may not have thought of their actions as political, but if we define as political all actions designed to effect larger social changes, they were indeed political. Clearly their actions challenged certain state-supported norms and thus positioned them as "bad girls." These young women used that position in interesting ways: they asserted their youthful difference and attempted to recast the dominant notions of masculinity and femininity, which were, as we have seen, at the heart of reconstruction in both states. Recognizing that cultural consumption took place in and reshaped the public sphere will allow us to examine how (re)constructions of (private) identities affected state politics. Certainly the reactions of authorities in East and West Germany left little doubt that female rock 'n' roll fans posed a political threat to the established order. . . . In spite of, perhaps because of, these [repressive] efforts, rock 'n' roll spread in West Germany during these years from working-class adolescents to middle- and upper-class youths. The shift of the working-class styles associated with rock 'n' roll to the middle and upper classes included a transformation—and taming—of these styles. Concurrently, the rhetoric against rock 'n' roll in West Germany turned more mild. Given the authorities' preoccupation in East and West Germany with the gender and racial ambiguities imported with rock 'n' roll, the taming of the "threat" of rock 'n' roll in West Germany rested on undermining the racial and gender transgressions in youth styles. As a result, race was effaced from discussions of rock 'n' roll. . . .

As rock 'n' roll caught on, a new West German female emerged: the "teenager." In Germany this American term had first been used to describe American female Presley fans, but from 1957 onward "teenagers" increasingly became a label for young German women of all classes. For many of these young women, the term "teenager" carried a much more modern image of femininity, one that included greater openness in sexual matters. It also had implications for female adolescent consumption: the image of the teenager ran counter to the traditional ideal image of the woman who exerted self-restraint in matters of consumption and sexuality. Initially used as a criticism, but quickly turned into a marketing tool, "teenager" carried less rebellious connotations than the term *Halbstarke.* . . .

This shift was certainly fostered by the systematic marketing of Peter Kraus and Conny Froboess as ideal teenagers. Initially, Kraus was sold as the "German Elvis." Racial ambiguity was not part of his image, and nobody referred to his thick lips (which he did have). Although Kraus, too, encountered "hysterical teenagers," he was mostly portrayed as a nice German boy, much "more likable in voice and behavior" than the American original. When he was joined by a female mate, "Conny," his domestication was almost complete. "Conny and Peter" made movies together and were celebrated as West German rock 'n' roll stars. The West German fashion industry used their popularity to market teenage fashions and claimed to direct the "not so complaisant" wishes of adolescents into "pleasant forms." "Conny" sweaters for young women, as well as "Peter Kraus pulls" (vests) intended for young men, stressed different cuts for women and men and thus tried to reinstate a larger measure of gender difference.

In the promotion of Conny Froboess and Peter Kraus traditional gender roles were partially resurrected. Thus Froboess had to be protected from association with too much "sexiness." Froboess's manager/father invoked the differences between *Halbstarke* and teenagers and criticized Kraus when he allegedly turned too "sexy": "That is something for *Halbstarke* and not for teenagers. . . . If teenager music declines into sex, then [it will do so] without me." On the one hand, the duo was part of a heterosocial teenage world where young men and women together challenged older standards of respectable dancing or clothing; but on the other hand, they tried to steer away from open challenges to sexual mores.

Newer styles of rock 'n' roll dancing also stressed gender differences, developing from a "wild" style, in which men *and* women threw their partners through the air, to a "tamed" version in which the male partner hardly moved at all. In 1960 *Bravo* published directions for dancing rock 'n' roll as part of a series on ballroom dancing. The man depicted in the photograph wore a dark suit and guided a young woman dressed in a petticoat skirt while apparently avoiding any excessive movements himself. This style of rock 'n' roll dancing could be safely adopted at the private house parties that became the fashion among middle-class youth. It effectively symbolized the ideal female teenager as the acolyte of the controlled and controlling man, avoided allusions to black culture, and made rock 'n' roll compatible with a bourgeois gender system.

While the subversive gender, racial, and class implications of rock 'n' roll consumption lessened, the greater acceptance of rock 'n' roll and sexuality as modes of "private" expression constituted a widening of options for West German adolescents, especially young women. The West German attempts to tame rock 'n' roll had only limited success. Many young Germans perceived the German rock 'n' roll songs as weak imitations and preferred the American originals. And fashion makers were hardly able or even willing to prevent girls from wearing Peter Kraus pulls along with James Dean jackets. Moreover, even with their tamed German version of rock 'n' roll, Froboess and Kraus introduced American words like "baby," "sexy," and "love" into the German vocabulary. And the practice of petting—sexual touching without actual intercourse—became more acceptable for young men and women, at least in West Germany. . . .

In retrospect, adolescents of the 1950s . . . probably did not worry about whether their actions were political or not. Later, when they constructed their life stories, a narrow view of politics in West Germany may have prevented them from understanding as political their informal and public resistance to the very gender, racial, and sexual norms that in fact had been at the center of political reconstruction in both Germanies.

We cannot understand the upheaval of the late 1960s in West Germany without grasping the particular dynamics of containing the youth rebellion of the 1950s. Female rock 'n' roll fans of that decade participated in a revolt that can now be seen to have had clear political implications. Depoliticization did not diffuse the rebellion completely. As in the United States, the 1950s youth cultures raised expectations for individual expression and sexual openness among many young women, and some of them expressed these expectations in explicitly political terms in the 1960s. At the same time, "the politicization of private life" and a slogan like "The personal is political" could appear radical and new in an emerging West German women's movement in the late 1960s only after the dramatic reformulation of the relation between politics and culture in the late 1950s and early 1960s. . . .

41

THE TWENTIETH-CENTURY WAY OF DEATH

PHILIPPE ARIÈS

The way that modern society views death is gaining increasing attention from social historians. All agree that attitudes and practices regarding death have changed greatly over the past two centuries, perhaps more than once. In this selection, an eminent French historian, previously known for his work on the development of modern attitudes toward children, describes what he sees as major weaknesses in the contemporary approach to death. A number of other studies of death, in American as well as European history, roughly coincide with his approach.

Modern values do not neatly harmonize with death, according to this general argument. In the nineteenth century, the clash was not yet clear—death received a great deal of attention. Even then, elaborate new funeral practices suggested a guilt about death—and so did new attitudes toward punishment (see Chapter 13). Then in the twentieth century modern hostility to death became clearer, as demonstrated by the reduction of earlier funeral practices and mourning.

Modern people seek pleasure, individual identity, control over their environment, and progress in secular terms. Death contradicts these values. Hence, Ariès discusses the various ways that moderns seek to conceal death, which he clearly believes weaken the quality of modern life. In more traditional societies—even in the nineteenth century—death was faced more directly, surrounded by powerful ceremonies; this approach may well have helped the dying and the bereaved to be better reconciled to fate.

The twentieth-century approach to death obviously involves our attitudes toward health and medicine. We look to doctors to cure, more than to priests to console. Is this a fault we should try to correct by returning to a more positive acceptance of death? Other explanations for modern attitudes also deserve exploration. Infant deaths were once common. Modern people, shaking off traditional resignation toward infant death, have increasingly confined high death rates to the very old. The nature of death has changed. In the past, lingering respiratory diseases were the major cause of death among adults. Now, quick deaths are somewhat more common, which may affect attitudes

From: Philippe Ariès, *The Hour of Our Death,* trans. by Helen Weaver (New York: Random House, 1982), pp. 575–79, 611–14.

quite apart from a general invocation of modern values and a desire to ignore the inevitable. In other words, the Ariès approach, although it is a powerful use of modern history, need not be accepted uncritically; his conclusions can be evaluated and explained in different ways.

In recent years, both in Europe and the United States, new efforts to deal with death have gained ground. A *hospice* movement, designed to help terminally ill people and their families come to terms with death rather than try to fight it through heroic medicine, is a key expression of this new approach. Is this movement likely to produce a radically new stance toward death—and if it does, will this suggest a major change in the overall outlook of modern Western people?

The beginning of the twentieth century saw the completion of the psychological mechanism that removed death from society, eliminated its character of public ceremony, and made it a private act. At first this act was reserved for intimates, but eventually even the family was excluded as the hospitalization of the terminally ill became widespread.

There were still two periods of communication between the dying—or dead—man, and society: the final moments, in which the dying man recovered the initiative that he had lost, and mourning. The second great milestone in the contemporary history of death is the rejection and elimination of mourning. The first complete analysis of this phenomenon was made by Geoffrey Gorer, who was led to the subject by a series of personal experiences.

Gorer lost his father and his grandfather almost at the same time. His father died on the *Lusitania* in 1915, so Gorer was not able to see his body, as was then the custom. Indeed, he did not see his first dead body until 1931. He did observe the conventions of mourning, although he says that these had started to break down during the war because of the high mortality at the front, and also because women were working in men's jobs. The death of a sister-in-law and in 1948 the death of a friend introduced him to the new situation of the bereaved, their behavior, and that of society toward them. He realized that the social function of mourning was changing, and that this change revealed a profound transformation in people's attitude toward death. It was in 1955 that he published in *Encounter* his famous article, "The Pornography of Death," in which he showed that death had become as shameful and unmentionable as sex was in the Victorian era. One taboo had been substituted for another.

In 1961 his brother died of cancer. He was survived by a wife and children. Gorer took charge of the burial and looked after his sister-in-law and nephews, and again he was struck by the rejection of traditional ways of behaving and by the harmful effects of this rejection. He told the whole story in a book. Then he decided to study the phenomenon, no longer as a memorialist but as a sociologist, in a scientific manner. In 1963 he began an investigation of mourning, which resulted in his major work, *Death, Grief, and Mourning in Contemporary Britain*.

His first observation was that death has been removed to a distance. Not only are people no longer present at the deathbed, but burial has ceased to be a familiar sight. Among those interviewed, 70 percent had not attended a funeral in five years. Children do not even attend the funerals of their parents. Of his nephews, Gorer writes, "Their father's death was quite unmarked for them by any ritual of any kind, and was even nearly treated as a secret, for it was very many months before Elizabeth could bear to mention him or have him mentioned in her presence." When Gorer went back to his sister-in-law's house after his brother's cremation, she told him very naturally that she had had a good day with the children, that they had gone on a picnic and after that they had watched the grass being cut.

Children have been excluded from death. Either they are not informed or they are told that their father has gone on a trip or that Jesus has taken him. Jesus has become a kind of Santa Claus whom adults use to tell children about death without believing in him themselves.

A questionnaire published in 1971 by the American magazine *Psychology Today* elicited the following letter from a woman of twenty-five: "When I was twelve, my mother died of leukemia. She was there when I went to bed and when I woke up the next morning, my parents were gone. My father came home, took my brother and me on his knee, and burst into screeching sobs and said, 'Jesus took your mother.' Then we never talked about it again. It was too painful for all of us."

In most of the surveys the proportion of those who believe in an afterlife is between 30 and 40 percent. This is only an indication, for it is very difficult to confine in the words of a questionnaire notions that are more sensed than defined. The belief decreases in the young, whereas we have seen that it increases among the very ill.

It is rather remarkable that in 1963, Gorer's investigation, and only among the old, one encounters the anthropomorphic eschatology of the nineteenth century. The subjects interviewed see their dead again and talk to them. "They are able to watch over us here and give us help and guidance." "Just before my brother died, he saw Mother standing at the foot of the bed." "He was killed in the Air Force, in the war, my youngest boy, and he often comes back and speaks to me." One day when the subject was in bed thinking and worrying about him, a voice said, "It's all right, Mum," and she thought, "Thank God he's all right; but he'd gone. Still, I think I'll see him someday. In fact it's kept me going." Heaven is "a place where there are no worries, and where we meet all our relatives and friends."

One notes also the complete disappearance of hell. Even those who believe in the devil limit his power to this world and do not believe in eternal damnation. This will not surprise us; we have already noticed the phenomenon since the beginning of the nineteenth century.

The answers to Gorer's survey also show that the clergy have abandoned their traditional role. It is not that they are being dismissed; it is now they who are reticent.

But the most important phenomenon brought out by Gorer's study is the decline in mourning and in the dignity of funerals. From now on, cremation is more popular than burial. Out of sixty-seven cases, there are forty cremations and twenty-seven burials. The most remarkable aspect is the meaning attributed to the choice. To choose cremation is to reject the cult of tombs and cemeteries as it has developed since the beginning of the nineteenth century. "In many cases, it would appear, cremation is chosen because it is felt to get rid of the dead more completely and finally than does burial." Some subjects refuse cremation as being too final. This attitude does not depend on the nature of the act itself (the ancients worshipped the ashes of their dead) but on the comparison with the tomb. For despite the efforts of the directors of crematoria, the families of the cremated generally avoid erecting a monument. Out of the forty cremations in the survey, only one was accompanied by a memorial plaque and fourteen by an inscription in the "Book of Remembrance," which is available for the consultation of visitors. But there are no visitors. Some, and this is even more radical, have their ashes scattered.

But the cemetery remains the place of memory and visits. Of the twenty-seven who were buried, only four have no monuments. The survivor goes to the tomb to lay flowers on it and to remember.

It would be a mistake, however, to interpret the disappearance of the body in cremation as a mark of indifference or neglect. The relative of the cremated person rejects the physical reality of the site, its association with the body, which inspires distaste, and the public character of the cemetery. But he accepts the absolutely personal and private nature of regret. For the cult of the tomb he has substituted a cult of memory in the home: "I'm not one to keep going to the cemetery—I believe in helping the living. On birthdays, I put a bunch of flowers by their photographs" (a woman of forty-four). "I think that's the finish as far as the body goes. I mean, I think you can preserve their memory more at home than where they're actually buried. I'll tell you one thing I always do— perhaps it's silly, but I always buy her a little present at Christmas of some azaleas or flowers of some description; I feel that she's still in the house, you see" (a widower of fifty-five). Sometimes the cult may tend toward mummification: The house, or the room of the deceased, is left exactly as it was during his lifetime. Thus, a profound sense of loss is perfectly compatible with the neglect of the tomb, which is sometimes the hated place of the body.

From now on there are two places to cultivate the memory of the dead: at the tomb, a custom that is disappearing more rapidly in England than on the Continent; and in the home. The Canadian sociologist Fernand Dumont reports the following anecdote, which must have taken place in the early twentieth century: "When I was a child, the whole family used to pray to-gether at home. . . . After the prayer, . . . my father would remain alone for a while, kneeling with his head in his hands. This intrigued me in a man who had never been 'pious' in the usual sense of the word. When I asked him about it, . . . my father admitted that at these times he often spoke to his father, who had been dead for a long time."

After the funeral and burial comes mourning in the true sense of the word. The pain of loss may continue to exist in the secret heart of the survivor, but the rule today, almost throughout the West, is that he must never show it in public. This is exactly the opposite of what used to be required. In France since about 1970 the long line of people offering their condolences to the family af-ter the religious service has been eliminated. And in the country the death no-tice, which is still sent out, is accompanied by the dry, almost uncivil formula, "The family is not receiving," a way of avoiding the customary visits of neigh-bors and acquaintances before the funeral.

But generally speaking, the initiative for the refusal to mourn is not taken by the survivors. By withdrawing and avoiding outside contact, the family is affirming the authenticity of its grief, which bears no comparison with the so-licitude of well-meaning relatives; it is also adopting the discreet behavior that society requires.

Geoffrey Gorer distinguishes three categories of bereaved: those who suc-ceed in completely mastering their grief, those who hide it from others and keep it to themselves, and those who allow it to appear openly. In the first case the bereaved forces himself to behave as if nothing had happened, to pursue his normal life without interruption: Keep busy, he has been told by the few people he has spoken to, the doctor, the priest, a few friends. In the second case, almost nothing shows on the outside, and mourning goes on in private, "as one undresses or goes to bed in private." Mourning is an extension of modesty. This is probably the attitude most acceptable to common sense, which realizes that one must tolerate some release of emotion, provided it re-mains private. In the last case, the obstinate bereaved is mercilessly excluded as if he were insane.

Gorer had occasion to experience the judgment of society firsthand after the death of his brother. "A couple of times I refused invitations to cocktail parties, explaining that I was in mourning; the people who invited me re-sponded to this statement with shocked embarrassment, as if I had voiced some appalling obscenity. Indeed, I got the impression that, had I stated that the invitation clashed with some esoteric debauchery I had arranged, I would have had understanding and jocular encouragement; as it was, the people whose invitations I had refused, educated and sophisticated as they were, mumbled and hurried away." They did not know how to behave in a situation that had become unusual. "They clearly no longer had any guidance from rit-ual as to the way to treat a self-confessed mourner; and I suspect they were frightened lest I give way to my grief, and involve them in a distasteful upsurge of emotion." . . .

If hell is gone, heaven has changed too. . . . We have followed the slow transition from the sleep of the *homo totus* to the glory of the immortal soul. The nineteenth century saw the triumph of another image of the beyond. The next world becomes the scene of the reunion of those whom death has separated but who have never accepted this separation: a recreation of the affections of earth, purged of their dross, assured of eternity. It is the paradise of Christians or the astral world of spiritualists and psychics. But it is also the world of the memories of nonbelievers and freethinkers who deny the reality of a life after death. In the piety of their love, they preserve the memories of their departed with an intensity equal to the realistic afterlife of Christians or psychics. The difference in doctrine between these two groups may be great, but it becomes negligible in the practice of what may be called the cult of the dead. They have all built the same castle, in the image of earthly homes, where they will be reunited—in dream or in reality, who knows?—with those whom they have never ceased to love.

In the nineteenth century the psychological landscape was completely transformed. . . . The situation that resulted did not last more than a century and a half. But the model of death that came next, our model, which I have called the invisible death, does not challenge the underlying tendency or the structural character of the changes of nineteenth century. It continues them, even if it seems to contradict them in its most spectacular effects. It is as if beyond a certain threshold, these tendencies produced the opposite effects.

Our contemporary model of death is still determined by the sense of privacy, but it has become more rigorous, more demanding. It is often said that the sense of privacy is declining. This is because today we demand the perfection of the absolute, we tolerate none of the compromises that romantic society still accepted beneath its rhetoric—or beneath its hypocrisy, as we would say. Intimacy must be either total or nonexistent. There is no middle ground between success and failure. It is possible that our attitude toward life is dominated by the certainty of failure. On the other hand, our attitude toward death is defined by the impossible hypothesis of success. That is why it makes no sense.

The modern attitude toward death is an extension of the affectivity of the nineteenth century. The last inspiration of this inventive affectivity was to protect the dying or the invalid from his own emotions by concealing the seriousness of his condition until the end. When the dying man discovered the pious game, he lent himself to it so as not to disappoint the other's solicitude. The dying man's relations with those around him were now determined by a respect for this loving lie.

In order for the dying man, his entourage, and the society that observed them to consent to this situation, the protection of the patient had to outweigh the joys of a last communion with him. Let us not forget that in the nineteenth century, death, by virtue of its beauty, had become an occasion for the most perfect union between the one leaving and those remaining behind. The last communion with God and/or with others was the great privilege of the dying.

For centuries there was no question of depriving them of this privilege. But when the lie was maintained to the end, it eliminated this communion and its joys. Even when it was reciprocal and conspiratorial, the lie destroyed the spontaneity and pathos of the last moments.

Actually, the intimacy of these final exchanges had already been poisoned, first by the ugliness of disease, and later by the transfer to the hospital. Death became dirty, and then it became medicalized. The horror and fascination of death had fixed themselves for a moment on the apparent death and had then been sublimated by the beauty of the Last Communion. But the horror returned, without the fascination, in the repellent form of the serious illness and the care it required.

When the last of the traditional defenses against death and sex gave way, the medical profession could have taken over the role of the community. It did so in the case of sex, as is attested by the medical literature on masturbation. It tried to do so in the case of death by isolating it in the scientific laboratory and the hospital, from which the emotions would be banished. Under these conditions it was better to communicate silently in the complicity of a mutual lie.

It is obvious that the sense of the individual and his identity, what we mean when we speak of "possessing one's own death," has been overcome by the solicitude of the family.

But how are we to explain the abdication of the community? How has the community come to reverse its role and to forbid the mourning which it was responsible for imposing until the twentieth century? The answer is that the community feels less and less involved in the death of one of its members. First, because it no longer thinks it necessary to defend itself against a nature which has been domesticated once and for all by the advance of technology, especially medical technology. Next, because it no longer has a sufficient sense of solidarity; it has actually abandoned responsibility for the organization of collective life. The community in the traditional sense of the word no longer exists. It has been replaced by an enormous mass of atomized individuals.

But if this disappearance explains one abdication, it does not explain the powerful resurgence of other prohibitions. This vast and formless mass that we call society is, as we know, maintained and motivated by a new system of constraints and controls. It is also subject to irresistible movements that put it in a state of crisis and impose a transitory unity of aggression or denial. One of these movements has unified mass society against death. More precisely, it has led society to be ashamed of death, more ashamed than afraid, to behave as if death did not exist. If the sense of the other, which is a form of the sense of the self taken to its logical conclusion, is the first cause of the present state of death, then shame—and the resulting taboo—is the second.

But this shame is a direct consequence of the definitive retreat of evil. As early as the eighteenth century, man had begun to reduce the power of the

devil, to question his reality. Hell was abandoned, at least in the case of relatives and dear friends, the only people who counted. Along with hell went sin
and all the varieties of spiritual and moral evil. They were no longer regarded
as part of human nature but as social problems that could be eliminated by a
good system of supervision and punishment. The general advance of science,
morality, and organization would lead quite easily to happiness. But in the
middle of the nineteenth century, there was still the obstacle of physical illness
and death. There was no question of eliminating that. The romantics circum-
vented or assimilated it. They beautified death, the gateway to an anthropomorphic beyond. They preserved its immemorial association with illness, pain,
and agony; these things aroused pity rather than distaste. The trouble began
with distaste: Before people thought of abolishing physical illness, they ceased
to tolerate its sight, sounds, and smells.

Medicine reduced pain; it even succeeded in eliminating it altogether. The
goal glimpsed in the eighteenth century had almost been reached. Evil was no
longer part of human nature, as the religions, especially Christianity, believed.
It still existed, of course, but outside of man, in certain marginal spaces that
morality and politics had not yet colonized, in certain deviant behaviors such
as war, crime, and nonconformity, which had not yet been corrected but which
would one day be eliminated by society just as illness and pain had been eliminated by medicine.

But if there is no more evil, what do we do about death? To this question
modern society offers two answers.

The first is a massive admission of defeat. We ignore the existence of a
scandal that we have been unable to prevent; we act as if it did not exist, and
thus mercilessly force the bereaved to say nothing. A heavy silence has fallen
over the subject of death. When this silence is broken, as it sometimes is in
America today, it is to reduce death to the insignificance of an ordinary event
that is mentioned with feigned indifference. Either way, the result is the same:
Neither the individual nor the community is strong enough to recognize the
existence of death.

And yet this attitude has not annihilated death or the fear of death. On the
contrary, it has allowed the old savagery to creep back under the mask of medical technology. The death of the patient in the hospital, covered with tubes, is
becoming a popular image, more terrifying than the *transi* or skeleton of
macabre rhetoric. There seems to be a correlation between the "evacuation" of death, the last refuge of evil, and the return of this same death, no
longer tame. This should not surprise us. The belief in evil was necessary to
the taming of death; the disappearance of the belief has restored death to its
savage state.

A small elite of anthropologists, psychologists, and sociologists has been
struck by this contradiction. They propose not so much to "evacuate" death
as to humanize it. They acknowledge the necessity of death, but they want it
to be accepted and no longer shameful. Although they may consult the ancient
wisdom, there is no question of turning back or of rediscovering the evil that

has been abolished. They propose to reconcile death with happiness. Death must simply become the discreet but dignified exit of a peaceful person from a helpful society that is not torn, not even overly upset by the idea of a biological transition without significance, without pain or suffering, and ultimately without fear.

Anti-racisim rally in Hamburg, Germany.

(SOURCE: Liaison Agency)

V

TRENDS AND PERSPECTIVES AT THE TURN OF THE CENTURY

What are the leading characteristics and issues in European society at the dawn of the twenty-first century? They include the kinds of consumerism, family patterns, and work/leisure mixture that had taken shape earlier in the century—the values and behaviors discussed in the previous section of this book. Attitudes toward death, similarly, continued to emphasize a decline of ritual, a heavy reliance on convenient practices such as cremation. But there were other trends as well that related the present to the past in ways that raise basic questions about the identity of European society.

Selections in this final section all offer historical perspectives on the contemporary. Some are quite recent, though two, a bit older, have something of a classic status. Thus, Henri Mendras wonders about the deeper impact of the steady decline of Europe's peasantry, while Johan Huizinga goes beyond specific historical considerations in modern leisure to lament a decline of the true spirit of play. Both these characterizations involve trends going back at least to the nineteenth century. Other selections deal with additional developments and issues. A recent German commentary updates the issues of postwar immigration, one of Europe's vital connections with the world at large; the selection insists on the importance of the issue in shaping contemporary Europe, but also its increasing obduracy as Europe faces growing global economic competition and seeks to limit pressure on jobs at home. Identifying a responsible policy toward immigrants may be a measure of Europe's spirit, as well as a determinant of social stability. A sociologist-historian comments on another, less tangible trend: the growing informality of manners and the resultant need for careful personal controls in social relationships. Here, the later twentieth century—Europe since the 1950s, which seems to be the turning point for intimate habits including standards of child rearing—sees a more complex approach to mastery over physical and emotional impulse than was true even a century ago, and across both class and national lines. Finally, a noted British historian looks at what he sees as a dramatically new social and economic structure, in which Western Europe participates along with the world's other advanced industrial societies—but with a distinctive welfare commitment that he views as vital to long-range success.

None of these statements adds up to a tidy package or a definitive determination of where Europe is heading. Will Europe manage to maintain its strong position in world affairs? Is it on the verge of another major social transformation? Some of the trends discussed—the basic quality of modern leisure, problems of racial mixing, and the replacement of more formal behavioral rules—also loom large in other industrial societies as the twenty-first century begins—societies like the United States. But European responses may prove distinctive. Social change continues, and with it the task of intelligent assessment.

BIBLIOGRAPHY

The twentieth-century French peasant has received considerable attention from scholars, many of whom disagree about the extent of traditional behavior in rural society. See Gordon Wright, *Rural Revolution in France: The Peasantry in the Twentieth Century* (Stanford, CA, 1968), and Robert T. and Barbara G. Anderson, *Bus Stop for Paris* (New York, 1966). Lawrence W. Wylie, ed., *Chanzeaux: A Village in Anjou* (Cambridge, MA, 1966), studies a particularly conservative region; see also Wylie's *Village in the Vaucluse* (Cambridge, MA, 1957). A fine study of leisure is Michael Smith, Stanley Parker, and Cyril Smith, eds., *Leisure and Society in Britain* (London, 1973); see also Alisdair Clayre, *Work and Play: Ideas and Experience of Work and Leisure* (New York, 1974).

On changes in contemporary society, see David Riesman, *The Lonely Crowd* (New Haven, CT, 1968); and Christopher Lasch, *The Culture of Narcissism* (New York, 1978), and *Haven in a Heartless World* (New York, 1977) on dominant attitudes.

On technology and social structure, see Daniel Bell, *The Coming of Post-Industrial Society* (New York, 1973); and Alvin Toffler, *Future Shock* (New York, 1971) and *The Third Wave* (New York, 1981). These studies refer to the United States primarily, and have been much debated. Some comparable analysis of Europe can be found in the special issues of *Daedalus,* Vol. 108 numbers 1 and 2 (1979), which also discuss the variety of problems that beset contemporary Europe. Older but more optimistic evaluations of Europe's revival include Michel Crozier, *The Renaissance of Contemporary Europe* (New York, 1968); and Stephen R. Graubard, ed., *A New Europe?* (Boston, 1963). On Europe's technocratic elite and social structure, see Michael Young, *The Rise of the Meritocracy* (London, 1958); and Ralf Dahrendorf, *Class and Class Conflict in Industrial Society* (Stanford, CA, 1959). For historical perspective, see Harold Perkin, *The Rise of Professional Society: England Since 1880* (London, 1989).

On twentieth-century emotional change, several American studies are useful (including the David Riesman and Christopher Lasch titles mentioned previously)— Peter N. Stearns, *American Cool: Developing a Twentieth Century Emotional Style* (New York, 1994), and Arlie Russell Hochschild, *The Managed Heart— Commercialization of Human Feeling* (Berkeley, 1983). See also Michael Crozier, *The World of the Office Worker* (Chicago, 1971).

42

THE VANISHING PEASANT

HENRI MENDRAS

Just as the peasantry epitomized the character of traditional society—to the extent that generalizations about the one may too easily be used to describe the other—so industrialization seems ultimately to destroy the peasant spirit. Some of the first societies to move toward basic change had a distinctive rural population early on—perhaps lacking a real peasant class at all; the earlier selection by James Sharpe (see Chapter 6) suggests that key aspects of the peasant mentality were being eroded in Britain as early as the seventeenth century. Elsewhere the peasant spirit was stronger, for example, as it confronted a modern educational system in France as late as the nineteenth century. But structural change, through expansion of the cities and industrial production, everywhere reduced the relative numbers and economic importance of the peasantry. Henri Mendras, a noted French sociologist, argues that in recent decades the final vestiges of the peasant mentality have been disappearing as well. Here indeed is one measure of how far change has gone and what it means in terms of traditional values: the farming population is converted to a market orientation and manifests the behavior, including the family relationships, that accompanies such orientation. It is important to recall that this process was not sudden, that an identifiable peasantry long held out against complete change. Indeed, against Mendras' argument, we may see remnants of the peasant outlook even in city dwellers who have preserved some of the habits of their ancestors—in reactions to health problems, for example.

Mendras does more than note the disappearance of a basic way of life. He mourns it. The erosion of the peasantry is not an unalloyed triumph of progress over superstition. Mendras reminds us that the peasantry had virtues whose absence may endanger the civilization that uprooted them. Certain kinds of family ties, an attachment to the soil and a willingness to conserve resources to protect future generations, a sense of continuity—these qualities and more may now be irrevocably lost. How much will we suffer as a result? Can we strive to restore some of the solidarity that a peasantry traditionally offered? Should we in fact abandon the basic course of modernization in

From: Henri Mendras, *The Vanishing Peasant* (Cambridge, MA: M.I.T. Press, 1970), pp. 5–61. Published in French by S.E.D.E.I.S., Paris, under the title *La Fin des Paysans, Innovation et Changement dans l'Agriculture Française.*

favor of a return to a more tested social structure, and can we do so even if we wish? The decline of the peasantry may also relate to the new pessimism about Europe's future, increasingly under the sway of shallow materialist values and growing American influence.

Most historians of agriculture in this country have admired the "French prudence" (*sagesse française*) that kept the nation from pushing the agricultural revolution of the eighteenth century to extreme social consequences and enabled us to conserve a large peasant class, while the British, yielding to the logic of the industrial economy, sacrificed their agriculture to the development of industry. In a way, France stopped in her tracks; she paused for a century and a half while her peasants, though slowly accepting technological innovations, remained peasants.

Today, the second agricultural revolution is upsetting every structure, and the dependable equilibrium has been disturbed. Agriculture, in its turn, is becoming "industrialized," and the French peasantry is being destroyed, one hundred fifty years later, by what we call industrial civilization. Suddenly we feel very close to the eighteenth century. We are rediscovering that nature can be subdued by technology, that agrarian history is marked by constant advances, innovations, and improvements, and that the farmers are living in turmoil.

We live essentially on ideas that were bequeathed us by the nineteenth century, and are today obviously anachronistic. It is important to revise these ideas and to look at the countryside with a new eye; otherwise we will remain blind to the great movement that is carrying the agrarian societies of the entire world toward a complete remodeling of their technology and their social equilibrium. The disappearance of the peasant in countries that have industrialized the most rapidly is due less to the force of economic circumstances than to the misapplication to agriculture of analytical methods, legislative measures, and administrative decisions that were not designed for it.

In countries such as England or the United States, where it was wholly subordinated to the logic of industrial society, agriculture remains an irreducible political and social problem, which seriously concerns leaders in Washington and London. . . .

Peasant society is subdivided into local communities that exist in relative demographic, economic, and cultural autarchy. According to Marx's famous image, the French peasantry of the last century resembled "potatoes in a sack," each community being a social entity, each being unique although all the communities were of the same kind.

Each community is a face-to-face group in which everybody knows everyone else in all his aspects. Its social relations are thus personal and not functional or segmentary. The community unites peasants (independent farmers, stockbreeders, landowners, cultivators, or salaried workers and their families) and nonpeasants (notables, artisans and merchants, and so on); but the dominant tone of the society is set by the peasants. Power belongs normally to the notables, who are in a marginal position between the local community and the broader society. The principal cleavages are often hierarchical in nature, according to a scale of socioeconomic prestige. If not, they can be of an ideological, ecological, or family nature in the larger sense: there is often no clear distinction between blood relatives and business connections. Finally, categories of age and sex are in general strongly individualized.

In communities as highly structured as this, everything contributes to the stability of the whole, and change can be introduced only by consensus, so slowly as to deny that it is change. These communities are not inflexible, but, except in a grave crisis, they evolve slowly to the rhythm of generations. Every innovation, whether it be technological, economic, or demographic, comes from the outside. In the words of Albert Dauzat, a man hardly to be suspected of prejudice on this subject, "The countryside has created nothing; everything comes to it from the city—dress, customs, songs. . . ." and one could add machines and technology.

In such a social system, the individual does not have to adapt himself to new decisions or make decisions himself; neither does he have to express or reveal himself to others, who know him from every point of view. Hence he has a tendency to remain true to himself and to the image others have of him. Showing or expressing sentiments and personal opinions is not encouraged by the code of values and norms. . . .

The agricultural revolution of the eighteenth century required more than a hundred years to carry its advances into the French countryside. It took place in the rhythm of a traditional society that industry had not yet modified. While it brought social change, supported and sometimes accelerated by political revolution, the essential character of village society remained unaltered. After a century of continual rural exodus, the present revolution in France is reducing the number of farmers at the bewildering rate of 160,000 per year, both through the death of farmers without successors and through the movement of young farmers into other professions. Those who remain become correspondingly richer and can meet the new exigencies of economy and technology, but not without completely upsetting village society. . . .

The ease with which peasants formed in the traditional world can move in a modern world is a source of constant surprise to the observer. Provided that they enter into a coherent and significant economic game, "economic motivations" come to young farmers with disconcerting rapidity. Moreover, when they travel from their farms, these untrained country bumpkins show an amazing aptitude for creating new institutions that are perfectly adapted to modern conditions, such as C.E.T.A. (Center for Technical Farm Studies). . . . Under their constant pressure, modern methods of farm accounting have been introduced in France, and it is in response to their demands that rural economics has come out of its age-old lethargy.

What truth is more self-evident, what fact better substantiated, than the peasant's individualism and love of his land? He gives his life's blood to enlarge his fields, and then fences himself in on his property with fierce independence, like a petty king in his kingdom. Nevertheless for half a century it is in the area of agriculture that cooperation has known its greatest success. Buying and marketing cooperatives, mutual insurance societies, farm credit associations . . . —no other sector of production can offer such a variety of cooperative organizations. Today some farmers are attempting the final step by joining their lands and grouping them into larger units where each product constitutes a workshop under the responsibility of one of the cooperating parties. Such experiments in "group farming" are not proceeding without difficulties, in the absence of legislation and established customs; for these pioneers must invent everything themselves until such time as economists, legislators, and public authorities have codified their experiments.

In devoting themselves enthusiastically to this total remodeling of their social and technical structures, the farmers have the feeling that they are making up for lost time and creating a place for themselves in the era of industrial civilization. Once the crisis of adjustment has passed, they hope in a confused way to rediscover the equilibrium their fathers knew. Having assimilated some new techniques and accepted some economic regulations, they expect to recreate a system of cultivation and independent farming as durable as the previous one. But modern technological civilization lives on continual change and dooms the quietude of immutable habits. Far from rediscovering traditional stability, the peasant will in his turn settle into the perpetual change of technological innovation and economic contingency. Furthermore, he is setting up, more or less consciously, the institutions that will help him to do this. Centers of management and rural economics study the evolution of markets and direct the management of farm workers accordingly. Services for agronomical research and agricultural extension complete the chain that progressively adapts the scientific discoveries of the laboratory so that they can be used by the farmer in his field.

Peasant values, so highly esteemed since the time of Xenophon and Virgil, and heretofore at the very heart of our Western civilization, will not be able to survive the shakeup of their ancient stability. The eternal "peasant soul" is dying before our eyes, just as is the patriarchal family domain founded on subsistence polycultivation. It is the final battle of industrial society against the last stronghold of traditional civilization. What we are undertaking here, then, is not simply a study of a new agricultural revolution but a study of the disappearance of traditional peasant civilization, which is a fundamental element of Western civilization and Christianity, and its replacement by the new modern technological civilization, which will often take on different forms in the country from those it presently assumes in the city. . . .

In most French regions the farmers are still . . . "real" peasants. The sentiments that tie them to their land have until now been the subject of only one pilot study of a limited region. . . . It is enough to point out here how impossible it is to isolate the land from its entire natural setting, human and social. For the farmer the word "land" evokes simultaneously the soil he works, the farm that has supported his family for generations, and the profession he follows, as well as the peasant condition and the whole body of the nation's farmers. During an interview he jumps from one meaning to another without seeming to realize that these meanings are separate and distinct; and at the same time he says repeatedly that the sentiments evoked by this word are ineffable, that they exist but cannot be expressed. To make them understood, he calls on the interviewer's experience: "If you're from the country, you know what I mean."

On the other hand, a big farmer from the Paris basin can refuse to purchase the fields he works because it is economically more advantageous for him to rent them and invest his capital in livestock and machinery. During an interview, his "economic rationality" is visibly in conflict with his "peasant sentiments," as when he seeks to justify his refusal to buy his land by showing his contempt for it: "It's a poor piece of land where a man wouldn't want to settle his family." Or again, by reducing it to nothing: "This piece of land is like any other . . . nowadays the land doesn't count any more. . . ." To reduce to naught or curse the land one refuses to own betrays sentiments similar to those the "peasant" feels but refuses to express. However, other farmers are able to analyze the origin of these sentiments, if not their content, in astonishingly lucid terms: "To know one's land, to improve it, takes a long time! And the more you know it, the more you become attached to it." Such statements, almost evangelical in tone, are an admission of the fact that sentiment and ownership go together: "What belongs, belongs . . . a peasant is a proprietor of the land. . . . When a man is a proprietor, he has a feeling and a concern for the land." As opposed to the big farmer, and contrary to all economic analysis, a small proprietor can state: "Rented land is expensive and amounts to nothing."

Thus the peasant has a deep conviction that his field is unique because he is the only one to know it, to love it and to own it: knowledge, love, and possession are inseparable. And even when the farmer behaves in a rational economic fashion with respect to land as capital, his feelings for the soil are no less diffuse or deep; he identifies it intimately with his family and his profession, thus with himself. It can be said that these feelings are largely the product of a historical situation that is on the way to extinction, and that they will outlive it by some years. Moreover, they are already disparaged by the ideology that the new generation is fashioning for itself. Young people think that the cultivators should be relieved of land ownership, and that the latter should be considered solely as a factor of production, by farmers as well as by public authorities and capitalists. . . .

As mechanization became general, the concept of technological and urban time invaded agricultural work and introduced into it the new unit of the hour. This concept came first with the threshing contractor, who asked to be paid by the hour; soon the farmer who came with his machine to plow his neighbor's field did the same; and today young farmers, mindful of how profitable their tractors or harvester-threshers can be, keep a notebook in which they carefully record their hours of work and the liters of fuel burned. For the first time abstract time, made up of equal units, has entered into agricultural work. It is tending gradually to modify the time scale of an ever-increasing number of tasks. Thus the process of replacing one concept of time by another can be seen through many easily-measurable indices and hence can be observed by the sociologist with exceptional clarity. . . .

Hourly time already existed in country life. Every farm kitchen displayed proudly a clock with a long pendulum, and most of the farmers had pocket watches. According to the French Institute of Public Opinion, 47 percent of farmers did not carry a watch on their persons in 1953 (compared with 34 percent of the population as a whole). In daily life these instruments served to indicate the progress of the day more than to fix the time exactly or indicate the beginning or end of some activity. Witness to an external civilization, they were employed to "tell time" only when in contact with this civilization, when one must be "on time": to send the children to school, to catch the train or bus, to attend a meeting. And in the latter case, if it was an appointment with neighbors or other country people, everyone knew it was not necessary to be punctual.

Today, on the contrary, as meetings become more frequent all the time, young people particularly want them to start punctually in order not to "lose time"; this is one of the indices which reveal the passage from the peasant to the modern concept of time. In the past, since the means of transportation were slow, people would go to town for the day or half a day if they had a meeting. The meeting began when everyone had arrived at the city hall, the cooperative, or the school. People took advantage of the trip to do other errands or to chat with each other. Now they take the car or the motorbike in order to arrive in time for the meeting and leave immediately afterward if work is pressing. This change in customs was surprising to the rural researcher who went from a French village to an American one in 1950; today it can be observed in every French village.

One must not, however, conclude from our analysis that this concept of "flowing, dreamy" time, vague and slow-moving, was of no value whatever [for traditional peasants]. . . . Most French peasants . . . do not allow themselves to waste time. Time is so closely connected with the work experience that wasted time is wasted work; it is laziness to put off till tomorrow what one can do today. These two examples suffice to show how dangerous it would be to settle for a simplistic contrast between two extreme types. In each civilization the notion of time is closely linked to the system of values and the organization of daily life. In France we would have to undertake a study, region by region, to try to explain why some have rapidly accepted certain elements of modern time and others have proved more resistant. . . .

But, some will say, how are our traditionalist peasants going to shed the old self so abruptly and take on a new self? The peasant soul will survive the cataclysm that you forecast, if, indeed, it is to come. One has only to open a newspaper to dismiss this objection: there one sees article after article on progressive young farmers, on demonstrations, on conferences where the vocabulary of technical and economic efficiency has replaced the political and moral vocabulary that was in style only a few years ago.

On this point our studies are convincing: if economic structures are changed within a region, they will within a few years change the mentality of the inhabitants. It is striking to see the ease with which peasants formed in a traditional economic and social system can be moved to a modern system, given a few conditions—particularly that the coherence of the new system be rapidly established, visible, and comprehensible. It does not take the young farmers long to acquire "economic motivations," if only these have a meaning and are part of a coherent economic game that permits a glimpse of a successful future.

With astonishingly sure intuition they create entirely new institutions perfectly adapted to modern conditions. . . . But in reconstructing a new society on the dismantled structures of family, farm, and village, they sound the knell of the last vestiges of the peasantry in France, who will not survive their generation.

Thus, with them, the peasantry will itself be extinguished. And what will a world without peasants be like?

43

Modern Man at Play

JOHAN HUIZINGA

There is little doubt that the values of modern society remain confused in the areas of play and leisure. In a period when more and more time is spent not working (due to shorter work days, longer vacations, and earlier retirement), we continue to define work as reality. Our schools, among other things, train students for the job with an often narrow passion. Yet there are observers who hold that leisure, defined as nonwork time in which an individual chooses among diversions, is a phenomenon of modernization.

In this selection, Johan Huizinga, a noted Dutch historian whose interests range from the Middle Ages to (rather pessimistic) assessments about modern life, judges that modernity has indeed brought about a distinct and unfortunate trend in the area of play. His views should be compared with the specific assessments of leisure and recreation in premodern societies and during the industrialization process. Some of the trends that developed when modern leisure was born, in the later nineteenth century, may still constrain leisure today. Did school sports, for example, permit play? Insofar as Huizinga focuses on play, which is by nature particularly childlike, his opinions relate also to changes in the treatment and conception of childhood and youth. Quite possibly, in our desire to find purpose in activity (of which education and educational toys are one expression), we have indeed limited the spirit of play.

But do we need play? What is it, in contrast to other uses of leisure? Huizinga ironically suggests that we are substituting play for seriousness in work. Yet one could argue that modern life is excitingly recasting the definitions of seriousness and nonseriousness. But, if this is the case, it is largely unwitting. The modern form of life is so new—for example, the amount of time available for nonwork—that we may have difficulty in defining our own mentality, in adjusting our values to our behavior.

Huizinga certainly points to an area far removed from most of the standard valuations of the gains and losses involved in developing an advanced industrial society. His own judgment coincides with a pessimistic modernization thesis: We have lost a valued part of our own tradition. It coincides also with many of the criticisms of contemporary leisure that are made without definite

From: Johan Huizinga, *Homo Ludens: A Study of the Play Element in Culture* (New York: Roy Publishers, 1950), pp. 195–200.

historical criteria: modern people do not know how to relax; we are dominated by remote commercial media rather than really choosing our own leisure; mass taste is degraded, regimented taste. Have we lost a vital capacity to enjoy, to indulge in purposeless expression, and with this a key source of mental balance? Or are we groping to use our undeniably increased material resources to make life itself a form of play?

One other point: Huizinga's judgment was written a half century ago. It remains widely cited as an interpretive framework in dealing with modern society, but it may now be dated. Western Europe, particularly, has seen an explosion of leisure in recent decades, including substantial annual vacations for the middle classes and portions of the working classes (see Chapter 38). Countries like France have "Ministries of Free Time," suggesting the importance of a new type of leisure commitment. However provocative Huizinga's judgment about play—and it is vital to remember he distinguishes it from mere leisure, which he acknowledges—has recent social change outstripped it? Might Huizinga's views better fit societies like the United States and Japan, that have lagged behind Western Europe in leisure commitments?

The question to which we address ourselves is this: To what extent does the civilization we live in still develop in play-forms? How far does the play-spirit dominate the lives of those who share that civilization? The 19th century, we observed, had lost many of the play-elements so characteristic of former ages. Has this leeway been made up or has it increased?

It might seem at first sight that certain phenomena in modern social life have more than compensated for the loss of play-forms. Sport and athletics, as social functions, have steadily increased in scope and conquered ever fresh fields both nationally and internationally.

Contests in skill, strength and perseverance have, as we have shown, always occupied an important place in every culture either in connection with ritual or simply for fun and festivity. Feudal society was only really interested in the tournament; the rest was just popular recreation and nothing more. Now the tournament, with its highly dramatic staging and aristocratic embellishments, can hardly be called a sport. It fulfilled one of the functions of the theatre. Only a numerically small upper class took active part in it. This one-sidedness of mediaeval sporting life was due in large measure to the influence of the Church. The Christian ideal left but little room for the organized practice of sport and the cultivation of bodily exercise, except insofar as the latter contributed to gentle education. Similarly, the Renaissance affords fairly numerous examples of body-training cultivated for the sake of perfection, but only on the part of individuals, never groups or classes. If anything, the emphasis laid by the Humanists on learning and erudition tended to perpetuate the old under-estimation of the body, likewise the moral zeal and severe intellectuality of the Reformation and Counter-Reformation. The recognition of games and bodily exercises as important cultural values was withheld right up to the end of the 18th century.

The basic forms of sportive competition are, of course, constant through the ages. In some the trial of strength and speed is the whole essence of the contest, as in running and skating matches, chariot and horse races, weight-lifting, swimming, diving, marksmanship, etc. Though human beings have indulged in such activities since the dawn of time, these only take on the character of organized games to a very slight degree. Yet nobody, bearing in mind the agonistic principle which animates them, would hesitate to call them games in the sense of play—which, as we have seen, can be very serious indeed. There are, however, other forms of contest which develop of their own accord into "sports." These are the ball-games.

What we are concerned with here is the transition from occasional amusement to the system of organized clubs and matches. Dutch pictures of the 17th century show us burghers and peasants intent upon their game of *kolf,* but, so far as I know, nothing is heard of games being organized in clubs or played as matches. It is obvious that a fixed organization of this kind will most readily occur when two groups play against one another. The great ball-games in particular require the existence of permanent teams, and herein lies the starting-point of modern sport. The process arises quite spontaneously in the meeting of village against village, school against school, one part of a town against the rest, etc. That the process started in 19th-century England is understandable up to a point, though how far the specifically Anglo-Saxon bent of mind can be deemed an efficient cause is less certain. But it cannot be doubted that the structure of English social life had much to do with it. Local self-government encouraged the spirit of association and solidarity. The absence of obligatory military training favoured the occasion for, and the need of, physical exercise. The peculiar form of education tended to work in the same direction, and finally the geography of the country and the nature of the terrain, on the whole flat and, in the ubiquitous commons, offering the most perfect playing-fields that could be desired, were of the greatest importance. Thus England became the cradle and focus of modern sporting life.

Ever since the last quarter of the 19th century, games, in the guise of sport, have been taken more and more seriously. The rules have become increasingly strict and elaborate. Records are established at a higher, or faster, or longer level than was ever conceivable before. Everybody knows the delightful prints from the first half of the 19th century, showing the cricketers in top-hats. This speaks for itself.

Now, with the increasing systemization and regimentation of sport, something of the pure play-quality is inevitably lost. We see this very clearly in the official distinction between amateurs and professionals (or "gentlemen and players" as used pointedly to be said). It means that the play-group marks out those for whom playing is no longer play, ranging them inferior to the true players in standing but superior in capacity. The spirit of the professional is no longer the true play-spirit; it is lacking in spontaneity and carelessness. This affects the amateur too, who begins to suffer from an inferiority complex. Between them they push sport further and further away from the play-sphere proper until it becomes a thing *sui generis:* neither play nor earnest. In modern social life sport occupies a place alongside and apart from the cultural process. The great competitions in archaic cultures had always formed part of the sacred festivals and were indispensable as health and happiness-bringing activities. This ritual tie has now been completely severed; sport has become profane, "unholy" in every way and has no organic connection whatever with the structure of society, least of all when prescribed by the government. The ability of modern social techniques to stage mass demonstrations with the maximum of outward show in the field of athletics does not alter the fact that neither the Olympiads nor the organized sports of American Universities nor the loudly trumpeted international contests have, in the smallest degree, raised sport to the level of a culture-creating activity. However important it may be for the players or spectators, it remains sterile. The old play-factor has undergone almost complete atrophy.

This view will probably run counter to the popular feeling of to-day, according to which sport is the apotheosis of the play-element in our civilization. Nevertheless popular feeling is wrong. By way of emphasizing the fatal shift towards over-seriousness we would point out that it has also infected the non-athletic games where calculation is everything, such as chess and some card-games.

A great many board-games have been known since the earliest times, some even in primitive society, which attached great importance to them largely on account of their chanceful character. Whether they are games of chance or skill they all contain an element of seriousness. The merry play-mood has little scope here, particularly where chance is at a minimum as in chess, draughts, backgammon, halma, etc. Even so all these games remain within the definition of play. . . . Only recently has publicity seized on them and annexed them to athletics by means of public championships, world tournaments, registered records and press reportage in a literary style of its own, highly ridiculous to the innocent outsider.

Card-games differ from board-games in that they never succeed in eliminating chance completely. To the extent that chance predominates they fall into the category of gambling and, as such, are little suited to club life and public competition. The more intellectual card-games, on the other hand, leave plenty of room for associative tendencies. It is in this field that the shift towards seriousness and over-seriousness is so striking. From the days of *ombre* and *quadrille* to whist and bridge, card-games have undergone a process of increasing refinement, but only with bridge have the modern social techniques made themselves master of the game. The paraphernalia of handbooks and systems and professional training has made bridge a deadly earnest business. A recent newspaper article estimated that yearly winnings of the Culbertson couple [winners of bridge competitions] at more than two hundred thousand dollars. An enormous amount of mental energy is expended in this universal craze for bridge with no more tangible result than the exchange of relatively unimportant sums of money. Society as a whole is neither benefited nor damaged by this futile activity. It seems difficult to speak of it as an elevating recreation in the sense of Aristotle's *diagoge*. Proficiency at bridge is a sterile excellence, sharpening the mental faculties very one-sidedly without enriching the soul in any way, fixing and consuming a quantity of intellectual energy that might have been better applied. The most we can say, I think, is that it might have been applied worse. The status of bridge in modern society would indicate, to all appearances, an immense increase in the play-element today. But appearances are deceptive. Really to play, a man must play like a child. Can we assert that this is so in the case of such an ingenious game as bridge? If not, the virtue has gone out of the game.

The attempt to assess the play-content in the confusion of modern life is bound to lead us to contradictory conclusions. In the case of sport we have an activity nominally known as play but raised to such a pitch of technical organization and scientific thoroughness that the real play-spirit is threatened with extinction. Over against this tendency to overseriousness, however, there are other phenomena pointing in the opposite direction. Certain activities whose whole *raison d'être* lies in the field of material interest, and which had nothing of play about them in their initial stages, develop what we can only call play-forms as a secondary characteristic. Sport and athletics showed us play stiffening into seriousness but still being felt as play; now we come to serious business degenerating into play but still being called serious. The two phenomena are linked by the strong agonistic habit which still holds universal sway, though in other forms than before.

The impetus given to this agonistic principle which seems to be carrying the world back in the direction of play derives, in the main, from external factors independent of culture proper—in a word, communications, which have made intercourse of every sort so extraordinarily easy for mankind as a whole. Technology, publicity and propaganda everywhere promote the competitive spirit and afford means of satisfying it on an unprecedented scale. Commercial competition does not, of course, belong to the immemorial sacred play-forms. It only appears when trade begins to create fields of activity within which each must try to surpass and outwit his neighbour. Commercial rivalry soon makes limiting rules imperative, namely the trading customs. It remained primitive in essence until quite late, only becoming really intensive with the advent of modern communications, propaganda and statistics. Naturally a certain play-element had entered into business competition at an early stage. Statistics stimulated it with an idea that had originally arisen in sporting life, the idea, namely, of trading records. A record, as the word shows, was once simply a memorandum, a note which the innkeeper scrawled on the walls of his inn to say that such and such a rider or traveller had been the first to arrive after covering so and so many miles. The statistics of trade and production could not fail to introduce a sporting element into economic life. In consequence, there is now a sporting side to almost every triumph of commerce or technology: the highest turnover, the biggest tonnage, the fastest crossing, the greatest altitude, etc. Here a purely ludic element has, for once, got the better of utilitarian considerations, since the experts inform us that smaller units—less monstrous steamers and aircraft, etc.—are more efficient in the long run. Business becomes play. This process goes so far that some of the great business concerns deliberately instil the play-spirit into their workers so as to step up production. The trend is now reversed: play becomes business. A captain of industry, on whom the Rotterdam Academy of Commerce had conferred an honorary degree, spoke as follows:

> Ever since I first entered the business it had been a race between the technicians and the sales department. One tried to produce so much that the sales department would never be able to sell it, while the other tried to sell so much that the technicians would never be able to keep pace. This race has always continued: sometimes one is ahead, sometimes the other. Neither my brother nor myself has regarded the business as a task, but always as a game, the spirit of which it has been our constant endeavour to implant into the younger staff.

These words must, of course, be taken with a grain of salt. Nevertheless there are numerous instances of big concerns forming their own Sports Societies and even engaging workers with a view not so much to their professional capacities as to their fitness for the football eleven. Once more the wheel turns.

44

REACTIONS AGAINST IMMIGRANTS

KLAUS J. BADE

The following selection, by a German historian specializing in the contemporary period, deals with the complex reactions to immigration in the 1980s and 1990s (see also Chapter. 39), while also looking to the future. Western Europe at this point was facing growing levels of economic competition from other parts of the world, leading to slower economic growth and rising unemployment. The earlier boom period, in which immigrant labor had been encouraged, if also discriminated against, had clearly ended. Various tensions, including racist reactions to immigrant populations, encouraged new political assaults and outright violence against foreigners. This problem surfaced in most European countries, and prompted worries about a right-wing political resurgence that would build on, but also exacerbate, these new targets for social tension.

Problems were not necessarily greater in Germany than elsewhere—France, for example, had the fastest-growing right-wing political party—but they were more noticeable. Germany's National Socialist (Nazi) past inevitably called attention to racist activity, and might also contribute some special causes to this activity. Germany's economic boom but also the dislocations after World War II had caused unusually large immigration waves. Finally, the reunification between West Germany (Federal Republic) and the previously communist East (German Democratic Republic, or GDR) caused relevant internal pressures and dislocations, which could lead to outbreaks against foreigners.

Germans worried about these complex issues and what they implied for the future. The following selection suggests how anti-foreign activities could be explained, and what policy moves had been attempted to deal both with immigration and with racism as problems. It ends with some obviously liberal suggestions for a recasting of outlook.

United Germany as a destination for immigrants raises hopes and fears. Dreams and nightmares collide at its borders: those who are outside dream of

From: Klaus J. Bade, "Immigration and Social Peace in United Germany," *Daedalus* 123 (1994): 85–87, 89–90, 94–96, 100–01.

entering; those who are inside fear outsiders will indeed come and demand a share of the imagined fortune at the center of the continent which, it is said, lies in Germany.

AGGRESSION AND VIOLENCE

At the start of the 1990s, public discussion in united Germany is marked by fear of a growing, aggressive xenophobia, acceptance of violence against foreigners, and, correspondingly, a growing number of perpetrators and victims. Young people are especially well represented among the aggressors, under the influence of the radical Right. After unification (in 1990), first in the Eastern and then also in the Western parts of Germany, foreigners were openly attacked and hunted down in the streets, with the slogans "foreigners out" and "Germany for the Germans."

In the beginning, the victims of such violence were primarily asylum seekers hoping to find refuge from political, racial, or religious persecution, from war, poverty, and destitution in the crisis areas of the world. Soon the daytime encounters became arson attacks at night: first, and still, mostly on shelters for asylum seekers, but also on domiciles of ethnic Germans from Eastern Europe. In addition, since 1992, attacks have increasingly been aimed at the Turks—the largest group of "local foreigners," originating from the former population of "guest workers," living in united Germany. "Hoyerswerda" (September 1991) and "Rostock-Lichtenhagen" (August 1992), where attacks on asylum seekers were applauded by the public, have become worldwide known catchwords for the new terror in Germany. Arson attacks on Turks, long-term residents of Germany, in Mölln and Solingen have been similarly commemorated. Aggression has also been directed against the Romanies [gypsies], who already in the darkest epoch of German history were victims of government-organized crime. Since the 1980s, they have immigrated to Germany in large numbers. In addition, a growing number of anti-Semitic offenses have been noted, however, they do not include physical attacks on Jews who have lived in Germany all along or who returned after the Holocaust or on those who immigrated from the former Soviet Union during the past few years, but rather attacks on memorials of the Holocaust and Jewish cemeteries. Even the homeless and the handicapped have become victims of right-wing aggression.

This is more than "simple" hostility toward foreigners and outsiders. It is xenophobic violence originating from a lack of perspective, lack of orientation, and social fear, as well as frustration and aggression. The search for the sources of this new threat to society has become a focus of social science research and of public and published discussion in united Germany.

The new xenophobia is neither "fascist" nor distinctly "German." It also exists in other European countries with similar problems. But in Germany it exists in the shadow of a history that makes brutality against minorities seem even more gruesome. This fact and pronounced media interest in xenophobic aggressiveness have led to distortions and misinterpretations. Normal peaceful coexistence in united Germany is thus overlooked as are the "foreigner friendly" countermovements and helpful initiatives: the human chains of candle light in the winter of 1992; the vast numbers of organized and spontaneous offers for help in daily life; the taking in and caring for refugees; and the provision of illegal hiding places for asylum seekers whose applications have been denied and who are to be extradited.

This highly complex set of problems is usually discussed in only partially accurate, and therefore highly simplified catchwords such as "hostility toward foreigners," "xenophobia," "right-wing extremism," or "youth violence." Apart from the socioanthropological, bioevolutionary, and even sociobiological assessments diagnosing as a "natural" state of social behavior fear of that which is foreign, which sometimes legitimize xenophobia in the simplistic and coarse versions of public discussion, a variety of more or less broad attempts at explanation and interpretation of the causes are in circulation. Of those, only a few can be mentioned here. An important motive undoubtedly lies in the continued disorientation of the population about social problems relating to immigration and integration. The reason lies in a kind of emphatic political denial that the Federal Republic has become a new kind of country of immigration—not in a legal but in a social and cultural sense. . . . Taking into account the 4.8 million foreign minorities in 1990, the total number of people who immigrated since 1945 corresponded to one-third of the West German inhabitants in 1990. No comparable situation exists among Western industrialized nations in the second half of this century. Since 1987, the Federal Republic has absorbed more immigrants annually than the two classic immigration countries, Canada and Australia, combined. Yet, government declarations insist that Germany is not an "immigration country."

Overall, three different processes of integration of foreigners can be distinguished in West Germany since World War II: (1) the integration of refugees and expellees; (2) the evolution of the "guest workers issue" into an immigration problem; and (3) the new immigration situation in united Germany.

Refugees and expellees from East Germany and from Eastern Europe fled or were expelled primarily because of National Socialist politics, the war initiated by Germany, and the horrors of German occupation. Many were still foreigners in their new homeland when the German-Italian treaty of 1955 gave the signal for the officially organized recruitment of a foreign work force for the labor market of the Federal Republic. In contrast to the "foreign migrant workers" of the German Empire and the "foreign workers" in National Socialist Germany, those affected by the treaty of 1955 were publicly called "guest workers." A "guest," however, is someone who does not stay permanently.

At no time in the history of the Federal Republic has a comprehensive and long-term concept existed for the permanent integration of an immigrant population. For decades, the "politics concerning foreigners" were characterized by reactive social repair work without long-term organizational principles.

Foreign workers, in the 1960s, established residence for increasingly longer periods. This led to a full fledged immigration problem, unsuccessfully "denied" by the government. After the construction of the Berlin Wall on the Western border of the GDR [East Germany], and in conjunction with the related termination of a steady influx of workers from East to West Germany, the number of foreign workers in West Germany quickly rose into the millions. Approximately fourteen million people came during that time, of which eleven million returned to their home countries. The official recruiting process lasted until the worldwide economic crisis of 1973. Of the foreign population in West Germany, numbering approximately 4.8 million in 1990, almost three million were guest workers (or descendants thereof) from former recruitment countries.

The guest worker period ended with the "Recruitment Stop" of 1973. It had a boomerang effect on German politics regarding foreigners: for a short time it decreased the numbers of foreigners, but by lowering the transnational flux of migrant workers, it further strengthened the already growing tendency toward permanent residence. Foreign workers who did not want to be separated forever from their families still living in the country of origin were faced with the alternative of permanently returning to the homeland or moving their families to the Federal Republic. Most remained in Germany, and by 1979, the migration of their families raised the foreign population in the Federal Republic beyond the level of 1973.

With the increasing length of residence came the transition from guest worker to immigrant. At the start of the 1980s, a significant part of the foreign minority already derived from the former guest worker population. They lived in the paradoxical situation of being permanently integrated immigrants without an immigrant country. Even at the start of the 1990s, the declaration "The Federal Republic is not a country of immigration" continued to be the common denominator transcending all party lines regarding not "immigration politics" but "politics concerning foreigners." . . .

The number of refugees from Eastern Europe and the Third World seeking asylum in the Federal Republic has strongly increased since the 1980s. As of July 1, 1993, a new, restrictive German asylum law is in effect. Those coming from "persecution-free" countries or entering Europe via "safe third countries" have, as a general rule, no chance of being granted asylum. This could increase the already high number of illegal immigrants and the periods of residence of those who have not filed an application for asylum. A relatively recent phenomenon in Germany is the immigration of Jews from the former Soviet Union. It is skeptically watched by Israel and in early 1993 already included an estimated fifteen thousand people.

In addition to immigration across German borders, there are two major problems of internal integration in united Germany. First, those who came to the West in great numbers at the end of the 1980s as GDR refugees still suffer identity problems. Once in the West, many of them suffered culture shock: it was evidence of how great the distance had become not only in terms of lifestyle and material culture, but also in ways of thinking. . . .

The pressure of immigration from the outside grew into a "new mass-migration," an "invasion of the poor," an "onslaught on Europe," and was frightfully exaggerated in sensational reports by the media and in widely distributed horror publications. The fear of foreigners grew accordingly, in an immigration situation without guidelines. In the summer of 1991, the government deputy in charge of immigration affairs, Liselotte Funcke, resigned, thereby protesting the continued absence of political direction. The government blatantly ignored the resignation and seemed in no hurry to replace the person in charge of this important, but insufficiently funded, office.

The unrest continued to grow in large parts of the population, inflamed by the demagoguery of press reports during the "summer doldrums." Responses by the government, primarily concerned with problems of unification, showed continued helplessness on issues of immigration and integration. But the polemic rebuttals between government and opposition signaled an ability, on both sides, to take action. The tension grew from day to day, while the fear-producing topics "migration" and "asylum" became talk-show hits. Within party politics, the lack of direction was replaced by the noise of polemical invectives such as "Social Democratic Party (SPD) asylum seekers," "hypocrites," "agitators," and "multicriminal society." The office of the administrator for immigrant affairs remained vacant in the autumn of 1991.

"We are warning of the danger of further neglecting the central political concern regarding immigration and integration of immigrant minorities," a committed professoriat from various sciences stated in an appeal at the end of August 1991. "The problems . . . must finally be understood as a decisive task for the future of German and European politics and must be determined by encompassing concepts. The situation will worsen if future oriented political action is not forthcoming." There was no political answer. Suddenly the repeated warnings which had been ignored by the political parties turned into a terrifying reality. It started with the attacks on an apartment house for foreigners in Saxon Hoyerswerda in late September 1992 and raged through Germany like an infernal wildfire. The events in the autumn of 1991 brought to the surface the xenophobic undercurrents of which experts had warned for a long time. They produced a worldwide reaction of horror, disgust, and memories of the darkest epoch in German history.

A second wave of xenophobic violence ensued following the terror-nights in Rostock in August 1992, where the withdrawal of a police without guidelines at the height of the riot could have been taken to be an invitation to escalate the attack. The flames of Rostock-Lichtenhagen sparked similar attacks; at various places in the East and the West, shelters of asylum seeking refugees went up in flames. Many arson attacks could be countered and the flames put out before it was too late, but in Mölln in Schleswig-Holstein in November 1992, two houses inhabited by Turks went up in flames. Three people burned to death and nine escaped with serious injuries.

Only then did a united front emerge throughout the country against the xenophobic aggression from the Right. In this country of highly nervous consternation, many intellectuals and other well-intentioned people had initially reacted with shock and helplessness. After the arson attacks in Mölln, human chains of light gathered in stunned protest against xenophobia, right-wing extremism, and violence. At that point, the well established government monopoly on force against the Left went into motion after appearing, until then, all-too hesitant toward the Right; far-Right organizations, well-known for years, were forbidden; house searches followed. The danger from the Right had become unmistakable and impossible to ignore.

The fact that the government was reacting much less systematically to the extremism of the Right than it had years ago to the extremism of the Left did not have to do with the frequently raised argument that state and law in Bonn, as in Weimar, was "blind in its right eye," although it is true that the far-Right danger had indeed been underestimated. Rather, it had primarily to do with the fact that the perpetrators were a large and growing number of poorly educated, unorganized individuals and small groups whose actions were less strategically planned than spontaneously executed, in contrast to the highly intelligent, tightly organized conspiracy of the "Red Army Faction" (RAF) of the Left. Evidence in 1992–1993, however, pointed to an increasingly tighter organization of numerous factions of the far-Right. . . .

Discussions about German migration and asylum, emotionalized and neuroticised through political polemics and demagoguery, must be put into a proper perspective. In evaluating the changes of the rights to asylum which went into effect in the summer of 1993, it is important to remember that the offer of individual asylum for the politically persecuted, like the Basic Law itself, was the historical reply of the West Germans to the experience of National Socialism. Thus, the debate about changing the asylum policy carried not only humanitarian but historical and political weight. What is needed in addition is international agreement and coordination of a collective, generally limited regulation of contingents for refugees from areas of war and crises.

With regard to united Germany, stronger efforts are needed for the integration and protection of immigrants and minorities. Comprehensive guidelines with long-term perspectives are required for the development of population and economy, society and culture. Experts agree that Germany is a country that fears an excess of immigration but which continually and for some time needs a minimum of immigration. Otherwise, there might well be the frightening scenario at the turn of the century of a central European bunker with a shrinking and aging crew, causing innumerable problems for the development of the labor market, the stability of social security systems supported through the "contract between generations" as well as for the entire social welfare state. Without such guiding principles, immigration politics would remain aimless or would be condemned to remain merely defensive. Answers must be sought not just for periods of legislation but for generations. Most importantly, a public discussion must no longer develop the mistaken notion that the pressure of immigration at the German borders can be remedied with changes to the Basic Law.

Germans must come to realize that they will have to live with the continued pressure and the resulting problems of immigration for decades to come; that it is a lasting and constantly changing political problem which cannot be "solved" with pat legal-technical solutions. It is all the more important to denounce scare tactics and horror visions in public discussions and to contribute to a positive, or at least a more relaxed attitude toward the problems of immigration, integration, and minorities. In coping with these problems, political consulting based on multiethnic studies and research on migration and conflicts in multicultural societies can no doubt make an important contribution.

45

THE CONTEMPORARY PERSONALITY

ABRAM DE SWAAN

Changes in emotional standards and definitions of acceptable personal behavior have been a recurrent part of European history for the past several centuries. Earlier selections have picked up shifts of many sorts: changes in recognition of love, or humanitarian sensibility, or disgust are key examples.

Advanced industrial society demands still further change, and personal styles actively promoted in the nineteenth century have come under new attack. In this selection a Dutch sociologist describes the new balance between permissiveness and repression, arguing that some changes maintain trends launched earlier, but that others reflect the very different kind of organizational structure and male-female relationships that matured during the later twentieth century. Certain kinds of spontaneous behaviors become more possible than before, but important (largely unperceived) constraints have increased as well. For example, manipulativeness plays a growing role in interpersonal relations, as hierarchy declines.

This characterization involves a number of important issues. Simply defining what is new about shifting emotional and behavioral standards is the first task. Further assessment of the causes prompting change might lead to speculations about the durability and future directions of the new personality styles. Finally, of course, De Swaan himself implies some evaluation of the quality of the new styles. Contemporary Europeans (and many Americans, responding to a similar, though not identical, framework) may particularly emphasize new freedoms and equalities, but De Swaan suggests some illusions and inadequacies as well. Are the new standards likely to work better than the redefinitions of acceptable personalities developed in earlier phases of Europe's modern march? Do they produce better social results? Sounder individual psyches?

How many global developments of society have altered the intimate relations between people? . . . The early development of capitalism resulted in a strong limitation on the presence in public of urban bourgeois women,

From: Abram de Swaan, "The Politics of Agoraphobia: On Changes in Emotional and Relational Management," *Theory and Society* Vol. 10 (1981): 368–74, 376–77.

whereas bourgeois men could continue to move wherever they wished and, possibly, could allow themselves greater liberty than before towards women in public and with public women, since their own daughters and wives had disappeared from the streets. In the past hundred years, however, women have begun to move more freely in public and, possibly, bourgeois men have lost some of their privileges in approaching women in public. On the balance, bourgeois urban men and women have become more equal, at least in this respect. This partial equalization of intimate relations in the course of the past hundred years, however, is not limited to this one aspect in the balance of dependencies between men and women, but covers almost all relations between the sexes. A degree of equalization has also occurred in the relations between parents and children, or between young and old in general. A similar decrease in social distance is developing between adjacent ranks in organizations between those who used to be called "superiors" and "inferiors," and now often prefer to be viewed as members of a "team." Social distances between adjacent ranks within organizations may have decreased, yet with the growth of these organizations the number of such ranks has increased, and with it the overall distance between the lowest echelons of production workers, consumers, clients and the top echelon of company presidents, secretaries-general, and so on. This double movement may explain the conflicting reports on "informalization" and "alienation," the former going on among adjacent ranks, the latter between lower and the uppermost strata. . . . Insofar as these equalizing developments have occurred, they represent an aspect of the increasing mutual dependency of ever greater numbers of people upon one another, as more and more of their strivings are being taken care of within large organizations of production, reproduction, and government. . . .

A second line of long-term development in European countries concerns the increasing control of infantile and bodily impulses. . . . The gradual process of state formation and the increasing control of domestic violence implied a more equitable automatic and long-term management of emotions, as Norbert Elias has suggested in *The Civilizing Process*. Undoubtedly, the relations between people have become less volatile, impulsive, spontaneous, and violent since the Middle Ages, and people have found themselves compelled to control their impulses more strictly, through external compulsion first, gradually through a social compulsion to self-compulsion, and finally mainly through self-compulsion. By the turn of the nineteenth century, this had resulted in rather strict and limiting patterns of intercourse among the bourgeoisie and in severe and restrictive superego formations in such middle-class citizens—very much the type of families and the type of patients with which Freud was familiar. Unmistakably, these patterns have changed in the course of the twentieth century. This presents a theoretical problem to historical sociologists concerned with problems of societal change, family life, and character formation: how is this recent shift in manners to be interpreted and how can it be explained in terms of societal transformations? . . .

A first survey of contemporary mores suggests that the margins and the variety of acceptable behavior have increased markedly since World War I and even more quickly since World War II. Examples about the relaxation of restrictions on the movement of women in public are only one case in point. Many others may be added, especially in the realm of intimate relations: the practice of contraception, abortion, concubinage, promiscuity, divorce, homosexuality, pornography, masturbation . . . a wide gamut of sexual relations with oneself and with others has become mentionable, acceptable in many circles, thinkable for most people. But this observation often leads to the conclusion that the relaxation of restrictions also applies to other spheres of life. Although most people believe that violent behavior is on the increase everywhere in the world, as a general statement this is unlikely to be true. Here, what is most relevant is not the violence between states, not the violence of a state apparatus against its own or a foreign citizenry, nor even organized violent opposition to a state apparatus, but especially violent actions by individuals. Statistics over long periods of time, covering all crimes of violence and comparing several countries are rare, the problems of interpretation well-nigh unsolvable. In France, for example, the homicide rate has varied with periods of social upheaval and tranquility, until in the early 1970s it reached a level as low as the lowpoint in the nineteenth century, around 1865. In the Netherlands, rates for violent crimes declined steadily throughout this century until the sixties when the number of assaults continued to decline, but the incidence of manslaughter increased (probably a result of the spread of lethal arms).

The social acceptability of violent behavior has probably not increased. In most countries fraternity initiation rites and bar brawls are quickly disappearing as male rituals. On the other hand, gangs of soccer supporters have become almost as violent as they used to be before spectator sports became organized and broadcast. Paradoxically, an increased aversion among the public against violent behavior may result in an increased visibility of such violence both in newspaper reporting of shocking incidents and in official statistics: indignant citizens are more prone to report, police to investigate, and courts to convict in cases that before went unremarked as routine toughness. Increasing sexual tolerance does not extend at all to violent forms of sexual conduct such as rape or flagellation; rather, the contrary is true: mounting indignation should not be interpreted as increasing incidence. People, including young, strong, and volatile people, are still being pressured to surrender the advantages and pleasures of physical strength and not to lay hands on others. . . .

People, then, are not only supposed to contain their violent impulses, but there are also other emotions they must inhibit; all those manners of feeling and conduct with which one puts oneself above others are increasingly becoming unacceptable. Scorn for the defects of others, for their ugliness, incapacity, or indigence only serves to discredit the scoffer in the eyes of most contemporaries. The self-satisfied awareness and ostentatious display of one's superior social position, be it through wealth, descent, rank, or education no longer add to the deference one will receive, but is held against one. Even the awareness that such rankings play a role at all in one's own and other people's thoughts is more and more denied. People pretend to be "colorblind," not to notice class differences in speech, dress and demeanor, not to prescribe behavior but to arrive at a definition of the problem together with the client, to discuss alternatives with coworkers rather than order their assistants around. Differences in social position are denied in every possible way, yet are betrayed in this very denial at the same time that this denial also contributes to diminishing the social distance. Equally, people are expected not to apply themselves in an effort to outdo others, through ambition and competition, because of a desire for fame, glory, honor, power, or the domination of others. This is not to say that people in fact no longer attempt to rise above others, but that they try to control the expression of these strivings in themselves, and especially in others, and that they attempt to convey the impression that they never sought aggrandizement—it just befell them. Nor is there much reason to suppose that people have relaxed their mutual pressure and self-discipline concerning habits of punctuality, reliability, discretion, cleanliness, hygiene, dietary restrictions, precision, and accuracy, whereas their meticulousness in operating and maintaining all sorts of machinery and in participating in automobile traffic has necessarily increased (the sociologically interesting development is not the incidence of road accidents, but their relative rarity and the imposition of a deadly discipline in traffic). A small minority within bohemia and academia may have abandoned some of these "anal virtues" to a degree and in so doing they have become highly visible to university professors commenting on the spirit of the epoch. But at the same time, and almost unnoticed, many millions have each year joined the rigidly timed and regimented life in schools, factories, large organizations, the world of traffic, and of taxes.

Undeniably, the management of affect is changing, but the widely held assumption that, all things considered, restrictions are loosening does not hold; not when it comes to the control of violence, nor with regard to the control of self-aggrandizement or of laxity. It does not even apply to the management of sexuality. . . .

Rape, roughness, scorn, and degradation, so common and acceptable for employers to inflict upon servants and factory girls, or customers upon prostitutes only a few generations ago, have become more distasteful to the contemporary public, even as the indignation of the women's movement against the remnants of these manners increases. Self-aggrandizement and violence have become less acceptable and are increasingly subject to social compulsion, social compulsion to self-compulsion and self-control, in that order. In sexual matters some canons of behavior have relaxed or disappeared, but people now compel others and themselves to take into consideration more aspects of more people at more moments, to arrange their relations accordingly and to subordinate their emotional management to these considerations. In this process, many intimate relations have become less predictable for they no longer depend as much as before on the commands of social canons and personal conscience, but are shaped in a process of negotiation between relatively equal and autonomous parties. This requires new and different forms of self-control. It requires a degree of insistence and sincerity in voicing one's demands (now called "assertiveness"), the surrender of means of physical or economic compulsion, and it requires a readiness to consider the desires of others and identify with them, along with a degree of patience and inventiveness to cope with them. At the very least, it requires the display of those qualities, for, in the history of morals, appearances are half the work.

Relations between people are increasingly managed through negotiation rather than through command. This applies to relations between the sexes, between parents and children, often to relations between people in adjacent ranks within organizational hierarchies, and sometimes to relations between local authorities and citizen groups. This makes for a larger variety of possible outcomes, but the process of arranging these relations imposes onerous restrictions upon the people involved. In a sense, this transition from management through command to management through negotiation represents an increase in freedom; freedom being taken to mean the possibility to do what one wishes insofar as it does not interfere with that possibility in others. . . .

The shift from management through command to management through negotiation has tied people to one another even more intricately, in more and more subtle ways, in all phases of life, at all moments of the day, with regard to many more activities and desires. It compels each person, in turn, to scrutinize his own longings and to speak up for them and, at the same time, to be ready to abandon them if they clash with the claims of others. Now a couple may negotiate a promiscuous relationship, but they must control jealousy and the fear of desertion, deny anger and rivalry with the partner's partner, and force themselves to play the game according to the rules imposed upon them by their own mutual consent. Clearly, in the course of this process some people have gained a larger margin of movement, and other have lost. . . . Older people have lost the means to chide, chastise, and command children, but young people can afford greater freedom of movement, expression, and consumption. Organizational superiors find themselves forced to listen to their immediate subalterns, instead of running the department as they see fit, and the lower echelons can sometimes exact their demands. Men can afford less liberties towards women than they used to and women have gained in opportunities for physical and social movement. No wonder that many white, middle-aged males in high academic positions who produce the social criticism of the era show a keen eye for the increasing oppression in society and worry about the decay and decadence that others would call freedom. . . .

The relaxation of manners in the twentieth century affects only a limited range of activities. The restraint on violent behavior has not lessened, the inhibition upon self-aggrandizement has probably increased, and the discipline in the handling of time, money, goods, and the body has grown. What has broadened are the margins of tolerance in sexual matters and in the expression of emotions and desires, especially in intimate circles. But even this relaxation is conditional upon the consideration of the wishes of others and upon their negotiated consent. Most aspects of human interaction are still ordered according to the canons of authority and the superego, managed through commands from without and within. But even where these orders have lost their sway, people do not abandon themselves to inconsiderate indulgence but negotiate some kind of arrangement with those close to them. This occurs in the family, between lovers, often among collaborators in organizations, and sometimes even in local politics. The burdens of poverty and tyranny may have lessened, but in other respects western society has lost little of its oppressive character, and in many respects discipline has increased. Yet, some limitations are not imposed, but rather incurred in relations managed through negotiation.

There is no guarantee whatsoever that such negotiations lead to dignified or fair arrangements: "Authenticity replaced morality and sincerity replaced judgment." Worse, negotiators may even relinquish authenticity or sincerity, and mislead or manipulate one another. More important, management through negotiation paralyzes rebellion: the dissident agreed himself to deal, of his own will, after ample consultation. Thus, the contract theory of citizenship and of economic man is extended to lovers, parents and colleagues: one may take them or leave them. And this points to the basic flaw in any view of human relations as the outcome of negotiated consent: such negotiations always occur within a wider social context in which one party generally holds better alternative options than another. Within their marriage a man and a woman may be equal to one another, but outside it job opportunities or chances for remarriage are very different. Moreover, the scope of negotiations, of what is negotiable, are narrowly prescribed, not by the partners, but in the social context in which they find themselves. Thus collaborators in an organization may bargain with one another, for example over the distribution of caseloads, until all of them together are transferred by the board of trustees, then they may negotiate over who is to go first. The shift towards management through negotiation represents a change in the manner in which people control themselves and one another, especially in face-to-face relations. Seen within a larger social context such negotiations appear limited in scope, their outcome biased by the options that each party has in society at large, whereas the very occurrence of such negotiations legitimizes the social order in which such mutual consent is being achieved. Judged within its immediate context management through negotiation seems to allow a greater variety of arrangements, better suited to the strivings of the partners that bring about the arrangement. But even in this context such a form of relational and emotional management forces people to take each other's demands into consideration and to relinquish some of their own. Some people, rather, forego these options and steer clear of such threatening involvements, or they avoid the negotiations and the ensuing engagements. They do not rebel but they reject, not with so many words, but tacitly, implicitly, with a strategy that denies itself until it is expressed in a vocabulary of psychic problems, as depersonalization, as a pleasureless promiscuity, . . . or as phobia. . . . The transition to management through negotiation is onerous and hazardous. Where no command can be heard within or without, people may adopt fears and compulsions to help them refrain from what they are now allowed to do by others but what they find too difficult, too dangerous, and too lonesome.

46

A POST-INDUSTRIAL EUROPE?

HAROLD PERKIN

The following selection argues that Western Europe, along with North America and Japan as post-industrial societies, has developed a dramatically new elite, based on education, knowledge and managerial position. Just as agricultural society had an elite drawn from the ranks of landowners, and industrial society a ruling class based on business ownership, so the radical new entity currently taking shape has its own distinctive structure. Power now lies with people receiving higher education at the most prestigious institutions, drawn by their academic talent—a group sometimes called a meritocracy, though with advantages still to those born in the existing middle and upper classes. Power extends through positions in government but particularly multinational corporations.

Harold Perkin uses the notion of a dramatically new kind of society to base his argument. The post-industrial concept is not undisputed, but many scholars would acknowledge that the nature and training of the elite have substantially changed. Even in the nineteenth century, professional groups like doctors and lawyers began to advance claims based on education and specialized knowledge. They were joined by new professions such as engineers. Now, Perkin contends, this pattern has spread to big business itself, as highly trained managers replace the older industrial owner-magnates, and become the basis of social and economic power.

The selection, like that on immigration, places Europe in a new global framework, changing in ways both shared with and affected by larger international patterns. But Perkin adds an important twist: he sees the French-German model of the post-industrial society as different from that of the more individualistic Britain and the United States. Commitments to welfare and government limitations on inequality create a different, and Perkin argues a better, version of the new power alignments from that which has taken shape in the English-speaking countries. In 1997, in fact, an interesting debate opened between American leadership and the socialist prime minister of France. American leaders argued that their national pattern of substantial employment and deregulation was producing the best system, while the French,

From: Harold Perkin, *The Third Revolution: Professional Elites in the Modern World* (London, Routledge, 1996), pp. 177–78, 179–80, 181, 182, 183–84, 190–92, 195–98.

admitting that they faced higher unemployment in recent years in response to growing international competition, contended that welfare protections against pure market forces limited inequality and created a more just society. This debate over what specific policies best suited the current international environment, for advanced industrial societies, was certain to continue, within Europe (between Britain and its European Union colleagues) and beyond, as Europe continued to define its role in a changing world economy.

The third great social revolution in the history of the world . . . even more than the first two [agricultural and industrial], is a worldwide phenomenon which is in process of embracing the whole world, partly through imitation but chiefly through the domination of the global economy by the giant multinational corporations that now operate across national frontiers and outflank governments in the corporate neofeudalism that is its most characteristic form. These are based mainly in the advanced countries of the West and East Asia, above all in the five leading professional societies we have identified: the United States, Britain, France, Germany, and Japan. Yet all five have absorbed the trends of professionalism in idiosyncratic ways, and they impact on the rest of the world, chiefly through their home-based multinationals, in ways peculiar to themselves. Whichever of them comes to dominate the global professional society of the future will proselytize its own version of professional society, and it is therefore important to see how they differ from each other. Each of the six or seven leading nations in the transition has shaped the major trends of professional society to suit itself and the elites who midwifed the changes, according to its own political structure, economic resources, cultural inheritance, and system of values. All have enjoyed the benefits of professionalism in a dramatic rise of living standards, better health and longer life, superior education, greater mobility and access to leisure, sport and entertainment, and all the expert services that go with the new plane of existence. Some have enjoyed more of them than others, and some, notably the old Soviet empire, have gone into reverse and are suffering a decline in living standards, health and welfare, public safety and crime prevention, associated with the collapse of communism and the failure of the market to replace it in a prompt and orderly manner. There, in fact, professional society never took a firm enough hold or, rather, took a pathological form that was bound to fail. But this was only the most extreme example of the diversity of response to the major trends of the revolution, and all of them transformed themselves into their own versions of the new society. . . .

One effect of this transition everywhere has been the decline of the industrial working class, the backbone of the traditional class struggle. Professional hierarchy has to a degree replaced class as the chief matrix of the new society. Of course, both class and hierarchy exist in all but the most primitive societies, criss-crossing each other like the weft and warp in the social fabric, but which of the two prevails on the face of the cloth depends on which dimension is predominant in the incomes and attitudes of the people. Class does not disappear altogether in professional society, and its importance differs from one to another. Britain is by far the most class-conscious, and this infects the whole of social life, politics, education, and industrial relations. Its existence, or at least its importance, is hotly denied by right-wing politicians, who prefer to believe that the free market offers equality of opportunity for all, while making sure that it gives their own children a head start in the race. Attempts to stamp out class protest in industrial relations have manifestly failed in Britain and the United States, where industrial disputes persist despite the efforts of Reagan and Thatcher to hobble the trades unions by legislation and administrative orders. Germany and France have not lost their class dimension, which raises educational and career barriers between the working and middle classes, and breaks out from time to time in occasional strikes. . . . But with the decline everywhere of the old manual working class and the rise of the professional segment of the service sector, class is becoming latent again, as it was before the second, industrial, revolution brought it to the surface.

Professional hierarchy favours meritocracy, which all professional societies espouse in varying degrees. They steer between the self-conscious versions of France and Japan and the more relaxed, *ad hoc* varieties of Germany and the United States, while Britain, as ever, is weighed down by its backlog of old class attitudes. Meritocracy is most institutionalized, but perhaps most skewed, in France and Japan, where the integrated political, bureaucratic, and economic elites come from the same handful of educational institutions. . . . But everywhere in professional society human capital still has to be earned, and it cannot be harnessed without some concession to merit wherever it can be found. The notion that it is concentrated in certain classes, groups, or races flies in the face of the evidence if individual success rather than factitious averages is measured.

Next, and for the same reason, all post-industrial societies have had to make concessions to able women, especially in higher education where they now form nearly half the intake though much less of the graduate students and teachers, but in none so far have women achieved equality in access to jobs or equal pay for equivalent work. . . .

The growth of government, . . . one of the most powerful trends in professional society, seems to be levelling off with the collapse of the command economies and the backlash against public ownership and welfare in the West. It was always greater in Europe with its traditions of state enterprise going back to the eighteenth century and welfare provision going back to Bismarck, than in the United States and Japan, where culture and ideology favoured private enterprise, though of different kinds. The collapse of communism and the wave of privatization in Europe, begun in Thatcherite Britain, have started to roll back the involvement of the state in the civil economy, but this has by no means reduced the scale of traditional government employment and expenditure. . . .

The welfare state . . . plays a large part in maintaining human capital, and it now costs on average a fifth of GNP, though nearly all of it is recycled into the economy. Unsurprisingly, it is now the prime target of the free-market economists and the politicians of the radical right, especially in Britain and the United States, where the think tanks are paid huge grants by the rich to blame the poor and cut their benefits. Yet their own policies create the very problems they complain about: unemployment as the chosen cure for inflation, poverty as the result of the widening gap between rich and poor produced by a deregulated market, crime, drug addiction, and mental illness in consequence of that poverty and the social malaise of the disinherited. All these cost far more money than the preventive welfare practised by the state in Europe and by the corporations in Japan. Right-wing solutions always turn out to be more expensive: the largest prison population in the world has not reduced the American crime rate, nearly twice as high as the European, up to five times as high for murder and rape. . . . The cheapest and most rational solution is to treat welfare, as in continental Europe, as an investment in maintaining human capital, the mainspring of professional society.

Higher education . . . the chief creator of human capital, is one of the leading items in government expenditure. The United States, with the largest private university sector, still spends more public money per student than any other country: $13,639 in 1991, compared with Britain's $9,621, Japan's $7,570, West Germany's $6,322, and France's $5,871. Its enormous investment in higher education has produced the largest proportion of graduates to population in the world, 36 per cent, compared to 15–22 per cent in the other four countries, and has given it the leading edge in scientific research and in many high-tech industries.

But money isn't everything, and the more focused meritocratic higher education of France, Germany, and Japan has enabled them to catch up with, and the last two to overtake, the United States in GNP per capita (at current exchange rates) by 1992. In professional society it is the quality rather than the quantity of higher education that counts, and the expensive American system, with its diffuse liberal arts first degrees followed by graduate school for about the same proportion as the whole intake elsewhere, is no more effective than the fewer but more intensive first degrees in Europe and Japan.

The rise in the scale of organization is what ultimately gives professional society the leverage to perform its many functions. Along with the expansion of government, welfare, and education, the scale of operation in the economy, the next major trend, has to rise to produce the gigantic flow of goods and services. The huge dinosaurs of state industries in the command economies manifestly failed, more because of mismanagement and corruption than ideology, but in the free world business has continued to concentrate increasingly in large corporations. In every advanced country in both West and East each major industry is led by three to five large companies that dominate production, employment, and prices; on average some 200 big corporations and their satellite subcontractors and suppliers account for the largest part of the Gross Domestic Product of each nation.

Yet industrial concentration does not stop at national frontiers. The globalization of the economy is the . . . final major trend of the third social revolution. The world economy, . . . is now dominated by some 37,500 transnational corporations (TNCs), which between them control 207,000 foreign affiliates. Nine out of ten are based in the developed countries of North America, Europe, and Japan. They employ directly at home and abroad around 73 million people, nearly 10 per cent of paid employees in non-agricultural activities worldwide, and close to 20 per cent in the developed countries alone. Indirectly, through subcontractors, franchisees and tied suppliers, they employ as many again, making a total of 150 million workers, or nearly one in five of the globe's non-farm paid workers. The largest 100 (excluding banking and finance) held $3.4 trillion in global assets in 1992, about a third outside their home countries, and employed 12.4 million people, nearly half of them overseas, about one in six (17 per cent) of the multinationals' total direct employment. Three quarters of them are based in the five countries addressed here: twenty-nine in the United States, sixteen in Japan, twelve in France, eleven in the United Kingdom (including two jointly with the Netherlands), and nine in Germany; another five were based in Canada, Australia, and New Zealand. On a wider view, 386 (77 per cent) of the 500 largest industrial (manufacturing and mining) companies were based in the five: 157 in the United States, 119 in Japan, forty-five in the United Kingdom, thirty-three in Germany, and thirty-two in France. They controlled assets in 1991 of $4.5 trillion and employed nearly 20 million workers, and dominated the global economy. . . .

[T]he continental European elites have for the most part maintained the trust and cohesion of their societies, by emphasizing their meritocratic recruitment, their concern for the common welfare, and by modifying the beneficial ownership of big business. Despite the corruption that infects French politics on both sides, among the friends of both ex-President Mitterand and ex-Prime Minister Balladur for example, the French bureaucracy's reputation for upright public service has survived and spilled over via *pantouflages* to the executives of the corporations. The West German elite, too, has a long-standing reputation for public service and what Ralf Dahrendorf has called "the habit of obedience," and the scandals have chiefly concerned not personal corruption but clandestine relations with the East German secret police, the Stasi. Above all, trust and cohesion have been maintained by the "social market economy," the modified version of the free market that offers codetermination, participation in corporate governance to all stakeholders including the employees, combined with a generous welfare state that guarantees security to all. Although unification has put a strain on resources and annoyed the "Wessies" with the costs of rebuilding the East and the "Ossies" with the loss of the food and rent subsidies and other social benefits, the German economy has already recovered, as shown by the strength of the

Deutschmark, the largest trade balance in the world, and the highest rate of industrial growth among the larger economies. It is once more the locomotive of the European economy and the standard bearer for the industrial and welfare directives of the Union. In their different ways, both the Japanese and continental European elites have offered guarantees that they will not grossly abuse their power.

The American and British elites have offered no such guarantee. Like the Soviet *nomenklatura*, they have been seduced by a crude, reductionist ideology into believing that they have the right to exploit their societies to the limit, without conscience or restraint. Free-market theory has convinced them that greed is good, that the market will give everyone their due, and that they have a moral right to whatever share of society's resources they can grab. By a brilliant intellectual stratagem, their guru Friedrich von Hayek equated political freedom with the free market and argued that any interference with the individual's right to make money at the expense of his fellows was the road to serfdom. The heart of his theory is a distinction between fundamental law, which gives the individual indefeasible rights to acquire whatever he can in this world, and mere rules, the political regulations by which government underpins that law with definitions of property rights, contract, theft, fraud, and so on, but has no right to go beyond that to redistribute income or tax the rich to support the poor. The concept of social justice he specifically rejected as a sentimental interference with the individual's right to maximize his or her share of society's resources: justice is what the market gives you, no more and no less. The state and the state alone is the enemy of freedom: threats to liberty from other directions, from "overmighty subjects" like powerful corporations, he simply ignored. The idealist concept of positive freedom, of government as the protector of the weak and defender of all against the bully and the overbearing institution, he laughed out of court. The market balances all interests and allocates society's resources in the fairest possible way. . . .

Why does this theory appeal to the English-speaking elites far more than to the rest of the civilized world? The answer is deeply embedded in English law and culture. It goes back, of course, to Adam Smith, Ricardo, Malthus and the classical economists, through to the near-anarchism of Herbert Spencer in *The Man versus the State,* but it can be found much earlier, in Alexander Pope—"true self-love and social are the same"—and Bernard Mandeville—"private vices, public benefits." It stems ultimately from a peculiar change in the English idea of property between the fourteenth and seventeenth centuries, from contingent property in which a hierarchy of owners, the king, church, barons, knights, and peasants, had claims to a share of the income, to absolute property, in which a single individual owned all the rights. This concept the English carried with them wherever they went, and applied it in all the English-speaking lands and in Ireland, India, and the colonies. Elsewhere the concept of shared property, with overriding claims by the community, was the norm, but in Britain, the United States, and the English-speaking dominions the notion of individual absolute property rights held sway. . . .

This is the fundamental contradiction at the heart of extreme free-market theory. Far from allocating society's resources equitably, it tends to reinforce success and failure exponentially, and so to produce an ever-widening gap between rich and poor. The Anglo-American experiment with Reaganomics and Thatcherism in the 1980s has proved this empirically. . . . [I]n 1980 the ratio between the top and bottom quintiles of household incomes was twelve-fold in the United States and eight-fold in Britain, compared with nine-fold in France, five-fold in West Germany, and four-fold in Japan. Since then the gap has widened considerably. By 1987 the American top decile had gained 16.5 per cent in aggregate income (and the top 1 per cent, 49.8 per cent) and the bottom decile had lost 14.8 per cent. In Britain by 1991 the top fifth of households received before tax 23.7 times the average income of the bottom fifth, and after tax and benefits (which doubled the poor's income and reduced that of the rich by a third) still 7.4 times. . . .

The contrast between the United States and Britain and the rest was equally striking. In the period 1950–73 the American and British rates of growth of per capita GDP were not much more than half that of the other leading countries: 2.5 per cent and 2.2 per cent per annum, compared with France 4.0 per cent, Germany 4.9 per cent, and Japan 8.0 per cent. In 1973–89 all five suffered from slower growth, but Britain (1.8 per cent) and the United States (1.6 per cent) along with France (1.8 per cent) still lagged behind Germany (2.1 per cent) and Japan (3.1 per cent). But that is not the end of the story. Although America and Britain made more rapid recovery from the recession of the early 1990s, they both in that second period became debtor countries on a massive scale, in terms both of national budget and of overseas trade. The American national debt rose to $4,083 billion by 1992, and the British to £207 billion ($327 billion), despite selling off some £50 billion worth of public property. In 1983–92 the American overseas trading deficit added up to $762 billion, and the British in 1988–92 to £74 billion ($117 billion) in an economy one sixth the size. . . .

The social effects of the experiment have been no less dire. In both countries there has been a widening gap, as we have seen, between rich and poor, an increase in unemployment (ineptly disguised by adjusting the official figures), a rise in poverty and homelessness, a wave of crime and violence, an increase in racial tensions, a neglect of public infrastructure, the "in your face" rudeness and incivility in the streets, and for the first time an upwelling of insecurity and discontent among the middle classes, who can no longer feel assured that their children will be as well off as themselves. Like Malthus and the classical economists before them, the right-wing politicians and neoclassical economists try to fob off responsibility by shifting the blame on to the victims, the poor, teenage mothers, "welfare scroungers," immigrants, and racial minorities, even women who are blamed for taking white male jobs. This tactic has worked in the past, together with scaremongering about the "tax, and spend" opposition, but it cannot work for ever. Sooner or later the British and American people will wake up to the fact that the free-market ideology is simply a device for justifying exploitation of the many by the few, and demand a return to a responsible civil society. If they do not, the two societies may go the same way as the Soviet Union and East Germany. . . .

The continental Europeans have devised a more formal counter-ideology along the lines of the German social market economy and built it into the Maastricht Treaty [intensifying the European Union]. This includes the Social Chapter which guarantees social security for all citizens of member states and the human rights of workers and trades union members. It also underwrites the industrial directive which will require all large companies (with more than 1,000 employees including 150 in at least two member states) by September 1996 to appoint works councils. The British government has opted out of the Social Chapter, to the chagrin of the rest who consider that Britain is trying to gain an unfair competitive advantage, but British multinationals cannot opt out of the works council directive, even in their domestic plants, if they wish to operate in Europe. Some British companies, like United Biscuits and Coats Viyella, have welcomed this, and others, like ICI, British Aerospace, Unilever, Allied Lyons, British Petroleum, and Bass are negotiating schemes with their staff and trades union representatives. About a fifth of the 5,000 British manufacturing companies will be affected. John Edmonds of the GMB trade union commented, "The Government can like it or lump it. Works councils are changing the face of UK industrial relations by giving employees a seat at the table." The directive compels companies to report on their economic and financial situation, business development, investment plans, employment prospects, relocation, closures, and collective redundancies. Presumably, this will give the employees the opportunity not only to negotiate pay and conditions more effectively and to discuss alternatives to firing workers and closing plants, but to oppose gross overpayments to directors. Enlightened companies expect to gain better communication with workers, improved industrial relations, and speedier decision making. Others of course fear the loss of the executives' right to manage and, more particularly, their power to control the flow of income and to overpay themselves. Either way, if they wish to operate in what will soon become the largest market in the world, they have no choice. Re-regulation of the market is returning to Britain through the back door of the European Union. . . .

Literary Credits

MUCHEMBLED - Reprinted by permission of Louisiana State University Press from *Popular Culture and Elite Culture in France, 1400–1750*, by Robert Muchembled, translated by Lydia Cochrane. Originally published in France as *Populaire dès Élites dans la France Moderne*, © Flammarion, 1878. English translation copyright © 1985 by Louisiana State University Press.

ZEMON DAVIS - Natalie Zemon Davis, "The Sacred and the Body Social in Sixteenth-Century Lyon." *Past and Present*, 1981, pp. 40–41, 52–57, 60–61, 67–68. Used by permission of Oxford University Press.

HOWELL - Martha C. Howell, *Women, Production, & Patriarchy in Late Medieval Cities*, pp. 85–94, 151–83. Copyright by The University of Chicago Press. Reprinted by permission of The University of Chicago Press.

RUBLACK - Ulinka Rublack, "Pregnancy, Childbirth and the Female Body in Early Modern Germany," *Past and Present*, vol. 150 (1996), pp. 84–86, 87–89, 90, 92–96, 97–100, 103, 108–10. Used by permission of Oxford University Press.

GRIFFITHS - Paul Griffiths, "The Structure of Prostitution in Elizabethan London," from *Continuity and Change*, Vol. 8, No. 1 (1993), pp. 39–63. Copyright 1993 by Cambridge University Press. Reprinted with the permission of Cambridge University Press.

SHARPE - James Sharpe, *Instruments of Darkness: Witchcraft in Early Modern England*. pp. 15–17, 18–21, 158–63, 172–3, 262–3, 269, 273–5, 191, 292–3, 300–1, 302. Copyright 1997. Reprinted by permission of The University of Pennsylvania Press.

HOROWITZ - Elliot Horowitz, "The Eve of the Circumcision: A Chapter in the History of Jewish Night-life," *Journal of Social History*, v. 23, #1, 1989, pp. 45–60. Reprinted by permission of the *Journal of Social History*.

GILLIS - John R. Gillis, "From Ritual to Romance: Toward an Alternative History of Love." From *Emotion and Social History: Towards a New Psychohistory*, edited by Carol Z. Stearns and Peter N. Stearns (New York: Holmes & Meier, 1988). Copyright © 1988 by Holmes & Meier Publishers, Inc. Reproduced with the permission of the publisher.

ROODENBURG - Herman W. Roodenburg, "The Autobiography of Isabella De Moerloose: Sex, Childrearing and Popular Belief in Seventeenth-Century Holland," *Journal of Social History*, vol. 18, 1985, pp. 520–25. Reprinted by permission of the *Journal of Social History*.

SMAIL - John Smail, "Manufacturer or Artisan? The Relationship Between Economic and Cultural Change in the Early Stages of the Eighteenth-Century Industrialization," *Journal of Social History*, vol. 25, 1992, pp. 791–2, 798–9, 800–01, 803–04, 806–08. Reprinted by permission of the *Journal of Social History*.

WATT - Reprinted from Jeffrey R. Watt: *The Making of Modern Marriage: Matrimonial Control & the Rise of Sentiment in Neuchatel, 1550–1800*. Copyright © 1992 by Cornell University. Used by permission of the publisher, Cornell University Press.

TROYANSKY - Reprinted from David G. Troyansky: *Old Age in the Old Regime: Image & Experience in Eighteenth-Century France*. Copyright © 1989 by Cornell University Press. Used by permission of the publisher, Cornell University Press.

SPIERENBURG - Pieter Spierenburg, *The Spectacle of Suffering*, pp. 183–196. Copyright Cambridge University Press. Reprinted with the permission of Cambridge University Press.

MacDONALD - Michael MacDonald, "The Secularization of Suicide in England 1600–1800," *Past and Present*, vol. 111 (9186), pp. 52–55, 58–60, 64, 84–85, 87–88, 93. Reprinted by permission of Oxford University Press.

McKENDTRICK/BREWER/PLUMB - Neil McKendrick, John Brewer, and J.H. Plumb, "The Birth of a Consumer Society: The Commercialization of Eighteenth-Century England." Copyright 1982. Reprinted by permission of the authors.

GOUBERT - Jean-Pierre Goubert, "The Art of Healing: Learned Medicine and Popular Medicine in France of 1790." From *Medicine and Society in France*, ed. R. Forster & O. Ranum. Copyright 1980 by The Johns Hopkins University Press. Reprinted by permission of The Johns Hopkins University Press.

SUBACCHI - Paola Subacchi, "Conjunctural Poor and Structural Poor: Some Preliminary . . ." from *Continuity and Change*, Vol. 8, No. 1 (1993); p. 65 ff. Copyright 1993 by Cambridge University Press. Reprinted with the permission of Cambridge University Press.

CHISTIANSEN - Pave Ove Christiansen, "Culture and Contrasts in the Northern European Village: Lifestyle Away Manorial Peasants in 18th-Century Denmark," *Journal of Social History,* vol. 29, 1995, pp. 275–6, 279–80, 283–4, 288–9. Reprinted by permission of the *Journal of Social History.*

LEE - R. J. Evans & W. R. Lee, "The German Family" from *The Family and Modernisation* by Robert Lee, pp. 84, 94–99, 104–109. Copyright Routledge Publishing Co. Used by permission of Routledge Publishing Co.

MAYNES - From *School for the People: Comparative Local Studies of Schooling History in France and Germany, 1750–1850,* by Mary Jo Maynes (New York: Holmes & Meier, 1985). Copyright © 1985 by Mary Jo Maynes. Reproduced with the permission of the publisher.

CORBIN - Reprinted by permission of the publisher from *The Foul and the Fragrant* by Alain Corbin, Cambridge, Mass.: Harvard University Press, Copyright © 1986 by the President and Fellows of Harvard College.

TILLY - Reprinted by permission of the publisher from *The Contentious French* by Charles Tilly, Cambridge, Mass.: Harvard University Press, Copyright © 1986 by the President and Fellows of Harvard College.

BERLANSTEIN - Lenard R. Berlanstein, "Manager and Engineers in French Big Business of the Nineteenth Century," *Journal of Social History,* vol. Winter 1988, pp. 218–23, 225–30. Reprinted by permission of the *Journal of Social History.*

BRANCA - Reprinted from Patricia Branca: *Silent Sisterhood: Middle-Class Women in the Victorian Home* by permission of Carnegie Mellon University Press © 1975 by Patricia Branca.

NOLAN - Mary Nolan, I. Katznelson & A.R. Zolberg, eds. "Working Class Formation: Nineteenth-Century Patterns in Western Europe and the United States." pp. 335, 359–60, 364–66, 380–81. Copyright 1986 by Princeton University Press. Reprinted by permission of Princeton University Press.

RADCLIFF - Pamela Radcliff, "Elite Women Workers and Collective Action: The Cigarette Makers of Gijón, 1890–1930," *Journal of Social History,* vol. 27, 1993, pp. 85–7, 88–9, 100–01. Reprinted by permission of the *Journal of Social History.*

BURKE - Joanna Burke, "Housewifery in Working Class England 1860–1914," *Past and Present,* vol. 143, (1994), pp. 167–69, 171–74, 179–81, 188–91, 194, 195–96. Used by permission of Oxford University Press.

WALVIN - J.A. Mangan & J. Walvin, "Symbols of Moral Superiority: Slavery, Sport and the Changing World Order" from *Manliness and Morality: Middle-Class Masculinity in Britain and America 1800–1940.* Copyright © J.A. Mangan and J. Walvin. Reprinted with permission of St. Martin's Press, Incorporated.

REARICK - Charles Rearick, *Pleasures of the Belle-Epoque.* (1985), pp. 83–84, 90–93, 95–96, 101–104, 110, 189–90, 193–95. Copyright Yale University Press. Used by permission of Yale University Press.

BROWN - Kenneth D. Brown, "Modelling for War? Toy Soldiers in Late Victorian and Edwardian Britain," *Journal of Social History,* v. #24, 1990, pp. 237–41, 243–7. Reprinted by permission of the *Journal of Social History.*

PARELLA - Reprinted from *The Journal of Interdisciplinary History,* XXII (1992), 627–628, 630–633, 635, 637–639, 641, 647–649, 650–651, 653–657, with the permission of the editors of *The Journal of Interdisciplinary History* and The MIT Press, Cambridge, Massachusetts. Copyright © 1992 by the Massachusetts Institute of Technology and the editors of *The Journal of Interdisciplinary History.*

SECCOMBE - Wally Seccombe, "Starting to Stop: Working Class Fertility Decline in Britain," *Past and Present,* vol. 126 (1990), pp. 153–54, 160–62, 165–66, 170–71, 173, 175–76, 184–86. Used by permission of Oxford University Press.

WEGS - J. Robert Wegs, *Growing Up Working Class: Continuity & Change among Viennese Youth 1890–1938,* (University Park: The Pennsylvania State University Press), pp. 66–81, 86–91. Copyright The Pennsylvania State University. Reproduced by permission of the publisher.

WINKLER - Heinrich August Winkler, "Nazism and the Lower-Middle Class." *Journal of Modern History* 48:1 (1976), pp. 7–18. Used by permission of The University of Chicago Press.

ROBERTS - Mary Louise Roberts, "Sampson and Delilah Revisited: The Politics of Women's Fashion in 1920s France," *AHR,* vol. 98, no. 3 (June 1993), pp. 657–684. Used by permission of the author and the American Historical Association.

WHITNEY - Susan B. Whitney, "Embracing the Status Quo: French Communists, Young Women and the Popular Front," *Journal of Social History,* vol. #30, 1996, pp. 29–32, 33, 34–6, 37–8, 43–5. Reprinted by permission of the *Journal of Social History.*

PAHL - Raymond E. Pahl, extracts from *Divisions of Labour.* Used with permission of Blackwell Publishers.

ARDAGH - Excerpt from A TALE OF FIVE CITIES by John Ardagh. Copyright © 1979 by John Ardagh. Reprinted by permission of Harper Collins Publishers, Inc.

CASTLES - From Stephen Castles, *Here for Good.* Reprinted by permission of Pluto Press.

POIGER - Excerpts from Uta G. Poiger, "Rock 'n' Roll, Female Sexuality, and the Cold War Battle over German Identities," *Journal of Modern History,* vol. 68, pp. 577–80, 586–7, 589, 594–6, 598–9, 607–8, 610–11, 615. Copyright 1996 by The University of Chicago Press. Reprinted by permission of The University of Chicago Press.

ARIÈS - From *The Hour of Our Death* by Philippe Ariès, trans. Helen Weaver. Copyright © 1980 by Alfred A. Knopf, Inc. Reprinted by permission of the publisher.

MENDRAS - Henri Mendras, *The Vanishing Peasant: Innovation & Change in French Agriculture.* Published in French by S.É.D.É.I.S., Paris, under the title *La Fin des Paysans, Innovation et Changement dans l'Agriculture*